LAW IN IMPERIAL CHINA

LAW IN IMPERIAL CHINA

Exemplified by 190 Ch'ing Dynasty Cases

(*Translated from the* Hsing-an hui-lan)

*With Historical, Social, and
Juridical Commentaries*

by

Derk Bodde

and

Clarence Morris

UNIVERSITY OF PENNSYLVANIA PRESS
Philadelphia

Published by arrangement with Harvard University Press
First Pennsylvania Paperback *edition 1973*

Library of Congress Catalog Card Number 67-27080

ISBN: 0–8122–1060–3

Printed in the United States of America

191774-150

PREFACE

Clarence Morris

The scholarly literature in Western languages on the traditional law of China is relatively meager. The materials, however, are voluminous. Over the centuries the Chinese developed a complicated, expanding legal system. This vast system was indigenous; only in the nineteenth and twentieth centuries has the legal thought of other countries influenced Chinese law. The first Chinese imperial code was promulgated in the third century B.C. Its draftsmen drew on still more ancient Chinese laws, some of which were in force at least three centuries earlier. Each successive Chinese imperial dynasty promulgated a new code—a revision, and elaboration, and sometimes a radical rearrangement of the code of its predecessor. The last of these, the Ch'ing Code, assumed definitive form in 1740. Like the earlier codes, it too was uniquely Chinese. Imperial China's legal documents were not, of course, restricted to codes. Orderly and large collections of reported cases also existed and Chinese scholars, from time to time, dealt in various ways with their heritage of legal history.

This volume starts with a survey of the main currents of these Chinese legal developments; it then presents translations of 190 illustrative Ch'ing cases; it concludes with a legal analysis throwing some light on how the Ch'ing Code worked.

This is the way we came to write this book. In September 1959, the University of Pennsylvania's Graduate Department of Oriental Studies embarked on a two year seminar to discuss oriental legal systems. Derk Bodde, Professor of Chinese, and I were members. Dr. Bodde lectured to our seminar on Chinese law for several months. His presentation opened a vista on law with wide cultural dimensions. It seemed to me that professional law students could profit from so rich a topic. I proposed, therefore, that with the help of Dr. W. Allyn Rickett (also a sinologist) we three offer a Chinese legal thought course in our law school. They accepted, and we commenced teaching the course in January 1961. It was, perhaps, the first course on Chinese law ever given in an American law school. We have repeated the course five times, developing teaching materials as we went along. This volume is an outgrowth of study materials prepared for the first half of the course. (The second half of our course deals with the law of Republican and Communist China, study materials for which are not yet ready for publication.)

We start our course with Dr. Bodde presiding. He deals with the history and theory of Chinese law from ancient times through the Ch'ing dynasty (1644–1911), by giving us systematic lectures on the origins, nature, attitudes, and procedures of Chinese legal systems and their relations to society. Part One of this book has grown out of his lectures. I then take the chair and preside over several meetings spent in discursive analysis of cases selected from the translations in Part Two. Such an analysis is presented in Part Three.

When first we offered the course, we gave our students a wide variety of reading assignments. Our case materials were at the outset brief summaries that I had gleaned from works in English such as Alabaster's *Notes and Commentaries on Chinese Criminal Law*, *The Peking Gazette* (in translation), and van Gulik's translation of the *T'ang-yin-pi-shih*. We soon came to see that these scattered materials were inadequate. They were illustrative rather than documentary. Though they had served well enough in the works from which I culled them, they were too sketchy for professional instruction in a law school.

We therefore decided to turn from imperfect summaries and paraphrases to Chinese originals; for this purpose Dr. Bodde selected the largest and best of all Chinese casebooks, the *Hsing-an hui-lan* or *Conspectus of Penal Cases*. This title is a cover designation for three successive compilations dated 1834, 1840, and 1886, and containing a total of more than 7,600 cases covering the years 1736–1885. Most of the cases were taken by the compilers directly from the archives of the highest judicial organ in Peking, the Hsing Pu or Board of Punishments. From this gigantic collection we undertook the difficult task of selecting for translation our

190 cases, initially for classroom discussion and then for inclusion in this book. We tried to select cases that are interesting and representative.

We started our translation program by asking one of our juniors to translate the table of contents of the *Hsing-an hui-lan* under Dr. Bodde's supervision. I, then, picked out sections that looked profitable and tried to guess which of these might be especially important. Next, our junior translators went to work on at least two cases in each section; they translated several more cases from those sections that I had rated as important. First drafts of translations were read by Dr. Bodde and then submitted to me for either elimination or approval for polishing. We operated on this plan for some time with the hope that supervisory review by Dr. Bodde and legal editorial revision by me would produce satisfactory case translations. Neither Dr. Bodde nor I planned to expend great efforts on the cases. We had each supposed that production of our teaching materials would not require us to work long and hard. The supposition proved true in my case. Although my part was not quite so simple as I thought it would be, my efforts have not much exceeded my expectations.

The demands on Dr. Bodde, however, mushroomed. Translation of the abstruse classical Chinese of the cases was hard going, especially so since our translators had neither a comprehensive overview of the Ch'ing Code nor a grounding in Chinese legal history. Although the first translations were initially helpful, Dr. Bodde found that he had to spend considerable time on each of them. He worked and reworked the cases repeatedly; many of the printed versions hardly resemble the first translations. Soon, too, he decided that our original selection needed supplementation, and many of the cases were translated first and last by him. The further Dr. Bodde developed the historical and procedural materials, the more demanding they also became. So what had started out as an interesting sideline absorbed Dr. Bodde's available energies for many months. Even then he was not done; his text and cases called for appendices, glossary, and bibliography which could not be delegated. These demands made Dr. Bodde the major contributor in this collaboration. I stand ready, of course, to share responsibility for the whole work, and especially for its legalistic aspects. Nevertheless, he pulled the laboring oar in the development of Parts One and Two of this book; once we developed the plan for these two parts my role became editorial and advisory. In the production of the short Part Three, our roles were reversed; I wrote the first draft which was brought to final form with Dr. Bodde's invaluable help. The appendices, glossary, and bibliography are wholly Dr. Bodde's, except for the correlating of the French and Chinese code references in Appendix A, which was largely the work of Dr. Werner Ning, now of the Law School of Northwestern University. The index was compiled by Mrs. Alice H. Frey, who also helped read proof.

We are mindful of our debt to those who translated for us. Their work contributed to and advanced the project. We want to express appreciation to the late Mr. F. S. Ch'ien, whose knowledge of the bureaucratic systems of both imperial and Republican China was particularly helpful; to Mrs. Nancy Sheng-wu Cheng, of the East Asian collection of the Van Pelt Library, University of Pennsylvania; and to Messrs P'ei-chih Hsieh and Wu-su P'an, now respectively on the faculties of the University of Saskatchewan and of Bates College. Mr. P'an also prepared a paper on aspects of Ch'ing legal procedure with special reference to the *Hsing-an hui-lan* which helped in the development of certain matters in Chapter V of Part One of this book. Dr. Jonathan Mirsky, now on the staff of Dartmouth College, spent a part of one summer in preliminary reworking of some of the translated cases, particularly from the point of view of English style.

Naturally we are pleased to have this book initiate the Harvard Studies in East Asian Law series of Harvard University Press. For their help in bringing the book into the series, we are grateful to Professor John K. Fairbank, Director of the East Asian Research Center at Harvard, and to Professor Jerome A. Cohen of the Harvard Law School. Professor Cohen and his assistant, Mr. Yung-fang Chiang, have also offered valuable suggestions on certain aspects of Parts One and Two. Others to whom we are indebted for items of bibliographical help include Professor M. H. van der Valk of the University of Leiden, Professor Hui-lin Li of the University of Pennsylvania, Professor A. F. P. Hulsewé of the University of Leiden, and Professor Hans Bielenstein of Columbia

University, as well as the librarians of the East Asian collections at Harvard and Columbia.

To Mr. Henri Vetch, Director of the Hong Kong University Press, we owe thanks for contributing the Chinese woodblock illustration of the courtroom scene which adds to the book's interest and attractiveness. Finally, we are happy to thank Mrs. Andrea Kimmelman, who prepared much of the manuscript with skill and patience.

The Institute of Legal Research of the University of Pennsylvania School of Law generously supplied funds we needed from time to time. We are very grateful for this essential support.

We also want to express our thanks to the American Philosophical Society for permission to reprint an article by Dr. Bodde, "Basic Concepts of Chinese Law," originally published in *Proceedings of the American Philosophical Society*, 107.375–398 (1963), and now, with slight revisions, reprinted as the first chapter of Part One of this book.

C.M.
Professor of Law

University of Pennsylvania
April 1967

CONTENTS

ILLUSTRATIONS

I. "Kao Yao Clarifies the Punishments"

This modern (1905) Chinese depiction of Kao Yao dispensing justice with the aid of the supernatural Hsieh-chai shows, in the center, two suspects kneeling before the legendary judge. One of them, his face evincing terror, is about to be butted by the Hsieh-chai. Guards and their prisoners appear in the foreground, the latter fettered or wearing the cangue around their necks. Lictors flank the dais, two of them with staves, and from the rear comes an attendant bringing tea for the judge.

This woodblock engraving comes from the *Ch'in-ting Shuching T'u-shuo* or *Imperially Compiled Edition of the Documents Classic with Illustrations and Explanations* (Peking, 1905). Although the text of the ancient *Documents Classic* itself makes no mention of the Hsieh-chai and refers only to Kao Yao, and though the scene here depicted is utterly unhistorical, it nonetheless provides an excellent idea of how an imperial Chinese court looked as late as the early twentieth century.

Photograph courtesy of Mr. Henri Vetch, Hong Kong.

Appendix F contains more information about Kao Yao.

II. The Hsieh-chai

This "life-size" bronze figure of the Hsieh-chai, no doubt unique in the world today, was made in 1962 by the Philadelphia sculptor Henry Mitchell and stands in the main hall of the University of Pennsylvania Law School. The bilingual inscription describes the Hsieh-chai's magical judicial powers.

Appendix F contains more information about the Hsieh-chai.

"Kao Yao Clarifies the Punishments"

HSIEH-CHAI
(Syeh-jai)

The Hsieh-chai is an ancient Chinese supernatural animal, goat-like in appearance but with only one horn. It is endowed with the faculty of detecting the guilty, and can distinguish between the crooked and the upright. In the days of Shun (legendary sage-ruler, circa 2200 B.C.), when the famous minister Kao Yao tried cases in which guilt was uncertain, he would order the Hsieh-chai to butt the guilty. Those who were in fact guilty it would butt, whereas the innocent it would not butt.

Bronze statue
by Henry Mitchell, 1962

獬豸乃中國之古靈獸，似羊而一角，性知有罪，能別曲直。舜之時，其名臣皋陶決訟時，罪疑者令觸之，有罪則觸，無罪則不觸也。

Slow and painful has been man's
progress from magic to law

緩哉困哉人類之由幻術而至於法律也

The Hsieh-chai and Inscription

Part One

PRELIMINARY ESSAY ON CONCEPTS AND PRACTICES

I · BASIC CONCEPTS OF
CHINESE LAW

1. Scope and Significance of Chinese Law

Western scholars on China, with only a few distinguished exceptions, have until recently shown but little interest in the study of Chinese law. Today, especially in the United States, the situation is changing, but the stimulus obviously comes much more forcibly from the China of Mao Tse-tung than from the law of pre-Republican (pre-1912) China, which, especially in its formal codified aspects, is the subject of this book.[1]

Good reasons can of course be found to explain the traditional indifference. They include the lack of legal training or interest among all but a handful of earlier Western sinologists, the formidable difficulties in style and vocabulary of the Chinese legal literature, and the fact that Chinese scholars themselves usually regarded this literature as utilitarian only and hence as little worthy of study on esthetic or inspirational grounds.

Behind this last point, however, lie other more basic considerations: the fact that the written law of pre-modern China was overwhelmingly penal in emphasis, that it was limited in scope to being primarily a legal codification of the ethical norms long dominant in Chinese society, and that it was nevertheless rarely invoked to uphold these norms except when other less punitive measures had failed. Chinese traditional society, in short, was by

[1] In the pre-modern field, nonetheless, a notable contribution is T'ung-tsu Ch'ü, *Law and Society in Traditional China* (Paris and The Hague, 1961), which is a revised English version of the author's 1947 work in Chinese. The most comprehensive study of Chinese law in a Western language is Jean Escarra, *Le Droit chinois* (Peiping, 1936); for an English translation, see Gertrude R. Browne, tr., *Chinese Law* (Cambridge, Mass.: Xerox reprint, 1961). This important pioneer work is made sketchy by its broad coverage and now requires revision. For the Ch'ing dynasty (1644–1911), which is the main focus of the present book, the most important previous work is Ernest Alabaster, *Notes and Commentaries on Chinese Criminal Law* (London, 1899), on which see Chap. II, sec. 1.

no means a legally oriented society despite the fact that it produced a large and intellectually impressive body of codified law.

The penal emphasis of this law, for example, meant that matters of a civil nature were either ignored by it entirely (for example, contracts), or were given only limited treatment within its penal format (for example, property rights, inheritance, marriage). The law was only secondarily interested in defending the rights—especially the economic rights—of one individual or group against another individual or group and not at all in defending such rights against the state. What really concerned the law—though this is to be surmised rather than explicitly read in the Chinese legal literature—were all acts of moral or ritual impropriety or of criminal violence which seemed in Chinese eyes to be violations or disruptions of the total social order. The existence of the norms of propriety was intended to deter the commission of such acts, but once they occurred, the restoration of social harmony required that punishment be inflicted to exact retribution from their doer. In the final analysis, a disturbance of the social order really meant, in Chinese thinking, a violation of the total cosmic order because, according to the Chinese world-view, the spheres of man and nature were inextricably interwoven to form an unbroken continuum.[2]

For these reasons, the official law always operated in a vertical direction from the state upon the individual, rather than on a horizontal plane directly between two individuals. If a dispute involved two individuals, individual A did not bring a suit directly against individual B. Rather he lodged his complaint with the authorities, who then decided whether or not to prosecute individual B. No private legal profession existed to help individuals plead their cases, and even in the government itself, because law was only the last of several corrective agencies, officials exclusively concerned with the law operated only on the higher administrative levels. On the lowest level, that of the *hsien* (district or county), which was the level where governmental law impinged

[2] See especially M. H. van der Valk, *Interpretations of the Supreme Court at Peking, Years 1915 and 1916* (Batavia [Jakarta]: University of Indonesia Sinological Institute, 1949), pp. 20–21, and M. J. Meijer, *The Introduction of Modern Criminal Law in China* (Batavia, 1949), pp. 3–4. For the Chinese concept of cosmic harmony, see sec. 11 below, Appendix G, and Chap. VI, end of sec. 3.

most directly upon the people, its administration was conducted by the *hsien* magistrate as merely one of his several administrative functions. Although he usually lacked any formal legal training, he was obliged to act as detective, prosecutor, judge, and jury rolled into one.

Fortunately for the operation of the system, however, the magistrate was commonly assisted in his judicial work by a legal secretary who *did* possess specialized knowledge of the law, and who, on behalf of the magistrate, could prepare cases for trial, suggest appropriate sentences, or write the legal reports which went to higher governmental levels. Yet it is indicative of the Chinese attitude toward law that this secretary did not himself belong to the formal administrative system. He was merely a personal employee of the magistrate, who paid his salary out of his own private purse. Hence the secretary was not permitted to try cases himself or otherwise to take an active part in the trials. However, to avoid miscarriages of justice on this lowest administrative level, a very carefully defined system of appeals existed which automatically took all but minor cases to higher levels for final judgment—in the case of capital crimes as far upward as the emperor himself.[3]

How law in imperial China became the embodiment of the ethical norms of Confucianism will be discussed later. Here it should be stressed that in China, perhaps even more than in most other civilizations, the ordinary man's awareness and acceptance of such norms was shaped far more by the pervasive influence of custom and the usages of propriety than by any formally enacted system of law. The clan into which he was born, the guild of which he might become a member, the group of gentry elders holding informal sway in his rural community—these and other extra-legal bodies helped to smooth the inevitable frictions in

[3] See Chap. IV, sec. 1. Good accounts of judicial procedure in imperial times appear in R. H. van Gulik, tr., *T'ang-yin-pi-shih*, *"Parallel Cases from under the Pear-tree"* (Leiden, 1956), Chap. 3 of Introduction and in Sybille van der Sprenkel, *Legal Institutions in Manchu China* (London, 1962), Chap. 6. Particularly valuable for its account of the legal secretary and of the legal machinery which operated at the magistrate's level and from there took cases up to higher levels is T'ung-tsu Ch'ü, *Local Government in China under the Ch'ing* (Cambridge, Mass., 1962), Chap. 6, "Private Secretaries," and Chap. 7, "Administration of Justice."

Chinese society by inculcating moral precepts upon their members, mediating disputes, or, if need arose, imposing disciplinary sanctions and penalties.[4]

The workings of such unofficial agencies were complemented by procedures on the part of the government, procedures which, despite their official inspiration, functioned quite separately from the formal legal system.[5] These extra-legal organs and procedures, then, were what the Chinese everyman normally looked to for guidance and sanction, rather than to the formal judicial system per se. Involvement in the formal system was popularly regarded as a road to disaster and therefore to be avoided at all cost. "Win your lawsuit and lose your money," runs a Chinese proverb. Or again: "Of ten reasons by which a magistrate may decide a case, nine are unknown to the public." [6]

One might conclude that the real reason for the Western neglect of Chinese formal law is that this law is not inherently deserving of much attention. Such a conclusion, however, would be unfortunate on several counts. In the first place, law is an important touchstone for measuring any civilization, and its differing role in China as compared with its role in the West points to basic societal differences between the two civilizations which deserve detailed analysis. In the second place, the various extra-legal bodies for social control mentioned above, despite their obvious importance and the generalized remarks about them to be found in many writings, are very difficult to study with precision because of their scattered and informal mode of operation, and the fact that what they did and said was often either not written

---

[4] On extra-legal mediation organs and techniques in Ch'ing times, see the excellent summary by Jerome Alan Cohen, "Chinese Mediation on the Eve of Modernization," *California Law Review*, 54:1201–1226 (1966).

[5] These procedures, which were of a police nature (the *pao-chia* system of registration and crime-reporting), economic (the *li-chia* system for encouraging tax payment and governmental distribution of grain in times of need), and ideological (hortatory lectures on moral duties, ceremonies in honor of the aged), are described in great detail in Kung-chuan Hsiao, *Rural China, Imperial Control in the Nineteenth Century* (Seattle, 1960). They are also summarized in Dr. Hsiao's article, "Rural Control in Nineteenth Century China," *Far Eastern Quarterly*, 12:173–181 (1953).

[6] See William Scarborough, *A Collection of Chinese Proverbs*, rev. C. Wilfred Allan (Shanghai: Presbyterian Mission Press, 1926), pp. 334 and 335, as quoted in van der Sprenkel, p. 135.

down at all or, if written, not readily available in published form.[7]

The literature on formal Chinese law, by contrast, is large in quantity, fairly readily available, and covers a longer time span than that of any other present-day political entity. It includes the legal sections in various encyclopedic compilations of governmental institutions, the chapters on legal development in many of the dynastic histories,[8] several large compendia of actual law cases,[9] and above all the voluminous law codes of successive dynasties. The codes, in particular, have a continuity and authoritativeness which make them unrivaled instruments for measuring precisely, dynasty by dynasty, the shifting configurations of Chinese social and political values as officially defined. So far this challenging task has hardly been attempted.[10]

The most recent of the dynastic codes is that of the Ch'ing or Manchu dynasty (1644–1911). It was compiled in definitive form in 1740 and consists of 436 sections that contain a greater number of statutes and approximately 1,800 sub-statutes.[11] For previous dynasties there also exists a sequence of earlier codes going back to the T'ang Code of 653, in 501 articles.[12] Before this

[7] It is possible to study the rules of many large clans, however, as preserved in their genealogies. See Hu Hsien Chin, *The Common Descent Group in China and Its Function* (New York: Viking Fund, 1938); Hui-chen Wang Liu, *The Traditional Chinese Clan Rules* (Locust Valley, N.Y.: J. J. Augustin for the Association for Asian Studies, 1959); and Hui-chen Wang Liu, "An Analysis of Chinese Clan Rules: Confucian Theories in Action," in D. S. Nivison and Arthur F. Wright, eds., *Confucianism in Action* (Stanford: Stanford University Press, 1959), pp. 63–96.

[8] On both of these categories see Chap. II, sec. 1.

[9] Notably the nineteenth-century *Hsing-an hui-lan* (Conspectus of penal cases; Shanghai, ca. 1886), from which 190 of the more than 7,600 cases have been translated in this book. A much smaller compilation of 144 cases, made in 1211, has been translated in full by van Gulik.

[10] One exception is Dr. Ch'ü's *Law and Society*, which, however, may be criticized on the grounds that it unduly emphasizes the unchanging nature of these attitudes. A different approach might reveal significant, although less immediately evident, changes in attitudes.

[11] The *Ta Ch'ing lü-li* is available in two partial translations: George Thomas Staunton, tr., *Ta Tsing Leu Lee, Being the Fundamental Laws . . . of the Penal Code of China* (London, 1810), and Gui Boulais, tr., *Manuel du code chinois* (Shanghai, 1924). See the end of Chap. II below on these translations. The translation by Boulais is far more complete and therefore will be cited regularly in this book.

[12] The *T'ang lü shu-yi* (T'ang Code with commentary) is as yet untranslated. Although it is traditionally said to contain 500 articles, the actual number is 501

date, no codes survive save for scattered quotations in other works. However, a study still in progress has already yielded a wealth of information on the code and judicial procedure of the first lengthy imperial dynasty, that of Han (206 B.C–.A.D. 220).[13]

Prior to the Han and its short-lived predecessor, the Ch'in dynasty (221–207 B.C.), no centralized empire yet existed in China. At that time there were only a number of independent and mutually warring principalities. This pre-imperial age, often called the age of Chinese feudalism because of its institutional similarities to medieval Europe, is also the age that saw the formative beginnings of Chinese written law. Excluding unreliable myth and legend, the earliest datable evidence of such written law is the promulgation in 536 B.C. of certain "books of punishment" in one of these principalities (see section 4).

2. Law, Religion, and Economics

A striking feature of the early written law of several major civilizations of antiquity has been its close association with religion. Not all of these civilizations, to be sure, actually produced systems of written law. When they did so, however, they commonly signalized this achievement by attributing, at least initially, a divine origin to the law they used—an origin signifying that such law had been given or revealed to mankind by a god or gods.[14]

This belief so obviously underlies Judaic and Islamic law that for them it requires no further elaboration. It is equally apparent, however, in the world's earliest written law as known to us from

according to a personal communication from Wallace S. Johnson, Jr., of the University of Kansas, who, as this book goes to press, is preparing a translation of the first three books of the T'ang Code. However, the number 502 is given in Karl Bünger, *Quellen zur Rechtsgeschichte der T'ang-Zeit* (Peiping, 1946), p. 31. The Code has been analyzed by Ou Koei-hing, *La Peine d'après le code des T'ang* (Shanghai, 1935). For a study and partial translation of one of the codes between Ch'ing and T'ang, see Paul Ratchnevsky, tr., *Un Code des Yuan* (Paris, 1937).

[13] A. F. P. Hulsewé, *Remnants of Han Law* (Leiden, 1955), one volume so far, to be followed by a second volume. For the dynasties between Han and T'ang, see the translation and commentary by Étienne Balazs, tr., *Le Traité juridique du "Souei-chou"* (Leiden, 1954).

[14] This theme figures prominently in the excellent study by William A. Robson, *Civilisation and the Growth of Law* (New York: Macmillan, 1935).

BASIC CONCEPTS

9

Mesopotamia. On the stele bearing the famed laws of Hammurabi (ca. 1728–1686 B.C.), for example, a sculptured relief shows Hammurabi receiving from Shamash, god of justice, a divine commission for his writing of the laws. And in the prologue to the laws themselves Hammurabi tells us: "Anum [the sky-god] and Enlil [the storm-god] named me to promote the welfare of the people, me, Hammurabi, the devout, god-fearing prince, to cause justice to prevail in the land, to destroy the wicked and the evil, that the strong might not oppress the weak." [15]

In Egypt, on the other hand, no written law has as yet been found, apparently because the pharaoh, as a living god on earth, needed no law other than his own spoken utterance: "He, as a god, *was* the state . . . The customary law of the land was conceived to be the word of the pharaoh . . . The authority of codified law would have competed with the personal authority of the pharaoh." [16] And in India, too, no real equivalent of our idea of law existed in early times. The nearest approach was the concept of *dharma,* a word translatable as "law," but more properly signifying "religious law," and hence ipso facto having a divine connotation. Only later did the idea of a purely secular law appear in Kautilya's *Arthasāstra* (ca. 323 B.C.), but this development was short-lived and failed to survive the political disruption following the death of King Aśoka. Since that time, therefore, we are told that the "religious basis of law predominates through the rest of Indian history until modern times." [17]

Turning from Asia to Europe, we find Plato, in the famous opening passage of the *Laws,* making one of his protagonists unhesitatingly attribute the origin of law "to a god." [18] In Rome,

[15] See translation by Theophile J. Meek, in James B. Pritchard, ed., *Ancient Near Eastern Texts* (Princeton, N.J.: Princeton University Press, 1950), p. 164. The same idea goes back to the earliest collection of laws so far discovered, that of Ur-Nammu (ca. 2050 B.C.), the fragmentary prologue of which names Nanna, tutelary deity of the city of Ur, as the god through whose guidance Ur-Nammu "established justice in the land." See Samuel N. Kramer, "Ur-Nammu Law Code," *Orientalia,* new series, 23:40–51 (1954), quotation on p. 46.

[16] John A. Wilson, *The Burden of Egypt* (Chicago: University of Chicago Press, 1951), pp. 49–50.

[17] Daniel H. H. Ingalls, "Authority and Law in Ancient India," in *Authority and Law in the Ancient Orient* (supplement to *Journal of the American Oriental Society,* No. 17, July–Sept. 1954), pp. 34–45 (quotation on p. 43).

[18] The Athenian in the book asks his companions: "Do you attribute the origin of your legal system to a god or a man?" To which the Cretan replies:

similarly, despite its early secularization of law, we find Cicero purporting to quote "the opinion of the wisest men of his day" to the effect that "Law is not the product of human thought, nor is it any enactment of peoples, but something which rules the whole universe . . . Law is the primal and ultimate mind of God." [19] Even in eighteenth-century England, indeed, after centuries of experience with a secularly based common law, we find a similar conception persisting in legal theory. Thus we are told concerning Sir William Blackstone, author of the famous *Commentaries* (1765), that he "regarded divine law as the corner-stone of the whole [legal] edifice," "declared that divine law had been specifically revealed to men through inspired writings," and "sought to make secular law approximate to the dictates of God and of nature." [20]

The contrast of the Chinese attitude to the belief in a divine origin of the law is indeed striking, for in China no one at any time has ever hinted that any kind of written law—even the best written law—could have had a divine origin.

Another point worthy of attention is the possible relationship of law to economic growth in certain civilizations. Mesopotamia, for example, early experienced a very considerable commercial development, reflections of which appear conspicuously in the Hammurabi code. Mesopotamian civilization, in the words of a specialist, was characterized by "the ubiquitous recognition of private property," and a concern for "the rights of the individual in relation to society and the cosmos." [21] The guess may be hazarded that in part, at least, Mesopotamian law may have arisen in response to this insistence upon private property and individual rights.

Here again the contrast with China is instructive. For in China

---

"To a god; undoubtedly we ascribe our laws to Zeus, while in Sparta, the home of our friend here, I believe Apollo is regarded as the first law-giver." Quoted in J. Walter Jones, *The Law and Legal Theory of the Greeks* (Oxford: Clarendon Press, 1956), p. 95; see also Robson, p. 32.

[19] Cicero, *De Legibus*, II, iv; tr. Clinton Walker Keyes, *De Legibus* (Loeb Classical Library; Cambridge, Mass., and London, 1948 reprint), p. 381. Also paraphrased in Robson, p. 3.

[20] Robson, pp. 47–48, summarizing the ideas of Blackstone as expressed in the Introduction to his *Commentaries on the Laws of England*.

[21] See E. A. Speiser, "Early Law and Civilization," *Canadian Bar Review* (October 1953), pp. 863–877 (quotations on pp. 873 and 875).

the initial stimulus for law was no more economic than it was religious. Economic growth, to be sure, no doubt played a role in transforming the society of feudal China to the point where it could no longer get along without a written law. When this law appeared, however, it was used neither to uphold traditional religious values nor to protect private property. Rather, its primary purpose was political: that of imposing tighter political controls upon a society which was then losing its old cultural values and being drawn by inexorable new forces along the road leading eventually to universal empire.

3. Ancient Chinese Theories of the Origin of Law

Before entering upon this topic, a brief discussion of terms is necessary. By far the most important word in the Chinese legal vocabulary is *fa*. *Fa* is the usual generic term for positive or written law as an abstraction ("law" or "*the* law"), but it may also be used to mean separate "laws." The word was already in common use before its appearance in legal contexts. Its root meaning is that of a model, pattern, or standard; hence of a method or procedure to be followed. From this root meaning comes the notion, basic in Chinese legal thinking, that *fa* is a model or standard imposed by superior authority, to which the people must conform.

Another important word, perhaps even more common than *fa* in early legal references, is *hsing*, signifying "punishment" (or "punishments"), but more specifically "corporal punishment." That the latter is its primary meaning is indicated, among other things, by the inclusion in the written character for *hsing* of the graph meaning "knife." There is every reason to believe that such punishments as nose-cutting, leg-cutting, castration, and the like were current in China well before the enactment of any systems of written law (*fa*). Once written law came into existence, however, the meaning of *hsing* was extended to include not only the punishments per se, but also the written prohibitions whose violation would result in these punishments. In this important secondary usage, therefore, *hsing* may be fairly understood in the sense of "penal law" (or "laws"). The frequency of its occurrence in the early legal passages—both alone and as an alternative for *fa*—is indicative of the antiquity of the Chinese view which sees written law, *fa*, as signifying primarily penal law, *hsing*. Until as recently as the administrative reforms of 1906, this idea was perpetuated in the name of the highest governmental legal organ, the Hsing Pu or Board or Ministry of Punishments.

A third term, *lü*, though very important in the law codes of imperial times (221 B.C. onward), appears only rarely in a legal sense in earlier texts. As used in these codes, it is the technical designation for the major articles into which the codes are divided, and as such may be translated as "statute." It can also, however, refer to the entire body of such statutes as a collective entity, in which case it may conveniently, though a little loosely, be rendered as "code." Aside from its legal significance, *lü* is also the technical designation for the individual "pitch-pipes" (*lü*), twelve in number and of graduated lengths, which were the basis for the Chinese twelve-tone scale. The question of how, from this meaning, *lü* came to acquire its legal connotation, is a very moot one.[22]

With these definitions behind us, let us now see how the ancient Chinese viewed the origins of law. A notable feature of Chinese historical and philosophical thinking, apparent already in early times, is its strongly secular tone. In general, it prefers to explain human events in terms of the rational (or what seems to it to be the rational) than in terms of the supernatural. A good example is the fate suffered by Chinese mythology already in the early literature: in case after case, as we read this literature, the fragmentary evidence suggests that what at one time must have been the gods, demigods, or monsters of full-fledged myth have since become "euhemerized" or "historicized" into the denatured sage–kings, heroes, or rebels of pseudohistory.[23]

When we turn to the legal sphere, therefore, it should not

---

[22] Answers are suggested by Hulsewé, *Remnants of Han Law*, I, 30–31, and by Joseph Needham, *Science and Civilisation in China* (London and New York, 1956), II, 229 and 550–552; Needham discusses (pp. 229, 544 ff., and elsewhere) the various meanings of *fa* at considerable length. See also on *lü* Chap. II below, sec. 3.

[23] See D. Bodde, "Myths of Ancient China," in Samuel N. Kramer, ed., *Mythologies of the Ancient World* (New York: Doubleday Anchor Books, and Chicago: Quadrangle Books, 1961), pp. 369–408, esp. 372–376.

surprise us that here too the atmosphere is secular. What is really arresting, however, especially when we remember the honored status of law in other civilizations, is the overt hostility with which its appearance is initially greeted in China—seemingly not only as a violation of human morality, but perhaps even of the total cosmic order.[24]

An excellent example of this attitude is a story—apparently the historicized fragment of what was once a longer myth—providing probably the earliest explanation for the origin of *fa*, written law. The story appears in a short text entitled *Lü hsing* (Punishments of Lü), itself a section of the important classic known as the *Shu ching* or *Documents Classic*, where it is placed in the mouth of a king who reigned around 950 B.C. Its actual date of composition must surely be several centuries later, but just how much later is hard to say with exactness. However, the fact that it is quoted and mentioned by name in another text of the fourth century B.C. provides us with at least a *terminus ante quem*.[25]

The remarkable feature of this story is that it attributes the invention of *fa* neither to a Chinese sage–king nor even to a Chinese at all, but rather to a "barbarian" people, the Miao, alleged to have flourished during the reign of the (legendary) sage Shun (traditionally twenty-third century B.C.). Thus the key sentence tells us: "The Miao people made no use of spiritual cultivation, but controlled by means of punishments (*hsing*), creating the five oppressive punishments, which they called law (*fa*)." Then the text goes on to say that many innocent people

[24] The relationship of Chinese law to the cosmic order will be discussed further in Chap. I, sec. 11, in Chap. VI, end of sec. 3, and in Appendix G. Here it should be mentioned that in purportedly early literature there appears a well-known tradition about a legendary administrator of justice, Kao Yao, which at first sight seems to run counter to the hostile attitude just mentioned. Closer examination, however, shows that the relationship of this tradition to actual written law is a dubious one. See Appendix F, "Kao Yao and Early Chinese Law."

[25] For the translation of the following story, which has been used here with modifications, see Bernhard Karlgren, tr., "The Book of Documents," *Bulletin of the Museum of Far Eastern Antiquities* (Stockholm, 1950), 22:74. For another translation, see James Legge, tr., *The Chinese Classics*, 5 vols. (Hong Kong, 1960), III, 591–593. The work in which the *Lü hsing* is later quoted is the *Mo-tzu* (compiled by followers of the philosopher of the same name, who lived sometime between 479 and 381 B.C.); Y. P. Mei, tr., *The Ethical and Political Works of Motse* (London: Arthur Probsthain, 1929), pp. 45–46, 51, and esp. p. 64 (quoting the same sentence which appears below).

were executed by the Miao, who were the first to administer such punishments as castration or amputation of the nose or legs. Shang Ti or the "Lord on High" (the supreme god of the ancient Chinese), seeing the resulting disorder among the people, felt pity for the innocent and hence exterminated the Miao, so that they had no descendants.[26]

The abhorrence of law expressed in this story no doubt reflects a period in legal development (sixth or fifth century B.C.) when written law was still a novelty and hence viewed with suspicion. In later centuries, when law became more prevalent and the need for its existence became increasingly recognized, various non-mythological and soberly "sociological" explanations of its origin appeared. Although their attitude toward law was no longer hostile, they all agreed with the unknown author of the Miao legend in explaining the origin of law in strictly secular terms. The following are three representative examples, the first of which dates from the pre-imperial age (third century B.C.), and the other two from the Han empire (second century B.C. and first century A.D., respectively):

In the days of antiquity, before the time when there were rulers and subjects, superiors and inferiors, the people were disorderly and badly governed. Hence the sages made a division between the noble and the humble, regulated rank and division, and established names and appellations, in order to distinguish the ideas of ruler and subject, of superior and inferior . . . As the people were numerous and wickedness and depravity arose among them, they [the sages] therefore established laws (*fa*) and controls and created weights and measures, in order thereby to prevent these things.[27]

Law (*fa*) has its origin in social rightness (*yi*). Social rightness has its origin in what is fitting for the many. What is fitting for the many is what accords with the minds of men. Herein is the essence of good government . . . Law is not something sent down by Heaven, nor is it

---

[26] Further fragments of this myth, as found in this and other texts, state that the Lord on High then separated Heaven from Earth so that people could no longer pass from one to the other; also that the Miao, instead of being exterminated, were banished to the extreme northwestern corner of the world, where they continued to exist as a race of winged beings who, despite their wings, were unable to fly. See Bodde, "Myths of Ancient China," pp. 389–394.

[27] *Shang chün shu*, Chap. 23 (a third century B.C. work belonging to the Legalist school); tr. J. J. L. Duyvendak, *The Book of Lord Shang* (London, 1928), pp. 314–315, slightly modified here by D. Bodde.

something engendered by Earth. It springs from the midst of men themselves, and by being brought back [to men] it corrects itself.[28]

The sages, being enlightened and wise by nature, inevitably penetrated the mind of Heaven and Earth. They shaped the rules of proper behavior (*li*), created teachings, established laws (*fa*), and instituted punishments (*hsing*), always acting in accordance with the feelings of the people and patterning and modeling themselves on Heaven and Earth.[29]

4. The Earliest Chinese "Code"

From myth and social theory we should now turn to the concrete beginnings of Chinese written law as recorded in authentic history. The Chou dynasty (ca. 1027–221 B.C.) functioned during its early centuries under a political system which has often been compared to European feudalism. At the top were the Chou kings, who exercised nominal sovereignty over the entire Chinese cultural world. Under them were vassal lords who held as fiefs from the Chou house a multitude of small principalities, which were subdivided in turn into the estates of subordinate lords and officials. At the bottom of the pyramid came the peasant serfs, hereditarily attached to these estates. In the course of time, however, the vassal principalities broke away from the Chou overlordship and became completely independent states. By the sixth century B.C., a combination of social, political, economic, and technological forces was bringing about an accelerating dissolution of the old order.

The new forces included, among others: new agricultural techniques which made increases in population possible; the

[28] *Huai-nan-tzu* (The Master of Huai-nan), ed. Liu Wen-tien, *Huai-nan hung-lieh chi-chieh* (Huai-nan's Great and Illustrious [Composition] with Collected Commentaries; Shanghai, 1933), 9:20. This work is of an eclectic philosophical nature and was composed by scholars attached to the court of Liu An, Prince of Huai-nan (died 122 B.C.). The chapter here quoted represents the Legalist school.

[29] Pan Ku, *Han shu* (History of the [Former] Han dynasty, ca. A.D. 80), Chap. 23, ("Treatise on Punishments and Law"); tr. Hulsewé, *Remnants of Han Law*, I, 321–322, slightly modified here by D. Bodde. Although the sages are here said to have "penetrated the mind of Heaven and Earth," they surely did so through their own intelligence and not with the aid of divine revelation. Chinese thinking regularly attributes the creation of civilization to the intelligence of the ancient sages but never suggests that they received divine revelation.

growth of commerce and rise of a money economy; the buying and selling of land and partial freeing of the peasants from their former serfdom; a growing administrative complexity in the state governments; and the appearance of competing schools of philosophy and politics. The final centuries of the Chou dynasty, appropriately known as the Period of the Warring States (403–221 B.C.), saw increasingly bitter warfare between the few large states still surviving, till one of them, the state of Ch'in, succeeded in swallowing up its rivals one by one, and in 221 B.C. finally created the first centralized empire in Chinese history.[30]

Such is the background of interrelated changes against which should be viewed the creation of the first "codes" of written law in the late sixth century B.C. The earliest reliably known to us is the "books of punishment" (hsing shu) which Tzu-ch'an, prime minister of the state of Cheng, ordered to be inscribed in 536 B.C. on a set of bronze tripod vessels. His action was followed by similar steps in this and other states in 513, 501, and later. Although the texts of these "codes" have in every case been lost, we may judge of the opposition they aroused from the famed letter of protest which the high dignitary of a neighboring state, Shu-hsiang, sent to Tzu-ch'an upon the promulgation of the Cheng laws: [31]

Originally, sir, I had hope in you, but now that is all over. Anciently, the early kings conducted their administration by deliberating on matters [as they arose]; they did not put their punishments and penalties [into writing], fearing that this would create a contentiousness among the people which could not be checked. Therefore they used the principle of social rightness (yi) to keep the people in bounds, held them together through their administrative procedures, activated for them the accepted ways of behavior (li), maintained good faith (hsin) toward them, and presented them with [examples of] benevolence (jen) . . .

But when the people know what the penalties are, they lose their fear of authority and acquire a contentiousness which causes them to

[30] For a survey of these developments, see D. Bodde, "Feudalism in China," in Rushton Coulborn, ed., Feudalism in History (Princeton, N.J.: Princeton University Press, 1956), pp. 49–92.

[31] The letter is preserved in the Tso chuan history (probably compiled mostly in the third century B.C. from earlier records); tr. Legge, The Chinese Classics, V, 609, modified here by D. Bodde. For a rather similar criticism by Confucius of the promulgation of penal laws in the state of Chin in 513 B.C., see ibid., p. 732.

make their appeal to the written words [of the penal laws], on the chance that this will bring them success [in court cases] . . . Today, sir, as prime minister of the state of Cheng, you have built dikes and canals, set up an administration which evokes criticism, and cast [bronze vessels inscribed with] books of punishment. Is it not going to be difficult to bring tranquility to the people in this way? . . . As soon as the people know the grounds on which to conduct disputation, they will reject the [unwritten] accepted ways of behavior (*li*) and make their appeal to the written word, arguing to the last over the tip of an awl or knife. Disorderly litigations will multiply and bribery will become current. By the end of your era, Cheng will be ruined. I have heard it said that a state which is about to perish is sure to have many governmental regulations.

To this criticism, Tzu-ch'an's brief reply was polite but uncompromising:

As to your statements, sir, I have neither the talents nor ability to act for posterity. My object is to save the present age. Though I cannot accept your instructions, dare I forget your great kindness?

This letter is eloquent testimony to the unchanging spirit of conservatism throughout the ages. Shu-hsiang's criticisms of dike and canal building and of bigness in government are recognizably those of any conservative legislator today whenever he attacks public spending and demands a balanced budget. What is uniquely Chinese and therefore most significant about the letter, however, is its insistence upon the moral and political dangers involved in the public promulgation of legal norms. This view of law seems to have no real parallel in any other civilization.

It should not surprise us that Shu-hsiang's letter is strongly Confucian in tone, notably in its use of such Confucian terms as *yi, li, hsin* and *jen*. For though Confucius was but fifteen when the letter was written, these terms and the ideas they connoted were surely already "in the air" when he was young, and were not complete innovations with himself.

5. Confucians and Legalists

Although Shu-hsiang himself cannot be formally counted a Confucian, his letter nevertheless epitomizes what may be termed the "purist" Confucian view of law. As we shall see shortly, the

Confucians were staunch upholders of the traditional "feudal" scale of values. Hence it is natural that they should be bitterly hostile to the new law, especially in its early stages. Later, however, as it became increasingly apparent that law had come to stay, the Confucians softened their attitude to the point where they accepted law—although grudgingly—as a necessary evil. Even then, however, they remained Confucian in their insistence that the public enacting of law is not necessary in the ideal state, and that even in the inferior administrations of their own times, government by law should always be kept secondary to government by moral precept and example.[32]

Opposed to the Confucians were men who, because of their ardent advocacy of law, eventually came to be known as the Legalists or School of Law (fa chia). Most of them were less theoretical thinkers than tough-minded men of affairs who, as administrators, diplomats, and political economists, sought employment from whatever state would use their services. Their aim was direct and simple: to create a political and military apparatus powerful enough to suppress feudal privilege at home, expand the state's territories abroad, and eventually weld all the rival kingdoms into a single empire. Toward this goal they were ready to use every political, military, economic and diplomatic technique at their disposal. Their insistence on law, therefore, was motivated by no concern for "human rights," but simply by the realization that law was essential for effectively controlling the growing populations under their jurisdiction. In thinking and techniques they were genuine totalitarians, concerned with men in the mass, in contrast to the Confucians, for whom individual, family, or local community were of paramount importance. Yet it would be unfair to regard them merely as unscrupulous power-hungry politicians, for they sincerely believed that only through total methods could eventual peace and unity be brought to their war-torn world. If asked why they did what they did, they would no doubt have echoed Tzu-ch'an's dictum: "My object is to save the present age."

[32] This shift in Confucian attitude, which it is easy to overlook, is rightly stressed by T'ung-tsu Ch'ü, Law and Society, Chap. 6, sec. 3, "The Confucianization of Law," pp. 267 ff.

6. Confucian Views of *Li* and Law

As against the Legalists' *fa* or law, the key Confucian term is *li*. This word has an extraordinarily wide range of meanings. In its narrowest (and probably original) sense, it denotes the correct performance of all kinds of religious ritual: sacrificing to the ancestors at the right time and place and with the proper deportment and attitude is *li;* so is the proper performance of divination. In this sense *li* is often translated as ritual or rites. In a broader sense, however, *li* covers the entire gamut of ceremonial or polite behavior, secular as well as religious. There are numerous rules of *li* for all customary situations involving social relationships, such as receiving a guest, acquiring a wife, going into battle, and the many other varied duties and activities of polite society. In this sense, *li* is often translated as ceremonial, politeness, etiquette, or rules of proper conduct. Finally, *li* in its broadest sense is a designation for all the institutions and relationships, both political and social, which make for harmonious living in a Confucian society. The *li*, in short, constitute both the concrete institutions and the accepted modes of behavior in a civilized state.

The Confucians believed that the *li* had been created by the ancient sages, and that the disorder of their own age resulted from men's failure to understand or live according to these *li*. A prime Confucian duty, therefore, was to study and interpret the *li* as handed down from antiquity so as to make them meaningful for the present day. This idea led the Confucians to prepare several written compilations of *li* which, however, did not assume final form until near the end of the feudal age and during the early part of the age of empire. During most of the Chou dynasty, consequently, the *li* were transmitted in unwritten form only. At the same time, their large number, complexity, and refinement meant that they were largely an upper-class monopoly. Indeed, what most readily distinguished the Confucian ideal gentleman (the *chün-tzu* or Superior Man) from ordinary men was his mastery of the *li*.

On the other hand, the Confucians believed that underlying the minutiae of the specific rules of *li* are to be found certain broad moral principles which give the *li* their validity because they are rooted in innate human feeling; in other words, they represent what men in general instinctively feel to be right. It is this interpretation of *li* which has caused some modern scholars to suggest that a comparison may be made between Confucian *li* and the Western concept of natural law in apposition to a comparison between Legalist *fa* and Western positive law.[33]

Finally, and this point is important, the early *li* were the product of a society in which hierarchical difference was emphasized. That is to say, the *li* prescribed sharply differing patterns of behavior according to a person's age and rank both within his family and in society at large (one pattern when acting toward a superior, another toward an inferior, still a third toward an equal). This idea of hierarchical difference, with resulting differences in behavior and privilege, has remained alive in Confucianism throughout imperial times, despite the disappearance of the pre-imperial feudal society that first gave it birth.[34]

Following is a summary of the main Confucian argument with the Legalists from the point of view of a "purist" Confucian:

1. Man is by nature good (Mencius, 371?–289? B.C.), or at least is a rational being capable of learning goodness (Hsün Tzu, ca. 298–ca. 238 B.C.). It is by inculcating the *li* that society shapes the individual into a socially acceptable human being. The *li* are thus preventive in that they turn the individual away from evil before he has the chance of committing it, whereas law (*fa*) is punitive in that it only comes into action to punish the individual for evil already committed.

2. A government based on virtue can truly win the hearts of men; one based on force can only gain their outward submission. The *li* are suasive and hence the instrument of a virtuous government; laws are compulsive and hence the instrument of a tyrannical government.

3. The *li* derive their universal validity from the fact that they were created by the intelligent sages of antiquity in conformity

[33] See especially Needham, II, 519, 530–532, 544 ff.
[34] This point is stressed by T'ung-tsu Ch'ü, *Law and Society*, in his excellent discussion of *li* on p. 230, note 11. See also his entire Chap. 6, "The Confucian School and the Legal School."

with human nature and with the cosmic order. Law has no moral validity because it is merely the ad hoc creation of modern men who wish by means of it to generate political power.

4. The five major relationships of Confucianism—those of father and son, ruler and subject, husband and wife, elder and younger brother, friend and friend—are instinctive to man and essential for a stable social order. The *li* reinforce these and similar relationships by prescribing modes of behavior differing according to status, whereas law obliterates the relationships by imposing a forced uniformity.

5. The *li* (meaning at this point primarily rites and ceremony) give poetry and beauty to life. They provide channels for the expression of human emotion in ways that are socially acceptable. Law, on the contrary, is mechanistic and devoid of emotional content.

6. A government based on *li* functions harmoniously because the *li*, being unwritten, can be flexibly interpreted to meet the exigencies of any particular situation. A government based on law creates contention because its people, knowing in advance what the written law is, can find means to circumvent it, and will rest their sophistical arguments on the letter rather than the spirit of the law.

7. Laws are no better than the men who create and execute them. The moral training of the ruler and his officials counts for more than the devising of clever legal machinery.

To give the flavor of the Confucian spokesmen themselves, the following are offered as a few representative quotations. Included, however, are two of non-Confucian origin, illustrative of the fact that the Confucian distrust of law was shared by other schools of thought, though sometimes for different reasons: [35]

In hearing cases I am as good as anyone else, but what is really needed is to bring about that there are no cases! [36]

Lead the people by regulations, keep them in order by punishments (*hsing*), and they will flee from you and lose all self-respect. But lead

---

[35] For another list of such quotations, see Balazs, Appendix 9.
[36] Confucius (551–479 B.C.), as quoted in the *Analects*, XII, 13.

them by virtue and keep them in order by established morality (li),
and they will keep their self-respect and come to you.[37]

The more laws (fa) and ordinances (ling) are promulgated, the
more thieves and robbers there will be.[38]

Goodness alone [without law] does not suffice for handling government. Law (fa) alone [without goodness] cannot succeed in operating
of itself.[39]

To have good laws (fa) and yet experience disorder—examples of
this have indeed existed. But to have a Superior Man (chün-tzu) and
yet experience disorder—this is something which from antiquity until
today has never been heard of.[40]

Laws (fa) cannot stand alone, and analogies cannot act of themselves. When they have the proper man, they survive; when they lack
the proper man, they disappear. Law is the basis of good government,
but the Superior Man (chün-tzu) is the origin of the law. Therefore
when there is a Superior Man, the laws, though they may be numerically reduced, succeed in being all-pervading. When there is no Superior Man, the laws, though they may be all-embracing, lose their power
of orderly enforcement, are unable to respond to the changes of affairs,
and suffice only to bring confusion.[41]

The Legalists (fa chia) make no distinction between kindred and
strangers, nor do they differentiate the noble from the humble. All such
are judged by them as one before the law (fa), thereby sundering the
kindliness expressed in affection toward kindred and respect toward
the honorable. Their program might perhaps be followed a single time,
but it is not one to be used for long. Hence I say of them that they are
stern and deficient in kindliness.[42]

---

[37] Confucius, in Analects, II, 3.

[38] Lao-tzu, Chap. 57. Although Lao Tzu is traditionally said to have been an
elder contemporary of Confucius, most scholars today believe that the book
bearing his name (also known as the Tao-te ching) dates from the late fourth
or early third century B.C.

[39] Mencius (ca. 371–289 B.C.), in the work bearing his name, IVa, 1, where
he quotes this as a saying of his time. This and the following passages belong to
an age when law was coming into wider use. Although they grudgingly accept
it as inevitable, they emphasize its secondary role in the government of the
Confucian ruler.

[40] Hsün Tzu (ca. 298–238 B.C.), Hsün-tzu, Chap. 9; tr. H. H. Dubs, The Works
of Hsüntze (London: Arthur Probsthain, 1928), p. 123, modified here by D.
Bodde. This passage is repeated in Chap. 14 (not translated by Dubs).

[41] Hsün-tzu, beginning of Chap. 12 (not translated by Dubs).

[42] Ssu-ma T'an (d. 110 B.C.) and Ssu-ma Ch'ien (ca. 145–86 B.C.), Shih chi
(Records of the historian), Chap. 130; tr. Burton Watson, Ssu-ma Ch'ien, Grand
Historian of China (New York: Columbia University Press, 1958), p. 46, modified here by D. Bodde. This translated item appears in the essay on the six
schools of philosophy by Ssu-ma T'an in this great history begun by himself and
completed by his son, Ssu-ma Ch'ien. Ssu-ma T'an, though something of an
eclectic, was more inclined toward Taoism than Confucianism.

A good government is one that takes benevolence (*jen*) and social rightness (*yi*) as its basic roots, and laws (*fa*) and regulations (*tu*) as its lesser twigs . . . He who gives priority to the roots, but only secondary place to the twigs, is termed a Superior Man (*chün-tzu*), whereas he who lets his concern for the twigs result in damage to the roots is termed a petty man (*hsiao jen*) . . . To ignore cultivation of the roots while devoting effort to the twigs is to neglect the trunk while giving water to the branches. Law, moreover, has its birth in the upholding of benevolence and social rightness, so that to lay great weight on law while discarding social rightness is to value one's cap and shoes while forgetting one's head and feet.[43]

The rules of polite behavior (*li*) do not reach down to the common people; the punishments (*hsing*) do not reach up to the great dignitaries.[44]

7. The Legalists and Law

The main arguments of the Legalist position are as follows:

1. Although a very few persons may be found who are naturally altruistic, the great majority of men act only out of self-interest. Therefore, stern punishments are necessary. Law is concerned only with the many who are selfish, not with the insignificant few who are good.

2. A government, if it is to be strong, must destroy factionalism and privilege. Hence it is imperative for it to publicize its laws to all and to apply them impartially to high and low alike, irrespective of relationship or rank.

3. Law is the basis of stable government because, being fixed and known to all, it provides an exact instrument with which to measure individual conduct. A government based on *li* cannot do this, since the *li* are unwritten, particularistic, and subject to arbitrary interpretation.

---

[43] *Huai-nan-tzu*, 20:21b–22. The chapter is Confucian.

[44] *Li chi* (Record of the *Li*), Chap. 1; tr. James Legge, in F. Max Müller, *Sacred Books of the East* (Oxford: Clarendon Press, 1885), XXVII, 90, slightly modified here by D. Bodde. This best known of the above mentioned Confucian compilations of *li* did not assume its final form until the first century B.C. but is based upon earlier materials. The statement made here, that the officialdom (to which the Confucians themselves belonged) is not subject to the penalties of the commoners, was to assume key importance, as we shall see, in imperial Chinese law.

4. A vital principle for reducing particularism and thereby strengthening the state is that of group responsibility. Let the population be grouped into units of five or ten families each, and within each such unit let every individual be equally responsible for the wrongdoing of every other individual, and equally subject to punishment if he fails to inform the authorities of such wrongdoing.

5. Because history changes, human institutions must change accordingly. In antiquity people were few and life was easy, but today the growth of population has resulted in a sharpening struggle for existence. Hence, the *li* of the ancients no longer fit modern conditions and should be replaced by a system of law. Law should certainly not be changed arbitrarily; yet if it is to retain its vitality it should equally certainly be kept ever responsive to the shifting needs of its time.

6. A state that is strong is one that maintains a single standard of morality and thought for its people. All private standards must be suppressed if they do not agree with the public standard as prescribed by law.

7. Men, being essentially selfish, cannot be induced merely by moral suasion to act altruistically. Only by playing on their own self-interest can the state induce them to do what it desires. Hence the wise ruler establishes a system of rewards and punishments in such a way that citizens—especially officials holding important positions—are rewarded if their performance accords exactly with the specific responsibilities attached to their position but punished when this performance either falls short or exceeds these specified responsibilities.

8. The importance of individual capabilities in government is lessened when there is good legal machinery. Thus even a mediocre ruler, provided he keeps to his laws, can have a good administration.

9. Laws that are sufficiently stringent will no longer have to be applied because their mere existence will be enough to deter wrongdoing. Thus harsh laws, though painful in their immediate effects, lead in the long run to an actual reduction of government and to a society free from conflict and oppression.

That the foregoing summary represents the Legalist position is supported by the following quotations:

For governing the people there is no permanent principle save that it is the laws (*fa*) and nothing else that determine the government. Let the laws roll with the times and there will be good government. Let the government accord with the age and there will be great achievement . . . But let the times shift without any alteration in the laws and there will be disorder. Let human capabilities multiply without any modification in the prohibitions and there will be territorial dismemberment. This is why, in the sage's governing of men, the laws shift with the times and the prohibitions vary with the capabilities.[45]

If the law (*fa*) is not uniform, it will be inauspicious for the holder of the state . . . Therefore it is said that the law must be kept uniform. It is out of this that preservation or destruction, order or disorder, develop, and this it is that the sage–ruler uses as the great standard for the world . . . All beings and affairs, if not within the scope of the law, cannot operate . . . When ruler and minister, superior and inferior, noble and humble, all obey the law, this is called great good government.[46]

What are mutually incompatible should not coexist. To reward those who kill the enemy, yet at the same time praise acts of mercy and benevolence; to honor those who capture cities, yet at the same time believe in the doctrine of universal love; to improve arms and armies as preparation against emergency, yet at the same time admire the flourishes of the officials at the court; to depend on agriculture to enrich the nation, yet at the same time encourage men of letters: . . . strong government will not thus be gained. The state in times of peace feeds the scholars and cavaliers, but when difficulty arises it makes use of its soldiers. Those whom it benefits are not those whom it uses, and those whom it uses are not those whom it benefits . . . What is today called wisdom consists of subtle and speculative theories which even the wisest have difficulty in understanding . . . Now in ordering current affairs, when the most urgent needs are not met, one should not con-

[45] Han Fei Tzu (d. 233 B.C.; chief theoretician of the Legalist school), *Han Fei-tzu*, Chap. 54; tr. W. K. Liao, *The Complete Works of Han Fei Tzu*, 2 vols. (London, 1939–59), II, 328, modified here by D. Bodde.

[46] *Kuan-tzu*, Chap. 45; tr. D. Bodde, in Fung Yu-lan, *A History of Chinese Philosophy*, 2 vols. (Princeton, N.J.: Princeton University Press, 1952–53), I, 322, with slight changes here by D. Bodde. The *Kuan-tzu*, although traditionally ascribed to the statesman Kuan Chung (d. 645 B.C.), is actually an eclectic work by anonymous writers. This Legalist chapter probably dates from the third century B.C.

cern oneself with what is of no immediate bearing . . . Therefore subtle and speculative theories are no business of the people.[47]

In his rule of a state, the sage does not rely on men doing good of themselves, but uses them in such a way that they can do no wrong. Within the frontiers, those who can be relied on to do good of themselves are not enough to be counted in tens, whereas if men be used so as to do no wrong, the entire state may be equably administered. He who rules makes use of the many while disregarding the few, and hence he concerns himself not with virtue but with law (*fa*).[48]

When punishments are heavy, the people dare not transgress, and therefore there will be no punishments.[49]

When a ruler wishes to prevent wickedness, he examines into the correspondence between performance and title, words and work. When a minister makes claims, the ruler gives him work according to what he has claimed, but holds him wholly responsible for accomplishment corresponding to this work. When the accomplishment corresponds to the work, and the work corresponds to what the man has claimed he could do, he is rewarded. If the accomplishment does not correspond to the work, nor the work correspond to what the man has claimed for himself, he is punished. Thus when ministers have made great claims while their actual accomplishment is small, they are punished. This is not punishment because of the smallness of the accomplishment, but because the accomplishment is not equal to the name of it. And when ministers have made small claims while the actual accomplishment is great, they are also punished. This is not because no pleasure is taken in the larger accomplishment, but because it is not in accord with the name given to it.[50]

In governing a state, the regulating of clear laws (*fa*) and establishing of severe punishments (*hsing*) are done in order to save the masses of the living from disorder, to get rid of calamities in the world, to insure that the strong do not override the weak and the many do not oppress the few, that the aged may complete their years and the young and orphaned may attain maturity, that the border regions not be invaded, that ruler and minister have mutual regard for each other and father and son mutually support one another, and that there be none of

[47] *Han Fei-tzu,* Chap. 49; tr. Liao, II, 287–288, modified here by D. Bodde.
[48] *Han Fei-tzu,* Chap. 50; tr. Liao, II, 306–307, modified here by D. Bodde.
[49] *Shang chün shu,* Chap. 18; tr. Duyvendak, p. 288. Although it is attributed to the Legalist statesman Shang Yang (died 338 B.C.), it is actually a composite work by anonymous Legalists, mostly of the third century B.C.
[50] *Han Fei-tzu,* Chap. 7; tr. Liao, I, 48–49, modified here by D. Bodde. For the rendition in the first sentence of the important Legalist term *hsing-ming* (punishment and name) as "performance and title," see H. G. Creel, "The Meaning of *Hsing Ming,*" in Soren Egerod and Else Glahn, eds., *Studia Serica Bernhard Karlgren Dedicata* (Copenhagen, 1959), pp. 199–211, esp. p. 205.

the calamities of death, destruction, bonds and captivity. Such indeed is the height of achievement.[51]

8. Legalist Triumph but Confucianization of Law

A reading of the Confucian and Legalist platforms should be enough to tell us what happened. The dynamic and ruthlessly efficient program of the Legalists, as adopted in Ch'in, helped that state to triumph successively over its rivals and in 221 B.C. to found the first universal Chinese empire. Under the new regime the nobles and officials of the former states were taken away from their territories and stripped of power. Their place was taken by a centrally appointed, nonhereditary, salaried bureaucracy which was to be the model for all dynastic governments from that time onward until the founding of the Republic in 1912. The Legalist law of Ch'in became the law of the entire empire. Finally, in 213 B.C., the Legalist program reached its logical climax with the notorious "Burning of the Books," expressly ordered by the government to destroy the classical texts of antiquity, the writings of the non-Legalist schools of thought, and the historical records of former states other than Ch'in.

Yet the Legalist triumph was amazingly short-lived. In 210 B.C. the founder of the Ch'in empire died, and within two years his empire dissolved into rebellion and disorder. Out of the subsequent civil war arose a new empire, that of Han (206 B.C.–A.D. 220), under which the Ch'in bureaucratic government was reestablished and elaborated. At the same time, however, in one of the amazing reversals of history, Confucianism replaced Legalism as the dominant ideology. Already by 100 B.C. Confucianism was beginning to gain recognition as the orthodoxy of the state, whereas Legalism was disappearing for all time as a separate school.

However, the Confucianism which triumphed in Han times was a highly eclectic thought system—one that borrowed extensively from its philosophical rivals. Because these rivals included Legalism, the eclipse of Legalism as a recognized school

[51] *Han Fei-tzu*, Chap. 14, tr. Liao, I, 124, modified here by D. Bodde.

by no means meant the complete disappearance of Legalist ideas and practices. On the contrary, Legalism continued to influence the political and economic thinking of Han and later times, probably a good deal more than has been traditionally supposed. Such economic policies, for example, as the "ever-normal granary," various government efforts to equalize private holdings of land, or governmental monopolies of salt, iron, and other products, all probably owe as much or more to Legalism than they do to early Confucianism. Recent study shows that the same may even be true of what has traditionally been thought to be a peculiarly Confucian institution: the civil service examination system used in imperial times to recruit government personnel on the basis of intellect rather than birth.[52]

It would be strange, therefore, if Legalism did not leave a lasting mark on law. Its influence probably explains, for example, the continuing penal emphasis found in all the imperial codes, and the resulting fact that their treatment even of administrative and other noncriminal matters usually follows a standard formula: "Anyone who does x is to receive punishment y." [53] Or again, the background of Legalism probably explains certain important features of imperial judicial procedure: the non-existence of private lawyers; the assumption (nowhere explicitly stated but everywhere implied in the treatment of defendants) that a suspect must be guilty unless and until he is proven innocent; [54] or the legal use of torture (within certain specified limits) for extracting confession from suspects who stubbornly refuse to admit guilt despite seemingly convincing evidence against them. Still another idea which probably owes much to Legalism is that of group responsibility (especially conspicuous

---

[52] See Creel, "The Meaning of *Hsing Ming*," and H. G. Creel, "The Fa-Chia: 'Legalists' or 'Administrators'?" *Bulletin of the Institute of History and Philology, Academia Sinica*, Extra Vol. 4 (Taipei, 1961), pp. 607–636, esp. pp. 632–634. Professor Creel is continuing his research on this important topic.

[53] See van der Sprenkel, p. 64.

[54] This point is made by van Gulik, p. 56, where he comments: "This principle is not based so much on harshness as on the idea that no really good citizen will ever become involved with the law; even a completely innocent person being falsely accused is guilty in so far that he is a party to a disturbance of the peace in the district—which is an affront to the magistrate's administration." After assessing all the factors, van Gulik concludes (p. 63): "All circumstances considered, the old Chinese judicial system worked tolerably well."

in treason cases and the like). Here, however, Confucian emphasis on family and communal solidarity has probably also contributed considerably. The earliest roots of the concept, indeed, may well go back to an early communal stage of Chinese social thinking predating either Confucianism or Legalism.

Despite these and other probable survivals from Legalism, the really spectacular phenomenon of imperial times is what has been aptly termed the Confucianization of law—in other words, the incorporation of the spirit and sometimes of the actual provisions of the Confucian *li* into the legal codes. This process got under way during Han times only gradually and thereafter continued over several centuries. By the enactment of the T'ang Code in 653, however, it had effectively closed the one-time breach between *li* and *fa*. Customary morality (*li*) achieved official status in the form of positive law (*fa*), or, to reverse the equation and use another scholar's interpretation (see text above note 33), positive law (*fa*) achieved moral status as the embodiment of natural law (*li*). As T'ung-tsu Ch'ü rightly points out: "To study the ancient Chinese law we must compare the codes with the books of *li;* only in this way can we trace its origin and real meaning." [55]

The reader is referred to Dr. Ch'ü's book for innumerable illustrations of the truth of this statement. Here we can only summarize the main directions of influence, illustrating each with a few examples drawn from the Ch'ing Code of 1740, the final product of some two thousand years of imperial legal tradition.

9. The Imperial Codes as Exemplifications of *Li*

Of all the differences between Legalist *fa* and Confucian *li*, none is more basic than the universalism of the former (its refusal to make exceptions for particular individuals or groups) as against the particularism of the latter (its insistence upon differing treatment according to individual rank, relationship, and specific circumstance). This particularism we find perpetuated in the imperial codes along four major lines.

[55] T'ung-tsu Ch'ü, *Law and Society*, p. 278. Dr. Ch'ü is the author of the term, "Confucianization of law."

"Let the Punishment Fit the Crime"

The codes always endeavor to foresee all possible variations of any given offense and to provide specific penalties for each. Homicide, for example, is differentiated by the Ch'ing Code in its treatment of the subject into well over twenty varieties; additional varieties also appear incidentally in other sections of the Code in conjunction with such crimes as brigandage or assault and battery.[56]

If we try to discover the reason for these manifold differentiations, we find that most of them seem to be classifiable according to one or another of three major principles. The first is that of the *motivation* for the homicide, and it is among the varieties belonging to this group that we find the closest analogies with the differentiations familiar to us in Western legal systems. Examples would include premeditated homicide, intentional (but unpremeditated) homicide, homicide in an affray, by mischance or accident, in roughhousing, or by inducing the victim to commit suicide. Other possible examples might include homicide for purposes of witchcraft (killing an individual in order to use his organs for magical purposes) or the killing (usually by a husband) of an adulterous wife or her paramour or both.

The second principle of differentiation seems to be that of the *status*, social or familial, of the killer vis à vis his victim. This criterion, while not commonly used in modern Western legal systems, is basic to Confucian social thinking and will be discussed in greater detail below. Examples of homicide thus differentiated in the Ch'ing Code include parricide, homicide of an official, of a senior by a junior within a family and vice versa, of a child by its father, of a husband by his wife and vice versa, of a slave by his master and vice versa, or of three or more persons belonging to the same family.

The third criterion seems to be the *means* or the *situation* through which or under which the homicide is committed. In this group occur what seem to us the least useful and most arbitrary

---

[56] See translation by Boulais, section on homicide, nos. 1211–1343, as well as, in other sections, nos. 1063, 1065, 1380, 1401, 1410, 1424, and others. (Here and below, all references to Boulais are to the statutes and sub-statutes of the Ch'ing Code as numbered by him, and not to his page numbers.)

forms of differentiation. Examples would include homicide caused by poison, by improper administering of medicine, by introducing harmful objects into the nostrils, ears, or other openings of the victim's body (shades of Hamlet's ghost!), by depriving the victim of food or clothing, by vehicles or horses, in the course of hunting, and so forth.

It should be emphasized that these three criteria are nowhere mentioned in the Chinese codes themselves, and have been suggested here solely for purposes of analysis. Thus the Ch'ing Code's listing of homicidal offenses seems to follow no readily evident principle of classification: it begins with premeditated homicide, continues with premeditated homicide of an official, and then goes on to parricide, homicide connected with adultery, of three or more persons within a single family, homicide done for purposes of witchcraft, by poison, in an affray, and so forth.

It should further be remarked that these and the other kinds of homicide mentioned above by no means exhaust all the possibilities envisaged by the Code. Typical of a "situational" homicide, for example, is the one covered in the following statute: [57]

> Whoever, knowing the ford of a river to be deep or miry, falsely asserts it to be level and shallow, or who, knowing a bridge or a ferry boat to be decayed or leaky, falsely asserts it to be firm and solid, thereby causing someone crossing the river to drown, will be sentenced as under the statute concerning homicide or injuries received in an affray.

The principle of minute differentiation exemplified in the treatment of homicide is generally characteristic of all the subject matter in the codes. Some might argue that in conception it really goes back to the Legalists rather than the Confucians because the Legalists were interested in maintaining an exact measurement of individual performance. In view of the universalistic nature of Legalist law, however, as against the Confucian interest in particular differences, a Confucian derivation seems much more likely.

The principle of differentiation was no doubt introduced into the codes with the aim of maximizing justice by enabling the law to fit as closely as possible every foreseeable circumstance. In

[57] Boulais, no. 1284.

actual fact, however, as we shall see repeatedly in the cases translated in this book, the principle often made justice more difficult because it compelled the judge, faced by a case involving circumstances not exactly covered by any existing statute, to choose as best he could between the several statutes most nearly applicable.[58]

The usual device for handling this situation was the judgment by analogy. That is to say, the judge would select whatever statute seemed closest to the circumstances of the given case and then pronounce sentence "by analogy to" rather than directly "under" this chosen statute. Such analogical use of a statute also permitted the judge, in accordance with particular circumstances, to raise or lower what would otherwise be the statute's hard-and-fast penalty. Without the flexibility thus provided, it would have been extremely difficult, in a legal system emphasizing specificity rather than generality, to deal with the ever-changing configurations of human wrongdoing. In Chapter VI, section 3, the technical aspects of this exceedingly important device will be discussed in greater detail.

Still another device providing for greater latitude in what would otherwise have been a relatively static body of law was what in this book is called the *li* or sub-statute (a word different from *li*, "rites"). In contrast to the statutes (*lü*), which constituted the primary framework of the dynastic codes and often passed from one code to another with little or no change, the sub-statutes (*li*) could be promulgated by imperial edict at any moment to meet a given situation. Although the term *li* or sub-statute did not itself come into common use until the Ming dynasty (1368–1643), clear prototypes of it are to be found in earlier dynasties. These *li* or sub-statutes, being commonly devised to deal with very particular circumstances, were often more particularistic than the statutes to which they were appended. Thus, their proliferation during the Ming and especially the Ch'ing dynasties by no means obviated the continued need for judgment by analogy.

---

[58] This fact has been pointed out in slightly differing terms by van der Sprenkel, pp. 64–65.

Differentiation by Social Status

In accordance with the spirit of the *li* (rites), the codes provide penalties which differ sharply according to the relative class status of the offender and his victim. As one of countless examples, let us see how the Ch'ing Code treats the offense of striking or beating another person. The lowest degree of this offense, as defined in the Code, is a blow or blows delivered solely by the hand or foot and resulting in no wound (defined as inflamation or discoloration of the skin or other more serious injury). Such an act, when occurring between equals (a commoner striking a commoner or a slave a slave), is punishable by twenty blows of the light bamboo. This punishment constitutes the standard or normal penalty.[59] For a slave who beats a commoner, however, this normal penalty is increased by one degree to thirty blows, whereas for a commoner who beats a slave, it is decreased by one degree to only ten blows.[60] Decapitation is the penalty for a slave who strikes his master (irrespective of whether injury results), whereas no penalty attaches to a master who injures a slave, unless the injury leads to death.[61] The penalty for beating the presiding official of one's own locality is three years of penal servitude, whereas for beating an official belonging to another district the penalty ranges from two years downward depending on the official's rank.[62]

It should be noted in this connection that the number of social gradations recognized in the Ch'ing Code is markedly smaller than that found in the T'ang Code of 653, owing to the partial social leveling which occurred between these dynasties. Thus the

[59] Boulais, no. 1344. Here and below, all references to beating with the light or heavy bamboo are to the *nominal* number of blows which the Ch'ing Code, in accordance with earlier codes, continues to prescribe in its statutes, despite the fact that in Ch'ing times the number of blows which was *actually* administered was sharply reduced according to the following ratio: the five degrees of light bambooing, nominally 10, 20, 30, 40 and 50 blows, were in actual practice reduced to 4, 5, 10, 15 and 20 blows respectively; the five degrees of heavy bambooing, nominally 60, 70, 80, 90 and 100 blows, were in actual practice reduced to 20, 25, 30, 35 and 40 blows respectively. For the explanation, see Chap. III, sec. 3.
[60] Boulais, no. 1381; see also Ch'ü, *Law and Society*, pp. 186–187.
[61] Boulais, nos. 1387 and 1390; Ch'ü, *Law and Society*, pp. 191 and 193.
[62] Boulais, nos. 1367–1368; Ch'ü, *Law and Society*, p. 183.

T'ang Code has much to say about various serflike groups, collectively known as "bondsmen" (*chien jen*, literally "mean persons"), whose status varied from group to group but always fell between commoners and slaves. Although these groups, or similarly depressed groups, still existed in Ch'ing times (see the examples in Chapter VI, section 2), they were by then numerically and socially far less important than they had been during the T'ang. In the Ch'ing Code, as a result, attention centers upon slaves as the major representatives of all sub-commoner groups, whereas the term *chien jen* hardly appears at all. Thus, slaves, commoners, and officials are left as the three major categories differentiated by law.

Privileged Groups

Besides providing penalties that differ individually according to the relative status of offender and victim, the codes recognize entire categories of persons as deserving of special judicial procedure which distinguishes and elevates them as a whole from the great mass of commoners (*liang jen*, literally "good persons"). These categories are known as the *pa yi*, a term literally signifying the "eight considerations," but more meaningfully rendered as the "eight groups qualified for consideration." The term originates in the *Chou li* (Rites or institutions of Chou), one of the major Confucian compilations of *li*.[63] Together with its connotations, it first entered the law of the Wei dynasty (220–265), and has remained in all subsequent codes. Among the eight groups in question are members of the imperial family, descendants of former imperial houses, "persons of great merit," and others, but by far the most significant category is that of high officials (the mandarins) and their immediate family members.

Although the scope of the *pa yi* system changed somewhat from dynasty to dynasty, its general significance was that members of officialdom (and their immediate relatives) could not be arrested, investigated, or tortured without permission of the emperor; that the sentences of those found guilty of an offense were subject to consideration by the emperor with a view to pos-

---

[63] See Edouard Biot, tr., *Le Tcheou-li ou Rites des Tcheou*, 2 vols. (Paris: Imprimerie Nationale, 1851), II, 321–322.

sible reduction; and that the usual punishments inflicted on commoners (light or heavy bambooing, penal servitude of one to three years, life exile, death) were for the officials often (though by no means invariably) commutable to monetary fines, reduction in official rank, or dismissal from the civil service. Thus the law gave formal recognition to the great gap which in other ways separated the mass of commoners (the majority of them illiterate) from the small, highly educated, and theoretically nonhereditary group of scholar-officials.[64]

However, Confucian morality expected members of the official class to set a moral example to those beneath them, and hence to live according to a code of *noblesse oblige* which for certain offenses exposed them to heavier punishments than were prescribed for the ordinary man. Officials who violated the sumptuary regulations, for example, were punished under the Ch'ing Code by 100 blows of the heavy bamboo, whereas the corresponding punishment for nonofficials was only fifty blows. An official who debauched a woman living within his jurisdiction would receive a punishment two degrees greater than the normal punishment for this offense. Likewise, officials who frequented prostitutes were subject to punishment, whereas the Code says nothing about commoners who might do the same.[65]

Differentiation within the Family

With the family or clan, especially the joint or extended family consisting of several generations and collateral lines living together (which, however, was always primarily an upper-class phenomenon), we reach the very heart of the Confucian system. It is not surprising, therefore, that the codes should recognize intrafamily distinctions based upon sex, seniority, and degree of kinship, which are even more complex than those they recognize for society at large.

Of key importance for determining these distinctions is the system of mourning relationships known as the "five degrees of

[64] For a detailed account of the *pa yi* system, see Ch'ü, *Law and Society*, pp. 177–182. In Chap. V, sec. 2, we shall see that according to our translated cases, communication to monetary fines for officials was perhaps not as common in real life as might offhand be supposed.

[65] Boulais, nos. 836, 1617, 1619.

mourning" (*wu fu*), the five kinds of mourning which, in descending order of duration and severity corresponding to the closeness of kinship, are to be observed by any given members of a family upon the death of any other members. Each of the five degrees (of which the second actually comprises four subdivisions, referred to below as *2a, 2b,* and so on) bears the name of the particular mourning garb prescribed for it. In duration, they range from a mourning period of nominally three years (actually only twenty-seven months) for the first degree, down to three months for the fifth.[66]

The major relationships covered by the first degree are those of a son or an unmarried daughter who mourn their parents, a wife who mourns her husband or husband's parents, and a concubine who mourns her master. Thereafter, for the lesser degrees, the circle of relationships widens rapidly until at the fifth degree it includes more than forty, among them such unlikely possibilities as male ego's grandfather's spinster first cousin, or female ego's husband's grand-nephew's wife.

An important aspect of the mourning system is that, being based primarily on the superiority of senior generation over junior generation and of male over female, the degrees are not necessarily reciprocal. A father, for example, because his generation is senior to that of his son, stands toward the latter in a degree 1 relationship (he is mourned by the son for twenty-seven months). The son, however, being of a junior generation, stands toward his father only in a degree 2b relationship (he is mourned by the father only for the single year prescribed by the second

---

[66] The five degrees are:
1. *Chan-ts'ui* (garb of unhemmed sackcloth)
   3 years
2. *Tzu-ts'ui* (garb of hemmed sackcloth)
   a. 1 year with staff (needed to support bereaved mourner)
   b. 1 year without staff
   c. 5 months
   d. 3 months
3. *Ta-kung* (garb worked with greater coarseness)
   9 months
4. *Hsiao-kung* (garb worked with lesser coarseness)
   5 months
5. *Ssu-ma* (garb of plain hempen cloth)
   3 months

sub-level of the second mourning degree). Similarly, a husband
stands toward his wife in a degree 1 relationship, whereas the
relationship of the wife toward her husband is only that of degree
2a.[67]
This system had its origin in the various Confucian compilations of *li*, notably that known as the *Yi li*.[68] Its application to
family law almost surely has no parallel elsewhere.

As a concrete example, let us once more examine the Ch'ing
Code's treatment of the offense of beating, this time within the
family. A son who strikes or beats a parent (degree 1 relationship) suffers decapitation, irrespective of whether or not injury
results. However, no penalty applies to a parent who beats his son
(degree 2b), unless the son dies, in which case the punishment
for the parent is 100 blows of the heavy bamboo if the beating
was provoked by the son's disobedience, and one year of penal
servitude plus sixty blows of the heavy bamboo if the beating was
done wantonly.[69] Likewise a wife who strikes her husband
(degree 1) receives 100 blows of the heavy bamboo, whereas a
husband who strikes his wife (degree 2a) is punished only if he
inflicts a significant injury (the breaking of a tooth, a limb, or the
like), and if the wife personally lodges a complaint with the
authorities; in that case the husband is subject to a punishment
two degrees less than the norm (he receives eighty blows of the
heavy bamboo).[70]

At this point it should be stressed that the legal codes go even
further than the five-degree mourning system in their differentiations because, in addition to the distinctions based upon generation and sex which are basic to the mourning system, the codes
also differentiate according to the respective *ages* of the parties
involved. No distinction between older and younger brother, for
example, appears in the mourning system; that is to say, since
both belong to the same generation, the mourning relationship of
each toward the other is identical (degree 2b). In the Ch'ing

---

[67] See, among others, Boulais, nos. 29–33; or, for a more extended account,
Li chi, tr. Legge, in *Sacred Books of the East*, XXVII, 202–208 and charts.
[68] Chap. 11; tr. John Steele, *The I-li or Book of Etiquette and Ceremonial*, 2
vols. (London: Arthur Probsthain, 1917), II, 9–44.
[69] Boulais, nos. 1419–1420; Ch'ü, *Law and Society*, pp. 24 and 43–44.
[70] Boulais, nos. 1401 and 1403; Ch'ü, *Law and Society*, p. 106.

Code, on the contrary, the ages of the two are decisive. Thus if a younger brother beats an older brother, he receives two and one half years' penal servitude plus ninety blows of the heavy bamboo, even if no injury results. If, however, an older brother beats a younger one, he incurs no penalty at all.[71] Or again, the penalty for beating a first cousin once removed (degree 4) is one year of penal servitude plus sixty blows of the heavy bamboo, which is increased to one and one-half years plus seventy blows for beating a first cousin (degree 3). These punishments apply, however, *only* if the beater is younger than the cousin; if he is older, he incurs no penalty unless injury results.[72]

An interesting exception to the general principle that closer relationships involve heavier punishments is the treatment of theft within the family: the penalties for this offense are graduated *inversely* to the closeness of relationship, and at the same time made consistently lower than the punishments for ordinary theft outside the family. Thus the penalty for stealing from a fifth degree relative is two grades less than the ordinary punishment; for stealing from a fourth degree relative it is made three grades less; for stealing from a third degree relative it becomes four grades less, and so on. The same principle applies even to servants who steal within a family: the punishment is made one grade less than the norm.[73] The explanation, almost surely, lies in the concept, undoubtedly of ancient origin, that within a family property exists for the joint use of everyone and is not the exclusive possession of any single individual. Such, in effect, is what the Official Commentary on the Ch'ing Code itself states. It is confirmed by the fact that should a family theft involve violence, it no longer falls under the statutes on theft but under those concerning the killing or injuring of a relative, wherein the usual principle of punishment increased in ratio to closeness of relationship is followed.[74]

[71] Boulais, no. 1411; Ch'ü, *Law and Society*, pp. 55 and 61.
[72] Boulais, nos. 1410–1411; Ch'ü, *Law and Society*, pp. 55 and 61.
[73] Boulais, nos. 1154 and 1156; Ch'ü, *Law and Society*, p. 68.
[74] Boulais, no. 1155 and note 2; Ch'ü, *Law and Society*, pp. 68–69. See also, among our translated cases, case 45.1. For further general discussion of the family, see Chap. VI, sec. 5 below.

10. Filial Piety, Loyalty, and Humanitarianism in Law

Central to the family values exemplified in the foregoing pages is the Confucian virtue of *hsiao* or filial piety. The importance of this virtue is illustrated by the provision in the T'ang Code requiring all officials, upon the death of a parent, to retire from office during the entire mourning period of twenty-seven months (reduced by Ch'ing times, however, probably for practical reasons, to one year only).[75] Still more extraordinary is another article, also in the T'ang Code, providing one year of penal servitude for any couple who conceived a child during the twenty-seven months mourning period. The fact that elsewhere in the T'ang Code the same prohibition is listed together with other prohibitions for officials strongly suggests that it was directed toward them rather than toward the general population.[76] If so, it would be a further example of that code of *noblesse oblige* which, as we have seen in the preceding section, was demanded of officials. The founder of the Ming dynasty (reigned 1368–1398) strongly criticized the prohibition as contrary to human nature, with the result that it disappeared from the Ming and Ch'ing codes.[77]

In the world of social relationships outside the family, the correlate of *hsiao*, filial piety, is *chung*, loyalty to superior (meaning above all, of course, loyalty to ruler). Confucianism lays heavy emphasis on both these virtues, but it also teaches that should a conflict arise between the two, *hsiao* is to hold priority; in other words, father and family are to take precedence over ruler and state. This choice is already exemplified in the well known story in the Confucian *Analects* in which Confucius was told about a

[75] See Ou Koei-hing, p. 43, and *T'ang lü shu-yi*, book 25, article 22; also Boulais, no. 862. The figure of twenty-seven months, though not explicitly stated in this article of the T'ang Code, is specified by it elsewhere (book 3, article 2) as the length of mourning for a parent.
[76] Ou Koei-hing, p. 43. See *T'ang lü shu-yi*, book 12, article 7, and (for the parallel reference) book 3, article 2.
[77] See John C. H. Wu, "Chinese Legal Philosophy: A Brief Historical Survey," *Chinese Culture*, 1.4:34 (April 1958), citing the Ming founder's preface (dated 1374) to the work known as the *Hsiao tzu lu* (Record of filial piety and parental kindness). The Ming Code assumed definitive form in 1397.

person so upright that he had informed the authorities of the fact that his father had stolen a sheep. "With us," Confucius commented drily, "uprightness is different from this. The father conceals the son and the son conceals the father. Therein lies uprightness." [78]

The Legalists, of course, held a contrary opinion. Thus we find the same story quoted by Han Fei Tzu with the added detail that the son was later executed by the authorities on the grounds that the loyalty he showed his ruler in reporting his father's crime was outweighed by the resulting disloyalty to his father. Han Fei Tzu's view of such a judgment is of course quite unfavorable. [79]

The strength of Confucian morality is demonstrated by the fact that what Han Fei Tzu cited as a theoretical possibility became a recognized principle in the law of imperial China. Thus we find that already in Han times close relatives were permitted to conceal the crime of one of their members without legal penalty and were not compelled to testify in court against him. This idea conflicted of course with the Legalist principle of group responsibility mentioned earlier. In itself it may not seem too unusual, in view of the seeming American parallel that a wife, in many (not all) types of cases, is not permitted to testify against her husband over his objection. Added to the Chinese principle, however, is the more extreme provision, also known from Han times onward, that a son who brings an accusation of parental wrongdoing before the authorities is thereby unfilial and hence subject to heavy punishment. Under the Ch'ing Code, for example, such an accusation, if false, was punished by strangulation, but even if true, it brought three years of penal servitude plus 100 blows of the heavy bamboo. The same punishments applied to a wife accusing either her husband or her parents-in-law, and lesser punishments applied to less close relatives. [80] Probably China is the world's only country where the true reporting of a crime to the authorities could entail legal punishment for the reporter.

---

[78] Confucius, in *Analects*, XIII, 18.

[79] *Han Fei-tzu*, Chap. 49; tr. Liao, II, 285–286.

[80] Boulais, no. 1495. An exception, however, was made for wives severely beaten by their husbands (see text of this book above note 70). In such a case, the wife was permitted to accuse the husband without incurring penalty. See Boulais, no. 181.

A notable exception to the right of concealment, however, was its denial in cases of treason or rebellion. When these occurred, the principle of group responsibility was applied with a vengeance, all close relatives of the offender being either executed or permanently exiled. Thus we see that when the Confucian state felt its existence to be *really* threatened, it was willing to forgo its Confucian precepts.[81]

Another remarkable instance of filial piety in law is the provision that a criminal sentenced to death or long-term servitude, should he be the sole support of aged or infirm parents, might have his sentence commuted in various ways (beating, monetary redemption, wearing of the cangue), in order that he might remain at home to care for the parents. In 1769 this principle was broadened to include criminals who were the sole male heirs of *deceased* parents; these too were permitted to remain at home so that they could continue the family sacrifices to the ancestors.[82]

In some respects, the law of imperial China was more humane and intelligent than its Western counterpart. Theft, for example, merited the death penalty only when the theft exceeded a value of 120 ounces of silver, or was thrice committed, the third time in an amount of more than fifty ounces.[83] This punishment compares favorably with that of pre-industrial England, where only in 1818, and then only after four Parliamentary rejections of the bill, the death penalty was abolished for stealing from a shop goods valued at five shillings.[84] In imperial China all death sen-

[81] Boulais, nos. 1024–1030. On the whole topic of concealment, see Ch'ü, *Law and Society*, pp. 70–74, where it is stated (p. 74): "It is clear that when there was no conflict between sovereignty and family, between loyalty to the state and filial piety, both principles were recognized and encouraged. But when the two were in conflict, sovereignty took precedence, and loyalty to the state was the crucial issue." This judgment seems extreme, for the concealment of such a crime as murder certainly imposed a considerable limitation upon the state's authority and hence conflicted with the principle of loyalty to the state, even though it did not necessarily, as did treason or rebellion, directly threaten the security of the state.

[82] Boulais, nos. 96–102. Discussed in Chap. VI, sec. 5, near beginning.

[83] Boulais, nos. 1119 and 1124–1125. Actually, the so-called death penalty consisted of "strangulation after the assizes," which meant, as we shall see a few sentences below, that it would often be reduced to a lower penalty (commonly exile). For details, see Chap. IV, sec. 4.

[84] See G. F. Hudson, *Europe and China* (London: Arnold, 1931), p. 328. Hudson goes on to comment bitingly: ". . . and soon it was possible to talk about the lack of humane feeling among non-Christian peoples." Likewise, as

tences (with a few specified exceptions), as well as many other major sentences, had to be confirmed by the highest judicial body in the capital and even by the emperor himself before they could be carried out. Many death sentences included the standard formula, "after the assizes," which meant that they could not be executed until reviewed at the Autumn Assizes annually held in the capital, at which time they were often, though not invariably, reduced to a lower sentence. Amnesties, either general or for specified groups or individuals, also occurred fairly frequently.

Confucian humanitarianism further showed itself in the special exemptions and penal reductions provided by law for the aged (seventy and above), the young (fifteen and below), and the physically or mentally infirm.[85] Women, too, were permitted the privilege of monetary redemption for many crimes.[86] The making of anonymous accusations was viewed with abhorrence and punished very severely: strangulation after the assizes for the person guilty of this act, even if the accusation were true; and 100 blows of the heavy bamboo for officials accepting and acting on such accusations.[87] And Confucian confidence in the possibility of human reform underlies the remarkable provision—one going back to T'ang and probably to earlier times—that a criminal who sincerely confesses his guilt to the authorities before his crime becomes known to them will (with certain specified exceptions) be eligible for a reduction or remission of punishment.[88]

In short, the harsher aspects of Chinese law were restricted and blunted more than might at first sight appear by the many exceptions and special circumstances which were the particular contri-

---

Hudson points out, Parliament in 1814, after one rejection of the bill, "consented to abolish disembowelling alive as part of the statutory penalty for treason, and henceforth the Englishman could express his disgust at the atrocities of the Chinese penal code."

[85] See Karl Bünger, "The Punishment of Lunatics and Negligents According to Classical Chinese Law," Studia Serica, 9:1–16 (1950). Discussed in Chap. VI, sec. 2.

[86] Boulais, nos. 127–130. Discussed in Bünger, "The Punishment of Lunatics and Negligents."

[87] Boulais, no. 1463. To us today, living in an age which not long ago added the word "McCarthyism" to its vocabulary, this statute seems particularly impressive. See further Chap. VI, sec. 4, near end.

[88] See George Alexander Kennedy, Die Rolle des Geständnisses im chinesischen Gesetz (Berlin, 1939).

bution of the *li*. Furthermore, the total role of formal law in ordinary life was limited by the prominence of the customary (and largely unwritten) law of clan, guild, council of local gentry, and other extra-legal organs.

However, excluding from consideration the sanctioning of torture and the other unpleasant aspects of judicial procedure mentioned earlier, it is above all the gross inequalities in the Chinese codes—their insistence upon the sanctity of rank, privilege, and seniority—that probably seem most distasteful to the modern Westerner. Indeed, as he observes the law's harsh punishment of even slight infractions of the system of legalized inequality, he cannot but wonder at the savagery with which the originally "suasive" *li* came to be enforced in Confucian China. He wonders, that is, until he remembers the equal savagery with which religious and political nonconformity have been and often continue to be punished in the Christian West.

11. Law and Cosmic Harmony

In the opening pages it was suggested that law was traditionally viewed in China—though perhaps not consciously—primarily as an instrument for redressing violations of the social order caused by individual acts of moral or ritual impropriety or criminal violence. It was further stated that such violations, in Chinese eyes, really amounted to violations of the total cosmic order because the spheres of man and nature were thought of as forming a single continuum.

This concept of law could hardly have started with the Confucians, at least the early Confucians, since law to them was itself a violation of the social order. Nor could it have started with the Legalists, since these men used law quite consciously to destroy and remake the old social order. It is, in actual fact, only a particular facet of the broader concept summed up in the phrase, "the harmony of man and nature." This concept of harmony or oneness, expressed with varying degrees of explicitness, underlies a great deal of Chinese thinking. It is very prominent, of course, in Taoist philosophy. As developed into an elaborate political theory, however, it is particularly the work of the "cosmologists" or "naturalists"—men who tried to explain all phenomena, both natural and human, in terms of the eternal interplay of the positive and negative cosmic principles (the *yang* and the *yin*) and of the five Chinese elements (soil, wood, metal, fire, and water).

The basic theory of these thinkers was that the human and natural worlds are so closely interlinked through numerous correlations that any disturbance in the one will induce a corresponding disturbance in the other. If the ruler, for example, shows an overfondness for women, this will lead to an excess of the *yin* principle in the human world (since the *yin* is feminine), which in turn will cause a corresponding excess of *yin* in the world of nature. Inasmuch as one of the many correlates of the *yin* is water, the concrete result may well be disastrous floods. In order to avoid this kind of situation, therefore, it becomes the ruler's prime duty to cultivate himself morally, to see that his institutions accord with the natural order, and to maintain cosmic harmony by the correct performance of ritualistic observances in which sympathetic magic plays an important part.

This theory developed gradually during the last two centuries of the pre-imperial period and reached a high point during the Han dynasty, when it entered the highly eclectic Confucianism which then achieved orthodoxy. By this time too, as we have seen, law had become an accepted feature of Confucian government and Confucianization of the law was gradually getting under way. Parallel to this Confucianization, which meant the subordination of law to Confucian *li*, we may therefore perhaps speak of an analogous "naturalization" of law, meaning by this the subordination of law to the movements of nature.

This "naturalization" process is far less immediately apparent than is that of Confucianization. It is easier to detect in certain features of executive action—the granting of amnesties, for example, which often involved cosmological considerations—than in the content of the laws themselves. Nevertheless, traces of "naturalization" may be found in the codes as late as Ch'ing times, notably in the concept of "requital" as applied by the Ch'ing Code to the judging of certain types of homicide (discussed in Chapter VI, section 3).

In the field of judicial procedure itself, however, another conspicuous example of the "naturalization" of Chinese law occurs which, in view of its history of over two thousand years, deserves discussion here. This example involves the belief that serious legal proceedings, and especially death sentences, should be carried out only during the autumn and winter months, inasmuch as these are seasons of decay and death, and should be totally avoided during spring and summer, these being seasons of rebirth and growth.

That the genesis of this idea predates the imperial age is strongly suggested by scattered statements found in the *Yüeh ling* or *Monthly Ordinances,* a calendrical text representative of "naturalistic" thinking which was probably written shortly before 240 B.C. The text tells us month by month what human activities are in accord with the natural conditions of that month, and what are the natural disasters that will occur if the wrong activities are carried out. Of legal interest are the following statements: under the second month of spring it is said that the fetters of prisoners are to be removed and criminal cases halted; under the first month of summer that only light sentences are to be pronounced; and under the second month of summer that officials are not to apply punishments. Under the first month of autumn, on the other hand, the text states that laws, prisons, and fetters are to be made ready, and punishments to be applied with firmness, because "Heaven and Earth now begin to be severe"; under the second month that the punishments are to be made more severe; and under the third month that judgments and punishments are to be expedited.[89]

There is abundant evidence that by the Han dynasty the restriction of executions and serious legal proceedings to autumn and winter was not only an idea but an accepted practice— apparently, however, one not always consistently followed because some of the evidence consists of protests against its violation. In 7 B.C., for example, an official complained that "recently great lawsuits have been tried during the three months of spring," which, he thought, would result in poor harvests. Between 125

[89] The *Yüeh ling* was originally a portion of the *Lü-shih ch'un-ch'iu* (comp. ca. 240 B.C.), and was subsequently also inserted into the *Li chi* as its fourth chapter; tr. Legge, in *Sacred Books of the East,* XXVIII, 259, 271, 275, 284–285, 288, 295.

and 120 B.C., on the other hand, the *Han shu* (History of the [Former] Han dynasty) tells us that the stern legal measures of a certain official were so effective that "at the end of the twelfth month there was not even a thief to set the dogs barking." Upon the arrival of spring, however, the official "stamped with his feet and said with a sigh: 'Oh, if winter could be extended by one month, that would have finished my business.' " [90]

In addition to this general ban on spring and summer executions, it seems probable that in Han times, as later, the summer solstice and especially the winter solstice were specifically included in a similar ban. Although this ban is not clearly stated for the Han dynasty itself, we do know that already then, as later, the solstices were regarded as crucially important days, because on them occurred the transition from the culmination of the *yin* principle (cold and darkness) to the rebirth of the *yang* (heat and light), and vice versa. In order, therefore, to prevent any possible human interference with these cosmic changes, governmental activities in general were halted during a period from several days before until several days after each solstice. It seems reasonable to conclude that among these activities executions were included.

Jumping forward to the T'ang Code of 653 (the earliest surviving code), we find in it a great proliferation of the periods tabooed to executions. Many of the new taboos are inspired by the then extremely powerful influence of Buddhism, with its opposition to the taking of life. With numerous overlappings, the specified taboos include the following: (1) An unbroken period from the Beginning of Spring (ca. February 4 in the Western calendar) to the Autum Equinox (ca. September 23). Thus are added the first six weeks of autumn to the previously tabooed seasons of spring and summer. (2) The first, fifth, and ninth lunar months, these being Buddhist months of fasting. (3) The twenty-four "breaths" or "joints" of the year, these being days occurring throughout the year at approximately fifteen-day intervals, the sequence of which is based on solar reckoning. The most important of them, apart from the already mentioned two solstices, are

[90] See Hulsewé, *Remnants of Han Law*, I, 103–109, esp. (for the cases cited) pp. 105 and 107.

the two equinoxes and the four days which officially begin the four seasons. (4) Other annual sacrifice days and holidays. A modern scholar has calculated that these totaled fifty-three per year in T'ang times.[91] (5) Days 1, 8, 14–15, 18, 23–24, and 28–30 of each lunar month, these being Buddhist fast days. Coinciding with some of them, but separately listed, are the four days in each lunar month of new and full moon and first and last lunar quarters. (6) Rainy days and nighttime.[92]

The many overlaps make it difficult to determine just how many days in a year were forbidden for executions. Even a cursory calculation, however, indicates that the remaining days on which executions *were* permitted must have totaled less than two months annually and probably did not greatly exceed a single month. If, therefore, one *had* to undergo capital punishment, T'ang China would certainly seem to have been the world's best time and place in which to suffer such a fate! It should be noted, however, that in line with usual Confucian thinking, the tabooed periods were not permitted to apply to cases of treason or of slaves who killed their masters. Presumably such acts were regarded as of such social and cosmic enormity that delay in punishing them would be even worse than failure to follow the natural pattern.

The taboos of the T'ang Code were retained virtually unchanged in subsequent codes through the Ming dynasty. Then, with the Ch'ing Code of 1740, we reach a sharp change in which the periods of taboo shrink to mere symbolic vestiges of what they had been. Thus they now consist only of the first month of spring and last month of summer (only the first and last months of what had once been a solid half year or more of taboo) plus a period from ten days before until seven days after the Winter Solstice, and another period from five days before until three days

[91] See Yang Lien-sheng, "Schedules of Work and Rest in Imperial China," in Yang Lien-sheng, *Studies in Chinese Institutional History* (Cambridge, Mass.: Harvard University Press, 1961), pp. 18–42, esp. p. 22.

[92] See Ou Koei-hing, pp. 85–86, which, however, omits two of the days under (5) and does not explain all entries clearly. Compare *T'ang lü shu-yi*, book 30, article 14. For a much more extended study of the facts here summarized, see A. F. P. Hulsewé, *Periodieke executie- en slachtverboden in de T'ang tijd en hun oorsprong* (Leiden, 1948). We are indebted to Professor Hulsewé for kindly presenting a copy of this work.

after the Summer Solstice. The total time forbidden to executions thus amounts to less than three months.[93]

It has been suggested that the successive dynastic codes provide exceptional possibilities for measuring progressive changes in social and political values. Here we see that they can be used to measure changes in cosmological beliefs as well. The dramatic shift just noted from the Ming to the Ch'ing Code reveals a weakening belief by Ch'ing times in the doctrine of the oneness of man and nature, such as accords well with what we know from other sources.[94] This loss of conviction may indeed underlie a parallel phenomenon well attested for a quite different field: the unmistakable stereotyping and loss of feeling found in the later stages of Chinese landscape painting—itself the crowning summation in graphic form of the Chinese belief in cosmic harmony.

12. Summary and Conclusion

In this first general chapter, devoted to an historical survey of the development of Chinese legal thinking, various topics have necessarily been omitted despite their inherent interest and importance. Examples are the handling of disputes in feudal China prior to the appearance of written law,[95] property and contractual relations as treated in the written and customary law of imperial times,[96] or even, within the sphere of ideas proper, the

[93] See Boulais, nos. 35 and 1694. There is some confusion in the Chinese sources on this matter. Further discussion will be found in Appendix G below.

[94] See D. Bodde, "The Chinese Cosmic Magic Known as Watching for the Ethers," in Soren Egerod and Else Glahn, eds., *Studia Serica Bernhard Karlgren Dedicata* (Copenhagen: Ejnar Munksgaard, 1959), pp. 14–35. This article traces the history of a curious cosmological theory from its beginnings in the first century B.C. until it was declared in the eighteenth century to have reached a "blind alley."

[95] See Henri Maspero, "Le Serment dans la procédure judiciaire de la Chine antique," *Mélanges Chinois et Bouddhiques*, 3:257–317 (1934–35). The give-and-take spirit apparent in these disputes distinguishes them sharply from the vertically oriented court procedures of imperial times and suggests a society closer in spirit to Western society than was later possible when Chinese government became bureaucratized. It should be noted, however, that our picture is necessarily one-sided because the disputes of which we have knowledge are all between members of the aristocracy, that is, between men who were more or less social equals, and do not involve any of the common people.

[96] See Pierre Hoang, *Notions techniques sur la propriété en Chine*, 2nd ed. (Shanghai, 1920); Henry McAleavy, "Certain Aspects of Chinese Customary Law

important but difficult question of whether or not parallels to the Western concepts of "natural law" and "laws of nature" ever existed in China.[97]

Chinese legal development is in many ways sharply different from that experienced in other civilizations. Through the systematic study of Chinese law, we can learn much of basic importance about Chinese attitudes toward state, society, and family, as well as Chinese views of the universe. Heretofore, apart from a few distinguished exceptions, Western scholars have shown little interest in such study.

We have seen that Chinese written law arose in the sixth century B.C. as a political instrument for coping with the sharpening disorders then resulting from the breakdown of the old social and political order. As such, the earliest law was primarily penal in emphasis, and the same has been true of all later enacted law until recent times. Unlike many other major civilizations, where written law was held in honor and often attributed to a divine origin, law in China was from the beginning viewed in purely secular terms. Its initial appearance, indeed, was greeted with positive hostility by many as indicative of a serious moral decline.

Following the earliest known promulgation of penal law in 536 B.C., the next three centuries witnessed a bitter controversy between Confucians and Legalists. The Confucians advocated the retention in government of the flexibly interpreted and hi-

in the Light of Japanese Scholarship," *Bulletin of the School of Oriental and African Studies,* 17:535–547 (London, 1955); H. F. Schurmann, "Traditional Property Concepts in China," *Far Eastern Quarterly,* 15:507–516 (1956); Jacques Gernet, "La Vente en Chine d'après les contrats de Touen-houang (IXe–Xe siècles)," *T'oung Pao,* 45:295–391 (1957); Edward Kroker, "The Concept of Property in Chinese Customary Law," *Transactions of the Asiatic Society of Japan,* 3d series, 7:123–146 (1959).

[97] This topic, obviously of the greatest importance for comparing Chinese societal and scientific development with that in the West, has been discussed with learning and brilliance but not absolute finality by Joseph Needham, *Science and Civilisation in China,* final chapter of Vol. II. His twofold conclusion is that in the human sphere the Confucian *li* formed a reasonably close Chinese counterpart to the Western concept of "natural law," but that the concept of "laws of nature" in the non-human sphere (laws governing the physical universe, such as the law of gravity) failed to develop in China. For possible exceptions to the second part of this conclusion, which, however, do not destroy its general validity, see D. Bodde, "Evidence for 'Laws of Nature' in Chinese Thought," *Harvard Journal of Asiatic Studies,* 20:709–727 (1957).

erarchically oriented body of traditional and unwritten rules of behavior known as *li*, whereas the Legalists wished to replace the *li* by a fixed system of written law (*fa*) which would be equally and sternly applied to all, and would suppress private privilege in favor of a powerful centralized government. The ideas of the Legalists, ruthlessly carried out in the state of Ch'in, helped that state to create the first unified Chinese empire in 221 B.C.

The Ch'in empire collapsed within fifteen years, however, and under the following Han dynasty, beginning around 100 B.C., Confucianism supplanted Legalism as the state orthodoxy. The result in subsequent centuries was a gradual Confucianization of law, in other words, an incorporation into the law codes of the social values originally contained in the Confucian *li*. Thus law in imperial China developed as a hybrid of Legalism and Confucianism. It retained the penal format of Legalist *fa* and something of its harshness, but from Confucianism it adopted the view of society as a hierarchy of unequal components, harmoniously functioning at different levels to form an ordered whole. Only in the present century was serious challenge made of the Confucian doctrine of the natural superiority of the high over the low, of the old over the young, of man over woman.

This Confucianization was paralleled by what might be called the "naturalization" of law. That is to say, law was fitted into the wider doctrine of the oneness of man and nature, which maintained that man should shape his institutions in harmony with the forces of nature. A conspicuous manifestation of this doctrine in the legal sphere was the idea that death sentences should be carried out only during autumn and winter and should be totally avoided during spring and summer.

In conclusion, it would be well to remind ourselves that the controversy between Confucians and Legalists still holds relevance for us today. The concern of the Legalists was political control of the mass man, for which reason they have been termed totalitarian. Yet in their insistence that all men high and low should conform to a single law, they were egalitarian. The concern of the Confucians was moral development of the individual man, for which reason they have been termed democratic. Yet in their insistence that for a graded society there has to be a graded law, they were undemocratic. Throughout history the failing of democracy has been its tendency to accept a double standard: equal rights for those who are its full-fledged members but discrimination or outright exploitation for those who are not. How to create a society which will uphold the rights of the few, yet not permit these rights to harm the welfare of the many, still remains a major problem.

II · THE CH'ING CODE AND ITS PEDIGREE

1. Bibliographical Note

The next three chapters will deal with the mechanics of imperial Chinese law: the structure of its codes, the nature of its punishments, the functioning of its judicial system. The discussion will necessarily be more technical than the one just completed. The focus will be upon the Ch'ing dynasty (1644–1911) because it is during the second half of this dynasty that the 190 legal cases translated in this volume were decided. Chapters V and VI will then deal respectively with the compilation from which the cases have been taken and with their social, political, and legal significance.

Before proceeding, it will be helpful to enumerate some of the major primary sources and secondary accounts. A major group of primary sources is, of course, the codes themselves and especially the Ch'ing Code of 1740. Much information on legal procedure is contained in their sections on arrests, prison administration, trial procedure, and the like, as well as in their introductory divisions dealing with terms and general principles.

Second and particularly important because they present their materials in historical sequence are the monographic chapters commonly entitled *Hsing-fa chih* or "Treatise on Penal Law," to be found in many of the dynastic histories. This title will hereafter be regularly referred to as "Legal Treatise" and will refer to the dynastic history under discussion. Several of the more important of these treatises, but not that of the Ch'ing, have been translated in Western works already cited in the first chapter.[1]

---

[1] See, for the Han dynasty (206 B.C.–A.D. 220), Hulsewé, *Remnants of Han Law*, I, 321–350; for the Sui dynasty (581–617), Balazs; for the T'ang (618–906), Bünger, *Quellen zur Rechtsgeschichte der T'ang-Zeit*, pp. 73–173. For the Yuan (Mongol) dynasty (1280–1367), there is a partial translation by Ratchnevsky, *Un Code des Yuan*, but the chapter there translated differs from the other "Legal

The Ch'ing "Legal Treatise," which is our primary concern, occupies Chapters 143–145 of the *Ch'ing shih-kao* or *Draft History of the Ch'ing Dynasty* (compiled by a board of scholars, 1914–1928). All citations to it will follow the small one-volume Chinese edition, with detailed annotations, published in Peking in 1957.[2] For the Ming and other untranslated "Legal Treatises," references will be to the large Chinese one-volume compilation of all treatises edited by Ch'iu Han-p'ing.[3]

The third group of source materials consists of the sections on law in the great encyclopedic compilations dealing with governmental institutions. There are several of these for the Ch'ing, but one in particular will be regularly cited: the monumental *Ta Ch'ing hui-tien* or *Collected Institutes of the Great Ch'ing Dynasty*, especially Chapters 53–57.[4]

Among modern Chinese students of Chinese law, by far the most important is Shen Chia-pen (1840–1913), whose lengthy career on the Board of Punishments was climaxed by a leading role in the reform and modernization of Chinese law during the first decade of the twentieth century.[5] Shen combined an unusual

---

Treatises" in that it consists of a text of an actual code of uncertain date and origin, rather than an historical survey of its subject. The late Professor Balazs has also left a manuscript translation of the "Legal Treatise" of the Chin dynasty (265–419) which one hopes may soon appear posthumously. Some decades ago a preliminary translation of the "Legal Treatise" of the Ming dynasty (1368–1643) was collaboratively prepared by Ssu-yü Teng and Cyrus Peake, but it apparently requires considerable further work before it can be ready for publication.

[2] *Ch'ing shih-kao Hsing-fa chih chu-chieh* ("Legal Treatise" from the *Ch'ing Draft History* with annotations), ed. Kuo-wu yüan, Fa-chih chü, Fa-chih shih yen-chiu shih (Legal Research Division, Bureau of Legal Affairs, Council of State; Peking, 1957). In this edition, Chap. 143 of the "Legal Treatise," dealing with successive editions of the Ch'ing Code and other texts, occupies pp. 3–43; Chap. 144, on the system of punishments, occupies pp. 44–83; and Chap. 145, on the judicial process, occupies pp. 84–122.

[3] *Li-tai hsing-fa chih* (Legal treatises of successive dynasties) (Changsha, 1938). In this edition, Ch'iu has punctuated and paragraphed what in the original dynastic histories consists of unbroken pages of text and has added helpful topical headings at the tops of pages. Unfortunately, he has not contributed a commentary.

[4] First published in 1690, and then in revised and enlarged editions in 1732, 1764, 1818, and 1899. The edition here cited is that of 1899 as reprinted with continuous pagination in Taipei in 1963.

[5] Treated in detail in Meijer.

degree of objectivity with an encyclopedic knowledge of all Chinese legal literature, past and present. His numerous legal studies, ranging from one-page notes to lengthy monographs, fill hundreds of pages in his collected writings.[6] Unfortunately, like the compilers of the dynastic histories, Shen did not choose to write systematically about his own dynasty. Valuable scraps of information on the Ch'ing, nevertheless, emerge here and there from some of his writings on other topics, especially from his prefaces and postfaces to the legal studies on the Ch'ing written by other scholars or to reprints of early Ch'ing texts.

Much of the work done by later Chinese legal scholars seems to be more or less a retelling of what Shen has already told. The later work tends to be highly factual, with a minimum of theoretical interpretation. Included are the general surveys and compilations of Ch'eng Shu-te, Yang Hung-lieh, and Ch'en Ku-yüan of the 1920's and 1930's,[7] as well as, more recently, the very brief and derivative, but nevertheless informative and clearly written, outline by Hsü Tao-lin.[8]

Although many Japanese scholars have contributed significantly to the study of Chinese law, virtually none has devoted primary effort to the Ch'ing dynasty or in particular to its codified law.[9] The most preeminent of these scholars, Nüda Noboru (1904–1966), is no exception. However, he does of course deal to some extent with the Ch'ing in several of his comprehensive studies, notably his monumental *Chūgoku hōsei-shi kenkyū* or *Study of Chinese Legal History,* hereafter referred to by the English title.

[6] *Shen Chi-yi hsien-sheng yi-shu, chia pien* (Bequeathed writings of Mr. Shen Chi-yi [Shen Chia-pen], first series; Peking, n.d. [1929]; reprinted, Taipei, 1964 in 2 vols. with continuous pagination). Hereafter referred to as *Bequeathed Writings.*

[7] Ch'eng Shu-te, *Chiu-ch'ao lü-k'ao* (Study of the codes of nine dynasties), 2 vols. (Shanghai, 1927); Yang Hung-lieh, *Chung-kuo fa-lü fa-ta shih* (History of the development of Chinese law), 2 vols. (Shanghai, 1930); Ch'en Ku-yüan, *Chung-kuo fa-chih shih* (History of Chinese legal institutions; Shanghai, 1934).

[8] *Chung-kuo fa-chih shih lun-lüeh* (Outline history of Chinese legal institutions; Taipei, 1953).

[9] The comprehensive bibliography, Hōsei-shi Gakkai (Society for the Study of the History of Law), comp., *Hōsei-shi bunken mokuroku, 1945–1959—Shōwa 20–34* (Catalogue of works on the history of law, 1945–1959—Shōwa 20–34; Tokyo, 1962), in the China portion of the section on East Asia (pp. 143–193), lists no items dealing exclusively or even primarily with the Ch'ing Code and Ch'ing legal procedure.

Of the four volumes so far published, the first, *Criminal Law*, is particularly pertinent for the present book.[10]

Among Western studies relevant to Ch'ing law, only three will be cited with much frequency in these chapters. They are Meijer's illuminating study of late Ch'ing legal reforms (see Chapter I, note 2), Chang Yü-chüan's good, but overly brief, article on the Chinese judiciary,[11] and, by contrast, Ernest Alabaster's bulky *Notes and Commentaries on Chinese Criminal Law*. The study by Alabaster is a lucid and readable survey of the entire gamut of Ch'ing codified law, highly praiseworthy as a pioneer study (1899) in a difficult field. It is extremely sketchy, however, on the institutional (as against the ideological) aspects of the Ch'ing legal system, suffers from looseness of scholarship, and, in the opinion of this writer, shows manifest bias in favor of its subject.

2. History and Anatomy of the Ch'ing Code

The historical development of Chinese legal codification may be schematized as follows: [12]

[10] The volumes are not numbered, but each bears a subtitle (in English as well as Japanese) and contains a short résumé both in English and in Chinese. The dates and English subtitles are: *Criminal Law*, 1959; *Law of Land and Law of Transaction*, 1960; *Law of Slave and Serf, and Law of Family and Village*, 1962; *Law and Custom, Law and Morality*, 1964. This great series supersedes Niida's much briefer *Chūgoku hōsei-shi* (A history of Chinese law; Tokyo, 1952). Yet even his 700 page *Criminal Law* (hereafter referred to by English title), owing to its differing focus, says considerably less about the topics covered in the present chapters than one might offhand expect. A large segment deals with dynasties before the Ch'ing, and another large segment with the Mongols and other peoples peripheral to China. It says extremely little about the evolution and structure of the Ch'ing Code, about certain of the Ch'ing punishments, about Ch'ing judicial procedure, or about the *Hsing-an hui-lan*.

[11] "The Chinese Judiciary," *Chinese Social and Political Science Review*, 2.4:68–88 (December 1917), esp. pp. 78–85 for the Ch'ing appellate system; a continuation of the same article appears in *ibid.*, 3:1–30 (1918), dealing with the judiciary in Republican China.

[12] Data based on Balazs, p. 207, with modifications and additions by D. Bodde. A very few of the dates that follow, because of the differing criteria used, differ slightly from those in Balazs or elsewhere. For example, 1723–1727 is given as the period when the Ch'ing Code underwent extensive revisions. Strictly speaking, the revision work occupied only the years 1723–1725, whereas the remaining time was spent printing the resulting new version of the Code, which finally came from the press in 1727. For the sake of simplicity, however, we prefer to consider the revising and the printing as successive phases of a single operation, for which the overall dates are 1723–1727.

Pre-Imperial China (before 221 B.C.)

536 B.C. "Books of punishment" (*hsing shu*) inscribed on bronze tripod vessels in state of Cheng

513   "Books of punishment" (*hsing shu*) inscribed on iron vessels in state of Chin

501   "Bamboo punishments" (*chu hsing*, punishments inscribed on tablets of bamboo) used in state of Cheng

ca. 400   "Canon of Laws" (*Fa ching*) said to have been promulgated by Li K'uei, prime minister of state of Wei

ca. 350   Shang Yang "changed" the laws of the state of Ch'in and made them applicable to everyone high and low

The First Empires (221 B.C.–A.D. 220)

Ch'in Dynasty (221–207 B.C.)

Ch'in's unification of China in 221 B.C. enabled laws of Ch'in to be made universal throughout the newly created Ch'in empire

Han Dynasty (206 B.C.–A.D. 220)

ca. 200 B.C. *Han lü* or Han Code (known also as *Chiu-chang lü* or Code in Nine Sections; assumed definitive form ca. 128 B.C.)

Period of Disunity (A.D. 220–580)

Wei Dynasty (A.D. 220–265)

ca. 230 *Wei lü* or Wei Code

Chin Dynasty (265–419)

268 *Chin lü* or Chin Code

Southern Dynasties	Northern Dynasties
Codes of Ch'i (489–491), Liang (503), Ch'en (ca. 567)	Codes of Northern Wei (481, 492, 495, 504), Northern Chou (563), Northern Ch'i (564)

The Later Empires (581–1911)

Sui Dynasty (581–617)

581–583 *K'ai-huang lü*

607 *Ta-yeh lü*

T'ang Dynasty (618–906)
> 653 *T'ang lü shu-yi* or T'ang Code with Commentary (achieved final form in 737; oldest surviving code, based largely on now lost Sui Code of 581–583)

Sung Dynasty (960–1279)
> 963 *Hsing-t'ung* (largely a copy of T'ang Code)

Yuan (Mongol) Dynasty (1280–1367)
> 1316–1323 *Ta Yüan t'ung-chih* (lost; its relationship to other still partially extant Yuan codes is uncertain)

Ming Dynasty (1368–1643)
> 1373–1374 First version of *Ta Ming lü* or Ming Code (largely a copy of T'ang and subsequent codes)
>
> 1397 Definitive version of Ming Code (radically revised from preceding, 1389 onward; this version of Ming Code represents a sharp break in format from all previous codes and is prototype of Ch'ing Code)

Ch'ing (Manchu) Dynasty (1644–1911)
> 1646 *Ta Ch'ing lü* (revised in 1670 and again more extensively in 1723–1727) resulting in:
>
> 1740 *Ta Ch'ing lü-li* (definitive version of Ch'ing Code, remaining standard until extensive legal reforms of 1905 onward)

Traditionally, Li K'uei's *Canon of Laws* of about 400 B.C. is said to have been the prototype of all later codes. It is also said to have consisted of the following six main divisions:

1. Laws on Theft (*tao fa*)
2. Laws on Violence (*tsei fa*) [13]
3. Laws on Criminals under Detention (*ch'iu fa*)
4. Laws on Arrests (*pu fa*)
5. Miscellaneous Laws (*tsa fa*)
6. General Laws (*chü fa*)

The Han *Code in Nine Sections* is likewise said to have been a direct descendant of Li K'uei's *Canon*, but with two major

[13] *Tsei* seems originally to have been a cover term for various acts of destructive violence, including wanton homicide, assault, vandalism, and the like. Later the word tended to be used more particularly to designate violence as associated with theft (for example, banditry and piracy). Hence in the later codes we find *tsei* and *tao* (theft) linked together as a compound term, either *tsei tao* or *tao tsei*.

changes: (1) for the generic term for law, *fa,* appearing in the division titles of Li K'uei's *Canon,* the Han Code (and all subsequent codes) substituted the more narrowly technical term *lü,* satute; [14] (2) to the *Canon's* six divisions, the Han Code added three further divisions as follows:

    7. Statutes on Corvée Levies (*hsing lü*)
    8. Statutes on Stables (*chiu lü*)[15]
    9. Statutes on the Family (*hu lü*)

The validity of the Li K'uei tradition, unfortunately, is seriously compromised by the fact that the first detailed account of it occurs only in the "Legal Treatise" of the Chin dynastic history, compiled in A.D. 644. This long interval throws into question the reliability of the details in the "Treatise" about the *Canon,* though not necessarily the existence of the *Canon* per se.[16]

From the Han Code onward, on the other hand, the formal changes in subsequent codes can be traced with fair exactness in the successive "Legal Treatises." [17] A major turning point is the now lost Sui Code of 581–583, whose format was adopted virtually unchanged by the earliest surviving code, that of T'ang of 653. The contents of the T'ang Code are grouped under 501 (traditionally said to be 500) articles,[18] which in turn are grouped under the following twelve divisions or books:

    1. Terms and General Principles (*ming li*)
    2. The Imperial Guard and Prohibitions [relative to the Imperial Palaces] (*wei chin*)
    3. Administrative Regulations (*chih chih*)
    4. The Family and Marriage (*hu hun*)
    5. [Government] Stables and Treasuries (*chiu k'u*)
    6. Unauthorized Corvée Levies (*shan hsing*)

[14] See the discussion of legal terms in Chap. I, beginning of sec. 3, and this chapter, sec. 3.

[15] The statutes on stables were laws having to do with the imperial stud and, more generally, with the care of all domestic animals, as well as with injuries (such as goring) caused by such animals.

[16] See Timoteus Pokora, "The Canon of Laws by Li K'uei, A Double Falsification," *Archiv Orientalni,* 27:96–121 (1959).

[17] A convenient synopsis is found in Balazs, p. 208. In addition to the "Legal Treatises" of the Ming and Ch'ing histories, what is said in the remainder of this section about the Ming and Ch'ing codes rests in large part upon direct examination of these codes.

[18] See Chap. I, note 12.

7. Violence and Theft (*tsei tao*)
8. Conflicts and Suits (*tou sung*)
9. Deceptions and Frauds (*cha wei*)
10. Miscellaneous Statutes (*tsa lü*)
11. Arrests and Escapes (*pu wang*)
12. Trial and Imprisonment (*tuan yü*)

Not only the general format of the T'ang Code, but many of its individual statutes as well, were adopted with only trifling changes by the codes of Sung and Yuan.[19] From these the statutes passed onward to the first Ming Code of 1373–1374, whose only major change was that what had been the 501 articles of the T'ang Code had by this time increased to 606. Thereafter, however, the extensive revisions made in 1389–1397 bring us to a major dividing line. In 1397, as a result of these revisions, a new Ming Code was published which in format, and to a lesser degree in content, broke decisively with all preceding codes.

In this new Code, we find the 606 articles of the 1373–1374 Code drastically reduced to 460. Conversely, the books or parts under which these articles are listed are increased from 12 to 30. Furthermore, these 30 parts are in turn grouped under seven larger divisions. These consist of an introductory division, entitled (as in the T'ang Code) "Terms and General Principles," followed by six others corresponding in name and subject to the six boards or ministries (*pu*) under which, ever since T'ang times, the central government had operated. Their names are: 1. Civil Office, 2. Revenue and Population, 3. Rites, 4. War, 5. Punishments, 6. Public Works. Because these boards cover a wide gamut of human activity, they provide an excellent classification according to which relevant statutes and articles may be grouped. In view of the heavy penal emphasis of Chinese law, it is not surprising to find most statutes in the Ming Code falling under the division corresponding to the Board of Punishments, whereas a far lesser number—covering what we would call civil law—go

[19] Although the Mongols, in view of their very different cultural background, might have been expected to make sweeping changes in Chinese law when they ruled Yuan China, their major "contribution" seems actually to have been that of using numbers ending in sevens instead of tens when specifying the number of blows of beating or other punishments (7, 17, 27, and so on, in place of 10, 20, 30). See V. A. Riasanovsky, "Mongol Law and Chinese Law in the Yuan Dynasty," *Chinese Social and Political Science Review,* 20:266–289 (1936–1937).

under the division corresponding to the Board of Revenue and Population. Still others, dealing with matters pertaining to the civil service (standards of official behavior, official promotions and demotions and the like), are placed under the division corresponding to the Board of Civil Office, and so on.

This arrangement, as found in the Ming Code of 1397, is important because it was adopted unchanged by the successive editions of the Ch'ing Code, save only that the Ming Code's 460 articles or sections—themselves a reduction from the T'ang Code's 501 articles—were further reduced in Ch'ing times to 436. This reduction, however, was made only gradually. The first Ch'ing Code of 1646 was largely a copy of the Ming Code. In 1670 it underwent superficial revisions (primarily corrections of misprints) followed in 1723–1727 by changes much more significant. It was in the course of the latter that the number of sections was reduced to 436. Further minor changes in 1740 (primarily the dropping of a commentary, as described in section 4 below) resulted in the final definitive edition of the Code, known as the *Ta Ch'ing lü-li* or "Statutes and Sub-statutes of the Great Ch'ing." Thereafter, aside from periodic accretions of sub-statutes (see the next section), the Code remained unchanged until almost the end of the dynasty.

Following is a list of the seven major divisions and thirty subdivisions found in the Ming Code of 1397 and all its Ch'ing successors. After each title appears, within parentheses, the number of its subsumed articles or sections (a total of 436 for all divisions) as found in the Ch'ing Code of 1740. (See Glossary for the Chinese characters for all titles.)

    I. Terms and General Principles (articles 1–46)
   II. Administrative Law (articles 47–74)
      (This corresponds to the Board of Civil Office.)

        A. Administrative Regulations (articles 47–60)
        B. Standards of Official Behavior (articles 61–74)

  III. Civil Law (articles 75–156)
      (This corresponds to the Board of Revenue and Population.)

    A. The Family and Corvée Services (articles 75–89)
    B. Landed Property (articles 90–100)
    C. Marriage (articles 101–117)
    D. Government Granaries and Treasuries (articles 118–140)
    E. Taxes and Tariffs (articles 141–148)
    F. Money Lending (articles 149–151)
    G. Public Markets (articles 152–156)

IV. Ritual Law (articles 157–182)
    (This corresponds to the Board of Rites.)

    A. State Sacrifices (articles 157–162)
    B. Ceremonial Regulations (articles 163–182)

V. Military Law (articles 183–253)
    (This corresponds to the Board of War.)

    A. Imperial Palaces and Guards (articles 183–198)
    B. Administration of the Armed Forces (articles 199–219)
    C. Frontier Guard Posts (articles 220–226)
    D. Horses and Cattle (articles 227–237)
    E. Postal Services and Transport (articles 238–253)

VI. Penal Law (articles 254–423)
    (This corresponds to the Board of Punishments.)

    A. Violence and Theft (articles 254–281)
    B. Homicide (articles 282–301)
    C. Affrays and Blows (articles 302–323)
    D. Abusive Language (articles 324–331)
    E. Accusations and Suits (articles 332–343)
    F. Bribery and Squeeze (articles 344–354)
    G. Deception and Fraud (articles 355–365)
    H. Sexual Violations (articles 366–375)
    I. Miscellaneous Offenses (articles 376–386)
    J. Arrests and Escapes (articles 387–394)
    K. Trial and Imprisonment (articles 395–423)

VII. Laws on Public Works (articles 424–436)
    (This corresponds to the Board of Public Works.)

    A. Public Construction (articles 424–432)
    B. River Conservancy (articles 433–436)

If we compare these headings with the headings of the twelve books or parts of the T'ang Code, a continuity at once emerges: seven of the T'ang headings pass unchanged into the Ming and Ch'ing codes, and the remaining five, with slight changes in wording, become progenitors of seven Ming–Ch'ing counterparts. In short, all twelve book headings of the T'ang Code seem to have been carried over into the Ming-Ch'ing codes, either unchanged or in bifurcated form.[20]

However, more than half of the Ming–Ch'ing titles are entirely new creations, thus providing a broader spectrum within which to classify statutes. The T'ang Code's rather haphazard sequence of materials has in its Ming–Ch'ing reincarnations been remolded into a much more meaningful sequence, centered around an introductory division of terms and general principles, followed by six other divisions corresponding to the six boards.

The Ming has often been charged with a general lack of creativity, and in the legal sphere its codifiers have been accused of producing inconsistencies in their efforts to harmonize statutes of their own making with others taken from earlier codes.[21] No doubt these strictures are true, but they should not blind us to the great advance of the Ming Code over its predecessors in terms of

[20] The filiation of the various headings may be portrayed as follows:

T'ang headings	Ming–Ch'ing headings
1	I (unchanged)
2	V–A (modified)
3	II–A (unchanged)
4	III–A (in part) / III–C
5	III–D / V–D
6	III–A (in part)
7	VI–A (unchanged)
8	VI–C / VI–E
9	VI–G (unchanged)
10	VI–I (unchanged)
11	VI–J (unchanged)
12	VI–K (unchanged)

[21] See Hsü Tao-lin, pp. 95–98. Hsü's concise analysis is based in large measure on remarks scattered through Shen Chia-pen, *Ming lü mu chien* (The Title sections of the Ming Code explained), in *Bequeathed Writings*, pp. 774–821.

logical arrangement. In other respects as well, the Ming displayed considerable creativity in the legal sphere.

3. Statutes and Sub-statutes

We have seen in the preceding section and earlier in Chapter I, section 3, that beginning in imperial times, *lü* replaced *fa* as the regular technical designation for the individual "statutes" collectively comprising a code. Properly speaking, and perhaps in part because of the absence of inflectional difference in Chinese between singular and plural, the word *lü*, in imperial times, appears in three different legal senses: (1) As a designation for an individual "statute." (2) As a collective designation for several such statutes when assembled to form a single larger article or section. The 436 sections of the Ch'ing Code, for example, are known as the 436 *lü*, even though each of them usually—not invariably—contains three or four or perhaps half a dozen separate statutes or *lü*. In the Chinese text these are separated from one another by small printed hollow circles perhaps an eighth of an inch in diameter. (3) Finally, the total body of individual statutes or individual sections is likewise known as *lü*, in which sense the word may be translated as "code."

A study of the individual statutes found in successive dynastic codes shows that many of them have survived unchanged from one code to another. It is one scholar's estimate, for example, that 30 to 40 per cent of the statutes in the Ch'ing Code go back unchanged to the T'ang Code of 653.[22] A good many others, of course, go back with only minor changes in· wording. No doubt this continuity reflects the Chinese view of law as the codification of moral truths retaining eternal validity irrespective of time or place. Of course such a view could be only partially realized in actuality. If, for example, 30 to 40 per cent of the Ch'ing statutes remained unchanged from the T'ang, the other 60 to 70 per cent *did* change or were perhaps Ch'ing creations.

---

[22] This opinion is held by Hsüeh Yün-sheng, *Tu-li ts'un-yi* (Concentration on doubtful matters while perusing the sub-statutes; Peking, 1905), in his introductory "General Remarks" (*Tsung lun*), p. 8b. This work will be discussed later in this section.

Actually, through the centuries, some statutes were dropped, others newly created, and still others were changed in varying degrees to meet changing conditions. Even among the unchanged statutes, in fact, some survived only by becoming dead letters, retained in the codes but rarely or never invoked.

Even so, had all Chinese law consisted only of statutes, the widespread view of Chinese civilization as a monolithic entity remaining unchanged from antiquity until today would be strongly reinforced. In reality, however, the *lü* of the codes were supplemented by other legal enactments of a more informal ad hoc nature. At any time an imperial edict, issued on the emperor's own initiative or prompted by a new legal case, might modify or sometimes even virtually nullify the application of a particular *lü*. Such imperial pronouncements might or might not exert lasting force. Sometimes they eventually became enshrined in the code (perhaps of the following dynasty) as *lü* in their own right.

The names of these less formal legal pronouncements, as current under earlier dynasties, are numerous and confusing and need not concern us here. Apparently it was in Ming times that a clear-cut system was gradually formulated for dealing legally with the problem of change within tradition. The key term appearing at this time is *li*, meaning in everyday language "principle, pattern, norm, or example." Above all, it signifies a "precedent," in the sense of a past act or statement that can be appealed to as a precedent for a present decision. Used as a technical legal term, the word will be regularly translated in this book, for the sake of convenience, as "sub-statute." (It is a different word from *li*, encountered in Chapter I, signifying the rites, polite behavior, traditional morality, and exalted by the early Confucians.)

Li (sub-statutes) are legal formulations, functioning as supplements to the basic *lü* (statutes) and having their origin in imperial edicts or, perhaps more commonly, in individual legal judgments pronounced by the Board of Punishments and then confirmed by imperial endorsement. In 1492, so we read in the Ming "Legal Treatise," the president of the Board of Punishments asked the throne for permission to compile a single list of the *li* (precedents or sub-statutes) that had accumulated up to that time.[23] This compilation, entitled *Wen-hsing t'iao-li* or *Itemized Sub-statutes for Pronouncing Judgments,* was completed in 1500 and embodied a total of 297 *li.* A memorial accompanying the completed work explained that during the century following the compilation of the Ming Code in 1397, many *li* (precedents) had been issued by successive emperors as instruments for dealing with particular situations not anticipated by the original framers of the Code. "These *li,*" the memorial continued, "are intended to bolster the *lü,* not to destroy them."

Thereafter the *Wen-hsing t'iao-li* functioned side by side with the Ming Code as a subsidiary collection of legal pronoucements, to which new *li* were added as they appeared. By 1549 the number of *li* had increased in this way from 297 to 349.[24] Then in 1585 the final logical step was taken of combining the *li* in the *Wen-hsing t'iao-li*—by this time a total of 382—with the relevant *lü* in the Code, to form a single text.

It is the 1585 edition of the Ming Code, in which *lü* and *li* are thus for the first time combined, that became the basis for the first Ch'ing Code of 1646. Not only did the Ch'ing Code adopt a great many *lü* (statutes) from its predecessor, some of which went back to the T'ang dynasty or conceivably even earlier, but, at the same time, it adopted no less than 321 of the Ming Code's 382 *li* (sub-statutes).[25] The combination of statutes and sub-statutes in the first version of the Ch'ing Code is reflected in its full title, *Ta Ch'ing lü chi-chieh fu-li,* which means *Great Ch'ing Code with Collected Commentaries and Appended Sub-statutes.*[26]

Thereafter, however, what had happened in the Ming was repeated in the Ch'ing. That is to say, no effort was made to incorporate the new sub-statutes appearing in subsequent

[23] See *Li-tai hsing-fa chi'.,* pp. 572–573, on this compilation and the facts that follow on the Ming dynasty.

[24] The text of the Ming "Legal Treatise" reads 249, which, as pointed out by Hsü Tao-lin, p. 93, is probably a mistake for 349 because 249 is less than the number of *li* originally compiled in 1500.

[25] For the figure of 321, see Shen Chia-pen, *Yung-cheng lü k'o-pen pa* (Postface to the printed edition of the Yung-cheng Code), in *Bequeathed Writings,* pp. 996–997.

[26] For this development and the other Ch'ing developments discussed in the remainder of this section, see, unless otherwise indicated, the Ch'ing "Legal Treatise," pp. 13 ff.

decades directly into the Code. Instead, in 1679, they were all brought together into a separate compilation called the *Hsien-hsing tse-li* or *Sub-statutes Currently Operative*, which in later years was progressively enlarged. In 1689 it was suggested that it be amalgamated with the Code to form a single work, and after many years' delay the task was completed in 1707. For unexplained reasons, however, the result was never printed but was limited to 42 manuscript copies. Thus, prior to the last major revision of the Code in 1723–1727, all sub-statutes other than those originally incorporated into the Ch'ing Code from the Ming in 1646 were circulated and used quite separately from the Code itself. A major result of the 1723–1727 revision was to combine all statutes and sub-statutes for the first time into a single printed work. The sub-statutes thus incorporated included: (1) 321 of Ming origin taken from the 1646 Code; (2) 290 taken from the *Hsien-hsing tse-li;* and (3) 204 others of later years, making a total of 815 sub-statutes.[27]

In 1736 it was decided that the Code should be revised every three years by a special body known as the Statutes Commission (see Chapter IV, section 2) in order to include in it whatever sub-statutes had come into being since the previous revision. In 1746 the tempo of revision was reduced to once every five years, but this schedule was only approximately adhered to.[28] By 1863, when the next-to-last revision was made, the sub-statutes reached their peak figure of 1,892. Thereafter no further revisions took place until the final spate of changes from 1905 onward, as a result of which the sub-statutes were reduced to 1,327.[29]

To trace the successive textual changes in the Ch'ing Code— the precise date when one sub-statute was added, another dropped, and still a third revised—would be almost impossible

[27] These figures are those given by the Ch'ing "Legal Treatise," p. 21. Shen Chia-pen, *Yung-cheng lü k'o-pen pa*, in *Bequeathed Writings,* gives a different figure for (2) of 299, resulting in a total of 824.

[28] During the Ch'ien-lung period (1736–1795), according to the Ch'ing "Legal Treatise," p. 23, revisions occurred "eight or nine times." Thereafter, between 1801 and 1863, there were no fewer than fifteen revisions, occurring in 1801, 1806, 1814, 1820, 1821, 1825, 1826, 1830, 1839, 1840, 1841, 1845, 1846, 1852, and 1863. See table on p. 40 of Liang Ch'i-ch'ao, *Chung-kuo ch'eng-wen fa pien-chih chih yen-ko* (Changing phases in the compilation of Chinese written law; Taipei, 1957).

[29] See Ch'ing "Legal Treatise," p. 32, note 1, and Meijer, p. 56.

were it not for the painstaking work of a late Ch'ing scholar, Hsüeh Yün-sheng. In his *Tu-li ts'un-yi* or *Concentration on Doubtful Matters While Perusing the Sub-statutes,* Hsüeh has appended numerous notes to most items in the Code, indicating their date of origin and subsequent revisions, if any.[30]

In a legal system resting upon statutes sometimes already centuries old when a code was first compiled, something like the sub-statute system was obviously necessary if any real effort were to be made to cope with a changing social environment. Being the outgrowth of edicts or court decisions that might initially have been based upon very particular circumstances, the sub-statutes tended to be more concrete and narrower in scope than the statutes to which they were attached. As a consequence, it was a regular principle in Ch'ing law that whenever a statute and a sub-statute were both applicable to a given case, the decision was to be based on the sub-statute rather than the statute, even though this might sometimes result in serious modification or even virtual nullification of the intent of the statute.

Undoubtedly, the sub-statutes proved helpful for dealing with situations unthought-of by the original framers of the Code. However, a good deal of confusion and difficulty sometimes resulted from the rather ad hoc manner in which the sub-statutes had often originated and from the fact that, once included in the Code, they tended, much like the statutes, to acquire a sanctity of their own, resulting sometimes in their retention long after their usefulness had ended. The Ch'ing "Legal Treatise" (p. 23) describes what happened:

If a sub-statute were available, the statute would no longer be used. The statutes in large part became empty words, whereas the sub-statutes ever proliferated and became more fragmentary. Between those of earlier and later date contradictions developed. Sometimes a sub-statute was used to increase the punishment beyond that provided in the statute, or sometimes it was used to destroy a statute. And sometimes a sub-statute was formulated in such a way that it could deal with a single occurrence only. The point was reached where because of one sub-statute, it became necessary to create another sub-statute.

[30] To Professor M.H. van der Valk of the University of Leiden I am much indebted for first calling my attention to Hsüeh's work.

A good example of how a sub-statute might survive for centuries, despite its bizarre and highly specific language, occurs in one of the cases (195.2) translated later in this volume. The Board of Punishments, in passing judgment on this case, cites the sub-statute merely as the one "on knavish fellows who rush into government offices in order to exercise coercion upon the officials there." If we examine the actual text of the sub-statute as printed in the Code, however, we find that it begins with a very colorful preamble: "If a knavish fellow from outside [the capital], with a yellow square of cloth on his back, a yellow banner planted upon his head, and accusations issuing from his mouth, rushes into a government office in order to exercise coercion upon the officials there . . ."

It would be interesting to determine what particular episode in the history of Peking prompted the framing of this particular sub-statute but extremely difficult too because, as was pointed out by Hsüeh Yün-sheng,[31] the sub-statute is one of uncertain original date that was taken over by the Ch'ing Code from its Ming predecessor. Curiously enough, a revision of the sub-statute made in 1771 did not go so far as to alter its colorful preamble about the yellow banner. Hsüeh remarks that modern jurists, when using the sub-statute, no longer quote this curious passage, and his remark is confirmed by the way the sub-statute is cited in our own case, the date of which, 1881, makes it chronologically next to the last in our sequence of cases.

4. Commentaries and Translations

We come now to the thorny question of the commentaries on the Ch'ing Code—thorny because so little seems to be known about them. These commentaries, as a rule, cover only the statutes but not the sub-statutes. Generically they are of two kinds: official commentaries, which are compiled by governmental boards of scholars commissioned to write them; and private commentaries, which are written by scholars acting purely on their own initiative without governmental sanction.

[31] Hsüeh Yün-sheng, 39:7b–8.

Only official commentaries are mentioned in the Ch'ing "Legal Treatise." Commonly, however, editions of the Code are annotated with both official and unofficial commentaries.

Depending upon their typographical arrangement on the page, all commentaries, whether official or private, also fall into two categories: (1) An interlinear commentary, dealing with specific statutes, which is to be found in all standard editions of the Code and happens at the same time to be an official commentary. It is located at the end of each individual statute as well as between the clauses or phrases of the statute. Being printed in smaller type, it is sometimes known as the *Hsiao chu* or Small Commentary. (However, in the Chinese text from which the cases in Part Two of this book were translated, it is simply called the *Chu*, Commentary.) (2) General commentaries, which are usually longer than the interlinear commentary, also occur and do not deal with each statute separately. Rather, they discuss all statutes in a given section of the Code as a whole. This kind of commentary, which may be either official or private, is printed at the end of the block of statutes to which it refers and in front of the related sub-statutes.

In the Chinese texts, the Code's pages are divided into two horizontal parts. On the lower half-pages, blocks of statutes, with interspersed interlinear commentary, are followed by general commentary and then by sub-statutes. The upper half-pages may or may not be occupied by miscellaneous materials, such as edicts thought to be relevant, summary reports of pertinent important cases, and additional comments, including in many editions long quotations from the private commentary of Shen Chih-ch'i (discussed below). The materials thus printed on upper half-pages are called the *Shang chu* or Upper Commentary. Even though some of these materials—such as edicts—emanate from official sources, private editors determine the content of the Upper Commentary. These additions to the materials printed on the lower half-pages have no official standing. The Upper Commentary is, therefore, much less important than the officially compiled interlinear commentary found below.

The authors of the Ming Code followed the practice of earlier codifiers in accompanying the statutes with an officially compiled interlinear commentary. Hence, when many of the Ming statutes were incorporated in the first Ch'ing Code of 1646, the Ming interlinear commentary on these borrowed statutes was taken over as well and has reappeared ever since in subsequent versions of the Ch'ing Code. This interlinear commentary, because of its official origin and the fact that it carries an authority equal to that of the statutes themselves, will be referred to in the rest of this book as the Official Commentary. It should be noted that though the commentary is in principle restricted to the statutes only, there are rare instances (cases 148.7, 175.6, 239.7) in which it covers sub-statutes as well. In our translations we shall find the judicial authorities citing it occasionally as a basis for pronouncing judgment (cases 17.1, 19.1, 161.3, 167.5, 191.1, 200.2, 239.7). In three other cases (149.2, 186.9, 191.1) they cite instead other nonofficial commentaries.

It must not be supposed that the Ch'ing codifiers simply took over the Ming interlinear commentary without change. On the contrary, the commentary underwent significant additions as well as changes both in 1646 and again during the extensive reworking of the Ch'ing Code in 1723–1727. The result is that the Ch'ing Official Commentary is a great deal bulkier than its Ming prototype. For the most part, the additions consist of words or phrases inserted to give greater clarity or precision to the statute. Occasionally, however, the additions make a significant change in the meaning of the statute as well and are able to do this without actually changing the text of the virtually sacrosanct statute itself.

For examples of how this happens, let us examine the two successive statutes (Boulais translation, nos. 1268 and 1269) dealing respectively with homicide during an affray and with intentional (but not premeditated) homicide. When these statutes are cited in reports of legal cases, they are represented as respectively specifying strangulation after the assizes and decapitation after the assizes for the two offenses. Examination of the Code itself, however, reveals that the words "after the assizes" are nowhere present in the statutory text proper, but appear only as part of the interlinear Official Commentary, printed in smaller type. Furthermore, comparison with the Ming Code shows the words to have been added by the Ch'ing codifiers; they appear neither in the text proper nor the commentary of the Ming Code, which speaks in unqualified terms only of strangulation and decapitation. Although the difference between statute proper and the added qualifying words in the Official Commentary is typographically evident to anyone personally examining the Ch'ing Code, this difference disappears as soon as the statute is cited in another document. In this manner the interlinear additions succeed in becoming, to all intents and purposes, integral parts of the Code itself.

Besides the interlinear Official Commentary, the Ch'ing Code formerly had another commentary, also officially compiled, that was appended to each section of statutes, where it provided an overall exposition of their general meaning. This commentary, known as the *Tsung chu* or General Commentary, was composed in or around 1695, but apparently not formally published until much later.[32] Only in 1727, as part of the extensive revisions made in 1723–1727, was it joined to the text proper of the Code in a single printed work. However, this union did not last long, for the General Commentary soon came to be regarded as superficial and superfluous. In 1740, when the definitive edition of the Code appeared, the one significant difference between it and the 1727 version was the elimination of the General Commentary. It has been omitted ever since, and so the term Official Commentary, as used in this volume, refers only to the interlinear commentary.

Besides this now abandoned General Commentary and the still surviving Official Commentary—both compiled at imperial command—numerous commentaries prepared at the initiative of private scholars are known to have existed as early as Ming times; one scholar has put the Ming works at "not less than several tens."[33] Most of them have disappeared as separate entities, but among the few that survive, one, known as the *Chien-shih Com-*

---

[32] For this date, which does not appear in the Ch'ing "Legal Treatise," see Hsüeh Yün-sheng, "General Remarks," p. 9b in *Tu-li ts'un-yi.*

[33] Yang Hung-lieh, II, 735, where he lists fourteen titles. See also the similar list in Shen Chia-pen, *Lü-ling* (Statutes and ordinances), 9:28b–29b, in *Bequeathed Writings,* pp. 489–490.

mentary (original preface dated 1612), is quoted in two of our translated cases (186.9 and 191.1).

In 1706 an anonymous book was published in Peking bearing the lengthy title of *Ta Ch'ing lü-li chu-chu kuang-hui ch'üan-shu* (Expanded classification of complete writings written as a red commentary on statutes and sub-statutes of the great Ch'ing). Here the important words to keep in mind are *chu-chu*, "red commentary," referring to an extensive commentary printed in red ink on the upper margins of this work, as well as, often, between the vertical columns of the text proper. Unlike the other commentaries we have encountered, this one covers most of the sub-statutes as well as the statutes. It is a broadly conceived work, quoting liberally from earlier commentaries, among which some eight are identifiable as being of Ming date. Others, however, are cited in abbreviated form only ("Li says," "Yao says," "the *Mirror* says," "the *Annotation* says"), and are completely un-identifiable. Presumably they may include comments by Ch'ing as well as Ming writers.[34]

In contrast to this anonymous work, which apparently never achieved wide circulation, another private commentary was pro-duced about a decade later which became much better known. This is the *Ta Ch'ing lü chi-chu* or *Great Ch'ing Code with Collected Commentaries,* compiled by Shen Chih-ch'i, whose preface is dated 1715. Like any other private commentator, Shen of course retains the Official Commentary, but he then inserts his own general exposition after each block of statutes. In printed editions, his exposition is differentiated from the Official Com-mentary by being printed at a slightly lower level on the page. In addition, a supplemental commentary, also by Shen, runs along the tops of most pages above the statutes. In later editions of the Code containing the Shen commentary, numerous segments from this supplemental commentary (each identified by the rubric *Chi-chu*, "Collected Commentaries") are interspersed with other later materials to constitute, in their totality, what has been described above as the Upper Commentary.

[34] For a convenient brief account of this commentary, see Shen Chia-pen, *Kuang-hui ch'üan-shu pa* (Postface to the *Kuang-hui ch'üan-shu*), in *Bequeathed Writings,* p. 998.

Shen states in his preface that his commentary is the outgrowth of more than thirty years judicial experience in various prefectural and district government offices, that it has taken six or seven years to complete, and that it makes use of fifteen earlier commentaries. Among these he lists nine by name, all of which, when identifiable, turn out to be Ming works. Shen's commentary has been reproduced in many later editions of the Code, including the two of the late nineteenth century used for the present volume.[35] Indeed, one wonders if its popularity may not have been one reason for discarding the officially compiled General Commentary after 1740. Of course, the Shen work did not have the authority of the Official Commentary, and it is cited only once (case 149.2) in the text proper of our translated cases. Occasionally, however, the translator has made use of it in writing his added annotations, referring to it then as the Shen Chih-ch'i Commentary.

The Code is commonly printed with certain texts appended to it, such as the standard "Instructions to Coroners" (see our translated case 199.4), and, at the beginning, certain important introductory tables. The tables include lists of the various punishments, the fines permitted in lieu of ordinary penalties for certain categories of persons when guilty of certain kinds of offenses (see Chapter III, section 2), the five degrees of mourning whereby family relationships are measured (see Chapter I, section 9), and so on. Like so much else, most of these tables have been inherited from the Ming Code.

Finally, a word about Western translations of the Ch'ing Code made in English by George Thomas Staunton (1810), and in French by P. L. F. Philastre (1876), and Gui Boulais (1924).[36]

The Staunton translation was a remarkable work for its day but

---

[35] The primary edition used is the *Ta Ch'ing lü-li hui-t'ung hsin-tsuan* (Comprehensive new edition of the *Ta Ch'ing lü-li*), ed. Yao Yü-hsiang (Peking, 1873; reprinted, Taipei, 1964 in 5 vols. with continuous pagination). This edition, however, has been compared from time to time with the *Ta Ch'ing lü-li tseng-hsiu t'ung-tsuan chi-ch'eng* (1878).

[36] Staunton, tr., *Ta Tsing Leu Lee* (London, 1810); P. L. F. Philastre, tr., *Le Code annamite, nouvelle traduction complète, comprenant: Les commentaires officiels du Code, traduits pour la première fois; de nombreuses annotations extraites des Commentaires du Code chinois . . .* 2 vols. (Paris, 1876; 2d ed., 1909 [adds a 20-page index]); Boulais, tr., *Manuel du code chinois* (Shanghai, 1924).

has been rendered largely obsolete by the other two. Its major defect is that under each of the Code's 436 sections it translates only the statutes and none of the sub-statutes.

The Philastre work, despite its title, actually translates most of the Ch'ing Code, since the Annamite Code of 1812 which it covers is very largely a reproduction of the 1740 Ch'ing Code. However, it includes only 398 of the latter's 436 sections. Philastre is careful to indicate at all times the places where the Annamite Code diverges from that of Ch'ing. The translation is not only of high quality but is also amazingly complete, including as it does all of the Annamite Code's 398 statutes and most of its sub-statutes, as well as commentaries on the former. Indeed, it seems almost incredible that the translator, a French naval lieutenant, could have completed this work of over 1,500 pages (see his introduction) in less than four years (June 1871–March 1875, according to Vol. I, p. 4). Unfortunately, the book is excessively rare, at least in the United States, and could not be regularly consulted while the present volume was being prepared.[37]

The translation by Gui Boulais, a Jesuit, is of good quality and has the very great convenience that the Chinese texts of each translated statute or sub-statute are placed at the bottom of the page. (Neither Staunton nor Philastre provides Chinese characters.) Boulais, unlike Staunton, translates sub-statutes as well as statutes. However, he is far less complete than Philastre, for he includes no commentaries, omits a very considerable number of sub-statutes, and translates a fair number of others in abbreviated form only, making it necessary to check his reproduced Chinese texts against the original versions in the Code. Furthermore, he omits no less than 64 of the 436 sections of the Code entirely.[38] Very occasionally, moreover, we have found him guilty—and

---

[37] To Professor M. H. van der Valk of the University of Leiden I am once more indebted for drawing my attention to the importance of Philastre. [In 1967, while the present volume was in press, a reprint of Philastre (2d ed.) was issued by the Ch'eng-wen Publishing Co., Taiwan.]

[38] As numbered by Staunton, they are secs. 28–29, 34, 40–41, 43–44, 46, 51, 68–70, 85, 156, 161, 216, 226, 228–232, 235, 237, 241, 244, 246–247, 253, 279–281, 286, 307–308, 326, 342–343, 362–363, 377, 391–393, 397, 400, 402–403, 405–408, 410, 414–415, 417–419, 421–423, 427–428, 430. Although many of these omissions are relatively unimportant, others are astonishing, for example, the vitally important sec. 44 on the use of analogy. Particularly glaring are the twenty omissions from the divisions on Arrests and escapes and Trial and imprisonment.

who is not—of serious mistranslations (see our cases 149.2, 210.2, 260.1). Despite these flaws, however, Boulais is far superior to Staunton and much more accessible than Philastre. Hence his numbering of statutes and sub-statutes has been used throughout this volume for all references to the Code.[39]

These divisions are, of course, of the utmost importance for anyone studying the concrete operation of the judicial system.

[39] Boulais has 1,738 numbered paragraphs corresponding to individual statutes and sub-statutes in the Code, and also including occasional paragraphs of comment by himself. All these numbered paragraphs are preceded by his translation of the introductory tables in the Code; this introductory material, which he did not number consecutively with his subsequent numbered paragraphs, must be referred to separately by page number. It should be remembered that the original Chinese text of the Code contains no numbering whatsoever, either for its 436 main sections or for the individual statutes and sub-statutes grouped under them. Thus a Chinese judge never cited a statute or sub-statute by number but simply quoted that portion of it which was essential to his purpose, often abbreviating it in so doing. To identify such citations, therefore, a close familiarity with the Code is required, the more so as its arrangement of materials often differs from what one might initially expect. In Appendix A of this book, wherein all statutes and sub-statutes cited in our translated cases are listed, each reference to Boulais is correlated with the corresponding pagination in the Chinese Code (according to the 1964 reprint edition cited in note 35 above).

III · THE PENAL SYSTEM

1. The "Five Punishments"

Wu hsing, "the five punishments," is the generic term used by the Chinese from antiquity until the present century to designate their major legal penalties. At first sight the number suggests a relationship with the many sequences in fives (the five colors, five notes, five tastes, five directions, and many more) constituting the Chinese politico-cosmic system dominated by the Five Elements. However, a correlation between the five punishments and these elements has never been stressed in Chinese writings and is first mentioned only relatively late (perhaps in the first century B.C.). Further, it seems possible that the term "five punishments" may already have been known before the Five Elements system was worked out—perhaps, indeed, even before the appearance of the earliest written "codes" of law in the sixth century B.C. According to tradition, for example (see Chapter I, section 3), it was the non-Chinese barbarian Miao people who, in the twenty-third century B.C., first created the five punishments (*wu hsing*), which they then called law (*fa*).

The content of the term has changed greatly through the ages. In pre-imperial China it referred exclusively to the corporal punishments of tatooing, amputation of the nose, amputation of one or both feet, castration, and death. Under the Han dynasty, however, the five punishments were greatly mitigated. Tatooing and amputation of the nose and feet were abolished by imperial edict in 167 B.C. Castration, probably abolished at a slightly earlier date but then again revived, was finally ended in the second decade of the second century A.D. During the Han, in short, all corporal punishments other than death and beating were replaced by varying forms of penal servitude.[1]

During the Period of Disunity (220–580), the five punish-

[1] Hulsewé, *Remnants of Han Law*, I, 124–128.

ments underwent further changes and each of them, instead of remaining a single punishment, became a category embracing graduated degrees of the same punishment. Finally, in the Sui Code of 581–583 (the prototype of the surviving T'ang Code of 653), the five punishments assumed the standard forms which, with minor changes and additions, they have held ever since.[2]

1. Beating with light stick (5 degrees: 10 to 50 blows)
2. Beating with heavy stick (5 degrees: 60 to 100 blows)
3. Penal servitude (5 degrees: 1 to 3 years)
4. Life exile (3 degrees: at distances of 2,000 to 3,000 li)
   (3 li = about 1 English mile)
5. Death (2 degrees: strangulation and decapitation)

Among later additions, the most important has been a third degree of death penalty, death by slicing; also, a more severe form of exile, known as military exile, was appended to the standard three degrees of life exile. In addition, the two standard death penalties of strangulation and decapitation came to be divided into two sub-categories known as "immediate" execution and execution "after the assizes" (see below). It will be helpful to tabulate at this point the five main categories of punishment as listed in the Ch'ing Code of 1740:

I. *Light Bamboo (ch'ih):* 5 degrees		II. *Heavy Bamboo (chang):* 5 degrees	
Nominal number of blows	Actual number of blows	Nominal number of blows	Actual number of blows
1. 10	4	1. 60	20
2. 20	5	2. 70	25
3. 30	10	3. 80	30
4. 40	15	4. 90	35
5. 50	20	5. 100	40

III. *Penal Servitude (t'u):* 5 standard degrees plus 3 supplemental degrees (Actual number of blows of heavy bamboo is shown in parentheses.)

1. 1 year plus 60 (20) blows
2. 1½ years plus 70 (25) blows

[2] The punishments of the Period of Disunity are conveniently tabulated in Balazs, pp. 210–211.

3. 2 years plus 80 (30) blows
4. 2½ years plus 90 (35) blows
5. 3 years plus 100 (40) blows
6. Total penal servitude (*tsung t'u*): 4 years plus 100 (40) blows
7. Authorized penal servitude (*chun t'u*): 5 years plus same
8. Transportation reduced to two-year authorized penal servitude (*ch'ien hsi pi liu chien pan chun t'u erh nien*): 2 years plus same [Often abbreviated to "transportation-authorized penal servitude" (*ch'ien hsi chun t'u*)]

IVa. *Life Exile* (*liu*): 3 standard degrees plus 1 preliminary degree [Each degree was accompanied by 100 (40) blows of heavy bamboo.]

Transportation (*ch'ien hsi*): life exile at a distance of 1,000 li (about 333 miles) from the offender's place of conviction
1. Exile at a distance of 2,000 li
2. Exile at a distance of 2,500 li
3. Exile at a distance of 3,000 li

IVb. *Military Exile* (*ch'ung chün*): 5 standard degrees plus 1 supplemental degree [Each degree was accompanied by 100 (40) blows of heavy bamboo.]
1. Very near (*fu chin*): 2,000 li
2. Nearby frontier (*chin pien*): 2,500 li
3. Distant frontier (*pien yüan*): 3,000 li
4. Farthest frontier (*chi pien*): 4,000 li
5. In a malarial region (*yen chang*): 4,000 li
6. Deportation (*fa ch'ien*): life service as a slave in a Manchu or other Tatar military post in northern Manchuria (Amur River, etc.) or western Sinkiang (Ili, etc.)

V. *Death* (*ssu*): 2 standard degrees plus 1 supplemental degree
1a. Strangulation (*chiao*) after the assizes (*chien hou*)
2a. Decapitation (*chan*) after the assizes
1b. Strangulation, immediate (*li chüeh*)
2b. Decapitation, immediate
3. Death by slicing (*ling ch'ih*)

2. Imprisonment and Fines

Before discussing the above punishments in detail, it is worth noting that neither imprisonment nor fining was formally recognized as a separate punishment. (Imprisonment, meaning confinement in a local prison unaccompanied by forced labor, is to be distinguished from the standard punishment of penal servitude, described in section 4 below, which involved removal to, and forced labor in, another region.) Wrongdoers, of course, might be detained for considerable periods (sometimes years) in prison before final execution of sentence, but their sentence per se never included imprisonment. (A similar situation, aside from debtor's prison, existed in the West until the late eighteenth and early nineteenth century.) The only exception, and it is a rare one, is that of women who, because of their sex, might have their sentences of exile or of death after the assizes commuted respectively to temporary or life imprisonment in their own district. Solitary examples of each are found among our translated cases (cases 12.2 and 159.3).

Fining, although a common penalty, was a substitute for one or another recognized punishment rather than an accepted punishment in itself. Hence, it should more properly be termed monetary redemption or simply redemption. Redemption was permitted for certain categories of wrongdoers (women, persons aged 70 or above, children of 15 or below, officials, wives of officials, and some others) for some—not all—offenses. Such redemption was not automatic, but had to be granted in each case. In several of our translated cases (cases 12.2, 61.1, 159.1, 171.5, 171.6, 203.5) we find redemption expressly withheld by the judicial authorities. When granted, however, it amounted to token punishment. The sum for a capital crime committed by women, the aged, and some others, for example, was only 0.525 ounces of silver.[3]

Redemption was standard for accidental injury or death, when it became a reparation paid to the victim or his family, for which reason it was much larger than the token redemption fees mentioned above. For accidental death, for example, the sum was 12.42 ounces of silver. Sometimes such reparation might be exacted in addition to some other standard penalty. In treason cases, certain relatives of the chief offender became slaves of the government, and all their property was confiscated. Stolen prop-

[3] See Boulais, tables on pp. 11–16 and main text, nos. 36–41.

erty or property otherwise illegally acquired was, of course, also subject to confiscation and restoration to its proper owner. For officials guilty of misdeeds other than major offenses, the usual penalties might be commutable to redemption, forfeiture of salary for a given period, reduction in rank, or—a very serious punishment for an officeholder—dismissal from the civil service. Such commutation, however, was by no means invariably forthcoming.

3. The Light and Heavy Bamboo

Beating was administered on the buttocks—bared for men, covered with underpants for women. Ever since the Sui Code of 581–583, with the sole exception of the Yuan dynasty (see Chapter II, note 19), the number of blows of the light or heavy stick had been calculated in units of ten. Following the Manchu conquest of 1644, however, the number for each degree of beating was halved (10 blows became 5 blows, 20 became 10). Still later, as recorded in the *Hsien-hsing tse-li* (the first Ch'ing compilation of sub-statutes, issued in 1679), the number was further reduced so that what had originally been 10 became 4, 20 became 5, 30 became 10, and so on, as shown in our table above.

The Ch'ing "Legal Treatise" (p. 44) characterizes these developments as examples of "a benevolence transcending the law." In actual fact, however, the real reason was probably somewhat less idealistic. During the Han dynasty and for several centuries thereafter, the sticks used for beating had been made of bamboo. Beginning probably in the Liang dynasty (502–556), however, they were instead made of a special kind of wood known as *ch'u*.[4] The diameters of these *ch'u* sticks, as fixed by law from the T'ang through the Ming dynasty, were, for the small stick, 0.2 Chinese

[4] Exact identity uncertain, but very probably to be equated with the *Vitex negundo* (for which there is no common English name). This is a small bush-like tree, of which one variety is common in North China, where its thin flexible branches are used by the peasants to plait baskets. See Yü Ching-jang, "Shih ching chi" (The Ching and Chi plants elucidated), *Ta-lu tsa-chih* (Continent magazine), 14.12:365–372 (June 30, 1957). I am greatly indebted to Professor Hui-lin Li, of the Morris Arboretum, University of Pennsylvania, for directing me to this carefully reasoned article and for confirming its identification of *ch'u* as probably *Vitex negundo*.

inches at the large end and 0.15 inches at the small end; for the large stick, 0.27 inches at the large end, 0.17 inches at the small end. But then, for inexplicable reasons (except perhaps the desire to imitate antiquity), the Manchus replaced these *ch'u* sticks once more with staves of bamboo. Their diameters were, for the small bamboo, 1.5 inches at the large end, 1 inch at the small end; for the large bamboo, 2 inches at the large end, 1.5 inches at the small end. They were thus "several times larger" than their predecessors. Almost surely, it is this physical enlargement of the sticks, rather than any growth of humanitarianism, that made necessary the reduction of the number of blows, so that offenders might not die under the beatings.[5]

Despite the reduction, all penalties continued to be expressed in terms of the traditional numbers. This fact—a good example of Chinese insistence upon continuity in name despite change in fact—should be kept in mind as we encounter beatings ordered in the cases translated in this book.

4. Penal Servitude

The basic meaning of *t'u* is "to walk on foot." The word occurs in certain early texts as a designation for "convict," probably in the sense of a criminal who was marched on foot to the place where he was to perform hard labor. Beginning in 564, the word became the formal designation for a legal punishment, and in this book it will be regularly rendered as "penal servitude" in order to bring out the fact that the punishment included hard labor for the offender as well as his removal from his place of origin to another area for a fixed term of years. In Ming times, persons thus sentenced were sent from the province of their conviction to another province where, during the term specified, they worked in an iron or salt works. In these establishments the daily quotas required of them consisted either of the smelting of three catties (about four English pounds) of iron or the production, through

---

[5] For the materials and dimensions of the sticks at various periods, see Shen Chia-pen, *Hsing-chü k'ao* (A study of the instruments of punishment), p. 23b, in *Bequeathed Writings*, p. 519. For the deduction that the enlarged dimensions made the reduced number of blows necessary, see Philastre, I, 114–116.

boiling, of the same amount of salt. Persons sentenced to penal servitude were not sent from their own province to another province haphazardly. On the contrary, for each province of origin there was a specific counterpart province to which its convicts were always to be sent.[6]

This system continued during the early Ch'ing until 1725 when, for reasons that are not clear, convicts stopped being sent to outside provinces and, instead, were thereafter kept within the province of their conviction, there being put to work in government postal stations or, failing that, in local government yamens (centers of administration). Just what kind of work they did in these establishments is not clearly indicated.[7]

Exceedingly rare, but requiring more explanation than the standard five degrees of penal servitude, are the special supplemental punishments of four-year total penal servitude, five-year authorized penal servitude, and "transportation reduced to two-year authorized penal servitude." All three of these curious punishments are carry-overs from the Ming to the Ch'ing. Among the offenses listed in the Ch'ing Code, there are only two under each of the first two of these punishments and only five under the third (see section 10, table). Among the cases translated in this book, the first punishment appears only twice (cases 151.11 and 199.7), the second not at all, and the third only once (case 44.1).

To understand the origin of total penal servitude and five-year authorized penal servitude, we should keep in mind that among the many offenses punishable either by exile or by death (see section 10), there were a few (15 under exile and 12 under death) known as "miscellaneous offenses" (*tsa fan*). These were offenses which, though nominally punishable by exile or by death respectively, were in actual fact and as specified by statute automatically commutable to lower penalties.

Among these lower punishments, five-year authorized penal

[6] See account and table in *Ta Ming hui-tien* (Collected institutes of the great Ming dynasty; reprint of 1587 ed., Taipei, 1963), 61:27b–28. Convicts from Fukien, for example, were to be sent to salt works (names given) in Kiangsu, and convicts from Kiangsi to iron works (names also given) in Shantung.

[7] See *Ta Ch'ing hui-tien shih-li* (Supplement to collected institutes of the great Ch'ing dynasty; reprint of 1899 ed., Taipei, 1963), 741:1–3b. See also Ch'ing "Legal Treatise," p. 45.

servitude was especially devised as a substitute for death with respect to some—far from all—of the "miscellaneous offenses" for which death was the nominal penalty. The word "authorized" (*chun*) in the title of this punishment expresses the fact that its form of penal servitude (indistinguishable from any other save for the exceptional length of five years) was an "authorized" substitute for the nominal death penalty. In the same way, total penal servitude was especially devised as a substitute for exile with respect to some—again far from all—of the "miscellaneous offenses" nominally calling for exile. However, the significance of the word "total" (*tsung*) in the title is not clear.

The third of the peculiar punishments, "transportation reduced to two-year authorized penal servitude," is a hybrid, deriving from the rare Ming punishment of transportation, that is, life exile at a distance of 1,000 li. Apparently it was felt by the codifiers that some of the offenses covered by transportation did not really deserve such a heavy penalty. In order to take care of these offenses, therefore, a formula was devised under which the punishment, although still retaining "transportation" as part of its title, was in actual fact reduced to a mere two years of "authorized penal servitude" (authorized for the same reason cited above). Apparently this penal servitude was in no way different from an ordinary two-year term of penal servitude.

Information on all three of these special punishments is sparse, scattered, and far from easy to interpret, whether found in the Ch'ing Code, the Ch'ing "Legal Treatise," or elsewhere.[8]

5. Life Exile

Liu, here rendered "exile" or sometimes "life exile" (to differentiate it clearly from the other kind of exile known as military

[8] On total penal servitude and five-year authorized penal servitude, see Shen Chia-pen, *Tsung k'ao* (Comprehensive study), 4:14b, in *Bequeathed Writings,* p. 28. Unfortunately, he fails to discuss "transportation reduced to two-year authorized penal servitude," which is the most obscure of the three. Casual references to it appear in the Ch'ing Code (Boulais, nos. 225, 381 and 1518, and another section which is omitted by Boulais, but, if included, would come between his nos. 1515 and 1516; it is no. 343 in Staunton). Still more important are the brief remarks in the Ch'ing "Legal Treatise," p. 49, and comments by the Peking editors in *ibid.,* p. 50, notes 4–5; also the even briefer, but important, remarks in *Ta Ch'ing hui-tien* (reprint of 1899 ed., Taipei, 1963), 53:6b.

exile), literally means "to flow" (as of a river). From this root meaning the word acquires the secondary meanings of "to disperse, to disappear," and so, in a legal context, "to go into exile" (to disappear from one's kith and kin). As used in the codes, however, the word has a limited connotation only: that of exile from one's own to another province rather than outside the country. In the next section, under the name of deportation, we will encounter the only form of exile actually taking the offender beyond the confines of China proper.

The word *liu* brings us face to face with one of the earliest phases of Chinese legal thinking. In Chapter I, we read the myth of the barbarian Miao who created the five oppressive punishments. According to one version of that myth, they were exterminated for so doing; according to another, however, they were merely banished to the extreme northwestern corner of the world.[9] This instance of exile is not the only one in early Chinese pseudo-history. On the contrary, we hear of other ancient "rebels" and refractory persons who, during approximately the same period (supposedly a golden age), committed such crimes against humanity that they had to be exiled beyond the habitable world.

There is no doubt that an important purpose of exile, in China as elsewhere, was to protect society against the criminal. At the same time, however, the antiquity of the concept in China and the fact that exile persisted there until the twentieth century as the most serious of all legal punishments short of death itself, point to something deeply rooted in the Chinese psyche, namely, their horror at the idea of being permanently detached from clan and natal community. This sentiment in turn rested upon a religious foundation: the common cult of the ancestors by the clan group and the consequent identification of the individual with his clan members both living and dead.

Of course, with the expansion of Chinese civilization and its growing contacts with outside peoples, this ancient sense of clan and communal solidarity weakened. Yet legal institutions—particularly those of China—are notorious conservers of tradition. Moreover, even in recent centuries, with the migration of millions of Chinese overseas, the tradition has persisted that at death one's body should be returned to the homeland for burial with the ancestors.

Once we understand this attitude, it becomes quite natural that the severity of exile should be measured in terms of its distance from the native community. Thus, in the Ch'ing and earlier codes, the three degrees of exile progress through distances of 2,000 li (about 666 English miles), to 2,500 li, and finally to 3,000 li.

By Ch'ing times, however, we may question whether the average Chinese really felt any material difference between going into exile at a distance of 2,000 li or being sent another 167 miles to the next distance of 2,500 li. In short, the whole system had become largely symbolic. Complications arose, moreover, because of the way in which the distances were calculated for different provinces. These distances were not merely based upon the provincial capitals as points of departure but more specifically upon each of the individual prefectures (*fu*) within each province. The resulting complexity can be imagined when we keep in mind that during the eighteenth century there were some 180 prefectures within the eighteen provinces of China proper.

As a guide to the places of exile for each of these prefectures, a good-sized work in two Chinese-style volumes, entitled *San-liu tao-li piao* or *Table of Road Distances for the Three Degrees of Life Exile*, was published in 1743 (with revised editions in 1784 and 1801). In this book, prefecture by prefecture under each province, destinations for each of the three degrees of exile are listed. Under the first listed province of Chihli (Hopei), for example, we find that convicts originating in Pao-ting fu (not far south of Peking) are, for 2,000 li exile, to be sent to T'ung-chou fu in eastern Shensi, for 2,500 li to Pin-chou fu in western Shensi, and for 3,000 li to Ch'in-chou fu in eastern Kansu. These allocations, however, are not reciprocal. T'ung-chou fu, for example, instead of sending its 2,000 li convicts to Pao-ting fu, sends them to Tung-ch'ang fu in Shantung. Similarly Pin-chou fu, instead of sending its 2,500 li convicts to Pao-ting fu, sends them to Yi-chou fu, also in Shantung.[10]

If all the places of origin and destination were plotted on a

[10] See *San-liu tao-li piao* (Hupei ed. 1872), under Chihli province, p. 1b, and under Shensi province, pp. 2 and 3.

map, an incredible network of lines would no doubt result. Very likely such a map would also reveal discrimination between favored provinces that were required to accept only a few convicts and others obliged to take them in numbers out of proportion to their own size and population. Probably, too, the map would further emphasize the symbolism of the whole exile system by revealing substantial differences between the actual distances of exile points and the nominal distances under which these points are listed in the table.

Labor services, it will be remembered, were required of persons sentenced to fixed terms of penal servitude within their own provinces. Although such services were likewise required of persons sent into exile, so little is said about them in the sources as to make it appear that they were largely pro forma (see the account near the end of this chapter). As we shall see later, exiled persons, aside from the requirement that they report twice monthly to the authorities of the locality to which they had been sent, enjoyed considerable freedom of movement. Apparently it was felt that the mere fact of life exile more than compensated for their relatively mild treatment.

In the functioning of the exile system we find a contradiction between its presumed original major aim of isolating the criminal from his family and community and Confucian insistence upon the moral need for family solidarity. During the early part of the Ch'ing, Confucian familism triumphed over Legalist strictness in a statutory provision (Boulais no. 79, a heritage from the Ming) obligating the criminal's wife to accompany him (at government expense) to exile and further granting permission to his parents and children, if they so desired, to do the same. Later in the dynasty, however, at a date on which there are differences of opinion, the requirement that a wife accompany her exiled husband was abrogated and the government ceased to supply travel funds for this purpose. In part, no doubt, the change was prompted by financial considerations, but other factors were the arduousness of the journey for the woman as well as her uncertain future should her husband die in exile and leave her a widow among strangers. However, until the end of the dynasty it still remained possible for a wife to go into exile with her husband provided he expressly stated he wanted to have her and that he had the funds to cover her travel costs.[11]

Finally, a word about transportation as a lesser supplement to the three regular degrees of exile. This punishment, consisting of exile at a distance of 1,000 li only, has a T'ang prototype, but did not assume final form until 1329 under the Yuan dynasty.[12] In Ch'ing times it was an excessively rare punishment, applied to only three offenses (see section 10 below). It does not occur in any of the cases translated in this book. A special variant of it, "transportation reduced to two-year authorized penal servitude," has been discussed at the end of the last section.

6. Military Exile

"Military exile" is a very loose rendering of the term *ch'ung chün*, "to fill the army." This penalty was an adjunct of the much older standard punishment of *liu*, "exile" or "life exile." Traditionally, military exile is said to have been a Ming invention. However, as Shen Chia-pen has demonstrated in a detailed study,[13] the idea of sending criminals into military service on the frontiers is an ancient one, sporadically practiced from the Ch'in and Han dynasties onward. Military exile began to be clearly

[11] The details of this matter are confusing and require further research. According to the Ch'ing "Legal Treatise," pp. 47–48, a sub-statute requiring the wife to accompany her husband into exile was abrogated in 1759, and the government at the same time stopped providing funds for that purpose. (This sub-statute, now no longer in the Code, apparently elaborated upon the brief statement in the main statute, Boulais, no. 79, to the effect that the wife was to accompany the husband.) However, the Peking editors of the Ch'ing "Legal Treatise" (pp. 47, note 2, and 48, note 1) assert this date to be in error. According to them, the sub-statute was abrogated in 1743, and the government stopped providing funds in 1766. From one of the cases translated in this volume and dated 1818 (case 9.1), we know that at that time the clause requiring the wife to accompany her exiled husband continued to operate with respect to slaves of Manchu households who became exiles. These, however, represented a special category. Case 187.1, dated 1826, concerns an ordinary husband whose wife did not accompany him when he was deported to Manchuria. Furthermore, we are told by an American describing the exile system in 1859 (see end of this chapter) that the families of exiles were allowed to accompany them, but not that they were compelled to do so.

[12] See Shen Chia-pen, *Fen k'ao* (Separate studies), 9:11–13b, in *Bequeathed Writings*, pp. 113–114.

[13] Shen Chia-pen, *Ch'ung-chün k'ao* (A study of military exile), in *Bequeathed Writings*, pp. 541–552.

distinguishable from ordinary exile during Sung times (960–1279), was further elaborated under the Yuan dynasty (1280–1367), and became really systematized and accepted as a major punishment during the Ming.

During the early Ming, military exile was primarily a substitute for ordinary exile in the case of military officers or soldiers guilty of crime; as such, it consisted of lifetime military service at some distant frontier military post or military colony (of which there were many facilitating the opening up of new lands). At the beginning of the dynasty, however, contemporary documents already refer to unauthorized sellers of salt, dishonest recipients of land or grain, cornerers of the market, instigators of false accusations, unregistered citizens, and numerous other non-military "persons without proper employment" as undergoing military exile. Increasingly, with the passage of time, military exile apparently became a punishment for civilians as well as for military personnel. At the same time, its scope was broadened to include service at military posts within, as well as along, the national frontiers. The 1585 edition of the Ming Code lists no less than ten varieties of military exile, some of them bearing the same names as their Ch'ing counterparts (such as "farthest frontier," "in a malarial region"); however, others (such as "along the sea," "outside the pass") failed to be perpetuated.[14]

When the Ch'ing adopted the system, it retained the name but significantly altered its content by divesting it of its military features. The ten descriptive varieties in use under the Ming were reduced to the five listed in our table in section 1, and in 1725 they were correlated with the fixed distances there indicated. In 1772 a work was compiled, the *Wu-chün tao-li piao* or *Table of Road Distances for the Five Degrees of Military Exile*, similar to the earlier mentioned *Table of Road Distances for the Three Degrees of Exile*.[15]

However, the military exile table is even more complex than its predecessor for two main reasons. In the first place, whereas the

---

[14] *Ibid.*, pp. 2–3b; p. 543. For instances in Ming times of high civilian officials punished by being stripped of rank and sent to "serve as a common soldier on the frontier," see Charles O. Hucker, *The Censorial System of Ming China* (Stanford, Calif., 1966), pp. 254, 261, 263, etc. (esp. p. 268).

[15] For this date, see the Ch'ing "Legal Treatise," p. 52.

table for life exile has to deal with only three degrees of punishment, the military exile table has to deal with five. Secondly, the table for life exile, under each prefecture from which exiles are to be sent, lists only a single destination point for each degree of exile. The military exile table, on the contrary, lists several places of exile for each of its five degrees, consisting of prefectures and districts distributed usually over two or more provinces. To show the complexity of the system, let us see the places of military exile used for convicts from Pao-ting prefecture (the same example as used in the last section). For the sake of simplicity, we shall, following the initial entry, list only the *provinces* to which military exiles from Pao-ting fu were sent, ignoring the several prefectures or districts which, in the original text, are named under each of these provinces.[16]

1. *Very near* (2,000 li). Eastward: Shantung province (under which are listed Teng-chou fu, P'eng-lai hsien, Fu-shan hsien; similar listings, here omitted, are likewise to be understood under each subsequent provincial entry); southward: Honan, Hupei, Anhui, Kiangsu; westward: Shensi; northward: no localities listed because the northern frontier of China proper is less than 2,000 li away from Pao-ting, and all the standard degrees of military exile are for places within China proper.

2. *Nearby frontier* (2,500 li). Eastward: no localities listed because China's eastern seabord is less than 2,500 li from Pao-ting; southward: Hupei, Anhui, Kiangsu; westward: Kansu, Shensi; northward: as above, no localities listed.

3. *Distant frontier* (3,000 li). Eastward and northward: no localities listed for either direction as above; southward: Hunan, Kiangsi, Chekiang; westward: Kansu.

4. *Farthest frontier* (4,000 li). Eastward and northward: again no localities listed; southward: Fukien, Kiangsi, Chekiang; westward: Kansu.

5. *In a malarial region* (4,000 li). Kuangtung and Kuangsi (no compass directions listed).

Even this sample listing, despite our omission from it of the many prefectures and districts given in the original under each province, is enormously more complex than the table for the three

[16] See *Wu-chün tao-li piao* (Hupei ed. 1872), under Chihli province, p. 2b.

degrees of exile. Combining the two tables in our minds, we are compelled to visualize gangs of convicted criminals being marched to places of exile over practically every road of China.

The military exile system raises other problems as well. For example, if Kuangtung is the province to which convicts from Pao-ting fu are to be sent when sentenced to military exile "in a malarial region," what then is to be done with convicts of Kuangtung who, already natives of "a malarial region," are nevertheless sentenced to this kind of military exile? For the answer, let us examine Nan-hsiung-chou, one of four localities in Kuangtung specified as being a malarial region for convicts from Pao-ting. The table informs us that convicts from Nan-hsiung-chou, when and if sentenced to a malarial region, are to be sent to Yunnan, where the governor of that province will assign them to a definite location.[17]

These technicalities, though curious and sometimes anachronistic (for example, it is quite possible that some of the regions listed in the table as "malarial" were no longer so by the nineteenth century), are less important than a fundamental objection voiced by Shen Chia-pen. He states that what had been real military exile in the Ming dynasty was, despite its name, no longer military in the Ch'ing. Shen, who has a very low opinion of the Ch'ing military exile system, summarizes the differences between the Ch'ing and the Ming systems as follows: [18] Military exile meant in Ming times going to actual military encampments, but these disappeared during the Ch'ing, leaving no significant difference between this punishment and ordinary exile. Military exile in the Ming was, at least originally, primarily intended for military personnel, whereas by Ch'ing times anyone might be sentenced to military exile. The various degrees of military exile remained vague and shifting during Ming times, and were not clearly correlated with fixed distances; during the Ch'ing they were reduced to five definite degrees which, in 1725, were correlated with fixed distances.

Shen then proceeds to point out the inconsistencies in the

---

[17] *Wu-chün tao-li piao,* under Kuangtung province, p. 2b.
[18] Shen Chia-pen, *Ch'ung chün k'ao,* Pt. 3, pp. 1–2, in *Bequeathed Writings,* p. 552.

Ch'ing system: Although military exile is ostensibly a heavier punishment than ordinary exile, its first three degrees are identical in distance (2,000, 2,500, and 3,000 li) with the three degrees of ordinary exile, which means that its first two degrees are actually less distant than the third degree of ordinary exile. Also, military exile convicts are, despite their name, under the jurisdiction of the local civilian (not military) authorities, just as are ordinary exiles, and enjoy equal freedom of movement.

In conclusion, we should remind ourselves again that neither military nor ordinary exile meant more than transfer from one province to another within China proper. The only real exile, in the sense of going beyond the national frontiers, was *fa ch'ien* or deportation. Deportation, apparently one of the very few Ch'ing additions to the penal heritage from Ming, was devised by the Manchus as a punishment higher than any other, short of death itself. It consisted of life slavery in the service of military personnel belonging to the Manchu and other non-Chinese garrisons stationed in northern Manchuria (mostly along the Amur River) or in the western part of Chinese Turkestan (Sinkiang), especially Ili. Toward the end of this chapter and again in one of our translated cases (241.9), we shall see the difficulties that deportees sent to these areas posed for the military authorities charged with supervising them. During the first part of the dynasty, such deportees were sent to Manchuria only; with the subjugation of the western reaches of Sinkiang in the eighteenth century, they were sent to these as well; but when the great Muslim rebellions broke out in the northwest around the middle of the nineteenth century, Sinkiang was blocked off and deportees were again sent only to Manchuria until the suppression of the rebellions.

7. The Death Penalties

Ever since the Sui Code of 581–583, the standard death penalties, in increasing order of severity, have been strangulation and decapitation. Describing the procedure for strangulation, Alabaster tells us:[19] "The executioner throws the victim down

[19] Alabaster, *Notes and Commentaries on Chinese Criminal Law*, p. 62.

upon his face, and then sits astride him twisting a cord around his neck; then, as speedily as he can—though slowly in effect—he strangles his victim. If the executioner is not skilful, the experience must be worse than that of hanging prolonged, bad as that is."

However, as may be seen from the text and pictures in Niida Noboru's *Study of Chinese Legal History,* this technique was only one of several. Among these illustrations, one, reproduced from a Chinese woodcut, shows the victim, tied to a post, being strangled by the executioner as he stands behind him; in another, two executioners stand on either side of the trussed-up victim, whom they strangle by twisting the rope looped around his neck in opposite directions.[20]

Concerning the procedure for decapitation, we are told by Alabaster: [21] "The criminal does not lay his head upon a block to be chopped off by an axe, but is placed kneeling with his hands tied behind him. One assistant holds him in position by the rope with which his hands are tied, another pulls his head forward [seizing his queue for this purpose], and with one stroke of his sword the executioner whips it off."

Although strangulation is thus a slower and more painful death than decapitation, it has always been regarded as a lesser punishment for socio-religious reasons: According to the tenets of Chinese filial piety, one's body is not one's own property, but a bequest from his parents. To mutilate one's body, therefore, or allow it to be mutilated, is to be unfilial. Strangulation, from this point of view, is superior to decapitation since it leaves the body intact. Furthermore, by the same token, strangulation is superior because it leaves the spirit of the executed man an intact body which it can continue to inhabit.

We have seen in the tabulation at the end of section 1 that both strangulation and decapitation are subdivided into the two categories of "immediate" and "after the assizes." As we shall see in detail later, "Immediate" strangulation or decapitation means a sentence that is certain to be carried out, whereas "after the

---

[20] Niida Noboru, *Criminal Law,* text and illustration on p. 120, text on pp. 162–163, and illustration on Plate II, 2, at beginning of the volume.

[21] *Ibid.,* p. 59.

assizes" means a sentence that will be reconsidered at the assizes held in Peking in early autumn, where there is considerable possibility of commutation, either at once or later, from execution to some lesser sentence (usually life exile or military exile).

Besides these standard forms of death, there is another, the severest of all, which does not go back to antiquity. This is *ling ch'ih* or "death by slicing," also sometimes referred to in Western writings as "lingering death." It is reserved as a punishment for treason and a very few other heinous crimes such as parricide, mutilation of a living person for purposes of witchcraft, murder of three or more persons belonging to the same family, and other offenses collectively known as the "Ten Abominations" (*shih ô*). In the words of Alabaster: [22]

Here the offender is tied to a cross, and, by a series of painful but not in themselves mortal cuts, his body is sliced beyond recognition . . . This punishment . . . is not inflicted so much as a torture, but to destroy the future as well as the present life of the offender—he is unworthy to exist longer either as a man or a recognizable spirit . . . As spirits to appear must assume their previous corporeal forms, he can only appear as a collection of little bits. It is not a lingering death, for it is all over in a few seconds, and the *coup de grace* is generally given the third cut . . . In short, though the punishment is severe and revolting, it is not so painful as the half-hanging, disembowelling, and final quartering, practised in England not so very long ago.

Shen Chia-pen remarks that the codes do not describe the procedure for carrying out the slicing death, which was an esoteric technique individually transmitted by each executioner. Hence, he says, even between such nearby cities as Peking and Pao-ting fu slight variations may be found. Generally speaking, however, the executioner inflicts "eight cuts" (*pa tao*) upon his victim, that is to say, he makes successive cuts upon the victim's face, his two hands and two feet, and his breast and stomach, with the final cut consisting of the cutting off of the head. [23]

From Niida Noboru's much longer discussion, however, it would seem that Shen's remarks cover only the bare essentials of the subject. According to Niida, the cuts suffered by the victim might be as many as 24, 36, 72, or even 120 in number. Among

[22] *Ibid.*, pp. 57–58.
[23] Shen Chia-pen, *Fen k'ao*, 2:17–19b, in *Bequeathed Writings*, pp. 47–48.

Niida's reproductions of several gory woodcuts, one shows the victim tied to a cross, with three of his limbs lying on the ground and the executioner hard at work severing the fourth. Particularly notorious was the execution of the Ming eunuch Liu Chin by slicing in 1510, in retaliation for the man's gross political machinations. According to Niida, the eunuch's body was sliced no less than 4,700 times, each cut being accompanied by a blow of the whip.[24]

It would seem that the slicing death represents a "barbarian" contribution to Chinese civilization, inasmuch as the earliest references to it are associated with a tribal people of Tungus stock (distant ancestors of the Manchus) who, under the dynastic name of Liao, ruled parts of North China from 907 to 1123. The dynastic history of the Liao, beginning with the year 912, records at least six instances of rebels against Liao rule (themselves members of the Liao) who underwent execution by *ling ch'ih*.[25] From Liao the punishment was then apparently transmitted to the contemporary Chinese Sung empire in the south, where references to it appear in 1028, 1075, and later.[26] Although it was used sporadically during the Sung as an extra-legal punishment,

[24] For Niida's lengthy discussion of all aspects of death by slicing (in which also appear general remarks on the former execution ground in Peking and the handling of executions there), see Niida, *Criminal Law*, pp. 153–171. For the particular points here cited, see pp. 158–159. The illustration is Plate II, 1, at the beginning of the book. Niida fails to document his account of Liu Chin's execution, which may well be based on popular tradition rather than sober history. It is not confirmed in Liu's biography in the *Ming shih* (History of the Ming dynasty), Chap. 304, near end.

[25] See *Liao shih*, 112:4 (year 912), 113:1b–4 (years 948, 951, 952, and 1063), and 114:2 (also 1063). These references are here cited in detail because, very curiously, neither Shen Chia-pen nor Niida Noboru refer to them in their studies cited above. Shen merely mentions *ling ch'ih* as one of several kinds of capital punishment listed in the Liao "Legal Treatise." Similarly, Niida cites, as probably the earliest indirect reference to *ling ch'ih*, a memorial of 953 addressed to the ruler of the short-lived Later Chou dynasty (951–959), in which "dismembering a man's flesh with a short knife" is mentioned as one of several illegal forms of execution that have originated on alien soil. See Niida, *Criminal Law*, p. 156. The memorial occurs in the "Legal Treatise" of the *Chiu Wu-tai shih* (Old history of the Five Dynasties), in *Li-tai hsing-fa chih*, p. 374. This memorial does indeed sound as if it were speaking about *ling ch'ih*, in which case the alien origin of this punishment would be confirmed. However, the reference is, of course, some four decades later than the first explicit reference to *ling ch'ih* itself in the Liao kingdom in 912.

[26] References cited in Shen Chia-pen, *Fen k'ao*, 2:17–19b, in *Bequeathed Writings*, pp. 47–48, and Niida Noboru, *Criminal Law*, p. 157.

death by slicing achieved legal status only in the Yuan and Ming Codes, from which it passed to that of Ch'ing.

Ling ch'ih is a linguistically peculiar term, and the early association of the punishment with the Liao people strongly suggests a linguistic borrowing from the Liao language. Although Shen Chia-pen, in the study already cited, tries to link the term with an ancient *ling ch'ih* (in which *ling* is written with a slightly different character), his effort is unconvincing.[27]

8. Supplemental Punishments

So far we have been discussing only the standard "five punishments," but there also exist several supplemental or substitute punishments, as follows:

Cangue (chia or chia hao).[28] This device was a rectangular collar made of heavy blocks of wood longer from front to back than from side to side. It encircled the neck and rested on the shoulders of the offender, projecting outward in such a way as to prevent him from reaching his face with his hand. (Two such offenders are shown in the courtroom scene illustrated in this book.) Worn for a fixed number of days, months, or, very rarely, years, the cangue was ordinarily a punishment supplemental to the standard five punishments. Often it was expressly provided for by statute. A thief, for example, if guilty for the second time of a theft punishable by 60 blows of the heavy bamboo, not only received the standard 60 blows for the amount stolen, but, as a recidivist, was additionally subjected to 20 days wearing of the cangue (see Boulais, no. 1122). On the other hand, it could also happen, in cases having particularly aggravating circumstances,

[27] The ancient phrase appears in a passage by Hsün Tzu (famed Confucian of the third century B.C.), in which he says that it is the *ling ch'ih* of a hill 100 cubits high that permits that hill to be climbed by a chariot. See the *Hsün-tzu*, Chap. 28, middle (not translated in Dubs). The literal meaning of *ling ch'ih* in this passage is "mound slow," which is explained by Hsün Tzu's commentator, Yang Liang (in his commentary dated 818), as referring to the hill's "gradual slope." Shen argues that when death by slicing became current as a punishment, a term had to be found to designate it, and the ancient *ling ch'ih* was selected in order to emphasize the "gradualness" of the punishment.

[28] See Ch'ing "Legal Treatise," pp. 56–60; *Ta Ch'ing hui-tien*, 53:4b–5; Shen Chia-pen, *Hsing-chü k'ao*, pp. 10b–13b, in *Bequeathed Writings*, pp. 513–514; Balazs, p. 67.

that the cangue might be imposed by the court as an addition to the usual penalty, even though not called for by statute, as in several of our translated cases (89.1, 93.2, 270.1, etc.).

For Manchus and other members of the hereditary armed forces known as Banners (which included Mongols and Chinese as well as Manchus), the cangue was a substitute for, rather than merely a supplement to, punishments ranging from penal servitude through military exile. One year of penal servitude, for example, was commutable for a Manchu or other bannerman to 20 days wearing of the cangue, and military exile in a malarial region was similarly communtable to 90 days.[29]

The word *chia* was apparently originally a designation for a flail-like agricultural implement. Used to designate an instrument for confining prisoners (in the same manner as manacles and handcuffs), it first occurs in an historical text referring to the first half of the fourth century A.D. Then in the 563 Code of the Northern Chou dynasty the word appears as the name of a legally recognized instrument, apparently intended to punish as well as to confine. Thereafter the cangue was long used as an instrument of confinement, but by Ch'ing times its primary usage was as a supplemental punishment. Its legally recognized weight changed considerably in the course of the dynasty. In the Code of 1740 the weight was fixed at 25 catties (1 catty=about 1.3 English lbs.), but either in 1812 or 1814 it was increased to 35 catties.

Tatooing (*tz'u tzu*).[30] As we have seen at the beginning of this chapter, tatooing was one of the five major punishments of antiquity (when it was known as *mo*). Following the abolition of it and other corporal punishments in 167 B.C., it was used only very occasionally during the rest of the Han dynasty and the four centuries of the Period of Disunity that followed. During the Sui and T'ang dynasties it was not used at all, but from about A.D. 940 onward it was revived as a means for marking some (not all) criminals sent into exile.

In Ch'ing times, tatooing was usually applied to robbers, vio-

[29] See case 4.3 among the translated cases.
[30] See memorial to the throne of April 16, 1905, by Shen Chia-pen and Wu T'ing-fang, concerning the need to reform several punishments, tr. Meijer, p. 168; Ch'ing "Legal Treatise," pp. 59–60; and case 144.17 of our translated cases.

lators of tombs, criminals deported outside China proper, and criminals recaptured after escaping from life or military exile. For an initial offense, the name of the offense was tatooed (either in Chinese or in Manchu, or sometimes in both) on the offender's right forearm. A second offense meant repetition of the tatoo on the left forearm. For a third or a fourth offense, the tatooing was repeated on the right and then on the left side of the face. Under special circumstances, such as an imperial amnesty or exemplary conduct on the part of the offender, it became legally permissible for him to have the tatoo removed, thus restoring him to the status of a respectable citizen.

Whip (*pien*). Whipping, used side by side with, or as a substitute for, beating with the stick, appears in the Code of 503 of the Liang dynasty, as well as in many subsequent codes.[31] In Ch'ing times, the whip replaced the bamboo as a punishment for Manchus, the designated number of blows of the light or heavy bamboo being convertible to the same number of blows of the whip. Otherwise, it did not constitute a legal punishment. Among our translated cases, 259.1 deals with its improper use.

Exposure of the head (*hsiao shih*). This punishment goes back to pre-imperial China. In Ch'ing times, it was reserved as a supplemental punishment for particularly notorious criminals, especially bandits or rebels. (It is mentioned in the description of bandit executions at the end of this chapter.) After decapitation or death by slicing, the severed head of the criminal would be hung up in a cage and left for days or weeks at the execution ground or other public spot for everyone to witness.

Legalized torture.[32] The Ch'ing Code sanctions the use of torture, within specified limits, for extracting confession from suspects who refuse to admit guilt. If deemed necessary, such torture may be applied to secondary suspects and to witnesses as well as to principals. Even if death results, the official conducting the investigation is not to be held responsible, provided he has acted according to statute. However, should he apply torture to an

---

[31] See Balazs, p. 40 and table of punishments on pp. 210–211.

[32] See Boulais, p. 6 and nos. 1671–1673 (in which several passages from the original text of the Code are omitted, as well as several entire sub-statutes); Alabaster, *Notes and Commentaries*, pp. 17–19; memorial to the throne of about April 29, 1907, from Board of Punishments, tr. Meijer, pp. 160–162.

innocent person because of personal enmity, so that death results, he is subject to decapitation after the assizes; if injury be the result, the punishment for him is the same as for inflicting injury in an affray. Furthermore, the torture must fall within certain legally defined limits: twisting the ears, slapping or beating, making the prisoner kneel on a chain, or squeezing the fingers or ankles with wooden compressors that are made for the purpose and conform to legally defined measurements. In actual practice, of course, other extra-legal forms of torture were also sometimes used.

It would seem that the use of judicial torture in Ch'ing times was in some respects less closely regulated than it had been during the T'ang. Thus it is stated in the T'ang Code (and omitted from the Ch'ing Code) that a suspect from whom a confession is desired may not be beaten more than three times for a total of 200 blows during any period of sixty consecutive days. Furthermore, this number is permissible only if the crime of which he is accused is punishable by penal servitude or more; if it is punishable only by beating, the number of blows allowable during the sixty-day period may not exceed the number given in punishment for his alleged crime.[33] By comparison, we read in the Ch'ing "Legal Treatise" (p. 108) that in Ch'ing times the maximum beating for any prisoner was 30 blows of the heavy bamboo daily.

9. General Comments on the Penal System

Archaism, symbolism, and nominalism (insistence upon name at the expense of reality) are all conspicuous in the final formulation of the penal system found in the Ch'ing Code of 1740. We have seen the archaistic thinking underlying the exile system, the complications entailed in trying to maintain symbolic distinctions between the various kinds of exile, and the gross inconsistencies that resulted (particularly evident in the overlaps of distances between ordinary and military exile).

Nominalism is manifest in the term "military exile" itself, retained despite the complete demilitarization of what it once stood for. It is apparent again in insistence upon continued citation of

[33] Ou Koei-hing, p. 27, citing *T'ang lü shu-yi* (T'ang Code), book 29, article 9.

light and heavy bambooing sentences in terms of the number of blows traditionally administered, despite drastic reduction in Ch'ing times of their actual number. Likewise we have seen that when the Ch'ing codifiers redrafted the Ming Code, they usually retained the traditional capital punishments of "strangulation" and "decapitation" if originally specified in the statutory text but then sometimes mitigated them unobtrusively by stating (in smaller type in the Official Commentary) that the sentence should be executed "after the assizes." This addendum, of course, set in action procedures that often resulted in commutation.

The reluctance of the codifiers to depart from the older expressions of horrible harshness, although in fact they provided for less inhumane punishment, exemplifies not only a typical Chinese reverence for tradition but also a hope that the terrifying words of black letter punishment clauses would deter wrongdoing. Emphasis on the deterrent function of the criminal law was central in the polity of the ancient Chinese Legalists, who believed that dire threats would forestall all wrongdoing. Even though by Ch'ing times "strangulation" often amounted only to exile, and "military exile" was actually a milder civilian form, and "100 blows of the heavy bamboo" meant 40 blows, the harsh verbiage probably was retained because of its supposed deterrent effect.

Some often used punishments seem to have appealed to the codifiers primarily or in good part as deterrents. Exile, for example, only disagreeably isolates the convict from his familiars; it provides no rehabilitation fitting the outcast for a better future role in society. The cangue, a punishment which, like the stocks of the West, humiliates the convict, was calculated to discourage wrong, but the codifiers ignored the fact that the cangue may unsettle, rather than improve, the wrongdoer. Tatooing robbers did warn others of their untrustworthiness; however, it went far beyond identification to differentiate them conspicuously from ordinary persons, thereby inhibiting their rehabilitation.[34] On all these points the underlying theory would seem to have come from

[34] See case 144.17 among the translated cases, in which a boy of 14, convicted of theft for which he was tatooed (improperly so, as he was a minor), was a year later convicted again of a second offense. We can imagine that the word "thief," tatooed on his forearm, was hardly calculated to dissuade him from repeating his offense.

the Legalists, in whose eyes man, as a selfish creature, can be deterred only by fear from committing wrongful acts. This point of view contrasts with that of the Confucians, according to which human nature is basically good, so that moral rehabilitation always remains possible. It is the varying symbiosis of Legalist and Confucian thinking at different points of the legal system that provides a prime focus for studying the system.

An important aspect of the Chinese world-view is its interpretation of the universe in terms of orderly arrays of things, concepts, and attributes, all neatly packaged, graduated, and correlated with one another. Already mentioned as a notable example of this kind of thinking is the Five Elements system with its numerous correlations in sets of fives. Illustrative of a similar mode of thinking in the legal sphere is the Chinese penal ladder, with its step-by-step progression from the lightest punishment of ten blows of the light bamboo all the way to death by slicing. We may interpret this system as a complex device for measuring morality with quantitative exactitude or again as constituting a graduated continuum whereby any offense, ranging from the most trivial to the most serious, may be requited with the utmost precision.[35]

So at least it may seem at first sight. A closer look, however, reveals that the symmetry of punishments is more apparent than real and, in particular, breaks down at the joints between the five major categories. For example, there is a very considerable gap, in physical fact if not in number, between the 50 blows of the light bamboo (the highest degree in this category) and the 60 blows of the heavy bamboo immediately following. Even when these nominal figures are converted into their concrete equivalents of 20 blows each, the difference between 20 light blows and 20 heavy blows remains considerable.

Similarly, there is a sharp jump from the highest degree of bambooing, that of 100 (actually 40) heavy blows, to the lowest degree of the next category of penal servitude, consisting of one year of penal servitude plus 60 (actually 20) blows of the heavy

[35] For an interesting attempt by the Ch'ien-lung Emperor (1736–1795) to break away from the overly mechanical measuring of morality, see case 172.4 among the translated cases.

bamboo. Again, between the maximum degree of penal servitude (three years) and the following category of life exile there is another serious gap, although it is bridged to some slight extent by insertion of the supplemental and very rare intermediate punishments of total and authorized penal servitude. Between life exile and military exile, on the other hand, there is, as we have seen, not a gap but a serious overlap. Finally, by the addition of deportation beyond China proper over and above the other five degrees of military exile, and by the subdivision of the two main death penalties into those that are immediate (certain) and those that come after the assizes, the Chinese codifiers have probably done as much as anyone could to provide a reasonably even progression from life to death.

Before ending this discussion, it is important to point out the differing formulas used to calculate increases and reductions of penalty among the three higher categories (penal servitude, life exile and military exile counted as a single category, and death). An increase by one degree means an increase of sentence from one year of penal servitude to one and one half years; from the highest degree of penal servitude to the lowest degree of life exile; from the highest degree of life exile to the lowest degree of military exile; from strangulation after the assizes to decapitation after the assizes, and so forth. (It should be noted that the special punishments of total penal servitude, deportation, and others, are not taken into account when calculating these one-degree increases.)

However, when it comes to *diminishing* the same punishments, the procedure is radically different: each entire *category* of punishment (death, exile both ordinary and military, and penal servitude) then counts as only a single degree. Thus a one-degree reduction from immediate strangulation does not, as one might expect, lead to the next immediately lower penalty, which is decapitation after the assizes. Rather it carries the penalty all the way down from death (the highest category) to *either* military or ordinary exile (because these two are regarded as jointly constituting the next highest category). Theoretically, therefore, the next lower degree from immediate decapitation *might* be the lowest level of ordinary exile (exile at a distance of 2,000 li), though in practice it would more probably mean one of the five levels of military exile. Likewise, a two-degree reduction could in theory bring the penalty all the way down from death to only one year of penal servitude, though here again the highest level of penal servitude, that of three years, would be more likely. "The acme of humanity" is the way the Ch'ing Code's Upper Commentary (see Chapter II, section 4) characterizes these differing formulas for increasing and reducing punishment, and no doubt they are indeed a reflection of Confucian humanitarianism.[36]

10. How Many Offenses Were Punishable under Chinese Law?

Shen Chia-pen has conveniently assembled figures for the number of offenses legally punishable by death under successive dynasties before the Ch'ing. Beginning with the T'ang, they are as follows: [37]

T'ang Code of 653

Strangulation: 144   Decapitation: 89

Total capital offenses: 233

Sung Code of 963

Same as T'ang Code, plus 60 other capital offenses gradually added during the dynasty, making a total of 293

Yuan Code (as recorded in the Yuan "Legal Treatise")

Total of 135 capital offenses (including, for first time, 9 punishable by death by slicing)

Ming Code of 1397

Death by slicing: 13   Decapitation after assizes: 98
Immediate decapitation: 38   Strangulation after assizes: 87
Immediate strangulation: 13

Total capital offenses 249

Added to above are 20 capital offenses separately enumerated in the Ming's collection of sub-statutes, plus 13 "miscellaneous" capital offenses (offenses for which the death penalty is nominal only, on which see section 4 above)

Grand total of all capital offenses: 282

[36] See Boulais, no. 111.
[37] See Shen Chia-pen, Ssu-hsing chih shu (The figures for the death penalty), in Bequeathed Writings, pp. 532–533.

Aside from the sharp dip for Yuan, not explained by Shen and particularly striking because of the Mongol reputation for harshness, these figures are remarkably consistent. By remaining always under 300, they compare favorably with those of eighteenth-century Britain, where "more than 300 crimes, from murder to petty thefts, were punishable death." [38] The comparison is particularly favorable to Ming China, among whose grand total of 282 nominally capital offenses, no less than 198 (those labelled "after the assizes" plus the 13 "miscellaneous offenses") were in actual practice commonly—though not invariably—commutable to something less than death.

For the Ch'ing dynasty we have the much more detailed statistics for *all* punishable offenses provided by the *Collected Institutes of the Great Ch'ing Dynasty*.[39] These figures are extremely puzzling because, in the category of capital offenses, the only category comparable with Shen's figures for earlier dynasties, they are so very much higher. In good part, no doubt, the discrepancy is explainable by the tremendous proliferation of sub-statutes in Ch'ing times (1,892 of them by 1863, as compared with 382 in the 1585 edition of the Ming Code). Even so, however, the increase is so great as to suggest a possibly different basis for the compilation of the Ch'ing figures.

According to the *Collected Institutes*, the grand total of all punishable offenses listed by the Ch'ing Code is 3,987. The fact that this figure falls just under 4,000 and hence remains within the general category of "3,000 plus" may very well stem from a deliberate attempt to conform to historical tradition. Thus in China's earliest legal text, the *Lü hsing* or "Punishments of Lü" (the same text containing the legend about the Miao barbarians who created the first written law), there is the famous sentence: "The offences falling under the five punishments are 3,000 in number." [40]

The statistics in the *Collected Institutes* are too detailed to

[38] See editorial, "Passing of the Death Penalty," *New York Times*, May 17, 1965.

[39] *Ta Ch'ing hui-tien*, 54:1a–b.

[40] Tr. James Legge, in *The Chinese Classics*, 5 vols. (Hong Kong, 1960), III, 606, modified here by D. Bodde.

reproduce here. By reducing them to totals for major categories, we arrive at the following figures:

Light bamboo: 363 offenses (ranging from 31 for 10 blows to 123 for 50 blows)

Heavy bamboo: 1,071 offenses (ranging from 124 for 60 blows to 505 for 100 blows)

Penal servitude: 721 offenses (ranging from 95 for one year to 352 for 3 years; also including 2 each for the rare penalties of total servitude and 5 years authorized penal servitude, as well as 5 for transportation reduced to 2 years authorized penal servitude)

Life exile: 400 offenses (ranging from 73 for 2,000 li exile to 301 for 3,000 li exile; also including 3 for the rare penalty of transporation as well as 18 nominal "miscellanec us offenses," on which see section 4 above)

Military exile: 619 offenses (ranging from 56 for very near exile to 100 for exile in a malarial region; also including 143 for deportation)

Death: 813 offenses (including 12 nominal "miscellaneous offenses")
  Strangulation after the assizes: 272 offenses
  Decapitation after the assizes: 218 offenses
  Strangulation, immediate: 71 offenses
  Decapitation, immediate: 222 offenses
  Death by slicing: 30 offenses

11. Western Glimpses of Chinese Punishments

How did the punishments we have been describing appear to the men and women who underwent them? The answer is extremely difficult because Chinese accounts of penal matters have almost always been written in the impersonal language of the bureaucrat rather than the living langugage of the sufferer. Most victims of the penal system were illiterate, and those who were not were rarely willing to describe in personal terms what they had experienced. There were exceedingly few Chinese equivalents of the Dostoevskys and others who have written so vividly about imprisonment and exile in Czarist Russia.[41]

[41] A possible exception is Fang Pao (1668–1749), who in his *Yü-chung tsa-chi* (Notes on prison life) is said to have written a terrifying account of life in a Peking prison. See Arthur Waley, *Yüan Mei* (London: Allen & Unwin, 1956), p. 115.

A few decades ago it would still have been possible to interview men who had personally participated in the Chinese imperial judicial system. Now, of course, these are gone for all time. As a substitute, what is needed is a search through pertinent Ch'ing and pre-Ch'ing writings, including the novels, plays, and short stories which, though fictional, often give realistic pictures of their time.[42] Another avenue might be via such casebooks as the *Hsing-an hui-lan* (source of the cases translated in this volume), concentrating upon those sections of it that particularly have to do with the machinery of the judicial system. For example, we find in one of our own translated cases (263.1) a rather vivid account of how the pressure of milling crowds at the execution grounds results in the mistaken decapitation of one criminal who should properly have been strangled and the strangulation of another who should have been decapitated.

To do all this ourselves, however, would have involved research far beyond what was possible for this book. As a partial substitute, we shall quote excerpts from the observations of three nineteenth-century Westerners, all of whom knew China well and seem to have been reasonably objective men. The first is Sir Harry S. Parkes, a British diplomat accompanying the Anglo-French forces that marched on Peking from Tientsin in 1860. Parkes went ahead under a flag of truce to negotiate, was captured by the Chinese (who probably did not understand what such a flag meant), taken by them to Peking, and there imprisoned, September 18 to 29, in one of the two prisons maintained by the Board of Punishments. On the latter date he was transferred to pleasanter surroundings and then, on October 8, he was released shortly before the allied forces entered and occupied Peking. Later he gave a brief account of his prison experience from which the following is an excerpt: [43]

As the massive door [of the prison] opened and closed on me I found myself in a throng of 70 or 80 wild-looking prisoners, most of them

[42] Much valuable material has already been collected by Niida Noboru, *Criminal Law*, pp. 615–675, where he quotes what is said in plays, stories, and other writings about judicial torture, instruments of confinement, imprisonment, and bambooing. Very strangely, he omits from his survey all materials having to do with the various degrees of penal servitude and life and military exile.

[43] See Sir Harry S. Parkes, article in *North-China Herald* (Shanghai, March 30, 1861), 557: 51.

offensive in the extreme, as is usual in Chinese gaols, from disease and dirt, and who were naturally anxious to gaze on the newcomer . . .

They then laid me on the raised boarding on which the prisoners sleep and made me fast by another large chain to a beam overhead. The chains consisted of one long and heavy one, stretching from the neck to the feet, to which the hands were fastened by the two cross chains and handcuffs, and the feet in a similar manner . . .

Most of them [the prisoners] were men of the lowest class and the gravest order of offenders, as murderers, burglars, etc. Those who had no means of their own were reduced by prison filth and prison diet to a shocking state of emaciation and disease, but those who could afford to fee the gaolers, and purchase such things as they wanted, lived in comparative fulness and comfort.

They explained to me that their prison system cost the government nothing more than the pay of the gaolers, and the supply of two bowls of boiled millet per day to each prisoner. All other expenses, such as water, lighting, fuel, tea, salt, vegetables for the prisoners, and good meals for the gaolers, etc., are defrayed by some one among the prisoners, who voluntarily undertakes the charge in redemption of a certain portion of his term of imprisonment.

The Mandarin of the Board [of Punishments] having ordered that I should be supplied with the food that I could eat, my maintenance, which cost, as I was told, 1s [one shilling] a-day, was carried to the charge of the man who held this position; but instead of taking a dislike to me on account of the increased expense which I occasioned him, he was one of the foremost in showing me kindness or consideration. My meals consisted of two meals a-day of boiled rice, or a kind of macaroni seasoned with a very sparing allowance of meat or vegetables; also cakes or the bread of the country, and a little tea and tobacco.

In the prison roll, which was hung up on the wall, I found myself returned as "a rebel," and that I was one of five out of a total of 73, who were ordered to wear the heaviest chains.

This account should not unduly shock persons who have read Dickens. What it says about shortening one's prison term by defraying the cost of meals seems based on a misunderstanding because, as we have seen, imprisonment was not one of the recognized punishments. However, its assertion that prisoners were obliged to defray part of their living expenses is important because it accords well with what we know in general about the Chinese governmental system. A major defect of this system was its failure to pay adequate salaries either to the officials or to the persons who worked under them. The inevitable result was squeeze, the only question being whether or not this squeeze remained within the limits of what was socially acceptable.[44]

Our second Western witness is D. J. MacGowan, an American medical missionary from Fall River, Massachusetts, who lived several decades in China where in 1859 he published an article, "On the Banishment of Criminals in China," much of it seemingly based on personal observation.[45]

Concerning penal servitude he has little to say, other than terming it (p. 299) a "slight punishment." Most of his remarks concern life exile and military exile, between which he first of all denies that a significant difference exists. (Throughout his article, he uses the word banishment to designate what we call exile.) Thus he writes (pp. 296–297):

At the present time little difference exists in practice between a modified form of military banishment and extra-provincial [ordinary] banishment; there being a class of exiles designated military, who are merely sent from their own to a distant province.

The law contemplates the employment of these criminals as in some sort slaves to the yamuns [yamens], or public offices, just as those in Ili are slaves to the army. In some places it is not unlikely that the banished of this class are to the present day to be found employed as runners or lictors to the authorities.

Indeed, he continues, vestiges of this service were to be found in the great city of Hangchow in connection with the civil service examinations, each lasting several days, that were periodically held there in a large special enclosure. Formerly the criminals undergoing military exile were mobilized on these occasions to bring food to the examination candidates and otherwise serve their needs. So lucrative, however, did the tips paid to them by the candidates prove to be that now, ironically, all such services

[44] See, among others, T'ung-tsu Ch'ü, *Local Government in China under the Ch'ing*, pp. 22–32.

[45] *Journal of the North China Branch of the Royal Asiatic Society*, 3:293–301 (December 1859). The article is partially based on a memorial to the throne from the military governor-general of Ili in Western Sinkiang (see *Peking Gazette,* June 19, 1857), petitioning that criminals no longer be deported to that distant area. Most of MacGowan's article, however, seems to be based on personal observation in Chekiang province and more specifically in the important port of Ningpo in central China. It is possible that MacGowan generalizes too broadly from what he saw in this particular area.

have been taken over by regular professional servants. MacGowan
continues (pp. 297–298):

There are then two classes of extra-provincial exiles, one coming under the military designation, and the other to whom the term is more
strictly applicable. These criminals are to be met with in every large
city of the empire, and opportunities therefore are not wanting of ob-
serving the operation of the system.

The whole number of banished criminals in the province of Chehkiang, assuming those of Ningpo as a basis of calculation, is about
eight hundred, which would give the eighteen provinces not much less
than twenty-five thousand. They are under strict surveillance, and by
rule should report themselves, or be reported by their sureties bi-
monthly, to the district magistrate; very little restraint is imposed
upon any save the new-comers. An allowance nearly sufficient to supply them with rice is made by the local government, and the privilege
accorded to beggars, is claimed by the exiles,—that of suing at every
shop daily for a cash. Like the mendicants the exiles have a responsible
chief who collects quarterly, or annually, this tax from the shopmen.
Compared with beggars, the poorest of these criminals is well to do.
All pursue some calling. Nearly all the dealers in second-hand articles
are of this class. They make much money as usurers, lending small
sums to the needy poor at the rate of twenty per cent *per mensum*.
They are notorious as receivers of stolen goods, and between them and
the thieves on the one hand, and detectives so called, on the other,
there is good understanding. They are always ready for a row that will
pay, and when hired as bullies are careful to have a show of law or
justice on their side; nevertheless, despite their sharpness and circum-
spection, they sometimes become involved in the meshes of the law, or
get roughly handled by the people. About twenty were killed a few
years since, to the east of Ningpo, in an attack on the villagers who
rose against the salt monopoly. They had been hired by the mandarins . . .

Some bring property with them. Their families are allowed to accompany them, or they may send for them. In this manner it happens
on the occasion of a general pardon [an imperial amnesty], that many
are found who decline availing themselves of it, preferring exile with
its certain means of subsistence, to the uncertainties of their old haunts.
There exists a strong community of feeling among them, and the whole
body are apt to resent an injury to a member . . . This will be understood when it is stated that the criminals in one province will be found
to hail from the same region of country in another:—thus the province
of Chehkiang is the place to which by law offenders from Shantung,
Chihli and Shansi are banished.[46]

---

[46] As we have seen earlier, the situation for military exile was not quite so

Concerning deportation outside China proper (the supplemental and most severe degree of military exile), MacGowan also writes as follows (pp. 294–295), relying at this point primarily on the above-mentioned memorial (see note 45) from the military governor-general of Ili:

During the thirty years reign of Taukwang [Tao-kuang, 1821–1850], between one and two thousand were banished to Ili at a cost of one hundred taels [ounces of silver] per head. Besides this expense to the imperial government, the districts through which criminals are conducted, are compelled to disburse money for the support of the convoy. And, moreover, on the journey they rob and oppress throughout the entire route. Inn-keepers and villagers dare not offer resistance, perhaps partly owing to the share that the military escort receive of the booty.

Arrived at their place of exile, these men form secret societies according to their natal province and

the confederations thus formed often intimidate officers and people, and thwart the course of justice. The Code contemplates their employment as agriculturalists on the military lands, and as menials in public offices, or, as they are sometimes designated, slaves to soldiers and officers. They seem however to be unprofitable servants. Last year there was a dearth in Ili, and these men were clamorous for support, engaging in bread riots.

Was MacGowan unduly biased? I think not in view of his concluding words (p. 300):

It were a mistake, and to the Chinese very unjust, to consider the disregard of human life exhibited of late at the tribunals, as illustrative of the criminal jurisprudence of this country. The present is an exceptionable period. Ordinarily the life of the subject is guarded with jealous care, capital punishment being inflicted only after obtaining the imperial warrant. In the expense and trouble involved in banishment, is afforded an evidence of a desire to spare the effusion of blood. It is but just to add also that since the reign of Kienlung [Ch'ien-lung, 1736–1795] there has been a gradual melioration of the Code. In no period of Chinese history have punishments been mitigated to the same degree.

---

simple as indicated in this last sentence because criminals from any given prefecture were liable to be sent not to one but to several localities, often situated in more than one province. Nonetheless, MacGowan's main contention that the exiles living in any given area tended to originate from another common area is basically true. The resulting cliques and gang loyalties may be imagined.

Our final witness is the British consul T. T. Meadows, very well known among nineteenth-century writers on China for his philosophical and sympathetic approach to Chinese civilization,[47] and for his favorable accounts of the Chinese civil service, which helped inspire the creation of the first British civil service around the middle of the century.[48]

On July 30, 1851, Meadows witnessed the execution of thirty-four bandits in Canton, an event recorded by him in detail in his "Description of an Execution at Canton." [49] This article begins by describing (p. 55) the place of execution: a short lane about fifty yards long from north to south, some eight yards wide at its northern end, from which it narrowed to five yards at the southern. The lane was flanked on the east by a wall and on the west by a row of shops selling coarse pottery. We are then told:

In this lane, not larger than the deck of a hulk, and almost surrounded by dead brick walls, upwards of four hundred human beings have been put to death during the past eight months of the present year. It is fetid with the stench of decomposing heads, and rank with the steams raised by the hot sun from a soil saturated with human blood. Sometimes the bodies of such criminals as have friends, are allowed to remain till these remove them for burial. The first time I entered the place I found four bodies so left, lying in various attitudes as they had fallen, their heads near them, and two pigs moving among them, busily feeding in the pools of blood that had gushed from the trunks. At the distance of about seven yards, and facing this scene, a woman sat at the door of one of the pottery workshops, affectionately tending a child on her knees, of one or two years old; both stared hard, not at a sight so common as pigs feeding among human bodies on human blood, but at the strangely-dressed foreigner.

Meadows goes on to describe the execution of the bandits (p. 56):

The criminals were brought in, the greater number walking, but many carried in large baskets of bamboo attached each to a pole and borne by two men. We observed that the strength of the men so carried was altogether gone, either from excess of fear or the treatment

[47] See especially his large work (still worth reading today), *The Chinese and Their Rebellions* (London, 1856; reprinted, Stanford, Calif., 1953).

[48] See Ssu-yü Teng, "Chinese Influence on the Western Examination System," *Harvard Journal of Asiatic Studies*, 7:267–312, esp. pp. 289–290 and 303 (1943).

[49] *Journal of the Royal Asiatic Society*, 16:54–58 (1856).

they had met with during their imprisonment and trial. They fell powerless together as they were tumbled out on the spots where they were to die. They were immediately raised up to a kneeling position and supported thus by the man who stands behind each criminal.

Each was executed kneeling, with his head extended, and pulled further forward if necessary by an assistant who held the victim's queue. Within three minutes the single executioner had executed thirty-three men, severing the heads of all but the first with a single blow. Then came the execution of the ringleader by the slicing method. First he was fastened to a rough cross set in a hole in the ground. Then, in the words of Meadows (pp. 57–58):

As the man was at a distance of twenty-five yards with his side towards us, though we observed the two cuts across the forehead, the cutting-off of the left breast, and slicing of the flesh from the front of the thighs, we could not see all the horrible operation. From the first stroke of the knife till the moment the body was cut down from the cross and decapitated, about four or five minutes elapsed. We should not have been prohibited from going close up, but as may be easily imagined, even a powerful curiosity was an insufficient inducement to jump over a number of dead bodies and literally wade through pools of blood to place ourselves in the hearing of the groans indicated by the heaving chest and quivering limbs of the poor man. Where we stood we heard not a single cry; and I may add that of the thirty-three men decapitated no one struggled or uttered any exclamation as the executioner approached him.

Immediately after the first body fell I observed a man put himself in a sitting posture by the neck, and with a businesslike air commence dipping in the blood a bunch of rush pith. When it was well saturated he put it carefully by on a pile of the adjacent pottery, and then proceeded to saturate another bunch. This so-saturated rush pith is used by the Chinese as a medicine.[50]

The fact that these accounts from north, central and south China have to do with events occurring respectively in 1860, 1857, and 1851 is important because all three dates fall within the period of the Taiping Rebellion (1850–1864). This conflict, probably the most destructive civil war of all time, devastated

---

[50] The superstitious belief here alluded to is the basis of a starkly realistic short story, "Medicine," by China's greatest modern writer, Lu Hsün (1881–1936). In this story a couple, desperately eager to save the life of their small tubercular son, feed him a roll soaked in blood that a professional collector has just gathered from the execution ground.

much of the richest land of China, killed twenty or more million people, and very nearly overthrew the Manchu government. These then were years of crisis, very different indeed from the period only thirty or forty years earlier to which the bulk of the cases translated in this book belong. Hence it may not be wholly fair to project what is said about penal institutions during the one age back to the earlier age of political stability. On the other hand, the accounts do seem to be accurate for their own day, and a reading of them helps give an understanding of the reasons for the biting attacks made by Shen Chia-pen and other jurists on the traditional penal system from 1901 onward—attacks leading to its radical revision just before the Revolution of 1911 was to destroy it entirely.[51]

[51] For an account of these changes, Meijer's often cited *Introduction of Modern Criminal Law in China* is invaluable. The three descriptions from which we have quoted at length were selected because of their seeming accuracy and objectivity, as well as detail. Illustrative of what may be found in the large nineteenth-century general works on China is the lively account of judicial procedure and punishments in John Henry Gray, *China: A History of the Laws, Manners and Customs of the People*, 2 vols. (London, 1878), I, 29–74. This study contains many accurate remarks based upon personal observation, coupled with serious errors and omissions. The book's air of infallibility, and its manifest disapproval of its subject (from a Christian missionary point of view), result in overall distortion.

The earliest European accounts of Chinese prisons and judicial procedure are those by: the Portuguese trader Galeote Pereira, based on personal experience, because much of his sojourn in south coastal China, 1549–1552, was spent in a Chinese prison; the Portuguese Friar Gaspar da Cruz, based in good part on Pereira, but also on a brief personal stay in Canton in 1556. Both accounts, though brief, contain much accurate observation and show remarkable objectivity. Tr. C. R. Boxer, ed., *South China in the Sixteenth Century* (London: Hakluyt Society, 1953), pp. 17–25 and 175–185.

IV · THE JUDICIARY

1. The Appellate System [1]

The center of our attention in this chapter will be the Hsing Pu or Board of Punishments in Peking because it is the organ that judged the cases translated later in this book. First, however, let us review the process whereby cases came to Peking from the lower levels. In so doing, it will be helpful to keep in mind some of the points made toward the beginning of the opening chapter of this book: the fact that the judicial system of imperial China, like the governmental system as a whole, was a centralized monolith with no division of powers; that there was no private legal profession; that on the lowest level of the *hsien* (district) or *chou* (department), where all cases originated (save those in the capital or in frontier regions), the magistrate rarely possessed any specialized legal training and handled the cases that came before him simply as one of many administrative duties; that, however, he often personally employed a non-civil service private legal secretary who did possess specialized knowledge of the law; and that all but minor cases automatically went upward from the *hsien* or *chou* to higher levels for final ratification, some as high as the emperor himself.

The government of China, as of the early nineteenth century (the period of most of our translated cases), operated on four main administrative levels. In ascending order, and with certain lesser administrative units ignored for the sake of simplicity,

---

[1] Useful for this section are T'ung-tsu Ch'ü, *Local Government in China under the Ch'ing*, Chaps. 6 and 7; Chang Yü-chüan, pp. 68–88; and Pao Chao Hsieh, *The Government of China* (*1644–1911*) (Baltimore, 1925), esp. Chaps. 4, 8 and 11. In the Ch'ing Code itself, the most important division on judicial procedure is that entitled "Trial and Imprisonment" (Bk. VI, Division K, in the table of contents given in Chap. II, sec. 2 above), which, however, is very inadequately covered by Boulais. Thus of the three statutes and 58 sub-statutes in the all-important sec. 411, "Jurisdiction Exercised by Tribunals of Different Levels," Boulais offers only three short paragraphs (Boulais, nos. 1692–1694).

these were: (1) On the lowest level, approximately 1,300 districts (*hsien*) and 150 departments (*chou*). (2) Approximately 180 prefectures (*fu*). (3) The 18 provinces (*sheng*) of China proper, each governed by a governor or a (higher ranking) governor-general or both. (Several of the governors-general exercised jurisdiction over two provinces, each of which at the same time had its own separate governor.) In addition, outside of China proper, there were Manchuria, whose three provinces were each governed by a military governor, and certain extra-provincial frontier regions along the north and northwest frontiers, among them Chahar and Jehol, each governed by a military lieutenant-governor. (4) The central administration in Peking.

The entire administration, from top to bottom, was highly centralized. All officials (the so-called mandarins) down to the lowest *hsien* level belonged to a single civil service and were appointed and controlled by Peking. The great majority entered the civil service by passing a series of examinations offered periodically by the government on the district, provincial, and national levels. These examinations were humanistic and Confucian in content and were open to almost all males educationally qualified to take them.[2]

The bureaucracy consisted of nine main ranks, each subdivided into two sub-ranks to make a total of eighteen divisions, with fixed insignia and salary for each. Throughout his civil service career, an official's conduct was carefully graded and recorded by his superiors, his dossier accumulating a growing number of merits or demerits that determined his promotions or demotions. Demerits might mean forfeiture of salary for a fixed term, reduction in rank, or, for very serious causes, complete dismissal from the civil service. There is much to admire in this system, the beginnings of which go back to the founding of the first Chinese empire in 221 B.C. and probably before. A major defect, already mentioned in the preceding chapter (section 11), was the inadequacy of the salaries paid to bureaucrats, which often compelled even honest men to supplement their salaries with income from other sources.

---

[2] However, certain groups were barred from taking the examinations. See the remarks on servants of officials near end of sec. 2 in Chap. VI.

Turning now to the court system, we find that it provided both for the automatic review of all but minor cases at various stages of the judicial ladder and for private individuals to appeal particular judgments if they so wished. Under the standard routine, all cases were initially investigated and heard on the lowest level, that is, in the yamen (government office) of the district or department magistrate. However, only in minor cases involving sentences of no more than bambooing could final judgment be pronounced at this level and sentence immediately carried out. These bambooing judgments were then collectively reported at fixed intervals to the prefecture to which the district or department was attached. In all other more serious cases, on the other hand, the magistrate could do no more than pronounce a provisional sentence and await confirmation from above before carrying it out. Such cases were then individually reported to the superior prefecture, which in legal matters seems often to have functioned merely as an agent for transmitting cases to a higher level.

From the prefecture the individually reported cases were in turn transmitted to the provincial capital where, for the first time, the system made use of full-time legal experts. These were the judicial commissioners (an-ch'a shih), of whom each province had one for the handling of its legal affairs, and who counted among the three or four most powerful officials in the province. Though subordinate to the provincial governor-general and governor, the fact that the judicial commissioner owed his first responsibility to the Board of Punishments in Peking gave him considerable autonomy. To his court (the Provincial Court) in the provincial capital came the defendants and witnesses, who were sent there for trial from their districts of origin. Sometimes, but probably much less often because of the great distances involved, these men might again be sent from the province to Peking for further hearings when their cases were transmitted there.

Judgments pronounced by the judicial commissioner required ratification by the governor-general or governor of the province. Thereafter, cases in which punishment was not heavier than penal servitude and which did not involve homicide, were periodically reported collectively by the governor-general or governor to the Board of Punishments in Peking, which normally did not review them individually. All more serious cases, however, as well as cases punishable merely by penal servitude but which *did* involve homicide, went as individual reports to the Board of Punishments. Among these, the Board exercised final jurisdiction over all except cases punishable by death, which went further upward through a body known collectively as the Three High Courts, and from it to the emperor himself for final ratification. The whole system can be portrayed more graphically in the following table:

ADMINIS-TRATIVE LEVEL	CATEGORY OF CASES (ACCORDING TO PUNISHMENT)			
	Capital	Exile or penal servitude involving homicide	Penal servitude	Bambooing
1. District or department	Investigated	Investigated	Investigated	Tried
2. Prefecture	Transmitted	Transmitted	Transmitted	Cases collectively reported
3a. Provincial court	Tried	Tried	Tried	Highest possible appeal
3b. Governor-general or governor	Confirmed	Confirmed	Confirmed	
4. Board of Punishments	Reviewed	Final judgment	Cases collectively reported	
5. Three High Courts	Final judgment			
6. Emperor	Ratification of judgment			

This table is necessarily an oversimplification. The Board of Punishments of level 4, for example, was, when it came to handling capital cases, at the same time one of the Three High Courts constituting level 5. Likewise, as we shall see in the next section, cases reaching the Board of Punishments passed through more than one level within the Board itself before receiving final approval. All sentences involving officials as offenders, even if punishable by bambooing only, had to be ratified by the emperor before they could be carried out.[3] All cases judged by analogy (see Chapter VI, section 3), even including bambooing cases, had to come to Peking for final judgment. And of course it often happened that bambooing sentences came to Peking as minor constituents of cases simultaneously involving more serious punishments.[4]

The ascent of cases through fixed channels from the *hsien* or *chou* upward to higher levels conformed to a series of deadlines that varied according to the gravity of the case. For an ordinary capital case originating in Chihli (the province in which Peking is located), for example, six months were permitted for the case to pass from initial investigation in district of origin to submission before the Board of Punishments (three months from district or department to prefecture, and one month each from prefecture to provincial court, from provincial court to governor-general or governor, and from the latter to the Board of Punishments). Often, however, these deadlines may have been violated in practice, at least to judge from a comment made in the Ch'ing "Legal Treatise": "Though the rules [for legal deadlines and the like] were strict, the cleverness of those who circumvented them remained as before."[5]

Once a case had been started on its upward course, its further

---

[3] See Boulais, no. 63.

[4] The 190 cases translated in this book generally confirm the truth of these statements. If, however, from among our bambooing cases, we eliminate those involving homicide or officials, those judged by analogy, or those coming to the Board directly from Peking itself, we are still left with one (case 183.3) in which bambooing is the only punishment, and which therefore should theoretically not have come to the Board of Punishments at all. As pointed out in our commentary, this case should by rights have been judged by analogy. The fact that it was not, coupled with the fact that the punishment pronounced in it is expressed ambiguously, suggests that the account of the case as we now have it may be inexact.

[5] See Ch'ing "Legal Treatise," p. 110, and, for the discussion of the deadlines, p. 109.

progress was automatic, to be abrogated only under most exceptional circumstances. Should a judge, for example, find the aggrieved party or defendant in a case to be his relative, former teacher, or former administrative superior, he was required to disqualify himself (Boulais, no. 1473). As we may deduce from the sub-statute immediately following (omitted by Boulais), the case was then transferred to another (presumably nearby) city of the same judicial level for trial.

Or again—and this situation was surely much more frequent, though still far from common—private individuals, if they found a lower tribunal unwilling to accept their case or were dissatisfied with the handling of the case by this tribunal, could then themselves appeal to a court of higher jurisdiction and there lodge an accusation or protest a decision. Two of the cases translated in this book (cases 171.3 and 260.1) involve appeals of this sort, which might go even as high as the emperor. The making of an appeal, however, was an uncommon and risky procedure because the complainant was himself subject to punishment either if he failed to exhaust all available legal procedures at the lower level before appealing higher, or if his accusation were found to be untrue (see Boulais, no. 1458 and following).

It seems reasonable to suppose, despite the apparent silence of the legislative sources on this point, that whenever someone appealed a sentence of bambooing—a punishment ordinarily carried out at once on the lowest level—this act automatically resulted in a stay of sentence until the appeal was decided. Otherwise there would seem little point in making an appeal. We may suspect, however, that sentences of bambooing were appealed only very rarely. Officials, who otherwise might have been the persons most ready to do so, enjoyed the privilege that any sentence against them had to be ratified by the emperor himself before execution.

In general, although the sources do not say so explicitly, there seems to have been little procedural difference, at least on the lower levels, between the handling of criminal and civil cases. Indeed, the law failed to distinguish clearly between the two categories, generally approaching them both from a penal point of view. Nonetheless, a pragmatic distinction was made by local magistrates between civil suits, that is, suits brought by one individual against another on matters concerning marriage, landed property, financial matters, and the like, as against criminal cases, that is, cases involving homicide, assault, robbery, and the like; the latter, especially if serious, would, unlike the former, be investigated and tried irrespective of whether or not one individual lodged a legal complaint against another. As we shall see in Appendix G, the hearing of *all* cases whatever (except under grave emergency) was halted during the first, sixth, and tenth months of the lunar year, as well as during the first two days of every month, and at certain stated annual holidays and festival periods (a total duration of five or more months per year). In addition, however, a further halt was placed upon the hearing of civil suits—which were regarded as less urgent—during the period of greatest agricultural activity, namely, from the fourth through the seventh lunar months.

At the provincial level, where most cases went to the judicial commissioner, those of a purely civil nature nevertheless commonly passed instead into the hands of an equally important colleague, the financial commissioner (*pu-cheng shih*). Although the primary responsibility of this official was to the Board of Revenue in Peking (just as that of the judicial commissioner was to the Board of Punishments), civil suits were almost invariably settled by him without going on to Peking. This handling of civil suits contrasts with cases other than civil suits, a large percentage of which, after reaching the judicial commissioner, moved on from him to Peking.

Once a case of the latter kind had been retried by the judicial commissioner, it was the record of this retrial and not the record made in the case from the court of first instance at the district level that passed on to Peking and became the basis for the final decision. This is why, in the reports of the Board of Punishments which are the basis for our translated cases, constant reference is made to the opinions and provisional findings made by the provincial court (the judicial commissioner) or by the governor or governor-general, but none at all to what might initially have been reported by the magistrate of the originating district. In fact, not even the names of such districts appear in these reports, which refer only to the province.

Should the Board of Punishments reverse a decision reached at the provincial level, the case would then be remanded to the provincial governor-general or governor with stated reasons for the reversal and instructions to reconsider the case accordingly. Thereafter, the resulting new judgment would again be submitted to Peking for approval. Once this approval had been given, however, the judgment would be sent downward level by level over the same channels along which the case had originally moved upward, until it finally reached the district or department in which the case had originated. So too the convicted offender would be returned if, as was usual, he had initially been sent with his case from the district or department of origin to the provincial court or, as was less likely, from there to Peking. Thus it was at the lowest administrative level, and not in Peking or in the provincial capitals, that capital or other punishment was finally administered (except for those cases that themselves originated either in Peking or in a provincial capital).

So far we have been discussing the routine channels along which the great majority of cases came to Peking. However, we should always remember that judicial activity might also originate, depending upon particular circumstances, from a variety of agencies other than those already mentioned. The Imperial Clan Court, for example, passed judgment upon any cases involving members of the Imperial Manchu Clan, which judgment was nominally subject to confirmation by the Board of Punishments. Each of the five boards, other than the Board of Punishments, likewise maintained its own set of written regulations for dealing with persons and activities falling within its particular sphere of jurisdiction; these too were often at the same time subject to the wider jurisdiction of the Board of Punishments. Among our translated cases, 263.1 illustrates the difficulties that could arise from such overlapping jurisdictions. In his *Government of China*, Pao Chao Hsieh, whose general opinion of the Ch'ing government is very unfavorable, summarizes the situation by saying: "The result of this confusion of jurisdiction was that 'everybody's business made it nobody's business,' or every one took up the case and a dispute arose out of, and among, the judges." [6]

[6] Pao Chao Hsieh, pp. 228–229. Among our 190 translated cases, the following references occur to various government organs as playing judicial or quasi-

Aside from the Board of Punishments, by far the most important agency of the central government to include judicial activities among its functions was the Censorate (*tu-ch'a yüan*).[7] This age old Chinese institution, staffed both by regular appointees and by *ex officio* functionaries from other governmental organs, had as its primary general purpose the investigating and impeaching of governmental wrongdoing or corruption wherever uncovered—theoretically, but unfortunately not always in practice, immune to any retributive punishment for its staff. On the topmost level, as we shall see in section 3, members of the Censorate cooperated with the Board of Punishments and a third judicial organ in the trying of capital cases. On a lower level, censors exercised jurisdiction over the five wards into which Peking was divided, and thus were responsible for bringing before the Board of Punishments some of the cases originating in Peking; others, however, came to it from another supervisory official, the general commandant of the gendarmerie of Peking.[8] Similarly, for dealing with provincial matters, the Censorate was divided into fifteen territorially-named departments known as circuits (*tao*), the staff members of which could at any time initiate legal action on matters pertaining to the area covered by their circuit. Such action might be entirely independent of the routine channels for legal activity within the area.[9]

Finally, a word must be said about the situation in Manchuria, which, as the original home of the Manchus before they conquered China in 1644, retained after the conquest a partially separate judicial system. The territory, with its capital at the city

judicial roles: Board of Civil Office (cases 49.1, 59.1, 263.1), Board of Revenue (40.1), Board of Rites (237.3), Imperial Household Department (124.1, 235.3), Imperial Clan Court (93.1), Salt Gabelle Administration of Tientsin (210.3).

[7] For this very important body as it functioned in Ming times, see the fine study by Hucker. For the Ch'ing Censorate there is the much more limited résumé by Li Hsiung-fei, *Les Censeurs sous la dynastie mandchoue (1616–1911) en Chine* (Paris: Imprimeries Les Presses modernes, 1936).

[8] Among our translated cases originating in Peking, six come from the ward censors (cases 92.1, 134.3, 150.19, 171.5, 223.4, 223.5), and eleven from the general commandant of the gendarmerie (cases 4.3, 9.1, 52.2, 52.3, 61.1, 82.6, 86.2, 171.6, 214.1, 214.4, 223.3).

[9] For references in our cases, see 49.1 (censorial Circuit of Kiangsi), 162.1 (Circuit of Chekiang), and 264.1 (Circuit of Shantung). Other references to judicial activities of the Censorate appear in cases 87.3 and 214.3.

of Mukden (called Sheng-ching in Chinese), consisted of the three provinces of Heilungkiang, Kirin, and Mukden (the latter also known in Chinese as Fengtien or Liaoning). Each province was governed by a military governor, and the capital by a prefect. The capital was the seat of a centralized administration for all of Manchuria which included among its organs a Board of Punishments for Manchuria quite separate from the Board in Peking. Cases, however, had to go from Manchuria to Peking for final approval just as they did from the provinces of China proper, though the precise channels of transmission are not wholly clear. Among our translated cases are several received by the Peking Board of Punishments from its counterpart in Mukden, but there are also cases received by it directly from the prefect of Mukden city or from one or another of the provincial military governors. Thus contrary to initial expectation, it would seem that not all cases originating in Manchuria had to pass through the Manchurian Board of Punishments before they could be sent on to Peking.

2. The Board of Punishments [10]

The Board of Punishments was one of six major boards or ministries (*pu*), the others being those of Civil Office, Revenue and Population, Rites, War, and Public Works. All of these, as well as other important government offices, were situated in the southern part of Peking east and west of a central north-to-south axis. To visualize their location, we must think of Peking as a walled and moated square, approximately four miles long on each side, and oriented from north to south in such a way that all major buildings face south. In its center stands another walled and moated square, approximately half a mile long on each side and similarly oriented, enclosing the vast complex of palace

[10] The main Chinese sources for this section are the Ch'ing "Legal Treatise," pp. 84 ff., and especially the *Ta Ch'ing hui-tien*, 53:1, 56:18b–21, and all of 57. In English, an extremely helpful parallel study, especially useful for its translation of technical terms, is E-tu Zen Sun, "The Board of Revenue in Nineteenth-Century China," *Harvard Journal of Asiatic Studies*, 24:175–228 (1962–63). Pao Chao Hsieh, Chap. 8, is generally useful but insufficiently detailed on specific points. Alabaster's *Notes and Commentaries* says almost nothing about the structure of the Board of Punishments, which is our present topic.

buildings known as the Forbidden City. Midway on the south side of the Forbidden City is its major entrance, the T'ien-an men or Gate of Heavenly Peace, which in turn faces south upon the vast T'ien-an Square. It is from the top of the T'ien-an Gate that China's present-day leaders review the parades passing through this square on May Day and October 1, the anniversary of the founding of the People's Republic of China. From the square's south side, and in line with the gate, a broad passageway or corridor, known as the Ch'ien pu lang or Esplanade of a Thousand Paces, leads southward toward the main south city gate of Peking, thereby evenly bisecting all of this portion of the city into an eastern and a western sector. In imperial times, the walls flanking the esplanade on its eastern and western sides effectively closed it off from the hurly-burly of ordinary city traffic. (These walls are gone today.)

The Board of Punishments formerly occupied a large walled compound some two hundred or more yards west of the Esplanade near its southern end. Immediately to the north of the Board was the Censorate, and immediately to its south the Court of Revision; the latter's judicial functions will be described in section 3. All of the other five boards, as well as other government offices, were ranged in a roughly similar manner to the east of the dividing Esplanade. This separation of the Board of Punishments from the other boards was almost certainly not fortuitous but was based upon geomantic considerations connected with the cosmological system of the Five Elements. According to this system, west is the direction of the element metal, which, because of its ability to cut other things, symbolizes the punitive functions of the judicial system. Likewise, west is the direction of autumn, the season of approaching death when, as we have seen near the end of Chapter I, capital punishment was annually reinstated after having been halted during the generative seasons of spring and summer.

Each of the six boards had a similar administrative structure. In contrast to the Ch'ing empire as a whole, in which the great majority of office-holders were Chinese, every effort was made on the higher administrative levels in Peking to maintain an even balance between Chinese and Manchus (with, very occasionally, a Mongol added because the Mongols had helped the Manchus in their conquest). The leadership of each major governmental organ thus usually consisted of two presidents and four vice-presidents, evenly divided according to race. The organization of the Hsing Pu or Board of Punishments conformed to this arrangement, being headed by one Chinese and one Manchu president, under whom were two senior and two junior vice-presidents, each pair likewise consisting of one Chinese and one Manchu. This august body of three Chinese and three Manchus was collectively known as the T'ang, a word literally meaning "hall" but in this book rendered as "Directorate."

Below the Directorate, the main core of the Board consisted of seventeen supervisory departments (*ch'ing-li ssu*), each named after one or more provinces as follows:

1. Mukden (or Fengtien, covering Manchuria)
2. Chihli (modern Hopei)
3. Kiangsu
4. Anhui
5. Kiangsi
6. Fukien
7. Chekiang
8. Hukuang (Hunan and Hupei)
9. Honan
10. Shantung
11. Shansi
12. Shensi (including also Kansu, plus Sinkiang after that area became a province in 1882)
13. Szechuan
14. Kuangtung
15. Kuangsi
16. Yunnan
17. Kueichow

Generally speaking, each department was staffed by two directors (one Chinese and one Manchu), two assistant directors (again evenly divided), and two secretaries (the same). Thus their organization was a replica, on a lower level, of the central Directorate. There were, however, a few minor variations for individual departments, resulting in the following totals covering official personnel for all seventeen supervisory departments: [11]

	Manchu	Chinese	Mongol	Total
Directors	16	19	1	36
Assistant Directors	22	19	1	42
Secretaries	17	17	0	34
Total	55	55	2	112

[11] Based on *Ta Ch'ing hui-tien*, 57:1–7b.

These figures, of course, represent only civil service officials of fairly high rank. They do not include lesser non-civil service personnel, such as clerks, servants, and messengers.

Each regional department was responsible for all cases coming to it from the province (or provinces) whose name it bore. In addition, Peking itself was administratively divided into five areas or precincts (Central City, West City, North City, and so on), cases from which were allocated among several of the departments. Central City cases, for example, were sent to the Department of Kiangsi, and West City cases to the Department for Shensi. In the same way, allocations were made of cases originating in other organs of the central government, such as the remaining five boards, the Imperial Astronomical Observatory, the Imperial Household Department, and the Court of Colonial Affairs. Matters having to do with Manchu nationals, whether in Manchuria or in other parts of China, were the particular concern of the Department for Mukden.

In Ch'ing times, the armed forces consisted of soldiers serving hereditarily in twenty-four units known as Banners, eight of which consisted of Manchus, eight of Mongols, and eight of Chinese descended from those Chinese who had collaborated with the Manchus in their conquest of China. (The term "bannerman," which will be encountered frequently in our translated cases, is thus in its broad sense a designation for any Manchu, Mongol, or Chinese member of one of these twenty-four Banners, though in popular parlance it is primarily a synonym for Manchu.) These Banners, designated Plain White Banner, Bordered White Banner, Plain Blue Banner, and so for several other colors, were permanently stationed in various parts of the country. Cases originating from them were likewise allocated among the various regional departments of the Board of Punishments. So too were cases coming from the extraprovincial frontier territories governed by military rather than civil administrators, such as Chahar, Jehol, and (prior to 1882) Sinkiang.

So many, indeed, were the government organs, military units, sectors of Peking, or other special territories from which cases could come and so few (hardly more than half a dozen) the officials attached to each of the Board's departments, that one

wonders how these possibly found time to do their work.[12]
A partial answer, perhaps, is that many of the government
organs—the Imperial Board of Astronomy, for example—were
not of the sort from which one might expect a large amount of
legal activity.

On the other hand, some of the regional departments were
saddled with additional responsibilities quite different from those
already listed. The Department for Kiangsu, for example, was
responsible for seeing to it that imperial amnesties, whenever
pronounced, were properly carried out among eligible convicted
criminals throughout the empire. The Department for Szechuan
had to check upon all government-used instruments of punishment and torture to see that they were of the legal size,
weight, and number. And the Department for Shensi was
responsible for issuing the food consumed in the prisons maintained by the Board of Punishments in Peking. (These were the
only prisons directly maintained by the Board. Prisons in the
provinces and districts were administered locally and so did not
come under the supervision of the Board.)

Until now we have been following what is said in our legislative sources, especially the Ta Ch'ing hui-tien. From our translated cases, however, we know that the allotment of cases in
actual practice often differed from the theoretical allotment as
described in the texts. Among our Peking North City cases, for
example, we find one going to the Department for Chekiang for
settlement (case 150.19), another to the Department for Yunnan
(case 92.1), a third to the Department for Kiangsu (case 223.5),
and still a fourth to the Department for Szechuan (case 223.4),
whereas all of them, according to the Ta Ch'ing hui-tien, should
properly have gone to the Department for Shensi. We have cases
from the Imperial Household Department going to the Departments for Kiangsi (case 124.1) and Shensi (case 235.2), whereas
both of them by rights should have gone to the Shansi Department. The Board of Revenue sends a case to the Department for
Kueichow (case 40.1) whereas its proper destination was the

[12] Pao Chao Hsieh, pp. 222–224, lists the seventeen supervisory departments
and enumerates under each the organs and areas from which it receives cases,
but this enumeration is far from complete.

Department for Fukien. The probable explanation is that, in order to equalize the flow of work, cases other than those originating in the provinces were allowed in actual practice to go to whatever departments were at the moment not too overloaded to accept them, regardless of theoretical allocations.

Before describing the procedure for handling cases after they reached a given department, it is well first to complete our survey of the remaining divisions of the Board. With few exceptions (notably the Registry Offices listed immediately below), their staffs were about the same in size as those for the regional departments. They included:

Manchu Record and Registry Office (ch'ing tang-fang) and *Chinese Record and Registry Office (han tang-fang)*. These two offices, with a combined staff of 40 copyist clerks (ranks 7 to 9 in the civil service) plus higher functionaries, made copies and translations in Chinese and Manchu of the memorials going to the throne from the Board, and the reports and memorials coming to the Board from the provinces.

Chancery (ssu-wu t'ing). This division received and made a file record of documents coming from the provinces, and distributed them to the supervisory departments. It likewise handled any prisoners who might have been sent to Peking for further interrogation.

Record Office (tang-yüeh ch'u). Just as the Chancery handled and distributed documents coming from the provinces, so the Record Office did the same with those coming from within the capital.

Expediting Office (tu-ts'ui so). This office had the important function of seeing that the bureaucratic machinery did not slow down. It established deadlines for the handling of various types of cases at various stages by the supervisory departments and saw to it that the memorials, reports, replies to the provinces, and so on, were prepared, circulated, and acted upon within the set timetables.

Supervisory Department on Arrests (tu-pu ch'ing-li ssu). This office is listed in the *Ta Ch'ing hui-tien* as an eighteenth supervisory department following the seventeen regional supervisory departments, even though it had very different functions. It was wholly concerned with the apprehension and punishment of bannermen who absconded from their Banners and became deserters and of other bannermen who might assist or harbor them. The several pages devoted by the *Ta Ch'ing hui-tien* (57/7b-12b) to this single Department suggest that the problem of deserting bannermen was an inordinately serious one. One suspects, however, that it was much more significant during the early decades of the dynasty when the Manchus were still consolidating their rule, than it was after they achieved political stability. By the mid-nineteenth century, when China was shaken by internal rebellion and external aggression, the bannermen had become so sedentary and parasitical that they were almost useless for fighting purposes, and had to be supplemented by large new-style conscripted armies.

Office for the Autumn Assizes (ch'iu-shen ch'u). This office handled arrangements for the important assizes to be described in section 4, and maintained deadlines for the receipt of cases from different parts of China so that they could be judged at the earliest possible autumn assizes.

Office for the Reduction of Sentences (chien-teng ch'u). This office was an ad hoc body appointed whenever an imperial amnesty was proclaimed. It handled the technical details involved in applying the amnesty throughout the empire. We have already seen that the Department for Kiangsu included similar duties among its responsibilities.

Statutes Commission (lü-li kuan). This extremely important body consisted of four Manchu and four Chinese proctors, appointed at irregular intervals, plus other officials skilled in jurisprudence appointed from other high governmental organs in the capital. Its head might be a Manchu prince of the blood appointed by the emperor himself, or some other very high official. Its continuing function was to select from the never-ending flow of completed cases and imperial edicts those that seemed to have particular legal significance, which it then (with imperial sanction, of course) incorporated in the form of new sub-statutes into successive editions of the Code. As we have already seen (Chapter II, note 28), during the period 1801–1863, such revised editions of the Code appeared on the average slightly more often than once every five years. Besides this primary function, the Commission also contributed its opinion on particularly difficult cases in a manner to be described later.

Office of Prisons (t'i-lao t'ing). This office administered the North and South Prisons in Peking maintained by the Board for persons held for trial in cases originating in Peking, as well as other persons sent there from the provinces with their cases. These prisons occupied respectively the northwest and southwest corners of the Board's compound.

Treasury (tsang-fa k'u). This body kept records of the confiscations and fines received by the Board in cases originating within Peking, as well as disbursements for food and clothing of persons under detention in the Board's prisons.

Food Costs Office (fan-yin ch'u). This office had charge of all the funds received and disbursed by the Board for its operation. (The funds were contributed by the provinces on a quota basis.) As pointed out by E-tu Zen Sun in connection with a similar organ in the Board of Revenue,[13] the officials serving in this office—the only one handling large sums of money—were appointed for short terms only: two years in the case of the Board of Revenue, and only one year in the case of the Board of Punishments.

Other personnel. An unspecified number of additional officials of high rank could be appointed as needed to the supervisory departments or elsewhere. About 125 lower-level clerks (ranks 7 to 9 in the civil service) were also employed as translators. Most of them were Manchu, but there were Chinese and a few Mongols as well. The *Ta Ch'ing hui-tien* fails to specify the number of non-civil service personnel who were also employed, but no doubt they exceeded the ranking officials in numbers. Although the total of all persons employed by the Board may have been under 1,000, our sources give the impression of a complex and busy bureaucratic machine at work, handling enormous amounts of paper work (numerous handwritten copies prepared of all major documents, and the added complication that many of them had to be bilingual). The existence of the Expediting Office testifies to a self-awareness of the difficulties of keeping the machinery going.

[13] E-tu Zen Sun, "The Board of Revenue," pp. 191–192.

Unfortunately, our sources give no clue as to its degree of success in coping with these difficulties. It becomes more and more evident, however, that China was probably the originator and developer of the most complex bureaucracy known to man prior to the Industrial Revolution. Now that the bureaucratization of the modern world proceeds apace, the Chinese experience becomes increasingly relevant.

We should end this section by telling what happened to cases after they reached the Board of Punishments.[14] If it was a case from the provinces, its report was transmitted by the Chancery to the proper supervisory department, or, if it was a Peking case, by the Record Office. The department in question then met and considered the case, interrogating the defendant and witnesses who might have accompanied it from the lower level, though, as we have suggested earlier, the long travel distances probably precluded this from being a common practice with respect to provincial cases.

Having reached a decision, the department wrote a report called a *shuo t'ieh,* translated in this book as "memorandum." Such a memorandum was submitted to the Board's Directorate, and, if approved by that body, was then returned to the department so that, on its basis, the department could prepare a reply for transmission to the governor-general or governor of the originating province. If, on the other hand, the Directorate found fault with the department's decision, it expressed this fact in a statement which, together with the department's memorandum, was then submitted to the Statutes Commission. The Commission's judgment, embodied in a further memorandum, was final, aside from the fact that the department presumably still had the right to argue its position before the Commission if it felt so inclined. Once the Commission had arrived at its final judgment, this was transmitted via the Directorate to the department, which on its basis sent a reply to the province, whence in turn it was transmitted to the originating district or department as described earlier.

[14] On this topic, in addition to the sources cited in note 10 above, remarks made *en passant* by Shen Chia-pen are helpful because of their clarity and the fact that they are based on his lengthy personal experience. See Shen, *Hsing-an hui-lan san-pien hsü* (Preface to a third compilation of the *Hsing-an hui-lan*), in *Bequeathed Writings,* pp. 976–977.

How many cases were annually handled by the Board of Punishments in this way? Nowhere, unfortunately, do we seem to have a clear-cut answer. Shen Chia-pen, however, writing in 1899 the brief preface to which reference has already been made (note 14 above), utters a remark made all the more remarkable by its casualness. During a career of some thirty years in the Board of Punishments, he says, he happened in the autumn of 1883 to serve in the Department for Mukden, where his task was that of writing the replies sent back to the three Manchurian provinces. Somewhat scornfully he comments: "The officials of the said provinces were for the most part not versed in legal matters, so that the replies that had to reverse their decisions amounted annually to as many as over 100." Unfortunately, Shen does not go on to tell us how many of the cases annually submitted from Manchuria *did* receive approval.

Until now we have been considering only the procedure for handling cases involving a punishment of less than death. In the next two sections we shall see that for capital cases the procedure was considerably more elaborate.

3. Capital Cases [15]

Noteworthy, and probably a heritage from Confucianism, is the insistence in Chinese law on careful scrutiny of every capital case at the highest level, including imperial ratification, before life may be taken. In A.D. 592 Emperor Wen of the Sui dynasty forbade the pronouncement of final judgment upon capital cases at

[15] The procedure for handling capital cases is extraordinarily complex, and on some points the sources either do not agree, are ambiguous, or remain silent. Therefore what follows in this and the next section may sometimes contain minor errors. To have stopped at each point to discuss discrepancies or alternative possibilities would have made the account impossibly long and technical. For the same reason, lesser details have been omitted. The major primary sources for the two sections are the same as before: *Ta Ch'ing hui-tien*, 53:1–3, and Ch'ing "Legal Treatise," pp. 85–98, to which should be added, from the Code, a great many of the almost 60 sub-statutes found under its sec. 411, "Jurisdiction Exercised by Tribunals of Different Levels." Most of these sub-statutes are omitted by Boulais, but, if included, would come between his nos. 1693 and 1694, and again between his nos. 1694 and 1695. See also, on the assizes, Boulais, no. 107, which is incomplete and contains inaccuracies. In English, see Chang Yü-chüan, and Alabaster, *Notes and Commentaries*, pp. 27–29. Also T'ung-tsu Ch'ü, *Law and Society*, p. 45, note 150.

the prefectural level. He ordered that such cases be transmitted to the capital for judgment there by the supreme judicial organ known as the Court of Revision (*ta li ssu*), this judgment then to be submitted in turn to the emperor for final ratification.[16]

Again in 631 Emperor T'ai-tsung of the T'ang dynasty was confronted by a case in which a high official, a member of the Court of Revision, defended another man who had been guilty of uttering improper remarks on the grounds that the accused was insane and hence not legally responsible for what he said. Another official immediately denounced this argument, saying it was prompted by the fact that its author was native of the prefecture of which the elder brother of the allegedly insane man was prefect. The emperor, exasperated, forthwith ordered the official who had defended the insane man to be executed. Later he regretted his act and uttered the oft-quoted remark: "Human life is of the utmost importance, for once dead, a man cannot live again." With these words he ordered that henceforth, before the execution of any capital sentence, memorials requesting approval must be submitted to the emperor two days before the execution, one day before, and no less than thrice on the day of the execution itself.[17]

There is thus a long-standing tradition behind the care with which capital cases were handled in Ming and Ch'ing times. By the latter period, the Board of Punishments had become increasingly powerful at the expense of the formerly important Court of Revision (*ta li ssu*). The Court still existed, however. Its main function was to participate in the making of decisions on capital cases by joining with members both of the Board and of another very important organ discussed in section 1, the Censorate (*tu-ch'a yüan*); these three bodies collectively constituted what were known as the Three High Courts (*san fa ssu*).[18] In practice, this

[16] See Balazs, p. 83. Balazs' own comment on this edict (p. 173, note 269) seems quite unjustified in view of the constant insistence upon this procedure during later dynasties. He says: "The procedure, with its multiple juridical guarantees, would be in absolute contradiction with autocracy—if it had ever been put into practice, which may be doubted. However, it is already remarkable that the idea of it had been conceived."

[17] See Bünger, *Quellen zur Rechtsgeschichte der T'ang-Zeit*, pp. 95–97 and 147–148.

[18] From certain references it would appear that the three bodies also sometimes jointly met to decide cases other than capital ones presenting special legal difficulties. Just how this may have happened (if indeed it did happen) and the

meant that whenever a department of the Board met to consider a capital case, its deliberations were attended by a secretary or an assistant secretary from the Court of Revision, and a censor from the Censorate. Inasmuch as the participants from all three bodies were not of the highest rank, the deliberations at this level were known as the Assemblage of the Lesser Judiciary (*hui hsiao fa*).

The decision emerging from these joint deliberations was then submitted to the Directorate of the Board of Punishments, which in turn enlisted participation of members of the Court of Revision and the Censorate in its deliberations. These deliberations, being conducted by men of much higher rank (including perhaps a director or a sub-director from the Court of Revision and a president or vice-president from the Censorate), were termed the Assemblage of the Greater Judiciary (*hui ta fa*). If this assemblage reached a decision different from that of the lower assemblage, it sent the case back to the lower body for renewed discussion. If, on the other hand, the two groups were in agreement, a memorial was prepared submitting the facts to the emperor and requesting his endorsement. This would normally be forthcoming in the form of a confirmatory rescript, though of course the emperor could always disapprove, in which event he would return a rescript of disapproval.

Should the judgment reached by the two assemblages differ from what had been provisionally suggested at the provincial level, the case might then, instead of immediately going up to the emperor for his approval, be remanded to the provincial court for reconsideration, followed by resubmission to Peking. Such a remand, however, as we learn from one of our translated cases (263.3), was mandatory for capital cases only if the sentence suggested by the provincial court had been a "light" one (strangulation), and had then been changed by Peking to a "heavy" one (decapitation). The reverse process—a change of sentence by Peking from "heavy" to "light"—did not normally require a remanding of the case to the provincial court. The only exception was, in the words of the sub-statute cited in our translated case,

---

relationship of such decisions to those made by the Board's Directorate or the Statutes Commission is not clear from the vague references.

when "something suspicious" was believed to exist behind Peking's softening of the sentence. Not surprisingly, however, the sub-statute fails to indicate how and by whom the existence of this suspicious something was to be determined. We may assume, therefore, that this part of the sub-statute was a dead letter.

Returning to the routine for handling capital cases in Peking, we should recall the fact (see Chapter III, section 7) that the two major death penalties, strangulation and decapitation, were, depending upon the seriousness of the crime, further qualified as either "immediate" (*li chüeh*) or coming "after the assizes" (*chien hou*, "awaiting [the assizes] in prison"). (The third rarely imposed death penalty, death by slicing, was ipso facto always classed as "immediate.")

If the penalty approved by the two assemblages and endorsed by the emperor called for immediate death, this fact was relayed down the line to the district or department where the case had originated, and where the execution was then carried out—not, however, under the jurisdiction of the Board of Punishments but of the Board of War, which was responsible for the executing of capital sentences. Of course, if the execution happened to coincide with one of the seasons or shorter periods annually tabooed for executions because of considerations of cosmic harmony, a delay until the end of the taboo period was necessary. Thus the sentence was not executed immediately in the sense that it was necessarily carried out at once, but only in the sense that such a judgment definitely closed the door to further consideration of the case and therefore made death inevitable.

If, on the other hand, a penalty approved by the two assemblages and endorsed by the emperor called for either strangulation or decapitation "after the assizes," this decision routed the case into an entirely new set of complicating and delaying procedures.

4. The Assizes

The assizes were of two kinds: Autumn Assizes (*ch'iu shen*) and Court Assizes (*ch'ao shen*). The Autumn Assizes handled all capital cases originating in the provinces which, having passed through the various stages of deliberation described in the last section, ended up with a sentence of execution "after the assizes" rather than "immediate" execution. The Court Assizes handled the same kind of cases when originating in Peking. Other than this, there was no difference between the two. The assizes system per se did not exist before the Ming dynasty. Nonetheless, it was an entirely natural outgrowth of a much earlier cautiousness toward the taking of human life such as we have seen exemplified in T'ang times in the insistence upon repeated memorializing to the emperor for his approval before the carrying out of execution. Likewise we have just mentioned the taboo upon executions until after the annual death of nature symbolized by the coming of autumn. This ancient taboo no doubt explains why both assizes were scheduled in autumn.

The earliest reference to the Court Assizes apparently belongs to the year 1459, when, according to the Ming "Legal Treatise," [19] the emperor ordered that annually thereafter, on a date following Frost's Descent (a point in the Chinese calendar coming two weeks before the beginning of the winter season and occurring approximately on October 23), representatives of the Three High Courts (the Board of Punishments, the Court of Revision, and the Censorate) should meet with members of the nobility to deliberate upon capital cases. This meeting apparently marked the formal beginning of the assizes system. The system was gradually elaborated and apparently the nobles were dispensed with. At any rate, we hear no more about them. Curiously, the term Autumn Assizes does not seem to appear in the main Ming sources. The reason, perhaps, is that the Court Assizes, at least during the early period of their development, apparently handled *all* capital cases, whether they originated in Peking or in the provinces. By the end of the Ming, however, some sort of differentiation between the two categories must have been established, and the term Autumn Assizes must have become at least verbally current, to judge from the casual reference to it that immediately follows.

This we find in the very first year of the Ch'ing dynasty, 1644, when a memorial to the throne referred both to Court Assizes and

[19] See the Ming *Hsing-fa chih*, in *Li-tai hsing-fa chih*, p. 588. The *Ta Ming hui-tien*, 177:11, gives the date as 1458.

Autumn Assizes as procedures for dealing with capital cases from Peking and from the provinces respectively. Both kinds of assizes continued throughout the dynasty, the docket of Autumn being, of course, considerably the more voluminous. The function of the assizes was to classify all "after-the-assizes" capital cases into several sub-categories. This classification was a complex undertaking in which it was easy to make mistakes. To rationalize the system, therefore, and make it as foolproof as possible, a set of forty rules was published in 1767 (augmented in 1784), entitled *Pi-tuei t'iao-k'uan* or *Articles for Matching [Capital Cases with Their Proper Categories]*. Other more elaborate guides of the same sort followed.

All capital cases, upon arrival in Peking, passed through the procedure described in the preceding section, but those provisionally labelled "after the assizes" had to reach the Board of Punishments by the middle of the fifth lunar month (in Western terms, sometime during July) if they were to be considered at the assizes that same autumn. If, as the result of review, they retained (or acquired) the designation of "after the assizes," they then had to undergo further processing in preparation for the Autumn Assizes themselves. Such processing included not only a tentative classification of them in terms of the several sub-categories to be described shortly, but also multiple reproduction of case reports for advance distribution to the prospective participants in the assizes.

The Autumn Assizes were scheduled for a day within the first ten days of the eighth lunar month (sometime during September in Western reckoning, by which time, according to the Chinese calendar, autumn was already about half over). Their locale was not far south of the T'ien-an men or Gate of Heavenly Peace, along the west side of the broad Ch'ien pu lang or Esplanade of a Thousand Paces which leads southward from the T'ien-an Square toward the main south gate of Peking.[20]

Although the walls flanking the east and west sides of the Esplanade were each lined on their inner face by a row of small

[20] For certain of the physical details in this and the next three paragraphs, use has been made, in addition to the sources listed in note 15, of the descriptive booklet by Chao Lo entitled *T'ien-an men* (Peking, 1957), pp. 24–25.

cell-like rooms, it would seem from the wording of the sources that the assizes were not held in these rooms at all (which would have been too small), but in the open air in front of them. There, on the appointed day, several tens of tables, topped by red cloth coverings, were set forth for the participating jurists, who included prominent officials from the Nine Chief Ministries (*chiu ch'ing*, that is, the six Boards together with the Court of Revision, the Censorate, and the Office of Transmission), as well as other dignitaries such as the tutors of the imperial heir apparent.

This mixed body examined the "after the assizes" cases and confirmed or altered their provisional classifications. From the *Ta Ch'ing hui-tien* (53/2a) we learn that the various stages of the proceedings were reported in a loud voice and "listened to by the multitude of the humble"—statements indicating that these highest judicial proceedings, like those in the lowest district court, were open to the public. The whole description carries a strongly archaic flavor, reminiscent of the tradition, as described by van Gulik, of "the Priest–King of hoary antiquity, holding court in the open, in the shade of a tree." [21] We may strongly suspect that in the overwhelming majority of cases, the judgments reached in public by this ad hoc body during its one-day session were little more than *pro forma* ratifications of the decisions already privately reached by the officials really professionally concerned.

The Court Assizes were the same as those of autumn save for the added feature that their condemned criminals, being all from Peking itself, were allowed to appear in person in order to utter a final plea for themselves. Our sources differ, however, concerning the date of the Court Assizes: either they were held on the day before the Autumn Assizes or on the tenth day after Frost's Descent, which would be more than a month later (around November 2 or 3).[22] We may reconcile this disagreement by assuming that the tenth day after Frost's Descent was the original date of

[21] See van Gulik, Introduction, p. 50.

[22] The Ch'ing "Legal Treatise," p. 93, says "the day preceding," and the Code, in sub-statute 48 under sec. 411 (one of the 58 sub-statutes on judicial procedure omitted by Boulais following his no. 1693), confirms this date by saying that the Court Assizes took place during the early part of the eighth month. The *Ta Ch'ing hui-tien*, 53:2, however, gives the date as the tenth day after Frost's Descent.

the Court Assizes during early Ch'ing times (thereby perpetuating the Ming date), but that in the course of the dynasty, for the sake of convenience, the date was shifted earlier so as to form an unbroken sequence with the Autumn Assizes.

What were the categories under which the assizes cases had to be placed? There were four of them: (1) Deferred execution (*huan chüeh*); (2) Worthy of compassion (*k'o chin*); (3) Remaining at home to care for parents or to perpetuate the ancestral sacrifices (*liu-yang ch'eng-ssu*); (4) Circumstances deserving of capital punishment (*ch'ing shih*). (This last term literally means "the facts are verified," but what it signifies in this context is that the facts of the case are not in question, and that they are of a sort calling for actual execution.)

1. *Deferred execution.* Certain common offenses nominally calling for capital punishment, such as killing by mischance or through roughhousing, or theft thrice repeated in an amount each time of 50 or more ounces of silver, were almost automatically placed in this category. Their nominal death sentences, as a result, were then reduced to one or another degree of military or ordinary exile. Other less usual offenses could also be placed in this category. Because of the greater difficulty of judging them, however, the Ch'ing "Legal Treatise" (pp. 93–94) states that they were set aside for final decision to be made only at the assizes two years later. During the intervening two years, therefore, the offenders were kept in prison. The "Legal Treatise" adds that though a change in their status was theoretically possible as the result of the decision reached two years later, such change was uncommon and as a rule the earlier tentative reduction of their nominal death sentence to a lower penalty was then confirmed. Thus in the overwhelming majority of cases, deferred execution meant commutation of execution to a lower penalty either immediately or after a waiting period of two years.

2. *Worthy of compassion.* Cases placed in this category were those involving the young, the aged, or other persons for whom particular extenuating circumstances existed. One of the Code's sub-statutes (no. 13 in the series cited in note 22) cites as an example of such extenuating circumstances the case of a husband who, in a sudden burst of anger, kills his wife because she has re-

viled or struck his father. Classification under this category meant reduction of death sentence to exile or penal servitude.

3. *Remaining at home to care for parents or to perpetuate the ancestral sacrifices.* Should an offender be the sole son of aged or infirm parents, or (from 1769 onward) should he be the sole male heir of *deceased* parents, he might, under appropriate circumstances, be classified under this category, thereby escaping death so as to care for the parents at home or, if they were deceased, to carry on the sacrifices to the ancestors. A person receiving this privilege commonly had his death penalty reduced to 40 blows of the heavy bamboo and two months wearing of the cangue. This remarkable injection of the principle of filial piety into the legal system has already been mentioned in our first chapter (section 10), and turns up several times in our translated cases (especially cases 11.1 and 11.2). From the latter it would appear that escape from death on these grounds, though sought rather often, was not readily granted. The reader is referred to these cases for details of the procedure involved.

4. *Circumstances deserving of capital punishment.* This final category, into which the more serious offenses were placed, was the only one of the four leading toward actual execution. Yet even here there remained a final procedure which might save some of the offenders from death. By way of preparation, offenders placed in this fourth category were further subdivided into: (a) officials; (b) persons guilty of family offenses (said to consist commonly of injuries or killings inflicted in affrays by junior relatives upon senior relatives belonging to the third degree of mourning); (c) all other persons.

Following the conclusion of the Autumn and Court Assizes, the results of the classifications then arrived at were submitted to the emperor so that he might examine them prior to a final climactic ceremony at which he confirmed the disposition of the various categories. For the Autumn Assizes this ceremony took place some sixty days before the winter solstice or around October 21, and for the Court Assizes some ten days before the solstice or around December 11. At dawn on these two days, high officials, including presidents or vice-presidents of the nine ministries mentioned earlier, representatives of the Grand Secretariat (a kind of inner cabinet), and others, assembled in the Hall of Earnest Diligence (Mou-ch'in tien) located in the northern part of the Forbidden City. To mark the solemnity of the occasion, all wore funeral garb of plain undecorated white, the Chinese color for mourning. Our sources describe in great detail each move that followed. We can summarize by saying that the sub-chancellor, kneeling, placed the lists of the condemned on a table in front of the dais on which the emperor was sitting. Apparently the lists included the names of all those placed in the three categories leading to reduced punishment, as well as the fourth category of "circumstances deserving of capital punishment." It was only for the latter, however, that the ceremony was of crucial importance.

Having received the lists, the emperor inspected them and indicated his approval either by marking them himself with his vermillion brush or having a grand secretary do this on his behalf. In particular, with regard to the list of persons in the category of "circumstances deserving of capital punishment," he checked off (yü kou, "gave a hook to") the names of those actually destined to die.

Curiously, the Chinese sources, despite their specificity on the steps leading up to this crucial moment, fail to explain how the checking itself was done. For this we have to turn to two of our English-language sources which, though differing slightly, obviously represent a common tradition. Alabaster [23] states that the names of the condemned were written on a large sheet (more probably it was several sheets) "not alphabetically, or by chance, but so that the names of those prisoners who are, in the opinion of the Board, less guilty than the others are placed either at the corners or in the centre. The list is then submitted to the Emperor who, with a brush dipped in vermillion, makes a circle on it at seeming, and to some extent real, hazard, and the criminals whose names are traversed by the red line are ordered for execution. The others remain on the list until the next year."

Chang Yü-chüan [24] writes somewhat differently that "on the day fixed, the Emperor held a Court, and ordered a Grand Secretary to use the vermillion pen and make a bracket on the list of

[23] Notes and Commentaries, pp. 28–29.
[24] Pp. 84–85.

the capital offenders . . . Those whose names were enclosed within that bracket were to be executed forthwith, while those whose names were outside the bracket remained in prison, and were again brought back to try their luck the following year."

Chang's account seems more probable than Alabaster's, since the procedure described by Alabaster would allow all names not actually touched by the brush to escape execution, and this would probably be an inordinately large number. Be this as it may, it is striking to see the long progression of highly rationalistic procedures in capital cases culminating in a ceremony resting upon magic and the charismatic insight of the emperor.

What happened to those whose names were not checked off? They were kept in prison to re-experience the ordeal a year later. Those guilty of family offenses, if they twice succeeded in escaping the vermillion brush, then had their classification changed to "deferred execution," and their death penalty was reduced to a lower punishment. If, however, the convicted belonged to the sub-categories of either officials or ordinary persons, they then had to escape the vermillion brush no less than ten times before achieving the status of "deferred execution." By the law of averages, obviously few persons could thus escape the brush ten times running unless, as seems likely, the names of some were in fact consistently arranged in such a manner as to insure that they would not be checked.

One conclusion emerging very clearly from all that has been said is that although imprisonment was not recognized as a formal punishment in China, a great many people must nonetheless have spent a great deal of time in prison. Before conviction, a defendant could conceivably spend several years awaiting the many moves up and down the legal ladder needed to conclude his case, and even after conviction, if placed among those "deserving of capital punishment," he might remain ten years in prison before the continuing threat of death was finally replaced by exile or possibly penal servitude.

How many persons were spared by the procedures we have been describing? Though firm statistics are unavailable, the general opinion is that the percentage was high. We have seen already (Chapter III, section 10) that in Ch'ing times a total of 490 offenses were punishable by strangulation or decapitation after the assizes, as against only 323 punishable by immediate execution. These figures, however, tell nothing about either the relative frequency of the different offenses or what proportion of persons sentenced to death after the assizes actually were executed. Limited help on the first point, but none at all on the second, is provided in Appendix A, which lists all punishments imposed in our 190 translated cases. The death penalties total 38, of which 24 are after the assizes, and only 14 are immediate. Among the assizes penalties, however, only in exceptional instances do our cases give any hint as to whether the circumstances point toward eventual execution or a lower penalty.

A subjective statement, but authoritative as the utterance of one of the greatest of Chinese jurists, Shen Chia-pen, occurs in a memorial made by him to the throne on October 3, 1907. In this document, having to do with the drafting of a new criminal code, he writes concerning offenders annually sentenced to death after the assizes: "Those who were really marked off for execution every year were no more than ten per cent of the total." [25]

From the rather narrow context of our modern Western background we may feel critical of the non-separation of powers in the Chinese legal system, of the absence of a private legal profession, of the archaisms preserved over a span of two thousand years, of the torture permitted as a contribution from the Legalists, or of the sharp social and individual inequalities written into law under the influence of Confucianism. Yet the appellate system in general and more particularly the system for handling capital cases should rightly be regarded as notable creations of the human mind. No doubt the system was complex and overrefined; perhaps it was unduly ritualized; and almost surely it was wasteful of manpower. Nonetheless, it constitutes a kind of "due process" which, different as it is from our own, certainly deserves admiration and respect.

Having said this, it is important to keep one final point in mind: the fact that the procedure governing capital cases was not universal. Bandits and rebels were literally outside the law in the sense that the safeguards normally covering the application of

[25] Tr. Meijer, p. 194.

capital punishment did not apply to them. They could be tried and executed in the locality where they were captured, with only a report of their case going to higher levels and with no need to wait for ratification. In times of political unrest, such as the Taiping Rebellion of the mid-nineteenth century, criminals of this kind might far outnumber ordinary offenders. It will be remembered, for example, that all of the thirty-four men whose execution Meadows witnessed in Canton in 1851 (see the end of the last chapter) were called "bandits." So, in all probability, were the "upwards of four hundred human beings" whose heads Meadows describes as having been left to decompose at the execution ground during the preceding eight months. None of these cases, presumably, had been sent to Peking.

V · THE *HSING-AN HUI-LAN* OR *CONSPECTUS OF PENAL CASES*

1. The *Conspectus,* Its Background and Purpose

The Chinese are perhaps the world's most inveterate compilers of documents. Their dynastic histories, compiled over a span of more than two millennia, are gigantic mosaics of imperial edicts, memorials to the throne, and other products of bureaucracy, linked together by threads of chronological narrative.[1] Their encyclopedias are even vaster repertories of earlier writings, and include what is still the largest encyclopedia known to man.[2]

It would be strange, therefore, if Chinese jurists had not taken the trouble to compile collections of cases. What is really surprising, in fact, is the relative paucity of such casebooks until recent centuries. Probably the earliest example is a casebook prepared near the beginning of the imperial age by the famed Confucian scholar Tung Chung-shu (179?–107? B.C.).[3] Unfortunately its 232 cases have all been lost save for half a dozen fragments. These are of interest, both because they epitomize Confucian moral problems (for example, what is to be done to a father who conceals an adopted son guilty of homicide) and because of the

[1] It has been estimated that a properly annotated English translation of the twenty-four standard histories would amount to something like 45 million words. See H. H. Dubs, "The Reliability of Chinese Histories," *Far Eastern Quarterly,* 6:23–25 (1946).

[2] This work, compiled in 1725, was estimated in 1911 as being from three to four times the size of the (then current) 11th edition of the *Encyclopaedia Britannica.* See Lionel Giles, *An Alphabetical Index to the Chinese Encyclopaedia Ch'in Ting Ku Chin T'u Shu Chi Ch'eng* (London: The British Museum, 1911), p. ix, note 2.

[3] The work is cited in later texts under several variant titles, among them *Ch'un-ch'iu chüeh-yü* or *Case Decisions Based on the Spring and Autumn Annals.* The *Annals,* a brief chronicle history of Confucius's native state of Lu, covering the years 722–481 B.C., was in Han times widely (but probably erroneously) believed to have been written by Confucius himself in order to express in esoteric language his ideas about good government and society. Thus Tung's treatise, based on this chronicle, would seem to be an early attempt to interpret law in terms of Confucian morality.

abstract manner of their presentation: the persons in them are not referred to by name but by the Chinese equivalents of A, B, C, and so on.[4]

It was not until much later, in the Sung dynasty (960–1279), that casebooks were published in any number. Three survive, of which the best, *Parallel Cases from under the Pear-Tree*, has been admirably translated by R. H. van Gulik.[5] This work, compiled in 1211 by an otherwise obscure scholar, is a collection of 144 selected criminal and civil cases ranging from about 300 B.C. to about A.D. 1100. The cases are arranged in parallel pairs embodying similar themes and are taken from a variety of sources, including, often, a biography in a dynastic history of the main protagonist (commonly a district magistrate or other official). This means that their form is anecdotal rather than juridical. Although supposedly based on true materials, some of them contain episodes that are apparently legendary. And many do not focus on legal points at all but serve to illustrate clever detective techniques used by a magistrate or other hero in catching the wrongdoer. The following example, aside from being a little shorter than most, is typical: [6]

When Li Hui of the Later Wei Dynasty (386–534 A.D.) served as Prefect of Yung-chou, a salt carrier and a wood carrier quarreled about a lamb skin, each claiming it as the very one he used to wear on his back. Li Hui ordered one of his officers: "Question this skin under torture, then you will know its owner." All the officers were dumbfounded. Li Hui had the lamb-skin placed on a mat, and had it beaten with a stick; then grains of salt came out of it. He showed them to the contestants, and the wood carrier confessed.

Many of the stories throw vivid light on operations of the law at the lowest district level.[7] However, if we wish to read cases from the archives of professional jurists rather than the anecdotal writings of amateurs, there is extremely little available before the Ch'ing dynasty—the greatest age of pre-modern Chinese scholarship.

---

[4] Translations of some appear in Escarra, pp. 279 ff.

[5] In his often cited *T'ang-yin-pi-shih*.

[6] *Ibid.*, p. 113, Case 26-B.

[7] The third chapter of van Gulik's introduction, "Court procedure in ancient China," is an excellent account of this subject.

Most of the half dozen or so major Ch'ing casebooks belong to the second half of the eighteenth and first half of the nineteenth centuries. We shall not try to list or evaluate them here,[8] other than to say that they are based on archive materials from the Board of Punishments, and that the cases reported are commonly ones raising contradictory rulings, involving judgment by analogy, or representing reversals by Peking of sentences proposed at the provincial level. Some of the collections are quite voluminous, and some are quite difficult to consult because of poor classification of materials (although successive collections show steady improvement in this respect). A good illustration, and perhaps also the earliest of the genre, is Hung Pin's *Po-an ch'eng-pien* (Compilation of reversed cases), covering the years 1736–1770. Use of the two hundred and sixty cases in this collection is impeded by their arrangement in chronological order without regard to subject matter.

Of all such collections, there is no doubt that the largest in size, broadest in subject matter and chronology, and best classified is the *Hsing-an hui-lan* or *Conspectus of Penal Cases*—the primary subject of the rest of this book.[9] The work actually consists of three separate publications: an initial very bulky compilation constituting the *Hsing-an hui-lan* proper; a considerably smaller but nevertheless substantial sequel, called *Hsü-tseng Hsing-an hui-lan* (Supplement to the *Hsing-an hui-lan*); and a quite small second sequel known as *Hsin-tseng Hsing-an hui-lan* (New supplement to the *Hsing-an hui-lan*). These three works will hereafter be collectively referred to as the *Conspectus* or (in text references) as HAHL; separately, they will be referred to as the *Conspectus* (or HAHL) proper, the *Conspectus* (or HAHL) Supplement, and the *Conspectus* (or HAHL) New Supplement. From the prefaces (*hsü*) and "General Principles" (*fan li*) heading the three works, we learn the following:

Conspectus proper. Compiled in 60 *chüan* (parts or books) by Chu Ch'ing-ch'i and Pao Shu-yün, with a preface by Pao dated

[8] The main ones are listed in T'ung-tsu Ch'ü, *Law and Society*, pp. 292–293.
[9] *Hsing* means "punishment" or "penal"; *an* means "case(s)"; *hui* means "the flowing together of waters," hence "to collect," "to bring together"; *lan* means "to observe," "to survey," "a general survey" or "view." Hence the title literally means something like "Penal cases brought together to be surveyed."

1834. It contains over 5,650 cases covering a total time span of 1736–1834 but most of the cases fall within the years 1784–1834.

Conspectus Supplement. Compiled in 16 *chüan* by Chu Ch'ing-ch'i, who died before the work was completed. Finishing touches were added by Pao Shu-yün, whose preface this time is dated 1840. It contains over 1,680 cases covering the years 1824–1838.

Conspectus New Supplement. Compiled in 16 *chüan* by P'an Wen-fang and Hsü Chien-ch'üan. The preface is by a third man, Ho Wei-chieh, and is dated 1886. It contains fewer than 300 cases for the years 1842–1885, of which most seem to belong to the final decade of this period.

The three compilations thus contain a grand total of over 7,600 cases, with a time span of 1736–1885. The great majority, however, belong to the first three decades of the nineteenth century, especially the second and third decades.

More than one edition of these compilations has been published.[10] The one used for this book is the relatively small but still misleadingly labelled "Pocket Size Edition" (*fang hsiu-chen pan-yin*).[11]

Concerning the authors of the three compilations, the several prefaces tell us but little. Chu Ch'ing-ch'i, the person primarily responsible for the first two of them, was a native of K'uei-chi, well known district in Chekiang, central coastal China. During long years of service in the Department for Yunnan of the Board of Punishments, he used his spare time to collect the cases forming the nucleus of the *Conspectus* proper "in order to save the world."

Meanwhile Pao Shu-yün, a native of Shê hsien, Anhui, also in central China, had been serving in the Board of Punishments since 1823, where, confronted by the ever increasing piles of completed cases and documents "spreading forth like a sea," he "constantly

[10] See T'ung-tsu Ch'ü, *Law and Society,* pp. 292–293, entries under Chu Ch'ing-ch'i and P'an Wen-fang.

[11] No date of publication, but the catalogue of the East Asian Library of Columbia University gives the date as 1886, I do not know on what ground. The edition is handsomely printed with movable type, and consists of 40 *ts'e* or Chinese-style stitched vols., of which the *Conspectus* occupies *ts'e* 1–28, the *Conspectus* Supplement *ts'e* 29–36, and the *Conspectus* New Supplement *ts'e* 37–40.

thought of compiling a book in which these would be classified according to category and group, so as to facilitate consultation." He was prevented by lack of time, however, until the death of his mother obliged him to retire to Yangchow (famed city in Kiangsu, central China) to mourn for her during the requisite period. There he came in contact with Chu Ch'ing-ch'i and read the compilation on which Chu had been working. Finding it in harmony with his own ideas, he joined Chu in the latter's efforts. The collaboration was interrupted when Chu became private secretary to the governor-general of Fukien, but resumed when he returned to Yangchow in 1832, and completed three years later. Pao, in his preface to the *Conspectus* Supplement, says that the total work on the *Conspectus* proper required more than ten years.

In this same preface, Pao writes that because of the continuing prolific output of the Board of Punishments, Chu Ch'ing-ch'i decided to carry his compilation further. He died, however, before it was brought to completion. Pao Shu-yün gave it the final touches, therefore, and the result was the *Conspectus* Supplement, the arrangement of which conforms exactly to that of the *Conspectus* proper.

We know still less about the compilers of the *Conspectus* New Supplement. Ho Wei-chieh, author of its preface of 1886, signs himself as a native of Ch'ü-yang in Chihli (Hopei) province, north China and describes himself as having held office in the Board of Punishments. The same was almost surely true of P'an Wen-fang, major compiler of the New Supplement, though Ho does not tell us this but merely identifies him as a native of Lanchow in Kansu, northwest China. Nor does Ho say anything about P'an's collaborator, Hsü Chien-ch'üan. We are merely told that during the more than forty years since Chu had compiled the original *Conspectus* and its sequel, China had been plagued with rebels (the Taiping Rebellion), changes had taken place in the legal system, and Western law had become known in China. These factors are what induced P'an to prepare a sequel to Chu's two compilations with the collaboration of his colleague Hsü Chien-ch'üan. At the end of the "General Principles" following this preface, we are told that whereas the original *Conspectus* required ten years and the Supplement three years to complete, the New Supplement was rushed to completion in only three months. The reader's indulgence is requested for any resulting errors.

In all three compilations cases are arranged according to the 436 titled sections of the Ch'ing Code. Classification of a case under a given section does not necessarily mean, however, that the judgment rests on a statute or sub-statute taken from that section. For example, a case involving improper sex relations culminating in homicide might very well be classed under the section on sexual violations yet be judged according to one of the statutes or sub-statutes on homicide.

Furthermore, not all of the Code's 436 sections are actually represented by cases in the *Conspectus*. For the most part, the omitted sections are ones that had become dead letters. For example, it is not surprising to find that section 163 of the Code, "Preparation of Imperial Medicine" (preparation of improper medical prescriptions for the emperor), is unrepresented by cases in the *Conspectus*. Another reason for the omission of some sections is that they consist of legal definitions rather than penal prohibitions. For example, section 41, "Divisions of Time," explains among other things that a legal day consists of 100 Chinese quarter-hours, and a legal year of 360 days.

The net result is that only 270 of the 436 sections of the Code are represented by cases in the *Conspectus*. Neither in the one nor in the other are these sections numbered. To facilitate references we have numbered the 270 sections in the *Conspectus* consecutively and thus the case numbering there differs from the Code numbering. "Marriage," for example, is section 101 in the Code but section 52 in the *Conspectus*.

Under various sections of the *Conspectus*, the quantity of cases ranges from one to 376 (see next chapter, section 1). In the larger sections, at least, the arrangement of cases is not necessarily chronological but rather according to variant types. The date and source of a case are regularly printed in smaller type immediately following the main text.

As with the sections, the cases are unnumbered in the original; they have been numbered by us to facilitate reference for this book according to their grouping under each section. An annotation such as "case 52.2," for example, means that we are talking about the second case (out of a total of nine) under section 52 of the *Conspectus* (equivalent, in the Code itself, to section 101). In this connection it should be noted that in any given section, the cases in the Supplement and New Supplement have been numbered consecutively after those in the *Conspectus* proper. If, for example, the *Conspectus* has ten cases under a given section, then the first case under the corresponding section in the *Conspectus* Supplement is numbered 11, and so forth.

In conclusion, let us turn from technicalities to the basic question of why the *Conspectus* was compiled. The answer, almost surely, is the same as the reason for case compilation in the West: to supply jurists with a body of precedents in readily accessible form. Pao Shu-yün practically states as much in his prefaces when he initially says of Chu Ch'ing-ch'i that he compiled the cases "in order to save the world," and then of himself that, overwhelmed by the proliferation of legal materials, he wished to produce a classified compilation "so as to facilitate consultation." Pao is by no means a very articulate speaker on this subject, however. A more extended exposition of the value of the *Conspectus* can be found in the philosophically minded Shen Chia-pen, who in 1899 wrote a preface for a planned new edition of the *Conspectus*—one that would have brought it up to date but was in fact never published. In this Shen says: [12]

The relationships between legal punishments (*hsing*) and terms (*ming*) are of the utmost importance. The facts involved, with their innumerable permutations, each has a thousand beginnings and myriad ramifications. The principles involved, with their minute differences, are like the threads of a silk-cocoon or the hairs on an ox. Suppose one assumes responsibility for all of these in one's own person, without seeking for the accepted pronouncements of earlier men or examining into the circumstances of previous cases, and suppose one relies merely on one's own thinking and on the viewpoint of one's own age. Then what had been firmness of mind will become obstinacy, and eagerness of spirit will become rashness. The result will surely be to "miss by a hair's breadth and thereby go astray by a thousand miles." [13] Again

---

[12] Shen Chia-pen, *Hsing-an hui-lan san-pien hsü*, in *Bequeathed Writings*, pp. 976–977.

[13] A well-known saying. Compare our "a miss is as good as a mile."

and again a mistake in a single case or a single sub-statute can lead to incalculable harm . . . Very definitely the *Conspectus* enables us to seek out the pronouncements of earlier men as standards [for our own pronouncements] and to look into the circumstances of previous cases as foundations [for our own cases].

2. The Sources

The cases contained in the *Conspectus* are taken, in overwhelming measure, from three main archival sources: memoranda, leading cases, and general circulars. In addition, a few cases come from printed sources.

1. *Memoranda* (*shuo t'ieh*). These are the reports of cases circulated among the various sectors of the Board of Punishments. A given regional department of the Board, having received a case, prepares a *shuo t'ieh* on it which, as we have seen in the last chapter, goes to the Board's Directorate for approval. From there, if the case presents special difficulties, it may go on to the Statutes Commission, which eventually returns it to the Directorate with an additional memorandum of its own. Some cases too, as we have seen, must go to the emperor for final approval. Manuscript file copies of these several kinds of memoranda were kept in the archives of the Board of Punishments, and make up a very large proportion—close to 40 per cent—of all cases included in the *Conspectus*.[14]

2. *Leading cases* (*ch'eng an*). It is important to note that these, in the *Conspectus*, are commonly referred to simply as *an*, "cases." [15] Literally, the term *ch'eng an* merely means "finished (or completed) case"; that it bears a further special legal significance, however, is indicated by the following definition: [16] "Leading Cases (*ch'eng an*) are cases to which no existing article exactly applies, and that are decided on the lines of some clause

---

[14] The East Asian Library of Columbia University possesses a manuscript copy of *shuo-t'ieh* of the Board of Punishments covering the period 1784–1883. No doubt there are many duplications between this series and the memoranda included in the *Conspectus*.

[15] See the twelfth of the "General Principles" (*fan li*) listed immediately after the Preface of the *Conspectus*.

[16] See fourth of the "General Principles" cited in the preceding note. The definition is also translated in Alabaster, *Notes and Commentaries*, p. 12.

more or less applicable, with increase or reduction of the established penalty." In other words, leading cases are either cases
judged by analogy (see Chapter I, section 9), or cases in which
special circumstances call for changes from the statutory penalty.
It is these special features, of course, that make leading cases
important as precedents and thus explain why they constitute
over 35 per cent of all cases included in the *Conspectus*.

3. *General circulars* (*t'ung hsing*).[17] These are leading cases or
imperial edicts (often inspired by leading cases) which, thought
to have particular importance, are designated *t'ung hsing* so that
they may be generally circulated among judicial authorities
throughout the country. From among these general circulars, in
turn, a relatively small proportion is subsequently selected by the
Statutes Commission for reincarnation as genuine new sub-statutes in the next edition of the Code (revised by the Statutes
Commission for this purpose, it will be remembered, approximately every five years). The number of general circulars in the
Conspectus is less than 10 per cent of the items in the total work.
For the years 1736–1809, a printed edition of general circulars
was prepared; because it was published in Kiangsu province, it is
referred to in our cases, when general circulars from this period
are cited, as the Kiangsu Printed Edition. Post-1810 general circulars, on the other hand, are copies from originals in the Board
of Punishments.[18] Subordinate to the general category of general
circulars (*t'ung hsing*) there is a very minor sub-category of documents known as circulars for compliance (*tsun hsing*). These
are case documents intended for circulation among the departments of the Board of Punishments only, and not for wider circulation outside the Board.

Of the printed publications also used by the *Conspectus* as
sources for cases, the two most important are:

1. *Peking Gazette* (*Ti-ch'ao*). This official daily publication

[17] For an explanation of this term, which is not formally defined in the
sources, I am happy to acknowledge help from a paper prepared for me by Mr.
Wu-su P'an, in which aspects of Ch'ing judicial procedure are discussed with
special reference to the *Conspectus*. The paper has also been helpful with regard
to certain other points discussed in this chapter.

[18] At least, this information is what is provided by the fifth of the *Conspectus*'s
"General Principles" (see note 15 above). That it is subject to minor qualification is indicated by the fact that of the three cases among our translations stated
to have come from the Kiangsu Printed Edition of General Circulars (cases 41.7,
59.1 and 162.1), the third embodies an imperial edict dated January 19, 1812.

might very loosely be described as a sort of Chinese *Congressional Record*, containing edicts, memorials to the throne, and other documents and news items of an official nature. The existence of this publication perhaps as early as the Sung dynasty gives China the distinction of having had the world's oldest newspaper.[19] A few cases in the *Conspectus* have been taken from reports of cases in the *Gazette*. Because these reports were intended for a wide audience, they lack legal details of the reports issued by jurists for jurists.

2. *Ch'eng-an so-chien-chi* (Collection of seen leading cases). This compilation of 1,138 cases, covering the years 1736–1805, was prepared by Ma Shih-lin in four successive collections. A very few of its cases have been reproduced in the *Conspectus*, where it is referred to under the abbreviated title of *So-chien-chi*.

In addition, the *Conspectus* editors took a small number of their cases (not more than 8 or 9 per cent of the total) from a variety of other sources, including more than 500 cases which Chu Ch'ing-ch'i personally copied from the files of the Board of Punishments. It is unclear from what is said whether there is any significant difference in type between these 500 cases (*an*) and the other "leading cases" (*ch'eng an*) which, as we have seen, are likewise usually referred to in the *Conspectus* simply as *an*, "cases."

For the 190 cases translated in this book, a breakdown of the sources will be found in Appendix E. Among leading cases there listed, one (case 172.4) bears the special designation, "Leading Case Selected for Redaction as a Sub-statute" (*an yi-tsuan li*). Likewise two of the general circulars (cases 175.6 and 198.7) are similarly termed "General Circular Selected for Redaction as a Sub-statute" (*t'ung hsing yi-tsuan an*). We may suppose that all three cases became the bases for new sub-statutes. No source at all is indicated for one case (267.2), presumably owing to editorial inadvertence. Incidentally, it is one of the most interesting of all our cases.

Two problems are raised by the 100 leading cases included in

---

[19] Translated excerpts from the *Peking Gazette* were published by the British *North-China Herald* (and its successors) of Shanghai from 1850 until the 1880's, and thereafter for a few years by the Tientsin *Chinese Times*.

our translations. In the first place, no less then ten of them do not seem to meet the criteria for leading cases presented above.[20] That is to say, these ten cases do not involve sentencing by analogy, increase or reduction of punishment, or other special features allegedly distinguishing leading cases from routine ones. Conceivably the explanation is that they are not really leading cases at all but belong to the "more than 500 other cases" (precise nature unspecified) which, as just noted, the *Conspectus* compilers added to their leading cases.

Another problem surrounds the term *hsien shen* which is found prefixed to eighteen of our *an*, "leading cases." Empirically, we know that all *hsien shen* cases had their origin in Peking. Hence, for the sake of convenience, the term *hsien shen an* is uniformly rendered in this book as "metropolitan leading case." Actually, however, the words *hsien shen* mean something like "exposed for judicial examination," and the sparse and unclear references seem to indicate that the term originally had to do primarily with the judicial investigation of Manchu matters and secondarily with that of matters originating from other government organs in Peking.[21] Among our own eighteen *hsien shen* cases, however, only five (cases 4.3, 124.1, 134.3, 235.2, 237.1) do in fact either deal with Manchu matters or come from other government organs. A similarly mixed picture is provided by the remaining thirteen cases (see Appendix D) which likewise originate in Peking, yet are not prefixed by the words *hsien shen.*

Irrespective of origin, not all of the so-called cases in the *Conspectus* are really cases in the sense of passing sentence upon acts of wrongdoing. Among our 190 cases, nine are actually procedural, that is, they provide directives on standards of official

[20] They are cases 134.2, 141.16, 144.7, 152.2, 152.4, 170.1, 170.2, 210.3, 224.10, 228.3.

[21] The Board of Revenue maintained a *hsien shen ch'u*, a title translated by Dr. E-tu Zen Sun as "Court of Manchu Affairs" and explained as a "court where civil cases among Manchus were adjudged." See Sun, "The Board of Revenue," p. 190. The Ch'ing "Legal Treatise" (p. 87) states that in 1723 *hsien shen* Courts of the Left and Right were established in Peking for the purpose of "making judicial investigation (*shen*) of homicides and robberies among the [Manchu] Eight Banners, as well as [other judicial] matters presented by the various government offices (*yamens*) [in Peking]." At a subsequent unspecified date, however, these two courts were abolished, leaving such matters in the hands of the Board's seventeen regional departments.

behavior or on the proper procedure for handling certain kinds of situations.[22] Still other "cases"—among them some of the most interesting—actually consist, either in whole [23] or in part,[24] of imperial edicts or rescripts.

Generally speaking, the reporting of the cases conforms to one of two standard patterns: (1) Most commonly, a case begins with the formula: "The governor (or the governor-general) of a certain province reports (or memorializes) that so-and-so has committed such-and-such an offense." ("Reports" means that the case will be decided by the Board of Punishments itself; "memorializes" means that it is a capital or other special case requiring transmission from the Board to the throne for final approval.) From this point the department of the Board of Punishments handling the case goes on to spell out the facts, cite the judgment provisionally arrived at on the provincial level, and agree or disagree with this judgment, adducing, if need be, its own arguments and relevant statutes or sub-statutes.

(2) Another less direct and less common procedure is for the department to begin by citing a series of statutes or sub-statutes having a possible bearing on the case. Then, as before, it narrates the facts of the case, what has happened to it at the provincial level, and arrives at a judgment of its own on the basis of the cited statutes or sub-statutes. This second procedure tends to be used for the longer and more complex cases in which not merely one or two but several conceivably relevant statutes or sub-statutes have to be considered.

Memoranda, inasmuch as they represent a pre-final stage in the processing of a case (one that must still be submitted to a higher level either within or above the Board for final approval), commonly end with variations of a standard formula: "This penalty being in accord with the facts of this case, we deem it appropriate to request a confirmatory reply." This formula signifies that the department of the Board, having approved of the provisional sentence proposed at the provincial level, requests the Directorate of the Board or other higher organ for final approval so

[22] See cases 9.1, 49.1, 166.2, 198.7, 203.7, 257.2, 264.1, and, in part, 260.1 and 263.1.
[23] Cases 198.7, 198.8, 203.7, 264.1.
[24] Cases 41.8, 162.1, 172.4, 263.1.

that a reply confirming the provisional sentence may be returned to the originating province. Of course the formula is avoided if the department disagrees with the provisional verdict.

3. Problems of Selection and Translation

From among the more than 7,600 cases in the *Conspectus,* covering 270 out of the 436 sections in the Ch'ing Code, space limitations have allowed only 190 cases covering 105 sections to be translated for this book. How was this tiny sampling effected?

It was quickly realized that it would be impossible to reach any statistically significant conclusions on the basis of such a small sampling. Therefore other criteria were used to make the selection: the comprehensiveness of the cases and their interest (sociological and political as well as purely legal).

Of the thirty-one sections in the *Conspectus* having fifty or more cases each, all but one have been included in our translations.[25] In addition, a very wide range of other smaller sections has been selected so as to provide a sampling of almost all of the major divisions of the *Conspectus.* The result is necessarily a disproportion between criminal cases proper, which are relatively much less numerous in the translations than in the original, and cases on other matters (marriage, property, fiscal matters, ritual, public works, and the like), which conversely are more prominent in the translations than in the original.[26]

With few exceptions, very lengthy cases have been excluded.

[25] The thirty-one sections are listed in Chap. VI, sec. 1. The omitted section is *Conspectus* sec. 27, "Localities Designated for Penal Servitude, Life Exile, and Military Exile," which contains 54 cases. It was decided not to translate any of these when it was found that they were not really penal cases at all, but highly technical and lengthy directives to the officials concerned as to procedures to be followed in sending convicts to their places of penal servitude or exile. Of course, an analysis of this section might reveal information of interest for the study of judicial procedure.

[26] The imbalance between different sections in their proportion of translated to untranslated cases is indicated by the fact that for no less than twelve of these sections, the single case selected for translation is the only one belonging to the section, whereas for others the proportion of translated to untranslated cases is as small as two out of 294 (sec. 172), or even two out of 376 (sec. 160). See the table of translated cases at the beginning of Part Two below. For the very laborious task of counting the number of cases under each section of the *Conspectus* and its supplements, I am again much indebted to the paper by Mr. Wu-su P'an cited in note 17 above.

Whenever possible, cases have been selected from or near the beginning of each represented section (so as to facilitate case numbering), and preference has been given to choices from the *Conspectus* proper rather than its supplements. This last point means that only eleven of the 190 cases come from the Supplement to the *Conspectus*, [27] and only another three from its New Supplement.[28]

Despite the heterogeneous materials in the translated cases, and their distributional divergence from the materials in the original compilation, the repeated occurrence in the cases of certain legal, social and political patterns seems to be a guarantee of their overall typicality. In the next chapter we shall attempt an analysis of some of these patterns. As far as looking in the *Conspectus* for interesting and vital materials is concerned, it does not seem to matter too much what particular procedure is used. Almost anywhere one chooses to probe, the chances are that something of interest will be uncovered.

The difficulties of translating from the *Conspectus* are formidable and no doubt help explain why no one has hitherto done more than prepare brief (and necessarily pallid) summaries of selected cases.[29]

A major barrier to translation, of course, is the large technical vocabulary. Despite specialized dictionaries and other aids,[30] it

[27] Cases 40.1, 44.1, 45.1, 50.1, 61.1, 82.6, 83.1, 86.2, 92.1, 171.12, 171.13.

[28] Cases 195.2, 196.1, 237.3.

[29] Such summaries appear in Alabaster, *Notes and Commentaries*, in Boulais, and—within more restricted compass—in George Jamieson, *Chinese Family and Commercial Law* (Shanghai, 1921). So far as known, the only scholarly study of a portion of the *Conspectus* is Judy Feldman Harrison's "Wrongful Treatment of Prisoners: A Case Study of Ch'ing Legal Practice," *Journal of Asian Studies*, 23:227–244 (Feb. 1964). This is an analysis (not a translation) of more than thirty cases contained in sec. 259 of the *Conspectus* (equivalent to sec. 413 of the Code). For comments, see our case 259.1.

[30] The major aids are: for legal terms, the translation of the Ch'ing Code by Boulais and Cheng Ching-yi, comp., *Fa-lü ta tz'u-shu* (Large dictionary of legal terms), 3 vols. (Shanghai, 1936); for bureaucratic terms, E-tu Zen Sun, tr. and ed., *Ch'ing Administrative Terms* (Cambridge, Mass., 1961); for official titles, H. S. Brunnert and V. V. Hagelstrom, *Present Day Political Organization of China* (Shanghai, 1912); for intricate family relationships, Han-yi Feng, "The Chinese Kinship System," *Harvard Journal of Asiatic Studies*, 2:141–275 (1937); for the names of edicts, rescripts, throne memorials, and other official documents, the glossary in John K. Fairbank and Ssu-yü Teng, "On the Types and Uses of Ch'ing Documents," in Fairbank and Teng, *Ch'ing Administration: Three Studies* (Cambridge, Mass., 1960), pp. 74–106.

has happened all too often that the terms of greatest difficulty were precisely those on which dictionary definitions were either inadequate or absent, compelling the translator to determine his own meaning for them according to context as best he could. A systematic glossary of terms of pre-Republican Chinese law would be a great help to future research in the field. As a tiny start in this direction, the Glossary at the end of the book contains Chinese characters for the names and terms whose transliterations are scattered through the pages of this text.

A second major obstacle to translation is the Code itself. As noted in Chapter II, the original has no numbering or index of any kind, and its arrangement of materials can sometimes be quite frustrating. What in the Code may be a lengthy and complex statute, covering many eventualities, will often, as cited in the *Conspectus,* be telescoped into a single relevant clause or phrase. Many weary hours have been consumed in tracking down each statutory reference, and it is cause for satisfaction that of the several hundred occurring in our 190 cases, only one has remained unidentified (see Appendix A). For future research, a concordance of the Code would be a great boon.

A third major difficulty is the literary Chinese style in which the cases are written. Ellipses, no doubt simple enough to the experienced Chinese jurist but seemingly designed to trip the tyro just where he most needs support, are countered by repetitions which, although natural to the style of literary Chinese, become redundant in translation. Worst of all is the frequent use of impersonal sentences wherein neither subject nor object is clearly specified. Throughout the text, as a consequence, there is a recurring struggle to determine to whom the case has come from where, and who is speaking at any given moment. Is it the governor or governor-general who has sent the case to Peking? The department of the Board to which it has been allocated? The Board's Directorate? The Statutes Commission? In the absence of quotation marks or any other punctuation in the original, the clues may be small indeed, resting on such set phrases as *kai ssu,* "the said department" (meaning that someone other than the department is speaking at this point), or *pen ssu,* "this department" (which identifies the department itself as the speaker).

Sometimes, indeed, even the geographical origin of the case remains uncertain.

These and other difficulties have been smoothed away in these translations. Being intended for legal historians and comparative jurists as well as for China specialists, it was not feasible for them to be equipped with the endless footnotes that would have been needed for linguistically justifying each interpretation. Repetitive clauses natural to the cadenced prose of literary Chinese have on occasion been omitted for the sake of simplicity. Terms or names have sometimes been added when their presence, though not explicitly stated in the original, seems clearly called for by context. For example, an ambiguous statement like "it is said" may perhaps be expanded in English into "the Department for Honan of the Board of Punishments says," if it is reasonably certain from the preceding remarks that this department is in fact speaking at this point. Many other explanations and clarifications have been added to the translation in the form of an interlinear and interparagraphed running commentary differentiated from the text proper by enclosure in square brackets. All Chinese dates have also been converted to the Western calendar. Although it would be folly to suppose that all this adjusting has been done without error, it is believed that whatever errors of detail may occasionally be present, they are not significant enough to detract seriously from the overall value of the translations.[31]

[31] A good example of the technical difficulties encountered in this kind of translation is the phrase *pu ying chung*, literally, "not ought heavy," occurring a number of times in the cases. This phrase becomes meaningful only when identified as an abbreviated reference to a common catch-all statute in the Code, Boulais, no. 1656, entitled: "Doing What Ought Not to Be Done." The statute is designed to punish any acts which, though deemed reprehensible by the authorities, are yet not specifically prohibited by the Code. A heavier punishment of 80 blows of the heavy bamboo is provided for graver acts of this kind, and a lesser one of 40 blows of the light bamboo for those of a minor nature. Hence pronouncement of the sentence, "not ought heavy," means that the offender, under the statute on doing what ought not to be done, is being sentenced to its heavier penalty of 80 blows of the heavy bamboo.

VI · CHINESE SOCIETY AND GOVERNMENT AS SEEN IN THE *CONSPECTUS*

1. Crime in Ch'ing China

This chapter is an impressionistic and subjective effort to bring together some of the highlights of our 190 cases, paying particular attention to what they may tell us about family, society, and government in imperial China. (For an analysis from a more technically juridical point of view, see Part Three, "Statutory Interpretation".) The great merit of these cases is that they give us a starkly realistic picture of actual happenings in China. Not surprisingly, what they portray differs considerably from what a Chinese philosopher, for example, might choose to write about his country. Like courtroom records anywhere, they are usually somber and depressing. Nonetheless, within certain recognizable limits they are true pictures, and very useful for correcting the highly idealized accounts of the old China still sometimes current.

To be sure, the cases suffer from overbrevity. Very often their focus on law blurs matters of great sociological or psychological interest. Yet with all their omissions, what they tell us—and sometimes what they do not—is deeply revealing. Their significance is not the fact that crime, including very terrible crime, existed in China—this is true in all countries. More important is the appearance in the cases of certain deep-rooted social and political attitudes, including some that have persisted until very recently. In short, it is hoped that a reading of the cases, despite the gap of more than a century between them and the present day, will help make clear why the Chinese monarchy had to give way to a republic in 1911, and why the republic in turn had to be torn by further revolution.

A glance at Appendix D will show that although the 190 cases cover a total time span of 1738–1883, most of them belong to the early decades of the nineteenth century. More specifically, 145, or just over 76 per cent, fall within a neat two-decade span of 1812–1831; in other words, they belong to the last nine years of the Chia-ch'ing reign and the first eleven years of the Tao-kuang reign following. Of the remainder, thirty-five cases cover the long preceding period of 1738–1811, and only ten belong to the subsequent span of 1832–1885. This means that what we are examining is the final phase of a legal tradition of two thousand years, just before the shaking and shattering of that tradition by the impact of the West.

The period of most of the cases was one of relative cultural and political stability, despite impending storm. In 1793, when Lord Macartney came to Peking on behalf of King George III to request formal diplomatic and trade relations between China and Britain, the Ch'ien-lung Emperor proudly replied in his letter to the king: "As your Ambassador can see for himself, we possess all things. I set no value on objects strange or ingenious, and have no use for your country's manufactures." In 1839, the Chinese government's destruction of 20,000 chests of opium brought to Canton by Western ships ushered in the Opium War with Britain, itself the beginning of a century of humiliation and aggression suffered by China from the West, coupled with disastrous rebellion and disintegration at home. The half century between 1793 and 1839, although actually a time of dynastic decline and marked by some minor rebellions, was for the most part outwardly impressive and constituted imperial China's last age of "normalcy." In its legal institutions we find an indigenous tradition untouched as yet by any Western influence.[1]

What were the most common crimes in the China of this age?

---

[1] The only Western touch in our cases is the reference in case 8.1 to dollars, no doubt the Mexican silver dollars brought to China via the Philippines. This case originated in the south coastal province of Fukien, where in 1803, the time of the case, such dollars were already current. Throughout other cases money is always calculated in terms of lumps of silver weighing one ounce each and known as taels, but referred to in our translation for clarity's sake as ounces of silver; 1,000 of the small copper coins with square holes, strung together and known as cash, constituted one such tael. Of course, if one were interested in the Western impact on Chinese law rather than the indigenous legal tradition, one would concentrate upon the cases in the *Conspectus* New Supplement.

Below is a list of all the sections in the *Conspectus* (31 out of a total of 270) having 50 or more cases each. They are numbered on the left margin according to order of magnitude, followed, after the slant, by their numbering in the *Conspectus*. After each title, in parentheses, is given first the number of cases translated in the present book, followed by the total number of cases for the section in the *Conspectus* itself: [2]

1/160 Killing a wife's paramour (2 out of 376 cases)

2/172 Pressing a person into committing suicide (2 out of 294 cases)

3/239 Wrongdoers who resist arrest (3 out of 237 cases)

4/199 False accusations (3 out of 206 cases)

5/164 Homicide committed during an affray or with intent (2 out of 164 cases)

6/60 Abduction of women of respectable family (1 out of 152 cases)

7/141 Robbery committed with violence (1 out of 145 cases)

8/161 Homicide of three or more persons in one family (2 out of 122 cases)

9/189 Assault on senior relatives of the third degree of mourning and below (1 out of 120 cases)

10/151 Violation of tombs (2 out of 112 cases)

11/144 Stealing (2 out of 111 cases)

12/190 Assault on senior relatives of the second degree of mourning (1 out of 107 cases)

13/11 Wrongdoers permitted to remain at home to care for parents (2 out of 106 cases)

14/166 Killing or wounding during roughhousing, by mischance, or by accident (3 out of 104 cases)

15/143 Plundering in broad daylight (2 out of 100 cases)

16/148 Extortion through intimidation (3 out of 98 cases)

17/222 Sexual violations (2 out of 96 cases)

18/201 Disobedience to parents or grandparents (4 out of 91 cases)

19/241 Escapees from penal servitude or exile (1 out of 86 cases)

20/150 Kidnapping and sale of human beings (2 out of 84 cases)

21/206 Acceptance of bribes by officials and their subordinates (2 out of 75 cases)

22/224 Incest (2 out of 75 cases)

23/194 Parents assaulted by outsiders (2 out of 72 cases)

24/187 Assault by a wife or concubine on her husband (1 out of 62 cases)

[2] Again I must express gratitude to Mr. Wu-su P'an for counting the number of cases in each section of the *Conspectus* and recording these figures in the paper referred to in Chap. V, notes 17 and 26. As was explained earlier (Chap. V, note 25), sec. 27 (no. 28 in the present table) was omitted from the translations because its so-called cases are not really cases at all but procedural directives.

25/186 Assault by a slave or servant on his master (2 out of 60 cases)
26/191 Assault by offspring on parents or grandparents (2 out of 59 cases)
27/175 Affrays and blows (4 out of 58 cases)
28/27 Localities designed for penal servitude, life exile, and military exile (none out of 54 cases)
29/80 Salt laws (2 out of 53 cases)
30/159 Premeditated homicide of parents or grandparents (3 out of 53 cases)
31/21 Wrongdoers who are fugitives from justice at the time of their trial (2 out of 50 cases)

Grouping these sections under broad categories, we find that crimes that are economically motivated, although conspicuous, by no means hold first place. They include nos. 6 (perhaps also a sex crime), 7, 11, 15–16, 20–21, and 29. The relatively low position of no. 21, official bribery, seems at first sight peculiar in view of the prevalence of this offence. A possible explanation is that bribery cases may often have been separately handled by the Censorate rather than passing through usual judicial channels.

Sex crimes occupy fewer sections than do those economically motivated, namely nos. 1, 6 (shared, as we have seen, by the economic category), 17, 22, and 24 (at the same time a family crime). Yet it is notable that the eternal triangle (husband killing wife's paramour) comes at the very top of the list. Even the strict canons of Confucian morality, it would seem, did not prevent crimes of passion from occurring in China as elsewhere.

Crimes of violence (homicide and assault, without specification of motives in the title), not surprisingly, form the largest category of all (nos. 5, 8–9, 12, 14, 18, 23–27, 30). In general, violence in China, as elsewhere, is punished much more sternly than non-violent crime, even though non-violent crime may result in greater material gain for the perpetrator, as is exemplified by our two translated cases under no. 15, "Plundering in broad daylight." In the first of these, 143.2, a gang of men who have systematically, but without violence, plundered a wrecked vessel while its owner shouted vainly to them from the shore to stop, receive only three years penal servitude. In case 143.9, on the other hand, military exile in a malarial region is the punishment for a man who, with his gang, sneaks up behind a victim, suddenly covers the victim's eyes with a cloth, and runs off with his bag. The heavier punishment is based on the fact that even the momentary covering of the victim's eyes is legally regarded as violence, even though no actual injury is inflicted.

Still a fourth category of offenses may be termed resistance to authority (wrongdoers who resist arrest, escaped convicts), and includes nos. 3, 19 and 31. Nos. 4 (false accusations) and 28 (largely procedural rather than criminal) are miscellaneous items. The false accusation group, because of its high position on the list and its seemingly peculiarly Chinese characteristics, deserves further study. Of the three cases from it in our translations (cases 199.4, 199.5, 199.7), the first two concern fathers who make false accusations to the authorities in order to save their guilty sons from conviction, and the third a father who does the same because he wrongly suspects foul play in the death of his son.

So far it would seem, at least superficially, that most of these crimes are not too unlike those familiar to us in the West. Uniquely Chinese, however, because of special provisions made for them in Chinese law, is the long list of crimes—mostly crimes of violence—that may be called family crimes inasmuch as they occur between members of the same clan or family. They include nos. 9, 12, 23, 24 (also classed under sex crimes), 25 (assuming, as the Chinese do, that servants and slaves are members of the family), 26, and 30. It should be noted that the titles of all of them (except no. 23) are phrased in terms of a junior family member who kills or injures a senior member. In other words, they all exemplify the principle (already stressed in Chapter I, section 9) of the superiority of senior over younger generation.

However, it should also be noted that with the exception of no. 18 (disobedience to parents), all sections are reciprocal. That is to say, despite their wording, they go on to prescribe further penalties (usually, of course, lighter penalties) for senior family members who kill or injure junior members. As a matter of fact, among our translated cases, all of those under nos. 24–26 and 30 concern the latter kind of offense, in contrast to the cases under nos. 9, 12 and 18, where the reverse is true. We may strongly suspect concerning some of these sections (no. 25, assault by a slave or servant on his master), that despite their wording, the offenses they cover much oftener involve violence by family seniors against juniors than vice versa, just as during the time of American slavery, there were probably far more slave owners who killed their slaves than the other way round.

Aside from family crimes proper, two other sections, each with more than fifty cases, are indicative of the intense Chinese preoccupation with family and ancestors. One of them, no. 13, "Wrongdoers permitted to remain at home to care for parents," has already been discussed (Chapter I, section 10, and Chapter IV, section 4). The other, no. 10, "Violation of tombs," is a crime regarded with particular horror in China because of the cult of the ancestors. At the same time, it is one made particularly tempting to the poor peasant by the large number of tombs visible everywhere in the Chinese countryside and by the fact that many of them may contain valuables.

Finally, it is somewhat astonishing to find the second highest position held by the section on "Pressing a person into committing suicide." (See discussion at end of section 4.)

2. Who Were the Criminals?

Some of our 190 cases are lurid enough. For example, a man who hates a married couple murders their four year old son, then persuades a friend to help him remove the corpse to the courtyard of the friend's enemy, in order to get that enemy into trouble (case 157.4). A father cuts his son's throat in order to silence the son's protests against the father's adulterous relationship with a married woman; in so doing, the father is aided by the woman's husband, whom he (the father) has been paying to tolerate the relationship (case 159.2). Two men go by night to a cave of three peasants whom they hate and murder all three as they sleep (case 161.2). A man who at the time of his apprehension is over seventy has in the course of sixteen years allegedly "licked and sucked out the vital marrow" of sixteen baby girls, of whom eleven died (case 162.1). An innkeeper, fearful lest a critically ill lodger might die and thereby get him (the innkeeper) into trouble, carries the sick man naked out of the inn and abandons him in a field, where he dies (case 165.4). A father, when his eldest son takes a knife to chase a younger son who refused to give the older boy money, seizes the eldest son and, with the coerced assistance of the younger one, buries him alive (case 191.1). Other such cases are not lacking.

There are also curious and unusual cases. A husband, believing his delirious wife to be possessed by the spirit of a dead person, probably a relative, pries open the latter's unburied coffin cover in order to drive the spirit away (case 151.8). A quack doctor, called in to perform acupuncture (probing with a long needle) upon a critically ill patient, finds the patient too weak for treatment, so performs it instead upon the patient's wife, who dies (case 171.12). A young Manchu officer, out of gratitude toward his deceased teacher, decides to commit suicide in order to serve him in the next world, and informs the head of his Banner in advance of his plans (case 237.1). A professional copyist of civil service examination papers is punished because a paperweight placed by him on a paper he was copying obscured two characters, so that he fails to copy them (case 237.3). More important than any of these—indeed, one of the most interesting cases sociologically and psychologically—is that in which a licentiate (holder of the lowest civil service examination degree) is punished for lèse majesté and possible subversive intent because of his improper use of two terms in a biographical memoir of his father and in a family genealogy, both written by him (case 267.2).

Rather than enumerate further cases, let us see now what kinds of people the offenders were. Rarely, unless the offender belonged to some very particular group—official, Buddhist monk, slave—was his social origin explicitly stated. Often, nonetheless, the general settings of the cases give us useful clues. A frequent background, of course, is that of a pre-industrial, rural society, in which poverty and a keen struggle for existence are conspicuous elements of life.

Rural China, for example, is obviously the setting for the rake with which a twelve year old boy kills his older brother's assailant (case 194.5), for the agricultural implement known as a "grain-spike" (otherwise unidentified) which figures as a weapon in case 175.9, or for the iron ploughshare which similarly appears in case 147.2. Again, rural China is the setting for three cases involving gleaning in the fields: the boy of fifteen who in case 14.1 picks up a handful of soybeans from a neighbor's field where harvesting is in progress; the boy of thirteen who in case 51.1 picks three pears while passing a neighbor's orchard; the old woman who, with her infant grandson, in case 260.1 picks up the wheat dropped by a neighbor along the wayside. Poverty is underscored by the fact that all three of these trivial acts lead to violence and homicide.

Although there must surely have been a number of tenant peasants among our offenders, the fact is judged sufficiently relevant for explicit mention in only two cases (148.7 and 184.2). In case 148.7 the tenant joins his landlord, a Buddhist monk, in defrauding another man, but then, on asking the monk for a share of the proceeds, is intimidated until he commits suicide. In case 184.2 the tenant is compelled by his landlord to beat a man to death.

In several of the cases poverty is explicitly named as the cause of the crime. A father, "because he was poor and found it hard to make a living, decided to murder his blind son, who could do nothing but eat, in order to lighten his own burden" (case 168.1). A husband sells his wife to another man, and "investigation shows that Wang's act was prompted by poverty and illness, which gave him no alternative" (case 223.2). A husband is coerced by his wife's lover to tolerate the affair between the two, whereupon the Board of Punishments finds that "were his children to remain solely in his care after dissolution of the marriage, his straitened circumstances would make it impossible for him to care for them alone, so that the consequences would be disastrous" (case 223.3). The fact that wife selling and the related offense of a husband's toleration for money of his wife's adultery not only appear several times in our cases,[3] but are also covered

[3] For further instances of wife selling, see cases 59.1, 223.4 and 223.5. For a husband's toleration of his wife's adulterous relationship, see cases 159.2, 160.10 and 172.3. See also cases 19.1 (abduction and sale of a young girl), 150.19 (attempted sale of a daughter into semi-slavery), and 150.21 (sale by a man of his elder sister to become someone's wife).

by specific articles in the Code, suggests that these were common crimes in a society in which a wife might be a man's only or almost only salable property.

Evidences of wealth, on the other hand, are relatively rare. References to the purchase of civil service examination degrees appear in three cases (41.7, 93.2, 200.4). Great fireworks displays, which must have cost large sums of money, are the subject of two (89.1 and 166.3). Case 201.8 deals with an entrepreneur who rents out land in order to finance a coal enterprise. In case 45.1, a Buddhist monk steals 270 ounces of silver (a very considerable sum) from an older monk, and in case 149.2 a merchant removes no less than 700 ounces from the trunk of his traveling merchant companion. The most striking evidence of wealth occurs in case 210.3, in which a man who is probably a salt merchant is arrested for an unstated reason and asked by a government clerk to pay 3,000 ounces of silver "to straighten matters out."

Persons who are recognizably merchants—including small shopkeepers as well as large entrepreneurs—appear in fewer than ten cases (87.3, 112.7, 149.2, 171.4, 184.1, 201.8, 210.3, 270.1). There are two references to innkeepers (cases 83.1 and 165.4).

By contrast, there is a score of references to officials, who thus constitute the largest group to be explicitly identified.[4] Holders of examination degrees—persons whose status is superior to that of commoners, but who have not become officials—figure in some half dozen cases.[5] About the same number of references apply to the clerks, guards, servants, and "runners" who work without civil service status in the yamens (offices) of the officials, and who are commonly referred to in the Code as "rapacious underlings."[6]

There are some ten cases in which Manchus, including imperial clansmen, appear, and half a dozen (some of them overlapping with the foregoing) having to do with bannermen (who include some Mongols and Chinese as well as Manchus). Mongols appear twice and Muslims once.

[4] Case references for this and the other groups mentioned below, unless cited directly in the text or notes, will all be found at the end of Appendix B.
[5] Cases 44.1, 59.1, 88.1, 133.1, 200.4, 267.2.
[6] Cases 40.1, 87.3, 206.19, 210.2, 210.3, 248.2, 248.3.

Among the great mass of commoners, there are eight references to Buddhist and Taoist monks—men who, though formally of commoner status, are distinguished from other commoners by their celibate lives and separate communities. Concubines appear twice and servants and slaves five times each. Other persons whose special treatment before the law requires them to be separately mentioned include women (twenty cases), and persons aged 70 or above and 15 or below (four cases each). Insane persons appear in three cases (152.2, 152.4, 196.1) but in a manner telling us nothing about their status in Chinese society, except that the mental illness of the official in the third case does not save him from being punished.

In our first chapter (section 9) we saw that officials enjoyed a privileged status under Chinese law. However, our twenty official cases yield a rather surprising result: in only five of them do these officials, because of their status, gain even a partial reduction of sentence. The five cases are: An official who beats to death a son guilty of a capital crime, is sentenced for this to 80 blows of the heavy bamboo, and is then permitted monetary redemption because of his status (case 4.2). An official who is sentenced to military exile for various rascally acts, but is exempted from tattooing because of his status (case 8.1). An official who has bought a married woman as his concubine, and has his punishment of 80 blows of the heavy bamboo commuted as an official to a three-degree reduction in official rank, which is then further commuted to a one-degree reduction only (case 59.1). A jail warden who, having been convicted of attempted extortion, is exempted, because of official status, from two months wearing of the cangue; however, he is not spared the major penalty of three years penal servitude (case 206.8). A Manchu hereditary officer who is permitted monetary redemption in place of the 80 blows of the heavy bamboo to which he is sentenced for having planned suicide in order to serve his deceased teacher in the next world (case 237.1).

Aside from these five, convicted officials are apparently punished like commoners without mention of any kind of redemption. Commonly, indeed, the very fact of their official status means that the normal punishment is supplemented by dismissal from the civil service (a very severe penalty for any official). In one case (195.2), the Board of Punishments explicitly states that the offender, precisely because of his official status, must be dealt with sternly. In another (196.1), a sub-prefect guilty of writing scurrilous anonymous letters to a superior is not only dismissed from government service, but also sentenced to 100 blows of the heavy bamboo despite the fact that he is known to have acted during a fit of insanity.

Among references to holders of civil service degrees, no single instance of redemption of the stipulated penalty is indicated. Similarly, the numerous references to Manchus and bannermen include only two (cases 4.3 and 170.2) in which commutation of bambooing and military exile to whipping and the cangue is mentioned. Another case (237.1) is that of the same Manchu officer mentioned above as being granted monetary redemption in place of bambooing, but this commutation comes to him as an official rather than a Manchu. By contrast, high ranking Manchus, apparently because of their rank, are severely punished: an imperial clansman receives 60 blows of the heavy bamboo, with redemption explicitly denied, for having taken a common singsong girl (woman of pleasure) as his concubine (case 61.1); two nobles of imperial lineage of the twelfth rank are deprived of their rank because of failure to perform the proper sacrifices at the imperial ancestral temple (case 93.1). And of our two Mongol cases, one (165.2) involves no redemption whatsoever, whereas the other (6.2) results in a sentence of military exile actually slightly *higher* than the offender (a Mongol police officer) would have received had he been an ordinary Chinese.

On the other end of the social ladder, Muslims (as well as certain other ethnic or religious minorities, such as the tribes people of south China) were discriminated against in Ch'ing China. Our single Muslim reference (case 144.7), for example, cites a sub-statute which had been expressly formulated to deal with robber bands consisting of Muslims.

Privilege is also not commonly accorded in our cases to women, the aged, and minors, despite statutory provisions for it in the Code. Thus only three of our twenty women offenders are permitted some kind of redemption. They include a woman who, having first been fined instead of being sent into military exile for forcing other women into prostitution, is then, as a repeater, given the very special punishment of three years imprisonment in her own locality in place of exile (case 12.2). Another woman is permitted monetary redemption for the 100 blows of the heavy bamboo to which she has been sentenced for falsely assuming responsibility for the death of her son in return for a bribe (case 208.5). Still a third is permitted redemption in place of penal servitude for having been privy to a homicide (case 257.2). Aside from these, none of the other women is apparently granted any special privilege on grounds of sex; four of them, indeed, have the privilege of redemption explicitly denied to them in their sentence.[7]

Of our four cases involving persons aged 70 or above, monetary redemption is permitted for two (cases 199.5 and 228.2), but denied for the two others (cases 162.1 and 203.5). Minors of 15 or less are treated even less favorably: one is allowed redemption (case 8.1), two are denied (cases 14.1 and 194.5), and the fourth (case 144.17) is in a situation where neither granting nor denying is applicable.

Among other groups listed earlier, we find that three of the eight cases concerning Buddhist or Taoist monks are ones in which these men have engaged in sex relations with married women. The first of them (case 89.2) is not clear cut because the basic offense is compounded by having been committed in a Buddhist temple, but in the other two (cases 228.2 and 228.3) it is evident that the penalties for the monks are heavier than they would be for the same offense committed by laymen. In the remaining five cases (45.1, 133.2, 148.7, 183.1, 183.3), however, the monks seem to be treated like others.

Of our two concubine offenders, one (case 186.8) is exonerated for beating and thereby inducing the suicide of a servant girl who, having been indentured for over three years, had by the time of the beating arrived at the same status as an ordinary slave. This case makes evident that concubine status, low though it be compared with that of wife, nevertheless remains well above

---

[7] See cases 159.1, 159.3, 171.5 and 171.6. Monetary redemption is also permitted in case 171.13, but this is a standard procedure for this particular kind of offense and has nothing to do with the fact that the offender is a woman.

that of slave. In the other case (186.9), a concubine receives three years penal servitude for beating to death her serving woman who, having been indentured for less than three years, had not yet fallen to slave status. Still other cases in which slaves are victims (185.1 and 185.3) clearly reveal, as might be expected, their lowly status as compared with commoners (*liang jen,* "good persons").[8]

Four of our cases (41.7–8 and 210.2–3) have to do with another depressed class known as *ch'ang sui* or "permanent attendants." This is a technical designation for servants in the private employ of district magistrates and other government officials. The legal status of these servants, despite their close association with officialdom, was extremely low, as is vividly illustrated by the first two of our cases. Like slaves and like certain occupational groups which included entertainers, prostitutes, and government "runners" (messengers, jailers, and other public employees in the government yamens), as well as certain regionally defined groups such as the "beggars" of Kiangsu and Anhui, the "lazy people" of Chekiang, and others, these servants of officials belonged among those having less than commoner status collectively known as *chien jen,* "mean persons." No "mean person" was allowed to take the civil service examinations for government office or to obtain office through purchase; this prohibition extended at least to his immediate descendant as well.[9]

The first of our cases, 41.7, shows that in this respect there was not much to choose between the son of a *ch'ang sui* servant and the son of a slave. The case punishes an official who was the son of such a servant for concealing his social origin; the precedent relied on was a case in which the son of a slave was punished for a similar offense. Likewise, case 41.8 concerns a commander of the gendarmerie in Peking who is deprived of rank upon discovery that his father, a prefect of Shensi, had once been an official's private servant. The governor-general of Shensi, on trying to speak on the son's behalf, is severely reprimanded by the emperor. The

[8] This term, which means commoner when used in apposition to other social groups, also appears in the Code when referring to a "decent woman" or a "woman of respectable family" as against a prostitute and the like.

[9] For a general account of these various disfavored groups, see T'ung-tsu Ch'ü, *Law and Society,* pp. 129–133, and for a detailed discussion of the *ch'ang sui,* see T'ung-tsu Ch'ü, *Local Government in China under the Ch'ing,* pp. 74–92, esp. 86–87.

existence of the *ch'ang sui* and other caste-like depressed groups as late as the nineteenth century should be kept in mind when the extent of social mobility in imperial China is considered.[10]

The general conclusion emerging from this section is that the privileged groups of Ch'ing society—notably officials, but also, for legal purposes, such special groups as women, the aged, and the young—did not derive as much benefit from their special legal status as one might theoretically assume. The law discriminated against certain disfavored groups such as servants and slaves, but it could also bear heavily upon the privileged. In short, entanglement with the law was to be feared in all sectors of society, including even those enjoying prestige and power.[11]

3. The Judicial Process

A major impression emerging from the cases is that of the great care and seriousness with which the Board of Punishments performs its work. By no means is its approval of sentences proposed by the provinces automatic. In Chapter IV, section 2, we noted the assertion by Shen Chia-pen that when he served in the Board's Department for Mukden in 1883, that department annually reversed as many as 100 or more of the cases coming to it from Manchuria. This figure, though amazingly high, is supported to some extent by the fact that among our 190 cases, no less than twenty-five are reversals by the Board of provincial decisions.[12] In four others, moreover, the Board's Directorate re-

[10] See, among several important studies, Ho Ping-ti's *The Ladder of Success in Imperial China* (New York: Columbia University Press, 1962). The ostensible reason for punishing the servant's son in case 41.7 is not that he purchased official rank, but that when so doing "he practiced deception by concealing his social origin." Obviously, however, there would have been no need for such deception were the rank as accessible to him as to other members of society.

[11] There is another hypothesis that could conceivably modify the conclusion here reached, namely that in some or many of the cases involving special groups, the Board of Punishments fails to mention monetary redemption or other commutation simply because these are taken for granted. Although this hypothesis cannot be disproved, it does not seem probable in view of the general carefulness with which the Board pronounces sentence and the considerable number of times that it does specifically refer to redemption or some other special consideration.

[12] The cases are 6.2, 11.4, 83.1, 133.1, 159.3, 160.10, 161.3, 166.1, 166.2, 166.3, 167.5, 168.1, 183.1, 184.2, 188.2, 191.1, 191.2, 200.2, 201.9, 208.5, 239.15, 241.9, 259.2, 260.1, 263.2.

verses in turn the decisions reached by its own regional departments.[13] A notable instance is case 184.1, in which the Directorate overturns the judgment of its own department in order to re-
affirm the original judgment reached in Manchuria.

Sometimes reversals are accompanied by rebukes ranging from
mild to stinging. An example of a mild rebuke is the conclusion to
case 166.1: "The Governor of Hupei has been careless in his failure to make explicit reference in his report to the payment of
funeral money. Let him add a clause concerning it." Much more
stinging are the remarks in the very interesting case 260.1, in
which the Board, after charging that "errors of fact occur in the
report of the Governor of Honan," reaches the conclusion several
pages later that "the disposition of this case has been hasty and
devious," so that the conviction of the defendant should be
voided.

It is only when the emperor himself intervenes in a case (which
happens but rarely) that the Chinese equivalent of "due process"
(see the end of Chapter IV) may succumb to arbitrariness. For
example, an absolute requirement at every judicial level is that
pronouncement of sentence must always be accompanied by citation of relevant statute or sub-statute. In only one of our cases is
this requirement violated by the Board of Punishments itself.[14]
However, when the emperor intervenes in one particularly heinous case (162.1) with an emotionally worded judgment, not
only does he make no effort to support his sentence with an appropriate statute, but he gives almost no details about the crime
itself and says nothing about what is to happen to the family
members of the chief offender.

Theoretically, of course, the emperor had the power to over-
turn any decision irrespective of law. Whether or not he actually
felt free to do so is interestingly illustrated in two further in-

[13] The cases are 9.1, 19.1, 183.3, 184.1.

[14] See case 235.1, where it is quite conceivable that the violation may be due
to faulty recording of the case rather than carelessness on the part of the Board
itself. Case 93.1, likewise, fails to cite a statute or sub-statute, but this is because the case is a special one concerning Manchu nobles and handled primarily by the Imperial Clan Court. Another case having no statute or sub-
statute is 230.1, but the probable reason is that it is a summary taken from the
Peking Gazette rather than the technical report by the Board itself. Still a fourth
instance is the imperial edict cited immediately below.

stances of imperial intervention. In the first of these (case 147.2), the Chia-ch'ing Emperor initially wishes to lighten the penalty for a homicide case but the Board, with remarkable pertinacity, insists that no leading case exists as a basis for so doing. The result is a second imperial endorsement issued by the emperor, in which he "agrees that in the absence of such a leading case, it is only possible to grant a confirmatory reply for the earlier sentence as requested."

A contrary result is reached in case 172.4, in which the strong-willed Ch'ien-lung Emperor (father of the Chia-ch'ing Emperor) overturns the Board's judgment on a suicide case in favor of a harsher sentence. The emperor's rescript, which becomes the basis for a new sub-statute, is legally important as a clear denial of the principle forbidding ex post facto law. It is also of psychological interest as indicating the emperor's opposition to the overly mechanical attempt to measure morality quantitatively, so often found in Chinese law.

A major problem of many legal systems is that of "letting the punishment fit the crime." In China, as we have seen (Chapter I, section 9), the problem was accentuated by the extreme specificity of many of the individual statutes. A system whose laws are formulated in general terms abstracted from particularities provides greater possibilities for the judge to find a law under which to class a crime but imposes greater demands upon his interpretive powers when so doing. Conversely, a system like the Chinese, in which the laws tend to be narrowly specific (and are accompanied by a minutely graduated series of punishments), reduces the judge's freedom of interpretation as long as a law can be found whose specific provisions correspond reasonably closely to the specific circumstances of the particular case. Difficulties arise, however, as soon as the judge is confronted by a case whose circumstances are not thus closely covered by any existing statute or sub-statute. It is this dilemma that no doubt helps in part to explain the enormous proliferation of sub-statutes during the Ch'ing dynasty, issued in an attempt to keep up with man's ingenuity in finding new ways to harm his fellowmen.

Aside from new sub-statutes, the major device for coping with this situation is the application of law by analogy (discussed briefly in Chapter I, section 9). The judge, instead of pronouncing sentence directly "under" or "according to" a given statute (*yi* or *chao*, literally "in reliance on" or "in the light of"), finds whatever statute or sub-statute seems to him most nearly applicable and then pronounces sentence "by analogy to" (and not directly "under") the chosen law. (The Chinese term used, *pi chao*, literally means "in the light of comparison with," which is sometimes shortened to *pi*, "in comparison with.") The key statute in the Ch'ing Code covering this vitally important principle goes back in embryonic form to the T'ang Code (Book 6, article 50). Rather than quote it, however, we prefer to translate the appended sub-statute in the Ch'ing Code, because of its added procedural details. This reads in part: [15]

When, because there is no precisely applicable statute or sub-statute, a statute or sub-statute which is most closely applicable is cited, the Board of Punishments will then assemble the Three High Courts [see Chapter IV, section 3] to deliberate and determine sentence. This sentence will then be submitted to the throne with detailed explanation that inasmuch as the Code lacks a precisely applicable article, the present judgment is being pronounced "by analogy to" (*pi chao*) a certain statute or sub-statute or that, in the same manner, a one-degree increase or reduction of the statutory penalty is being pronounced. The imperial rescript will then be awaited and action taken accordingly.

Among our 190 cases, the use of analogy occurs no less than sixty times—more often than can be conveniently recorded here —and it is among these sixty cases, not surprisingly, that the greatest opportunities for disagreement arise. Sometimes it is unclear why the Board of Punishments chooses to apply a particular statute or sub-statute analogically rather than another or even why it feels obliged to use analogical judgment at all, the more so as it by no means invariably explains the reasons for its choice.

Examination of our sixty analogical cases in the light of the sub-statute just quoted raises two major problems. In the first place, contrary to the sub-statute's insistence that analogy cases are to go up to the Three High Courts and from there to the throne for final approval, there is no evidence of such procedure in three

[15] Curiously enough, neither the statute nor the sub-statute is translated by Boulais. If included, they would come between his nos. 194 and 195. The section is no. 44 in Staunton's translation.

fourths of our sixty cases. Only in fifteen of them does terminology appear (*tsou* or *t'i*, words both meaning "to memorialize," that is, to submit a memorial to the throne) from which we may conclude that the cases are destined for the emperor. All fifteen of them, moreover, have to do with officials, capital crimes, or other major matters, so that their submission to the emperor would be routine in any event.[16]

Secondly, despite the provision in the quoted sub-statute that increase or reduction of a statutory penalty requires analogical judgment, and despite adherence to this procedure in many of our cases, there are many others, likewise involving changes of penalty, in which citation is made directly rather than analogically.[17] In a good number of these cases the absence of express recognition that a statute is used analogically seems merely to be a formal departure from the requirement; it is clear that the Board intended and in effect carried out an analogical use. In a few of the cases, however, the Board has clearly departed from prescribed statutory penalties.

As with almost everything else in Ch'ing times, attempts were made to systematize, and thus to render foolproof, the analogy system. In 1779 a list of thirty rules for applying statutes analogically was drawn up, and has since been appended to the Code. The first of them (not among the fifteen translated in Boulais, nos. 1724–1738) is as good an example as any: "If a disciple of a Buddhist or Taoist monk commits a crime jointly with nis preceptor, he will escape punishment by comparison with the statute on members of the same family guilty of a crime."

The statute in question (Boulais, no. 112) tells us that if members of the same family are jointly guilty of a crime, it is the family head, and not the others, who is to be held responsible and punished.[18] Of course, formulated rules of this sort could take

---

[16] See cases 41.7, 87.3, 134.3, 160.15, 162.1, 165.5, 171.12, 195.2, 203.2, 206.8, 222.31, 224.22, 235.1, 263.1, 267.2.

[17] See cases 52.3, 60.5, 112.7, 133.1, 143.2, 165.2, 165.4, 171.6, 183.3, 190.2, 199.7, 203.4, 203.5, 206.19, 235.2, 239.14, 248.2, 269.1.

[18] From cases 45.1, 183.1, and 183.3, we may see that the relationship between a Buddhist monk and his disciple, although considered sufficiently close under law to be treated as analogous to that between a senior and junior member of the same family, is not regarded as close enough to be analogous to a father–son relationship.

care of only a small proportion of the endless cases requiring analogical treatment. Among our sixty, we believe that none falls under any of the thirty rules.[19]

Besides analogy, another common device for handling offenses not readily subsumed under an existing law is the catch-all statute. There are several of these, of which all but the last one named below are intended for relatively minor infractions. The commonest of them, already mentioned at the end of the last chapter, is "Doing what ought not to be done" (Boulais, no. 1656). This statute conveniently provides alternative punishments of 80 blows of the heavy bamboo or 40 blows of the light for offenses which, though deemed reprehensible, are nowhere explicitly banned in the Code. As can be seen in Appendix A, this statute is cited in ten of our cases.

Another statute, invoked with almost equal frequency and performing a very similar function, is Boulais no. 274, providing 100 blows of the heavy bamboo for "violating imperial decrees." Its functioning as a catch-all is clearly shown by the fact that in the Code itself the Official Commentary severely limits the scope of the statute by adding the qualifying word *ku*, "deliberately," to the main text, whereas in every one of our nine cases in which the statute is cited, this key word is omitted. It seems that the term *chih shu*, "imperial decree," need not always refer to a specific existing decree. In our cases, at least, the statute seems to be used to penalize a wide variety of conduct of which it can merely be said that, if known to the emperor, it would no doubt run counter to his imperial will. Among the kinds of misconduct in these cases are improper use of certificate of official appointment, sale or handling of unauthorized texts, failure to dismount before the Confucian temple early enough, combining of quack medicine with magic, and use in printed works of certain phrases conceivably having a subversive connotation. As against these and other rather bizarre kinds of offenses, the statute on doing what ought not to be done is commonly applied to a diverse, but much more

---

[19] Niida Noboru, *Criminal Law*, devotes a lengthy section (pp. 265–292) to the use of analogy from T'ang through Ch'ing times. However, he is less concerned with its general theory than with the technical details of how, at various times, it has functioned in the form of specific rules similar to the thirty just mentioned.

run-of-the-mill, range of misdemeanors, often involving physical actions.

Another catch-all, cited only once in our cases, is Boulais no. 1655, providing 50 blows of the light bamboo for "violating ordinances." Its infrequent use is probably because its penalty so nearly coincides with the lighter of the two specified under "doing what ought not to be done." There are also two other articles, much narrower in scope but, within their particular fields, used to cover an astonishing variety of offenses. They are Boulais no. 1503, "Disobedience by offspring to the instructions of parents or grandparents" (100 blows of the heavy bamboo), and the much more serious appended sub-statute, Boulais no. 1504, providing exile at a distance of 3,000 li for offspring "whose poverty prevents them from supporting their parents, so that the latter commit suicide." The reader is referred again to the citations in Appendix A for examples in our cases of the curious workings of these two articles, especially the citation on poverty.

In a civilization as historically minded as the Chinese, one would expect precedent to loom large in the judicial process, and indeed we find it appealed to in various of our cases. Some citations are exceedingly generalized, as in case 175.9: "Grain-spike cases in other provinces have always been considered to be like those in which an ordinary knife is used." More often, however, the citation is quite specific: "In reviewing past cases, we have found none analogous to the one at bar, except for a case occurring in Honan in 1800 . . ." (case 17.1). Or again: "Our search for comparable earlier cases reveals one in Honan in 1820, in which Liu Yü-lin strangled his adulterous daughter . . ." (case 191.2). Rarely are the cited precedents more than a decade or so older than the cases in which they appear. One famous precedent case in 1732, however, as embodied in a sub-statute, is cited in our case 14.1 of 1826.

It is a little surprising, nonetheless, that only sixteen of our cases contain explicit references to precedents.[20] Our limited sampling seems to suggest that though Chinese jurists no doubt searched carefully for helpful precedents when faced by difficult

[20] The cases are 9.1, 11.1, 11.4, 14.1, 17.1, 41.7, 42.1, 51.1, 161.3, 166.2, 172.3, 175.9, 191.2, 199.4, 236.1, 257.2.

cases—after all, the need for a convenient repertory of such precedents was probably the primary reason for compiling the *Conspectus*—they apparently did not feel obliged to cite them explicitly as often as this is done by Anglo-American judges.

The Board's concern for correctness and precision in sentencing is illustrated in various ways. In case 168.1, for example, we find it making an interesting distinction between "killing a son and *then* falsely imputing the act to another person," as against "killing a son *in order* to impute the act falsely to another." Or again, in case 51.1, the Statutes Commission goes to great lengths, including analysis of two precedent cases, to determine whether an offender's crime was that of killing in an affray or of "unauthorized killing"—despite the fact that the penalty for either offense is the same: strangulation after the assizes. In cases 183.1 and 239.15, likewise, the Board rejects the sentences proposed by the provincial courts and replaces them with others based on a different statute, even though the resulting penalties remain unchanged. Or yet again, the Board in three cases (157.4, 164.1, 208.5) takes great pains to pronounce sentence itself or to confirm sentences proposed at the provincial level, upon offenders who have already died before the cases even reach Peking.

Another impression emerging from these cases is that of the Board's omniscience. It *always* seems to know all the relevant facts—to its own satisfaction, at least, if not always to ours—even when they are of such a private nature as to make us wonder how the Board can feel so certain about them. A partial answer, no doubt, lies in the judicial right to apply torture to recalcitrant defendants or witnesses if deemed necessary (a topic not treated in our cases). But there is another factor that is probably more basic: the psychological need, in a society consisting of an illiterate majority dominated by a small elitist bureaucracy, for that bureaucracy always to possess superior knowledge. Under a judicial system permitting no challenge from private legal practitioners, it simply would not do for the judicial authorities to confess to ignorance or error.

Yet another characteristic of the Board's handling of our cases is its extreme reluctance ever wholly to acquit a defendant. The small list of complete acquitals will be found toward the end of

Appendix B. One of the few examples of readiness to ignore the letter of the law in order to forgo punishment is case 223.2 (closely paralleled by 223.3), in which a husband has sold his wife to another man. The statutory penalty for this offiense is 100 blows of the heavy bamboo for each of the three parties, dissolution of the wife's marriage to her first husband, her return to her natal family, and confiscation by the state of the gift money given the first husband. Yet here we find the Board disregarding the statute on the grounds that the husband's sale of his wife was prompted by poverty and illness rather than wilfulness. It reaches the decision—extraordinary in the general context of these cases —that the wife should remain with the second husband (since the first cannot support her), and that the first husband should in recompense be permitted to keep the gift money given him. No doubt the Board's judgment is prompted not only by compassion but by the practical consideration that the wife had no natal family to which to return. Unless, therefore, she were allowed to stay with the second husband, she would become a homeless woman.

This and the parellel case, 223.2, are almost the only ones in which the Board cites but then ignores the provisions of what is clearly the relevant statute. Almost always, once it finds a statute to have been violated, it feels obliged to exact at least token retribution, and at this point it makes little apparent difference whether the offender is a man of high or low degree. A striking illustration is case 93.2, in which a district magistrate, riding in his sedan chair at dawn through a driving rain to participate in the sacrifices at the Confucian temple, was borne before he knew it beyond the outer enclosure where, according to ritual, he should have dismounted. The Board's conclusion is that "his failure to dismount from the chair in time, though occasioned by the great accumulation of rain water on the ground and the error of the chair bearers, nevertheless constitutes a violation of the established regulations." It accordingly sentences him to 100 blows of the heavy bamboo and dismissal from his position.

The insistence upon punishment for any violation, no matter how occasioned, no doubt goes back in part to the ancient Legalists. More than this, however, it may well reflect a very ancient concept, according to which a criminal act is not merely a violation of the human order, but also ipso facto of the total cosmic order of which the human order forms part. In order to restore the original state of cosmic balance, therefore, a punishment precisely corresponding to the original violation must be exacted in return. We would not want to suggest that this concept was consciously sensed or expressed by the jurists of the Ch'ing dynasty, but merely that it lies behind certain features of Chinese law continuing into Ch'ing times. We have noted, for example, the Board's insistence upon pronouncing sentence even after the offender has already died. Such procedure becomes understandable if we interpret it as a means for concluding a case whose continued presence upon the books would otherwise render impossible the task of repairing the breach in cosmic harmony originally caused by the offense.

The same idea is illustrated still more clearly in those kinds of homicide to which the Code applies the terms *ti* or *ti ming*. *Ti ming*, literally "requital-life" or "requiting a life," signifies the kind of homicide for which, according to statute, another life must be offered in requital. On the basis of cases 164.1 and 164.2, we may conclude that it is the fact of requital itself that really counts in the judgment of such cases, rather than who precisely is the person who has to make the requital. This conclusion is deducible from a principle enunciated in the two cases, to the effect that should several persons be under arrest for having participated in an affray resulting in death, and should one of them die in prison while they are all awaiting sentence, his death, even though fortuitous, will cancel out, so to speak, the death of the victim or victims for whom the several offenders are jointly responsible. The result, for the other offenders, is a sentence of life exile in place of the retributive capital punishment otherwise required from them. Of course, the concept becomes highly symbolic in late times: strangulation after the assizes replaces earlier actual strangulation, and the death of a single assailant is accepted as requital for the deaths of even two victims.

Another illustration of requital occurs in case 185.1, involving the killing of a slave. Here we learn that as long as a slave is merely injured by a commoner, the penalty for so doing is one degree less than that for a commoner injuring another commoner. As soon, however, as the violence leads to the slave's death, the penalty thereupon becomes the same as it would be for killing any commoner in an affray, namely strangulation after the assizes. In the words of the Board of Punishments: "For any destruction of a human life there has to be a proper requital *(ti)*."

Still another glimpse of the same idea from a different angle appears in case 187.1. There we learn that a husband who merely injures but does not kill his wife receives a penalty two degrees less than he would for inflicting the same injury on an outsider. (Because the penalty for doing the same to a slave is only one degree below the norm, it would thus appear that a wife's status vis à vis her husband is lower than that of a slave vis à vis a commoner.) If, however, the husband actually kills his wife, the penalty, as in our preceding case (and presumably for the same reason), becomes strangulation after the assizes, just as it would for homicide in an ordinary affray. Or yet again, we learn in case 194.3 that strangulation after the assizes is likewise the penalty for a son who kills an outsider attacking his (the son's) parent, whereas should the son merely injure the attacking outsider, his penalty would be three degrees lower than for doing the same in an ordinary affray not involving his parents.[21]

The life-for-a-life idea breaks down, however, in cases of accidental homicide (because, being accidental, the homicide is not the result of evil intent); also, as we shall see, in certain homicide cases occurring within the family, for which the justification is deemed to be overriding.[22]

[21] See also cases 194.5, 239.7, and 239.15 for further references to the concept of requital. It should be emphasized that what has here been suggested about this concept is at present a theory only, for which further study along historical lines would be highly desirable. Furthermore, the concept, as here presented, should be distinguished from that discussed by Lien-sheng Yang, "The Concept of *Pao* as a Basis for Social Relations in China," in John K. Fairbank, ed., *Chinese Thought and Institutions* (Chicago: University of Chicago Press, 1957), pp. 291–309.

[22] Niida Noboru, *Criminal Law*, pp. 146–152, discusses manifestations in Chinese legal thought of the concept of retaliation or *lex talionis* ("an eye for an eye, a tooth for a tooth"). Although traces of it unquestionably can be found in the codes (under Boulais, no. 1474, for example, anyone who through false accusation brings about the execution of an innocent man will himself suffer the same fate), it is also evident that there are material differences between it and the principle of requital discussed by us: (1) Retaliation requires that if *A* de-

4. The Regularization of Society

A central goal of imperial Confucianism is a regularized society: one ideally consisting of a well defined hierarchy of social and political units, governed from above by a humanistically educated civil service bureaucracy headed by an all-wise emperor. What is prized above all in this kind of society is social and political stability. Government is for but not by the people, and persons other than those belonging to the small ruling elite are encouraged to remain wherever they may have been brought up, there to carry out to the best of their ability the particular tasks that are theirs to do. The rural peasantry are looked upon as the economic backbone of society; merchants are distrusted as an unstable and often itinerant group whose private interests run counter to those of society at large; the cities function primarily as centers of bureaucratic power rather than of commercial development; and the government exercises broad controls over a variety of economic activities.

Such, at least, is what imperial Confucianism wanted in theory, though it was necessarily modified in actual practice. Every major dynasty of imperial China has tried with varying success to impose political, economic, social, and ideological controls upon its people. Certainly, the Ch'ing dynasty attempted to do so dur-

---

stroys the eye of B, A and only A must lose his own eye as retaliation. Requital, on the contrary, merely requires that one life be requited by another but does not insist that the requital must necessarily come from the person most directly responsible for the original homicide. (2) Retaliation is invoked to cover many kinds of injury, great and small, whereas requital, at least in the Ch'ing Code, becomes operative only when homicide is involved, and then only when it is a motivated homicide; accidental homicide is thereby excluded. In short, the principle of retaliation serves primarily to correct the individual imbalance arising when A commits a wrongful act against B, whereas the principle of requital is intended to correct the total situational or environmental imbalance resulting from major acts of deliberate wrongdoing. From the point of view of requital, therefore, the center of interest is the wrongful act per se: its nature and motivation. Little importance attaches to the agent and his victim, considered as individuals. What is important about them is their social status vis à vis each other, because this relationship bears significantly upon the seriousness of the wrongful act itself and hence upon the extent to which it disturbs the environment, both human and natural.

ing its period of grandeur, prior to its rapid decline from the 1840's onward.[23]

Evidences of the regularization of society appear repeatedly in our cases. The contrast between the sedentary grain-producing society of rural China and, let us say, the American West of the nineteenth century, is strikingly illustrated in our cases dealing with weapons and gunpowder or its constituents. From these cases we learn that the private manufacture and sale of gunpowder is punishable by three years penal servitude (case 115.6; see also cases 115.7 and 115.8, dealing with graphite and saltpeter). A careful distinction is made between "dangerous weapons" (swords, spears, maces, and the like) and ordinary household cutting implements (sickles, kitchen knives, and the like); injuries inflicted by the former are punishable two degrees more heavily than those inflicted by the latter (case 175.6 and three following cases in same section).

Among the several examples of economic controls, one of the most striking is case 86.2, in which we learn that rural persons who come to Peking and there buy and take back with them more than one *shih* (about 2.75 English bushels) of rice, are liable to 100 blows of the heavy bamboo. To understand this prohibition, we must remember that north China is a wheat- and millet-producing and not a rice-producing area, so that the rice consumed in the capital had to be transported hundreds of miles from central China over the Grand Canal. The purpose of the prohibition, in the words of the Board, "was to prevent improper trafficking by dishonest merchants." An assistant magistrate of a department some fifty miles outside Peking, however, being apparently ignorant of the prohibiton, sent his underlings to the capital to buy twelve *shih* of rice for feeding his soldiers; the latter, at the time, were engaged in important public construction. The Board, after admitting that "his act was intended for the public good," nevertheless concludes that in view of the violation of the prohibition, "it would be impolitic to grant complete exemption of penalty." It accordingly reaches a very unusual judgment —one that completely sidesteps the sub-statute containing the

[23] How these controls operated on the local level is excellently described by Kung-chuan Hsiao.

prohibition and uses quite a different statute instead to sentence the assistant magistrate to what was probably the lightest feasible penalty, namely 40 blows of the light bamboo under "doing what ought not to be done."

A major offense, of course, in such a society is any kind of insubordination, especially if accompanied by physical violence. In republican times the Chinese have shown great ability in using the strike and boycott as economic and political weapons. Students of modern China should be interested to learn from our cases that, a century or more earlier, incipient strike movements were already being attempted from time to time for the economic betterment of certain occupational groups.

In 1778, in the earliest of these strike movements among our cases, a sailor belonging to the fleet bringing tribute rice to Peking on the Grand Canal organizes ten or more of his fellow sailors to strike for better wages just as the boats are being taken through a lock. A fracas arises, in which he injures a lieutenant who has been stationed at the lock precisely in order to repress any such disturbance (case 87.1). For this the sailor is sentenced to immediate decapitation and exposure of his head on the bank of the Grand Canal. Or again (1825), a boat-tracker (a man who tows rice boats) working at the terminus of the Grand Canal near Peking, "finding that food prices were rising to a point where his wages no longer met the cost of living," similarly organizes a group of fellow trackers to hold a demonstration, which results in conflict with a presiding lieutenant (case 87.2). This time the punishment is unexpectedly light: only three years of penal servitude. Still a third case in 1812 (case 269.1) deals with the "emergency workers" living in a village on the banks of the Yungting River not far from Peking. These men, in return for government allocated plots of river land of approximately one acre each, are obligated, when needed, to do river conservancy work at the rate of 0.04 ounces of silver for every ten cubic Chinese feet of earth removed. One of the workers organizes a mass slowdown for better wages; the agitation spreads to other river villages; and money is collected from the workers for possible legal use in the event of court action against them. In the end, however, the movement is broken by the arrest of the ringleader, who receives life exile.

In another comparable yet different kind of case (112.7), a shopkeeper urges his fellow shopkeepers to close their shops in protest against the detention by the authorities of one of their number on grounds of alleged implication in a crime. The commercial strike collapses, however, when only eight out of the 300 shops in the city close their doors, and the ringleader is sentenced to maximum life exile.

The limited range of economic opportunity in a pre-industrial society such as that of China combined with powerful political and ideological pressures to encourage a high degree of social conformity. Several of our cases raise an age-old problem still very much with us: how responsible is a subordinate for acts he knows to be wrong but nevertheless carries out because of compulsion from a superior? The usual answer implied by these cases is that the subordinate, simply because he is a subordinate, has no alternative but to obey even if he commits a criminal act. This answer appears most clearly in the Board's judgments in cases 184.1 and 184.2. In the former, a shop owner's two shop clerks and his servant are ordered by the owner to beat another man, which they do with fatal results. The Board reduces their punishment on the grounds that, as employees of the shopkeeper, "all three of them were therefore dependent upon him, and thus subject to a pressure on his part which they could not but follow." In the second case, likewise, a tenant farmer joins his landlord in a fatal attack upon another man, but the Board changes the farmer's penalty from strangulation after the assizes to life exile because his "normal obedience to whatever was ordered by Niu [the landlord] was the result of subjection to pressure which he could not but follow."

Confucianism, ever since it achieved orthodoxy in the second century B.C. and indeed even earlier, has shown itself deeply suspicious of "heterodox" ideologies. Religious groups and sects, especially of an esoteric kind, have repeatedly been persecuted in imperial China, not so much because of religious ideas per se as because of the fear—not infrequently justified—that their religion was a cloak for anti-dynastic political activities. Aside from such occasional persecutions, the major organized religions of Buddhism and Taoism were traditionally subject to a variety of governmental controls. Thus in Ch'ing times, as we learn from case 183.1 (citing various provisions in the Code), Buddhist and Taoist matters throughout the empire were supervised by religious dignitaries who were at the same time ranking members of the government's civil service and were responsible to the government for the conduct of their coreligionists. A person could not legally become a monk if he were already an adult (age sixteen and above), or if there were fewer than three adult males in his family; even then, he was required to obtain a special certificate of monkhood issued by the government. Once a monk, furthermore, he could not legally recruit disciples for himself until he reached the age of forty. New temples or monasteries could not be constructed without governmental permission.

Governmental fear of possible subversion, a frequent phenomenon throughout imperial times, was compounded during the Ch'ing by the fact that the ruling Manchus were an alien group. The tensions arising from this situation culminated in the second half of the eighteenth century in a widespread governmental proscription and destruction of allegedly anti-Manchu as well as other "dangerous" or "immoral" writings. As a result, much literature was totally lost.[24] Echoes of this fear and suspicion sound clearly in several of our cases. In two of them (133.2 and 133.3), the propagators of so-called "non-canonical writings" (precise nature unspecified) are punished by three years penal servitude. In another (case 92.1), someone is given 100 blows of the heavy bamboo for having "bought miscellaneous small texts [again precise nature unspecified] from an unknown person and sold them within the city [Peking] with the aim of making a profit." Most interesting of all is an early case of 1779, coming at the height of the literary proscription. In this a licentiate, that is, a man belonging to the lower fringes of the gentry, is sentenced to three years penal servitude for having inadvertently used, in a biography of his grandfather and in a family genealogy, a word and a

---

[24] The movement has been described in detail by L. Carrington Goodrich, *The Literary Inquisition of Ch'ien-lung* (Baltimore: Waverly Press, 1935).

phrase respectively which, by a highly suspicious government, *might* be regarded as possibly having subversive connotations.[25]

We have already mentioned (Chapter I, section 10) the severe punishment provided in the Ch'ing Code for making anonymous accusations. This subject is the concern of three of our cases (198.7-9). The first of them is an 1818 edict from the Chia-ch'ing Emperor in which, after ostensibly upholding the prohibition against anonymous accusations, he weakens it by declaring in his final sentence: "Should it [such an accusation], however, pertain to matters of grave concern to the state, only then may it be secretly memorialized for Our private consideration." It is a pleasure to report that in the following case of 1829, in which a high official does precisely what the emperor suggested, the succeeding Tao-kuang Emperor, in his reply, rebukes the official and unconditionally upholds the original prohibition.

Among the most interesting cases for the jurist are four (cases 203.2, 203.4, 203.5, 203.7) dealing with the persons known as "litigation tricksters" *(sung kun,* "litigation sticks"). These were the occasional individuals who, in rural China, in the absence of a formally recognized legal profession, were ready from time to time, with or without a fee, to prepare a legal petition or accusation for a relative, friend, or client. In a society whose population was four fifths or more illiterate, it is difficult to see how the ordinary man could hope to apply for legal justice without the aid of such an educated person. The "litigation tricksters," however, were regarded by the government as troublemakers, ever ready, for a price, to stir up disputes and corrupt the simple country folk.

In case 203.5 we find a person of this kind sentenced to three years penal servitude for having drafted five litigation documents, despite the fact that "all of these documents were of an ordinary nature, and there is no evidence that he conspired with government clerks, tricked ignorant country folk, or practiced intimidation or fraud." Furthermore, despite the offender's age of over 70,

---

[25] This case, 267.2, has already been alluded to in sec. 2, beginning. See also case 248.3, in which a man is held for investigation "because of having written some queer characters." The jail keeper's suspicion of him causes him to commit suicide in his cell.

the privilege of monetary redemption is explicitly denied him. The next case, 203.7, is of even greater interest as an authoritative pronouncement by the Chia-ch'ing Emperor on the subject. The sentiments in this edict of 1820 may profitably be compared with the criticism expressed by a statesman in 536 B.C. of China's earliest "books of punishment" (quoted in Chapter I, section 4).[26]

Finally, a word about the apparent prevalence of suicide—perhaps indicative of the tensions and restraints existing in Confucian society. Among the most frequent crimes in the *Conspectus,* as we have seen, "pressing a person into committing suicide" is second on the list. This formulation, however, is only the most generalized statement of an offense of which many much more specific varieties are enumerated in sub-statutes scattered throughout the Code. In a single case (17.1), for example, we find references to statutes and sub-statutes covering the following ways of committing suicide: making improper verbal advances to a woman which cause her to commit suicide; committing adultery with a woman, the exposure of which shames her into killing herself; robbing someone and thereby pushing him into suicide; suicide resulting from falsely accusing a person of theft, from deceptions practiced by knavish fellows, from extortions practiced by rapacious governmental underlings, or by impersonators of servants of government officials; beating which inflicts fatal injuries upon the victim, thereby inducing him to kill himself before the injuries take effect (the same sub-statute enumerates four other kinds of beating, all inducing the same fatal result). These by no means exhaust all the possibilities recognized by the Code. For others, see especially cases 148.2, 201.6–9, 224.10, and 248.2–4.

Among our 190 cases, no less than 23 refer in one way or another to suicide.[27] Some of the suicides they describe are quite

---

[26] An analogous case is 44.1, concerning a military student who "prepared public notices announcing plans for establishing an office for himself, wherein he hoped to fish for profit by handling taxation matters for people and settling their litigations." For this infringement of constituted authority he received two years' penal servitude.

[27] See cases 17.1, 83.1, 147.1, 147.2, 148.2, 148.6, 148.7, 165.3, 172.3, 172.4, 185.3, 186.8, 201.6–9, 224.10, 237.1, 248.2–4, 259.2, 260.1.

familiar in terms of Western patterns of behavior: the daughter-in-law who kills herself after hearing abusive language from her mother-in-law (case 148.6), the two slave girls who commit suicide after being beaten (cases 185.3 and 186.8), the three male prisoners who hang themselves in jail or otherwise kill themselves after being heavily manacled and otherwise abused by their jailors (cases 248.2–4), the girl who commits suicide after her love affair with a distant cousin is discovered (case 224.10).

Other suicides, however, strike the average Westerner as decidedly bizarre. Case 83.1, for example, recounts the story of a man who, on asking for the return of money he has entrusted to an innkeeper for safekeeping, is told by the latter that he (the innkeeper) must consult his business partner before repaying. "This statement put Chao [owner of the money] into such a nervous state that he went off and hanged himself." In case 147.2, "Sun Lun-yüan surreptitiously sawed off and took away tree branches belonging to Sun Shou-chih, was beaten by the latter in reprisal, and then committed suicide." In case 172.3 a husband, after allowing his wife to sleep with another man in return for money and after repeatedly dunning the other man for increasing sums of money until the latter struck him, "fell into such a state of uncontrollable passion that he hanged himself." And in case 260.1, a woman, having had a fight with a farmer in whose field she was gleaning wheat, rushed home in a rage, then went to the farmer's house to get even with him, and finding no one there, "in her passion hanged herself from a beam of the house"; her daughter-in-law, on hearing the news, also unsuccessfully tried to jump into a well. Particularly curious is the group of four cases (201.6–9) of mothers whose suicide results from worry over the activities—legal or illegal—of their sons, resulting in fear of legal involvement.

Some suicides, especially those committed by the weak and lowly, are, as might be expected, escapes from the troubles of life. However, these seem to be a minority; only ten of our twenty-three suicide cases, for example, involve women. Others appear to be attempts to retaliate against an enemy or an oppressor by placing on him the onus for one's death. (A theme sometimes found in Chinese literature is that of the ghost of a suicide returning to molest the person who induced the death.) Still other suicides, including most of the bizarre examples, are occasioned by seemingly trivial causes and appear to be compulsively motivated by psychological factors in which loss of face is important.

The psychology of Chinese suicide is far from clear and deserves detailed study. Unfortunately, there is no apparent method for statistically measuring the incidence of suicide in pre-modern China. Hence, its place in Confucian China, no matter how significant, cannot be meaningfully compared with that of suicide in modern America, where, according to a recent study, "suicide is the fourth-ranking cause of death among Americans in the productive years of 18 to 45." [28]

5. The Family

Any serious account of Chinese society must begin or end with the family. The Chinese family system has been a source of great social stability, historical continuity, and individual security. It has also been the cause of untold strain, frustration, and unhappiness. More than any other factor, it has been a major instrument for insuring social conformity and discouraging personal initiative. A very large number of cases in the *Conspectus* have to do with family relationships. As we look through our own cases, nowhere do the tensions of Confucian society emerge more clearly than in the hierarchical differences maintained within the family—differences carefully measured in terms of the five degrees of mourning.[29]

Of focal importance, of course, is the parent–child relationship and its corollary, the relationship between parents-in-law and daughter-in-law. Confronted by these and analogous senior–junior relationships (grandparent–grandchild, uncle–nephew, and so on), some of the principles normally operative in the legal

[28] Associated Press dispatch of July 1, 1965, from Washington, D.C., in the *New York Times* of July 2, reporting research on suicide being conducted by a psychiatrist, Dr. William E. Bunney, Jr., and others, at the U.S. National Institute of Mental Health. Compare the assertion made in 1878 by John Henry Gray, Archdeacon of Hong Kong: "The Chinese are perhaps more prone to commit suicide than the people of any other country in the world." This is the opening sentence in Gray's interesting chapter on suicide; see Gray, I, 329–341.

[29] On this very important system, see Chap. I, note 66.

sphere seem, as we shall see, no longer to function fully. A widespread example is the provision permitting wrongdoers, under special circumstances, to remain at home to care for aged parents for whom they are the sole support. This provision, which in effect suspends the normal functioning of the law in favor of filial piety, is thirteenth on the list of sections having the most numerous cases in the *Conspectus* and appears seven times in our own cases.[30]

What do the Chinese jurists mean when they speak of *chia,* a word usually translated in this volume as "family" and occasionally as "household"? The clearest answer comes in our cases 161.2 and 161.3. A passage from the Code's Official Commentary, quoted in the second case, states unequivocally that the *chia* need not necessarily be confined to blood relatives. " 'Single family' (*yi chia*)," it says, "means those who live together, including even slaves and servants." However, it becomes evident from the rest of this case as well as from the case preceding it that the fact of living together, although a necessary condition for establishing membership in a single family, is not by itself decisive; it must be accompanied by the existence of an economic relationship among the persons thus maintaining a common residence. That is to say, there must be a common pooling of their economic resources.

This fact emerges clearly in case 161.2, in which three peasants living in a single cave are brutally murdered in the middle of the night by two other men. The crime of killing three or more persons belonging to a single family constitutes one of the Ten Abominations (*shih ô*) and is punishable by death by slicing. This, then, is what the two murderers would have undergone had the three peasants, because of their common residence, been adjudged to constitute a single family or household. The Board of Punishments, however, rules otherwise on the decisive grounds that "though the three murdered men lived together in a single cave, they each farmed their land separately and did not share their resources, so that they differed from a single household (*yi chia*)." The murderers, in consequence, are condemned to decapitation after the assizes instead of death by slicing.

Confirmation of the same point is found in the subsequent case,

161.3, in which two distant merchant cousins, whose relationship to each other lies outside of the five degrees of mourning, are traveling together on a business trip. Their hired baggage-carrier tries to abscond with their money, is apprehended, and, while awaiting delivery by them to the authorities, poisons the two in their inn room. The governor-general, on the grounds that the victims were too distantly related to belong to a common family, sentences the murderer to decapitation after the assizes. The Board, however, decides otherwise. It argues that the two victims, despite their distant relationship, may properly be regarded as belonging to a single family because: (1) they were traveling together and stayed overnight together, and "between this and living together there is no essential difference"; (2) the baggage transported for them by the baggage-carrier and the money stolen by him was their joint property, so that "they may thus be regarded as men who jointly shared their resources."

In the preceding section we discussed the problem of a subordinate's responsibility for criminal acts committed by him at the behest of a superior. The Board's attitude, as we have seen, is that the pressure to which the subordinate is subjected leaves him no freedom of choice. The same problem, intensified by the sanctity of family ties, arises in two of our family cases, where, however, it is further complicated by the injection of an equally weighty conflicting principle: the absolute evilness, from a Chinese point of view, of any violence committed by a junior against a senior relative. What, then, is to be done with a junior relative who, on the orders of a senior relative, commits violence against yet another senior relative?

In the first case, 189.1, an older brother, learning that his younger brother has been a robber, intimidates his two nephews once removed into joining him to tie up the younger brother, carry him to a pond, and there drown him. The two nephews are sentenced to decapitation after the assizes, with, however, a recommendation that this sentence be reduced to life exile because of the uncle's coercion. Nothing is said about punishment for the uncle himself. (Conceivably, however, this may have been handled by the Board in a separate memorandum.)

In the other case, 190.2, an older brother, angered by the refusal of his younger brother to loan him money, climbs over the younger brother's wall while drunk, falls, injures himself, has his head bandaged by an uncle of the two, makes a ruckus, brandishes a knife, and is finally stopped from committing serious violence only by being hit on the legs with a stick by the younger brother at the shouted orders of the uncle. The uncle bandages the older brother's wounds a second time and sends him home. However, the older brother pulls off his bandages and dies eight days later from infection. Although it is proved that the cause of death is the older brother's self-induced wound suffered when he fell and not the lesser injury inflicted by the younger brother, and although it is recognized that the younger brother was acting under the uncle's orders, the Board concludes that the younger brother is nevertheless guilty of assaulting and injuring the older one, for which the statutory penalty is three years penal servitude. Without explaining why it does so, the Board thereupon increases this penalty for the younger brother to life exile, but, as in the preceding case, says nothing about the uncle.

We have seen in section 3 that insistence upon at least token punishment for anyone becoming entangled with the law, regardless of circumstances, is a feature of our cases. This principle remains operative in those of our family cases in which the offender is of junior status—indeed, the punishment administered in such cases is usually much more than token. Case 194.5, for example, concerns a boy of twelve who, seeing his older brother attacked by an outsider, hits the outsider with a rake, fatally wounding him. The Board points out that although there is a sub-statute providing for a reduction of the normal punishment when a son or wife fatally wounds the attacker of a parent or husband, there is no such sub-statute for a younger brother who similarly acts to save an older brother. The Board therefore finds that the boy, despite his age of twelve, must receive the customary punishment for homicide resulting from an affray, namely strangulation after the assizes. In so doing it considers, but then rejects, the possibility of applying one or another sub-statute to gain clemency for the boy as a minor. Why the Board chooses to cling so inflexibly to the letter of the law is not clearly explained, but Professor Morris, in his "Statutory Interpretation" (see his note 25), has offered a plausible interpretation.[31]

Another concept discussed in section 3 was that of requital: the imperative need to requite a life for a life, which we suggested originated in the idea of thereby restoring the cosmic harmony ruptured by the original homicide. Among our family cases, however, we find that this idea of requital breaks down as soon as it comes up against a situation in which the killing is that of a child by his parent. Here the necessity to uphold parental authority seemingly overrides all other considerations. The result, for the parent, is token punishment only or even no punishment at all.

An excellent example is case 159.2, in which a father maintains an adulterous relationship with the wife of another man, whom he pays for the privilege. The father's son strongly criticizes the arrangement until the father, in connivance with the willingly cuckolded husband, lures the son to a secluded spot and kills him. The Board comments: "We find it extremely cruel of Wu Ta-wen to have killed his son with premeditation because of lustful desire for an adulterous relationship." Yet it sentences the father, as a father, to a mere year of penal servitude, even though it is he who struck the fatal blow. The cooperating husband, on the other hand, is sentenced, as an unrelated conniver, to life exile, despite the fact that "he did not himself play a physical role in the killing."[32]

[31] See also case 201.9: A neighbor argues with a son, and when the son's mother tries to reason with the neighbor, the latter attacks her. The son, hearing the mother's screams, stabs the neighbor (but not seriously), who then decides to take the matter to court. The mother, brooding on the idea of being dragged into a court case, hangs herself, and the son is sentenced to life exile at a distance of 3,000 li. Although an imperial amnesty has meanwhile been proclaimed, the son is explicitly denied any reduction of punishment on its account. There is no mention of any penalty for the attacking neighbor, who has meanwhile recovered from his wound.

[32] See also case 4.2: A father kills his son because the boy had appropriated money and beaten a donkey-boy to death. The father is sentenced to 80 blows of the heavy bamboo, primarily because he tried to conceal his offense from the authorities. As an official, however, he is permitted monetary redemption for the bambooing. Again in case 191.1: A father buries his older son alive because the boy chased the younger son with a knife. The father is exempted from any punishment whereas the younger son, having become a fugitive after helping the father to bury the older brother at the father's command, will probably, when apprehended, receive life exile. Yet again in case 191.2: A father, con-

Finally, what happens when the reverse situation occurs, that is, when it is a son or his wife who kills one of the son's parents? Case 262.3 gives us the graphic answer. Here a Mrs. Han has by mischance fatally injured her father-in-law. Although the circumstances of the death, not being central to the case, are unfortunately not told us, we do know that "by mischance"(*wu*) means, as a technical term, that the woman had the intention of injuring someone else but by error injured her father-in-law instead. Such injury of a father-in-law, when resulting in death, nominally calls for the heaviest of all penalties, death by slicing. Eighteen years prior to Mrs. Han's case of 1831, however, a similar case had occurred in which a son by mischance killed his parent. The circumstances of the case had so aroused the compassion of the Chiach'ing Emperor that he had issued an edict reducing the penalty to immediate decapitation. On the basis of this precedent, therefore, we find Mrs. Han's penalty similarly reduced.

Mrs. Han's case is further complicated, however, by the fact that while awaiting sentence she has given birth to a child. According to statute, a woman guilty of a capital crime who gives birth to a child while awaiting execution is allowed to live and care for the child for 100 days before undergoing execution— unless, that is, her crime is so heinous as to call for death by slicing, in which case her execution is postponed for 30 days only. We therefore find the Board of Punishments solemnly deliberating whether, in Mrs. Han's case, she should live for 100 or only 30 days. Its decision is that because the punishment of immediate decapitation has superseded that of slicing, she may be allowed the full 100 days. Apparently no one questions or probably even senses the enormity of either of the two punishments.

In this chapter we have examined the major categories of crime in Ch'ing China and the kinds of persons responsible for them. We have seen that the law discriminated against certain dis-

---

fronted by the adultery and subsequent elopement of his daughter, "felt it to be such a disgrace to the ancestors that in his fury he ordered his son to chop her to death." The father is exonerated and the son, being *older* than his sister, is likewise sentenced as an accessory merely to 100 blows of the heavy bamboo. (Compare with the preceding case, in which it is a *younger* son who helps the father to bury the older one, and who, in consequence, is doomed to probable life exile.)

favored groups, but that even for privileged groups legal involvement was something to be feared and avoided whenever possible.

In discussing the judicial process, we have noted the care and
precision with which the Board of Punishments performed its
work, its readiness, on occasion, to maintain its opinion even
against the emperor himself, and its extreme reluctance ever
wholly to acquit a defendant. We have discussed the major
devices used for facilitating the fitting of punishment to crime,
notably catch-all statutes and judgment by analogy. We have also
examined the concept of "requital" as a probable exemplification
of the ancient belief that when the state of cosmic balance has
been upset by a wrongful act, restoration of that balance requires
the carrying out of a compensating punishment.

From this we have gone on to review many examples of the
varied controls used in a Confucian state to maintain social and
political stability. They include prohibitions on the private use of
"dangerous weapons," harsh repression of all acts of insubordination, especially if accompanied by physical violence, restrictions
upon both economic and religious activities, and measures of
thought control that include prohibitions against the legal activities of so-called "litigation tricksters." We find in Confucian
China a legal acceptance of the doctrine that lesser responsibility,
and hence lesser punishment, attaches to a crime if committed by
a subordinate acting on command of his superior rather than on
his own initiative. We also find an apparently high incidence of
suicide.

Finally, we have found that the word "family" connotes something vastly broader in Confucian China than it does in the West.
So powerful are the demands made by the hierarchical family
relationships upon the individual that they may on occasion even
partially supersede for him the normal functioning of the legal
system. And so extreme are the differences maintained between
senior and junior family generation that they enable an adulterous
father to suffer only one year of penal servitude for murdering his
critical son, in contrast to the daughter-in-law whose sentence of
immediate decapitation for having fatally injured her father-in-
law "by mischance" is a mitigation from death by slicing.

Confucianism has long been officially dead in China, but the social and political patterns here summarized have never ceased to influence the painful process of change during the past half century. Indeed, their influence has by no means wholly disappeared even today.

Part Two

190 CASES FROM THE
HSING-AN HUI·LAN

TABLE OF CASES

Under each section, following the list of translated cases, the number of such cases is given in parentheses together with the total number of cases contained in the given section of the *Hsing-an hui-lan* proper or its two supplements or both.

Explanation of Headings

At the beginning of each section of the cases that follow, the following information is provided:

Line 1. Number and title of section in the *Hsing-an hui-lan* (HAHL). (Total of 270 sections; numbering done by translator.)

Line 2. Numbering of the statutes and sub-statutes comprising the corresponding section in the Ch'ing Code (total of 436 sections). Numbering is in accordance with the numbering of sections given in two Western translations of the Code: George Thomas Staunton, *Ta Tsing Leu Lee*—this translation is of the statutes only, so that its 436 numbered sections correspond exactly to the 436 divisions of the Code; Gui Boulais, *Manuel du code chinois*—this translation includes many sub-statutes as well as most statutes, so that it contains a total of 1,738 numbered paragraphs. (For a discussion of these two translations, see Chapter II, section 4.)

Line 3. (a) Number and date of the case. For example, "Case 4.2, 1789," means that this is the second of several cases contained in the fourth section (out of 270) in the HAHL, and that it occurred in 1789. (Numbering is by the translator, and does not appear in the original.) (b) Type of document from which the case is taken, such as "memorandum," "leading case," "from the *Peking Gazette,*" and others (on these sources, see Chapter V, section 2).

Line 4. Location of the case in the HAHL proper or in the HAHL Supplement or New Supplement. For example, "Reported in HAHL 3.1/8b–9a" means that the case is contained in the HAHL proper, where it is to be found in *ts'e* (Chinese-style stitched volume) 3, *chüan* (book or part) 1, pp. 8b–9a. (For the edition used, see Bibliography or Chapter V, section 1.)

Note on the Translations

In the translator's annotations (in square brackets) that accompany these translations, a great many procedural or technical matters—judgment by analogy, the Autumn Assizes, what a "Banner" is, and many more—are usually not explained and sometimes not even explicitly mentioned if they have already been explained in the Preliminary Essay. The reader should consult the Index for references.

Of the more than 300 statutes and sub-statutes cited in these cases, 60 or almost twenty per cent are not translated by Boulais. In order to facilitate citation of these items (almost all sub-statutes), they are each given the number of the item that would immediately precede them in Boulais, followed by the letter *a* (or rarely *b* or *c* if two or more untranslated items occur together). Thus the citation "Boulais 1664a" refers to a sub-statute in the Code which, though not actually appearing in Boulais, would, if it were included there, occur between Boulais no. 1664 and the immediately following no. 1665. So too would "Boulais 1664b," but the suffix *b* shows that its position in the original Code comes after that of Boulais 1664a.

In Appendix A, where every statute and sub-statute mentioned in these cases is listed, each Boulais citation is correlated with the corresponding page in the Chinese edition of the Code that has been used for preparing this volume (the 1964 Taipei reprint, with continuous pagination, of an 1873 edition of the Code). This makes it readily possible to identify the Chinese original of every statute or sub-statute which, in these translations, is cited according to the numbering in Boulais, including even those that have not actually been translated by Boulais.

TRANSLATIONS OF CASES

4. OFFENSES COMMITTED BY OFFICIALS
[Statutory References: Staunton 6, Boulais 63–687]

Case 4.2, 1789. Memorandum.
Reported in HAHL 3.1/8b-9a.

The Department for Chihli of the Board of Punishments finds, according to statute [Boulais 71], that a civil or military official who commits a "private offense" meriting 100 blows of the heavy bamboo is to have his punishment commuted to deprivation of official rank.

[Officials, unlike commoners, were commonly privileged to have punishments entailing bambooing commuted to forfeiture of salary or reduction or deprivation of official rank. The offenses of officials, however, were classified as either "official" (*kung*) or "private" (*ssu*). The former are offenses committed in an official capacity but without any premeditation or thought of personal gain; the latter, whether committed in an official or a private capacity, are designed to serve the private ends of the official concerned. The penalities for official offenses are, as a consequence less severe than those for private ones. See Boulais 69–71]

In the present case, Hsing-hai, [a Manchu] who through examination had gained the position of official writer [having a civil service rating of seventh to ninth rank], found that his son Santing had appropriated money entrusted to him for buying sacrifices to be used in worshipping the ancestors. At the same time he had beaten a donkey-boy to death. In the course of questioning the son, Hsing-hai beat him with a club and stabbed him with a knife, so that he died. Then he secretly buried the body.

The fact that the son had committed a capital crime means that the father's act of beating him to death is no longer the same as that of a parent who beats to death a child guilty of disobedience. [See Boulais 1420, which provides 100 blows of the heavy bamboo for the latter offense. The implication here is that a parent who beats a child to death because the child has committed a capital crime is in such a case not to incur punishment. This implication does not appear to be explicitly supported by any actual statute. Under Boulais 1421, however, wherein it is stated that a parent who kills a child because the child has struck or reviled him is not to suffer penalty, the Shen Chih-ch'i Commentary explains that the child's act of striking or reviling the parent has made the child guilty of a capital offense (because of which, we may deduce, the killing becomes justified). See citation in case 191.1, and similar sentiment underlying case 191.2.]

However, the father erred in failing to report the matter to the authorities and secretly burying the corpse. The governor-general of Chihli has accordingly recommended that he be sentenced under the statute on doing what ought not to be done to the heavier punishment therein provided of 80 blows of the heavy bamboo. [This catch-all statute (Boulais 1656) provides 40 blows of the light bamboo or 80 blows of the heavy one for lesser or greater offenses which, though not expressly forbidden under any specific statute, are regarded as reprehensible.] However, the governor-general further inquires whether, inasmuch as the penalty is under 100 blows, this means that the culprit's commutation should be deprivation of official status or simply payment of a fine.

This Board finds that inasmuch as the son had committed a capital crime, the father's beating him to death in the course of questioning was an act committed during a momentary fit of rage and as such was different from such criminal acts as theft, forgery, etc. [The distinction here between an act of passion and a premeditated crime also underlies the judgments recorded in case 191.2.] Because the father holds the position of official writer, and his penalty of 80 blows is not severe enough to call for removal from the civil service, it seems fitting that, in accordance with the sub-statute, he be permitted to pay a monetary redemption. [According to Boulais 71, however, the redemption for 80 blows is neither outright dismissal from the civil service (as it would be for 100 blows) nor a mere monetary fine, but rather a middle course of a three-degree reduction in rank and transfer to

another position. See also case 59.1. The term *na shu* normally
means to pay a monetary fine. Possibly, however, as used here, it
may include undergoing reduction in rank as well.]

*Case 4.3, 1820. Metropolitan Leading Case from the Depart-
ment for Mukden of the Board of Punishments.
Reported in HAHL 3.1/9a.*

The general commandant of the gendarmerie of Peking has reported a case in which Private Fu-tseng-ê, of the Guards Division
[a crack Manchu force which guarded the imperial palace], asked
Corporal Fu-k'ang [of the same division] for a loan and got into a
fight with him.

On investigation, we find that Fu-tseng-ê, fearing that the incident might cost him his money and grain allowances and hearing that Yi-ch'ing-ê was a younger brother of Commissioner Feng-
shen-tai, therefore appealed to the younger brother to put in a
good word for him to the commissioner. For this he promised him
100 strings of cash. [A "cash" is a small Chinese copper coin with
a square hole; approximately 1,000 such cash, strung together to
form ten "strings," constitute one tael or ounce of silver. See also
Chapter VI, note 1.]

Yi-ch'ing-ê, however, seized the opportunity to make further
extortionary demands, and though no money actually entered his
hands, it would be improper to let him off easily.

Accordingly, Yi-ch'ing-ê should be sentenced to military exile
at a nearby frontier, under the sub-statute [Boulais 1174] which
provides this penalty for anyone who, by using the name of some
official, swindles another person out of a sum which, if it had
been stolen, would merit a punishment of penal servitude or
more. [According to the table of penalties for theft given in Boulais 1119, a theft of 40 to 50 ounces of silver merits the lowest degree of penal servitude, namely one year.] Since, however, Yi-
ch'ing-ê belongs to the [Manchu] Guards Division, this punishment is to be commuted, under the supervision of the division, to
loss of money and grain allowances, wearing of the cangue, and a
whipping.

[On the commutation of offenses committed by Manchus (as well as by Mongols and those Chinese who were members of the armies known as Banners), see Boulais 74, which, however, only summarizes the original statute. According to this statute, any specified number of blows of the bamboo is to be converted to an equal number of blows of the whip. (The number, in the case of Yi-ch'ing-ê, would be 100, since this is the number of blows of the heavy bamboo which regularly accompanies military exile.) Likewise the various degrees of penal servitude or life exile are commutable to varying lengths of time of wearing of the cangue; for military exile to a nearby frontier, it would be worn for 70 days.]

6. WRONGDOERS EXEMPTED FROM DEPORTATION [1]
[Statutory References: Staunton 9, Boulais 74]

Case 6.2, 1816. Leading Case from the Department for Shansi of the Board of Punishments.
Reported in HAHL 3.1/9b.

The military lieutenant-general of Chahar has reported that Police Officer Chung-lu, a Mongol now already stripped of official rank, had, despite his official position, been guilty of frequenting prostitutes, arresting innocent people, and practicing deception and extortion. The military lieutenant-general has accordingly recommended that he be deported under the sub-statute [Boulais 1169] concerning molestations committed by scoundrels. [This important sub-statute is used to punish a wide variety of offenses when successively committed by a single individual. It provides military exile to the farthest distance of 4,000 li for any "vicious scoundrel" (*hsiung-ô kun-t'u*) who repeatedly and causelessly commits molestations against decent citizens. See case 8.1 for examples, and case 239.15 for discussion of criteria for adjudging a person to be a "scoundrel" (*kun-t'u*).]

---

[1] This section covers the special legal treatment (usually but not invariably preferential) extended to Manchus, Mongols, and to Chinese bannermen. (On the armed forces of the Manchu government known as bannermen, see Chap. IV, sec. 2.) For the differential treatment of bannermen, see also Chap. VI, sec. 2, and T'ung-tsu Ch'ü, *Law and Society in Traditional China*, pp. 204–206.

This Board, however, finds it inappropriate to apply to an official a sub-statute that is intended for commoners. Instead, Chung-lu should be sentenced under the sub-statute which states that a bannerman official, if guilty of practicing false accusation and deception and of worthless and reckless behavior, is to be deported as a slave to such a place as San-hsing in Heilungkiang. [See Boulais 74a. San-hsing is located on the Amur River, downstream from modern Harbin.]

[In case 8.1 (1803), we find Boulais 1169 (sub-statute on molestations by scoundrels) used against a Chinese official who, by way of preparation, is stripped of official rank and thus reduced to commoner status. In the present case (1816), the same sub-statute is ruled inapplicable to a Mongol official on the alleged ground that it is intended only for commoners—despite the fact that he too has already been deprived of official rank. It would seem that the real basis for the differing interpretations is racial rather than hierarchical. Noteworthy, however, is the fact that the Mongol does not benefit from the resulting different treatment accorded him. On the contrary, his deportation to Heilungkiang is the severest of all kinds of military exile, which means that it is one degree higher than the military exile to a distance of 4,000 li which he would have received under Boulais 1169. Probably, therefore, the real reason why he is not judged under this sub-statute is the fact that another sub-statute was available which, being expressly intended for bannermen officials, was therefore deemed applicable. For the Chinese official of case 8.1, on the other hand, only the more generalized Boulais 1169 could be used.]

8. OFFENSES COMMITTED BY OFFICIALS BEFORE THEY ASSUME OFFICIAL STATUS
[Statutory References: Staunton 13, Boulais 77]

Case 8.1, 1803. From the Collection of Seen Leading Cases. *Reported in HAHL 3.1/18a–b.*

The governor-general of Fukien has memorialized concerning the case of Li Wei-t'ang, who in 1794 gained the degree of *chü-*

jen (Promoted Man) in the provincial government examinations, thereby qualifying for appointment in 1801 as a district magistrate, first class, in Honan province. Before assuming his post, however, he was obliged, because of the death of his mother, to return to his native place for mourning.

Previously, in 1794, he had bought a young girl as a slave. Her mother often came to his house to visit her daughter, and in the course of time he enticed the mother into sex relations. Last year, when he returned home for mourning, he brought this adulterous woman with him and kept her in an empty room near his house. His purpose was to use her as a prostitute and to profit from her earnings.

Again, in 1797, Li went to buy candles at a shop and demanded a reduced price. When the shopkeeper refused, Li decided to take revenge. He put four dollars in counterfeit money into a letter and asked the shopkeeper to take it to a friend. Before it was delivered, he asked to have the letter back in order to add a few words, and on opening it in the presence of the shopkeeper, accused the latter of having substituted counterfeit money for real. To avoid a lawsuit, the shopkeeper paid Li four silver dollars.

Later, in 1799, Li met an acquaintance, Yang Pa-ying, who was on his way to the provincial capital to participate in a military examination. Taking advantage of Yang's youth, Li enticed him to drink wine and to gamble at his home. When Yang lost $25 and was unable to pay in cash, Li kept him a prisoner until Yang wrote a promissory note for $100; upon his release, Yang actually paid Li $60 in cash.

Another time, a neighbor lost a hen and thought it might have run into Li's house. While he was asking Li's maid to look for it, Li arrived on the scene, accused the neighbor of making love to the maid, and forced him to pay $10 in settlement.

On being brought to trial, Li Wei-t'ang confessed to everything without exception. He should first be deprived of his official rank and then exiled to the farthest frontier at a distance of 4,000 li in accordance with the sub-statute concerning molestations committed by scoundrels [Boulais 1169. See also discussion in case 6.2.] Because he has had official rank, he may be exempted from face-tatooing.

[Such tatooing, though it often accompanied the severest grades of exile (Boulais p. 4), could be countermanded for officials, owing to its physical humiliation. Bambooing, for the same reason, was commutable in the case of officials to a monetary fine or reduction or deprivation of rank, whereas more serious punishments (penal servitude, exile, death) were not thus commutable except under extenuating circumstances (Boulais 37 and 70–71). Before an official underwent the latter, however, he would (as in the present case) be stripped of official status (Boulais 69), so that he would thus be technically a commoner when he received these punishments. Essentially the same privileges and procedures were applied to officials who (as in the present case) were punished for offenses committed prior to acquiring official status (Boulais 77).]

As for the young cadet, Yang Pa-ying, he was enticed into gambling, for which, according to the sub-statute on gambling, he is liable to 100 blows of the heavy bamboo and one month wearing the cangue. [See Boulais 1636, which, however, specifies two months of the cangue; "one" in the text may be a misprint.] But at the time he committed the crime, he was only 15 and thus not yet an adult. According to statute [Boulais 131], therefore, he is entitled to redemption of the penalty by paying a fine.

Imperial Edict: It has been reported that a district magistrate, Li Wei-t'ang, having harbored prostitutes, gambled, and made himself an evil to decent people, has been recommended for exile. Even contracting a legal marriage is improper during mourning, yet this man, while mourning for his mother, kept an adulterous woman in his house and profiteered from prostitution. His act is base and utterly shameful. In addition, he is known to have cheated, committed fraud, and practiced coercion. [For sexual offenses committed while in mourning, see Boulais 1624, and for cheating, etc., Boulais 1171.] He should be sentenced to two months wearing the cangue, during which he is to be publicly exhibited. After that he may be permanently deported, as recommended by the governor-general.

9. RELATIVES OF WRONGDOERS SENTENCED TO LIFE EXILE
[Statutory References: Staunton 15, Boulais 79–87]

Case 9.1, 1818. Memorandum.
Reported in HAHL 3.1/18b–19a.

The Department for Fukien of the Board of Punishments has pronounced judgment upon a case reported to it by the general commandant of the gendarmerie of Peking, in which a slave belonging to Prince Hui [a Manchu] has been drunk and disorderly.

This Board finds, according to sub-statute [Boulais 83a], that if a slave belonging to a Banner household has acted violently under the influence of liquor, his master is to report him, through the Banner to which the master belongs, to this Board for deportation. The slave's wife and children, moreover, are to be deported with him so that they may all be given as slaves to the frontier troops. If, however, there are some who because of age, youth, or infirmity are unable to accompany him, they are to be permitted to live with relatives or, in the case of the wife, to remarry. In no event are they to be permitted to continue in the service of their original master.

In the present case, the slave Su Lo-pi, because of frequent drunkenness, disorder, and violation of his master's regulations, has been reported by his master for deportation. Under the sub-statute quoted above, the deportation of the said slave should be accompanied by that of his wife and children. In contradiction with this sub-statute, however, the judgment reached by the Department for Fukien is that the wife and children should be handed back to their original master. It is therefore requested [by the Directorate of this Board] that the Department now correct this judgment so as to accord with the sub-statute. [On the Directorate, a body composed of the Board's highest administrative heads, see Chapter IV, section 2.]

We have reexamined a case handled earlier this year by the Board's Department for Chekiang, concerning a slave, Liu En-pao, whose drunken and disorderly behavior caused his [Manchu] master, Huo-shen-wu, to report him for deportation. The Department for Chekiang, on being informed in the same report that Liu's wife and children were willing to accompany him to become slaves at a frontier garrison, learned through further inquiry that the criminal himself wanted them to go with him. Accordingly, it gave them permission to do so, but at the same time added the proviso that the government would be unable to defray their costs of transportation.

In thus basing its decision upon the wishes of the criminal and of his family, while at the same time announcing the government's unreadiness to pay for the latter's transportation, the Department has contravened the meaning of the relevant sub-statute. Arbitrariness of this sort, moreover, may lead to future cases in which a department, hearing that a certain criminal prefers not to be accompanied by his wife and children, may order the latter on this account to remain in the service of their original master.

The several departments of this Board, therefore, are requested to note that hereafter, whenever a slave may be reported to this Board by his bannerman master for deportation, the slave's wife and children are always to accompany him in accordance with the sub-statute, thereby preventing any possible recurrence of inconsistent and erroneous judgments.

[The conditions under which relatives—especially wives—of criminals sentenced to life exile did or did not accompany the convicts into exile are complicated and unclear. See Chapter III, section 5, especially note 11. During the first century of the Ch'ing, wives were required to accompany convicted husbands into exile at government expense. Somewhere around the mid-eighteenth century, however, the government stopped providing travel funds and thereafter the question of whether a wife accompanied her convicted husband depended on whether he wished her to do so and could himself supply travel funds for the purpose. This situation seems, at least, to have prevailed for ordinary exiles, but the present case indicates that the earlier provision continued to apply with respect to the exiled slaves of Manchu households. However, the present case also demonstrates that the varying directives on the subject could result in confused and inconsistent judgments.]

11. WRONGDOERS PERMITTED TO REMAIN AT HOME TO CARE FOR PARENTS [2]
[Statutory References: Staunton 18, Boulais 96–106]

Case 11.1, 1826. Memorandum.
Reported in HAHL 3.2/1a.

[Two matters appear conspicuously in this and the following case. The first is the system of family mourning relationships known as the "five degrees of mourning" (*wu fu*), often cited here and in later cases for classifying family relationships when dealing with intrafamily offenses. It is described in Chapter I, section 9, and especially note 66. The second matter is the differentiation of all capital sentences into "immediate" execution and execution taking place "after the assizes," with the latter category being further subdivided, at the assizes themselves, into the four sub-categories of "Deferred execution," "Worthy of compassion," "Remaining at home to care for parents or to perpetuate the ancestral sacrifices," and "Circumstances deserving of capital punishment." The whole procedure is described in detail in Chapter IV, section 4.]

The governor-general of Szechuan has petitioned that Liao Hsing-shou, a criminal whose sentence is that of deferred decapitation ["deferred execution," one of the four sub-categories just mentioned], should now be permitted to remain at home to care for his parents.

It should be pointed out that the practice of allowing criminals to remain at home to care for their parents originated as an extra-legal manifestation of kindness, designed to provide comfort for

---

[2] This section exemplifies the Chinese emphasis upon filial piety. Its basic provision (hedged with various limitations) is that a criminal sentenced to death or other serious punishment may, if he be the sole adult son of parents aged 70 or more, have his punishment commuted to bambooing and wearing the cangue so that he may thereby be enabled to remain at home and care for his parents. The cases that follow indicate, however, that this privilege is by no means to be enjoyed automatically.

the parents during their declining years. It was not intended to be a loophole for escaping punishment. Moreover, in all capital cases involving crimes between relatives belonging to the five degrees of mourning, any changing of sentence from "immediate execution" (*li chüeh*) to "execution after the assizes" (*chien hou*) is to be granted in the first place only because of special circumstances calling for compassion. Therefore, the fact that the offender may happen to be the only adult son of aged parents does not at this initial stage suffice to allow him in addition [to having his sentence changed from "immediate execution" to "execution after the assizes"] to be permitted to remain at home to care for the parents. If, however, [as a result of the deliberations made at the assizes] his case should then be placed in the category of those whose "circumstances are deserving of capital punishment" (*ch'ing shih*), and if in that form the case should pass through two subsequent autumn assizes without execution of sentence actually taking place, thereby enabling it thereupon to be transferred to the category of "deferred execution" (*huan chüeh*), it then finally becomes permissible to petition that the criminal be allowed to remain at home to care for his parents. [For the sub-statute describing this procedure, see Boulais 101a.]

In the present case, Liao Hsing-shou got into a fight with another man and fired a musket in order to frighten him. By mistake, however, the shot struck and fatally wounded Liao's father's younger cousin, who accordingly was Liao's own relative of the fourth degree of mourning. Liao was therefore sentenced to immediate decapitation under the statute which provides this penalty for a junior relative assaulting and killing a senior relative belonging to the fourth degree of mourning. [See Boulais 1410, where the penalty is wrongly translated as "decapitation after the assizes." In the Code's Official Commentary on the statute, it is explained that decapitation after the assizes is to take the place of immediate decapitation only if the fourth-degree relative who is killed is a junior (and not a senior) of the relative who does the killing.]

In accordance with the relevant sub-statute [see above], this sentence of immediate decapitation was memorialized to the throne, which issued an imperial rescript changing it to decapitation after the assizes, and, within that category, classified it among cases whose "circumstances are deserving of capital punishment." The case having then passed in this form through two successive autumn assizes without execution of sentence, it was thereupon, once more in accordance with the same sub-statute, changed in status to "deferred execution." At this juncture the governor-general of Szechuan has now petitioned this Board that inasmuch as the criminal's father is presently aged 71 and there is no other adult son in the family, the criminal should accordingly be permitted to stay at home to care for his parents.

In 1822, in Chihli province, there occurred the case of Kuo Li-chen, who in defense of his mother fired a pistol which fatally wounded an elder cousin of the third degree of mourning. For this he was sentenced to immediate decapitation, which, however, in the manner described above, was successively changed to decapitation after the assizes, category of "circumstances deserving of capital punishment," and finally, after two assizes, to "deferred execution." Being the only son of an aged mother, the offender was then accordingly permitted to stay at home to care for her.

In the present case, the original report stated that the killing was done unintentionally and accidentally and thus was different from a senseless act of murderous violence. Therefore, in view of the fact that the case has now reached the status of "deferred execution," it is proper that the criminal be permitted to go home and care for his parents. [However, the criminal does not consequently escape all further punishment. On the contrary, as pointed out in the revelant sub-statute, Boulais 99, the death penalty is to be commuted to 100 blows of the heavy bamboo and 60 days wearing of the cangue; military or life exile are similarly commuted to lesser amounts of bambooing and the cangue.]

Case 11.4, 1819. Memorandum.
Reported in HAHL 3.2/2b.

The governor of Shantung has memorialized concerning a case in which Kuo Ching-hsia, acting upon his father's shouted order, beat and fatally wounded an elder cousin once removed who belonged to the fourth degree of mourning, and who had unsuccessfully tried to rape the cousin's younger sister-in-law. In his report the governor has stated that the criminal is the only adult son of aged parents.

Investigation shows that even in cases involving the beating to death of a senior relative on the paternal side belonging to the fifth degree of mourning, the question of allowing the criminal to stay at home as the sole support of aged parents must wait upon disposition of the case at the autumn assizes. It naturally follows, therefore, that should there be a case involving the beating to death of a senior relative on the paternal side who belongs to the fourth [rather than the fifth] degree of mourning, a petition asking for special treatment for the offender may not be submitted simultaneously with the initial report itself on his case.

In 1809 in Kiangsu there was a case in which Chang A-t'i fatally beat his elder brother [mourning degree 2b]. Again in 1817 there was a case in Shantung in which Yao Heng-chieh fatally beat his elder cousin of the third degree of mourning. Both men, under the respective relevant statutes [Boulais 1410–1411], were sentenced to immediate decapitation, which, however, was then changed, through imperial rescript, to decapitation after the assizes and entered among those cases, in which relatives are involved, whose "circumstances are deserving of capital punishment."

In the present case, Kuo Ching-hsia's elder cousin once removed, belonging to the fourth degree of mourning, attempted unsuccessfully to rape the cousin's younger sister-in-law, who was also of the fourth degree of mourning [to the cousin]. Upon the shouted order of his father, Kuo thereupon struck the would-be rapist, but then kept on beating him until he died. There is no doubt that the deceased cousin was guilty of the crime of attempted rape. It is likewise true that Kuo's act, being done at his father's command, was different from a senseless act of murderous violence. Nevertheless, it is also a fact that the deceased was Kuo's senior relative on the paternal side of the fourth degree of mourning. According to sub-statute, if a junior relative, obeying the command of his father, beats another senior relative, but then continues the beating until the latter dies, the penalty is decapitation after the assizes. [This sub-statute, Boulais 1410a, specifies the above penalty for such a beating when committed by a junior relative against any senior relative who, vis à vis the junior relative, belongs to either the third or fourth degree of mourning. The resulting punishment of decapitation after the assizes is less than that of immediate decapitation given for the same offense when done without command from a senior relative. See Boulais 1410.]

Between an initial sentence of decapitation after the assizes, and sentence which initially calls for immediate decapitation but is subsequently changed to decapitation after the assizes, there is an unquestionable difference with regard to the respective offenses which have provoked these sentences. Assuming, however, that in both instances the offenses have been committed against relatives belonging to the mourning system, there is then no procedural difference whatever as to the actual handling of the two kinds of sentence. That is to say, should the offender in either instance happen to be the sole adult son of aged parents, it is not legally permitted [see case 11.1] for a petition to be presented on his behalf asking permission for him to stay at home with them, unless and until his sentence, after having passed through two autumn assizes among cases whose "circumstances are deserving of capital punishment," has then finally been converted into a sentence of "deferred execution." Thus the Shantung Provincial Court, in presenting a petition of this kind at the very time when it submitted the case itself, has acted inappropriately. It should accordingly make correction.

12. OFFENSES COMMITTED BY GOVERNMENT ARTISANS AND MUSICIANS, AND BY WOMEN
[Statutory References: Staunton 20, Boulais 127–130]

Case 12.2, 1830. Memorandum.
Reported in HAHL 3.3/16b.

The Department for Yunnan of the Board of Punishments has examined the case of Mrs. Chang née Ch'en, who had previously forced several women into prostitution, for which she was sentenced to military exile. [The sub-statute covering this offense, Boulais 1630a, specifies a punishment of three months wearing the cangue, 100 blows of the heavy bamboo, and military exile in a malarial area in south or southwest China.] For this offense, being a woman, she was allowed to pay a redeeming fine [Boulais 127]. However, she later enticed other women to become prostitutes in order to profit from the earnings. Such a wicked woman should not, this time, be allowed to redeem her crime, and should be made to suffer what she deserves.

The governor of Yunnan has recommended that she be imprisoned for three years, by analogy to the sub-statute concerning women who, out of hate or jealousy, bring false accusations against another person in court. This recommendation should be approved.

[In this case, for the first time, we encounter the common practice of applying a statute or sub-statute analogically rather than directly. For details, see Chapter VI, section 3. Most of the sub-statute here referred to appears in Boulais 129, which, however, omits the opening section here cited in telescoped form. Combining this opening section with what is contained in Boulais 129, the sub-statute may be summarized as stating that military exile to a malarial area in south or southwest China is the prescribed punishment for a woman bringing false accusations against another person in court or for one who commits a theft and thus induces her own or her husband's parents or grandparents to commit suicide out of fear of criminal involvement. This nominal punishment is, however (because of the sex of the offender), to be commuted to the unusual punishment of three years' imprisonment (presumably so that she may be kept near her home, rather than, as in the case of the usual penal servitude, sent elsewhere). If, at the end of three years, the offender shows signs of repentance, she is then to be released. Here we have a good example of the use of certain statutes or sub-statutes as catch-alls: a sub-statute purporting to cover only the crimes of women who make false accusations and of women whose thefts induce parental suicide is applied analogically to a defendant whose crime is repeatedly bringing women into prostitution.]

14. MONETARY REDEMPTION PERMITTED TO THE AGED, THE YOUNG, AND THE INFIRM
[Statutory References: Staunton 22, Boulais 131–135]

Case 14.1, 1826. Memorandum.
Reported in HAHL 4.4/1a–b.

The governor of Kiangsu has memorialized concerning a case in which Tai Ch'i stabbed and thus caused the death of P'eng Po-tzu.

This Board finds, according to sub-statute [Boulais 134], that if a child of fifteen or less, on being insulted and ridiculed by someone older than himself, strikes that person and thereby causes his death, it should then be determined whether the deceased was four or more years older than the offender and whether his wrongful behavior was indeed the cause provoking the offender to his murderous action. If this be so, a petition may be submitted requesting clemency, in accordance with the holding in the case of Ting Ch'i-san. [This case, which occurred in 1732, is summarized in Boulais 138 and described below. It is exceptional for a sub-statute, as here, to refer by name to a precedent case.]

Ting Ch'i-san, a boy of fourteen, had been carrying basketloads of earth together with Ting Kou-tzu, a youth four years his senior. The older boy, taking advantage of his age, ordered Ting Ch'i-san to carry the heavier loads and also insulted him by throwing clods of earth at him. Ting Ch'i-san threw clods back, and happened to hit the older boy, thereby killing him. At the trial, however, Ting Ch'i-san was granted a reduced penalty on the grounds that he had suffered abuse from someone older than himself.

[Here and in case 14.2 (untranslated), where Ting Ch'i-san's case is cited in greater detail, it is evident that the ambiguous phrase "reduced penalty" means that Ting's punishment was reduced from strangulation after the assizes to life exile. The different interpretation in Boulais 138, that the boy was permitted the privilege of monetary redemption, seems arbitrary and wrong. Strangulation after the assizes is the normal punishment for homicide in an affray. See Boulais 1268.]

Therefore, when cases of assault resulting in homicide arise, in which the offender, like Ting Ch'i-san, is aged fifteen or less, and has, like him, been provoked into his murderous action, petition may be made for a reduction of punishment to life exile.

In the present case, Tai Ch'i, aged fifteen, had gone with his sickle to the fields to cut grass. On his way he saw P'eng Po-tzu, aged twenty-five, and others harvesting soy beans. Noticing a few beans scattered along the side, Tai Ch'i collected a handful and put them in his basket. P'eng, on seeing this, swore at him and tried to grab his basket. Tai became frightened and ran away, but P'eng overtook him and began beating him. Tai wielded his sickle to scare off P'eng, but in so doing he stabbed P'eng in the heart, killing him.

The Provincial Court of Kiangsu has accordingly sentenced Tai Ch'i to strangulation. [Boulais 1268 specifies strangulation after the assizes for homicide resulting in an affray.] At the same time, however, it has petitioned for clemency, citing the case of Ting Ch'i-san. In its report, it has pointed out that poor people are customarily permitted to glean scattered wheat or beans left on the ground, that at the time in question other persons were in fact doing just this in neighboring fields, and that even in P'eng's own field, Tai Ch'i was not the only one who was thus gleaning beans. Hence it was unreasonable for P'eng to single out Tai alone as the one to forbid, to curse, and to want to take his basket. P'eng, moreover, by chasing and beating Tai after the latter had tried to avoid a fight by running away, showed himself particularly ready to commit outrageous violence, taking advantage of his own seniority.

We find that, even though the details of this case are not too similar to those in the case of Ting Ch'i-san, the arguments advanced by the Provincial Court of Kiangsu nevertheless provide grounds for leniency inherently sufficient to enable this case to become classified at the Autumn Assizes among the ones designated as "worthy of compassion" (*k'o chin*). [This category, one of the several under which capital cases were classified at the Autumn Assizes, was expressly intended for the young, the aged, and other persons for whom particular extenuating circumstances existed. The death sentences of such cases were commonly reduced to life exile or penal servitude.]

Further interchange of discussion between this Board and the Provincial Court of Kiangsu would merely prolong the offender's imprisonment until the Autumn Assizes when, his case then being entered among those classed as "worthy of compassion," he would in any event receive an identical reduction of sentence, namely from strangulation to life exile. In order, therefore, to spare the offender further imprisonment, it seems appropriate to follow the precedent of the Ting Ch'i-san case and grant approval to the provincial court's plea for clemency.

17. VOLUNTARY CONFESSION BY WRONGDOERS
[Statutory References: Staunton 25, Boulais 115–125]

Case 17.1, 1818. Memorandum.
Reported in HAHL 4.4/20a–b.

[This case is of interest on several counts: (1) It illustrates the workings of the principle of voluntary confession (touched on in Chapter I, section 10, near the end). (2) It illustrates the conscientious efforts of the Board of Punishments to look for earlier precedent—in this case a precedent rejected in the end as not really relevant. (3) It develops a theory of causation, according to which some crimes consist of unitary criminal acts only, whereas others are composite combinations of an initial criminal act A, followed by a resultant criminal act B. The technical term for A is *yin*, literally "cause," but here rendered as "antecedent causal act." In actual practice it would seem often difficult to maintain a clear-cut distinction between unitary and composite criminal acts.]

The governor of Kuangtung has presented a memorial concerning a case in which Liang Ts'ai-hsien hanged himslf as a result of being reviled in foul language by Liang Ya-ju. The latter, learning that he was wanted by the authorities, then gave himself up.

This Board finds, according to statute [Boulais 115], that criminals who confess to the authorities before their crime is discovered are to have remission of punishment. However, another statute [Boulais 118] provides that the foregoing statute is inapplicable to cases of irreparable bodily injuries. The Code's Official Commentary [cited in Boulais 124 in the course of outlining a case] explains that criminals who have committed homicide and then confess are permitted remission of punishment for whatever causal act may have led up to the killing but still remain liable for the penalties provided under the homicide laws themselves. A sub-statute [Boulais 122a] further provides that if a criminal, upon hearing that he is wanted, then turns himself in, he will be granted a one-degree reduction of penalty for all crimes except those specified above to which the principle of remission for voluntary confession does not apply. The term "irreparable bodily injuries" mentioned above is to be understood as including all forms of death as well as other kinds of injury. In other words, even if a homicide has not been directly occasioned by physical injuries [inflicted on the victim by another person], it is nevertheless irreparable, and therefore is to be judged like any other kind of irreparable injury, provided only that it has truly stemmed from the act of some wrongdoer.

In the present case, Liang Ya-ju dirtied the clothing of Liang Ts'ai-hsien with unclean water, for which he was upbraided by the latter. Thereupon he retaliated with such foul language that Liang Ts'ai-hsien, in a state of shame and rage, killed himself. Liang Ya-ju's use of foul language, which caused the other man to commit suicide, falls into the same category as inflictions of physical injury by one man upon another. In the circumstances of the death of Liang Ts'ai-hsien, there is no antecedent causal act (*yin*) for which remission of punishment may be granted to an offender because of his confessing. [In other words, the use of abusive language and the death resulting therefrom are to be regarded as constituting a single nexus of events, wherein the use of abusive language cannot be isolated from the resulting homicide. Hence the offender, even if he confess, cannot thereby obtain remission of punishment for the abusive language while still remaining liable for the homicide. (Of course, such remission would in any event be academic, inasmuch as homicide is punishable by a much heavier penalty than that for abusive language.)]

By way of comparison, we may cite the example of a thief who resists arrest, kills someone while so doing, and then, on hearing that he is wanted, surrenders himself. By reason of his surrender, the thief is granted remission of punishment for his antecedent causal act of resisting arrest, and so is permitted to be sentenced simply on the charge of killing in an affray. [For killing done by a thief while resisting arrest, the penalty is decapitation after the assizes (Boulais 1063); for ordinary killing in an affray, it is one degree less, or strangulation after the assizes (Boulais 1268).]

If, however, the case from the start is simply one of killing in an affray, there then exists no antecedent causal act for which the offender may gain remission of punishment through confession. Hence, despite such confession, he still remains liable for the full punishment for killing in an affray. [The argument is that such killing involves only the single criminal act of the killing itself, whereas killing while resisting arrest involves the two criminal acts of resisting arrest and then of killing. The former of these is thus regarded as the antecedent causal act (*yin*) for the latter —what in Western logic would be called the necessary cause for the killing, though not its sufficient cause. This differentiation enables the Chinese jurist to deal with the two acts separately.]

Although a suicide occasioned by foul language and a killing during an affray are nominally different, they are alike in that the inflicting of bodily injury takes place in both.

In reviewing past cases, we have found none analogous to the one at bar, except for a case occurring in Honan in 1800, in which a certain Chang Ch'eng, having committed adultery with a Mrs. Lin, ran off with her. On the road, however, he became afraid and sent her back to her husband. Whereupon, she was reviled by her husband and committed suicide out of shame. Chang Ch'eng was not punished for the seduction and abduction that led up to the homicide but was sentenced because of the latter to penal servitude under the sub-statute on homicide resulting from adultery. [For seducing and abducting a woman, the penalty is strangulation after the assizes (Boulais 1185). For having an adulterous relationship, the exposure of which shames the woman into committing suicide, the penalty is three years penal servitude (Boulais 1334). In the case cited, the return of the woman to her husband seems to be equated by the Board of Punishments to confession and surrender, thus entitling the paramour to exemption of punishment for seduction and abduction, and leaving him liable only for the lesser offense of adultery resulting in suicide.]

Death occasioned by adultery and death occasioned by foul language fall into a common category. Nevertheless, between the cases of Chang Ch'eng [the cited adultery case] and Liang Ya-ju [the principal case] there is the distinction that the homicide occasioned by Chang occurred only after his confession [that is, after he sent the woman home], whereas that occasioned by Liang occurred before his confession. Thus these cases are not congruent.

[It is regrettable that the Board does not expand its argument here. Apparently it rejects the relevancy of the Chang Ch'eng case on the grounds that Chang's "confession" (his return of the woman) necessarily relates only to his act of seduction and abduction and cannot relate to the offense for which he is actually convicted—that of homicide resulting from adultery—because the homicide occurred only subsequently to the confession. In the case at bar, on the other hand, the confession does relate directly to the suicide itself. This fact, however, makes the confession inadmissible in the eyes of the Board, because suicide, when induced by an outside person, is included by the Board among the kinds of death falling under the category of irreparable bodily injury, to which confession does not apply.]

We have reviewed various kinds of homicide punishable by decapitation or strangulation, for example, pressing a person into suicide by robbing him [Boulais 1325], suicide resulting from a false accusation of theft [Boulais 1486], from deceptions practiced by knavish fellows [Boulais 1170a], from extortions practiced by rapacious governmental underlings [Boulais 1522], from extortions practiced by impersonators of the servants of government officials [Boulais 1572a], and from improper verbal advances made to women [Boulais 1327].

We have further reviewed crimes punishable by military exile or by penal servitude, such as beating which inflicts fatal injuries upon the victim, thereby inducing him to commit suicide before the injuries take effect, or beating which inflicts serious but nonfatal injuries, thereby likewise inducing suicide. [The sub-statute covering these two possibilities, Boulais 1327a, prescribes as respective punishments military exile at a distance of 2,500 li and three years penal servitude.]

In none of the items reviewed is there any antecedent causal act for which confession may bring about a remission of punishment. In this basic respect they are the same as the case at bar, even though as kinds of criminal conduct they are individually distinguishable. [It is noteworthy that all the instances cited are single criminal acts, each resulting in the suicide of another person. Herein lies the difference between them and such composite offenses as killing while resisting arrest. Surely, however, the Chinese jurist must have found it difficult at times to maintain a clear-cut distinction between what is unitary and what is composite.]

In these kinds of crimes, if a criminal were allowed a one-degree punishment reduction simply for giving himself up after learning that the authorities wanted him, he would accordingly be entitled to a two-degree reduction when, having learned a charge was about to be made against him, he voluntarily surrendered himself in advance. [Boulais 117 specifies a two-degree reduction under these circumstances. But, as we have seen above, Boulais 118 withholds all leniency for confession whenever the victim has suffered irreparable bodily injuries.] Furthermore, according to statute [Boulais 115], it would be possible for such a criminal, by turning himself in before the crime became at all known to the authorities, to gain complete remission of punishment. But if such remission were permitted for major crimes of homicide punishable by decapitation or strangulation, there would then be no means to deter the violent. It follows that despite Liang Ya-ju's voluntary surrender, he should not on this account be granted a reduced punishment.

19. JOINT FLIGHT BY WRONGDOERS
[Statutory References: Staunton 27, Boulais 170]

Case 19.1, 1791. Memorandum.
Reported in HAHL 4.5/3a–b.

The governor of Kiangsu has reported a case in which Mrs. Ch'en née Shen, a matchmaker, aided Hsü Tsai-keng in abducting and selling a young girl. Because Hsü surrendered himself to the authorities on hearing that he was wanted, and therefore had his punishment reduced from strangulation to life exile [under Boulais 122a], Mrs. Ch'en's punishment was correspondingly reduced by the governor from life exile to penal servitude.

The Department for Kiangsu of the Board of Punishments finds that, according to the statute concerning joint flight by criminals [Boulais 170], the penalty for persons "implicated" (*lien-lei*) in a crime of a principal offender will, when the principal receives a reduced sentence as the result of making a confession, be correspondingly reduced. The Code's Official Commentary explains that "implication in the crime of a principal offender" means hiding, transporting, or aiding the criminal, or giving false testimony concerning him, or negligence on the part of frontier guards or prison attendants. From this it is evident that the statute applies solely to persons becoming accessories after the fact; it does not apply to accomplices who actually joined the principal in committing the crime.

If anybody, knowing someone else is kidnapping and selling children, participates in promoting such a sale for the sake of gain, the participant becomes a co-principal in the crime, and differs from one merely "implicated" in the crime of another. Such a co-principal, therefore, should be judged in his own person, that is, according to his own offense; he is not entitled to a reduced sentence on the ground that his co-principal has confessed and thereby received a reduced penalty.

We [members of the Board's Directorate] find that in the present case, the matchmaker, Mrs. Ch'en, knowing that Hsü Tsai-keng was abducting and selling a young girl, suggested to him that he change the child's name and that they jointly sell the child and divide the proceeds. This constitutes a personal violation of the law as a principal, for which she should be sentenced to life exile, this being the reduction from strangulation, which is the proper punishment for Hsü. [Boulais 1185 prescribes strangulation after the assizes for the principal in such a crime and life exile at a distance of 3,000 li, plus 100 blows of the heavy bamboo, for an accomplice.]

The governor's sentence is not justified by the meaning of the statute concerning joint flight of criminals [Boulais 170, which extends leniency only to accessories after the fact, and not to a person like Mrs. Ch'en who was a co-principal even though a secondary participant in the crime].

Therefore the Department for Kiangsu should accordingly make correction.

21. WRONGDOERS WHO ARE FUGITIVES FROM JUSTICE AT THE TIME OF THEIR TRIAL
[Statutory References: Staunton 31, Boulais 171–172]

Case 21.38, 1810. Memorandum.
Reported in HAHL 4.5/25b.

The Department for Kiangsi of the Board of Punishments finds that Li Mao-erh was guilty of raping an eleven year old girl, for which, according to sub-statute [Boulais 1588], he should have received decapitation after the assizes. However, he remained a fugitive for ten years before being captured.

The fact remains, nonetheless, that his crime was not one of homicide. This is why the Provincial Court of Kiangsi, in now passing judgment, has adhered to the original sub-statute governing his case. [In other words, it has disregarded his ten years as a fugitive by giving him merely the same sentence of decapitation after the assizes for which he would originally have been liable.] This judgment being in accord with the relevant sub-statute, it would seem that a confirmatory reply may be given.

[The relevant sub-statute here mentioned is not the same as the above-cited Boulais 1589, under which the penalty for raping a girl under twelve is decapitation after the assizes. Rather, the sub-statute specifies the procedure for dealing with offenders who have been fugitives. See Boulais 172a. For a criminal whose offense calls for a death penalty, and who has been a fugitive for "two or three years" or more before being captured, the sub-statute provides as follows: (a) If the criminal has been guilty of a serious homicide calling for immediate execution, such execution is to be carried out unchanged following his capture. (b) If the criminal has been guilty of a lesser kind of homicide calling only for execution after the assizes, this sentence is, upon his capture, to be increased to immediate execution. (c) If the criminal is guilty of an offense other than homicide, for which the penalty nonetheless likewise consists of execution after the assizes, such penalty is to be carried out unchanged, following capture. It is this last clause that forms the basis for judgment in the present case, whereas the next case is decided under clause (b).]

Case 21.40, 1812. Memorandum.
Reported in HAHL 4.5/26a.

The governor of Honan has memorialized concerning a case in which Chang Hu-ni killed with premeditation the husband of a woman with whom he had committed adultery, this husband having tolerated the affair. For this offense, according to statute [Boulais 1211], the punishment is decapitation after the assizes. [The husband's toleration is important, because it turns his killing into an ordinary case of premeditated homicide, punishable by decapitation after the assizes, whereas the killing of a husband who does not tolerate his wife's adultery is punishable, under Boulais 1241, by immediate decapitation.]

After committing the murder, Chang did away with the corpse and obliterated all traces of the crime, so that although it had occurred in January, 1806, it was not finally exposed until December, 1811. The offender, while not actually a fugitive during these several years, was indeed lucky to have enjoyed such a delay in execution. [He would have been subject to execution had his guilt been known.]

The Honan Provincial Court has therefore sentenced Chang Hu-ni by analogy to the sub-statute on an offender who, being guilty of a homicide punishable by decapitation after the assizes, remains a fugitive for two or three years before being captured. Consequently, Chang's punishment, which would originally have been decapitation after the assizes, has now been raised by the Court to immediate decapitation. This judgment being equitable, it is proper to request a confirmatory reply.

[The judgment is based upon clause (b) of the same sub-statute discussed in detail in the preceding case, Boulais 172a. The sub-statute has to be applied analogically in the present case because it deals with fugitives from justice, whereas Chang Hu-ni was not technically a fugitive.]

40. IMPROPER MANIPULATION OF OFFICIAL SEALS
[Statutory References: Staunton 73, Boulais 303]

Case 40.1, 1824. Leading Case from the Department for Kueichow of the Board of Punishments.
Reported in HAHL Supplement 30.3/3b.

[In China, at least until very recently, seals were very widely used on letters and all kinds of documents for purposes of authentication. In the 1930's, for example, when I lived in Peking, it was necessary for me, when cashing a check at my bank, not only to endorse it with my signature but also to stamp it with my personal seal. Boulais 303 provides 60 blows of the heavy bamboo for anyone who stamps a seal upon an official circulating document (an official letter, petition, or notice) in an improper manner (for example, impressing a seal upside down would, as explained in the Shen Chih-ch'i Commentary, constitute such improper use); 80 blows is the punishment for failing to use the seal at all on a circulating document; 100 blows if the document thus improperly stamped or not stamped at all deals with military matters; and decapitation after the assizes if such misuse of the seal results in errors in military operations.]

The Board of Revenue has reported a case in which Ts'ui T'ai-hung, one of its departmental clerks in charge of registration records, neglected to stamp one of the Board's registration books of 1822 with the official seal. Although investigation shows no evidence of deliberate wrongdoing on his part, he is certainly guilty of negligence. Furthermore, even though the Board's registration records are not intended to circulate, but are merely kept on file for reference purposes, there is no vital difference [as far as their official status is concerned] between them and other government documents which do circulate. Therefore, by analogy to the statute on improper manipulation of official seals [Boulais 303], Ts'ui T'ai-hung should receive 60 blows of the heavy bamboo, without, however, being dismissed from his employment.

[The decision of the Board of Punishments to apply Boulais 303 analogically rather than directly probably stems from two factors: (1) The documents specified in Boulais 303 are ones intended for circulation (official letters and the like), whereas those involved in the present case are non-circulating file records (records of population figures, land holdings, etc.); this factor may have been influential despite the Board's insistence that, at least in the context of this case, there is no really vital difference between the two kinds of document. (2) The Board apparently wished to let the clerk off as easily as possible, as demonstrated by the fact that it imposes upon him the lowest punishment of 60 blows provided by Boulais 303, instead of the 80 blows which that statute specifically provides for one who, like him, fails to use a seal at all.]

As for the other responsible functionaries in the said department who failed to detect the mistake in time, they, being guilty of doing what ought not to be done, should accordingly receive 40 blows of the light bamboo without, however, being dismissed from their employment. [For this catch-all statute, which provides 40 blows of the light bamboo or 80 blows of the heavy one for lesser or more serious actions which, though deemed to be improper, are not precisely covered by any statute or sub-statute, see Boulais 1656.]

41. DETERMINATION OF STATUS ACCORDING TO HOUSEHOLD REGISTRATION
[Statutory References: Staunton 76, Boulais 350–363]

Case 41.7, 1751. General Circular from the Kiangsu Printed Edition.
Reported in HAHL 5.7/14a.

[This and the next case are of great sociological interest for the light they throw on the legal discrimination shown toward a depressed occupational group known as *ch'ang sui*. This term, literally "permanent attendants," is the technical designation for the privately employed servants of district magistrates and other officials (as against the government-paid subordinates of such officials). As these cases show us, even the sons of these servants, let alone the servants themselves, were, like the sons of slaves, barred from taking the civil service examinations or acquiring official rank through purchase. For further details, see Chapter VI, end of section 2.]

The Board of Civil Office, in a memorial, has sent to the Board of Punishments a case concerning the status of Tu Shih-ch'ang, a sub-prefect, first class, of Szechuan province.

This Board finds that there is no statute concerning a privately employed servant of an official (*ch'ang sui*) or a hired hand who under false pretenses buys official rank. However, there has been the case of Yü Ch'üan, son of a household slave, who bought the rank of sub-prefect, first class, and who was sentenced for this to military exile by analogy to the sub-statute concerning concealing an offense or a name in order to obtain a government post. [Boulais 244 specifies such a punishment for this kind of fraud, and Boulais 356 states that manumitted slaves and their descendants to the third generation are not allowed to take the civil service examinations or hold official rank.]

As for the defendant Tu Shih-ch'ang, he is the son of a private official servant (*ch'ang sui*) who had served in the household of a lieutenant-governor who had been deprived of official rank. Thus there is indeed a difference between him and a household slave. Yet it is nonetheless a fact that when he obtained the rank, he practiced deception by concealing his social origin. He may, therefore, be dealt with by analogy to Yü Ch'üan, but with a one-degree reduction in punishment, namely: deprivation of rank, 100 blows of the heavy bamboo, and penal servitude for three years. [The sub-statute (Boulais 244) is applied analogically both because of the reduction of punishment, and because the sub-statute includes "yamen servants" but not *ch'ang sui* among the dismissed officials, degraded holders of examination degrees, and others, who are potential practitioners of this kind of fraud.]

Two other men were also involved in this case. They signed papers as guarantors, receiving for this more than two ounces of silver. Their punishments may be calculated as follows: (1) For bribes of one to ten ounces of silver, involving, however, no contravention of the law, the punishment is 70 blows of the heavy bamboo. [See Boulais 1519. "No contravention of the law" means that though bribes are given, their purpose is simply to insure the performance of a lawful act rather than to bring about the performance of an illegal one.] (2) However, because the offenders happen in this instance to be official clerks, their punishment should be increased by one degree to 80 blows. [This is peculiar, because no differentiation of punishment is specified in Boulais 1519 as between officials and the clerks of officials.] (3) However, because they are clerks who are not salaried by the government, one degree is to be reduced, making a final punishment of 70 blows. [See Boulais 1517. "Not salaried by the government" means that they are the personal employees (not, however, the menials, like the *ch'ang sui*) of the official who uses them, and are paid by him rather than from government funds.]

The 70 blows are to be administered by the Board of Civil Office.

Imperial Rescript: Let it be as has been deliberated.

Case 41.8, 1831. From the Peking Gazette.
Reported in HAHL 5.7/14a.

The governor-general of Shensi has memorialized concerning Lo Han-pao, former commander of the gendarmerie of the East City of Peking, who was deprived of official status when it was learned that his father, a department prefect in Shensi, had once been the privately employed servant of an official *(ch'ang sui)*. [Boulais 356 prohibits manumitted slaves and their descendants to the third generation from taking the government examinations, and the present case indicates that the prohibition was applied to *ch'ang sui* as well.] Recently, however, Lo Han-pao distinguished himself while in military service at Kashgar. May he, then, be permitted to regain his status and participate in the imperial examinations?

Imperial Edict: If Lo Han-pao has really performed outstandingly in the army, it is proper for the governor-general to confer honors upon him accordingly. If, however, he were on this account to be allowed to participate in the examinations for official rank, how could the proper distinctions between menials and persons of honorable parentage be maintained? The governor-general's request is denied and he himself is rebuked.

42. ILLEGAL APPOINTMENT OF AN HEIR
[Statutory References: Staunton 78, Boulais 386–408]

Case 42.1, 1827. Memorandum of Metropolitan Leading Case.
Reported in HAHL 5.7/15b.

[In order to understand this case, it is essential to keep in mind that, as explained in Boulais 386, the primary purpose of establishing a legal heir in China is to insure the continuity of the family line and its cult of the ancestors; in other words, the dominant considerations are religious and sociological. The selection of such an heir (known as *chi-tzu,* "successor" or *ssu,* "perpetuator") must, if at all possible, be made from within the same clan to which the person making the adoption himself belongs. Otherwise, the adoptee must at least come from a family bearing the same surname as that of the adoptor, even though there is no clan relationship. (This insistence upon a common surname as a minimum requirement reflects the deep-rooted belief that some kind of affinity does in fact exist between persons of common surname, even though of unrelated clans—a belief exemplified in the traditional prohibition of marriage between persons of the same surname. See Boulais 582.) At the same time it is also necessary, in order to prevent a scrambling of the family genealogy, for the adopted heir to belong to a generation lower than that of his adoptor. The heir can, for example, be a son of the adoptor's brother or cousin but not the brother or cousin of the adoptor. In contrast to these strict requirements for a legal heir, it was of course also possible for a family to adopt a person who was totally unrelated and had a different surname, but this adoption, when it took place, was done primarily for the sake of that person and in no way met the needs of the family for its formal perpetuation. The adoptee, though supported by this family, enjoyed no legal rights within it, did not participate in its cult of the ancestors, and was known as an *yi-tzu* or "charity son."]

The Department for Szechuan of the Board of Punishments has

been examining a case in which Li Ssu assaulted Mao Pu-erh, thus inflicting wounds which led to the latter's death sixteen days later as the result of infection.

[For "infection," the Chinese text reads *feng*, "wind" or "air." This reflects the prevalent belief in pre-modern China that the infecting of a wound is caused by exposure to wind or air. For the sake of convenience, the same rendition will be followed in later cases whenever the term *feng* occurs.]

Li Ssu has accordingly been sentenced to life exile under the relevant sub-statute. [Boulais 1361 specifies life exile at a distance of 3,000 li for the inflicting in an affray of wounds which, though not serious themselves, lead to death from infection after five days; should such death occur in less than five days, the penalty is increased to strangulation after the assizes.] Investigation has revealed, however, that because of the early death of the offender's father and the consequent remarriage of his mother, he himself was brought up since infancy as the adopted son of Mrs. Li née Liu, now the widow of the late Li Shuang-huai. The latter, though sharing a common surname with the offender, came from a different clan. On this basis it has been petitioned that the offender Li Ssu, instead of being sent into exile, should be permitted to remain at home as the sole support for the widowed Mrs. Li, his aged foster mother. [See cases 11.1 and 11.4, as well as below, for discussion of this privilege.] However, in the absence of any leading case covering the precise relationship and circumstances here involved, this Department now submits the case to the Board's Directorate, requesting this body to transmit it to the Statutes Commission [see Chapter IV, section 2] for a decision.

Statutes Commission: This Commission finds, according to sub-statute [Boulais 102], that if a criminal who has been sentenced to military or life exile should happen to be the sole adult son of aged parents and if there be no brothers or nephews or progeny of his own who can take his place in perpetuating the family, he will then be permitted to remain at home himself in order to care for his parents. A statute [Boulais 392] also states that whoever adopts as a legal heir someone with a surname different from his own, thereby contaminating his own clan, will receive 60 blows of the heavy bamboo; the person thus adopted will likewise be returned to his own clan. Finally, there is a sub-statute [Boulais 396] stating that a person, if childless, is permitted to adopt as a son someone on the paternal side of his own clan belonging to a younger generation than himself, preference first being given to a son of his own brother, and then successively to a son of a first paternal cousin, of a second paternal cousin, or of a third paternal cousin. If none of these is available, he is then permitted to adopt a son from a still more distant branch of his clan, or, finally, from a family having the same surname.

In the present case, the offender, Li Ssu, now sentenced to exile at the age of forty-one, has for no less than forty years been cared for by Mrs. Li née Liu, widow of the late Li Shuang-huai. The latter, though having the same surname as the offender, belonged to an unrelated clan. It is further found that Mrs. Li, who is now seventy-one, has no descendant within the clan line of her late husband who could serve as an heir.

In the final sub-statute quoted above, it is evident that its final phrase, "family having the same surname," can in the context of the preceding words only be understood as meaning: "family having the same surname but not belonging to the same clan." Since, therefore, according to this sub-statute on adoption [Boulais 396], adoption of a person bearing the same surname but belonging to an outside clan is permissible and does not contaminate the adoptor's own clan, it would certainly seem that the same kind of adoption would be accepted as equally valid within the context of the sub-statute [Boulais 102] concerning criminals who, being the sole support of aged parents, are permitted to remain at home to care for them.

Our conclusion, then, is that even though the precise circumstances of the present case are not explicitly covered by the foregoing sub-statute on criminals who are permitted to care for aged parents, a weighing of the circumstances nevertheless leads to the judgment that the present offender may indeed be permitted to remain at home in this instance, so as to care for his foster mother. [From cases 11.1 and 11.4 it is evident that the granting of this privilege to a criminal guilty of a capital offense is accorded much less readily than to one who, as here, is guilty only of an offense calling for exile.]

44. PROHIBITION AGAINST UNAUTHORIZED ASSUMPTION OF RURAL HEADMAN'S POSITION [3]

[Statutory References: Staunton 83, Boulais 381]

Case 44.1, 1827. Leading Case.
Reported in HAHL Supplement 30.3/4b.

The governor of Honan has reported a case in which a government military student, Wang T'ing-chü, now dismissed, prepared public notices announcing plans for establishing an office for himself, wherein he hoped to fish for profit by handling taxation matters for people and settling their litigations. He is accordingly now sentenced to 100 blows of the heavy bamboo and two years of penal servitude, by analogy to the statute [Boulais 381] which provides 100 blows of the heavy bamboo and transportation reduced to two-year authorized penal servitude for anyone who falsely terms himself a *pao* or *li* head, thereby creating trouble and annoying the people. [On this rare and curious hybrid punishment, see Chapter III, section 4.]

As for Ho Wan-ch'ao, a man who revised the text of Wang's notice, made multiple copies of it, and distributed these, he as an accessory [Boulais 110] should receive a punishment one degree less, namely 70 blows of the heavy bamboo and one and one half years penal servitude.

[Here it is necessary to apply Boulais 381 analogically rather than directly because the military student was not actually guilty

[3] In order to facilitate the maintenance of good order and collection of taxes in rural China, the Ch'ing government divided the local populace into one series of units known as *pao* (each *pao* consisting of 1,000 households) and another series of units known as *li* (each *li* consisting of 110 households). The *pao* and *li* heads were appointed annually by the government from the local population and were responsible to the government for the good order and payment of taxes of the people within their respective units. Yet they were unsalaried, and the whole system operated outside of, and on a lower level than, the formal governmental system with its salaried civil service personnel. Thus, being a *pao* or *li* head could be a real hardship unless, as of course could happen, the headman took improper advantage of his position to squeeze profits for himself. No doubt it is this possibility that provides the rationale for the present statute. See Kung-chuan Hsiao, *Rural China, Imperial Control in the Nineteenth Century* (Seattle, 1960), Chaps. 2–4.

of calling himself a *pao* or *li* head, which is what the statute prohibits, but merely of planning to perform functions analogous to those performed by such a head. The case should be compared with cases 203.2, 4, 5, and 7. These cases well illustrate how activities which in a different kind of society would seem quite innocent were viewed with official hostility in the highly regularized society of imperial China.]

45. PRIVATE APPROPRIATION OF FAMILY PROPERTY BY A JUNIOR MEMBER
[Statutory References: Staunton 88, Boulais 412–422]

Case 45.1, 1826. Leading Case.
Reported in HAHL Supplement 30.3/4b.

The governor of Hunan has reported a case in which the Buddhist monk Ch'ang-lien, having since childhood been the disciple of the monk Wen-yüan, with whom he lived together and shared a common purse, stole from him 270 ounces of silver.

Sentence should be pronounced by analogy to the statute [Boulais 414] which states that if a junior member of a family privately appropriates family property for himself, he is to receive 10 blows of the light bamboo for the first 10 ounces thus appropriated, with a one-degree increase in punishment for each additional 10 ounces, stopping, however, at a maximum punishment of 100 blows of the heavy bamboo. Monk Ch'ang-lien is accordingly sentenced to 100 blows of the heavy bamboo.

[Boulais 414 is here used analogically rather than directly because the relationship of the older monk to his disciple is analogous to, but not identical with, that of a senior to a junior member of the same family. As pointed out earlier in this book (Chapter I, section 9), theft within the family is punished much more lightly than ordinary theft, owing to the ancient concept that what exists within the family is owned in common by everyone, so that no one member of the family can really steal it from another. The distinction between the two kinds of theft is reflected in the fact that whereas ordinary theft of 120 or more ounces of silver would be punishable by strangulation after the assizes (Boulais 1119), the theft here of 270 ounces merits only 100 blows of the heavy bamboo.]

49. PURCHASE BY AN OFFICIAL OF LAND OR BUILDINGS IN AN AREA UNDER HIS JURISDICTION
[Statutory References: Staunton 94, Boulais 502–504]

Case 49.1, 1832. General Circular.
Reported in HAHL 5.7/21a.

The censor of the Kiangsi Censorial Circuit has submitted a memorial in which he quotes a sub-statute [Boulais 502a] to the effect that if any official, on being sent out on assignment, takes with him his family dependents and numerous servants, or, before undergoing investigation by the Board of Civil Office upon his return from assignment, purchases land or houses or engages in money lending or usury in the area under his jurisdiction, he is accordingly to be handed over to the Board of Civil Office for determination of his punishment. Likewise, should a yamen [government office] underling go on his own initiative to the capital in order there to meet an official and escort him to his provincial post, or should an official request an extension of time before leaving on assignment, on the pretext that his departure will leave his present post vacant, such persons are likewise to be handed over to the Board of Civil Office for determination of punishment.

The censor, after citing this sub-statute in his memorial, points out that the sub-statute fails to provide specific penalties for these offenses, and that it would be appropriate to deliberate upon the matter with a view to repairing this omission.

We of the Board of Punishments find, however, that this sub-statute was drafted in the fear that an official who is thus sent on assignment, if guilty of these relatively minor offenses, might also be guilty of such graver offenses as embezzlement or misappropriation of taxes or public funds. As soon as cases arise, therefore, involving these minor offenses, investigation naturally has to be made as to whether evidence for the more serious offenses of embezzlement, and so on also exists. If it does, the offender will then accordingly be given the specific punishments prescribed for each or several of these more serious offenses. It is to be feared, however, that if hard-and-fast penalties were to be specified in advance for the lesser offenses mentioned in the sub-statute, this would merely interfere with the handling of the more serious related offenses.

Imperial Rescript: The censor's memorial requesting that this matter be deliberated upon requires no further discussion.

50. DESTRUCTION OF TOOLS, CROPS, AND SO ON
[Statutory References: Staunton 98, Boulais 514–515]

Case 50.1, 1833. Leading Case.
Reported in HAHL Supplement 30.3/6a.

The governor-general of Szechuan has reported a case in which Chou Tzu-tao, a [non-civil service] functionary connected with the civil service examinations, after having been refused a loan by Teng Fa-hsien, was moved by hatred to destroy the stone lining of the channel which carries the water used to irrigate Teng's fields.

This Board finds that this subsidiary channel with its stone lining is distinct from the main [government-maintained] dike system, so that Chou, when he destroyed the stone lining of this channel, caused no damage to the main dike itself. Therefore, his offense is not identical with that of someone who deliberately cuts a [government-maintained] river dike. [The penalty for which, according to Boulais 1716, is 100 blows of the heavy bamboo and three years penal servitude. Note here the characteristic emphasis upon the seriousness of destroying public as against private property.]

Chou should be sentenced by analogy to the statute [Boulais 515] which states that if someone destroys or damages the house, walls, or other property of another person, the cost of restoration will be calculated, and the offender will be sentenced as he would for taking the same amount in squeeze *(tsang)*. [The following sentence of the statute, unquoted, goes on to say that the offender must also carry out (pay for) the work of restoration.]

The sum spent by Teng in repairing the stone lining amounts to 160 ounces of silver, which, halved, comes to 80 ounces. This means that Chou Tzu-tao should accordingly be sentenced to 100 blows of the heavy bamboo.

[The reason for applying Boulais 515 analogously rather than directly is that the statute deals with the destruction of houses and walls, whereas Chou's offense is that of destroying an irrigation channel. *Tsang*, the word here rendered as "squeeze," more generally signifies loot, booty, property acquired improperly. In the present context, however, "squeeze" seems to be the best rendition, as may be deduced from what is said about the word in Boulais 1528–1529, where the offense of taking *tsang* is discussed. In contrast to an ordinary bribe (a sum paid to an official or other person in authority to induce him either to do or refrain from doing a certain action), *tsang* or squeeze is simply what such an official keeps for himself when money or other wealth passes through his hands. An example given in Boulais 1528 is the recovery through official action of stolen goods and then the retention by the responsible official of a portion of the goods before making restitution of them to their rightful owner. Boulais 1529 provides a table of the punishment to be given for taking varying amounts of squeeze. To use the table, it is necessary to divide in half the amount of actual squeeze in a particular case and then to use the resulting figure as the basis for calculating the punishment. The lightest punishment listed, for example, is 20 blows of the small bamboo, which corresponds to a single ounce of silver. Since the single ounce, in turn, represents only half of the amount squeezed, the 20 blows are actually a punishment for having squeezed two ounces. Likewise, the maximum punishment of 100 blows of the heavy bamboo and three years penal servitude is specified for 400 or more ounces, or, translated into actual fact, this is the punishment for having taken 800 or more ounces in squeeze. This table is the basis for the 100 blows of the heavy bamboo given to the offender in our case, as per the procedure specified in Boulais 515, applied to him analogously.]

[We have seen that the Board of Punishments, before applying Boulais 515, rules out the applicability of Boulais 1716, under which 100 blows and three years penal servitude is the punishment for anyone deliberately cutting a (government-maintained) river dike. Curiously enough, however, the Board ignores the very next sentence in the same statute, in which a two-degree lesser punishment (80 blows and two years penal servitude) is specified for anyone who similarly cuts the irrigation dike of ·a private person. Why does the Board disregard this clause of the statute, which directly concerns the damaging of private irrigation systems, and sentence the offender instead by analogy to Boulais 515, which seems much less germane, thereby reducing his punishment to 100 blows? Is it because the offender, under Boulais 515, is obligated in addition to pay the restoration cost of 160 silver ounces, whereas Boulais 1716, rather strangely, makes no mention of any such reparation? Or is there some other less creditable motivation?]

51. UNAUTHORIZED EATING OF FRUITS TAKEN FROM FIELDS AND ORCHARDS
[Statutory References: Staunton 99, Boulais 516]

Case 51.1, 1792. Memorandum.
Reported in HAHL 5.7/21a–b.

The governor of Kiangsi has memorialized concerning a case in which Teng Yü-shu beat to death Wen Shui-tzu. In accordance with imperial edict, the case has now been transmitted to the Statutes Commission for determining whether it should be treated as a killing in an affray or an unauthorized killing.

[For killing in an affray (Boulais 1268) the penalty is strangulation after the assizes. "Unauthorized killing" *(shan sha)*, although not the subject of detailed discussion in any single statute or sub-statute, is mentioned a number of times in the Code, usually in conjunction with "unauthorized injuring" *(shan shang)*. Imperial Chinese law categorizes two ways in which a private individual may take the law into his own hands to kill a wrongdoer: (a) the individual may kill the wrongdoer in the heat of passion or under the pressure of emergency, in which case the punishment for so doing is minimal or nonexistent; (b) he may kill the wrongdoer later on in cold blood, in which case his act constitutes "unauthorized killing" and is punishable usually—though not invariably—as would be killing in an affray, by strangulation after the assizes. Examples are: the master of a house who kills a nocturnal intruder immediately upon detecting him incurs no penalty, but if after apprehending him he then "unauthorizedly" kills him, the penalty is 100 blows of the heavy bamboo and three years penal servitude (Boulais 1199); a husband who kills on the spot the would-be rapist of his wife incurs no penalty, but if he unauthorizedly kills him later, the penalty for so doing is strangulation after the assizes (Boulais 1238); someone who kills a wrongdoer while that wrongdoer resists arrest incurs no penalty, but if he unauthorizedly kills him following arrest or kills him despite the wrongdoer's nonresistance to arrest, the penalty is the same as that for killing in an affray (Boulais 1659 and, for the clauses on unauthorized killing, 1659a). Other similar references may be found, especially in the sections on adultery, rape, and arrest of wrongdoers. Many of them, however, do not appear in the abbreviated Boulais translations or belong to sub-statutes that have been completely omitted by Boulais.]

The Commission has accordingly examined two similar cases. The first, reported from Honan in the fifth month of this year, is one in which Ch'eng Jen-wu, having been scolded by Chao Wen-k'o for picking some persimmons growing on the land of a third person, reviled Chao in turn until the latter, enraged, gave Ch'eng a kick from which Ch'eng died. The report makes clear that Ch'eng had picked only a few persimmons in broad daylight in open land so that his act is not comparable to that of genuine theft. Chao was therefore sentenced to strangulation [after the assizes] for having killed Ch'eng in an affray.

A second case from Shensi is that of Wu Hsiao-meng who, on finding Liu Yang-erh and another person picking beans from his (Wu's) field, gave Liu a kick from which Liu died. Wu was accordingly sentenced to strangulation [after the assizes] for unauthorized killing. Both these sentences have received imperial endorsement.

The two cases are similar in that both involved the picking of fruit or vegetables from another person's fields, and both resulted in the offender's death through assault. Careful analysis, however, also reveals significant differences. Thus, the act of Ch'eng Jen-wu consisted merely of picking a few persimmons from a field as he was passing along a road and so was not comparable to genuine theft. Hence, Chao was convicted of killing him in an affray. [See Boulais 1268 above. Had Ch'eng been adjudged a thief and thereby a wrongdoer *(tsui jen)*, his reviling of Chao would have placed him in the special category of a wrongdoer who resists arrest, which in turn, according to the relevant statute (Boulais 1659), would have caused Chao to be exempted from any penalty for killing him.]

Liu Yang-erh's case, on the other hand, did constitute genuine theft, since he and Liu Fa-erh [perhaps his brother?] had planned in advance to steal the beans and had each brought separate bags with them for that purpose. Hence Wu was convicted of un-authorizedly killing a wrongdoer. [Liu's status as a thief made him ipso facto a wrongdoer, but he was not a wrongdoer who offered any resistance to arrest. Hence Wu's killing him falls under the above-mentioned statute Boulais 1659a, which provides strangulation after the assizes for one who unauthorizedly kills a wrongdoer who does not resist arrest.]

In the present case the person who was killed, Wen Shui-tzu, was a mere boy of 13 when, happening to pass Teng Yü-shu's pear orchard along the road, he picked three pears from it for himself. On hearing Teng's shouts, Wen threw the pears away. Teng, however, then tried to drag Wen to court, whereupon Wen raised his rake against Teng. Teng then hit Wen back and killed him.

The governor of Kiangsi, in reporting this case, has pointed out that Wen's deed in picking the pears was that of a young ignorant boy, and therefore he may not properly be adjudged a wrongdoer *(tsui jen)*. Hence, the governor has sentenced Teng for killing Wen under the statute on killing in an affray. In view of the similarity between this case and that cited above in which Chao was likewise convicted under the same statute, it would seem that the governor's sentence may be approved.

[The present Wen-Teng case agrees with the above cited Ch'eng-Chao case in that the victims in both (Wen and Ch'eng) offered resistance to their killers (Wen by raising his rake, Ch'eng by reviling), but neither of them was adjudged to be a thief and therefore a wrongdoer; hence both were the victims of a simple killing in an affray. In the second cited case, on the contrary, the victim, Liu, offered no resistance, but he was in fact adjudged to be a thief and therefore a wrongdoer. Hence his killing properly fell under the statute on unauthorizedly killing a wrongdoer who does not resist arrest. It is remarkable to find the eminent Statutes Commission going to such pains to analyze the difference between the two offenses because the punishment for both is identical: strangulation after the assizes.]

[Gleaning in another person's field as a cause leading to homicide appears also in cases 14.1 and 260.1. That homicide could result from the taking of three pears perhaps reflects the economy of scarcity of the average Chinese peasant, for whom every bit of foodstuff is precious.]

52. MARRIAGE
[Statutory References: Staunton 101, Boulais 538–554]

Case 52.2, 1822. Metropolitan Leading Case from the Department for Kuangsi of the Board of Punishments.
Reported in HAHL 5.7/22b.

The general commandant of the gendarmerie of Peking has reported a case in which Erh-niu, a daughter of the Chao family, had sex relations with her fiancé, Chang Hsüeh-erh, prior to entering his family as a bride. The Chao family therefore broke off her engagement and betrothed her to another party, but when this happened, Chang secretly eloped with her.

The Code prescribes no specific punishment for elopement by a couple prior to marriage. Were the case to be judged by analogy to the sub-statute dealing with the situation in which a girl's family breaks off her engagement, thereby causing the family of her fiancé to abduct her, this would merely result in a punishment of light bambooing. [Fifty blows of the light bamboo is the punishment stipulated by Boulais 547 for the head of a family which thus abducts a previously engaged girl.]

Because Chang Hsüeh-erh has now taken Chao Erh-niu for himself, it would seem best to sentence him to 100 blows of the heavy bamboo, under the sub-statute [Boulais 553, repeated in 1725] which provides that if an engaged boy and girl have sex relations prior to marriage, they are to be punished by analogy to the statute [Boulais 1503] concerning disobedience shown by offspring to instructions of parents or grandparents. [Here (and again in case 52.3) only the boy is punished, though the substatute stipulates punishment for boy and girl alike. Boulais 1725 quotes a commentary to the effect that inasmuch as the couple are not being punished directly for sexual immorality, but only by analogy to a case of disobedience to parental instructions, the girl is therefore permitted to pay a monetary redemption for the punishment of 100 blows which she, like the boy, would otherwise receive. However, no statement to this effect appears in the sub-statute itself.]

Case 52.3, 1822. Metropolitan Leading Case from the Department for Kuangtung of the Board of Punishments.
Reported in HAHL 5.7/22b.

The general commandant of the gendarmerie of Peking has reported a case in which Niu-erh, a daughter of the Tai family, had sex relations with her fiancé, Hu Liu-wu [prior to formal marriage but] after she had entered his family as a *t'ung-yang hsi.* [Literally, "Daughter-in-law cared for in youth (by her future husband's family)," in other words, a girl who from an early age lives in the family of her prospective husband. The primary reason for this institution, which was widespread in China, was the poverty of the prospective bride. Although she was thus taken care of from an early age, her status in her future husband's family was sometimes little better than that of a slave.]

Because, as a *t'ung-yang hsi,* the girl had already entered the family of her future husband, her situation is different from that of the usual engaged girl who has not yet entered her future husband's family. Hu Liu-wu should therefore be sentenced under the sub-statute [Boulais 553, repeated in 1725] which provides that if an engaged boy and girl have sex relations prior to marriage, they are to be punished by analogy to the statute [Boulais 1503] concerning disobedience by offspring to instructions of parents or grandparents; however, this punishment of 100 blows of the heavy bamboo shall be reduced by one degree to 90 blows because of the above-mentioned special circumstances. [See comments at end of preceding case. In order to effect this reduction of punishment, it would seem that the judgment should have been made "by analogy to" rather than directly under Boulais 553.]

59. MARRIAGE OF AN OFFICIAL TO A WOMAN UNDER HIS JURISDICTION [4]
[Statutory References: Staunton 110, Boulais 602]

Case 59.1, 1798. Approved Case from the Kiangsu Printed Edition of General Circulars.
Reported in HAHL 5.8/4a.

The Board of Civil Office has noted the disposition of a case by the Board of Punishments, in which Mrs. Wang née Shih, a housewife of Ta-hsing hsien, induced Mrs. Hsü, wife of Hsü Ch'ao-t'ai, a Kuangtung military provincial graduate, to state falsely of herself that she (Mrs. Hsü) was a widow, in order thereby to be sold as a concubine to Sun Huai-fen.

[The interest of the Board of Civil Office in this case stems from the fact that the offender, Sun, is an official. The locale of the case is Peking, Ta-hsing hsien being the eastern of the two *hsien* or districts into which Peking in Ch'ing times was administratively divided.]

The Board of Punishments has found that, according to statute

[4] This statute, intended to reduce the occurrence of nepotism or other corruption in local administration, prohibits any prefect or magistrate of a prefecture (*fu*) or district (*hsien*) from marrying or taking as a concubine a woman belonging to the said prefecture or district.

[Boulais 602], an official who marries a woman under his jurisdiction or takes her as a concubine is to be punished by 80 blows of the heavy bamboo. Moreover, according to statute [Boulais 71], if an official commits an offense in a private rather than an official capacity and such offense is punishable by 80 blows of the heavy bamboo, the said punishment is to be commuted to a three-degree reduction in official rank and transfer to another position.

In the present case, Sun Huai-fen relied upon a go-between [Mrs. Wang] for buying Mrs. Hsü as his concubine. However, when he learned that Mrs. Hsü still had a husband, he at once sent her back again. Being a newly appointed subprefect, second class, for grain and horses for Shun-t'ien fu, his position, although not identical with those of ordinary prefects or magistrates, is nonetheless comparable with them. Moreover, he did in fact purchase a concubine pertaining to the area in which he held office. In view of these circumstances, it seems appropriate that his punishment should be somewhat reduced [from the standard penalty cited above] and therefore consist of a one-degree reduction in official rank [instead of three degrees], coupled with transfer to another position.

[Because Shun-t'ien fu was the metropolitan prefecture in which Peking was situated, Sun's position as a secondary official in this metropolitan center was indeed different from, though still analogous to, the positions of the usual prefects or magistrates in rural China (the officials who are specifically referred to in Boulais 602). This distinction no doubt explains the lighter than usual punishment given to Sun, which theoretically should have required the Board to apply the statute analogically rather than directly. It is strange that the judgment includes no punishment either for Mrs. Hsü's husband, the military provincial graduate (without whose acquiescence the sale of Mrs. Hsü as concubine could hardly have been carried out) or for the go-between in the affair, Mrs. Wang. Although Boulais 602 does not itself refer either to husband or go-between, Boulais 1595, on the contrary, specifies 90 blows of the heavy bamboo for a husband who tolerates his wife's adulterous affair with another man, and Boulais 1597 also states that a husband who, in return for money, permits his wife to be taken by another man, is to receive 100 blows, and that a one-degree lesser punishment of 80 blows is to go to any go-between involved. In the present case we are told only that Mrs. Hsü was sold to Sun for money, but not to whom the money went. In short, there seems to be more to this case than the official record reveals.]

60. ABDUCTION OF WOMEN OF RESPECTABLE FAMILY
[Statutory References: Staunton 112, Boulais 605–618]

Case 60.5, 1819. Leading Case.
Reported in HAHL 5.8/5a–b.

The governor of Fukien has reported a case involving a feud between the Chan and Yeh clans. [Such clan feuds were not infrequent in Fukien and some other southern provinces.] A male member of the Chan clan, Chan Chin, happening to see a female member of the Yeh clan, Mrs. Yeh née Ch'en, passing through his village, ordered a woman of his own clan, Mrs. Chan née Yeh, to intercept Mrs. Yeh and bring her into his house. [Although it is not stated, we may strongly suspect that this Mrs. Chan was in fact Chan's own wife. This would explain why she was at his house and why he could order her to do what she did. Her maiden name indicates that she had been born a member of the rival Yeh clan.]

Once Mrs. Yeh was inside the house, Chan raped her. This, however, he had not originally intended to do. It only came about through his having had her intercepted and brought inside.

Chan Chin is to be sentenced under the statute [Boulais 606] on abducting and having sex relations with a woman, with, however, the penalty therein stipulated [strangulation after the assizes] reduced by one degree to maximum exile [exile at a distance of 3,000 li]. As for Mrs. Chan, since she played no leading part in the abduction and rape, but only obeyed the command to detain the other woman, she should be given a sentence one degree less than that given to Chan, that is, maximum [three years] penal servitude.

[An accomplice normally receives a punishment one degree less than the ringleader. See Boulais 110. If Mrs. Chan was indeed Chan's wife, she was punished for doing what she had no alternative but to do: obeying her husband and then, in all likelihood, witnessing him rape the other woman who belonged to the rival clan from which she herself had originally come. Why the Board grants Chan a reduction from the normal penalty is unclear. In so doing, it neglects here, as in many other instances, to apply the statute analogically instead of directly, as it theoretically ought to do.]

61. MARRIAGE OF AN OFFICIAL TO A SINGSONG GIRL

[Statutory References: Staunton 113, Boulais 603]

Case 61.1, 1828. Leading Case from the Department for Hunan and Hupei of the Board of Punishments.
Reported in HAHL Supplement 30.3/18b.

The general commandant of the gendarmerie of Peking has reported that Te-ying-ê, an imperial clansman, has bought as a concubine for himself a singing girl [a female entertainer] from the streets who is no better than an ordinary singsong prostitute. By analogy to the statute [Boulais 603] concerning officials who marry singsong girls or take them as concubines, Te-ying-ê is sentenced to 60 blows of the heavy bamboo, the said blows to be actually administered without any privilege of monetary redemption. [Boulais 603 also provides, of course, for the dissolution of the improper liaison.]

[This case, involving as it does the actual corporal punishment of an imperial clansman, illustrates how strictly the code of noblesse oblige could operate for members of the ruling group, especially on matters of sexual morality. The fact that the clansman was sentenced "by analogy to" rather than directly under Boulais 603 presumably means that, despite his imperial blood, he held no official position himself, whereas the statute explicitly names officials as the object of its prohibition.]

80. SALT LAWS [5]
[Statutory References: Staunton 141, Boulais 704–716]

Case 80.20, 1819. Leading Case.
Reported in HAHL 6.10/10a.

The governor-general of Hunan and Hupei has reported a case involving the private sale of salt by Liu Heng-ch'uan. Although none of Liu's individual sales ever exceeded 50 to 60 catties [1 catty = about 1⅓ lbs.], he has already been doing this for twenty years, thus truly being a habitual offender.

Therefore, by analogy to the sub-statute on an unlicensed private sale of 3,000 or more catties of salt [Boulais 713a], Liu Heng-ch'uan is now sentenced to military exile at a very near distance [2,000 li].

[The reason for the application of this sub-statute analogically rather than directly is that, although none of the offender's sales of salt individually equalled the figure of 3,000 catties mentioned by the sub-statute, they cumulatively, in the course of twenty years, no doubt greatly exceeded this figure.]

Case 80.23, 1825. Leading Case.
Reported in HAHL 6.10/10a.

The governor-general of Chihli has reported a case in which Wang T'ing-hsüan, a native of another province, dug up salt-impregnated soil from which, by boiling, he extracted unlicensed salt for his own consumption. Investigation shows that he sold none of this salt to others for profit. However, when approached by a salt examiner, he resisted arrest by the examiner and inflicted on him some injury.

By analogy to the statute [Boulais 708] on buying and consuming unlicensed private salt, Wang T'ing-hsüan is now sentenced to

[5] For more than two thousand years salt has been a monopoly commodity in imperial China, the private production and sale of which has been controlled by government licensing. Thus this section, like others (see especially case 86.2), illustrates the extent to which economic activity was subjected to governmental controls in the old China.

100 blows of the heavy bamboo. Furthermore, under the statute on resisting arrest [Boulais 1658], said punishment is to be increased by two degrees, making a total punishment of 70 blows of the heavy bamboo and one and one half years of penal servitude.

[Probably Wang lived near the salt flats flanking the North China coast near Tientsin, which would make it easy for him to produce salt for his own use. We may suspect that there would have been no trouble had he not resisted the salt examiner. The statute is applied to Wang analogically because it deals only with the buying and consuming of unlicensed salt but not its manufacture. Boulais, in an introductory "observation" to this section (Boulais 704), asserts that ordinary people were permitted by the government to produce salt without licensing, even though licenses were required for its sale. The present case contradicts this assertion, however, and also to some extent runs counter to a sub-statute (Boulais 714) stating that soldiers and civilians who are impoverished and in difficulties may be permitted to carry unlicensed salt on their backs and exchange it for grain in order to support themselves. The ambiguity of the sub-statute lies in its failure to define "impoverished and in difficulties." The phraseology suggests, however, that it may have been framed to deal with temporary emergencies rather than long-term conditions.]

82. VIOLATION OF PROHIBITION OF USURY
[Statutory References: Staunton 149, Boulais 729–739]

Case 82.6, 1831. Leading Case from the Department for Kuangtung of the Board of Punishments.
Reported in HAHL Supplement 30.4/4b.

The general commandant of the gendarmerie of Peking has submitted a memorial in which he reports that Wang Hsün, a lieutenant appointed to the garrison at Suchow [in Anhui], now already dismissed, had [while still in Peking] used his certificate of official appointment [his document of official credentials] as a pledge with which to secure repayment of a loan from a certain person. There being no article specifically covering this offense, Wang Hsün has been sentenced to 100 blows of the heavy bam-

boo under the statute on violating imperial decrees [Boulais 274].
Since he has already been removed from his position, there is no
need for further deliberation on his case.

[The classification of this case under the section on usury seems
peculiar since it has nothing to do with usury as such. It would
seem from this case that the statute on violating imperial decrees
functions as a catch-all for offenses not otherwise clearly inter-
dicted, in a manner not unlike the more commonly cited catch-all
statute on doing what ought not to be done (Boulais 1656). A
third statute, also, seems to be used similarly, viz., Boulais 1655,
penalizing violation of ordinances (*ling*) of less force than a formal decree or law.]

83. SALE OR USE OF PROPERTIES GIVEN IN TRUST
[Statutory References: Staunton 150, Boulais 740–744]

Case 83.1, 1834. Memorandum.
Reported in HAHL Supplement 30.4/4b–4a.

The Department for Honan has examined a case in which Chao
P'an-ming, an innkeeper, used money entrusted to him for safekeeping by Chao Te-ch'üan with which to buy flour, intending to
return the money as soon as he had resold the flour. When Chao
Te-ch'üan asked to have the money back, however, the defendant
was not yet in a position to repay it. At the same time he was
fearful that if word got around that he was making private use of
money belonging to the guests at his inn, it would harm his business. He therefore falsely told Chao Te-ch'üan that he would
have to consult his business partner about repaying the money.
This statement put Chao into such a nervous state that he went
off and hanged himself.

This Department's investigation indicates that when Chao P'an-
ming used the money entrusted to him by Chao Te-ch'üan, he
definitely intended to repay it, so that his act differs from that of
deliberate appropriation of money [committed without intention
to repay]. Likewise the fact that his act put Chao Te-ch'üan into
such a nervous state as to bring him to suicide was entirely un-

foreseen by the defendant. Under the statute [Boulais 740] concerning a person who falsely claims to have lost the property entrusted to him by another, the penalty for so doing is one degree less than that for ordinary theft. Certainly the defendant's unauthorized use of money entrusted to him by one of his inn visitors, thereby leading to the latter's suicide, was detrimental to the welfare of travelers. Nonetheless, the defendant may be sentenced only by analogy to the sub-statute concerning a thief whose act of theft induces his victim to commit suicide. The punishment therein provided will be adequate as a public warning. [Boulais 1128 specifies 100 blows of the heavy bamboo and three years penal servitude as the normal penalty for this offense, with, however, the possibility of higher penalty if the amount stolen is very large, if the thief has been guilty of previous thefts or if the theft is committed by a band rather than a single individual.]

The governor of Honan, however, has added one degree of punishment to the penal servitude [provided by the foregoing sub-statute], thereby sentencing the defendant to life exile. Thus, the penalty for inducing a person to commit suicide by selling or using the properties which one has received in trust from him is made even more severe than the penalty for inducing a person to commit suicide by stealing from him. Such a sentence cannot be accepted as fair.

Chao P'an-ming's sentence should accordingly be changed to 100 blows of the heavy bamboo and three years penal servitude, by analogy to the foregoing sub-statute concerning suicide occasioned by theft. Furthermore, according to the defendant's testimony, he is the sole adult son of aged parents and therefore, under statute, eligible for the privilege of remaining at home in order to care for them. [Cases 11.1 and 11.4 indicate how difficult it was to obtain this privilege in capital cases. The present case and case 42.1 make it evident that the privilege was accorded much more readily in cases involving less than capital punishment.]

The proposal, already presented by the governor in his report, that the defendant's punishment be increased by one degree to 100 blows of the heavy bamboo and life exile at a distance of

2,000 li and that he be denied the privilege of remaining at home to care for his parents, need not be deliberated upon further.

[Note the analytical or systematic insistence that the penalty for inducing suicide by breach of trust be no greater than the penalty for inducing suicide by theft.]

86. STABILIZATION OF COMMODITY PRICES BY MARKET SUPERVISORS
[Statutory References: Staunton 153, Boulais 754]

Case 86.2, 1831. Leading Case from the Department for Kuangtung of the Board of Punishments.
Reported in HAHL Supplement 30.4/6b.

The general commandant of the gendarmerie of Peking has presented a memorial concerning K'ang Kao, assistant department magistrate, first class, for Pa-chou [about 50 miles south of Peking], who ordered his underlings to go to Peking and there buy for him 12 *shih* [about 33 English bushels] of rice.

Investigation by this Board reveals a sub-statute [Boulais 754b] in which limits are imposed upon the amount of rice a rural person coming to Peking is permitted to buy. [Among many other provisions, this sub-statute states that a rural person who enters Peking and there buys more than one *shih* (about 2.75 English bushels) of rice is liable to 100 blows of the heavy bamboo.] Neither this nor any other sub-statute, however, says anything about officials close to the capital who may do the same, nor is this possibility touched upon in the regulations of the Board of Civil Office.

The original purpose of the sub-statute prohibiting rural people from buying more than one *shih* of rice in the capital was to prevent improper trafficking by dishonest merchants. The official under consideration, however, bought the rice simply in order to feed his soldiers who were engaged in important public construction. Thus there is no indication of any improper trafficking on his part. On the contrary, his act was intended for the public good and as such was quite different from that of an ordinary rural person buying more than the allowed amount of rice in the capital.

The fact remains, nonetheless, that more than one *shih* of rice was as a consequence taken out of the capital, so that it would be impolitic to grant complete exemption of penalty. Deliberation leads us to conclude that K'ang Kao should, under the statute on doing what ought not to be done, be sentenced to the lighter penalty there provided, namely 40 blows of the light bamboo. [See Boulais 1656 for this catch-all statute, under which 40 blows of the light bamboo or 80 blows of the heavy one are provided for lesser or greater offenses not otherwise covered in the Code.] We transmit this case to the Board of Civil Office for its consideration in accordance with regulations.

[This case is a good illustration of the high degree of social regularization attempted by all major Chinese dynasties, which in the economic sphere led already in early times to such institutions as the "ever-normal granary." Because the rice used to feed the population of the capital was almost entirely transported from the distant south over the Grand Canal, the government inevitably objected to any kind of free market participated in by outsiders which might upset the planned balance between supply and demand. The imposition of economic controls in a city the size of Peking was facilitated in part by the inspection of commodities entering or leaving the city at the several city gates. In part it was also made possible by the official appointment—made in other large cities as well as in Peking—of prominent local merchants to serve as "market supervisors" (*shih ssu*). These supervisors, who are mentioned in the title of this section and explained in Boulais 749–750, were members of various branches of trade who represented their fellow merchants in dealings with the authorities. They were responsible to the authorities for collecting taxes from their business colleagues, whose numbers and activities they also controlled by issuing licenses to them without which they were not permitted to conduct business. The fees from these licenses provided the supervisors with an important source of income. Like the heads of the *pao* and *li* units into which the population at large was divided (see case 44.1), these business heads served as important links between their respective groups and the governmental apparatus, even though they themselves were quite outside of the formal official hierarchy. The political technique of thus using extra-official agents to control various segments of the population is of long standing in China and has clear analogues today. In 1949, for example, when the Chinese Communists occupied the important port of Tientsin, they imposed tax quotas upon various commercial groups, including Western businessmen, and then left it to the representatives of these groups to collect as best they could the amounts required from their colleagues.]

87. RESTRAINT OF MARKET TRANSACTIONS [6]
[Statutory References: Staunton 154, Boulais 755]

Case 87.1, 1788. From the Collection of Seen Leading Cases. *Reported in HAHL 6.10/20b–21a.*

The governor-general of Kiangsu, Kiangsi, and Anhui has memorialized concerning Hou Ming-chang, a native of Shao-hsing, Chekiang, and sailor on the Grand Canal rice boats. [The so-called "tribute rice" sent to Peking from Central and South China was transported in government boats over the Grand Canal until the development of maritime traffic in the nineteenth century made the canal obsolete.] When his fleet had arrived at the Li-yün lock at Su-ch'ien, Kiangsu, and was about to pass through, it occurred to Hou Ming-chang that since the boat cargoes were heavier than in previous years, it might be a good idea to demand increased wages. He accordingly assembled ten or more other sailors, went with them to bannerman Sung Ping-ho on the first boat, and insisted on increased compensation before taking the boats through the lock. [A Chinese canal "lock" does not operate hydraulically, but consists of a ramp leading from one water level

---

[6] As becomes evident from the cases that follow, this title has a much wider connotation than would be expected from it in a Western context, so that wage disputes and attempted strikes are included among "restraints on market transactions." It is striking that contrary to what one might expect from the title, all three cases have to do with public rather than private enterprise—the first two with transportation of government grain on the Grand Canal, the third with fraudulent removal of grain from a government granary.

to another, up or down which the boats must be dragged by man- or animal-power.] Having no alternative, Sung Ping-ho offered to pay an additional 3,600 cash [about 3.6 ounces of silver] per boat, but Hou Ming-chang said it had to be 6,000 cash. On being refused, Hou ordered his sailor band to start an uproar, which continued even after Lieutenant Ts'ai Luan, an officer of the grain transport escort, rushed to the scene and shouted to them to stop. He was followed by Yün T'ien-pao, a lieutenant expectant who had been commissioned to be at the lock to repress any possible disturbances and expedite the flow of traffic. After shouting to the troublemakers to stop, Lieutenant Yün advanced to make arrests, whereupon Hou Ming-chang beat him with a stick and inflicted many injuries. This is certainly the height of lawlessness.

As a functionary of the grain transport escort especially commissioned by it to repress any possible disturbances at the lock, Yün T'ien-pao's status was in no way different from that of the lock's permanent commanding officer. Hou Ming-chang is accordingly sentenced under the sub-statute [Boulais 1369a] on civilians or soldiers who, unwilling to submit to arrest, attack and injure a presiding official. Under this sub-statute he, as the wicked ringleader, is to suffer immediate decapitation, with his head to be exposed in a cage on the bank of the Grand Canal.

[The extreme severity with which resistance to authority is here punished is noteworthy and should be compared with the treatment contained in the somewhat similar following case. The sub-statute's death penalty for a ringleader is applicable regardless of whether he kills or merely wounds an official. However, it makes no mention of exposure of the head as here specified. This added punishment, intended to have a deterrent effect upon the general populace, was most commonly applied to bandits and pirates.]

Hou's accessory, Liu Ssu, who joined with him in the attack but is now a fugitive, will be dealt with as soon as apprehended. [Strangulation after the assizes is the penalty provided by the same sub-statute for an accessory.]

Investigation indicates that another sailor, Yao Kuei, though not an actual participant in the attack, had previously helped

Hou Ming-chang to make the disturbance against bannerman Sung Ping-ho, which he then continued without any show of fear even after Lieutenant Ts'ai Luan shouted to him to stop. His penalty should be one degree less than the strangulation prescribed for the immediate accessory, which means that he is to be sentenced to exile. Under this category of punishment, however, he is to be given its most severe variety, namely deportation to Heilungkiang as a slave. Prior to deportation, moreover, he is to wear the cangue at the bank of the Grand Canal until the boats of his fleet repass the lock empty on their return trip southward.

The other offenders who belonged to the group but did not actually join in the disturbance itself are each to wear the cangue for two months and to receive 100 blows of the heavy bamboo.

Case 87.2, 1825. Leading Case.
Reported in HAHL 6.10/21a.

The governor of Chihli has reported a case concerning Tsou San, a boat tracker for the lighters of the grain transport administration who comes from another province. [The Grand Canal over which the "tribute rice" passed from the south to Peking had its terminus at T'ung-chou, where the rice was transshipped to lighters and taken by them the remaining ten miles over a lesser canal to Peking.] Finding that food prices were rising to a point where his wages no longer met the cost of living, Tsou San got the idea of assembling a group of fellow trackers and going with them to the supervisory bannerman to demand money. Going to the bannerman with his group and being ordered to stop by Lieutenant Jen Ta-heng, Tsou, brooking authority, outrageously started a disturbance which culminated in his and his followers' striking the lieutenant and tearing his official clothing.

The disturbance happened, however, only after the lighters had been brought to their final moorings, so that the grain transport suffered no interference in consequence. Nor was the offender's scheme to get more money in the nature of an obstructionist act done in order to extort money. Thus he is still deserving of leniency.

Tsou San should therefore be sentenced under the sub-statute

[Boulais 755a] which provides that if rowdies among grain-boat trackers form a group to press for money, and if this group attacks somebody, their ringleader will be sent into military exile at a nearby frontier. For Tsou San, however, this punishment is to be reduced by one degree to 100 blows of the heavy bamboo and three years penal servitude. [For the manner of making one-degree reductions among the three highest categories of punishment, see Chapter III, end of section 9.]

As for Tsou's accessories, Wang Wu and others, they are each [under the same sub-statute] to receive 100 blows of the heavy bamboo and to wear the cangue for two months on the bank of the Grand Canal.

[In view of the many close similarities between this case and the preceding one, the differing attitudes toward them on the part of the judicial authorities are particularly striking. In the present case, the trackers are sentenced under a sub-statute especially designed for unruly trackers, whereas the sailors of the preceding case have no such sub-statute and are sentenced instead under a more general and, incidentally, severer sub-statute. Aside from this difference between the two cases, the question arises whether other differences are adequate to explain the differing attitudes of their respective judicial authorities.]

Case 87.3, 1831. From the Peking Gazette.
Reported in HAHL 6.10/21a–b.

A junior censor of the Office for Scrutiny of Metropolitan Officials, Section for the Board of Revenue, has memorialized concerning Hsü Chiu, a former non-civil service employee of the Wan-an government granary [in Peking]. Following his dismissal from the granary, Hsü joined with Chang Lao to open a grain shop. Previous to this, beginning in 1829, there had been repeated instances of members of the Banner troops selling the grain coupons issued to them for obtaining food rations from this granary. Hence Hsü Chiu, acting in concert with Chang Lao, conceived the idea of buying up more than 300 of these coupons with which they were able to obtain more than 1,000 *shih* [close to 3,000 English bushels] of grain from the granary under false pretenses.

Examination [by the Board of Punishments] reveals no statute or sub-statute specifically covering this offense. The offender, however, by buying grain coupons while yet employed by the granary and before his establishment of a grain shop and by then holding on to them in order later to acquire grain through them under false pretenses, has been guilty of dishonest trading, monopolistic practices, and fraud. His acts differ in no essential particular from those involved in imposing restraints on market transactions in order thereby to acquire monopolistic profits [Boulais 755]. The testimony indicates that on every *shih* of grain he made excess profits of more than 200 cash, amounting in all to more than 120 ounces of silver.

Hsü Chiu is further guilty of having hoarded 440 *shih* [about 1,200 English bushels] of millet, but since the penalty for this is merely bambooing, it requires no deliberation by this Board. [A sub-statute, Boulais 754a, states that private grain shops in Peking are legally permitted to store only 160 *shih* (about 440 English bushels) of each separate grain; hoarding a greater amount exposes the grain proprietor to punishment under the statute (Boulais 274) on violating imperial decrees (100 blows of the heavy bamboo).]

Irrespective of this offense, however, Hsü Chiu could be sentenced by analogy to the statute on restraint of market transactions in order to acquire monopolistic profits under the clause stating that punishment is to be calculated according to the amount of profit, this calculation being the same as that used for determining punishment for theft, with the one exception that the highest punishment is to be restricted to maximum life exile. This means that Hsü Chiu should be sentenced to 100 blows of the heavy bamboo and life exile at a distance of 3,000 li. [This statute, as given in Boulais 755, is so greatly telescoped as to omit all the details given here (as well as several other clauses). For the table of punishments for theft, see Boulais 1119. Hsü Chiu's illegal gains of more than 120 ounces of silver would, if he had committed theft, make him liable to strangulation after the assizes, but because the corresponding punishment for restraint of market operations is, as we have just seen, limited to maximum life exile, this is accordingly what Hsü Chiu received.]

Chang Lao, since he collaborated in buying the coupons and getting grain for them from the granary, and also shared in the profits, ranks as an accessory. He should accordingly be sentenced to 100 blows of the heavy bamboo and three years penal servitude. [The penalty for an accessory is normally one degree less than for a principal. See Boulais 110.]

Neither man is to be permitted to remain at home to care for his aged parents as their sole adult son. [For this privilege, see Boulais 96–106 and cases 11.1 and 11.4. The blanket denial of it here in advance, as well as references to it elsewhere, suggest that it was a device invoked fairly frequently in order to escape full punishment.]

As for the granary employee Hou Wu [presumably the person immediately responsible within the granary for allowing the grain coupons to be used improperly], his failure to detect the false pretenses under which the grain was taken makes him liable to punishment. He is presently a fugitive but will be dealt with as soon as he is apprehended.

As to the granary superintendent and granary inspector who showed themselves wanting in vigilance, it is requested that they both be handed over to the Board of Civil Office for judgment. [This board, in cooperation with the Board of Punishments, commonly determined the penalties for offenses committed by officials.]

The names of the members of the Banner troops who sold the coupons are unavailable so that there is no way of tracing them. Lest, however, such selling of grain coupons become an established custom, notices should be circulated to all Banner forces, stating that whenever such coupons are issued, special deputies are to be sent by the Banners to receive them, who are to be forbidden to sell them.

88. DESTRUCTION OF ALTARS DEDICATED TO MAJOR SACRIFICES
[Statutory References: Staunton 158, Boulais 767–771]

Case 88.1, 1819. Leading Case.
Reported in HAHL 6.10/22a.

The governor of Chekiang has reported a case involving Yeh Lin, a licentiate [holder of a first degree] in the civil service examinations who, because of some offense, was denied the right of wearing the cap and gown going with this degree [that is, was deprived of his degree] and who also was expelled from his father's house because he had incurred a private debt. At this juncture he unauthorizedly entered the Temple of Confucius, where he wailed and complained until he reached such a state that he finally hit and damaged the altar tablet of the Highest Sage and First Teacher [Confucius].

By analogy to the statute on destroying or damaging altars dedicated to major sacrifices [Boulais 767], Yeh Lin is sentenced to 100 blows of the heavy bamboo and life exile at a distance of 2,000 li.

[It is unclear why sentence is pronounced only "by analogy to" rather than directly under the statute. Conceivably it may have been done on the narrowly literal grounds that the statute applies only to altars, whereas Yeh's act was against the tablet of Confucius standing on the altar. A more likely explanation is that the "major sacrifices" are those to Heaven, Earth, the ancestors of the imperial house, and the Gods of Soil and Grain, whereas the rites to Confucius constitute only a second class sacrifice (Boulais 758).]

89. SACRILEGE TOWARD THE SPIRITS
[Statutory References: Staunton 161, Boulais 774–778]

Case 89.1, 1817. Leading Case
Reported in HAHL 6.10/22a.

The governor of Kiangsi has reported a case in which Liu Chen-yao honored the birthday of Hsü the True Man by putting on theatricals for the public and setting off fireworks from a pavilion on East Mountain which were viewed by a vast crowd. [Hsü the True Man was a Taoist saint, Hsü Hsün (died ca. A.D. 280), noted for his use of Taoist arts to ward off harm from the people. His home was in Nanchang, capital of Kiangsi, and it was probably there that this birthday celebration took place.] At the conclusion of the fireworks a sudden downpour of heavy rain caused the crowd to flee in disorder, whereupon, owing to the crowding of the people along the steep and narrow mountain ledge, many fell to the ground and seventeen persons were trampled to death.

This Board finds that Liu's celebration of the birthday did not involve any religious procession in honor of the saint, nor did the trampling to death of the people take place until after the fireworks were over. [Boulais 781 states that the chief organizer of such a procession is liable to 100 blows of the heavy bamboo. The statute reflects the governmental dislike of popular religious observances attracting large crowds of people because of possible resulting disturbances; also the fact that many secret societies which were religiously based were at the same time politically anti-dynastic. This statute, nonetheless, was probably often tacitly ignored.]

The fact remains, however, that the defendant did put up a pavilion where fireworks attracting a large crowd were set off late at night. Accordingly, by analogy to the statute on violation of imperial decrees [Boulais 274], Liu Chen-yao should be sentenced to 100 blows of the heavy bamboo and wearing of the cangue for one month. [For the use of this statute as a convenient catch-all for offenses not otherwise clearly delimited by law, see case 82.6. Application of the statute analogically rather than directly permits its stipulated punishment of bambooing to be supplemented by wearing of the cangue.]

Yü Chung-mo and others, who bought and set off the fireworks at the orders of the defendant, should, as accessories, receive a one-degree reduction in penalty, namely 90 blows of the heavy bamboo and 25 days wearing of the cangue.

[This case does not involve overt sacrilege to any spirit, so that its classification under this section seems peculiar. A possible explanation, however, is that a birthday celebration which ends so disastrously brings ill fortune rather than honor to the saint or spirit for whom it is intended, and therefore is sacrilegious. Another fireworks case, also involving several deaths, is classified under a very different section (see case 166.3), and one that seems more relevant.]

Case 89.2, 1818. Leading Case.
Reported in HAHL 6.10/22a–b.

The governor of Shantung has reported that the Buddhist monk Ta-ch'ao, a native of another province, took advantage of the coming to his temple of the concubine of Wang Chia-hsiang to get her to go inside, where he spent the night with her. Sexual enticement, when done at such a place, is still worse than that done elsewhere. However, the fact that the offender did not in addition use his wiles to get possession of the woman's belongings means that he may be allowed a punishment less than the norm. Ta-ch'ao, therefore, should be punished one degree less than the punishment of military exile provided by the sub-statute [Boulais 777; repeated in part with verbal changes in 1626] concerning a Buddhist monk who entices a woman into sexual relations at a temple and then uses his wiles to gain possession of her belongings. Accordingly, Ta-ch'ao is sentenced to 100 blows of the heavy bamboo and three years penal servitude.

[This sentence is peculiar, since Boulais 777 (though in rather oblique and unclear language] specifies: (a) 70 blows of the heavy bamboo and one and one half years penal servitude for a monk who entices a woman into sexual relations at a temple; (b) military exile at a distant frontier for a monk who does the same and furthermore uses his wiles to gain possession of the woman's belongings. The Board of Punishments, by disregarding (a) in the present case and sentencing the offender instead under the first half of (b) to a punishment which for this reason is made one degree less than the punishment therein provided, is as a result giving the offender three years penal servitude when he should in actual fact receive only one and one half years under (a).]

[In this case, the emphasis is upon the *locale* of the offense; consequently, the penalty is correspondingly heavy. In cases 228.2 and 228.3, what is essentially the same offense, but minus the sacred locale, is punished by only one year of penal servitude and two months wearing of the cangue.]

92. PRIVATE POSSESSION OF PROHIBITED BOOKS
[Statutory References: Staunton 165, Boulais 816]

Case 92.1, 1832. Leading Case from the Department for Yunnan of the Board of Punishments.
Reported in HAHL Supplement 30.4/11b–12a.

The Censorate of the North City of Peking has transferred to this Department the case of Kuan Sung-t'ing, who bought miscellaneous small texts from an unknown person and sold them to bookstores within the city with the aim of making a profit. Because there is no article specifically covering this act, Kuan Sung-t'ing is sentenced to 100 blows of the heavy bamboo under the statute on violation of imperial decrees.

[For the use of this statute (Boulais 274) as a convenient catch-all for offenses not otherwise clearly delimited by law, see cases 82.6, 89.1, etc. One hundred blows of the heavy bamboo is the punishment prescribed in Boulais 816 for the private possession of "prohibited books," but the statute fails to define the term. There has been a long history of governmental attempts at thought control in China, however, notably in the eighteenth century, when allegedly anti-dynastic, anti-Manchu, anti other racial groups ethnically related to the Manchus, anti-Confucian, or pornographic books, were all banned by imperial decree and destroyed in large numbers. See L. C. Goodrich, *The Literary Inquisition of Ch'ien-lung* (Baltimore: Waverly Press, 1935). In the present case, the texts sold to and by Kuan were apparently innocuous in content, otherwise the statute on prohibited books would have been used against him. Yet it would also seem that his private buying and selling of texts was viewed with official suspicion (perhaps in part because it bypassed the proper channels for entering business; see case 86.2). Hence some kind of punishment was deemed advisable, and the statute on violating imperial decrees was a convenient means for providing it.]

93. MISBEHAVIOR IN CEREMONIES
[Statutory References: Staunton 168, Boulais 819]

Case 93.1, 1830. From the Peking Gazette.
Reported in HAHL 7.11/1a.

The Imperial Clan Court [an organization for handling all matters relating to members of the Ch'ing imperial clan] has memorialized that on the first day of the tenth month of this year, which is a day of sacrifice to the ancestors at the beginning of winter, Yung-k'ao and Hua-ying, both nobles of imperial lineage of the twelfth rank, neglected to make the offerings of silk expected of them at the sacrifices performed at the Imperial Ancestral Temple. The memorial requested that the two men be handed over to the Imperial Clan Court for judgment of guilt, and an imperial rescript approved this request, pointing out that the negligence of the two men was not comparable with [was worse than] ordinary carelessness.

The Imperial Clan Court has accordingly examined the regulations concerning sacrifice and requests that, as a warning to others, Yung-k'ao and Hua-ying be deprived of their positions as nobles of imperial lineage of the twelfth rank. An imperial rescript has approved this request and ordered the Imperial Clan Court to transmit the case to the Board of Punishments for judgment.

[Note that no statute is cited to support this sentence, nor does the punishment conform to the usual pattern of punishments. The reason, of course, is the special status of the offenders and the special organ which judges them. Even though the case is then passed to the Board of Punishments, the latter's judgment may safely be assumed to be concurring and nominal only. The punishment received by the offenders, though severe, is no more so than might be expected for a ritualistic violation, especially one having to do with the imperial ancestors.]

Case 93.2, 1834. From the Peking Gazette.
Reported in HAHL 7.11/1a–b.

The governor-general of Hupei and Hunan has memorialized concerning Chang Lei, the now dismissed district magistrate of Huang-p'o hsien [near Hankow, Hupei], who has been guilty of violating the regulations for the state sacrifices.

The Temple of Confucius of the said district has, outside its main gate, an outer enclosure surrounded by a secondary wall, through which pass two outer gates. An official coming to the Temple of Confucius to participate in the sacrifices must dismount from his sedan chair when it arrives outside one or the other of these outer gates.

On the occasion of the biannual spring and autumn sacrifice to Confucius, Chang Lei, as district magistrate, was being carried at dawn in a small sedan chair toward the Confucian temple. The curtain of the chair was closed because of heavy rain. On arriving outside of one of the two above-mentioned gates to the outer enclosure, the two chair bearers saw that so much rain had accumulated on the ground that there was no place to set down the chair. They therefore wrongly carried Chang Lei onward through the gate. Through the lowered curtain Chang caught a glimpse of what was happening and shouted to the bearers to stop, but so loud was the rain that they failed to hear him as they hurried forward. The magistrate at once got out of the chair in a terrific hurry, but by then it had already been brought as far as the main entrance to the temple.

The district director of schools and others were inside the temple at the time, arranging the sacrificial offerings. However, a first degree licentiate [holder of the lowest degree in the civil service examinations] was present to watch the ceremony and happened to glimpse the incident. He reported it to the director of schools. Subsequently, two other persons who had also witnessed it, Hu Ch'i-ch'üan and Yeh Mai-k'uei, presented written charges which judicial examination has failed to disprove.

The Board of Punishments finds that Chang Lei was lacking in respect when he participated in the sacrifice at the Temple of Confucius. His failure to dismount from the chair in time, though occasioned by the great accumulation of rainwater on the ground and the error of the chairbearers, nevertheless constitutes a violation of the established regulations. Accordingly, he should be sentenced to 100 blows of the heavy bamboo under the statute on violation of imperial decrees [Boulais 274]. Because he has already been dismissed from his position [and hence is now technically a commoner], this sentence requires no further deliberation.

As to the two chairbearers, they are to receive the heavier punishment provided under the statute on doing what ought not to be done, namely heavy bambooing and wearing the cangue for one month. [This catch-all statute (Boulais 1656) provides 40 blows of the light bamboo for lesser offenses and 80 blows of the heavy bamboo for more serious ones but says nothing at all about the cangue here specified. It has a broader application than the above-cited statute on violating imperial decrees, which, though also something of a catch-all, tends to be applied only to civil or administrative, but not to penal, infractions.]

It has been found that Hu Ch'i-ch'üan, one of the two persons who presented written charges against the magistrate, although a purchaser of official rank and belonging to the category of unclassed officials, was yet improperly wearing the golden button of the seventh rank. His case will receive separate consideration. [There were nine main ranks in the official hierarchy, but below them there was also an inferior category of "unclassed" officials. It was this category to which Hu had gained entry through purchase of official rank (a practice always looked down upon but one that became widespread during the nineteenth century, when the Manchu government needed additional revenues). The penalty for an official wearing insignia other than that to which he is entitled is 100 blows of the heavy bamboo and deprivation of official rank. See Boulais 836.]

As for the other person, Yeh Mai-k'uei, who also brought written charges against the magistrate, because these charges have been proved to be correct, there is no need to deliberate further concerning him. [Heavy penalties are provided by Boulais 1474 for deliberately bringing a false charge against another person in court. The person so doing usually receives a punishment three degrees heavier than would be received by the person he accuses if the accusation were correct. This statute, though having the laudable intention of reducing false testimony, probably also had the practical effect of inhibiting the readiness of witnesses to offer testimony.]

112. INCITING CITIZENS TO DISORDER [7]
[Statutory References: Staunton 210, Boulais 924–925]

Case 112.7, 1819. Leading Case.
Reported in HAHL 7.11/13b.

The governor of Shensi has reported the case of Li Hsüeh-lung and other [shopkeepers] who, when their neighbor shopkeeper

---

[7] The basic statute of this section (Boulais 924) provides decapitation after the assizes for an administrative official whose severity causes the people under his jurisdiction to revolt, whereas the main sub-statute (Boulais 925) punishes people in general (other than officials) who incite others to commit disorders. It is perhaps significant that the overwhelming majority of the seventeen cases recorded in HAHL under this section pertain to the second possibility rather than to the first.

Ma Yüan-te was implicated in the testimony given by a criminal and consequently summoned to the District Court for investigation, petitioned for his release under their guarantee. When the petition was denied, Li led his associates in urging shopkeepers to close their shops in protest. Out of more than 300 shops in the city, however, only the eight shops of Li and his followers actually closed. Thus their act was a commercial strike which failed.

Li Hsüeh is accordingly sentenced under the sub-statute [Boulais 925] on enticing people to carry out a commercial strike, but with its specified punishment of immediate decapitation reduced, for him, by one degree to maximum life exile.

[Thus, a sentence of life exile at a distance of 3,000 li. The sub-statute also covers other forms of strike or boycott, such as refusal to pay the land tax or boycotting of the civil service examinations. (In Republican times the strike and boycott became potent means of expressing social and political protest.) The original text of the sub-statute destinguishes clearly between the ringleader, who receives immediate decapitation, and his followers, for whom the penalty is strangulation of the assizes. It must be assumed that the same differentiation is intended in the present case between Li and his followers, even though it is not explicitly stated. The reason for reduction of punishment by one degree is that the commercial strike was only attempted but not accomplished. Theoretically the Board, in order to make the modification of punishment, should have applied the sub-statute analogically rather than directly.]

115. PRIVATE POSSESSION OF PROHIBITED ARMS [8]
[Statutory References: Staunton 214, Boulais 938–940]

Case 115.6, 1815. Leading Case.
Reported in HAHL 7.11/20a.

The governor of Kuangtung has reported a case in which Feng Hsüeh-chou, native of another province, planned with Lo Hui-

---

[8] This section, like a good many others, reflects the fears of the imperial government of sedition or other disorders and its consequent attempts to regularize society.

ch'üan and others to manufacture and sell gunpowder privately. Before any sale was made, however, they were arrested.

Feng Hsüeh-chou is to be sentenced by analogy to the sub-statute [Boulais 940] specifying military exile for the production of gunpowder and its sale to salt smugglers. The sentence, however, is to be reduced for Feng by one degree to 100 blows of the heavy bamboo and three years penal servitude.

[The application of this sub-statute analogically rather than directly, thus permitting Feng to be given a sentence one degree less than he would otherwise receive, is based on the fact that his intended sale of gunpowder did not actually take place and, if it had, would not have been to salt smugglers. The lack of mention of any sentence for Feng's associates is peculiar. Perhaps it means that they, unlike Feng, escaped arrest (and the lack of inflection in Chinese permits the phrase, "they were arrested," to be rendered equally well as "he was arrested"), yet if this were so, it would probably have been explicitly mentioned. More likely, therefore, is that their punishment is unmentioned because, as accessories, they would automatically receive a sentence one degree less than that for Feng as principal (see Boulais 110).]

[Note that the specificity of the crime of sale to salt smugglers leaves the Board no choice but analogical application. However, because sale to them is a special evil, and because provisions of the Code usually carry one specified punishment for one crime, the specificity of the sub-statute is natural and understandable. What is more surprising is that no more general sub-statute was enacted to cover other types of private sale of gunpowder.]

Case 115.7, 1823. Leading Case.
Reported in HAHL 7.11/20a.

The governor of Yunnan has reported a case in which Wang Hsüeh, native of another province, accumulated a private supply of graphite. There is no article in the Code specifically covering this act. However, insofar as graphite and saltpeter are both used in the manufacture of munitions, they in this respect do not differ. Therefore Wang Hsüeh is to be sentenced by analogy to the sub-statute [Boulais 940] which, for accumulating but not selling saltpeter, provides a punishment one degree less than it would for [both accumulating and] privately selling it. The punishment for private sale of more than 100 catties [about 133 lbs.] of saltpeter is maximum [three years] penal servitude, which, reduced by one degree [for only accumulating it without selling], results in a punishment for Wang Hsüeh of 90 blows of the heavy bamboo and two and one half years penal servitude.

[This judgment seems to be based upon a version of the relevent sub-statute which differs both from the later version found in our Chinese edition of the Code and the still further changed and abbreviated version given in Boulais 940. To explain and reconcile the various differences (presumably the result of progressive revisions of the Code) would require more effort than the subject seems worth. Here again, as in the preceding case, the application of the sub-statute analogically rather than directly makes possible a one-degree reduction in punishment.]

Case 115.8, 1816. Leading Case.
Reported in HAHL 7.11/20a.

The governor of Shantung has reported a case in which Ch'en Ch'üan-kuei, native of another province, privately sold 287 catties [about 383 lbs.] of "earthy" [unrefined] saltpeter, which, on examination by the authorities of Chang-ch'iu hsien, was found to contain a considerable amount of clay. When refined into pure saltpeter, it amounted to only 95 catties. Because the amount is less than 100 catties, Ch'en Ch'üan-kuei is to be sentenced by analogy to the statute [Boulais 274] which provides 100 blows of the heavy bamboo for violation of imperial decrees, with, however, a one-degree increase in this penalty for Ch'en, thus resulting in a sentence for him of 60 blows of the heavy bamboo and one year penal servitude.

[Here again, as in the preceding case, the judgment seems to rest on a version of the relevant sub-statute antecedent both to the version contained in our Chinese edition of the Code and to the still further revised one found in Boulais 940. The basis of the present judgment appears to be a judgment pronounced in 1751 on a Kuangtung case and printed in our Chinese edition of the

Code as part of the Upper Commentary. In this judgment, the
private sale of less than 100 catties of saltpeter is punished under
the statute on violation of imperial decrees, whereas the later
versions of the sub-statute drop any reference to this catch-all
statute and replace it by a series of graded punishments corresponding to the amounts of saltpeter involved. The basis for
invoking the imperial decree statute here analogically rather than
directly is not too clear. It has the evident practical effect, however, of enabling the Board to impose a one-degree heavier sentence than it would otherwise have done.]

124. REARING OF DOMESTIC ANIMALS IN AN
IMPROPER MANNER
[Statutory References: Staunton 227, Boulais 987]

*Case 124.1, 1820. Metropolitan Leading Case from the Depart-
ment for Kiangsi of the Board of Punishments.*
Reported in HAHL 7.12/8b–9a.

The Imperial Household Department has memorialized concerning the escape of a tiger from the tiger cage [in one of the
imperial parks]. Investigation reveals that Te-t'ai, a [Manchu]
member of the park personnel, had been on duty at the tiger cage
at the time. Although it had previously been reported to a deputy
inspector of the park that the iron bars of the cage were badly
worn, there had been no immediate request for repair nor any
added attention to guarding the cage during the night in question. The tiger, as a consequence, managed to slip out, causing
loss of life. This is certainly the result of negligence on the part of
the park personnel, which, in view of the cage's proximity to the
palace quarters, might have had even more serious consequences.

It would be overly lenient [continues the memorial] were the
offender to be punished merely under the statute [Boulais 997]
which, just as for accidental homicide, permits monetary redemption to be paid for a homicide resulting from having left an
animal improperly tied up. [The redemption sum for accidental

homicide, according to Table III, no. 4, in Boulais pp. 13–14, is 12.42 ounces of silver.]

There is also a statute [Boulais 987] providing up to three years penal servitude for one who, while caring for government horses [or oxen or camels], allows them to perish. Yet even were Te-t'ai sentenced by analogy to this statute, with its penalty increased for him to life exile, this would still not serve as an adequate public warning. Therefore Te-t'ai should be sentenced to two months wearing of the cangue, followed by deportation to Kirin as a slave.

[The Imperial Household Department, in its memorial, has here arrived at the heaviest punishment possible within the general category of exile. In order to do this, it has had to discard what seems the really analogous statute (Boulais 997) and replace it by another (Boulais 987) which, because it has to do with the death of horses caused by men, rather than the death of men caused by animals, seems hardly analogous to the present case. Furthermore, the Imperial Household Department has gone on to apply this statute analogically to raise the proposed penalty above the statutory maximum of three years penal servitude. The formula given in the statute itself, moreover, indicates that for an offender to incur even this statutory maximum, he would have to allow no less than 72 horses to perish.]

A rescript written upon receipt of this memorial has, as an act of imperial grace, exempted the offender from the deportation proposed for him and ordered him instead simply to wear the cangue for two months.

[Why this act of imperial grace after the Imperial Household Department has tried so hard to give the offender (a Manchu, to judge from his name) the heaviest possible punishment? Why no apparent punishment for the deputy inspector to whom the worn out condition of the cage had previously been reported? Why the failure to identify the victim (or victims?) of the tiger's escape? Although no definite answers can be given, we may suspect that had the tiger's victim been a prominent individual, he would indeed have been named and the final outcome of the case would have been very different. It should be added that the imperial rescript of course makes of the judgment subsequently reached by the Board of Punishments nothing more than a formal confirmation.]

126. PERSONS BITTEN OR KICKED BY DOMESTIC ANIMALS
[Statutory References: Staunton 234, Boulais 997–998]

Case 126.1, 1821. Memorandum from the Department for Mukden of the Board of Punishments.
Reported in HAHL 7.12/9b–10a.

The military governor of Heilungkiang has reported a case in which two Manchu bannermen, Ssu-kuo-an and Ch'ing-pao, each tried to seize a lost horse for himself, with the result that Ch'ing-pao was dragged and kicked to death by the horse.

This Department finds, according to the statute on the goring or kicking of persons by horses or oxen [Boulais 997], that if the animal in question has been released deliberately, thereby resulting in human death or injury, the penalty for having thus released the animal is to be one degree less than that for causing human death or injury in an affray. Turning to the statute on committing homicide during an affray [Boulais 1268], we find that the penalty for so doing is strangulation after the assizes.

In the present case, Ssu-kuo-an erroneously supposed that a colt tied up in Ch'ing-pao's paddock was the one which his own family had lost. He wanted to lead it away and make a report to the authorities, but Ch'ing-pao at once objected and each man thereupon tried to seize it for himself. Ssu-kuo-an, seeing that the colt was plunging and rearing, thought of releasing it in the expectation that it would run off to his own house. He accordingly relaxed his hold and at the same time frightened the colt with a shout. Meanwhile, however, Ch'ing-pao had tied the animal's reins around his own waist so that when the colt ran off in fright, it dragged and kicked Ch'ing-pao to death.

The military governor, in making his report, has raised the question whether the defendant should be sentenced to life exile under the above-cited statute on homicide resulting from the deliberate release of a horse or ox or should rather be sentenced to strangulation [after the assizes] under the statute, also cited, on homicide resulting from an affray.

This Department finds that the action between Ssu-kuo-an and Ch'ing-pao consisted simply of each trying to seize the colt for himself and thus did not constitute a direct affray between the two men themselves. Ch'ing-pao's death from being kicked and dragged took place only after Ssu-kuo-an had released the colt. Moreover, Ssu-kuo-an's purpose in so doing was solely that the colt might thereby be free to run off to his (Ssu-kuo-an's) house. Thus the situation differs from that of an affray directly between two parties, so that it would be inappropriate to find Ssu-kuo-an guilty of committing homicide during an affray.

However, the defendant did in fact, on seeing the colt plunging and rearing, deliberately release and startle it, thereby causing it to run away and to drag and kick Ch'ing-pao to death. According to the testimony, the defendant did not then know that Ch'ing-pao had tied the reins around his own waist. Nonetheless, it is a fact that Ch'ing-pao's death was, in the final analysis, occasioned by the defendant's releasing of the colt.

This Department accordingly sentences Ssu-kuo-an to 100 blows of the heavy bamboo and life exile at a distance of 3,000 li, this being the penalty, made one degree less than that for committing homicide during an affray, which is provided by the statute on the goring or kicking of persons by horses or oxen, when the animal in question has been deliberately released so as to inflict death. This being an equitable decision, we deem it appropriate to request a confirmatory reply.

Case 126.2, 1822. Leading Case.
Reported in HAHL 7.12/10a.

The governor of Shensi has reported a case in which Wu Pao-wa, while driving a mule loaded with charcoal, encountered Mrs. Wen née Huang on a narrow path. The latter's attendant shouted to Wu to give way, but Wu simply continued to whip his mule forward until, through its kicking, it caused loss of human life. [Although the text does not specify who was killed, it was probably the attendant because he would normally have been ahead of Mrs. Wen. Moreover, if she had been killed, the report would surely have stated as much.]

What happened was neither unforeseeable nor unavoidable. Therefore, by analogy to the statute [Boulais 997] concerning the owner of a domestic animal who deliberately releases the animal, thereby causing homicide—the penalty for which is one degree less than that for homicide committed during an affray [strangulation after the assizes]—Wu Pao-wa is sentenced to 100 blows of the heavy bamboo and life exile at a distance of 3,000 li.

[The statute is applied to Wu analogically rather than directly, presumably because he did not actually "deliberately release" his animal but simply continued driving it forward. As a maker of charcoal, Wu was probably of humbler status than was Mrs. Wen, who was accompanied by an attendant. If so, this may explain why no question is raised in the case as to whether Mrs. Wen did, in actual fact, enjoy the right of way on what was quite probably a narrow mountain path.]

131. HIGH TREASON [9]
[Statutory References: Staunton 254, Boulais 1024–1026]

Case 131.1, 1824. Memorandum from the Department for Shantung of the Board of Punishments.
Reported in HAHL 7.12/11b.

With regard to the case in which Ma Chin-chung and others preached heresy and plotted subversion in Lin-ch'ing and other departments and districts of Shantung, the governor-general of

[9] The literal title, "Plotting Revolt and Great Subversion," combines into a single title the titles of the first two of the Ten Abominations (*shih ô*). These are the most serious crimes in the Code (listed in Boulais 45) and therefore most heavily punished, sometimes with mass extermination of the offender's relatives. The statute on high treason (Boulais 1024), for example, provides the following punishments: death by slicing for the principal offender (whether he actually commits or merely plans to commit treason); decapitation (save for those under sixteen) for the offender's father, grandfather, sons, grandsons, brothers, brother's sons, paternal uncles, and others living with him in the same household (including more distant relatives on father's side, as well as maternal grandfather, father-in-law, and brothers-in-law); slavery in the families of meritorious ministers for any of the above who are aged fifteen or less, as well as for the offender's mother, unmarried sisters and daughters, wife and concubine (or concubines), and wives and concubines of his sons.

Chihli has reported the request of Li Erh-hsiao and T'ien Mang-chung that their implication in this affair be voided.

This Department finds that according to the statute on high treason [Boulais 1024], sons or grandsons of a principal offender, if aged fifteen or less, are to be handed over as slaves to the families of meritorious ministers, unless prior to the act of treason they have already been adopted into some other family, in which case they are not to be implicated in the crime of the principal offender.

The statute makes no mention of a son or grandson who, likewise prior to the act of treason, has been sold as a slave to someone. Such a one, however, has ceased to be a son or grandson of the offender, just as much as if he had been adopted into another family. It naturally follows, therefore, that he should not be implicated in the latter's crime.

In the present case, Li Erh-hsiao is the son of one of the principal offenders, and T'ien Mang-chung is the son of another. Both of them, therefore, would normally be implicated in the treasonable activities of their fathers. In infancy, however, Li Erh-hsiao had left his own family for adoption in the family of a distant cousin of his father, while T'ien Mang-chung had likewise, prior to the recent treasonable activity, been contractually sold as a slave to a Shansi shopkeeper. We therefore find the judgment of the Chihli Provincial Court in voiding the implications of Li and T'ien and allowing them to retain their status of adopted son and of slave respectively to be in accord with the statute. This being so, we request the sending of a confirmatory reply.

Case 131.2, 1796. Memorandum.
Reported in HAHL 7.12/11b.

The Department for Fukien of the Board of Punishments finds that Cheng Liu, because of the treasonable activities in Taiwan of his younger brother Cheng Ho, has himself been sentenced to immediate decapitation under the statute on high treason [Boulais 1024], and that Cheng Ho's wife and daughter have, under the same statute, been implicated and accordingly made slaves. There is also Cheng Liu's wife, however, who by this very fact is the sister-in-law of the principal offender Cheng Ho. The statute says nothing about implicating the sister-in-law of a principal offender, and it is presumably for this reason that the governor of Fukien has not taken her into account in his deliberations.

This decision being appropriate, we request the sending of a confirmatory reply.

133. FABRICATING MAGICAL WRITINGS AND SPELLS [10]
[Statutory References: Staunton 256, Boulais 1031–1038]

Case 133.1, 1816. Leading Case.
Reported in HAHL 7.12/20b–21a.

The governor of Honan has reported concerning Yang Ying-ch'en, a licentiate [holder of the lowest degree in the civil service examinations] whose title has already been taken from him because after becoming drunk, he imagined that he would get a concubine for himself and claimed that a fairy princess (*niang-niang*) appeared before him out of Great Gulch (Hung Kou). This being an instance of the reckless propagation of wild words, Yang has accordingly been sentenced to deportation as a slave under the sub-statute [Boulais 1033] providing this penalty for recklessly propagating wild words without, however, reaching large numbers of people. [The word translated "large numbers of people" (*chung*, "masses") is not defined. Decapitation after the assizes is the penalty for the same offense when the propagation does reach large numbers of people. See Boulais 1032.]

This Board, however, is returning the case to the governor for re-examination on the ground that Yang's words were spoken in jest after drunkenness with no intent of wantonly spreading them

---

[10] This section is another illustration of the government's fear of rebellion (see also sec. 92). Magical writings and spells could be invoked (as in the Boxer Rebellion) to give supernatural powers to insurgents. There were also writers of the Nostradamus type in China, predicting in esoteric language the rise and fall of dynasties. Generally speaking, governmental persecutions of religion, when they occurred, were not directed against religious doctrines per se, but against the alleged or actual use of religion, especially by esoteric sects, for anti-dynastic movements.

to delude people. Yang Ying-ch'en should accordingly be sentenced under the same sub-statute as above, but with a one-degree reduction from its penalty of deportation to that of 100 blows of the heavy bamboo and three years penal servitude.

[For the mechanics of reduction from capital punishment or life exile, see Chapter III, end of section 9. The reduction would normally require application of the relevant statute analogically rather than directly; in the next two cases, under similar circumstances, the Board does apply the identical sub-statute analogically.]

Case 133.2, 1815. Leading Case.
Reported in HAHL 7.12/21a.

The governor of Shensi has reported a case in which a Buddhist monk, Ni Tao-yüan, when his former disciple had returned from an itinerant tour bearing noncanonical magical writings, not only failed to report them immediately to the authorities but even lent a hand to their copying and propagation.

By analogy to the statute [Boulais 1033] providing deportation for one who fabricates magical writings and spells without, however, reaching large numbers of people, Ni Tao-yüan is to receive a one-degree lesser sentence, namely 100 blows of the heavy bamboo and three years penal servitude. [See remarks at end of preceding case.]

Case 133.3, 1815. Leading Case.
Reported in HAHL 7.12/21a.

The associate governor of Hupei has reported a case in which Chou Wen-ts'ai, wishing to avoid calamities, copied noncanonical writings obtained from a released criminal and then took them to a neighboring district (*hsien*) to have further copies made of them. Investigation indicates that he had no intention of deluding other people by so doing nor did he fabricate the writings himself. Therefore, by analogy to the sub-statute [Boulais 1033] providing deportation for one who fabricates magical writings and spells without, however, reaching large numbers of people, he is to receive a one-degree lesser sentence of 100 blows of the heavy bamboo and three years penal servitude. [See remarks at the end of case 133.1.]

The individuals who did allow themselves to be deluded are to be sentenced, by analogy to the statute on violating imperial decrees [Boulais 274], to 100 blows of the heavy bamboo and two months wearing of the cangue. [For the use of this statute as a catch-all device, see case 82.6. The statute specifies only 100 blows as a punishment, but its application analogically rather than directly makes possible the inclusion of the wearing of the cangue as an additional punishment. See also case 89.1.]

134. THEFT OF OBJECTS FOR IMPERIAL WORSHIP
[Statutory References: Staunton 257, Boulais 1039]

Case 134.1, 1817. Leading Case from the Department for Mukden of the Board of Punishments.
Reported in HAHL 7.12/21a–b.

The Board of Punishments of Manchuria [which maintained for Manchuria a juridical organization somewhat similar to that of the Board of Punishments in Peking] has memorialized concerning a case in which Kuo Liang gained the collaboration of Chang Wen-kuei in robbing one of the state temples, the Hall of the Glorious Protector. [This temple, the Hsien-yu Kung, was dedicated to one of the most popular protective divinities of Ch'ing times, Kuan Ti or Lord Kuan (commonly but misleadingly referred to in English as the God of War). He is the deification of a famed historical general, Kuan Yü (died A.D. 219), who played an important role in the events ushering in the Three Kingdoms period (220–280).] The two men used knives to gouge out the silver ornaments embedded in the sacred statues and also stole the silver vessels used for making offerings to Lord Kuan.

This Department finds that although the cult of Lord Kuan does not belong to the major state sacrifices [enumerated in Boulais 758 and case 88.1], he is a divinity very highly respected by our dynasty. The two culprits should therefore be sentenced to immediate decapitation by analogy to the statute [Boulais 1039] which provides this punishment for both principals and accessories guilty of the theft of objects used for imperial worship. [The statute is applied analogically rather than directly because it does not specifically refer to state sacrifices of the second rank (including that to Lord Kuan), but only to the major state sacrifices (for example, to Heaven and Earth).]

An imperial rescript replying to this memorial has changed the penalty to decapitation after the autumn assizes, with classification of the case among those whose "circumstances are deserving of capital punishment." [See case 11.1 for explanation of this term.]

Case 134.2, 1813. Leading Case from the Department for Mukden of the Board of Punishments.
Reported in HAHL 7.12/21b.

The section of the Board of Punishments which is currently accompanying His Majesty [perhaps to Jehol or elsewhere to escape the summer heat] reports that according to a memorial from the Board of Punishments in Manchuria, Chi Erh is guilty of having stolen yellow satins from the Imperial Shamanic Temple in Mukden. [Shamanism was a cult which the Manchus brought with them when they conquered China, and for which temples were maintained by them both in Peking and Mukden.]

The memorial recommends that Chi Erh, under the statute on the theft of objects used for imperial worship [Boulais 1039], should be sentenced to immediate decapitation.

An imperial rescript replying to the memorial has confirmed this sentence. [Note the differing treatment of the offender here as compared with the preceding case. Probably the difference reflects the psychological closeness of shamanism to the Manchus as compared with the cult of Kuan Ti, a non-Manchu Chinese divinity.]

Case 134.3, 1823. Metropolitan Leading Case from the Department for Chihli of the Board of Punishments.
Reported in HAHL 7.12/21b.

The Censorate of the South City of Peking has reported and transferred to this Department the case of Ch'en Hei-tzu and Tu

Ch'ang-kuei, who, while assisting in work being done at the Imperial Yü Mausoleum, happened to glimpse the bronze gilt stud nails covering the gate of glazed tiles leading into the Hall of Surpassing Kindness (Lung-en tien). [The Yü Mausoleum is that of the Ch'ien-lung Emperor (1736–1795), and is one of several located 80 miles northeast of Peking and collectively known as the Tung Ling or Eastern Imperial Mausolea.] The two men, thinking that these nails were made of gold, crawled into the enclosure at night and gouged out more than ten of them. Then they sneaked away to Peking to sell them, where, however, they were apprehended.

There being no article specifically covering this offense, the offenders should be sentenced to immediate decapitation by analogy to the statute [Boulais 1039] which provides this punishment for both principals and accessories of the theft of objects used for imperial worship.

A third person, Wu Niu-tzu, simply stayed outside on guard without following the others into the enclosure. Thus he to some extent deserves leniency, concerning which the imperial will is respectfully awaited.

An imperial rescript replying to this memorial has changed Wu Niu-tzu's sentence [from immediate decapitation] to decapitation after the assizes.

141. ROBBERY COMMITTED WITH VIOLENCE
[Statutory References: Staunton 266, Boulais 1061–1084]

Case 141.16, 1815. Leading Case.
Reported in HAHL 7.13/13b.

The associate governor of Hupei has reported a case in which Liu Wu-erh and Ts'ai Ta-erh were stealing money and property [in a certain house] for their gang when the property owner woke up and began to shout for help. Liu warned him that if he dared leave the house after them, they would kill him, and Ts'ai joined in similar threats. The property owner, as a result, was afraid to go out so that they were able to leave, divide the booty, and each go his own way.

Under the sub-statute on thieves who momentarily resist arrest but inflict no injury, Liu Wu-erh and Ts'ai Ta-erh are now sentenced, as ringleader and accessory, to military exile and penal servitude respectively.

[More specifically, to military exile at a nearby frontier (2,500 li) and to three years penal servitude. This sub-statute, Boulais 1080b, includes several other provisions covering the killing or injuring of the property owner in various ways by the thief while the latter, still at the scene of the crime, momentarily resists arrest.]

143. PLUNDERING IN BROAD DAYLIGHT
[Statutory References: Staunton 268, Boulais 1092–1116]

Case 143.2, 1823. Leading Case.
Reported in HAHL 8.15/11b–12a.

The governor-general of Hunan and Hupei has reported a case in which, after the vessel of Shuai Ch'eng-fa had been sunk by a storm, Chou Heng-yü and others went out to it in small boats and dredged boxes and other things from it out of the water. Because this act was done only after the vessel had already sunk, it does not, strictly speaking, constitute plundering which is carried out at the moment of, and takes advantage of, a crisis. However, though Shuai Ch'eng-fa shouted from the shore to Chou and the others to stop, they went right ahead salvaging the boxes without paying any attention. This behavior is enough to give their act the character of plundering (*ch'iang-to*). Each of them moved to and fro and dredged up the boxes without distinction as to ringleader and accessories.

Therefore Chou Heng-yü and his associates, in accordance with the sub-statute [Boulais 1107] on taking advantage of a crisis to plunder property, without, however, inflicting injury on anyone, are all to be sentenced to maximum [three years] penal servitude, a punishment one degree less than that prescribed by the sub-statute.

[This sub-statute, which deals wholly with shipwrecks and other maritime disasters, provides life exile at a distance of 2,000 li for this particular offense. The fact that the plundering occurred only after, rather than during, the shipwreck, plus the one-degree reduction of the sub-statute's stated penalty, would seem to require the sub-statute to be applied analogically rather than directly. Yet, as in so many other cases, the full technical term *pi chao*, "by analogy to," is not used, but only the reduced form *chao*, here translated as "in accordance with." In some other cases likewise involving a change of statutory penalty, not even the word *chao* is used.]

Case 143.9, 1814. Leading Case.
Reported in HAHL 8.15/13a.

The associate governor of Hupei has reported a case in which Chang T'ien-kuei, on seeing Huang Shih-lung carrying a heavy bag on his back, supposed it to contain silver. He accordingly gathered his own associates and with them overtook Huang from behind, when he suddenly covered Huang's eyes with a cloth, snatched away what he was carrying, and ran off.

Chang T'ien-kuei is accordingly sentenced to military exile by analogy to the sub-statute [Boulais 1100] on plundering involving injury to the victim, which, however, is not caused by a metal blade and is so slight that the victim wholly recovers.

[The particular part of the rather lengthy sub-statute here cited is omitted from Boulais 1100. The military exile it prescribes for the stated offense is of the harshest sort, that is, exile in a malarial region at a distance of 4,000 li. The fact that the sub-statute deals with plundering involving killing or injuring the victim in various ways, whereas the victim of the present case merely had his eyes momentarily covered over, explains why the sub-statute has to be applied analogically rather than directly. Apparently the Board of Punishments selected this particular sub-statute because it felt that even this slight show of force required a punishment sterner than the mere three years penal servitude provided by Boulais 1093 for ordinary plundering unaccompanied by violence or injury. Again and again in the Code we see the enormous importance attached to violence (especially when involving the use of weapons) as a primary criterion for determining severity of punishment.]

144. STEALING
[Statutory References: Staunton 269, Boulais 1117–1134]

Case 144.7, 1818. Leading Case.
Reported in HAHL 9.16/15a.

The governor-general of Chihli has reported a case in which several Muslims were invited to join a band of Muslim robbers. One of those invited, Yang Ta-pao, was at first unwilling, until Ch'ang San, as an incentive, indicated to him how the booty would be shared.

According to statute [Boulais 1577], anyone who entices another person to break the law is equally guilty with that lawbreaker himself. Therefore, Ch'ang San as well as Yang Ta-pao should both be sentenced to military exile under the sub-statute on Muslims who form a band and take up weapons to practice robbery.

[This sub-statute, Boulais 1122a, provides military exile in a malarial area in Yunnan, Kueichow, Kuangtung, or Kuangsi for Muslims forming an armed band of three or more persons for purposes of robbery. Scattered through the Code occur a number of laws dealing, often in a discriminatory fashion, with Muslims, Miao, and other minority groups.]

Case 144.17, 1796. Memorandum.
Reported in HAHL 9.16/19b.

The Department for Chekiang of the Board of Punishments has examined the case of Chu Sheng-erh, who last year, at the age of fourteen, committed a theft for which, according to sub-statute, he should have been exempted from tatooing. [The penalty for theft, as prescribed by Boulais 1117, includes not only a primary punishment dependent upon the amount stolen, but also, for a first offender, the tatooing of the Chinese term for thief, *ch'ieh-tao*, upon his right forearm. For a second offense, the same is tatooed upon the left forearm. In the present case, however, the fact that the offender was under fifteen should have given him (though, as we shall see, it failed to do so) exemption from tatooing as well as the privilege of monetary redemption in place of his major punishment. See Boulais 131 and 135.]

However, when Chu was brought to trial by the Censorate of the North City of Peking, he was wrongly subjected to beating with the heavy bamboo and tatooing upon his forearm. [One would like to know, but we are not told, what was the punishment given to the municipal judicial authorities responsible for this mistake. Because the main punishment they administered was only bambooing (which means that the amount stolen by the boy did not at most exceed 40 ounces of silver; see Boulais 1119), the case could be settled by them without going up to the Board of Punishments.]

Now, in the sixth month of the present year, the same offender has again committed theft, this time of a table drape and other articles. His case [as a second offender] has therefore been sent to this Board. This makes him a second offender, for which, according to rule, he should again be tatooed on the forearm. There is therefore no need now to eradicate the tatooing wrongly undergone by him last year. Instead, it may serve in place of the second tatooing to which he would now otherwise be subjected for his new robbery.

[In finding this convenient solution to the difficulty, the Board seems oblivious to the fact that had this boy of fourteen not been wrongfully subjected to tatooing for all the world to see in the first place, he might conceivably not have committed a second offense a year later. The private eradication of tatooing by a tatooed criminal was of course illegal, but under special circumstances, such as an imperial amnesty, eradication might be permitted by the authorities. The subject of tatooing—its various sorts for various offenses, as well as its removal—is discussed in a section of the Code, "Eradication of Tatooing," which is the last of three successive sections omitted entirely by Boulais. It is covered in part by Staunton 281, and would be 1210a in Boulais.]

147. STEALING BETWEEN RELATIVES
[Statutory References: Staunton 272, Boulais 1154–1165]

Case 147.1, 1826. Memorandum.
Reported in HAHL 9.18/12b–13a.

The governor of Anhui has reported a case in which Ch'en Chih-shuang forcefully seized an ox from Mrs. Ch'en, wife of Ch'en Chih-shuang's father's first younger cousin, thereby pushing her to the point where she committed suicide.

In this case Mrs. Ch'en, whose relationship to Ch'en Chih-shuang was that of the fifth degree of mourning, was leading her ox on the road when she encountered him. The idea came to him of stealing her ox, so together with a distant younger cousin who was with him, Ch'en Shou-kuo, he seized the ox from her and the two men then disappeared. After trying in vain to recover it, Mrs. Ch'en returned home, where she announced that she was ready to give up her life because of Ch'en Chih-shuang and his associate and with a knife slashed herself on the forehead. Furthermore, when someone snatched the knife from her and tried to console her, Mrs. Ch'en went off and hanged herself.

For plundering from a relative of the fifth degree of mourning, thereby pushing that relative into suicide—as Ch'en did when he seized the ox of Mrs. Ch'en—there is no specified penalty in the Code. In the absence of such a penalty, judgment should be made on the basis of the statutes [Boulais 1166 and 1167] on extorting property through intimidation. One of these statutes [Boulais 1167] provides that intimidation, when applied by a junior relative to a senior relative, is subject to the same punishment as ordinary intimidation occurring between non-relatives. [It should be remembered that in the present case, the offender, Ch'en Chih-shuang, was a junior relative of the victim, Mrs. Ch'en.] The other statute [Boulais 1166] further states that the punishments for intimidation between non-relatives are to be graded according to the varying amounts of booty obtained in the same way as are the punishments for ordinary stealing [Boulais 1119], save that the punishments for intimidation are in each instance to be one degree greater than the corresponding punishments for stealing.

It follows that when a junior relative plunders from a senior relative and thereby pushes the latter into suicide, the punishment for so doing should likewise be calculated by analogy to the statute [Boulais 1128] on committing a theft which causes the victim to commit suicide, the punishment for the plundering junior relative, however, to be one degree higher than that for the thief [causing the suicide, just as the punishment for getting something through intimidation is to be one degree more than for getting the same thing through ordinary stealing].

The statute on stealing resulting in suicide provides a penalty of maximum penal servitude [three years]. By analogy to this statute, the governor of Anhui has sentenced Ch'en Chih-shuang to a one-degree higher punishment than the foregoing, namely 100 blows of the heavy bamboo and life exile at a distance of 2,000 li. As for Ch'en's collaborator, Ch'en Shou-kuo, the governor has sentenced him to [three years] penal servitude, in accordance with the statute providing a one-degree lesser penalty for an accessory than for a principal [Boulais 110]. Both men, under the relevant statutes, have been exempted from tatooing. [Under the statute on stealing (Boulais 1117), a convicted thief is to have the Chinese two-character term for "thief" (ch'ieh-tao) tatooed on his right forearm. However, though this statute is basic to the parallel statutes on robbery between relatives (Boulais 1154) and on extortion through intimidation (Boulais 1166), the latter two both specifically exempt the guilty party from tatooing.]

These punishments being in accord with the facts of the case, it is proper to request the sending of a confirmatory reply.

Case 147.2, 1796. Memorandum.
Reported in HAHL 9.18/13a.

The governor of Shansi has reported a case in which Sun Lun-yüan surreptitiously sawed off and took away tree branches belonging to Sun Shou-chih, was beaten by the latter in reprisal, and then committed suicide. [The branches were stolen and the two men were distant relatives. Hence the classification of this case under the section on stealing between relatives.]

Sun Shou-chih, with respect to Sun Lun-yüan, was a grandson of the latter's paternal male third cousin. As such, his relationship to Sun Lun-yüan was outside [more remote than] the five degrees of mourning. When Sun Shou-chih discovered the loss of his branches, he beat Sun Lun-yüan with an iron ploughshare, breaking the latter's right thigh and shinbone. So ashamed was Sun Lun-yüan of having been thus beaten for theft that he went off and hanged himself.

This Board finds that the circumstances surrounding Sun Lun-yüan's death include his commission of a theft, the exposure thereof, his despisal of life, and suicide. Nonetheless, as he was a senior relative of Sun Shou-chih, belonging to the same paternal clan (even though outside the five degrees of mourning), the distinction between senior and junior still holds for them. On this ground the governor of Shansi has sentenced the offender to 100 blows of the heavy bamboo and life exile at a distance of 2,000 li, this being a punishment one degree higher than that provided by statute for disabling someone, which is maximum penal servitude. [Boulais 1347 provides three years penal servitude for breaking someone's hand, foot, haunch, or destroying an eye.] This one-degree increase being in accord with the relevant statute, a confirmatory reply is requested. [According to Boulais 1409, the penalty for a junior relative who strikes a senior one, even when the relationship between the two is outside the five degrees of mourning, is one degree higher than for the same act occurring between non-relatives.]

His Majesty, on receiving the foregoing report, has sent back an imperial endorsement pointing out that what happened in the case all started with the theft committed by the senior relative, and that therefore a reconsideration of the case is in order. [Apparently the emperor felt the sentence of the junior offender to be too severe and therefore wanted to mitigate it by balancing the junior's offense against the initial theft committed by the senior. Though such a balancing is a common feature of Chinese legal procedure, there is no statutory justification for it in the present instance, as is pointed out below.]

This Board has accordingly examined the statute on stealing between relatives [Boulais 1154] and found that, there being a

duty between relatives to support one another, this statute therefore provides for reductions of penalty in accordance with closeness of relationship, as well as for elimination of tatooing. The
same statute also provides, however, that if the stealing leads to
killing or wounding, priority is to be given to these more serious
offenses [when judging a case]. Thus less weight is to be given to
the stealing and more weight to the killing or injuring.

We have examined this matter and have jointly reached the
conclusion that in the absence of any previously formulated
leading case [providing a basis for revising the judgment], we
should still request a reply confirming the earlier decision.

A second imperial endorsement, issued later, agrees that in the
absence of such a leading case, it is only possible to grant a confirmatory reply for the earlier sentence as requested.

[This is an interesting example of the Board of Punishments
sticking to its decision based on promulgated law despite imperial
pressure, and the emperor finally yielding to the Board's judgment despite his theoretically absolute power.]

Case 147.3, 1826. Memorandum.
Reported in HAHL 9.18/13a–b.

The governor of Kuangtung has memorialized concerning a
case in which Li Mai-hou conspired to steal articles of silver from
the house of Mrs. Hsieh née Ho and also tried unsuccessfully to
rape her.

This Board finds that according to statute [Boulais 1154], stealing between relatives (both consanguinal and affinal), when the
relationship is that covered by the fifth degree of mourning, is to
be punished two degrees less [than ordinary stealing between non-
relatives]; it is to be one degree less when the relationship is outside [remoter than] the five degrees of mourning. However, a sub-
statute limits the scope of this statute by saying that the one
degree reduction for relatives outside of the five degrees of
mourning is to apply only to members of the paternal clan; it is
not to apply to other relatives (either consanguinal or affinal) if

they are not listed in the Code's mourning charts. [Boulais, Table IV, pp. 17–22. For the sub-statute, see Boulais 1159, which, however, abbreviates the original text in such a way as to obscure its true import as a limitation on Boulais 1154.]

In these charts a given individual's male first cousin, whether he be the son of the individual's paternal aunt or of his maternal uncle, is listed as belonging to the fifth degree of mourning with respect to that individual. The accompanying text further explains that the wives of these cousins or of other males related to the given individual through the female members of his family are always one degree of mourning further removed from him than are their husbands. Finally, the Code contains a sub-statute [Boulais 1080a] specifying strangulation after the assizes for theft eventuating in attempted but unsuccessful rape.

In the present case, Mrs. Hsieh, the victim of Li Mai-hou's theft, is the wife of Li's older first maternal cousin [Mrs. Hsieh is the wife of the son of Li's mother's brother]. The relationship of this cousin to Li is, as indicated above, that of the fifth degree of mourning. Therefore Mrs. Hsieh's relationship to Li, she being the wife of this cousin, is one degree further removed, which places it entirely outside of the five degrees of mourning. Hence, as indicated in the sub-statute cited above, the reduction of penalty provided by statute for members of the same paternal clan, even when their relationship is outside of the five degrees of mourning, does not apply to the relationship between Mrs. Hsieh and Li. Consequently, Li's theft of Mrs. Hsieh should be judged as an ordinary stealing from non-relatives, and his resulting attempt to rape Mrs. Hsieh should be considered no differently from rape committed by an ordinary thief.

Thus the governor of Kuangtung, in sentencing Li Mai-hou to strangulation [after the assizes] under the above-cited sub-statute on theft eventuating in attempted but unsuccessful rape, has reached an equitable decision for which a confirmatory reply should be sent.

[This case, with its careful analysis of family relationships before finally ignoring these relationships to reach a decision, well illustrates the overriding dominance of the family in China.]

148. EXTORTION THROUGH INTIMIDATION
[Statutory References: Staunton 273, Boulais 1166–1170]

Case 148.2, 1801. Memorandum.
Reported in HAHL 10.19/2a–b.

The governor of Chekiang has reported a case in which Ch'en Ch'ao-tsung enticed Ch'en Ch'ao-hsiu into gambling and then intimidated him, causing him to hang himself.

In this case, Ch'en Ch'ao-tsung, being in financial difficulties, enticed Ch'en Ch'ao-hsiu into repeated gambling and, when the latter lost and had no money to pay, forced him to write a promissory note putting up his land as collateral. When the note fell due and the money was still not paid, Ch'en Ch'ao-tsung made threatening demands of Ch'en Ch'ao-hsiu, who begged for deferment. Ch'en Ch'ao-tsung replied that if the money was not forthcoming, he intended to take over the land put up as collateral. Ch'en Ch'ao-hsiu's father, on hearing of this, upbraided his son and wished to beat him. Under these various pressures, Ch'en Ch'ao-hsiu hanged himself. Now the governor of Chekiang has sentenced Ch'en Ch'ao-tsung to military exile by analogy to the substatute on scoundrels who repeatedly commit molestations. [See Boulais 1119, which specifies military exile to a distance of 4,000 li for this offense.]

This Board finds that it was Ch'en Ch'ao-hsiu's weakness that enabled Ch'en Ch'ao-tsung to lead him into gambling, to force him to put up his land as collateral, to press him for payment, and to berate and beat him. Truly what Ch'en Ch'ao-tsung did was as hateful as causing the death of a man by bringing false charges or demands against him. Crimes in this category include, for example, falsely accusing a decent citizen of being a thief, thereby pushing him to suicide [Boulais 1483a]; bringing false accusations in court against a person that result in his death [Boulais 1482a]; or extortionate demands made by the rapacious underlings of an official upon someone until that person commits suicide [Boulais 1522]. All these offenses are punishable by strangulation [after the assizes].

However, there is no sub-statute providing the same penalty for ordinary acts of extortion leading to the victim's death. [It is strange indeed that the section on extortion through intimidation contains no article on suicide as the result of extortion, since the Chinese legislator is usually careful to provide for every conceivable contingency.]

Moreover, although Ch'en Ch'ao-hsiu was enticed into gambling, his death certificate shows that he had already reached the age of thirty, so that he was no mere ignorant child. Thus his sliding into gambling may also be said to have been of his own choosing.

The governor of Chekiang, finding Ch'en Ch'ao-tsung to have been previously guilty of robbery and rape, has sentenced him to military exile, as stated above, by analogy to the sub-statute on scoundrels who repeatedly commit molestations. It would seem that nothing further can be added to this penalty, and that therefore the only course is to send a confirmatory reply.

Case 148.6, 1803. Memorandum.
Reported in HAHL 10.19/4b.

The Department for Kiangsu of the Board of Punishments reports on a case in which the daughter-in-law of Mrs. Li née Hsüeh committed suicide after suffering abusive language from her mother-in-law. No report of the death was made to the authorities. Yen Cheng then conceived the idea of practicing blackmail on Mrs. Pu née Chu, landlady of Mrs. Li, and when he failed, pressed Mrs. Li to report the death to the authorities, hoping thus to involve Mrs. Pu. Mrs. Li asked a neighbor to promise to pay Yen 2,400 cash [about 2.4 ounces of silver], but Yen demanded immediate money and pressed her to borrow this sum from Mrs. Pu. In the end Mrs. Li drowned herself in the river.

This Department finds that Mrs. Pu was the [primary] one against whom Yen practiced his extortion. Had she committed suicide in consequence, Yen would have been sentenced to strangulation [after the assizes] by analogy to the statute [Boulais 1522] on rapacious underlings of officials who make extortionate demands on someone until he commits suicide. [It will be remembered from the preceding case that there is no article covering suicide resulting from extortion when practiced by an ordinary person. This is why analogical resort must be made to the statute on rapacious underlings.]

However, Mrs. Li, the person who in actual fact did die, was not herself the direct object of Yen's extortions, and her death came unexpectedly. Therefore the governor of Kiangsu, in sentencing Yen Cheng to military exile under the sub-statute on scoundrels who repeatedly commit molestations [Boulais 1169], has rendered a verdict which accords with the facts of the case and for which a confirmatory reply should be sent.

[The fact that Yen's blackmail activities against one woman were enough to bring death to a second probably explains why he was sentenced under this sub-statute on repeated molestations. Nothing is said here about the daughter-in-law's suicide which started the whole train of events. Presumably this is because the mother-in-law who had induced the suicide was herself already dead. Apparently there is no article in the Code covering a mother-in-law who induces her daughter-in-law to commit suicide, although this must have been a relatively common occurrence and although the Code (Boulais 1323) does provide strangulation after the assizes for the reverse offense (a daughter-in-law whose lack of filial piety causes her mother-in-law to commit suicide).]

Case 148.7, 1828. Memorandum.
Reported in HAHL 10.19/4b.

The governor of Kiangsu has reported a case in which P'ei Ya-tzu, a tenant farmer renting land from the Buddhist monk Yi-ho, excavated bricks from a certain tomb and then pretended to Li Ch'ang-fu that the bricks had come from his own wall. In this way Li was persuaded to buy them for paving his road. Monk Yi-ho thereupon conceived the idea of falsely claiming that the bricks came from the tomb of the founder of his monastery and then using his tenant farmer P'ei to deceive Li with this story. Thus they extorted money from Li. Meanwhile the caretaker of the tomb learned what had happened and was about to report it to the authorities. At this juncture, however, when P'ei asked the monk for a share of the money extorted from Li, the monk came back at P'ei with such intimidating threats that P'ei committed suicide by drinking lye.

There is no article in the Code on using an accomplice to practice deception and then causing the accomplice to commit suicide. The Provincial Court of Kiangsu has therefore sentenced Monk Yi-ho by analogy to the sub-statute [Boulais 1169] providing military exile for scoundrels who molest decent people, which penalty, however, is to be reduced by one degree for Yi-ho to penal servitude. [Application of the sub-statute analogically rather than directly permits, of course, this reduction.]

This Board finds that Monk Yi-ho took advantage of Li Ch'ang-fu's wealth, his fear of getting into trouble, and his timid stupidity, to deceive him by means of P'ei and thus extort money from him for the construction of a building. This already puts Yi-ho in the category of a molesting scoundrel. On top of this, however, he, when asked by P'ei for a share of the extorted money, verbally intimidated P'ei until he committed suicide. Yi-ho has failed as a monk to maintain his monastic rules of purity. His practice of deception has led to loss of life, and he has shown himself evil in nature and wicked in deed. It would certainly not be fitting to permit him leniency.

Monk Yi-ho, therefore, should be resentenced to military exile [at a distance of 4,000 li], under the sub-statute providing this penalty for scoundrels who at every time and occasion have shown themselves to be evil in nature and wicked in deed. [This is the same sub-statute previously used to sentence the monk, minus, however, the earlier reduction of penalty. The new phraseology of the sub-statute is taken from the exposition of it in the Code's Official Commentary (one of the very rare instances of the Commentary being attached to a sub-statute) and no doubt is used deliberately by the Board of Punishments because of its more forceful expression of moral disapproval.]

149. ACQUISITION OF PUBLIC OR PRIVATE
PROPERTY THROUGH DECEPTION
[Statutory References: Staunton 274, Boulais 1171–1177]

Case 149.2, 1821. Memorandum.
Reported in HAHL 10.19/22b–23a.

The governor of Kiangsu has reported a case in which Yang Hui-chi embezzled money from Wang Kuan-ch'ün to an amount exceeding the maximum [listed in the Code for calculating punishment].

This Board finds that, according to statute [Boulais 1173], the penalties for embezzling the property of another are calculated, in a manner comparable to those for theft, according to the amount of loot acquired [see table in Boulais 1119], but the offender does not undergo tatooing as he does for theft. The Shen Chih-ch'i Commentary on the statute further explains that "to have someone else's property in one's hand and then, when a favorable opportunity presents itself, to take this property for oneself is called embezzlement (*kuai-tai*)." From this definition it may be seen that although there is a seeming similarity between embezzlement and theft (*ch'ieh-tao*), the two are actually not identical. Between their respective penalties, for this reason, there is likewise a distinction of life for the one as against death for the other. The act of embezzling someone's property, to be sure, resembles theft in that it involves taking something which is not one's own. In the final analysis, nonetheless, it springs from the fact that the property owner has placed his trust in the wrong person. Hence embezzlement may not be placed in the same category as genuine theft. [It is considered a lesser offense because it is committed under the influence of temptation.] That is why the punishment for embezzlement stops at maximum exile [life exile at a distance of 3,000 li] even when the amount of loot exceeds the maximum [listed in the Code for calculating penalties].

[This statement at first sight seems mysterious. Boulais 1119 gives a sliding scale of punishments for stealing, culminating with strangulation after the assizes for stealing 120 ounces or more of silver, and Boulais 1173, as we have seen above, states that the penalties for embezzlement are calculated in a manner comparable to those for theft (save for exemption from tatooing). It does not state that any exception is to be made (maximum exile as against strangulation after the assizes) when the amount of loot embezzled reaches the maximum (120 ounces of silver) listed in the table for stealing. The key to the mystery lies in the word *chun*, "comparable," occurring in the phrase from Boulais 1173 cited above, "comparable to those for theft." This is a very special technical meaning of *chun*, whose much more common meaning of "authorized" we have already encountered in the phrase "authorized penal servitude." See Chapter III, sections 1 and 4.]

[For further explanation we must turn to a statute ignored entirely by Boulais (if included, it would be 188a), and, although included in Staunton 39, translated there in a manner that slurs over the technical point involved. From this statute we learn that the word *chun*, when used in the Code to delimit punishments said to be either "comparable *(chun)* to those for theft," or "comparable *(chun)* to those for bribery contravening the law," signifies that these punishments are only "comparable" to, and therefore not invariably identical with, those for theft and bribery. This is because, so the statute informs us further, the offenses covered by these "comparable" penalties (namely embezzlement and a special variety of bribery, for which see Boulais 1530) are regarded as less serious than their counterpart offenses of stealing and bribery per se. The statute says expressly that these "comparable" penalties never exceed exile at a distance of 3,000 li (in contrast to strangulation after the assizes, which is the highest punishment prescribed for theft and bribery alike) nor (for embezzlement) do they include tatooing (as prescribed for all levels of stealing). Boulais, having ignored this statute, likewise ignores the technical meaning of *chun* in his 1173, where, in consequence, his translation gives no hint of any difference of maximum punishment between embezzlement and stealing.]

In the present case, Yang Hui-chi and Wang Kuan-ch'ün were returning home together on a rented boat. Wang went ashore at a certain spot, accompanied by the boatman, to collect a minor debt. While he was away, he entrusted his trunk and its key to Yang. Yang got it into his head to open the trunk and on doing so found six or eight bank drafts and over 700 ounces of silver inside. These he transferred to his own trunk. Fearing lest the lightness of Wang's trunk might betray what had happened, Yang filled it with 5,000 copper cash. Then five days later he pretended that his father was seriously ill at Ch'ing-p'u and that he must go to see him. Taking with him the silver in his trunk, he departed for Yangchow, there bought sorghum (*kao-liang*) at a certain shop, loaded it on a boat which he hired, and started up the Yangtse river to sell it. At this point he was overtaken by Wang, who had Yang arrested and brought before the authorities.

This Board, on examining the circumstances of the case, finds that the offender is a merchant and not a habitual thief. He is well acquainted with Wang, moreover, and his use of opportune circumstances for taking Wang's money was prompted, in the final analysis, by Wang's mistaken trust in him and unfortunate consignment to him of his trunk and key. There is a difference between this act and a genuine act of theft.

The governor of Kiangsu, basing himself on the amount of loot taken by Yang Hui-chi, has sentenced him to life exile, but without tatooing, under the statute already cited [Boulais 1173] on embezzling another's property. This sentence accords with the statute in question, and also with the case of Chang Tseng-shou, tried earlier this year in Chekiang, reexamination of which led to a revised sentence of life exile. It would therefore seem that a confirmatory reply should now be given. [The case in question, 149.1, has not been translated because of its length.]

150. KIDNAPPING AND SALE OF HUMAN BEINGS
[Statutory References: Staunton 275, Boulais 1178–1190]

Case 150.19, 1822. Metropolitan Leading Case from the Department for Chekiang of the Board of Punishments.
Reported in HAHL 10.20/7b.

The Censorate of the North City of Peking has transferred to this Board a case in which Wang Erh, when his daughter was divorced by her husband, planned to sell her to Mrs. Chao née Chang to become the latter's "charity child."

[A "charity child" or "son" (*yi-tzu*) is one who is adopted, ostensibly out of kindness, by a family of different surname, in which family, as a result, the child enjoys no legal rights. See case 42.1. Here the term seems to be used to cover up the sale of a woman into virtual slavery.]

Wang Erh is to be sentenced by analogy to the statute [Boulais 1182] providing 80 blows of the heavy bamboo for deceitfully selling a child or grandchild as a slave, and stating that this penalty is to be reduced by one degree [to 70 blows] if the sale has been made with the consent of the person sold. For Wang Erh the latter penalty is to be reduced one more degree to 60 blows.

[Presumably the statute is applied analogically rather than directly, and the penalty is reduced because Wang merely *planned* to sell his daughter, but did not actually carry out the plan. Obviously, the act here being penalized is one that would rarely occur except in very poor families, and Wang Erh's own name, which means "Wang the Second," strongly suggests a humble origin. Indicative of the father's great authority over his children in a Confucian society is the lightness of punishment here given for selling a child into slavery, as contrasted with another clause of the same statute stipulating 80 blows of the heavy bamboo and two years penal servitude for similar sale of one's younger brother or sister or various other lesser relatives.]

Case 150.21, 1818. Leading Case.
Reported in HAHL 10.20/7b.

The governor of Kiangsu has reported a case in which Shih Fa, native of another province, deceitfully sold his already married elder sister, with her consent, to Huang Sung-mao to become the latter's wife. Prior to this event, the relationship of this sister to her brother had already, because of her previous marriage, fallen to the third degree of mourning. [Before her first marriage, her relationship to her brother had been that of degree 2*b*. On the way in which marriage reduces the strength of relationship of a daughter to her natal family, see also case 172.4.]

Shih Fa, therefore, should be sentenced to 90 blows of the

heavy bamboo and two and one half years penal servitude, as he would under the statute [Boulais 1180] on selling, with the woman's consent, a woman of respectable family to become someone's wife or concubine.

[The basis for punishing Shih as if the woman he sold were unrelated to him is presumably Boulais 1183 (not cited), which states that the sale of any relative of a degree 3 relationship or lower to become a slave (and, therefore, we may suppose analogically, to become a wife as well, though this is not stated) is to be punished as would the similar sale of an unrelated person. Although, as we have seen in the last case, the Code stipulates punishment for sale of a *younger* brother or sister, it apparently does not visualize the possibility of selling an elder (unmarried) sister. Hence we cannot be certain what the punishment would have been had the elder sister whom Shih sold been unmarried and therefore stood to him in a degree 2b relationship, instead of being married and therefore reduced in relationship to degree 3.]

151. VIOLATION OF TOMBS
[Statutory References: Staunton 276, Boulais 1191–1198]

Case 151.8, 1813. Leading Case.
Reported in HAHL 10.20/19a–b.

The governor of Kiangsu has reported a case concerning Chang Fu-kuan, an offender from another province, who, on hearing his sick wife talking incoherently during delirium, thought she had become possessed by the ghost of a dead person. He accordingly pried open the cover of a not yet permanently buried coffin containing the body of Chang Wei-ning, without, however, actually exposing the corpse itself.

[Presumably he was interrupted before he could do this. His obvious intention was, by acting against the corpse, to drive away its ghost—perhaps that of a relative to judge from the surname—which he believed had possessed his wife. It was common in China for a deceased person's coffin to be stored for some time above ground before being permanently buried in a propitious spot and time determined by geomancy.]

By analogy to the sub-statute [Boulais 1194a] on attempting to rob, but not actually succeeding in opening, the coffin of a not yet permanently buried deceased person, Chang Fu-kuan should be sentenced to 100 blows of the heavy bamboo and three years penal servitude.

[The sub-statute is applied analogically rather than directly because, in the present case, the offender had in fact partially opened the coffin, even though he did not actually expose the corpse. Had he committed the latter act, his much graver penalty, under the same sub-statute, would have been military exile at a distant frontier (3,000 li).]

Case 151.11, 1824. Leading Case.
Reported in HAHL 10.20/20a–b.

The governor-general of Chihli has reported a case in which Kung Yu-kuei and a follower dug up the corpse of Mrs. Ma née Kuo after it had been permanently buried. The corpse had previously been merely wrapped in a rush matting without a coffin and because of the difficulty of digging far into the ground, which was frozen, had simply been covered with a layer of light soil. [Obviously, the burial was that of an extremely poor family.]

Kung and his follower were led [to meddle with the corpse] by the fact that the wind had already blown away the light soil covering the outer mat, and the digging of dogs had then exposed the corpse itself.

By analogy to the sub-statute [Boulais 1194a] on violating an old disintegrated tomb, opening its coffin, and exposing its corpse, Kung Yu-kuei is sentenced to military exile at a distant frontier, this being the punishment provided under this sub-statute for a ringleader who is a first offender. By analogy to the same sub-statute, Kung's follower, Sun Wen-ch'eng, is likewise sentenced as an accessory to total penal servitude of four years. Both men are furthermore to have the two words, "violating tombs" (*fa chung*), tatooed on their face.

[The sub-statute is applied analogically because the "tomb" of the case was not old and had already been laid open by wind and dogs prior to its disturbance. Although the sub-statute does not specifically call for tatooing, this supplementary punishment was commonly applied to various kinds of robbers (including grave robbers), as well as escapees from penal servitude or exile. The punishment of "total" or four years penal servitude is a very rare one, found only in one other of our cases (199.7). See also Chapter III, section 4.]

152. NOCTURNAL ENTRY INTO DOMESTIC RESIDENCES WITHOUT PROPER CAUSE
[Statutory References: Staunton 277, Boulais 1199–1204]

Case 152.2, 1813. Leading Case.
Reported in HAHL 11.21/16b.

The governor of Fukien has reported that Liu Fu-pang, under the influence of a recurring fit of insanity, came late at night without proper cause to the house of Huang Ning-t'ai and tried to break down the door as if he were about to plunder the interior. Huang, being unacquainted with him, beat him until he died.

Under the statute on unauthorized killing of a nocturnal intruder after he has already been seized for entering a private residence without proper cause, Huang Ning-t'ai should be sentenced to 100 blows of the heavy bamboo and three years penal servitude. [See Boulais 1199, which provides 80 blows of the heavy bamboo for a nocturnal intruder who enters a private residence without proper cause, exempts from punishment the domicile's proprietor if he kills the intruder immediately upon detecting him but sentences the proprietor to the above-mentioned penalty if the killing occurs only after the intruder has been seized.]

Case 152.4, 1815. Leading Case.
Reported in HAHL 11.21/17a.

The governor of Chekiang has reported a case in which Ho Kuo-fu, because of insanity, happened to be lying in the bed of Mrs.

Fu née Wang with naked breast and bare feet. Mrs. Fu entered the room with a lamp, saw him, and screamed, whereupon he embraced her and would not let her go. On hearing the screams, Mrs. Fu's nephew, Fu T'ien-hsiang, rushed to her rescue. He saw what looked like rape and in a paroxysm of rage stripped Ho of his clothes, beat him, and drove him outside. Because of the cold weather, Ho froze to death.

Fu T'ien-hsiang is sentenced to 100 blows of the heavy bamboo and three years penal servitude under the sub-statute [Boulais 1659b] which provides this penalty for one who, being related within the five degrees of mourning to a woman who is the object of attempted rape, kills the would-be rapist in a paroxysm of rage.

The father of the insane man is sentenced to 80 blows of the heavy bamboo under the sub-statute [Boulais 1287] which provides this penalty for relatives of an insane person who fail to report that person to the authorities, thereby allowing him finally to kill himself.

157. PREMEDITATED HOMICIDE
[Statutory References: Staunton 282, Boulais 1211–1222]

Case 157.4, 1812. Memorandum.
Reported in HAHL 11.22/12a.

The governor of Shantung has submitted a memorial on a case concerning Ch'ang Kuang, who was an accomplice of Ch'ang Lo-san in the premeditated homicide of a little boy. The accomplice has since died of illness in jail.

This Board finds, according to sub-statute [Boulais 1216], that in the premeditated homicide of a child aged ten or less, the penalty for the principal offender is immediate decapitation, and that for an accomplice who does not himself physically participate in applying the force is 100 blows of the heavy bamboo and life exile at a distance of 3,000 li. A statute on the same subject [Boulais 1214] states further that an accomplice who is not actually present at the killing is to receive a punishment one degree less than that for an accomplice who does attend but who, in so doing, does not himself physically participate in the killing.

In the present case, Ch'ang Lo-san resented being reviled by Chang Shih-neng and his wife and resolved to murder their four year old son. He informed Ch'ang Kuang who, being on bad terms with another man, Wang Feng-hsiang, told Ch'ang Lo-san that if he murdered the boy, he should take the corpse to Wang's courtyard so as to make trouble for Wang. Ch'ang Lo-san accordingly seized an opportunity to murder the child, following which Ch'ang Kuang appeared on the scene to see what had happened. Ch'ang Lo-san told Ch'ang Kuang to go ahead of him to Wang's courtyard so as to keep an eye out for people, while he himself would follow with the corpse. Having done this and left the corpse in the courtyard, the two men separated but shortly afterward were apprehended.

This Board finds that though Ch'ang Lo-san twice told Ch'ang Kuang of his plan to kill the child, Ch'ang Kuang never tried to stop him but on the contrary told him to take the corpse to Wang's courtyard in order to implicate Wang. Such conduct on Ch'ang Kuang's part actually constitutes joint conspiracy (*t'ung mou*) and so differs from being merely aware of somebody's plans to harm a third person and not trying to stop him. However, Ch'ang Kuang was not actually present when Ch'ang Lo-san murdered the child so that, though he was an accomplice, he was not an accomplice attending the crime.

The governor of Shantung has accordingly sentenced Ch'ang Kuang to penal servitude under the above-cited statute [Boulais 1214] on a person who, though an accomplice in a case of premeditated homicide, is not himself actually present at the killing. [It will be remembered that under this statute and Boulais 1216, an accomplice who does not physically participate in applying the force but is present at the crime receives life exile, and that an accomplice who is not present receives one degree less. The resulting punishment for Ch'ang Kuang is (three years) penal servitude.]

The governor has also announced the decease of the offender through illness so that there is no need to deliberate the case further. We find that the punishment fits the circumstances and that it is appropriate to ask for a confirmatory reply.

[The emphasis on giving the offender a legal sentence, despite his intervening death, should be noted. The reason no sentence is specified for the principal offender is, presumably, that his case has already been handled separately. The legal punishment for him, as indicated above, is immediate decapitation.]

159. PREMEDITATED HOMICIDE OF PARENTS OR GRANDPARENTS [11]
[Statutory References: Staunton 284, Boulais 1224–1231]

Case 159.1, 1792. Memorandum.
Reported in HAHL 11.23/1a.

The governor of Anhui has memorialized concerning a case in which the elder Mrs. Chiao, having committed adultery and fearful that her act would be reported to her husband by her daughter-in-law, got into a fight with the latter in the course of which the latter died.

The Department for Anhui of the Board of Punishments finds that among sub-statutes on the intentional killing of a junior by a senior relative, there is that on the mother-in-law who, having been detected in adultery by her daughter-in-law, tries to compel the latter to acquiesce in her lewdness, and when this attempt fails, commits a planned murder of the girl in order to seal her mouth. The prescribed penalty for this offense is the same as that prescribed in the statute concerning premeditated homicide in general, namely, decapitation after the assizes for the principal offender, and strangulation after the assizes for an accomplice. [For premeditated homicide, see Boulais 1211, and for the particular sub-statute here referred to, Boulais 1226a.]

Last year this Board memorialized to the throne a case in which an adulterous couple had murdered the woman's son to seal his mouth. In so doing it enunciated the principle that hereafter any woman who, having committed adultery, thereupon kills a son or daughter in order to seal their mouths, is, if she is the actual mother, to be sentenced to strangulation after the assizes irrespective of whether or not she originated the idea of

[11] This section, despite its title, deals with premeditated homicide *by* as well as *of* parents or grandparents.

the killing. We then memorialized to have this case go out as a general circular. Permission being granted, the result is that the death penalty is now to be applied only to cases in which a son, daughter, or daughter-in-law have been killed with premeditation or intent in order to conceal adultery; it is not to apply to those cases, involving no premeditation, in which the progeny or daughter-in-law of an adulterous mother or mother-in-law, having learned of the latter's adultery, become involved in a fight with the mother or mother-in-law, in the course of which they die. [The sub-statute resulting from this general circular, Boulais 1423a, is cited in case 159.3.]

In the present case, the elder Mrs. Chiao, having committed an adultery which was discovered by her daughter-in-law, got into a fight with the latter in which she used a pronged fire poker to beat the younger woman. This poker was seized by the daughter-in-law at the sharp end and then pulled to and fro by the two women until the younger Mrs. Chiao was stabbed and killed. Thus this homicide, though arising out of adultery, was not premeditated. Hence it should not be judged under the usual statute on premeditated homicide.

The governor of Anhui has proposed that the elder Mrs. Chiao be given a punishment one degree higher than that provided for unreasonably beating a daughter-in-law and thereby causing her death, the penalty for which is three years penal servitude [Boulais 1420]. He has accordingly sentenced her to 100 blows of the heavy bamboo and life exile at a distance of 2,000 li. He further requests that this punishment be actually carried out, without permission to commute it to a monetary fine. Because this sentence constitutes the heaviest suitable punishment, it would seem that approval may be given.

[This final paragraph raises several points: (1) The homicide committed by Mrs. Chiao, though not premeditated or intentional, was evidently felt to be so heinous as to deserve the heaviest punishment possible. Hence the increase in her sentence one degree above the punishment normally provided in Boulais 1420. Hence also the refusal to permit commutation of the sentence to a monetary fine, as Boulais 127 specifies may be granted for women convicted of crimes entailing penal servitude or life exile. (2) It is thus evident that the privilege provided for in Boulais 127 was not invariably forthcoming as a matter of right. (3) The legal justification for increasing Mrs. Chiao's sentence by one degree is unclear. Boulais 1420, having pre-scribed three years penal servitude for beating a daughter-in-law to death without justification, goes on to prescribe the increased penalty of life exile for the same offense, but only when this offense is committed with premeditation. Yet premeditation, as we have seen, was disproved in Mrs. Chiao's case. In order to in-crease her sentence, the Board, properly speaking, should have applied the statute analogically instead of directly.]

Case 159.2, 1810. Memorandum.
Reported in HAHL 11.23/1a–b.

The associate governor of Hupei has reported a case in which Wu Ta-wen, with the connivance of Ch'a Ch'uan-kuei, killed his own son, Wu Yen-hua.

In this case, Wu Ta-wen committed adultery with the wife of Ch'a Ch'uan-kuei. Ch'a tolerated the situation for the sake of money he was receiving from Wu. Wu's second son, Wu Yen-hua, however, refused to keep silent and spread the news. On hearing about it, Wu's landlord ordered Wu to move from his premises. Wu accordingly moved to another rented house, taking with him his son and his son's wife, as well as Ch'a Ch'uan-kuei and his wife. In the new house, however, Wu's son and Ch'a Ch'uan-kuei continued to quarrel frequently, until Ch'a decided that he and his wife would have to move elsewhere. Wu as a result became fearful that his affair with Mrs. Ch'a would come to an end. He therefore resolved to kill his son so that he might continue to keep the Ch'a couple in his house. Accordingly, Wu schemed with Ch'a to lure the son to a secluded place, where Wu seized his son by the queue, cut his throat, and killed him.

We find it extremely cruel of Wu Ta-wen to have killed his son with premeditation because of lustful desire for an adulterous relationship. The Hupei Provincial Court has already sentenced him to penal servitude under the statute on parents who inten-tionally kill a son. [See Boulais 1420, which provides 60 blows of the heavy bamboo and one year penal servitude for this crime. The Code says nothing about a parent who kills a son with premeditation (*mou*) as against one who merely does so with immediate intent (*ku*).] As for Ch'a Ch'uan-kuei, it has been ascertained that though he was a party to the plan for the killing, he did not himself play a physical role in the killing. Hence the associate governor of Hupei has sentenced him, under the statute on premeditated homicide, to life exile as an accomplice but not as a physical participant in the homicide. [See Boulais 1211, which provides decapitation after the assizes for the person who originates the idea of a premeditated homicide, strangulation after the assizes for an accomplice who physically participates in the homicide, and 100 blows of the heavy bamboo and life exile at a distance of 3,000 li for an accomplice who does not physically participate. See also Boulais 1214, which provides that the originator of the idea of a homicide is to be considered as the principal in the crime, even though he does not physically take part in the killing, and that accomplices who do not directly participate will be given a punishment one degree less than that of accomplices who do.] These being fair decisions, it would seem that a confirmatory reply for both may be given.

[These judgments raise two points: (1) The father, though he initiated and carried out the murder of his son, received only 60 blows of the heavy bamboo and one year penal servitude, whereas Ch'a Ch'uan-kuei, although only an accomplice, received 100 blows and life exile. This disparity illustrates the Confucian emphasis upon seniority within the family, under which crimes of parents against offspring are punished much more lightly than are the same crimes when committed outside the family, whereas crimes of offspring against parents are punished with correspondingly greater severity. Premeditated parricide, for example, constitutes one of the Ten Abominations (see Boulais 45), and is punishable by death by slicing (Boulais 1224). (2) Murder is not the only crime of which Wu Ta-wen and Ch'a Ch'uan-kuei were guilty. Thus Boulais 1595 provides 90 blows of the heavy bamboo each for a husband who tolerates the adultery of his wife with another man, for his wife, and for the other man. Likewise Boulais 1597 states that if a husband accepts money from another man so that that man may take the husband's wife in marriage, the three parties concerned are each to receive 60 blows of the heavy bamboo and one year penal servitude. That Wu and Ch'a were nevertheless punished only for murder illustrates the principle (Boulais 153) that a person who is simultaneously accused of two or more offenses is to receive punishment only for the most serious of these offenses.]

Case 159.3, 1817. Memorandum.
Reported in HAHL 11.23/1b–2a.

The governor of Shantung has memorialized concerning a case in which Mrs. Kao née P'an murdered her stepson with premeditation in order to seal his mouth concerning her adulterous relations with another person. Besides this murder, she also, out of hatred, strangled her niece to death.

This Board finds, according to sub-statute [Boulais 1423a], that any woman who, having committed adultery, then kills a son or daughter in order to seal their mouth is, if she be their stepmother, to be sentenced to decapitation after the assizes, irrespective of whether or not she originated the idea of the killing.

[The genesis of this sub-statute has been described in case 159.1. As there cited, it prescribes strangulation after the assizes for a mother who, to conceal adultery, kills her child, whereas it here prescribes a one-degree heavier penalty, decapitation after the assizes, for a stepmother who does the same. The difference no doubt reflects the Confucian idea that a mother, being more closely related to her child than is a stepmother, thereby enjoys greater authority over the child and is permitted wider legal scope to do as she wishes with it. See the discussion at the end of case 159.2.]

The sub-statute further states that it should be ascertained whether or not the murdered child, if a son, is or is not the sole heir of the murderess's husband. If he is, the murderess's death sentence should, at the Autumn Assizes, be placed in the category of those whose "circumstances are deserving of capital punishment," whereas if he is not, it should be placed in the category of "deferred execution," resulting in commutation of sentence to perpetual imprisonment. [See Chapter II, section 4, for explanation of these terms. In case 12.2 we find another instance of the exceedingly rare punishment of imprisonment for women.]

In the present case, Mrs. Kao committed adultery with Kao San, a distant cousin whose relationship to her lay outside of the five degrees of mourning. Upon discovery of the affair by her nine year old stepson, Mrs. Kao decided to strangle him with a rope. Afterwards, when her husband's elder brother and his wife announced their intention to report the matter to the authorities, she was moved by hatred to strangle their seven year old daughter as well.

This Board finds that, according to statute [Boulais 1432], the premeditated murder of a husband's [nephew or] niece is to be punished by strangulation after the assizes. Also according to substatute [see above], the premeditated murder of a stepchild to conceal an adultery is to be punished by decapitation after the assizes. That the Provincial Court of Shantung has sentenced Mrs. Kao to the heavier of these two punishments is in due accord with the statutes [see Boulais 153 and preceding case]. In failing to ascertain, however, whether or not the murdered stepson was the sole heir of Mrs. Kao's husband, the Court has been guilty of an oversight.

Regardless of this, however, Mrs. Kao, through the premeditated killing of her seven year old niece, has already made herself deserving of having her sentence entered at the assizes among those whose "circumstances are deserving of capital punishment." Her further premeditated killing of her young stepson, moreover, done in order to conceal her adultery, is an act of extreme cruelty. Thus it would be unjust if, in accordance with the ordinary procedure in cases of the killing of a stepchild by a stepmother, investigation were to show that the murdered stepson was not the sole heir of the stepmother's husband, thus paving the way for entering her sentence under "deferred execution" and resulting commutation to perpetual imprisonment. We therefore recommend that regardless of whether or not the murdered stepson was in fact the sole heir, Mrs. Kao's death sentence should, as originally proposed by the Provincial Court, be entered at the assizes among those whose "circumstances are deserving of capital punishment" [so that it may more probably be carried out]. In this way it may serve as a warning to lewd and evil persons.

160. KILLING A WIFE'S PARAMOUR [12]
[Statutory References: Staunton 285, Boulais 1232–1248]

Case 160.10, 1816. Memorandum.
Reported in HAHL 12.24/5b.

The governor of Shantung has memorialized concerning a case in which Wang Fang-chung strangled Yang Ch'ang with premeditation.

This Board finds that in cases in which a husband, having tolerated his wife's adultery, is then killed with premeditation by the wife's paramour, it is necessary to determine carefully whether the husband did in fact really tolerate the adultery. If he did, the paramour guilty of the killing is to be sentenced to decapitation after the assizes, whereas the adulterous wife, provided she had no knowledge of her paramour's plot, is to be punished for adultery only, as under the basic statute on adultery tolerated by a husband. [See Boulais 1595 which, if a husband tolerates his wife's adultery, specifies 90 blows each of the heavy bamboo for him, the wife, and her paramour. For the sub-statute covering the premeditated killing of a husband who tolerates his wife's adultery, see Boulais 1235a.]

If, on the other hand, no substantial proof of the husband's toleration is to be found, other than the verbal assertions made by the wife and her paramour, it then becomes necessary to examine the circumstances further with utmost care. If nothing new is discovered, the paramour is then to be sentenced to immediate decapitation, whereas the adulterous wife, provided she has been ignorant of her paramour's plot, is to be sentenced to strangulation after the assizes. [These are the penalties specified by the main statute on this topic, Boulais 1233. The multiple increase in penalty for the wife, as compared with the one-degree increase for the paramour, is noteworthy. However, the one-degree in-

[12] This section, despite its title, also covers adultresses and their paramours who kill the woman's husband.

crease is no doubt more decisive because it takes the offender across the borderline from uncertain to certain execution.]

In the present case, the judgment reached by the Shantung Provincial Court, namely that the murdered husband had tolerated the adultery, rests wholly on the assertions of the two adulterers. No other person, not even the adulteress's mother-in-law, who lived with her, had knowledge of the alleged toleration. More than this, however, it is also difficult to find any solid support for the assertion that the adulteress herself was ignorant of her paramour's murderous plot. Yet the Shantung Provincial Court, without investigating to get the exact facts, has [accepted these assertions and accordingly] sentenced Wang Fang-chung, the paramour, to decapitation after the assizes, and Mrs. Yang, the adulteress, to bambooing. We [members of the Directorate of the Board of Punishments] find that the Department for Shantung of this Board has acted properly in reversing the Provincial Court's decision and returning the case to it for retrial.

[Aside from the Board's sharp criticism of the Provincial Court, this case has sociological interest as one of several (see also 159.2, 172.3, 223.3) involving toleration by a husband of his wife's infidelity. That this and the somewhat related offense of wife-selling by a husband (see cases 223.2, 223.4, 223.5) are covered by specific statutes in the Code no doubt reflects a society whose low standard of living could induce a fair number of its members to commit such acts for financial gain.]

Case 160.15, 1813. Leading Case.
Reported in HAHL 12.24/8a.

The governor-general of Hunan and Hupei has memorialized concerning a case in which Ma T'ung-kuei committed adultery with Mrs. Liu née Yang and then, at Mrs. Liu's inducement, killed her father-in-law with premeditation. [The fact that it was not the husband who was killed suggests that Mrs. Liu may have been a widow.] The governor-general, by analogy to the statute [Boulais 1233] on adulterous couples who jointly plan and carry out the killing of the woman's husband, has sentenced Ma to decapitation after the assizes.

However, the adulterous love which drove this criminal into his wrongdoing was a motivating force more powerful than that found in the generality of cases, and his resulting crime is especially serious. This Board therefore requests [the throne] that his sentence be raised to immediate decapitation.

[No doubt the Board's abhorrence is prompted by the fact that the person killed is not the wife's husband but—even worse—her father-in-law. It is because of this that Boulais 1233 has to be applied analogically rather than directly, which in turn permits the board to ask for increased punishment. That this request was granted by the throne may be assumed from the fact that, without further mention of the throne's reply, the case is listed as a leading case. The penalty for Mrs. Liu, although unmentioned, must have been death by slicing because this is the specified punishment in Boulais 1233 for an adultress who kills her husband. The heavier punishment for her, as compared with that of her paramour, reflects of course her family relationship to husband or father-in-law, which caused this crime to be placed among the Ten Abominations (see Boulais 45).]

161. HOMICIDE OF THREE OR MORE PERSONS IN ONE FAMILY [13]
[Statutory References: Staunton 287, Boulais 1249–1255]

Case 161.2, 1811. Memorandum.
Reported in HAHL 13.28/1a–b.

The governor of Shensi has memorialized concerning a case in which Fang Hsing-kuei caused the death of Wen Shang-lien and Shen Lao-hsiao, and Chang Chih-lung killed Hu Lao-ta with premeditation.

The Board's investigation reveals the following facts: Wen Shang-lien, Shen Lao-hsiao, and Hu Lao-ta all lived together in a single cave, though each farmed his land separately. [In Shensi, where much of the land is covered with the cohesive soil known as loess, large numbers of peasants live in caves dug out of the

---

[13] This crime is one of several listed in Boulais 45 as comprising the fifth of the Ten Abominations.

sides of the loess hills. So did the Chinese Communists during their sojourn at Yenan, Shensi, during the 1930's and 1940's.] On one occasion Wen had forcibly seized Fang Hsing-kuei's clothing and bedding to pay for gambling losses and threatened to do the same with Fang's wheat land. Fang, as a result, developed an uncontrollable hatred for Wen and decided to kill him. It so happened that Hu Lao-ta, a second member of the trio, had likewise inflicted a vicious beating on Chang Chih-lung, who consequently also nursed the idea of killing Hu. When Fang revealed his intention to Chang, the two men that very night, around midnight, went to the cave of the trio. There they found Wen and Shen sleeping on one large platform-bed (*k'ang*) and Hu sleeping separately on a smaller one. Chang at once killed Hu with an axe, but Fang only wounded Wen with his axe, whereupon Shen woke up and began to shout. In order to silence the witness, Fang then killed both him and Wen.

This Board finds that although the three murdered men lived together in a single cave, they each farmed their own land separately and did not share their resources, so that they differed from a single household. [See the next case for extended discussion of what constitutes a household or family.] Likewise, with regard to the two murderers, each had separately suffered an affront, each had separately developed his own hatred, and each separately came to the idea of murder. It is therefore fitting that each should be punished separately for his own crime. In the case of Fang, one of his two victims was killed by him with premeditation (*mou*) and the other with intent (*ku*) but without premeditation. Therefore he should be sentenced for one killing only. [See Boulais 153, which states that if an individual is simultaneously guilty of two offenses, he is to be punished only for the more serious of them, and that if the two offenses are equally serious, he is to be punished as if he had committed only one of them. In Fang's case, the more serious crime of premeditated homicide leads to the other crime of intentional homicide being ignored when sentence is pronounced on him.]

The governor of Shensi has accordingly sentenced both Fang Hsing-kuei and Chang Chih-lung to decapitation after the assizes under the statute on premeditated homicide [Boulais 1211]. This sentence being in accord with the statute, it would seem that a confirmatory reply may be sent.

[Had the three victims been regarded on the contrary as forming a single household, and had the killings of them by Fang and Chang been regarded as a single crime instead of being judged separately, the two murderers would each have received death by slicing under the statute on killing three or more persons in a single family (Boulais 1249), instead of merely decapitation after the assizes for premeditated homicide.]

Case 161.3, 1832. Memorandum.
Reported in HAHL 13.28/1b–2a.

The Department for Yunnan of the Board of Punishments finds, according to sub-statute [Boulais 1252], that if two persons, neither of them guilty of a capital crime, are killed within a single family, the punishment for so doing is immediate decapitation and exposure of the head. The Official Commentary, in its remarks on the statute on killing three or more persons in a single family [Boulais 1249], explains: " 'Single family' *(yi chia)* means those who live together, including even slaves and servants." And in the Code's first book on General Principles, the following definition appears in the Official Commentary: " 'Jointly' *(t'ung)* means relatives who jointly share their resources and live together, irrespective of where they may have been born. Even those outside [more remote than] the five degrees of mourning are to be included." [This definition appears under the opening phrase in Boulais 173, which states: "All who jointly *(t'ung)* live together, such as . . . (here follows a long list of relatives) . . . are mutually permitted, should any among them commit a crime, to conceal one another" from prosecution.]

In the present case, two fourth-degree cousins, Wu Teng-chü and Wu Teng-tien, were traveling together on a business trip and hired Chang Ch'ing to carry their baggage. At the inn where they stopped for the night, Chang saw money in their baggage and made off with it. The two Wus quickly captured him, however, and, intending to bring him before the authorities the next day, chained him by the neck overnight to a table in their room, while they themselves spread their sleeping mats against the door and lay down to sleep. During the night, however, Chang decided to poison them. He accordingly dropped medicine which he had with him for anointing sores into the soup left over by them from the evening meal. The next morning the Wus heated up the soup for breakfast, ate it, and both died.

The governor-general of Yunnan and Kueichow, inasmuch as the two Wus were distant cousins beyond the five degrees of mourning, has assumed that they did not belong to a single family. He has therefore deemed it proper to convict Chang Ch'ing for a single killing only [see Boulais 153 and comment near end of preceding case] and has accordingly sentenced him to decapitation after the assizes by analogy to the statute on a criminal who, while resisting capture, kills the person trying to capture him [Boulais 1658].

Our examination of cases of multiple homicide, however, indicates that if the victims are persons who have lived together and jointly shared their resources, they should then be properly regarded as belonging to a single family irrespective of whether or not their relationship to each other lies within the five degrees of mourning. Therefore, when these circumstances exist, one may not apply the statute on sentencing for a single offense only [see reference to Boulais 153 above] in order to give a lighter sentence to the killer.

In the present case, Wu Teng-chü arranged with his fourth-degree younger cousin Wu Teng-tien to go on a business trip together, during which time they traveled together and stayed overnight together. Between this and living together there is no essential difference. The load carried by Chang Ch'ing for the two Wus was baggage belonging to both of them, and what he stole from them was likewise money belonging to both of them. They may thus be regarded as men who jointly shared their resources.

The fact that Chang's poisoning of the two stemmed from their discovery of his theft makes his crime even worse than that of someone who decides to kill two persons in a single family because of some other kind of quarrel. How then can Chang nonetheless be given a sentence still lighter than the latter's? The governor-general has failed to examine the precedent cases with care and has evinced confusion in hastily deciding that the two victims did not belong to a single family. To use a statute analogically in order to sentence the offender to decapitation after the assizes would very definitely not suffice as an equitable decision, involving as it does a change of sentence from immediate decapitation with exposure of the head.

It would not be proper for this Board to issue a confirmatory reply for such a judgment. The governor-general should be instructed to arrive at a satisfactory judgment in accordance with precedent and to present it anew.

[This case exemplifies even better than the preceding one the meaning of "family" in China.]

162. MUTILATION OR MAIMING OF A LIVING PERSON [14]
[Statutory References: Staunton 288, Boulais 1256–1258]

Case 162.1, 1812. General Circular from the Kiangsu Printed Edition.
Reported in HAHL 13.28/31b–32a.

Previously, the Censorial Circuit of Chekiang submitted a memorial transmitting information received by it from Fang Ta-ch'uan, a former censor now retired to his native place, concerning his fellow townsman, Chang Liang-pi, who has been killing people by mutilating them. The memorial requested that the governor of Anhui, Ch'ien K'ai, be instructed to investigate and handle the matter. [The provinces of Anhui and Chekiang adjoin each other, but such investigation by the governor of one province of the affairs of another is of course an extraordinary procedure.] The governor has, accordingly, since submitted a memorial, reporting the facts of his investigation and his resulting

---

[14] This crime is one of several listed in Boulais 45 under the fifth of the Ten Abominations. Boulais 1256 explains that the crime is not committed deliberately in order to kill people, but rather in order to obtain the organs or other parts of (usually living) human beings for magical purposes—for example, in order to make from them an anthropomorphic figure which can then do one's bidding or can be sacrificed to some evil spirit, or in order to concoct from the organs medicines of extraordinary efficacy and so on.

judgment. An imperial edict, dated January 19, 1812, has now been issued in answer to his memorial.

Imperial Edict: Governor Ch'ien K'ai has submitted a memorial concerning the investigating and convicting of Chang Liang-pi for committing homicide by mutilating people. He has also requested that the magistrate and prefect of the respective local district and prefecture, because of their failure to investigate and prosecute the case, be summarily dismissed so they may undergo strict examination.

In this case Chang Liang-pi licked and sucked out the vital marrow of sixteen baby girls, eleven of whom died as a result while one was left disabled. [The translator is unable to explain the physical details of this extracting of feminine "vital marrow" (*ching sui*). The man, if actually guilty (see final comment), was probably a sex pervert.] Surely such horrible deeds were done by one who though human in form is a beast in nature. The offender already began his evil as early as 1796, and although in the beginning he perhaps could have claimed not to have realized the consequences of his acts, could he still have remained unaware after causing a death or two? For sixteen years he was familiar with evil, thus bringing death to more than ten persons.

The governor has recommended sentencing the offender by analogy to the statute on mutilating or maiming living persons [Boulais 1257], with, however, a reduction from its penalty of death by slicing to that of immediate decapitation. What is his purpose in thus secretly aiding such a human devil? The penalty for killing two persons in the same family, neither of them being guilty of a capital crime, is immediate decapitation [Boulais 1252], and for killing three or more such persons it is death by slicing [Boulais 1249]. How then can mere immediate decapitation cover the crime of destroying more than ten baby girls? Let Chang-Liang-pi at once undergo death by slicing.

The offender has already reached the age of seventy. Lest he die of illness or escape execution through suicide, it is ordered that this edict be sent by the 400 li per day post to Governor Ch'ien K'ai, who on its receipt must first of all have the offender executed by slicing. The execution is to be viewed by the masses, including all families of the sixteen victims, thus cheering men's hearts and purging them of their anger. Chang's family belongings are all to be confiscated and divided under official supervision among the sixteen families of the victims. A memorial on what has happened is then to be presented. [The edict fails to mention that, according to the same statute (Boulais 1257), the criminal's wife, children, and other family relatives living with him are to undergo life exile at a distance of 2,000 li, even though they may have been ignorant of his crimes.]

The matter of Governor Ch'ien K'ai's wrong judgment should be given to the Board of Punishments for consideration [as to possible punishment]. The local prefect and local magistrate are both to be dismissed from office and put in the hands of the governor for him to determine through strict investigation whether or not they received bribes to let the matter go unnoticed. If indeed they did, then there surely must be persons through whom the bribes passed, such as the servants and clerks of their yamens [government offices], or the members of Chang Liang-pi's own household. All of these persons can supply testimony, without any need to delay Chang's own execution. The governor must handle the matter strictly and impartially, avoiding the least bit of favoritism. After the investigation has been concluded, he is to submit another memorial reporting it. As to whether Fang Ta-ch'uan [the retired censor who first reported the matter] should also undergo investigation [concerning possible connivance or other wrongdoing], there will be time enough to consider this when the case reaches its final stage.

[The summary and emotional tone of this edict illustrates what may happen when the emperor personally intervenes in a case arousing his strong feelings. Thus the edict, in contrast to the normal judicial report, provides no details about the crimes of the offender. Indeed, its vagueness in this respect even suggests the possibility that the charges brought against the defendant were perhaps no more substantial than those made in the many witchcraft trials in the West. (Conceivably, doubts on this score may have caused Governor Ch'ien K'ai—otherwise rather inexplicably—to apply the relevant statute to the offender only analogically, with reduction of penalty, rather than directly. This, if so, would also explain the earlier failure of the local prefect and magistrate to take any action.) No statute is cited by the edict when sentencing the offender, nor is anything said about the disposition of his family members (who, as we have seen, are subject, according to statute, to life exile). Punishment is threatened for the governor who suggested an overly lenient punishment and even, perhaps, for the retired censor who originally brought the case to light. (It should be noted, however, that a legal basis, Boulais 1682–1691, does exist for punishing an official if he has been guilty of deliberately rendering a wrong judgment.) The understandably strong reaction of the emperor toward this case should be compared with the hands-off attitude of the same Chia-ch'ing Emperor toward the much less explosive case 147.2.]

164. HOMICIDE COMMITTED DURING AN AFFRAY OR WITH INTENT
[Statutory References: Staunton 290, Boulais 1268–1278]

Case 164.1, 1826. Memorandum.
Reported in HAHL 14.29/1a.

The governor of Hunan has reported a case in which Wang Ssu and others jointly assaulted Yang Ta-ho and Li Hung-huai, causing their deaths. [For discussion of another aspect of this same case, see case 166.1.]

This Board finds, according to sub-statute [Boulais 1276a], that if several persons have planned a joint assault resulting in the death of two persons not belonging to the same family, and if the original planner of the assault should die of illness while awaiting sentence in prison, his death will be acceptable as requital for the deaths of the victims, the result being that any of the other assailants guilty of having actually inflicted fatal blows and therefore normally punishable by strangulation [after the assizes] shall have this penalty reduced by one degree to life exile [at a distance of 3,000 li].

[To be properly understood, this sub-statute should be read in conjunction with the basic statute on homicidal group affray (Boulais 1270), according to which the person (or persons) who actually strike the mortal blows in such an affray are to suffer strangulation after the assizes, in contrast to its original planner who, irrespective of whether or not he has physically participated in the fight, is merely to receive life exile at a distance of 3,000 li—unless, that is, he too has been one of those striking the fatal blows. (The explanation for this differentiation given in the Shen Chih-ch'i Commentary is that the original planner merely intended to injure his prospective victim, and that therefore if the victim nevertheless dies, this is the fault of those who mortally wounded him and not of the planner.) With this statute in mind, we can now better understand the sub-statute, according to which, should the original planner die in prison while awaiting sentence, his death expiates, so to speak, the capital crime committed by his associates in fatally injuring the victim. Their punishment of strangulation after the assizes is therefore cancelled for them, and in its place they receive the punishment of life exile which otherwise would have gone to the original planner.]

[Despite its comparative modernity (it was promulgated in 1801), this sub-statute embodies a cosmological conception of very early origin. The key term here is *ti ming*, "requital-life" or "requiting a life," the meaning of which is that one life (or death) is to be given as requital for another. The term appears in the clause of the sub-statute rendered freely but accurately above as "his death will be acceptable as requital for the deaths of the victims." To the ancient Chinese, with their insistence upon a basic harmony existing between man and nature, a human crime —particularly a homicide—was regarded as a disruption of the total cosmic order. This disruption could be repaired only by offering or sacrificing adequate requital for what had been destroyed—a life for a life, an eye for an eye. Precisely how this should be done was less important than the fact of requital per se. Thus, in the sub-statute, the death of the original planner of the affray, even though fortuitous, is reckoned as cancelling out the death of the victim or victims, and therefore as releasing the planner's guilty associates from undergoing the retributive capital punishment otherwise required from them. Of course the concept in late times becomes highly symbolic: the penalty for striking the fatal blows, once a straightforward strangulation, has now become mitigated to strangulation after the assizes and thus no longer precisely balances the death of the victim; likewise the death of the original planner is accepted as adequate requital for the deaths of even two victims. For further analysis see the next case, citing a closely related sub-statute, Boulais 1275 (promulgated, like this one, in 1801 and containing the same term, *ti ming*). See also the discussion in Chapter VI, section 3.]

In the present case, Wang Ssu and Hu Teng-k'o, the latter now a fugitive from justice, accepted the invitation of Tseng Li-fang to join in an attack on Yang Yung-tso because Tseng was angry at Yang for having prevented him (Tseng) from collecting grass in waste lands belonging to the state. The ensuing fight resulted in the death of Yang's son, Yang Ta-ho, and of an unrelated neighbor, Li Hung-huai. Investigation has shown that Hu Teng-k'o was the one who fatally wounded Li Hung-huai, and Wang Ssu was the one who did the same to Yang Ta-ho. Since the attack did not involve any unusual circumstances, the offenders were sentenced under the ordinary statute on assault [Boulais 1270, outlined above].

Now, inasmuch as the original planner of the affray, Tseng Li-fang, has subsequently died of illness while in prison, the governor of Hunan has therefore sentenced Wang Ssu under the sub-statute cited above, according to which the death of the original planner while in prison is acceptable as requital for the death of the victim, thereby allowing a one-degree reduction of sentence for the actual striker of the fatal blow. Accordingly, the governor has sentenced Wang to bambooing and life exile instead of strangulation after the assizes. [Presumably the other chief assailant, Hu Teng-k'o, would have similarly benefited had he not become a fugitive.]

As for Tseng Li-fang himself, it happens that he surrendered himself to the authorities on learning that he was wanted. The governor has accordingly reduced his sentence by one degree from the life exile for which he would otherwise have been liable to [three years] penal servitude. In view of his subsequent death, there is no need to discuss his case further.

Both of these verdicts being appropriate, it is proper to request a confirmatory reply.

[The sub-statute here used is Boulais 122a from the section on confession by criminals. Note that Tseng's surrender to the authorities, unlike his death in prison, results in no transferral of reduced punishment to the assailant Wang Ssu because only the death itself serves as a requital for another death. Note also the Board's emphasis here, as in case 157.4, on confirming the legal sentence given to the offender by the governor, despite the offender's intervening death.]

Case 164.2, 1818. Memorandum.
Reported in HAHL 14.29/1a–b.

The governor of Kuangtung has memorialized concerning a case in which Ts'ai Niu-tsai and others joined in an affray which led to the death of Yüan Wu-shou and ten others. Among the persons guilty of attack, Ts'ai Ssu-ching and Mai Shu-hsin were each responsible for one death. Two other men, Ts'ai Fa-tsai and Ts'ai Ch'ien-fu, who were each guilty of striking fatal blows, have since successively died, the first in prison, the second while free on bail because of illness.

This Board finds, according to sub-statute [Boulais 1275], that if, in a case of joint assault resulting in homicide, an assailant who has struck mortal blows should encounter a situation in which either the original planner of the affray or the other assailants guilty of having struck mortal blows should die from illness either while awaiting sentence in prison or while en route to the trial, such death will be accepted as a requital for the death of the victim, thereby entitling the above-mentioned first assailant to have his normal penalty of strangulation [after the assizes] reduced by one degree to life exile [at a distance of 3,000 li. See preceding case for the significance of this sub-statute and of the similar sub-statute there cited.].

According to another sub-statute, however, if in a case of joint assault resulting in the homicide of three persons or more, the original planner should die of illness either while awaiting sentence in prison or while en route to the trial or should commit suicide out of fear of impending punishment, such death shall not warrant any reduction of punishment for the assailants guilty of having actually struck the fatal blows. [This sub-statute, Boulais

1276a, is a continuation of the portion already cited in case 164.1. In its original form it is a complex statement which, for the sake of clarity, has been reduced in translation to its essential point, namely, that it in effect denies the applicability of the earlier-cited Boulais 1275 to any case of affray involving the homicide of more than two persons.]

Whereas the earlier sub-statute permits a reduction of penalty for an assailant guilty of mortal blows either in the event of the death of the original planner or of any of the other guilty assailants, the second sub-statute, covering affrays involving the homicide of three or more persons, bars any such reduction in the event of the death of the original planner but makes no mention at all of the course to be followed should any of the other guilty assailants die prior to sentencing. Consistency, however, requires us to conclude that in such an event, also, a reduction of penalty would still have to be denied.

The present case, involving as it does the homicide of eleven victims, falls within the category of joint affrays resulting in the homicide of three or more persons [and therefore comes under the jurisdiction of the second of the two cited sub-statutes]. Hence, even though two of the assailants guilty of having struck fatal blows have since died, one of them in prison, the other out on bail, it would not be proper on this account to permit any reduction of punishment for the two remaining guilty assailants, Ts'ai Ssu-ching and Mai Shu-hsin. Therefore both of these criminals should, as already suggested by the governor of Kuangtung, be sentenced to strangulation after the assizes.

165. DEPRIVING A PERSON OF CLOTHING OR FOOD [15]

[Statutory References: Staunton 291, Boulais 1281–1282]

Case 165.2, 1816. Leading Case from the Department of Chihli of the Board of Punishments.
Reported in HAHL 14.31/12a–b.

The military lieutenant-governor of Jehol has reported a case in which Ho-ch'i-erh-pu-ni [a Mongol], after capturing Na-mu-sa-lai

---

[15] This section, despite its title, also contains a clause covering the introducing of foreign objects into a person's nostrils, ears, and other body openings. See case 165.5.

[another Mongol], who had been cutting wood on a mountain watched over by Ho-ch'i-erh-pu-ni, tied him up, took off his outer robe, and spread it over him, but with its collar firmly held down by something else. He later said that this was done so the offender might be taken to the authorities [without escaping, as he might have done if he were either wearing the robe or free to take it with him], and that he had no thought of letting him freeze. Na-mu-sa-lai nonetheless managed to escape on the road and [without his robe] froze to death.

This Department finds that this death, resulting as it did from Na-mu-sa-lai's escape, was of his own choosing. Hence Ho-ch'i-erh-pu-ni should be sentenced, under the statute on causing death by depriving a person of clothing or food [Boulais 1281], to 100 blows of the heavy bamboo and life exile at a distance of 3,000 li, this being one degree less than the punishment of strangulation [after the assizes] provided by the statute. [Here, as in some other cases, the Board, in order to justify its reduction of statutory penalty, ought in theory to apply the statute analogically rather than directly.]

[In the present case, as in the two that follow, the Board shows great reluctance to apply the full penalty of the relevant statute, and uses what may seem to some rather narrowly technical grounds to find excuses for the offender. Nonetheless, it then goes on in each case to sentence the offender to what is still a severe punishment, even though one degree less than that provided by statute. In China it was always difficult for anyone even remotely involved in a chain of circumstances resulting in death to escape at least some degree of responsibility. See, for example, the severe sentences handed out for the traffic deaths recorded in cases 170.1 and 170.2.]

Case 165.3, 1822. Leading Case.
Reported in HAHL 14.31/12b.

The governor-general of Chihli has reported a case in which P'eng Lo-wan, having vainly asked Ch'en Hua-tzu to pay him his gambling debt, put pressure (*pi*) upon him until Ch'en took off his clothing as collateral security for the debt. The consequence was that Ch'en became so cold that he committed suicide by jumping into a well.

This Board finds that it was Ch'en himself who took off his clothes and tossed them to the ground and not P'eng who stripped them off by force (ch'iang). Ch'en's death, moreover, resulted from his own suicide and thus was not the same as death due to exposure. Therefore P'eng Lo-wan should be sentenced, by analogy to the statute on causing death by depriving someone of clothing or food [Boulais 1281], to 100 blows of the heavy bamboo and life exile at a distance of 3,000 li, this being one degree less than the penalty of strangulation [after the assizes] provided by the statute.

[In this, unlike the preceding and the following case, the statute is applied analogically, thereby correctly permitting the reduction of sentence. Note the important distinction made in this case between pi, "pressure, pressingly, to exert pressure," and ch'iang, "force, forcibly, to exert force." The former has reference solely to verbal and psychological pressures (it appears commonly, for example, in cases in which the victim has been "pressed" into committing suicide), whereas the latter refers to outright physical force. In China, as in other civilizations, crimes of physical violence are usually punished more severely than those causing harm by applying only verbal and psychological pressures.]

Case 165.4, 1819. Leading Case.
Reported in HAHL 14.31/12b.

The governor-general of Chihli has reported a case in which Li Chung-lin, an innkeeper, became alarmed lest a lodger, Tu Chih-pang, being critically ill, might die in the inn and thereby involve him (Li) in trouble. Li accordingly carried the sick man naked outside and left him in a field, where Tu, as a result of illness and exposure, died.

This Board finds that Tu had himself already taken off his clothing [when he first became ill] and that therefore Li was not guilty of doing this [when he carried Tu out of the inn]. Moreover, Tu had already been critically ill so that his death was not due solely to exposure. Therefore, under the statute on causing death by depriving someone of clothing or food [Boulais 1281], Li Chung-lin should be sentenced to 100 blows of the heavy bamboo and life exile at a distance of 3,000 li, this being one degree less than the penalty of strangulation [after the assizes provided by the statute. Here again, as in case 165.2, the statute is not expressly applied analogically when reducing the sentence.]

Case 165.5, 1824. Leading Case.
Reported in HAHL 14.31/12b.

The governor-general of Chihli has memorialized concerning a case in which Su T'ing-hsiu, after being scratched by Mao Ming-ho, had ordure spread over his mouth and face by Mao Hua-hsia, with the result that, revolted by the stench, he vomited until he died.

By analogy to the statute on introducing foreign objects into someone's ears, nostrils, or other openings of the body, thereby causing his death [Boulais 1281], Mao Hua-hsia should be sentenced to strangulation after the assizes. [Presumably the man who first scratched the victim was punished separately.]

[There are two probable reasons why the statute is here applied analogically rather than directly: (1) The offense specified by the statute is that of inducing homicide by "introducing foreign objects *into*" the victim's ears, nostrils, etc., whereas the victim of the present case died as the result of having had ordure "spread *over*" (but not into) his mouth and face. (2) The statute's reference is to the "ears, nostrils, or other openings of the body," whereas the case mentions only the "mouth and face" of the victim. Although the statute does not further define what it means by "other openings," we may almost certainly assume that the term does not include the mouth, because, in view of its importance, it would surely be specified separately just as are the ears and nostrils. (Homicide by poisoning, which of course *does* normally involve the mouth, is dealt with elsewhere in the Code. See Boulais 1263.)]

166. KILLING OR WOUNDING DURING ROUGHHOUSING, BY MISCHANCE, OR BY ACCIDENT

[Statutory References: Staunton 292, Boulais 1283–1297]

Case 166.1, 1826. Memorandum.
Reported in HAHL 14.31/13a.

The governor of Hunan has memorialized concerning a case in which Wang Ssu and others assaulted Yang Ta-ho, thereby causing his death, after which the original planner of the assault died in prison while awaiting sentence. Wang Ssu, as a result, was given a sentence reduced by one degree [from strangulation after the assizes] to life exile. The governor also stated that Wang should pay funeral money to the family of the victim. [See case 164.1, where this affair, and the reason for the reduced sentence, have already been discussed, without, however, touching upon the payment of funeral expenses, which is the aspect of prime concern here.]

In another case, however, the governor of Hupei has reported that Yao Tso-lun and others assaulted Lo Yen-chün, thereby causing his death, after which one of the other assailants who had, like Yao, been guilty of striking mortal blows, died in prison while awaiting sentence. Yao Tso-lun, as a result, was given a sentence reduced by one degree [from strangulation after the assizes] to life exile, but the governor failed to say anything about his paying funeral money to the victim's family.

This Board finds, according to sub-statute [Boulais 1285a], that any criminal guilty of a capital crime, but then saved from death by an imperial amnesty, is thereupon required to pay 20 ounces of silver to the family of his victim. Another sub-statute [Boulais 166a] likewise states that if, in a case of homicide, the offender's sentence is reduced from death to a lower penalty [as in the two cases cited above], he is required to contribute a fixed sum for the funeral expenses of his victim and to complete the payment of this sum within a three-month period.

There is thus no doubt that an offender guilty of a capital crime, irrespective of whether he then receives an amnesty or otherwise gains a reduction of his penalty from death to military or life exile, is required to pay funeral money to the family of his victim. The two cases cited above both equally involve a one-degree reduction of penalty from strangulation [after the assizes], so that it would be improper to treat the one differently from the other. The governor of Hupei has been careless in his failure to make explicit reference in his report to the payment of funeral money. Let him add a clause concerning it.

Case 166.2, 1826. Memorandum.
Reported in HAHL 14.31/13a–b.

The Department for Shantung has been examining the kinds of homicide for which the offender is required to pay fixed sums of money to cover the funeral expenses of the victim. Aside from those cases in which such payment is explicitly required by statute [see among other examples Boulais 154, 1285–1286, 1312–1313, 1316, 1319], the question of whether or not payment is required for other kinds of cases depends upon whether they are homicides for which the standard penalty is or is not capital punishment.

Among kinds of homicide requiring the payment of funeral expenses, we find, for example, that though homicide resulting from an affray is normally a capital offense, this offense is reducible to life exile if the death, instead of occurring within a stipulated period coming immediately after the affray, takes place only at a later time as the result of infection. [See Boulais 1361, which stipulates that, immediately following an affray in which injuries have been inflicted, there shall be a "healing period" of five or ten days (depending upon the seriousness of what, under this sub-statute, are in general relatively minor injuries). If, within this healing period, the injuries prove fatal, the offender is then given the death penalty. If, on the other hand, the injuries do not result in death until after the expiration of the healing period, the offender's penalty then becomes reducible from capital punishment to life exile.]

Besides the foregoing, there are also cases in which a son kills someone in order to rescue his parents. [A sub-statute, Boulais

1445a, provides that if a son kills someone who is attacking his parents, thereby saving them from a really critical situation, he may use this ground to appeal to the emperor for a reduction of his death sentence for killing.] There are also cases of assault with resulting homicide in which either the original planner or one of the assailants who actually struck the fatal blows dies in prison while awaiting sentence. [See cases 164.1 and 164.2 for explanation.] In all such instances the primary offender, who would otherwise be guilty of a capital crime, is permitted through special circumstances to receive a reduced sentence. In all of them, as a consequence, he is thereupon obliged, because of his changed status, to pay money to the family of his victim.

If, on the other hand, an injury suffered in an affray leads to death through infection but does so only after the standard healing period has elapsed, yet still within the duration of a supplemental period immediately following, the person who has inflicted the injury will then, as under the statute on disabling somebody [Boulais 1347], be sentenced merely to [three years] penal servitude. [This is the second part (omitted by Boulais) of the sub-statute cited above as Boulais 1361. Unlike the first part, which concerns relatively minor injuries, the second part concerns broken bones and the like, the healing period for which is therefore much longer (50 days), and is followed by yet another supplemental period of 20 days. Death of the victim during the healing period proper means death for the offender, whereas death during the supplemental period means only penal servitude.] This kind of sentence differs from that of a death sentence which for special reasons becomes reducible to life exile, and therefore it carries with it no obligation to pay the funeral expenses of the victim.

In 1796 and 1797, this Board examined two cases coming to it from Shantung, in each of which the victim of an assault eventually died of wounds which became infected only after the expiration of the standard healing period. This Board, following the considerations noted above, therefore notified the governor not to require the offenders to pay the funeral expenses.

Now, however, according to reports recently received from the governor of Shantung, two men guilty of assault resulting in eventual death have both been sentenced to penal servitude under the sub-statute just cited and under the sub-statute cited by it in turn on disabling someone. Yet the governor has recommended that these men both pay the funeral expenses of their victims. Were this now to be approved by this Board, it would conflict with the disposition of earlier cases.

The relevant arguments should therefore be examined, and the meaning of the various sub-statutes clarified, so as to notify the governor that hereafter, for the sake of consistency, no payment of funeral expenses should be considered in cases of this kind.

[The underlying principle involved may be summarized as follows: (1) no payment of funeral expenses if the offender's homicide is of a sort for which he is actually executed; (2) payment to be made if the homicide is of a sort for which, under special circumstances, the normal death penalty is legally reducible to life exile; (3) no payment if the homicide is of a sort which, from the very beginning, is punishable by less than a death penalty. From the fact that it is only under the conditions of (2) that payment is to be made, we may deduce that such payment was originally thought of as an indemnity made by the offender for the fact that the reduction in his sentence no longer permits him to expiate with his own life the life of his victim. The practical result, however, as regards the family of the victim, is that it is better for them if the offender's sentence is reduced than if he actually undergoes execution.]

[It should be further noted that the foregoing principle is violated by those kinds of homicide (see listed examples in first paragraph) for which payment of funeral expenses is explicitly required by the relevant statutes or sub-statutes. All of these homicides seem to belong to category (3), namely, homicides for which the normal penalty, to start with, is less than death. It is presumably precisely because they contradict the general principle that the relevant articles in the Code explicitly stipulate the paying of funeral expenses in respect to them. No such stipulation, on the other hand, is made with regard to the kinds of homicide belonging to category (2), for which payment is actually obligatory but is taken for granted and therefore is not mentioned.]

Case 166.3, 1813. Memorandum.
Reported in HAHL 14.31/13b.

The governor of Fukien has reported a case in which Wu Ch'i-li set off fireworks, thus causing fire resulting in the deaths of four persons. The occasion was one on which Wu [and other family members] had gone to the mountains to offer sacrifices at the tombs of his ancestors. The charred remnants of the fireworks set fire to a thicket, and four people died as a result. [Probably this was at the Ch'ing-ming or "Clear and Bright" festival, about April 5, a day for visiting the graves of the ancestors in the countryside, there to offer sacrifices, to picnic, and to engage in general merry-making.]

This Board finds that what happened was neither foreseeable nor avoidable. From this it follows that the sentence should be based upon the statute on killing by accident, under which redemption by fine is permitted. [See Boulais 1285, which states that accidental killing or injuring is to be punished as would killing or injuring in an affray but then explains further that the resulting punishments are, in the accident cases, redeemable by monetary fines, to be paid to the families of the victims. For the table of such fines, of which the highest is 12.42 ounces of silver for accidental death, see Boulais, pp. 13–14.]

["Neither foreseeable nor avoidable" (literally, "what the ears and eyes do not reach, what thinking and planning do not arrive at," *erh-mu so pu chi, ssu-lü so pu tao*) is the formal definition offered by the Official Commentary, under Boulais 1285, to explain the meaning of "accident" or "accidental" (*kuo-shih*). The commentary then provides examples of accidental homicide or injury, among them: throwing a brick or tile at something and unexpectedly killing or injuring a person; falling while climbing in a precipitous place and thereby dragging one's companion to his death; being the unwitting collaborator with an uncontrollable force, such as the wind blowing upon one's boat, a runaway horse, or a vehicle rolling down a hill; joining with someone in lifting a heavy object which falls and crushes the other person. In all of these cases, the Commentary concludes, there is a resulting death or injury without any initial thought of doing harm on the part of any of the persons involved.]

In cases of multiple accidental killings, however, the relevant sub-statute [Boulais 154] states that the amount of redemption money depends upon the number of persons killed. Yet in the present case the governor has ordered Wu Ch'i-li merely to pay a single sum of 12.42 ounces of silver, which is a mistake. He should instead order Wu to pay four times this amount, the total to be divided equally among the families of the four victims.

[This and case 89.1 are very similar in that they both involve multiple deaths resulting from the setting off of fireworks. Yet the two cases are classed very differently. In both of them, however, the penalties seem slight considering the large number of fatalities involved.]

167. HUSBAND BEATING TO DEATH A CULPABLE WIFE OR CONCUBINE
[Statutory References: Staunton 293, Boulais 1298–1301]

Case 167.5, 1809. Memorandum.
Reported in HAHL 15.33/3a–b.

The governor of Kuangtung has reported two cases in which Su Jung-kuei and Hsü Hsien respectively killed their wives in anger.

This Board finds, according to statute [Boulais 1298], that if a wife or concubine strikes or reviles her parents-in-law and if the husband thereupon takes it upon himself to kill her, his penalty for so doing shall be 100 blows of the heavy bamboo. The Official Commentary, in its annotation on this statute, adds that for judgment to be made under it, the parents of the husband must personally bring an accusation against the woman in court. [If they fail to do so, the statute with its special mitigating circumstances will not be applied, and the husband will be sentenced instead under another statute (Boulais 1403) which provides strangulation after the assizes for the wanton killing of a wife by her husband.]

It may well happen that a husband, having beaten his wife to death because of some secret factor in their marital life or for some other reason, will then allege as justification that the wife had reviled or struck his parents. The latter too, because they dote upon their son, may go along with his fabrication of false testimony. Thus the Official Commentary's annotation on the statute is made with the purpose of preventing collusion and deceit from being practiced to exculpate the son of his crime.

Now as to the cases of Su Jung-kuei and Hsü Hsien: Su, angry that his wife had contradicted his mother and even pushed her to the ground, inflicted knife cuts on the wife so that she died; Hsü did the same to his wife because she too had used foul language against his mother and pushed her to the ground. Su's mother thereupon told the local constable about her daughter-in-law's behavior to her. [This constable, it is important to note in connection with what is said below, was not a formal member of the administration but was usually a relatively lowly commoner who, though appointed by the authorities to perform certain local supervisory tasks on their behalf, received no pay for this other than what his position might enable him to squeeze from his fellow community members.] As to the similar incident between Hsü's wife and his mother, this had been witnessed by a neighbor.

The governor of Kuangtung apparently supposes that there is no essential difference between such evidence and the personal bringing of formal charges before the court by the two mothers. He has accordingly sentenced both husbands to bambooing, using the above-cited statute on a husband who takes it upon himself to kill his wife because she has reviled or struck his parents.

This Board finds, however, that despite the considerations stated above, the ultimate fact remains that the two mothers failed to go in person to court to lodge an accusation and thereby failed to fulfill the stipulation laid down in the Official Commentary. Moreover, the possibility still exists that the offenders may have killed their wives for reasons other than those alleged, and then trumped up false evidence in order to avoid retribution. The governor, by accepting unsubstantiated evidence obtained at a later time and on that basis sentencing the husbands to 100 blows of the heavy bamboo, has rendered a definitely unsuitable judgment. He should be instructed to act again on the basis of law so as this time to reach a satisfactory judgment. [The strong implication is that he should sentence the husbands, under the above-mentioned Boulais 1403, to strangulation after the assizes for wanton wife killing.]

Case 167.11, 1819. Leading Case.
Reported in HAHL 15.33/5a.

The governor-general of Szechuan has reported a case in which Chang K'ai-p'eng, because his concubine had worked herself up into a tantrum, beat and injured her with a stick, and then tied her in her room, hoping she would repent. Later he heard her in her room reviling his parents. This so enraged him that he refused to give her food or drink, with the result that she suffered a recurrence of a former illness from which she died.

This Board finds that inasmuch as the concubine died from illness, it would not be proper to sentence the husband under the statute [Boulais 1403] which provides maximum [three years] penal servitude for a man who beats to death his concubine. On the other hand, Chang not only beat her but also tied her up and deprived her of food and drink after having heard her revile his parents, thereby occasioning the illness which led to her death. It would therefore likewise not be proper, simply because she died from illness, to disregard the fact that he deprived her of food and drink, and merely sentence him under the statute [also Boulais 1403] which frees a husband from any punishment if in beating a wife [or concubine] he does not break any of her bones [such as an arm or leg].

Accordingly, Chang K'ai-p'eng is to be sentenced to 100 blows of the heavy bamboo, by analogy to the statute [Boulais 1298] concerning a husband who takes it upon himself to kill a wife or concubine because she has reviled or struck his parents.

[The statute is applied analogically rather than directly because, according to the argument given, Chang's treatment of his concubine was a relatively remote cause of her death. In contrast to the preceding case, where the applicability of this same statute hinged upon whether or not the mothers-in-law had personally gone to court to report the unseemly behavior of their daughters-in-law, this factor is completely ignored in the present case. Moreover, it might seem that a statute at least equally apposite for sentencing the offender would be Boulais 1281, which provides strangulation after the assizes for anyone guilty of having deprived someone of food, thereby causing his death. Chinese emphasis on the family, however, means that a statute or sub-statute handling a crime in terms of family relationships, in a case in which such relationships occur, usually takes precedence over another statute in which family relationships are not considered (even if it be a statute dealing with such a specific offense as that of depriving someone of food).]

[The net result, as far as the present case is concerned, is that a man who not only beat his concubine, but also confined and deprived her of food—acts of considerable duration and therefore not attributable to sudden uncontrolled anger—received only 100 blows of the heavy bamboo. This punishment contrasts with the treatment of the two husbands of the preceding case, whose killing of their wives may in fact have sprung from sudden anger but whose initial sentencing to the same punishment of 100 blows was nevertheless reversed and replaced by another sentence which, though unspecified, probably consisted of strangulation after the assizes. Of course, there is a considerable difference of status between a wife and a concubine. As we have seen in the two cases, the penalty provided by Boulais 1403 for wantonly killing a wife is strangulation after the assizes, whereas for doing the same to a concubine it is only three years penal servitude.]

168. KILLING OFFSPRING OR SLAVES AND IMPUTING THE CRIME TO AN INNOCENT PERSON
[Statutory References: Staunton 294, Boulais 1302–1310]

Case 168.1, 1826. Memorandum.
Reported in HAHL 15.33/5b–6a.

The governor-general of Chihli has reported a case in which Wang Wu choked his son to death. Wang had often borrowed money and rice from Keng Yü-ts'ai and never kept an account. Finally, after being constantly annoyed, Keng refused to lend him any more. At this juncture Wang, because he was poor and found it hard to make a living, decided to murder his blind son, who could do nothing but eat, in order to lighten his own burden. He choked the boy to death.

Afterwards Wang remembered Keng's refusal to lend him money and rice and conceived the idea of leaving the corpse at Keng's doorway, intending thus to impute the crime to Keng and extort money from him. He did in fact carry the corpse there but failed in his attempt at extortion. When Keng reported the matter to the authorities, Wang was arrested.

This Board finds that it was Wang's own poverty that caused him to dislike his son for his blindness and uselessness. Only after Wang had choked the boy to death did he remember with dislike Keng's unwillingness to loan him money, so that it was only then that the idea occurred to him of leaving the corpse at Keng's door and in this way falsely imputing the crime to Keng. Thus when Wang killed his son, he had no idea of attempting extortion on Keng, so that his crime differs from that of killing a son in order to practice extortion. It would not be right, in a case in which someone has intentionally killed his son but only then has thought of using the corpse to practice extortion, to convict that person instead of the different crime of killing his son in order to bring false imputations against another person.

The crime of killing a son and *then* falsely imputing the act to another person is, according to statute [Boulais 1302], punishable merely by [two and one half years] penal servitude, whereas the crime of killing a son *in order* to impute the act falsely to another is, according to sub-statute [Boulais 1307], punishable by military exile [at a very near frontier]. There is a considerable difference between these two punishments. The governor-general should therefore restudy the offender's case to determine whether the idea of falsely imputing his crime to another person really occurred to him before or after he killed his son. When his intent has been made clear, the offender may be resentenced.

[Regardless of which sentence the offender eventually receives, this case illustrates the lenient attitude shown in imperial China toward a father who kills his son. If he kills him without due cause, the punishment is merely 60 blows of the heavy bamboo and one year penal servitude (Boulais 1420), and should he do so because the son has been disobedient (a term interpreted very flexibly), the punishment is further reduced to 100 blows of the heavy bamboo (Boulais 1503).]

169. INJURIES CAUSED BY SHOOTING ARROWS [16]
[Statutory References: Staunton 295, Boulais 1311]

Case 169.1, 1826. Memorandum.
Reported in HAHL 15.33/10a.

The governor of Shantung has reported a case in which Fang Hsiao-liu by mischance wounded Ma Ch'eng-t'ung by firing a musket. Ma died thirteen days later from infection.

In this case, Fang Hsiao-liu went to watch a funeral procession leaving a certain house. He noticed a man who had been engaged for the purpose load a musket and place it, ready for action, near the entrance to the house. [Presumably the musket was to be fired so that, as with firecrackers, the noise might scare away evil spirits who might otherwise molest the procession.] Fang picked up the musket and it went off, wounding Ma Ch'eng-t'ung by mischance on the right temple just as he was emerging from the house. Thirteen days later, Ma died from infection. According to the coroner's report, the wound leading to death was a light one.

[The text specifies the dimensions of the wound.]

This Board finds, according to sub-statute [Boulais 1274a], that death, when it results from a firearm being discharged during an affray, is to be punished as if it were intentional homicide. [For intentional (but unpremeditated) homicide (Boulais 1269) the penalty is decapitation after the assizes.] Because such a death is treated as intentional homicide, no reduction in penalty can be permitted, even though the death is not immediate, but comes only later as a result of infection of the wound.

[A sub-statute, Boulais 1361, provides, among other things, that

---

[16] This section, despite its title, deals with injuries caused by firearms as well as by arrows.

if the wound is light (which Ma's was) but is in a vulnerable part of the body (which Ma's also was) and more than ten days intervene between the wounding and death by infection (13 days intervened), then commutation from strangulation to life exile is proper. This sub-statute, however, does not apply to intentional homicide; it is limited by its terms to death resulting from injuries perpetrated in an affray or beating; the court is referring to this limitation.]

Another sub-statute [Boulais 1311a] states, however, that the penalty for discharging firearms toward inhabited buildings and thereby wounding someone by mischance is one degree less than that for injuring someone with boiling water or fire. [For injuring (but not killing) someone with boiling water or fire during an affray, Boulais 1345 specifies 100 blows of the heavy bamboo, which, reduced by one degree, would mean 90 blows for injury caused by shooting.] The same sub-statute further states that if the shooting results in death, the penalty is to be life exile at a distance of 3,000 li. [This too is a one-degree reduction from the penalty for killing in an affray, which in Boulais 1268 is given as strangulation after the assizes.]

Not only does the present case not fall under the sub-statute stating that death caused by shooting during an affray is to be penalized as intentional homicide [because there was no affray when this defendant fired the musket], but, as seen in the second sub-statute cited above [the sub-statute penalizing firing toward inhabited dwellings], its violation is even less serious than the corresponding offenses committed during an affray. When, during an affray, a light injury is inflicted and results in eventual death through infection but the death occurs only after the expiration of a ten day period, it is then permissible to reduce the usual penalty for killing in an affray—that of strangulation after the assizes —to one of life exile. [Such a reduction for death ensuing only after a ten-day waiting period is to be granted, according to Boulais 1361 (the statute earlier referred to as not applying to intentional homicide), either for a light wound inflicted on a vulnerable part of the body (as in the present case), or for a serious injury inflicted on a less vulnerable part.]

By the same token, a light injury which accidentally results from shooting and which leads to death, but only after a ten-day period, should receive a lesser punishment than the life exile provided for an ordinary killing resulting from the discharge of firearms toward inhabited buildings. The Provincial Court of Shantung has in fact, under the above-cited sub-statute on fatal injuries resulting by mischance from the discharge of firearms toward inhabited buildings, sentenced the offender to maximum penal servitude [three years], this being a one-degree reduction from the maximum life exile [exile at a distance of 3,000 li] provided by this sub-statute. [For the manner in which reductions from capital punishment or life exile are calculated, see Chapter III, section 9.]

This decision being equitable, it is proper to request a confirmatory reply.

170. HOMICIDE OR INJURY CAUSED BY VEHICLES OR HORSES
[Statutory References: Staunton 296, Boulais 1312–1314]

Case 170.1, 1815. Leading Case.
Reported in HAHL 15.33/10b.

The governor of Kiangsu has reported that Wang Liu was rapidly riding his horse on West Avenue when he encountered Lu Tsai-lung coming out of an alley. Wang shouted at Lu to give way, but Lu, being old and hard of hearing, did not hear him. Wang could not draw rein in time, and his horse knocked Lu to the ground. Lu died from the resulting injury to his left temple. In accordance with the statute [Boulais 1312] on fatal injuries caused by persons who ride horses or drive vehicles quickly through city streets, Wang Liu has been sentenced to 100 blows of the heavy bamboo, and life exile at a distance of 3,000 li.

[What seems to Westerners a heavy punishment is based upon the fact that Wang was riding fast and was doing so in a populated place (probably Nanking, the provincial capital of Kiangsu, since otherwise more than the mere name of the street would presumably have been mentioned). According to the same statute, if such a fatality occurs in the thinly populated countryside, the punishment is reduced to 100 blows of the heavy bamboo and a payment of ten ounces of silver to the victim's family for funeral expenses. Even so, however, the principle of responsibility rests heavily upon the rider or driver. Indeed, the principle still remains strong today, as many Westerners who have driven cars in modern China can testify. In the *Chieh-fang Jih-pao* (Liberation Daily), Shanghai, June 6, 1949, p. 1, a report is published of a death sentence for a (Communist) army truck driver who killed a bicyclist. This report inspired pleas for clemency. *Ibid.*, June 7. The military court reduced the penalty to three years of penal servitude. *Ibid.*, June 16.]

Case 170.2, 1815. Leading Case from the Department for Mukden of the Board of Punishments.
Reported in HAHL 15.33/10b.

The military governor of Heilungkiang has reported that Chi Ch'ang-ch'un, a Manchu, was entering the city in his cart, when he encountered a five year old boy running head on toward him. The defendant could not stop in time, and the boy was crushed to death.

What happened was neither unforeseeable nor unavoidable; it was a case of negligence. Therefore, in accordance with the statute [Boulais 1312] concerning fatal injuries caused by persons who ride horses or drive vehicles quickly through city streets, Chi Ch'ang-ch'un should be sentenced to 100 blows of the heavy bamboo and life exile at a distance of 3,000 li. However, because he is a Manchu, his sentence is to be commuted to wearing the cangue and a whipping.

[Here we see that the defendant was still held responsible, despite the fact that the boy himself ran head on toward the cart. Presumably the defendant's negligence consisted either in the very fact that the boy ran directly toward him, so that he should have seen the boy in time to stop his cart, or his excess speed (though the latter is not explicitly mentioned). For the commutation of offenses by Manchus, see Boulais 74 (also discussed in case 4.3), which, however, only summarizes the original statute. According to this statute, any specified number of blows of the light or heavy bamboo is to be converted to an equal number of blows of the whip, and life exile at a distance of 3,000 li is to be converted to 60 days wearing of the cangue.]

[In the preceding case, the victim was an old man hard of hearing; in the present one, he is a boy of five. One wonders what the verdict would be if the victim were an able-bodied adult. Unfortunately, and rather strangely, the HAHL reports only these two cases under this section.]

171. DOCTORS WHO KILL OR INJURE PATIENTS
[Statutory References: Staunton 297, Boulais 1315–1318]

Case 171.3, 1812. Memorandum.
Reported in HAHL 15.33/11a–b.

The governor of Anhui has reported on a case, previously appealed to Peking by Hsüeh Chuan-nien, concerning a medical practitioner, Yeh Chung-kuang, who had treated Hsüeh's son with acupuncture, so that the latter died. [The treatment known as acupuncture consists of pushing thin needle-like probes deeply into various determined spots of the patient's body, thereby relieving muscular soreness, nervous tension, and other conditions. The technique, known in China since antiquity, is used to treat many ailments and has enjoyed something of a renaissance since the Chinese Communists came into power.]

This Board finds the case to be one in which Hsüeh Chuan-nien's son had been suffering from an internal congestion. Yeh Chung-kuang, on finding the patient's pulse to be faint, diagnosed this to be cholera, the treatment for which, according to medical writings, is acupuncture. To Hsüeh's objection that the day was an unlucky one and therefore unpropitious for acupuncture, Yeh replied that if the illness were allowed to continue, it might well prove incurable. He accordingly performed acupuncture on the hands and feet of the patient, gave him medicine, and administered drops of ginger juice into his eyes, the result being that the patient perspired profusely until he passed away.

Some time ago Hsüeh came to Peking to present an accusation, which was then transmitted to Anhui for handling. After due consideration, the Provincial Court, acting under the statute on doctors who kill their patients, sentenced Yeh Chung-kuang to strangulation, this to be commuted to monetary redemption. [See Boulais 1316, which states that if a doctor has killed a patient through improper use of medicine or acupuncture and if his negligence has been attested through examination of the case by another doctor, he is to be sentenced as if guilty of accidental homicide, the penalty for which (Boulais 1285) is strangulation after the assizes, which, however, is commutable to a redemption sum of 12.42 ounces of silver (see table in Boulais, p. 13). He is also barred from further practice of medicine.]

As for Hsüeh Chuan-nien himself, the Provincial Court likewise sentenced him to bambooing under the statute [Boulais 1459] on presenting an accusation which proves to be false. It then submitted a report to the Board of Punishments so as to conclude the case. [This statute provides 100 blows of the heavy bamboo for an accusation which, though presented in good faith, proves to be false. However, it also limits this punishment to persons who actually bring their accusation before the emperor himself. This limiting clause, based on a tradition which by Ch'ing times had become anachronistic (see case 260.1 for details), was ignored by many officials who used the statute as a convenient device for disposing of importunate petitioners. See the strong criticism voiced at a much later time (1870) in case 260.1, as a result of which it was ordered by edict that the statute could be applied only with strict attention to its limiting clause.]

Thereafter, however, Hsüeh again came to Peking and submitted an accusation, on the grounds that Yeh's sentence did not pay for his offense, whereas Hsüeh himself had been unfairly subjected to bambooing. This appeal was once more transmitted to the Provincial Court, which after examination has now reaffirmed its original decision.

The governor of Anhui, in reporting on this to the Board of Punishments, states that Yeh Chung-kuang's faulty use of acupuncture for treating the patient, with resulting death, was intended to achieve beneficial results, and there is no evidence whatever that he harbored any ill will toward the patient. It is therefore proper that he should be convicted under the statute on doctors who kill their patients. [Had he acted with malicious premeditation, presumably he would have been sentenced to decapitation after the assizes under the statute on premeditated homicide, Boulais 1211.]

As for Hsüeh Chuan-nien's sentence of 100 blows of the heavy bamboo, perusal of the original report indicates that his conviction under the statute on presenting false accusations is based on the fact that the language used by him in his complaint embellished the facts.

We of this Board find these judgments to accord with the circumstances of the case and therefore deem it proper to request a confirmatory reply.

Case 171.4, 1816. Leading Case.
Reported in HAHL 15.33/11b.

The governor-general of Szechuan has reported a case in which [a shopkeeper] Liu Wu-shou by mistake sold the wrong medicinal drug to Liu Shih-keng, so that the latter died from poisoning.

This Board finds nothing in the Code covering homicide resulting from the sale by a shop of a drug which it has failed to identify correctly. Therefore, by analogy to the statute [Boulais 1316] on doctors who by mistake administer medicines not conforming to the correct prescription, thereby causing the death of their patient, Liu Wu-shou is now sentenced to the same penalty as for accidental homicide [strangulation after the assizes], which, however, is commutable to a monetary redemption. [The amount is 12.42 ounces of silver. See preceding case. The present case is summarized in Boulais 1321.]

Case 171.5, 1818. Metropolitan Leading Case from the
Department for Chekiang of the Board of Punishments.
Reported in HAHL 15.33/11b.

The Censorate of the South City of Peking has referred to this Department the case of Mrs. Tu née Chang, who treated illness by watching the burning of incense, and who swindled and performed acupuncture upon Mrs. Su, thereby causing injuries leading to death.

On investigation, this Department finds that the suggested sentence [unspecified] errs on the side of over-severity, for though Mrs. Tu's wrong action led to injuries, she had no thought of deliberately doing harm. On the other hand, she was not content with her status as an ordinary woman but conceived the idea of treating illness by watching the burning of incense, hoping thus to swindle people out of their money. Therefore, should she be sentenced merely under the statute on doctors who kill patients [Boulais 1316], the penalty for which, according to the statute, is commutable to monetary redemption, this would not suffice to serve as a public warning.

Mrs. Tu née Chang should, therefore, be sentenced to 100 blows of the heavy bamboo, under the statute on violating imperial decrees, and no commutation of this penalty to monetary redemption should be permitted. [For this catch-all statute, see Boulais 274.]

Case 171.6, 1817. Metropolitan Leading Case from the Department for Honan of the Board of Punishments. Reported in HAHL 15.33/11b.

The general commandant of the gendarmerie of Peking has referred to this Department the case of Mrs. Feng née Chang, who worshipped a paper image left to her by her aunt and also used such things as tea leaves and dragon-embracing pills (*paolung wan*) to treat sick patients.

The testimony refers only to her schemes for swindling and makes no reference to any religous sect, aside from mentioning the patriarch of the Wu-tang sect. In addition, it states that she drew pictures and used charms to cure illness. [The Wu-tang sect is named from the mountain of this name in northern Hupei. The sect specialized in the physical exercises known incorrectly to Westerners as Chinese "boxing." Its patriarch or founder, Chang San-feng, is said to have lived in the twelfth century.]

Mrs. Feng née Chang should be sentenced under the sub-statute [Boulais 785a] which specifies military exile for followers of the Red Male sect who worship the Patriarch Who Soars Aloft on the Whirlwind. For Mrs. Feng, however, this sentence is to be reduced by one degree to 100 blows of the heavy bamboo and three years penal servitude, without the privilege of commuting the penalty to a monetary redemption.

[The Red Male or Hung-yang sect and its founder, the Patriarch Who Soars Aloft on the Whirlwind (P'iao-kao Lao-tsu), are touched upon in J. J. M. de Groot, *Sectarianism and Religious Persecution in China*, 2 vols. (Amsterdam: Johannes Müller, 1903–1904), I, 146–147. The founder lived in the sixteenth century, and his sect was one of the esoteric religious groups which was proscribed during the Ch'ing dynasty because of its allegedly anti-dynastic political activities. We have already seen (case 133.1) the way in which the imperial government was suspicious and oppressive toward heterodox religious activities and especially toward organized religious groups. Note the harsher punishment given Mrs. Feng in this case as compared with the punishment given in the last case to Mrs. Tu, who only practiced magic, but did not, like Mrs. Feng, have any organizational ties.]

[As in a number of earlier cases, the sub-statute here used to sentence Mrs. Feng is applied to her directly, whereas strictly speaking it should have been applied analogically, in order to permit her the one-degree reduction of sentence and to correlate its topic of interest—the Red Male sect—with the Wu-tang sect, to which Mrs. Feng may possibly have belonged.]

Case 171.12, 1828. Leading Case.
Reported in HAHL Supplement 33.9/14a.

The governor of Honan has memorialized concerning a case in which Han Chung, while treating the illness of Sun Chü-ni, failed to follow proper methods and instead performed acupuncture, basing himself as he did so on uncanonical old books, pictures, charms, and invocations. Furthermore, because of the weakness of the patient, Han did not perform the acupuncture on Sun himself but on Sun's wife, who died as a result.

There is no article in the Code on treating the illness of one person by performing acupuncture on another with fatal results. Therefore, by analogy to the sub-statute [Boulais 1318] specifying strangulation after the assizes for sorcerers or Taoists who use heterodox arts to treat illness and thereby cause death, Han Chung is now sentenced to this penalty.

Case 171.13, 1824. Leading Case.
Reported in HAHL Supplement 33.9/14a–b.

The governor of Shensi has reported a case in which Mrs. Chang, being commissioned to help Mrs. Shih in her parturition and not knowing the principles of midwifery, reached her hand into the pregnant woman's vagina and forcibly extracted the child. Mother and child both died as a result.

Accordingly, Mrs. Chang is now sentenced by analogy to the statute [Boulais 1316] on doctors who kill their patients through faulty methods, and who, provided there has been no indication of harmful intent on their part, are to be sentenced as if for accidental homicide. In accordance with the statute covering the latter offense [Boulais 1285], the resulting penalty [strangulation after the assizes] is to be commuted to a monetary redemption of 12.42 ounces of silver, which Mrs. Chang is to pay to the family of the victim.

172. PRESSING A PERSON INTO COMMITTING SUICIDE
[Statutory References: Staunton 299, Boulais 1322–1339]

Case 172.3, 1827. Memorandum.
Reported in HAHL 15.33/14b.

The governor of Shensi has reported a case in which Wang Fu beat Lin K'o-chin and pressed him to the point where he committed suicide.

This Board finds, according to sub-statute [Boulais 1325a], that if a husband, because of the adulterous relationship [of his wife], is pressed to the point of committing suicide, care must be taken to examine whether he has really been subjected to intimidation and insult. If he is finally pushed by shame into committing suicide only after having first tolerated the adultery, his case may not be judged under the statute on pressing somebody, through adultery, into suicide. [The statute here referred to, Boulais 1325, provides decapitation after the assizes for a paramour who, through his adultery with another man's wife, presses another person (the wife herself, her husband, or the husband's parents) into committing suicide.]

We have examined a case reported from Mukden in 1813, in which Ma Huan-lung tolerated an adulterous relationship between his wife and Ch'i Ta. Later, when Ch'i saw Ma stealing hemp stalks from Ma's landlord for fuel, he (Ch'i) reproved Ma and injured him by striking him on the left temple. On top of this, Ch'i also ran away with Ma's wife. After searching for them in vain, Ma, afflicted by shame, committed suicide. Ch'i was then sentenced under the sub-statute on seduction. [This is the second half of a sub-statute of which only the first half is reproduced in Boulais 1185. It provides military exile for a man who seduces and abducts a woman with her acquiescence. The reason for citing the case is to show that despite the husband's suicide, the paramour was sentenced under an article other than that on inducing suicide through adultery.]

The present case is one in which Lin K'o-chin, because of greed, tolerated the adulterous relationship between his wife and Wang Fu, in return for which he repeatedly received money from Wang. Finally, however, Wang was unable to meet Lin's numerous demands, whereupon Lin forbade Wang to sleep with Mrs. Lin. At this, Wang demanded restoration of the money he had previously given Lin. Lin berated Wang in return, and Wang then struck Lin with his fists, injuring him on the left eye and elsewhere. Lin, after proclaiming the fact that Wang had not only been unwilling to give him money, but had also struck him, fell into such a state of uncontrollable passion that he hanged himself.

The Board finds that Lin was shameless in tolerating the affair between his wife and Wang and that by demanding money from Wang and picking a quarrel with him leading to being struck by Wang, Lin brought disgrace on himself which was of his own choosing. Under these circumstances, the sub-statute on pressing somebody into suicide through adultery may not be applied to Wang.

The Provincial Court of Shensi has sentenced Wang Fu under the sub-statute [Boulais 1327a] which provides 60 blows of the heavy bamboo and one year penal servitude for a person who, in the course of beating another person, inflicts injury which, though neither fatal nor serious in itself, pushes that person into committing suicide. This sentence being in accord with the case, we deem it appropriate to request a confirmatory reply.

[What is here cited from this sub-statute is one of five kinds of beating, each inflicting a different degree of injury, but all alike leading eventually to the victim's suicide. For a listing of all five kinds of beating, see case 260.1.]

Case 172.4, 1791. Case Selected for Redaction as a Sub-statute.

Reported in HAHL 15.33/14b–15a.

[Three key terms, *fu, nü,* and *tzu,* are involved in what follows. *Fu* and *nü* ordinarily mean respectively "woman" or "wife" and "girl" or "daughter." When jointly used in a legal context, however (as in Boulais 1326 below), *fu* means "married daughter" and *nü* means "unmarried daughter." As we shall see below, when an unmarried daughter, *nü,* becomes a married daughter, *fu,* her ties to her natal family are automatically weakened in favor of new ties to her husband's family. The third term, *tzu,* primarily means son but can also, in a broader sense, signify progeny of either sex. When thus broadly used, however, the coverage of *tzu,* as legally defined, extends on the distaff side only to *nü,* unmarried daughter, but not to the more remote *fu,* married daughter. (See the definition in Boulais 187.) Hence, within a legal context, *tzu* may refer to a son either married or unmarried, to an unmarried daughter, or to both collectively, but not to a married daughter. These distinctions are essential to the discussion that follows.]

The governor of Honan has memorialized concerning a case in which Mrs. Ch'en née Chang committed adultery with Wang Chieh and was abducted by him. The result was such shame and indignation on the part of her father that he killed himself. The governor has recommended strangulation after the assizes for Mrs. Ch'en, under the sub-statute providing this penalty for a married daughter (*fu*) or an unmarried daughter (*nü*) whose parents, after learning that she has entered into an illicit sexual relationship unsanctioned by themselves and after trying in vain to kill her seducer, commit suicide out of shame and indignation. [See Boulais 1326, where the identical wording appears save that the specified punishment is immediate strangulation rather than strangulation after the assizes. The increase in penalty came, as we shall see, as the direct result of the emperor's intervention in the present case.]

An imperial rescript on this memorial has been issued as follows:

Imperial Rescript: In the case in which Mrs. Ch'en committed adultery with Wang Chieh and thereby occasioned her father's suicide, the governor, inasmuch as she is married [and therefore no longer a member of her parents' family], has sentenced her [under the sub-statute cited above merely] to strangulation after the assizes. The Board of Punishments has now also confirmed this sentence, which certainly accords with the cited sub-statute. Nonetheless, the fact that the father's death was occasioned by his daughter's adultery puts the offense into the same category as that in which a parent or grandparent, because his child (*tzu*) or grandchild has committed an act of moral turpitude or of theft, ends his own life out of chagrin and indignation. Therefore, the punishment should be the same as that for the latter offense, namely immediate strangulation.

[See Boulais 1506. By "moral turpitude" (*chien*) are meant adultery, rape, and other kinds of illicit sexual relationships. See case 201.6. We have seen above that *tzu*, commonly rendered either as "son" or "child," means in legal context either "son" or "unmarried daughter" or both. The difference is important for distinguishing Boulais 1326 from 1506. Both statutes punish offspring whose illicit sexual relationships cause one or both parents to commit suicide. Until the present case, Boulais 1326 provided strangulation after the assizes for either a married or an unmarried daughter (but not a son) guilty of this offense. Boulais 1506, on the other hand, provides the higher penalty of immediate strangulation for a *tzu* (meaning either a son or an unmarried daughter but not a daughter already married) guilty of a similar offense. The problem in the present case is whether the offender, despite her married status, may still somehow be given the punishment provided under the harsher sub-statute.]

Under the mourning system [the system of the five degrees], we may accept that a daughter's relationship to her natal family will be stronger while she is still unmarried than after she has been married [and thereby has become a member of her husband's family]. When such a matter enters into the death of a parent, however, it is no longer allowable, as in ordinary offenses, that a married daughter's lower degree of mourning toward her parents, as compared with that of an unmarried daughter, should enable the married daughter to enjoy a lesser sentence for an offense committed against them.

[Under the mourning system, a father stands to his unmarried daughter in a degree 1 relationship, whereas as soon as she marries, the relationship diminishes to degree 2b. Conversely, the daughter prior to marriage stands to her father in a degree 2b relationship, whereas after her marriage the relationship diminishes to degree 3. The same principle can be differently illustrated by the statute on high treason (Boulais 1024), according to which the daughter of a man guilty of treason, if unmarried, is sent into slavery (together with many other members of his family), whereas if married she receives no punishment, being then legally a member of her husband's rather than of her parents' family.]

Moreover, the aim in clarifying the punishments is thereby to assist the spread of moral teachings. [This sentence is quoted with minor changes from the chapter entitled "Counsels of the Great Yü" (*Ta Yü mo*) in the *Documents Classic* (*Shu ching*).] Because the child's relationship to the parents derives from Heaven, no differentiation in that relationship should be made with respect to a daughter simply on the basis of whether or not she happens to be married. Why indeed should the mere fact of marriage enable a daughter who has caused the death of a parent to escape on that account the penalty of execution by slicing which she would otherwise receive? [Of course, death by slicing is not the penalty for all kinds of parental killings, but only for premeditated parricide. See Boulais 1224.]

Hereafter, if a daughter engages in illicit sex relations, thus

causing the parents to commit suicide out of shame and indignation, let it be ordered that the girl, no matter whether married or
unmarried, be sentenced to immediate strangulation. Let this rescript be transmitted to the Board of Punishments for inclusion in
the register of new sub-statutes, and let Mrs. Ch'en be sentenced
in accordance with it.

[This case illustrates the way in which sub-statutes were born
out of imperial edicts. The Code was re-edited approximately
every five years to allow the incorporation of such new sub-
statutes. The case also demonstrates clearly that the principle forbidding ex post facto law was not recognized in China. Finally,
the case illustrates how a strong-willed ruler (the Ch'ien-lung
Emperor) dared to reassert the primacy of natural family ties
("the child's relationship to the parents derives from Heaven"),
as against the strongly established but overly mechanical measurement of morality in exact amounts and degrees which appears
so conspicuously in Chinese law. The result of this attempt to
"humanize" quantitative justice, however, was in effect an added
burden for the already well burdened married daughter, since it
meant that in addition to the utter submissiveness required of her
toward her husband and his family, she was now held closely ac-
countable, not simply until her marriage but throughout her life,
for any act of hers that might seriously affect her own parents.]

175. AFFRAYS AND BLOWS
[Statutory References: Staunton 302, Boulais 1344-1355]

*Case 175.6, 1817. General Circular Selected for Redaction
as a Sub-statute.*
Reported in HAHL 16.37/3a.

The governor of Shansi, concerning the case in which Chang
Hsüeh-san and others assaulted and killed Li Meng-lin, has submitted a memorial raising the question of one of these other men,
Chang Ssu-wa, who seized a dangerous weapon from the hand of
the victim and used it to help in the killing.

The Board finds that in the sub-statute [Boulais 1350a] on
ruffians who, being stirred to anger on some pretext, plunge into

fights, mention is made of "dangerous weapons," and it is explained that these are distinct from implements used in everyday life by the people.

[Among the many dangerous weapons (*hsiung ch'i*) enumerated in this sub-statute are daggers, swords, spears, battle-axes, and maces *(chien,* a kind of four-edged iron club which is the weapon figuring in the present case). In contrast to these, the possession of which is illegal, the Official Commentary on the sub-statute (one of the very rare instances of the Commentary being attached to a sub-statute) explains that implements of everyday use include sickles, kitchen knives, firewood axes, and the like.]

Thus, anyone possessing such a dangerous weapon is by that very fact not a law-abiding citizen, so that even though his use of the weapon in an affray may lead to injury no greater than that caused by an ordinary knife or other ordinary implement, his offense in so doing is nevertheless more serious than that connected with an ordinary affray. For this reason, the sub-statute goes on to say that any injury whatever, when caused by use of a dangerous weapon in an affray, is to be punished by military exile [at a distance of 2,500 li]; even if no injury at all results, the penalty is still to be 100 blows of the heavy bamboo.

[These penalties are considerably heavier than those for use of ordinary implements in an affray. The latter penalties differ according to the extent of the injury, ranging from 30 blows of the light bamboo when no injury at all is inflicted, to 100 blows of the heavy bamboo and life exile at a distance of 3,000 li for causing blindness in both eyes or inflicting other comparable injuries. See Boulais 1344–1348. This last punishment, though severe, is still two degrees less than the military exile meted out for inflicting *any* kind of injury by a dangerous weapon.]

When, however, a dangerous weapon is used in an affray by one who does not himself initially possess the weapon but who seizes it during the affray from the hand of his opponent, it is evident that this act, if not resulting in injury, should not be punished by 100 blows of the heavy bamboo. Nor, if it results in any kind of injury, should it therefore be punished by military exile. Otherwise the act would be indistinguishable from that of the actual possessor of such a dangerous weapon.

In the present case of the assaulting and killing of Li Meng-lin by Chang Hsüeh-san and others, Chang Ssu-wa seized a mace from Li and used it to help beat him. For this, Chang Ssu-wa should certainly not be sentenced merely to 100 blows of the heavy bamboo, as he would were he a secondary participant in an ordinary case of joint assault by several persons resulting in death [Boulais 1270]. On the other hand, he should also not be sentenced to military exile as he would under the sub-statute on injuries inflicted by dangerous weapons, because, as already indicated, the distinction between possessing a dangerous weapon and seizing it from an opponent would then be lost.

It follows that Chang Ssu-wa may properly receive a one-degree reduction in penalty from that of military exile, as specified in the sub-statute on dangerous weapons. He is therefore sentenced to 100 blows of the heavy bamboo and three years penal servitude.

[Here it would seem that the Board of Punishments exercises flexibility in arriving at a compromise between the punishment for using dangerous weapons and that for ordinary assault. For the manner in which reductions in punishment are computed, see Chapter III, end of section 9.]

Case 175.7, 1819. Leading Case.
Reported in HAHL 16.37/3a–b.

The governor of Kiangsu has reported a case in which Chou Ssu and others, at the prompting of Liu Pa, assaulted Wu Hsiang and inflicted wounds which caused death.

This Board finds that during the affray Chou Ssu took over an "iron footrule" from a fellow participant who had brought it with him and used it to injure the wrist of Wu Hsiang. [An "iron footrule" (*t'ieh ch'ih*) is a small club-like military weapon shaped like a footrule; it constitutes one of the "dangerous weapons."] This act is different from seizing such a weapon from an opponent. Hence, in accordance with the sub-statute on inflicting injuries with dangerous weapons, Chou Ssu is sentenced to military exile

[at a distance of 2,500 li. See preceding case for this sub-statute, Boulais 1350a, and the distinction it makes between possession of a dangerous weapon and seizure of such a weapon from an opponent during an affray. In the present case, acquisition of the weapon from a fellow participant is accounted the same as possession of it.]

Liu Erh, another participant in the same affray, took over a knife from the chief instigator, Liu Pa, which the latter had previously seized from Wu Hsiang, the opponent. With this knife, Liu Erh wounded Wu Hsiang. His act is essentially the same as if he had seized the weapon directly from the hands of his opponent. Hence he is sentenced to 100 blows of the heavy bamboo and three years penal servitude, this being a penalty one degree less than that provided for inflicting injuries with dangerous weapons. [On such a reduction of penalty when the dangerous weapon has been seized from the opponent, see again the preceding case.]

Case 175.8, 1816. Leading Case.
Reported in HAHL 16.37/3b.

The governor of Honan, concerning the case in which several men assaulted and killed Ho Yü-p'ei, has submitted a memorial raising the question of one of these men, Liu Tien-ch'eng, who picked up an "iron footrule" [see the preceding case] on the spot and used it to injure the victim's left leg.

The Provincial Court of Honan has sentenced Liu Tien-ch'eng to [three years] penal servitude, this being a penalty one degree less than that for inflicting injuries with dangerous weapons [see the two preceding cases]. This Board maintains, however, that inasmuch as the culprit did in fact use a dangerous weapon to wound another person, the mere fact that he picked the weapon up on the spot cannot differentiate him from any other handler of such dangerous weapons. We accordingly change the penalty for Liu Tien-ch'eng to military exile [at a distance of 2,500 li], as stipulated in the sub-statute on inflicting injuries with dangerous weapons [Boulais 1350a].

Case 175.9, 1810. Memorandum.
Reported in HAHL 16.37/3b.

The governor of Honan has reported a case in which Chiao Ying-shan wounded Hsü T'i-chung with a spear. Chiao had wished to join a gambling group, but was forcibly ejected by Hsü. Out of revenge, Chiao then rounded up several people, among them Liu Hui-yüan, and attacked Hsü.

The facts show that Chiao used a long-handled spear and wounded Hsü in the left leg. The Provincial Court of Honan has sentenced Chiao to military exile [at a distance of 2,500 li] under the sub-statute [Boulais 1350a] on inflicting injuries with danger-ous weapons. This sentence accords with the sub-statute [see the last three cases].

In the same affair, Liu Hui-yüan wielded a grain-spike, which is an agricultural implement and so cannot be considered a "dan-gerous weapon". [See case 175.6. It has not been possible to deter-mine the precise nature of this "grain-spike" (*ho-ch'iang*).] Fur-thermore, grain-spike cases in other provinces have always been considered to be like those in which an ordinary knife is used. Ac-cordingly, the Provincial Court has sentenced Liu to penal servi-tude under the statute on inflicting injury with a knife. [Boulais 1346 provides 80 blows of the heavy bamboo and two years penal servitude for this offense.]

We deem it appropriate to send a confirmatory reply for both these sentences.

183. ASSAULT BY A DISCIPLE ON HIS MASTER [17]
[Statutory References: Staunton 311, Boulais 1375–1379]

Case 183.1, 1817. Memorandum.
Reported in HAHL 17.38/14b.

The governor of Fukien has memorialized concerning a case in which the Buddhist monk Yü-ching inflicted injuries upon his

---

[17] Despite its title, this section also covers the offense of a master beating his disciple.

disciple Cheng-shun, from which the latter died. This memorial, submitted to the throne, has been answered by an imperial endorsement, in which it is pointed out that, according to substatute [Boulais 371], disciples may not be accepted by a monk if he is under forty. For this reason this case should be referred to the Board of Punishments to determine whether or not the offender should be treated as would a layman guilty of the same offense.

This Board now finds that under the above-mentioned substatute, Buddhist and Taoist monks are not permitted to accept disciples indiscriminately, so that if a monk recruits disciples before he is forty, he is to suffer 50 blows of the light bamboo as he would under the statute on violating ordinances [Boulais 1655], and the disciples themselves are to be returned to lay life.

In the present case, the monk Yü-ching violated the above substatute by accepting Cheng-shun as his disciple when he himself had not yet reached forty. Therefore, Cheng-shun, at the time he was struck and killed by Yü-ching, was legally not Yü-ching's disciple, since he should have been returned to lay life. This in turn means that any offense committed against him by Yü-ching should be judged as if committed against a lay citizen.

Now, however, the Provincial Court of Fukien has sentenced the offender to strangulation after the assizes, under the substatute [Boulais 1377] which states that if a Buddhist or Taoist monk, because his disciple has disobeyed his instructions, beats that disciple in a reasonable manner yet thereby causes his death, the monk is to receive the same punishment as provided under statute [Boulais 1410] for a senior relative who beats a junior relative of the third degree of mourning, thereby causing his death.

Citation of this sub-statute is, in the final analysis, erroneous. The monk Yü-ching should properly be re-sentenced to strangulation after the assizes under the statute [Boulais 1268] on killing somebody in an affray.

[Noteworthy here is the care with which the Board of Punishments determines the correct offense committed by the offender, even though the resulting punishment actually turns out to be the same as that originally proposed for another crime by the Provincial Court. The case also illustrates the high degree of governmental control of religious life found in such a regularized society as that of imperial China. From Peking down to the local districts, Buddhist and Taoist matters were supervised by religious dignitaries who were at the same time ranking members of the government's civil service and were responsible to the government for the conduct of their co-religionists (Boulais 364). A person could not become a monk if he were already an adult (age 16 and above), or if there were fewer than three adult males in his family (Boulais 368); even then, he was required to obtain a special certificate of monkhood issued by the government (Boulais 366). New temples or monasteries could not be constructed save with governmental permission (Boulais 365 and 370).]

Case 183.3, 1794. Memorandum.
Reported in HAHL 17.38/17a–b.

The Department for Kueichow of the Board of Punishments finds, according to sub-statute [Boulais 1377], that a Buddhist male or female disciple guilty of striking his or her Buddhist master is to receive the same punishment as provided by statute [Boulais 1410] for a junior relative who strikes a senior relative of the third degree of mourning. Thus, the act of a Buddhist disciple who strikes his master is not analogous to that of a child who strikes his parents.

The present case concerns the Buddhist monk Ch'e-pang and his disciple Lang-yüeh. Ch'e-pang asked the disciple to clean up the manure, but the disciple, being afflicted with an eye disease, wished to postpone the job until early morning or evening, when it would be cool and pleasant. Ch'e-pang scolded him for laziness and, on receiving back-talk from him, beat him with a stick on his arms and legs. The disciple then fled into a room, pursued by Ch'e-pang, and there, in desperation, seized a vegetable chopper with which he cut open the left crown of his own head. Therefore, the Department for Kueichow has now sentenced the disciple to bambooing under the statute on a son or grandson who disobeys the instructions of his parents or grandparents. [See Boulais 1503, which provides 100 blows of the heavy bamboo for this offense.]

We [members of the Board of Punishments' Directorate, to whom the Department for Kueichow has submitted this report], find that even if Lang-yüeh, as a disciple, had been guilty of striking his master, Ch'e-pang, the relevant sub-statute, cited above, would only permit him to be punished as would a junior relative who strikes a senior relative of the third degree of mourning. In actual fact, however, it was the disciple himself who was struck by his master, rather than the other way around, and who then in desperation inflicted injury upon himself. In view of this, it would be forcing matters to sentence him under the statute on disobeying parental instructions. Moreover, the Code says nothing about a junior relative who, on being beaten by a senior relative, inflicts injury upon himself out of desperation. Yet, since this is what Lang-yüeh, the disciple, did in effect do, he should properly be sentenced under the statute on a person who deliberately injures himself.

[Boulais 1576 provides 100 blows of the heavy bamboo for an arrested person who injures himself in order to avoid official interrogation and 80 blows for an ordinary person who does the same in order to frighten someone or falsely to impute to that person his act of self-injury. Curiously, the Board's Directorate fails to specify which of these two alternatives it intends for the disciple. Although neither of them fits this case exactly, the second one seems more germane. Because of this lack of exactitude, the Directorate ought to have used the statute only analogically rather than by direct application.]

184. COERCION THROUGH APPLICATION OF INTIMIDATING POWER
[Statutory References: Staunton 312, Boulais 1380]

Case 184.1, 1785. Memorandum.
Reported in HAHL 17.38/19a–b.

The Department for Mukden of the Board of Punishments finds that, according to statute [Boulais 1380], if someone uses his intimidating power (*wei li*) to instigate an attack by someone else who attacks and kills a third person, the instigator shall be

370 LAW IN IMPERIAL CHINA

treated as the primary offender, and the one who actually strikes the blows as an accessory. [The respective punishments for the two are strangulation after the assizes and 100 blows of the heavy bamboo with life exile at a distance of 3,000 li.] However, another statute also states [Boulais 1270] that if several persons jointly plan an attack upon another man, resulting in his death, the person who actually strikes the fatal blows shall suffer strangulation after the assizes, whereas the original planner shall receive 100 blows of the heavy bamboo and life exile at a distance of 3,000 li. [For the reasoning underlying the second statute, see case 164.1. Notice that its punishments are precisely the reverse of those specified by the first statute.]

In the present case, Liu Wan-lu, after winning money from Liu Lao-wu in gambling, refused to gamble again when asked to do so by Liu Lao-wu. The latter, getting drunk, berated Liu Wan-lu for his unwillingness and thus upset him. Being a cripple, Liu Wan-lu was afraid he could not win a fight himself. Therefore he instigated an attack on the other Liu by two of his employees who slept in his shop, Li Hu-shan and Ch'en Ssu-hai, together with his servant, Wang Chi-kuei. During the fight, Liu Wan-lu went out to look and, finding Liu Lao-wu still unwilling to admit defeat, pulled off the latter's shoes and stockings and ordered Li and the others again to beat him on his legs and wrists. It was only when Liu Lao-wu finally begged for mercy and promised to kowtow, that Liu Wan-lu ordered the beating to stop. Ten days later Liu Lao-wu died from his injuries.

We [members of the Directorate of the Board of Punishments, to whom the case has been submitted by the Department for Mukden], have carefully studied the distinction between the terms "original planner" *(yüan mou)* and "instigator" *(chu shih)* [as used in the two statutes cited above]. The decisive point is whether an individual involved in a fight does or does not actually issue orders at the scene of action. If he merely conceives and plans the attack but does not issue any orders while it is actually in progress, he should then be judged as the original planner. If, however, in addition to conceiving and planning the attack, he also issues orders at the actual scene of the fight, he should then be judged as the instigator. [Under Boulais 1270, as noted above, the penalty for being an original planner is life exile, whereas under Boulais 1380 the instigator is regarded as being the primary offender and therefore is punished by strangulation after the assizes.]

In the present case, Liu Wan-lu, in order to assuage his anger, conceived and planned the attack on Liu Lao-wu. Then, while it was in progress and when the latter refused to submit, Liu Wan-lu took off Liu Lao-wu's shoes and stockings and ordered Li Hu-shan and the others to beat him. Still later, when Liu Lao-wu begged for mercy, Liu Wan-lu ordered them to stop. Thus, everything that happened was an outcome of his instigation.

Liu Wan-lu is a cripple; Li Hu-shan and Ch'en Ssu-hai are both attached to his shop, and Wang Chi-kuei is his servant. All three of them were therefore dependent upon him, and thus subject to a pressure on his part which they could not but follow.

Under the earlier-cited statute according to which the instigator of an attack shall be considered the primary offender [Boulais 1380], the vice-president of the Board of Punishments of Manchuria has sentenced Liu Wan-lu to strangulation [after the assizes]. This being appropriate, it would seem that a confirmatory reply should be sent.

After receiving the case from Manchuria, however, the Department for Mukden of the Board of Punishments in Peking has concluded that inasmuch as Liu Wan-lu did not strike any blows himself, his subordinate Li Hu-shan, who is presently a fugitive, should replace him [as the primary offender]. It has therefore sentenced Liu Wan-lu to life exile [under Boulais 1270] as the original planner of the attack, whereas in actual fact he was not only its original planner but also its instigator. [Under the same statute, as noted above, Li, being the actual inflictor of the fatal blows, would, when apprehended, suffer strangulation after the assizes, that is, he and Liu would exchange the punishments meted out to them under Boulais 1380.]

We find this an unfair judgment and therefore request [the throne] that it be nullified in favor of the earlier judgment from Manchuria.

Case 184.2, 1809. Memorandum.
Reported in HAHL 17.38/19b–20a.

The Department for Mukden of the Board of Punishments has examined a report concerning a case in which Niu Chung instigated the death by beating of Ssu T'ing-fang at the hands of Ts'ui Kuang-ta.

According to a previous report by the military governor of Mukden, this Department finds that Niu Chung, in order to assuage his anger, conceived and organized a joint attack with Ts'ui Kuang-ta upon Ssu T'ing-fang, in which Ts'ui agreed to participate. In the attack, Niu went forward first to seize Ssu, but was thrown by the latter to the ground. Then Ts'ui clubbed Ssu on his shinbones, bringing about his death. The military governor then recommended that Niu and Ts'ui be respectively sentenced to strangulation [after the assizes] and to life exile, under the statute on using intimidating power to instigate a fatal attack [see Boulais 1380 and preceding case]. A report of the case was then sent to this Board.

In this initial report it was merely stated that Niu had wished to assault Ssu in order to assuage his hatred and, being fearful that he might not be able to handle him alone, had ordered Ts'ui to help him. Nothing was said about Ts'ui being subjected to pressure which he could not but follow or about Niu really possessing a power of intimidation. It seemed, therefore, as if the case might actually be one in which the two men had equally planned together to commit a joint attack. [Under the statute, Boulais 1270, covering this kind of crime, the penalties for the two men would be precisely the reverse of what they would be under Boulais 1380. See the preceding case.]

On receiving this report, therefore, this Board sent back instructions to have the case re-examined. This has resulted in a new report now received from the military governor of Mukden, from which it is evident that Niu was Ts'ui's landlord, and that Ts'ui, as Niu's tenant farmer, was therefore normally obedient to Niu. When Niu, relying on his position as landlord, ordered Ts'ui to help him in attacking Ssu, it would seem that he was exercising intimidation. Likewise it would seem that Ts'ui, living as he did with his whole family on Niu's land and cultivating it for Niu, had no alternative but to do what he was told to do. In his second report, therefore, the military governor of Mukden has asked whether the case should be handled as one in which the fatal attack took place because the one man used his intimidating power (*wei li*) to instigate the joint action or whether it was simply a case of joint action through mutual agreement by the two. [See preceding case for detailed discussion of these two alternatives.]

This Board finds that Niu was exercising his intimidating power as a landlord when he ordered Ts'ui to help him in the attack, and that Ts'ui's normal obedience to whatever was ordered by Niu was the result of subjection to pressure which he could not but follow. This situation, not clearly brought out in the earlier report, is established beyond a doubt by the second investigation. It follows from this that the case should be judged under the statute on use of intimidating power to instigate someone to attack a third person, thereby causing homicide [Boulais 1380]. Under this statute Niu Chung, as the instigator and therefore the primary offender, is sentenced to strangulation after the assizes, whereas Ts'ui Kuang-ta, as the person who actually struck the blows and therefore the accessory, is given a sentence one degree less, namely 100 blows of the heavy bamboo and life exile at a distance of 3,000 li.

[This case (like case 183.1) illustrates the conscientiousness of the Board of Punishments in trying to establish the precise facts. It and the preceding case both touch upon a problem still very much with us: how responsible is a subordinate for acts which he knows to be wrong but which he carries out under the orders of a superior? In a highly authoritarian society or organization (such as the army), the pressures for conformity of subordinate to superior, irrespective of circumstances, are well-nigh overwhelming. As shown by the two cases of this section, however, they may also be exceedingly powerful in a society whose underdeveloped or pre-industrial economy permits only a minimum of economic choice to the individual. The tenant farmer of the present case was obliged to be "normally obedient" to his landlord because the pressure of population upon the land would have made it difficult for him to find new land to cultivate had he been ousted by his landlord. The shop employees and the servant of the preceding case would likewise have experienced trouble finding new jobs if they had been discharged by their employer. For all these men, therefore, the combination of social and economic forces was such as to make them "subject to pressure which they could not but follow." So overwhelming, indeed, was this pressure, that it was explicitly recognized as a compelling factor by the judicial authorities.]

185. AFFRAYS BETWEEN COMMONERS AND SLAVES
[Statutory References: Staunton 313, Boulais 1381–1386]

Case 185.1, 1806. Memorandum.
Reported in HAHL 17.39/1a.

The Department for Mukden of the Board of Punishments finds, according to statute [Boulais 1381], that if a commoner (*liang jen*, "good person") beats and injures another person's slave, he shall receive a penalty one degree less than that for beating and injuring a commoner. If death results or if he kills the slave intentionally, he shall suffer strangulation after the assizes. Premeditated homicide shall be dealt with in the same manner as intentional homicide. [The last sentence does not appear in the original statute. Apparently it is a projection by the Department for Mukden of the fact that the Code, rather curiously, prescribes only a single punishment—decapitation after the assizes—for either premeditated or intentional homicide when these involve ordinary persons. See Boulais 1211 and 1269.]

Thus, as long as only injury is involved, this statute provides a penalty one degree less than the standard penalty for this offense, whereas when death occurs, its penalty of strangulation after the assizes is the same as that for ordinary homicide in an affray [see Boulais 1268]. Truly, this is because for any destruction of a human life there has to be a proper requital. [A life must be given for a life. This statement reflects the ancient idea (see discussion in case 164.1) that the act of homicide ruptures the human order and therefore the cosmic order, in reparation for which a life must be given as requital for the life taken away. (The technical term for requital, *ti*, occurs both here and in cases 164.1 and 164.2.)]

That the penalty for either premeditated or intentional killing of a slave stops at strangulation after the assizes [whereas the corresponding penalty for killing a commoner in these ways is decapitation after the assizes] is based on the idea that in requiting [a life for a life] a distinction between commoner and slave must still be maintained.

The Code provides no penalty for a commoner who premeditates the murder of another person's slave but only succeeds in injuring him. It does contain a statute, however, covering the same offense when it occurs between ordinary persons. [See Boulais 1212, which provides strangulation after the assizes for this offense.] If this statute, intended to cover such an offense between ordinary persons, were likewise to be applied to a case involving a slave, not only would the distinction between commoner and slave thus be obliterated, but the result would be to set a single penalty of strangulation after the assizes for the premeditated attempt to kill a slave, whether this attempt proved successful or unsuccessful. This too would certainly destroy a necessary distinction.

We find again, according to statute [Boulais 1225], that the penalty for a senior relative who plans to kill a junior relative and succeeds in the attempt is strangulation [after the assizes], whereas if he succeeds only in injuring him, the penalty is reduced by one degree to life exile. If, therefore, the statutory penalty for a commoner who kills another man's slave with premeditation is strangulation [after the assizes], it would seem through comparison with the foregoing statute that the penalty for merely injuring but not killing him ought to be reduced by one degree [to life exile].

In the present case, Wu Wen planned to kill Liu Han-yün, a criminal who had been sentenced to transportation to Manchuria, there to be the slave of Tatar troops. However, the attempted killing was not successful. As noted above, there is no article in the Code specifically covering this offense when a slave is concerned.

Therefore, the military governor of Mukden has requested that the offender be sentenced instead in accordance with the statute [Boulais 1212] on an ordinary person who premeditates but fails to achieve the killing of another ordinary person; this sentence, however, to be reduced by one degree [for the reasons given above from strangulation after the assizes] to life exile [at a distance of 3,000 li]. It would seem that a confirmatory reply should be sent to him.

Case 185.3, 1816. Leading Case.
Reported in HAHL 17.39/1b–2a.

The governor of Kueichow has reported a case in which Wu Ying-ming beat and injured another person's slave girl. The consequence was that the girl committed suicide in a fit of passion.

According to statute [Boulais 1381], a commoner who beats and injures another person's slave suffers a penalty one degree less than that for the same act when done to another commoner. Accordingly, Wu Ying-ming is now sentenced to [three years] penal servitude, this being a penalty one degree less than that of military exile provided for an ordinary person who uses force to beat [and seriously injure] another ordinary person, thereby putting that person under such pressure that he commits suicide. [This sub-statute, Boulais 1327a, covers five categories of beating, each resulting in the victim committing suicide. This is the first of them. For the others, see case 260.1.]

186. ASSAULT BY A SLAVE OR SERVANT ON HIS MASTER [18]
[Statutory References: Staunton 314, Boulais 1387–1399]

Case 186.8, 1789. Memorandum of Metropolitan Leading Case.
Reported in HAHL 17.39/9b–10a.

The Department for Mukden of the Board of Punishments finds, according to statute [Boulais 1431], that a concubine who

---

[18] This section, despite its title, also deals with masters who beat a slave or servant. This situation—probably much more common than its reverse—is the nexus for both the cases that follow.

strikes any of her husband's senior relatives [exclusive of his parents] whose relationship to him ranges from degree 2*b* to degree 5 in the five-degree mourning system, shall receive the same punishment as would her master had he struck them. If, on the other hand, she strike one of her master's junior relatives, another statute [Boulais 1432] provides that she shall receive the same punishment as would a person involved in an ordinary affray [Boulais 1344–1348]. The charts depicting the mourning relationships [Boulais, p. 19] also indicate that a concubine is to observe one year of mourning for her master's eldest son and his other sons, including those borne by her. [Their relationship to her is that of degree 2*b* in the mourning system].

Again, with respect to slaves, we find that a slave addresses his master's eldest son as a "one-year mourning relative." [That is, a relative for whom he would observe one year of mourning (degree 2*b* in the mourning system). I have been unable to locate this statement, either in the Code's mourning charts or elsewhere.] If a slave strike any relatives for whom his master observes one year of mourning, his penalty, even if he fails to injure them, is strangulation [after the assizes]; if he injures them, it becomes decapitation [after the assizes]; for intentionally killing them it is execution by slicing [see Boulais 1387].

Finally [Boulais 1437], if a concubine strikes the son of her master's wife, the concubine's penalty is the same as for striking an ordinary person; if homicide results, the penalty is strangulation [after the assizes]; for intentional killing it is decapitation [after the assizes]. From these various citations, it is quite evident that a master's slave or slave girl cannot, for legal purposes, be considered on the same level as his concubine.

In the present case, the Department for Mukden has found that Chang Te-jung's concubine, née Kuan, had beaten and injured her waiting maid, Fu-erh, so that the maid later committed suicide by jumping into a well. A cousin of Chang Te-jung had originally purchased Fu-erh's contract as an indentured servant, but when the cousin's wife died, the cousin handed Fu-erh and her contract over to Chang Te-jung. She had already been employed in Chang's household for three years prior to her death, so that there was then no longer any difference between her and an ordinary slave. [Many slaves in China probably originated as indentured servants, who could regain their freedom if able to repay to their master the sum stipulated in their contract. After three years of service, however, and if the servant had been given a wife by his master, his status changed to that of a permanent slave. See T'ung-tsu Ch'ü, *Law and Society in Traditional China*, p. 194.]

Fu-erh had always been wilful by nature, and toward Chang's concubine, Miss Kuan, she turned out to be disobedient and disrespectful. This is why the latter beat her with a bamboo, inflicting injury on her right arm and shoulder. It was after this that the maid committed suicide out of indignation.

We have found that Chang Te-jung's wife, in contrast to Chang himself who now lives in Peking, has remained behind at his native place. Thus, his concubine, Miss Kuan, is the one who maintains discipline over his household here in the capital, so that when Fu-erh was disobedient, it was Miss Kuan's responsibility to beat her. This beating, moreover, did not itself cause Fu-erh's death, which, on the contrary, resulted from the girl's own drowning of herself. Thus the case is different from one in which one person presses another to the point where that other person commits suicide [Boulais 1323]—an offense punishable by [100 blows of] the heavy bamboo.

Because examination has revealed no further relevant facts, it seems to us that the charge against the concubine, Miss Kuan, may be dropped.

[This case indicates that the status of a concubine, low though it was compared with that of a wife, was considerably above that of a slave. In China, as elsewhere, it is the oppressed who in turn oppress the oppressed. For a discussion of concubinage, see Ch'ü, *Law and Society*, pp. 123–127, and for slaves and other lowly groups, see the same, pp. 186–200.]

Case 186.9, 1802. Memorandum from the Department for Mukden of the Board of Punishments.
Reported in HAHL 17.39/10a.

The Board of Punishments of Manchuria has reported a case in which Mrs. Yang née Chang, who belongs to a Chinese Banner, beat and injured her serving woman, Mrs. Wang née Huang, resulting in the latter's death. [Chinese bannermen were descendants of those Chinese who had collaborated with the Manchus in overthrowing the Ming dynasty in the seventeenth century. Like the Manchu and Mongol Banner troops, they were stationed in garrisons throughout the country, held their status hereditarily, and enjoyed special privileges. By the nineteenth century, however, all these Banner forces had become almost useless for fighting purposes.]

The Department for Mukden of the Peking Board of Punishments finds that Mrs. Yang had been the concubine of Yang Yü-chüeh, a former captain in the Chinese Banner forces, and had borne him an heir. When Yang's wife died, Yang announced to his fellow clansmen that he was establishing his former concubine to be his proper wife. In her new position as wife, Mrs. Yang employed an indentured servant couple, Wang Kuo-tung and his wife née Huang, whose service, however, had lasted less than three years when the trouble started. [As we have seen in the preceding case, if an indentured servant is not redeemed within three years, his status sinks to that of slave. This had not yet happened in the case of the Wang couple.]

Because Wang's wife proved to be disobedient and contrary, Mrs. Yang clubbed her on her feet and elsewhere so that she died. The vice-president of the Board of Punishments of Manchuria, on the ground that between Mrs. Yang and the servant woman there existed a recognizable distinction as between the honorable and the lowly, and inasmuch as Mrs. Yang's beating of the woman has been provoked by the latter's disobedience, maintains that the case should be judged as that of a master beating to death a servant. However, Mrs. Yang had been a concubine before becoming established as wife, and there is no article in the Code which states whether, for determining sentence under such circumstances, she should be adjudged a wife or a concubine. The vice-president has therefore asked this Board for a ruling.

We have found that, although no sub-statute deals with the establishing of a concubine as wife, there is the following statement in the *Chien-shih Commentary:* "If, after a wife has died, a concubine is made wife in her stead, a verdict of having done what ought not to be done is to be pronounced [against the responsible husband], and the concubine is to be restored to her former status."

[For the statute on doing what ought not to be done (Boulais 1656), see below, and for the *Chien-shih Commentary*, see Chapter II, section 4. This is perhaps the only private commentary of Ming date on the Code that still survives as a separate entity. The passage here quoted will be found in *Wang K'en-t'ang Chien-shih* (Wang K'en-tang's *Chien-shih Commentary*), 6/6b, under the statute (Boulais 562) which prohibits the promotion of a concubine to position of wife *during* the lifetime of the actual wife but says nothing about such promotion *after* the wife's death.]

Thus, the establishing of a concubine as wife fundamentally violates the Code's intention. [This seems an arbitrary conclusion to reach on the basis of a passage from a private commentary which by 1802 (the date of this case) did not appear at all in most editions of the Code. There is no doubt that a great many Chinese concubines did in actual fact achieve wifely status through the process here described.]

However, we find in the Code's charts depicting the mourning obligations [Boulais, pp. 18–19] that the sons of a family head are to mourn the family head's concubine for one year, provided she has borne him children [her relationship to them is degree 2a in the five-degree mourning system] and that the concubine, in turn, is to mourn them for one year [their relationship to her is degree 2b]. Again, a slave is to address his master's eldest son as a "one-year mourning relative." [This statement, already quoted in the preceding case, has not been located, and its precise relevance, either here or there, is not clear.] It may thus be concluded that a family head's concubine should be included among the relatives for whom one year of mourning is to be observed. [Does this mean that the family head himself should mourn her for one year? This seems to be the implication of what follows, yet the interpretation is made difficult by the fact that even for his own wife the family head mourns only one year. The concubine's lowly status is indicated by the fact that whereas, according to the mourning charts, she is to mourn her master for three years (he stands to her in a degree 1 relationship), no period of mourning at all is prescribed for him to her (her relationship to him is not included within the five degrees of mourning).]

Mrs. Yang, as a concubine who has borne children to Yang Yü-chüeh, would seem, according to the foregoing references, to be among those relatives for whom one year of mourning is to be observed by the head of a household. Inasmuch as her maid, the late Mrs. Wang, had been Mrs. Yang's indentured servant, Mrs. Yang thereby had the responsibility of disciplining her. Faced by the woman's disobedience, Mrs. Yang beat her in a reasonable fashion, which, however, resulted in her death. Accordingly, Mrs. Yang should be sentenced to 100 blows of the heavy bamboo and three years penal servitude, this being the punishment provided by statute [Boulais 1391] for a relative for whom a family head observes one year of mourning, should that relative beat to death a servant of that household.

As for Yang Yü-chüeh, we have seen that he was violating precedent by establishing his concubine to be his wife. He should, therefore, under the statute on doing what ought not to be done [Boulais 1656], be sentenced to the heavier of the two penalties therein provided, namely 80 blows of the heavy bamboo. [This catch-all statute also punishes by 40 blows of the light bamboo other lesser offenses which, like those punishable by 80 blows, are deemed objectionable by the authorities and are not covered elsewhere in the Code.] Having been a former captain, he is therefore, according to statute, permitted to commute this penalty to a monetary redemption. Mrs. Yang, however, must be returned to her status as a concubine. [For monetary redemption permitted to officials and former officials, see Boulais 37 and 76. According to the table of fines found at the beginning of the Code (but omitted from the several such tables included in Boulais), 80 blows of the heavy bamboo are redeemable for four ounces of silver.]

Imperial Endorsement: This being an equitable judgment, let it be carried out accordingly by the Department for Mukden of the Board of Punishments.

[Both here and in the preceding case, the offender is a concubine whose beating of her serving maid for alleged disobedience leads to the latter's death. At this point, however, the resemblance between the two cases ceases. In the first case, the concubine remains formally a concubine, even though for all practical purposes she has supplanted her master's wife as the mistress of his household; in the second case, the concubine has succeeded the deceased first wife as wife and has further enhanced her position by bearing children for her master. In the first case, the serving maid has passed in status from indentured servant to ordinary slave; in the second, she still remains an indentured servant. In the first case, the maid commits suicide because of the beating received from her mistress; in the second, her death is the direct physical result of the beating itself. These differing circumstances result in differing verdicts. Thus the concubine of the first case, despite her continuing formal status as concubine (and apparent failure to bear children, judging from the lack of reference to this fact), escapes all punishment. The concubine of the second case, despite her advancement to wifely status, the fact that she has given children to her master, and the efforts of the Board of Punishments to demonstrate that even a concubine enjoys honorable status, ends up with three years penal servitude and a return to her original position as concubine.]

187. ASSAULT BY A WIFE OR CONCUBINE ON HER HUSBAND [19]
[Statutory References: Staunton 315, Boulais 1400–1408]

Case 187.1, 1826. Memorandum.
Reported in HAHL 17.40/1a.

The governor of Honan has memorialized concerning a case in which Yün Ta-hsiao stabbed his wife, causing her death.

This Board finds, according to sub-statute [Boulais 642], that if a husband leaves his wife and disappears for three years, the wife, upon reporting this fact to the authorities, shall be given a certificate allowing her to remarry. However, there is no comparable sub-statute concerning remarriage by a wife whose husband, hav-

---

[19] This section, despite its title, also covers a husband's assault on his wife or concubine.

ing been sentenced to exile for a criminal offense, has for a prolonged period failed to give her any news of himself.

The present case is one in which Yün Ta-hsiao suffered deportation to Heilungkiang in 1809 for attempted sodomy. [This offense is punishable by 100 blows of the heavy bamboo and life exile at a distance of 3,000 li. See Boulais 1588, which, however, omits this particular clause near the end of the sub-statute it translates.] Thereafter nothing at all was heard from him. In 1813, therefore, his father, not knowing whether the son was still alive or dead and because of a deficient harvest and his family's poverty, arranged a new marriage for his daughter-in-law for money. In 1820, however, an imperial amnesty resulted in a pardon for Yün Ta-hsiao and his return home. Learning that his wife had remarried, he went to see her and tried to induce her to come back to him. She replied, however, that this was impossible because of the new marriage his father had arranged for her. During the night Yün came to her again and bade her flee with him. She, however, refused to go and upbraided him instead for having remained silent during all his years of exile. Enraged, Yün reviled her and so stabbed her with a knife that she died.

This Board finds that although Mrs. Yün was indeed Yün's wife, and although his deportation for crime is not to be compared with true desertion, it is nevertheless a fact that during five years he never sent a single word to his family, so that his behavior did indeed bear a semblance to desertion. When Yün's father, not knowing whether his son was still alive, and faced by a bad harvest, arranged for his daughter-in-law's remarriage, he acted thus because he had no alternative. Moreover, as a father-in-law, he had the right, according to statute [Boulais 574], to arrange for his daughter-in-law's remarriage. Once this marriage had been effected, therefore, the bond of affection formerly linking her with Yün Ta-hsiao was thereby severed.

The governor of Honan, therefore, under the statute on death resulting from an ordinary affray [Boulais 1268], has sentenced Yün Ta-hsiao to strangulation after the assizes. This decision being fair, we deem it appropriate to request a confirmatory reply.

[Aside from the nullification of Yün's marriage to his wife, the sentence he thus received—strangulation after the assizes—was no different from what he would have received had he been sentenced under the statute (Boulais 1403) on a husband who beats his wife to death. This sentence is rather remarkable because the same statute provides a penalty reduced by two degrees from the norm for a husband who only injures his wife seriously but does not actually kill her. The insistence in this and other comparable statutes on retention of the death penalty (even if softened by the words "after the assizes") probably reflects the ancient idea (see cases 164.1, 164.2, 185.1) that only through the sacrifice of a human life can a criminally caused homicide be adequately requited and cosmic harmony thereby restored.]

188. AFFRAYS BETWEEN RELATIVES OF THE SAME SURNAME [20]
[Statutory References: Staunton 316, Boulais 1409]

Case 188.2, 1828. Memorandum.
Reported in HAHL 17.40/23a.

The governor of Shantung has reported a case in which Liu Hu-ch'en attacked and maimed Mrs. Liu née Cheng, a distant clan aunt whose relationship to him lies outside the five degrees of mourning.

This Board finds that since Mrs. Liu belongs to a senior generation as compared with the offender and since they are fellow clan members but outside the five degrees of mourning, Liu Hu-ch'en should be sentenced under the statute on affrays between relatives of the same surname [Boulais 1409], according to which a junior relative who attacks a senior relative outside the five degrees of mourning is to receive a sentence one degree higher than that for the same offense occurring between non-relatives.

The governor of Shantung, however, has sentenced Liu Hu-ch'en to maximum [three years] penal servitude under the statute [Boulais 1347] on an ordinary affray resulting in maiming. [He has thus disregarded the distant relationship between the two parties.] This sentence is in error. It should be changed to a sen-

[20] This section covers relatives belonging to the same clan but whose relationship is so distant that it lies outside of the five degrees of mourning. Thus the section supplements others in which closer family relationships are considered.

tence one degree higher than the maximum penal servitude provided above for breaking someone's limb and thereby maiming him. That is to say, it should be 100 blows of the heavy bamboo and life exile at a distance of 3,000 li. The governor should be instructed to submit a further special report on this matter.

[A one-degree increase from three years penal servitude means the lowest degree of exile, at a distance of 2,000 li, whereas here, inexplicably, the alleged one-degree increase raises the penalty all the way to the highest level of ordinary exile, 3,000 li. This procedure seems clearly to violate the standard formula used for increasing penalties (as against the differing standard formula used for reducing those belonging to the three highest categories). See Boulais 111 and discussion in our Chapter III, end of section 9. See also case 266.1 for another unexpectedly large increase of penalty.]

189. ASSAULT ON SENIOR RELATIVES OF THE THIRD DEGREE OF MOURNING AND BELOW
[Statutory References: Staunton 317, Boulais 1410]

Case 189.1, 1826. Memorandum.
Reported in HAHL 18.41/1a.

The governor of Kuangtung has reported a case in which Pi Ch'i-chang, finding that his younger brother had been committing robbery, induced his two nephews once removed to help him in tying up the younger brother and throwing him into a pond, where he drowned. The governor has requested this Board to determine whether, when sentencing the two junior relatives, he may add a petition for clemency.

[The two nephews once removed were both sons of Pi Ch'i-chang's cousin (or cousins). Therefore their relationship to Pi and his brother was that of degree 4 in the five-degree mourning system. Accordingly, unless extenuating circumstances could be found, their killing of a senior relative of the fourth degree would, under Boulais 1410, be punishable by decapitation after the assizes.]

This Board finds that if a junior relative has been coerced and intimidated by a senior relative into going along with him in attacking and killing another senior relative of the third or fourth degrees of mourning, the usual statutory penalty for the junior relative [decapitation after the assizes] shall be reduced by one degree to life exile [at a distance of 3,000 li. See Boulais 1410a.] Again, there is no doubt that the premeditated drowning of a person is a more serious offense than that of assaulting him at the behest of someone else. [Under Boulais 1211, the penalty for premeditated homicide is decapitation after the assizes. Under Boulais 1380, a person who commits homicide because he has been coerced by someone into doing so receives a penalty one degree less than does the instigator, that is, in a case of premeditated homicide he receives life exile.] To commit a crime because of compulsion is different from doing it without cause.

In the present case, the two junior relatives had been intimidated by Pi Ch'i-chang into carrying his brother to the side of the pond and there joining with him in pushing the brother into the water. Thus their act, stemming as it does from Pi himself, is very different from killing a senior relative with wilful premeditation.

From this it follows that in order to give proper emphasis to the cardinal human relationships, the two junior relatives should be sentenced under the statute basic to their case [Boulais 1410, providing decapitation after the assizes. The five cardinal relationships are those of father and son (under which all ties between senior and junior relations would be subsumed), elder and younger brother, husband and wife, ruler and subject, and friend and friend.] In order, however, to display compassion as well, this sentence should be accompanied by a petition for clemency, with citation made of the relevant sub-statute [the one cited above providing a reduced punishment of life exile at a distance of 3,000 li if the killing is done under coercion]. The governor of Kuangtung should be instructed to act accordingly.

[This case, like a number of others, demonstrates the unquestioned power exercised by a senior relative over even a somewhat removed junior one. Apparently it occurred to no one connected with the case that the two junior relatives could have refused to join their uncle once removed in killing his brother. Concerning the fate of the uncle himself, the Board's memorandum makes no mention. Were he guilty of killing his brother intentionally (but without premeditation), the penalty under Boulais 1413 would be strangulation after the assizes. However, the references in the discussion to premeditated drowning and killing, plus the objective facts of the case themselves, make it probable that Pi's crime was adjudged to be premeditated and that he therefore suffered decapitation after the assizes.]

190. ASSAULT ON SENIOR RELATIVES OF THE SECOND DEGREE OF MOURNING
[Statutory References: Staunton 318, Boulais 1411–1418]

Case 190.2, 1738. From the Collection of Seen Leading Cases. *Reported in HAHL 18.42/15b.*

The governor-general of Chihli has reported a case in which Li Ch'ang, after injuring himself in an accidental fall, received further injuries when assaulted by his younger brother, Li Mao, and finally died of infection from the injury suffered in the fall. The governor-general has recommended that Li Mao be sentenced to life exile, this being a punishment one degree higher than the norm. [The relationship of an older to a younger brother is degree 2 in the five-degree mourning system. Boulais 1411 specifies 100 blows of the heavy bamboo and three years penal servitude as the normal penalty for beating and injuring an older brother.]

However, inasmuch as it was unclear from the governor-general's first report whether the evidence really shows that the victim was injured in his own fall, this board asked the governor-general to conduct a further investigation. The second report now received provides the following information:

Li Ch'ang, being angered at the refusal of his younger brother Li Mao to give money for "bean stone flowers" (*tou shih hua*) [unidentified but possibly the colloquial name of an alcoholic beverage], seized a knife while drunk and sought a quarrel. From the top of a manure pile he scaled his brother's wall into the brother's courtyard but lost his grip while climbing and fell, injuring the right side of his crown on a stone below the wall. The younger brother ran to his uncle Li Shu-pin, who rushed to see what had happened, urged the two brothers to stop quarrelling, and bandaged the elder brother's wound. Thus, there is good evidence that Li Ch'ang did in fact injure himself in a fall, the more so as examination conducted at the time of the autopsy revealed traces of blood on the stone below the wall.

Li Ch'ang, however, continued his disorderly conduct by smashing an iron cooking pot belonging to his brother, and when his uncle shouted to him to stop, he began to brandish his knife. The uncle shouted to Li Mao, the younger brother, to get the knife away from Li Ch'ang by hitting him. At first Li Mao beat him on the ribs with his fists but was unable to grab the knife, so he then hit him on the shins with a stick, causing him to fall and thus got the chance to wrest the knife from him.

Thereupon the uncle again bandaged the older brother's wounds and sent him home. There, however, Li Ch'ang pulled off the bandages, exposing the wounds to air. As a result, he died from infection eight days later. There is no doubt whatever that Li Ch'ang's injury to the crown of his head resulted from his accidental fall and that the infection of this injury led to his death.

Nonetheless, when Li Mao struck and injured his older brother on the ribs and shins, even though he was acting under his uncle's orders, and even though the inflicted injuries were not fatal, his action was nevertheless a violation of one of the cardinal relationships. [See preceding case for these relationships, five in number, of which the one intended here is, of course, that between older and younger brother.]

Accordingly, Li Mao should be sentenced, as recommended in the original report, under the statute on a younger brother who assaults and injures an older brother [Boulais 1411], with, however, the penalty therein specified of 100 blows of the heavy bamboo and three years penal servitude to be increased for Li Mao by one degree to 100 blows of the heavy bamboo and life exile at a distance of 2,000 li.

[Here again, as in several earlier cases, the Board, in order to raise or lower a statutory penalty, should have applied the relevant statute analogically rather than directly but neglected to do so. Why it increased the penalty at all is anyone's guess, aside from the obvious fact that the older brother eventually died (even though from self-inflicted injuries). Note the absence of any reference to the uncle. Apparently the fact that he belonged to a senior generation and struck no blows himself but merely ordered the younger brother to do so was enough to absolve him of any guilt. In the preceding case, we have seen that two junior relatives who tied, carried, and helped drown an uncle once removed—a series of actions requiring some premeditation—received a sentence one degree less than the norm because they had acted under the orders of another (and still older) uncle once removed. In the present case, almost a century earlier, a younger brother, confronted by a drunken older brother brandishing a knife, strikes that brother at the orders of an uncle, and therefore, even though the resulting injuries are not fatal, is given a sentence one degree higher than the norm—life exile.]

191. ASSAULT BY OFFSPRING ON PARENTS OR GRANDPARENTS [21]
[Statutory References: Staunton 319, Boulais 1419–1430]

Case 191.1, 1826. Memorandum from the Department for Mukden of the Board of Punishments.
Reported in HAHL 19.44/1a.

The military governor of Kirin has reported a case in which Wang Ch'i, a father, killed his son by burying him alive.

This Department finds, according to statute [Boulais 1420], that if parents or grandparents unreasonably beat and thus kill a son or grandson who has violated their commands, the penalty for so doing is 100 blows of the heavy bamboo; if the killing is intentional, the penalty becomes 60 blows of the heavy bamboo and one year penal servitude. Another statute [Boulais 1421] also states that if parents or grandparents beat and thus kill a son or grandson by whom they have been assaulted or reviled, they are to incur no penalty at all.

Concerning the second statute, the *Chien-shih Commentary* explains that the son or grandson who assaults or reviles a parent

---

[21] Despite its title, this section also deals with assaults by parents or grandparents on offspring.

or grandparent has thereby already committed a capital crime, which is why the parent is to incur no penalty. [This commentary, already cited in case 189.6, is discussed in Chapter II, section 4. The passage quoted will be found in *Wang K'en-t'ang Chien-shih* (Wang K'en-t'ang's *Chien-shih Commentary*), 20/39a.]

Concerning the first statute, the Official Commentary likewise explains [and, therefore, provides] that the term "intentional killing" (*ku sha*), as used in it, refers exclusively to the killing of a son or grandson who has not been guilty of any disobedience. Thus, for any case involving disobedience, even one in which the killing may in fact have been quite intentional, the sentence given cannot be more than 100 blows of the heavy bamboo, this being the penalty, under the statute on unreasonably beating and killing a son or grandson who is disobedient. It follows that if a son or grandson, in addition to being disobedient, also assaults or reviles a parent or grandparent, there obviously cannot be, conversely, an increased penalty for killing him.

In the present case, the older son of Wang Ch'i had wanted to borrow money from the younger son and, when he refused, the older son became so enraged that he chased the younger son with a knife. The father, on hearing this, dragged the older son home, tied his hands with a rope, and upbraided him. The older son reviled his father in turn, which so enraged the father that he buried his son alive.

Thus, although the killing was done intentionally, it was the killing of a son who had committed a capital crime by reviling his father. Such a killing is therefore not an intentional killing because this term is used to designate the killing of a son who has not been disobedient. Likewise, since the son had reviled his father, there is a distinction between such killing and what is termed "unreasonably beating and killing a disobedient son." The military governor of Kirin has been unjust, therefore, in sentencing Wang Ch'i to beating under the statute covering the latter offense, and his sentence should be changed to no punishment at all, in order to accord with the meaning of the law.

As for the younger brother, he was coerced by his father to help bury alive his older brother. At present he is a fugitive. When apprehended, however, and brought to trial, if the facts prove to be as they have been reported, it will be permissible, according to sub-statute [Boulais 1415a], to accompany his sentence with a petition for clemency.

[According to Boulais 1411, decapitation is the punishment for a younger brother who kills an older one, and the Official Commentary adds that this punishment is to be given whether the younger brother acted as a principal or an accomplice. The above-mentioned Boulais 1415a states, however, that if the killing of the older brother has been done by the younger brother at the command of his father because the father has either been struck or reviled by the older brother, a petition to the throne may be submitted, asking that the younger brother's sentence—ordinarily decapitation—be reduced to 100 blows of the heavy bamboo and life exile at a distance of 3,000 li. This sub-statute derives from a case of 1800, involving a certain Wang Chung-kuei, which is summarized in Boulais 1416.]

Case 191.2, 1826. Memorandum.
Reported in HAHL 19.44/1a–b.

The governor of Shantung has reported a case in which K'ung Ch'uan-li, a father, killed his daughter who had committed adultery and then eloped.

This Board finds, according to statute [Boulais 1420], that if a father unreasonably beats and thus kills a son or daughter who has violated his commands, the penalty for so doing is 100 blows of the heavy bamboo. A sub-statute [Boulais 1415] also states that if a senior relative kills a junior relative guilty of an offense which does not deserve death, but if the senior has really committed the homicide because of anger against the junior for having disgraced the ancestors, then, even though the senior is the principal in the homicide and commits it with premeditation or intention, his punishment will be one degree less than the punishment which, according to the closeness of relationship, is provided by statute for the ordinary beating to death of a junior by a senior relative.

[See Boulais 1410–1411, which provides punishments ranging from strangulation after the assizes (for the intentional killing of, for example, a first cousin) to no punishment at all (for accidental homicide). In citing the sub-statute on the killing of a junior relative who has disgraced his ancestors (Boulais 1415), the Board of Punishments has omitted an important clause to the effect that the junior relative must "really be a habitual good-for-nothing, whose obduracy and inability to reform are publicly known and have been definitely attested."]

The same sub-statute states also that any senior relative, other than the principal, who participates in such a killing, will, as under the statute on accessories in an affray [Boulais 1270], be punished by 100 blows of the heavy bamboo. [This sentence of the sub-statute is omitted in Boulais 1415.]

Of the above statute and sub-statute, the former refers only to parents who "unreasonably" *(fei li)* beat to death their disobedient children, whereas, in the latter, the terms "senior" and "junior" refer only to mourning relationships of the second degree or lower and therefore do not include the closer relationship of parent to child. [This fact is explicitly indicated by the complete terminology given in the original sub-statute (here only paraphrased). Among the various relationships of the second or lower degree of mourning specified in Boulais 1410–1411, there are those of elder to younger sibling, uncle or aunt to nephew or niece, and first cousins.] Thus, should a case arise of a father killing a licentious daughter, such killing cannot be termed unreasonable, inasmuch as the daughter's crime, by which her death has been provoked, is more serious than one of mere disobedience. However, because the killing is that of a daughter by a father, it cannot be placed under the sub-statute on the killing of a junior relative by a senior relative whose status toward the victim is that of the second degree of mourning or below.

Our search for comparable earlier cases reveals one in Honan in 1820, in which Liu Yü-lin strangled his adulterous daughter and was acquitted because the killing had been induced by his rage at her shamelessness. Another case is that of Chao Chung-yüan, who also strangled his adulterous daughter and was likewise acquitted.

In the present case, K'ung Ch'uan-li's daughter committed adultery and then eloped. The father sent his son [who was older than the daughter] to bring her home, and the matter, because of its unsavoriness, was then hushed up. Subsequently, however, the daughter, because of her husband's poverty, ran off again and appealed to people to find her a new husband. The father, on hearing this, felt it to be such a disgrace to the ancestors that in his fury he ordered his son to chop her to death.

The daughter's paramour, Chou Kuang, has been sentenced by the Provincial Court of Honan to military exile for seduction. [The pertinent sub-statute provides strangulation after the assizes for the seducer when the woman involved is an unwilling party and military exile at a distance of 4,000 li when, as here, she consents. This second provision of the sub-statute is omitted from the version of it given in Boulais 1185.] The Court has also sentenced the son to 100 blows of the heavy bamboo as a senior relative who acts as an accessory in the killing of a junior relative. These sentences both accord with their respective sub-statutes.

[Here a son who kills his younger sister at the command of his father is sentenced to 100 blows as an accessory. In case 191.1, a son who kills his older brother at the command of his father is promised, once he has been arrested, a probable reduction of sentence from the normal penalty of decapitation to life exile at a distance of 3,000 li. These differing sentences rest upon differences of age rather than of sex. Thus Boulais 1411 provides decapitation for the killing of an older by a younger sibling, irrespective of the sex of the sibling, but only three years penal servitude for the killing of a younger by an older sibling (further reducible in Boulais 1415, as we have seen, to 100 blows of the heavy bamboo if the older sibling acts merely as an accessory).]

As to the father, K'ung Ch'uan-li, however, his act in ordering his son to kill his daughter, inspired by anger at the latter's licentiousness, does not constitute an "unreasonable" beating to death of a son or daughter for mere disobedience. Nor, as we have seen, is it the killing by a senior relative of a junior relative who has disgraced the ancestors. The Provincial Court is therefore mistaken in applying here the sub-statute which provides a penalty for such an offense one degree less than that provided for the ordinary killing of a junior by a senior and in therefore sentencing K'ung Ch'uan-li to bambooing. This sentence needs to be corrected.

[The implication, clear though unstated, is that K'ung Ch'uan-li, like the fathers in the two cases cited earlier, should escape punishment entirely. (An almost identical result has already been encountered in cases 4.2 and 191.1.) There seem to be only two statutes and one sub-statute in the Code dealing specifically with the killing of a child by a blood parent: (1) Boulais 1420, which provides 100 blows of the heavy bamboo for "unreasonably" beating to death a disobedient child and 60 blows plus one year penal servitude for doing this to a child who is not disobedient; (2) Boulais 1421, which provides acquittal for the killing of a child when the child has struck or reviled the parents, when the killing has resulted inadvertently from the "reasonable" (*li*) beating of a disobedient child, or when the killing is accidental; (3) a sub-statute, Boulais 1423a, which provides decapitation after the assizes for an adulterous mother who kills her child in order to prevent the child from reporting the adultery.]

194. PARENTS ASSAULTED BY OUTSIDERS [22]
[Statutory References: Staunton 323, Boulais 1444–1446]

Case 194.3, 1815. Leading Case from the Department for Mukden of the Board of Punishments.
Reported in HAHL 19.44/19a.

The Board of Punishments of Manchuria has reported in a memorial to the Board of Punishments in Peking a case of multiple deaths resulting from a mass affray. In this case, four members of the Chia family, namely Chia Erh and his three adopted sons, Chia Ssu, Chia Wu, and Chia Shih, made an attack on Lu Ch'un, who, at the time, was accompanied by his son, Lu Ch'üan-hai, and another man, Wang Ho. Lu Ch'un, in return, fought with and killed the Chia father, Chia Erh, and one of his adopted sons, Chia Ssu. A third Chia, Chia Wu, then attacked and killed Lu Ch'un, whereupon Lu's son, Lu Ch'üan-hai, in turn killed both Chia Wu and the remaining foster brother, Chia Shih. Thus the son became responsible for the killing of two persons in a single family.

[22] This section, as becomes evident below, concerns the punishment to be given to offspring who, when rescuing their parents or grandparents from an attack made by an outside party, themselves injure or kill that outside party.

Under the relevant sub-statute, Lu Ch'üan-hai has been sentenced to immediate strangulation. [This is the penalty provided by Boulais 1251a for the killing of two persons within a single family during a mass affray. Boulais 1252, by contrast, provides the severer penalty of immediate decapitation for the same crime when committed by an individual acting on his own initiative independently of any general affray.]

However, a petition for clemency accompanying this judgment points out that Chia Wu, one of the two persons killed by Lu Ch'üan-hai, had just previously killed Lu's father. Hence, there is a difference between this act of Lu and an ordinary wanton killing of two persons in the same family.

Imperial Rescript: Let judgment be made in accordance with the memorial resulting from the deliberations between the Board of Punishments and high ministers from other boards, to the effect that sentence for the accused should be reduced [from immediate strangulation] to strangulation after the assizes.

[Under Boulais 1444, a child or grandchild who rescues a parent or grandparent from attack by an outside party and in so doing injures that outside party himself, is to receive a punishment three degrees less than the ordinary punishment for such an injury; if, however, he kills the outside party, his punishment is to remain the same as the ordinary punishment for killing in an affray, that is, strangulation after the assizes. In this insistence upon retention of the death penalty, even for a homicide committed under such mitigating circumstances, there is perhaps again a reflection of the idea (see cases 164.1, 164.2, 185.1) that maintenance of cosmic harmony requires that a criminal homicide always be requited by another human life (at least nominally, since strangulation after the assizes was often, though not invariably, eventually reduced to life exile).]

As for the other offender, Wang Ho, though he too fought with Chia Ssu and Chia Wu, the injuries he thereby inflicted were light and non-fatal. Therefore, under the statute [Boulais 1270] on a joint and fatal affray which involves subsidiary participants [other than the original planner and the persons actually striking the fatal blows], Wang Ho, as such a subsidiary participant, is to be sentenced to 100 blows of the heavy bamboo.

Case 194.5, 1812. Memorandum.
Reported in HAHL 19.44/20a.

The governor of Kiangsu has memorialized concerning a case in which P'u Yung-sheng attacked and fatally injured Chang Chiu-lin.

This Board finds, according to sub-statute [Boulais 1445a], that if grandparents, parents, or husband suffer attack [from an outside party], and the son, grandson, or wife acts to save them in the emergency [thereby injuring or killing the outside party], a reduction of punishment is forthcoming. However, there is nowhere any reference to such a reduction for a younger brother who is similarly acting to save an elder brother who is under attack.

In the present case, Chang Chiu-lin dragged P'u Ssu-pao down to the ground, sat on him, and began to beat him with his fists. P'u's younger brother, P'u Yung-sheng, seeing what was happening, seized a rake and hit Chang on the left ear, fatally wounding him.

As stated above, there is no sub-statute providing reduced punishment for a younger brother like P'u Yung-sheng who, to save his elder brother, kills another person. Although it is true that the offender is only twelve years of age, it is also true that the person he killed was not taking advantage of his own greater age to revile him. Thus it follows that the offender should be sentenced under the statute [Boulais 1268] on homicide resulting from an affray [without any reduction of penalty].

The governor of Kiangsu has indeed sentenced P'u Yung-sheng to strangulation after the assizes, this being the punishment under the aforesaid statute. Because this judgment accords with the law, we deem it appropriate to request a confirmatory reply.

[Boulais 131 (on offenses committed by the young, the aged, and the infirm) states *inter alia* that a child aged 11 to 15 may pay a fine as monetary redemption for an offense meriting life exile or less, but the statute denies this privilege for a capital offense. (Provisions for clemency for the latter exist if the child is under 11.) Boulais 134 adds that if a child aged 11 to 15 kills another person who is at least four years older than himself and who has been reviling him, a petition for clemency may then be addressed to the throne (for a reduction of sentence, not a complete pardon; see case 14.1). It is this statute to which the Board of Punishments is alluding when it says of the victim that he "was not taking advantage of his own greater age to revile" the killer. The Chinese wording of this clause makes it uncertain whether the Board rejected the statute because the person killed was less than four years older than the child killer or because, though four years older, he had not been guilty of reviling.]

[Be this as it may, it would seem at first sight that had the Board really wanted to give the twelve year old offender a sentence less than strangulation after the assizes, it could have done so by applying to him, analogically rather than directly, the sub-statute on a son or wife who saves a parent or husband from attack—the same sub-statute whose direct applicability it begins by denying. That on the contrary it expressly notes the absence of younger brothers from the relatives named by this sub-statute, suggests that the Board was thinking here in terms of a Western canon of statutory interpretation which states: "The expression of one thing is the exclusion of another." In other words, the Board believed that the omission of younger brothers from the list was deliberate and that had the framers of the sub-statute really intended younger brothers to receive the same consideration as the other named relatives, they would surely have stated as much. See discussion in Part Three, "Statutory Interpretation," note 25.]

195. ABUSIVE LANGUAGE USED AGAINST AN IMPERIAL COMMISSIONER OR ONE'S OWN PRESIDING OFFICIAL
[Statutory References: Staunton 325, Boulais 1450]

Case 195.2, 1881. Leading Case.
Reported in HAHL New Supplement 39.12/1a.

The Board of Punishments presents a memorial concerning To Fu, a [Manchu?] captain, now already dismissed, who, being a troublemaker by nature and despite the fact that he had no grievance of his own and was not personally concerned, often went to the residence of his top commanding officer, where under various excuses he would seek an interview to present a complaint. When stopped from entering, he would run around shouting and act violently. Truly his conduct was that of one wanting to coerce his superior officer.

There is, however, a difference between an official's private residence and his governmental office. Therefore To Fu should be given a sentence less than that called for under the sub-statute [cited immediately below]. Accordingly, he should be sentenced by analogy to [rather than directly under] the sub-statute on knavish fellows who rush into government offices in order to exercise coercion upon the officials there [Boulais 1461a]. His sentence, therefore, should be 100 blows of the heavy bamboo and three years penal servitude, this being one degree less than the military exile stipulated by the sub-statute. In view of his [former] official status, he should be dealt with sternly and therefore should be sent to a military post, so that he may there through efficacious labor redeem his crime.

[In the absence of any indication of an external origin, this case probably occurred in Peking. Despite its classification under Boulais 1450 (use of abusive language against a presiding official), it is judged under an entirely unrelated sub-statute (belonging to the section on lodging accusations without going through proper channels), probably because the Board felt that this was a more adequate punishment than the mere 100 blows of the heavy bamboo provided by Boulais 1450. It would seem from the colorful language contained in the sub-statute in its full unabridged form in the Code itself that it must have originated from some very specific individual incident. (See discussion in Chapter II, end of section 3.) Thus the text begins: "If a knavish fellow (*tiao t'u*) from outside [the capital], with a yellow square of cloth on his back, a yellow banner planted upon his head, and accusations issuing from his mouth, rushes into a government office in order to exercise coercion upon the officials there . . ." (Yellow was the color used for petitions and other documents destined for a superior.) The sub-statute then goes on to say that his complaint will be investigated. If found to represent his own personal grievance, it will be acted upon, but he himself, for his unruly conduct, will be punished by the heavier of the two penalties (80 blows of the heavy bamboo) provided under the statute on doing what ought not to be done (Boulais 1656). If, on the other hand, the complaint is found to represent something other than his own grievance, he and the instigator of his misconduct will both be sent into military exile at a nearby frontier.]

196. ABUSIVE LANGUAGE USED BY A SUBORDINATE OFFICIAL AGAINST AN IMMEDIATE SUPERIOR
[Statutory References: Staunton 326, Boulais 1450a]

Case 196.1, 1881. Leading Case.
Reported in HAHL New Supplement 39.12/1a.

The governor of Shantung has memorialized concerning Ch'en Ch'ü-mo, a sub-prefect of the first class, now already dismissed, whose fits of insanity led him into reckless behavior including the writing of anonymous letters. Such a letter was by mistake delivered to the governor by Ch'en's groom. Being a product of his mental illness, it apparently was not intentional. Neither did it accuse anyone of any crime but simply, for no reason at all, used abusive language against the upper hierarchy. Later Ch'en became sorry and afraid and came in person to explain what he had done. On reaching the office, however, he became embroiled in a noisy quarrel with the guard on duty. His conduct was unseemly and deserves punishment in accordance with law.

This Board, under the statute on an official who uses abusive language against an imperial commissioner [Boulais 1450], finds that Ch'en Ch'ü-mo should be sentenced to 100 blows of the heavy bamboo. Since he has already been dismissed from government service, there is no need to discuss his case further.

[Staunton 326, under which this case is classified, provides from 30 to 80 blows of the bamboo for subordinate officials who use abusive language toward their immediate superiors (the precise punishment depending upon the respective rank of the two).

Boulais 1450, under which the case is judged, provides 100 blows for an official who uses abusive language toward an imperial commissioner (and the same for a commoner who abuses the magistrate of his district, as well as certain others). Why the case is classed under the one statute but judged under the other is unclear. Perhaps Boulais 1450 is felt to be more apposite because the ambiguous term *shang ssu,* rendered as "upper hierarchy," implies a higher and wider range of officialdom than just the offender's own immediate superior. Another consideration may be the heavier punishment permitted by Boulais 1450 as compared with Boulais 1450a. However, in the absence of any specific mention in the text of an imperial commissioner, it would seem that the cited statute should have been applied analogically rather than directly.]

198. ANONYMOUS ACCUSATIONS
[Statutory References: Staunton 333, Boulais 1463–1467]

Case 198.7, 1818. General Circular Selected for Redaction as a Sub-statute.
Reported in HAHL 20.46/10a.

The Department for Shansi of the Board of Punishments has received the following imperial edict dated May 16, 1818:
Imperial Edict: Anonymous accusation is extremely harmful to morality and custom, its prime motivation being private hatred and desire for revenge. Investigation of accusations of this sort serves not only to smear the accused, but through its repercussions also ruthlessly implicates innocent outsiders. With a few anonymous words, the schemer induces officials to poison the lives of ordinary people, while he himself looks on with folded hands, thereby satisfying a private grudge. The resulting evil is worse than that caused by demons.

According to statute [Boulais 1463], strangulation [after the assizes] is provided for anyone who lodges an anonymous written accusation, 80 blows of the heavy bamboo for anyone who, on seeing such an accusation, fails to destroy it and brings it instead before the authorities, and 100 blows of the heavy bamboo for any official who accepts and acts upon it. The accused person himself, even if the accusation be true, is not to be tried. [The statute further specifies that a reward of ten ounces of silver is to be paid to anyone who detects and arrests a person in the act of lodging an anonymous accusation.]

Because this law is extremely clear, anyone hereafter who finds an anonymous accusation is to destroy it forthwith and is forbidden to memorialize its contents. Should it, however, pertain to matters of grave concern to the state, only then may it be secretly memorialized for our private consideration. [The most significant portion of this edict is its final sentence.]

Case 198.8, 1829. From the Peking Gazette.
Reported in HAHL 20.46/10a.

Imperial Edict of May 18, 1829: Sung Yün [a high official of Mongol birth, at that time a lieutenant-general] has memorialized stating that he has received an anonymous accusation, the contents of which, because they bear upon the administrative integrity of an entire province, he is reporting secretly. In his memorial he recognizes that lodging of anonymous accusations is extremely harmful to morality and custom, and cites the edict of the Chia-ch'ing Emperor [see preceding case] to the effect that anyone finding an anonymous accusation is to destroy it forthwith and is forbidden to memorialize its contents. He then goes on to say, however, that since this particular accusation brings charges against the highest officials in the said province, he has felt it his duty to acquaint us secretly with its contents.

By citing the relevant sub-statute [Boulais 1466a], Sung Yün has kept himself within the bounds of propriety. If, however, the accusation's charges are really true, why has the accuser not attached his name to them? His conduct is like a demon's tricks in hatefulness.

[What the emperor calls a sub-statute is the above-mentioned edict, for the full text of which see preceding case. The edict bears a date corresponding to May 16, 1818. In 1821 it was formally added to the Code as a sub-statute.]

The accusation submitted by Sung Yün is to be returned to him for destruction. Hereafter, in accordance with the sub-statute, anyone who finds an anonymous accusation is to destroy it and is forbidden to memorialize its contents. [The emperor who here upholds the sub-statute without qualification is the Tao-kuang Emperor (1821–1850), successor to the Chia-ch'ing Emperor (1796–1820) who issued the edict of the preceding case.]

Case 198.9, 1822. Leading Case.
Reported in HAHL 20.46/10b.

The governor-general of Szechuan reports that Li Hua-lin, a copyist in the provincial Office of Punishments, was dismissed by his superior for indulging in philandering. Out of revenge, he filched documents from the office and then wrote an anonymous letter about the theft to the higher authorities. Subsequently, however, on hearing that he was wanted, he voluntarily turned himself in. It is therefore proper that strangulation, which is the usual penalty for making anonymous accusations [Boulais 1463], should be reduced by one degree in his case to maximum exile.

[Strangulation was reduced to life exile at a distance of 3,000 li. For discussion of the sub-statute, Boulais 122a, which provides such a one-degree reduction for criminals who, on learning that they are wanted, turn themselves in, see case 17.1.]

199. FALSE ACCUSATIONS
[Statutory References: Staunton 336, Boulais 1474–1494]

Case 199.4, 1811. Memorandum.
Reported in HAHL 20.46/14b.

The governor of Shantung has memorialized concerning a case in which T'eng Ch'üan-ching, being anxious to save his son from punishment, uttered wild accusations whose verification or disproof required that the corpse of a slain man, Chiang An-chou, be subjected to post-mortem examination by steaming. [If a corpse is badly decomposed and foul play is suspected, the corpse is exposed to steam created by pouring vinegar over a charcoal fire, whereupon, so it is claimed, the marks of any injury will become apparent on the body. See Boulais, p. 641, note 5, and especially the standard thirteenth-century treatise on forensic medicine, *Hsi yüan lu*, Bk. I, Chap. 5; cf. H. A. Giles, trans., "The 'Hsi Yüan Lu' or 'Instructions to Coroners,'" *China Review*, 3:92 (1874).]

This Board finds that T'eng's son, after having murdered the dead man for his money, claimed that the man had died in a fall. It was after this false testimony was rejected that the elder T'eng made his wild charges in order to save his son, thus bringing on the need to exhume and steam the corpse.

There being no article specifically covering this offense in the Code, the Provincial Court of Shantung has taken the viewpoint that to cause a corpse to be needlessly steamed is as grievous an act as to mutilate or destroy it wantonly. The Court has accordingly sentenced T'eng Ch'üan-ching, by analogy to the statute on destroying the corpse of someone outside one's own family [Boulais 1193], to life exile [at a distance of 3,000 li].

This judgment accords well with the facts. Moreover, there has been an earlier case in Shantung which involved virtually the same circumstances and was judged by analogy to the same statute. There can be no question, therefore, of anything but a confirmatory reply. [This earlier case does not seem to be included in the HAHL. The present case, however, almost surely led to the drafting of the sub-statute (partially contained in Boulais 1487) which is the basis for judgment in our next case, decided twelve years later.]

Case 199.5, 1823. Leading Case.
Reported in HAHL 20.46/14b.

The governor of Yunnan has memorialized concerning a case in which Li Yi-k'ai fatally stabbed Ho Yü-jung, for which, under the statute on homicide in an affray [Boulais 1268], he should be sentenced to strangulation after the assizes. His father, however, Li Huan-ts'ai, was anxious to save the son from punishment, and therefore falsely maintained that the victim had committed suicide by hanging. This charge necessitated the exhumation and steaming of the corpse for post-mortem examination. [The result was to disprove the charge.]

The Yunnan Provincial Court has accordingly sentenced the father, Li Huan-ts'ai, to military exile at a nearby frontier, under the sub-statute on false charges, concerning a homicide, that are not motivated by revenge but consist simply in questioning the interpretation of the victim's wounds made at the autopsy. [In charges of this sort, no specific individual is accused of having committed the homicide, but the autopsy's findings are nevertheless challenged. This is the second half of the sub-statute of which only the first half is given in Boulais 1487. This first half provides strangulation after the assizes for one who, in a spirit of revenge, falsely accuses another person of homicide, thereby making necessary the steaming of the victim's corpse. The entire sub-statute was almost surely enacted to meet the issues raised by the preceding case.]

The offender, however, has already passed the age of 70, and is therefore permitted, according to statute, to pay a monetary redemption for his offense. [Boulais 131 permits such redemption for persons of 70 or above, except for capital offenses or implication in a very few major crimes such as treason. The redemption for military exile is the purely nominal sum of 0.45 ounces of silver. See table in Boulais, p. 11.]

There is no need to decide now whether Li's son may be granted the privilege of remaining at home to care for his father [instead of undergoing the statutory penalty] on the grounds that he is the sole adult son of aged parents. [See Boulais 96 for the specific provisions of this statute and cases 11.1 and 11.4 for its practical application.] However, nothing in the Code states that when father and son are both guilty in a single case, and when the father because of age is permitted to redeem his punishment, the son may not also be permitted [as the sole adult heir] to remain at home to care for him. In the present case, however, whereas Li Huan-ts'ai may be permitted to redeem his punishment now, the disposition of his son should await the Autumn Assizes for final decision. [The wording here strongly suggests that at that time the son will be permitted to forgo his slated punishment, even though, as may be seen from cases 11.1 and 11.4, the privilege of staying at home to care for aged parents was, in capital cases, by no means accorded easily or automatically.]

Case 199.7, 1821. Leading Case.
Reported in HAHL 20.46/15a.

The governor of Shansi has memorialized concerning a case in which the son of Wang Pen-chih, having lost money in gambling to another man and then being pressed for payment, finally committed suicide by jumping off a cliff. The father suspected that his son had really been killed by the other man and so went to Peking to lodge an accusation, thus necessitating exhumation and steaming of the corpse to verify or disprove his charges.

This Board's investigation has revealed that Wang's accusation [despite its lack of foundation] was motivated by a genuine feeling of suspicion, and therefore was different from ordinary false accusations [those deliberately fabricated in order to implicate an innocent person]. For what he has done, therefore, Wang Pen-chih should be sentenced under the statute [Boulais 1474] on falsely accusing another person of having committed a capital crime but with the accusation being disproved before the accused person actually undergoes punishment. For Wang, the penalty provided under this statute is to be reduced by one degree to 100 blows of the heavy bamboo and total penal servitude of four years.

[On this very rare punishment, see Chapter III, section 4. In the present case it is merely a lesser substitute for the statute's stipulated penalty of life exile at a distance of 3,000 li—itself made into an unusual penalty by the special provision that its first three years are to be devoted to hard labor of the sort ordinarily imposed in penal servitude sentences. In this case, again, the Board applies the statute directly rather than analogically, as strictly speaking it ought to do when reducing the statutory punishment.]

200. ACCUSATIONS BY JUNIOR AGAINST SENIOR RELATIVES
[Statutory References: Staunton 337, Boulais 1495–1502]

Case 200.2, 1823. Memorandum.
Reported in HAHL 21.48/20b–21a.

The governor of Shantung has reported a case in which Chang Chih-ch'ien falsely accused his older brother of acting like a rapacious scoundrel toward the people.

This Board finds, according to statute [Boulais 1495], that a junior relative who brings an accusation against a senior relative of the second degree of mourning [an older brother, a paternal uncle or aunt, and the like] is to receive 100 blows of the heavy bamboo, even if his accusation prove correct. Should he falsely accuse the senior relative of an offense for which the punishment is heavier than is the basic punishment given to the junior relative for making the accusation, then this heavier punishment, increased yet again by three additional degrees, shall revert to the junior relative. The Official Commentary on this explains that as in the case of a false accusation made by a non-relative, there is a limit to how far the three-degree increase may raise the punishment.

[We have just seen that the punishment for a junior relative accusing a second-degree senior relative is 100 blows of the heavy bamboo. This is the basic punishment, irrespective of whether the charge is true or false. (For relatives of other degrees it varies from three years penal servitude down to 70 blows of the heavy bamboo.) Suppose, however, that the accusation is a false one and that the offense it imputes to the senior relative calls for a punishment greater than 100 blows, let us say one year penal servitude. Then the junior relative making the accusation will receive this same one-year punishment, plus a further increment of three degrees, making a total punishment of two and one half years penal servitude. However, as deducible from the Official Commentary and the statute cited below, such a three-degree increment may not raise the accuser's punishment beyond the highest level of ordinary life exile, that is, exile at a distance of 3,000 li. Above this level, as indicated by the statute on military exile quoted immediately below, there is no increment of punishment for the accuser; he receives exactly the same punishment as that called for by the offense which he falsely imputes to the senior relative. The procedure here outlined follows, with minor variations, that provided in Boulais 1474 for the handling of ordinary false accusations made between non-relatives.]

Elsewhere, it is also stated that any person who falsely accuses another person of a crime deserving military exile, shall himself undergo military exile of the same degree and distance as that specified for the falsely imputed crime. [This statute is among the few completely omitted by Boulais. It constitutes Staunton 343, and would, if included by Boulais, be his 1515a.]

If we look at the statute on ordinary false accusations between non-relatives [Boulais 1474], we see that even when the punishment given to a false accuser is raised three degrees above the punishment destined for the person he has falsely accused, it still may not exceed 100 blows of the heavy bamboo and life exile at a distance of 3,000 li. If, for example, he falsely accuses another person of a crime meriting life exile, the punishment which he thereby receives in return may not exceed maximum life exile. And should the falsely imputed crime involve a yet higher punishment of military exile, we have seen from the relevant cited statute that the corresponding punishment thereby going to the accuser must remain on the same level and therefore not go beyond military exile. This being true in cases involving non-relatives, it clearly applies as well to junior relatives who falsely accuse senior relatives.

In the present case, Chang Chih-ch'ien reported to the authorities that his older brother had been acting like a rapacious scoundrel toward the people. The punishment for such an offense, if proved correct, is military exile [at the farthest distance of 4,000 li], as provided under the statute [Boulais 1169] on scoundrels who wantonly and repeatedly molest decent people. Investigation, however, has shown the charge to be baseless. Therefore, under the statute cited above [Boulais 1515a, on false accusation of a crime deserving military exile], the punishment to be given to the maker of the charge, Chang Chih-ch'ien, should be military exile of the same degree and distance [as specified for the offense falsely charged by him].

The governor of Shantung, however, has still further increased this punishment by three degrees, thereby raising it to deportation as a slave among the troops in Sinkiang. [This is the harshest of all kinds of military exile. The next higher grade of punishment would be strangulation after the assizes.] This verdict is erroneous and should be rectified in accordance with the foregoing statute.

[This case, involving rather complex calculations of punishment, has been further complicated in the Chinese original by the inclusion of considerable discussion which seems only marginal to the central argument. For the sake of clarity and brevity, this discussion has been trimmed to the bare essentials in this English version.]

Case 200.4, 1816. Leading Case.
Reported in HAHL 21.48/21b.

The governor of Anhui has reported a case in which Sung Ch'ien, because of personal animosity, falsely accused his two elder cousins, both of the third degree of mourning, of having practiced deceit when purchasing civil service degrees, by using dual registration. [A candidate for the civil service was required to take the lowest level government examination in the locality in which he was registered as having been born (Boulais 342). Unless especially provided otherwise, purchase of a civil service degree likewise had to be done in one's place of birth. (Governmental sale of degrees to persons who could pay for them became a growing abuse in the nineteenth century, when the government was hard pressed for money.) Apparently the two cousins were accused of maintaining registration in more than one locality and buying their degrees in a locality other than that in which they had been actually born.]

The two cousins, when subjected to court hearings as a result of this accusation, became so wrought up that they both fell ill, had to be carried home, and there died. Not only this, but Sung Ch'ien, the accuser, had previously once collected a crowd with which he invaded their home in search of trouble. He pretended that he had suffered injuries on that occasion so that he could thus bring false charges against them.

Truly, Sung Ch'ien is one of those scoundrels who wantonly and repeatedly molest decent people. Therefore, under the statute on such scoundrels [Boulais 1169], he is now sentenced to military exile [at the farthest distance of 4,000 li. This statute was used against him rather than the one on false accusations by a junior against a senior relative (Boulais 1495), probably because of the much heavier punishment it permits.]

201. DISOBEDIENCE TO PARENTS OR GRANDPARENTS

[Statutory References: Staunton 338, Boulais 1503–1509]

Case 201.6, 1816. Leading Case.
Reported in HAHL 22.49/2b–3a.

The governor-general of Szechuan has reported a case in which Ch'en Yü-mei, after vainly trying to borrow money from P'eng Tsung-ming, carried his father's coffin to the rear of P'eng's house and there buried it. P'eng thereupon lodged a complaint with the authorities, causing Ch'en's mother such worry over the possibility of becoming legally involved that she killed herself.

Granted that the son was not guilty of any act of moral turpitude or theft, his becoming involved in a court action with P'eng nonetheless was the cause in the last analysis of his mother's death. [The reference here is to Boulais 1506: immediate strangulation for a child or grandchild whose act of moral turpitude or theft causes a parent or grandparent to commit suicide. By "moral turpitude" (*chien*) are meant adultery, rape, sodomy, or other illicit and improper sexual relationships (see Boulais 1580 *et seq.*).]

Ch'en Yü-mei, therefore, is now sentenced to maximum exile [life exile at a distance of 3,000 li] by analogy to the sub-statute [Boulais 1504] on a son whose poverty makes him unable to support his parents, so that they commit suicide.

[As remarked by Boulais in a note, the unspoken assumption is that the poverty is due to the son's own indifference and laziness, rather than to force of circumstances. Here and in the next three cases, we find this same sub-statute used analogically to cover an astonishing variety of circumstances. Even granted the greater latitude permitted when a statute or sub-statute is applied analogically rather than directly (see case 12.2), how is this broad coverage possible? The answer lies in a general circular (*t'ung hsing*), issued in 1762 by the Board of Punishments with the approval of the emperor, which supplies the basis for the decisions in this and the next three cases, and is referred to explicitly in case 201.9. (Not being itself a formal sub-statute, but simply a directive for legal procedure, the circular does not appear among the sub-statutes in this section, though a portion of it is printed in the Chinese edition of the Code as part of the Upper Commentary at the beginning of the section. It also appears in full in case 201.1, untranslated.)]

[The circular was issued in response to criticism that the laws on unfilial conduct resulting in parental suicide were too restricted and arbitrary in their operation. (An example is the above-cited statute, Boulais 1506, which punishes a son whose moral turpitude or theft induce parental suicide but which fails to list other offenses.) In reply to this criticism, the circular provides: (1) If a son, being normally of good conduct, "unexpectedly happens to commit some other offense" besides those explicitly listed in the various relevant sub-statutes, thereby inducing parental suicide, he is to be sentenced to life exile by analogy to the sub-statute, Boulais 1504, on sons whose poverty makes them unable to support their parents. This sub-statute is used in this and the next three cases. (2) If, on the other hand, the parents commit suicide because the son habitually follows any one of a number of named undesirable kinds of conduct (fighting, gambling, and falsifying are among those listed in the circular), he is then to be sentenced to immediate decapitation under another sub-statute (Boulais 1329) on sons whose lack of filial piety pushes their parents into suicide. The issuing of the 1762 circular perhaps reflects a growing desire to facilitate the exaction of legal retribution for any kind of conduct by children deemed to be harmful to the parents and to challenge their authority.]

Case 201.7, 1820. Leading Case.
Reported in HAHL 22.49/3a.

The governor of Kiangsu has reported a case in which Chü Te-li, ordinarily a man of good behavior, beat and injured his sister-in-law, thereby causing his mother so much worry about a possible lawsuit that she committed suicide.

Chü Te-li is now sentenced to maximum exile [life exile at a distance of 3,000 li], by analogy to the sub-statute [Boulais 1504] on a son whose poverty makes him unable to support his parents, so that they commit suicide.

Case 201.8, 1820. Leading Case.
Reported in HAHL 22.49/3a.

The governor of Shansi has reported a case in which Li Wen-ch'ing, wishing to develop a coal enterprise, rented out some of his land to finance the project. His mother became so afraid that the project might fail and leave them destitute that she stopped eating and in her melancholy anxiety committed suicide.

Li Wen-ch'ing is now sentenced to maximum life exile, by analogy to the sub-statute [Boulais 1504] on a son whose poverty makes him unable to support his parents, so that they commit suicide.

Case 201.9, 1831. Memorandum.
Reported in HAHL 22.49/3a–b.

The Department for Kuangtung of the Board of Punishments finds this to be a case in which Huang Hsing-chou went at twilight to the house of his neighbor, Wei Ching-ch'ao, in order to borrow a light from Wei's wife. Wei himself, returning unexpectedly, suspected an affair between Huang and his wife and loudly demanded an explanation. However, when Huang tried to give him one, Wei rushed into Huang's house and started an uproar. There Huang's mother tried to reason with Wei, whereupon Wei accused her of shielding her son and seized her by her collar, pushing her backward. The mother screamed for help, and her son came to the rescue with a knife, with which he wounded Wei in the abdomen. Thereafter, when Wei decided to take the matter to court, Huang went into hiding, while Huang's mother, brooding on the idea of being dragged into a court case, hanged herself. As for Wei himself, he recovered from his wound.

The governor of Kuangtung has sentenced Huang Hsing-chou to 100 blows of the heavy bamboo and three years penal servitude, by analogy to the sub-statute [Boulais 1506] on parents who, having instructed a son to commit an act of moral turpitude or of theft, then become fearful that this may be discovered and so commit suicide.

[This clause is a variant of the earlier and better known clause in the same sub-statute in which these acts are performed against the will of the parents. The remarkable thing is that the son is punished for the parents' suicide even when the immoral acts committed by him and inducing their suicide have been done at their express instruction. In the present case, the governor's suggested penalty for Huang is unchanged from that prescribed by Boulais 1506. Therefore the "analogy" in the application of this sub-statute (rejected, as we shall see, by the Board of Punishments) seems to rest upon other considerations. These are that Huang's mother, in shouting to Huang to save her, was not telling him to do anything immoral, nor was Huang's response in wounding her assailant an act falling under the usual interpretation of "moral turpitude"; yet this act did in fact lead to his mother's suicide. It is important to note here that the causation of parental suicide is what Huang is being tried for, and not his incidental wounding of a neighbor.]

This Department, however, finds that Huang's use of a knife to wound another person, thereby leading his mother to commit suicide out of fear of legal involvement, differs from an act of moral turpitude or of theft, even though the latter may likewise result in parental suicide. Moreover, Huang's wounding of the other man was not an act done at his mother's bidding. [She had only shouted to him to save her but not actually to stab Wei.]

It follows that Huang should be dealt with in the manner detailed in the general circular of 1762, according to which life exile should be given to a son who is guilty of some other offense [besides those explicitly listed in the relevant sub-statutes. For the explanation of this often-cited 1762 general circular, see case 201.6.] The governor's proposed sentence, on the other hand, namely penal servitude, given by analogy to the sub-statute on sons who commit acts of moral turpitude or of theft, is quite inappropriate. Rather, [in accordance with the procedure laid down in the 1762 general circular], Huang Hsing-chou should be sentenced to 100 blows of the heavy bamboo and life exile at a distance of 3,000 li, by analogy to the sub-statute [Boulais 1504] on a son whose poverty makes him unable to support his parents, so that they commit suicide.

This case, though it came before the authorities during the present year and prior to the imperial amnesty proclaimed on the twelfth day of the first month (February 24, 1831), is not on that account to be permitted any reduction of punishment. [At the end of the Code's section on offenses to which amnesties do not apply (Boulais 88–93), there appears an 1862 list (not included in Boulais) of such excluded offenses. Second on the list is the crime of the son whose poverty (no doubt self-induced in the eyes of the authorities) prevents him from supporting his parents. The Board's insistence on giving Huang the highest possible punishment is difficult to understand here.]

203. INCITING LITIGATION
[Statutory References: Staunton 340, Boulais 1512]

Case 203.2, 1817. Leading Case.
Reported in HAHL 22.49/25a.

[This section (discussed also in Chapter VI, section 4) is of major interest from the point of view of legal psychology. From it we see that after more than two millennia of a highly developed legal tradition, the Chinese continued to view law primarily as a governmental instrument applied from above to punish infractions of the social and political order, rather than as a means theoretically, at least, within reach of anyone wishing to assert a claim against someone else or against the government itself. In a society dominated by such an attitude it is not surprising that there was no formally recognized private legal profession. Individuals could occasionally be found in rural China, however, who, with or without a fee, were sometimes ready to prepare a legal petition or accusation for a relative, friend, or client. This section makes it evident that such individuals were regarded by the government as troublemakers and corruptors of the simple country folk. They are commonly referred to as "litigation tricksters" (*sung kun*, "litigation sticks"), and the punishment uniformly meted out to them is three years penal servitude.]

[Case 203.2 strongly suggests, without explicitly stating, that in order to escape punishment as a "litigation trickster," one should be a close relative of, and therefore have a legitimate interest in, the person for whom or about whom one initiates legal action. Case 203.4 indicates that as few as six or seven legal petitions written for as many persons are enough to make one punishable as a professional litigation trickster.]

[Case 203.5 is particularly notable because its offender receives exactly the same punishment as the others, despite the Board's admission that the five litigation documents written by him are all of an ordinary nature, involving no wrongdoing, and the fact that, by statute, his age of more than seventy makes him eligible for the privilege of monetary redemption. In a largely illiterate society, it is evident that few people could apply for legal justice unless an educated person could be found to prepare the necessary written legal documents. This fact is recognized in one clause of the major statute under this section (Boulais 1512), wherein the preparation of such legal documents on behalf of "ignorant" (illiterate) persons is held permissible so long as it involves no attempt to "doctor" or falsify the charges. Disregard of this clause in this case makes it appear that the authorities were more interested in halting the preparation of legal documents by persons not personally involved, than in the truth or falsity of the averments per se.]

[Finally, case 203.7 is an admirably lucid and forceful presentation of the official point of view, given importance by the fact that it is actually not a case at all, but rather an edict issued by the Chia-ch'ing Emperor.]

The governor of Honan has memorialized concerning a case in which Hsia Fang-chüeh, when his fellow clansman belonging to the same generation as his own grandfather, but beyond the five degrees of mourning, was fatally beaten, reported the affair to the district authorities and requested them to apprehend the murderer. Hsia, when he did this, received two ounces of silver from the victim's son and falsely assumed the name of the victim's nephew.

Investigation has shown beyond the shadow of a doubt that the real murderer must be sought for otherwise [than as suggested by Hsia]. Hsia, furthermore, when he failed to derive further profit from the affair, heaped up additional empty charges and incited the son to bring his accusation to Peking.

Hsia Fang-chüeh, by analogy to the sub-statute providing military exile for litigation tricksters, is sentenced to a penalty one degree less, namely maximum [three years] penal servitude.

[This sub-statute, Boulais 1512a, provides military exile at the most distant malarial regions of Yunnan or Kueichow for "habitual litigation tricksters" who conspire with government clerks, trick ignorant country folk, or practice intimidation or fraud.]

Case 203.4, 1813. Leading Case.
Reported in HAHL 22.49/25b.

The governor of Anhui has reported a case in which Ch'en Yü-t'ien, an offender from another province, wrote a legal petition on behalf of Chang Ming-yü, falsely charging that Sun Yung-sui had violated the statute against taking excessive interest. [Boulais 730 states that interest on loans should not exceed 30 per cent per annum, nor should the total interest ever exceed the total amount loaned.]

Investigation has shown that it was Chang who supplied the general outline of the petition and asked Ch'en to write it accordingly. Ch'en had previously composed petitions of this sort for six other people. He should be sentenced under the sub-statute which provides military exile for litigation tricksters, but with this punishment reduced by one degree to maximum [three years] penal servitude. [For details on this sub-statute, Boulais 1512, see preceding case. In that case, in order to permit the reduction of penalty from military exile to penal servitude, the sub-statute is applied, as it properly should be, analogically rather than directly. Here and in the following case, however, this is not done.]

Case 203.5, 1820. Leading Case.
Reported in HAHL 22.49/25b.

The governor of Anhui has reported a case in which Hsü Hsüeh-ch'uan, an offender from another province, drafted five litigation documents for other persons. All of these documents were of an ordinary nature, and there is no evidence that he conspired with government clerks, tricked ignorant country folk, or practiced intimidation or fraud. [This repeats the wording of the sub-statute on litigation tricksters, for which see case 203.2.]

He should therefore receive a one-degree lesser penalty, namely maximum [three years] penal servitude, than the military exile which is prescribed for habitual litigation tricksters. [This again refers to the sub-statute on litigation tricksters, Boulais 1512a.]

Although the offender is past the age of 70, since he is a litigation specialist who brings harm to rural communities, he may not be allowed the privilege of monetary redemption for his offense.

[Boulais 131 states that persons aged 70 or above, if guilty of a crime punishable by life exile or less, may be permitted monetary redemption. The Official Commentary adds that the privilege extends to crimes punishable by military exile, but not to capital crimes nor to secondary involvement in a very few major offenses such as treason and the like.]

Case 203.7, 1820. General Circular.
Reported in HAHL 22.49/25b–26a.

Imperial Edict received August 17, 1820, by the Department for Chihli of the Board of Punishments:

The censor Chu Hung is extremely correct in what he says in his memorial about the need to check abuses of unbridled litigation and so extinguish vicious habits. The multiplication of lawsuits among the people brings much harm to rural communities, and the machinations of the litigation tricksters are what produce all the inconsequential verbiage going helter skelter into these accusations. These rascally fellows entrap people for the sake of profit. They fabricate empty words and heap up false charges. At their bidding plaintiffs are induced to bring up stupid nonsense in their accusations whose empty falsity, when exposed at the trial, brings blame upon the plaintiffs themselves while the litigation tricksters stand to one side.

The victims of these false accusations, once they have been dragged in, remain entrapped and their livelihood is gone. Even should they have the luck to be completely exonerated as a result of the trial, their families will by then have become ruined. No one knows how many lives have thus been damaged or brought to an end at the same time that the tricksters look on from the side and chirp their satisfaction. All these devilish doings certainly deserve our bitter detestation.

In all yamens [government offices] in Chihli where cases are heard, let it now be ordered that whenever magistrates encounter a false trumped-up accusation, they must investigate to find out who has instigated the accusation, who has guided it, who has planned it, who has publicized it. As soon as all this has been determined, the persons responsible must be immediately arrested, severely punished, and not allowed to escape. In addition, the local officials, whenever accepting any legal petition, should always find out first whether the petitioner himself actually composed and wrote it. Either they may compare the document with the petitioner's own handwriting, or they may take a section of it and ask him to expound its meaning. If the petitioner is unable to expound the section, they must press him for the name of the litigation specialist who prepared the petition and by no means allow the petitioner to claim that it was written for him by some itinerant fortune-teller or medicine peddler.

As soon as the litigation specialist has been arrested and brought to account, all the circumstances of how he planned and perpetrated the false accusation must be strictly investigated. Heavy punishment should always go to him, whereas the person tricked by him into presenting the accusation may be shown leniency. Let the investigation thus be probing and painstaking, and then these rascally fellows will go into hiding, the multitude of lawsuits will diminish daily, and decent respectable people will gain security.

206. ACCEPTANCE OF BRIBES BY OFFICIALS AND THEIR SUBORDINATES
[Statutory References: Staunton 344, Boulais 1516–1527]

Case 206.8, 1822. Leading Case.
Reported in HAHL 22.50/3b–4a.

The governor of Fukien, apropos the case involving mutual accusations between District Magistrate Ch'in Yu-su and Major

Hsü Shuang-kuan, has memorialized concerning Liu Wen-huan, a jail warden of the prefecture [superior to Ch'in's district or *hsien;* as such, Liu was a member of the civil service, holding a 9*b* rank]. Liu had been commissioned to bring a proclamation to the district and while there to conduct a secret investigation. On ascertaining after arrival that there was indeed truth in the talk about Magistrate Ch'in having padded his budget, Liu should have posted his proclamation and placed several persons under detention. Instead of this, however, he secretly informed Ch'in of the situation and suggested in a private letter that Ch'in [who had been absent] should return to the district for mutual consultation. In this letter, which talked about mediation, the language used was vague and ambiguous. Liu's purpose in writing it was to induce the magistrate to give money as the price for hushing up the scandal.

It would obviously not be proper to sentence Liu under the sub-statute [Boulais 1173a] which merely provides bambooing for an unsuccessful attempt at extortion in which no precisely stipulated sum of money is involved. [More precisely, the punishment is 100 blows of the heavy bamboo and one month wearing of the cangue.]

Accordingly, it would be better to sentence Liu Wen-huan by analogy to the sub-statute [actually another clause of the one just cited] providing [two months of] the cangue, 100 blows of the heavy bamboo, and three years penal servitude, for an unsuccessful attempt at extortion which *does* involve a precisely stipulated sum of money and is connected with a proposed evasion of the law. In view of the offender's official status, however, he may be exempted from the cangue.

[Because Liu's attempt at extortion was evidently expressed in the form of vague hints only, without mention of any precise sum of money, it would seem to fall more aptly under the first clause of the cited sub-statute than the second. That the Board nevertheless insists on placing it analogically under the second seems to be calculated to insure a heavier punishment for Liu than he would otherwise receive. The resulting judgment, while no doubt pragmatically desirable, is legally questionable.]

Case 206.19, 1820. Leading Case.
Reported in HAHL 22.50/7b.

The governor of Chekiang has submitted a memorial concerning a case in which a leg-band [a kind of gaiter] lost by Liu Chang-ming on the road was picked up by Ch'en Kuang-yü. The owner, on seeing this act, told Ch'en to return the band and at the same time accused him of stealing it. Ch'en's denial of the charge led to a quarrel in the course of which a third person, Jen Shih-tsai, asserted that Liu had made his accusation wrongly and that he should offer Ch'en a drink as forfeit.

Liu did not take kindly to this, and only repeated his trumped up charges, with which he even went to the local yamen [the government's administrative office] to launch an accusation. As a result, Ch'en Liang, a low-rank yamen employee, took Ch'en Kuang-yü into custody for bringing to the yamen for questioning. On the way, this yamen employee demanded money from Ch'en Yü-kuang, who, though promising to give it, had no means of doing so on the spot and therefore seized an opportunity to run away. With the yamen functionary in pursuit, Ch'en Yü-kuang fled onto a ferryboat from which, in his excitement, he jumped into the river and drowned.

Ch'en Liang, the yamen employee, is now sentenced to strangulation after the assizes under the sub-statute [Boulais 1522] on rapacious government underlings [see case 210.2] whose extortionate monetary demands upon others bring about loss of life. As for Liu Chang-ming, he should be sentenced according to the sub-statute [Boulais 1484] prescribing military exile [at a distant frontier] for one who falsely accuses a respectable person of theft and thereby brings about the person's arrest for questioning. This penalty, however, is to be reduced for Liu by one degree to 100 blows of the heavy bamboo and three years penal servitude.

[Here, as so often, the penalty is reduced even though the relevant sub-statute is not applied analogically. The reduction, though technically of one degree only (see case 87.2), is in actual fact very considerable, especially for a man like Liu, who appears to have been a born troublemaker. Psychologically, we may suspect that Liu's implacable hounding was more responsible for the victim's death than was the yamen employee's demand for money which, after all, was probably not particularly unusual. We see this case moving with the inexorability of fate from the trivial to the tragic. The case again illustrates (see especially case 51.1) how even a trifling object may, in an economically underdeveloped society, lead to violence and death.]

208. USE OF BRIBES TO GET SOMETHING DONE
[Statutory References: Staunton 348, Boulais 1532–1534]

Case 208.4, 1814. Leading Case.
Reported in HAHL 22.50/22a–b.

The governor of Yunnan has memorialized concerning a case in which Chang Hsiao-hsü, after his younger brother beat somebody to death, obeyed his mother's command to take the younger brother's crime upon his own head and sign a confession.

The sub-statute on a person within the culprit's family who does such an act provides that he is to receive a penalty one degree less than that due the actual criminal, which means for him in the present case a sentence of life exile. [The penalty for killing in an affray is strangulation after the assizes (Boulais 1268), which, reduced by one degree, comes to life exile at a distance of 3,000 li. The sub-statute here cited, Boulais 1532a, provides varying penalties for relatives or non-relatives who, with or without bribe, take upon themselves another person's crime and sign or do not sign a confession, thus enabling or not enabling the actual criminal to escape punishment, and so on.]

When, however, Chang thus took his younger brother's crime upon himself, he was acting under the pressure of his mother's orders. Hence his deed differs from that of an ordinary man who is bribed to assume another person's guilt. Accordingly, his sentence should be further reduced by one degree to 100 blows of the heavy bamboo and three years penal servitude.

[Nothing is said about the mother's role in this affair, but presumably she receives no punishment. Nor is it clear from the wording whether or not the younger brother is a fugitive from justice and is or is not successful in escaping punishment. Finally, the translator is unaware of any article specifically prescribing a lower penalty for a son if he commits a crime at his parent's bidding.]

Case 208.5, 1829. Memorandum.
Reported in HAHL 22.50/22b.

The Department for Szechuan of the Board of Punishments finds that Lo Shao-ch'eng beat and injured Lo Hsi-hua, who subsequently died through infection of the injuries. Accordingly, the penalty for Lo Shao-ch'eng should be life exile. [Boulais 1361 provides that if a person dies after five days from infection of wounds received in an affray which are neither serious nor situated in a vital part of the body, or if he thus dies after ten days either from wounds which are not serious though situated in a vital spot, or from wounds which are serious but not situated in a vital spot, the punishment for the inflictor of the wounds will in every case be life exile at a distance of 3,000 li.]

However, Lo also offered somebody a bribe to take the crime on his own head. Accordingly, Lo's penalty should be increased by one degree from life exile to military exile. [This refers to one of the several clauses in Boulais 1532a, the sub-statute already cited in the preceding case (on assumption by one person of another person's guilt). This clause states that a criminal bribing another person to assume his (the criminal's) guilt shall receive a punishment one degree heavier than the regular punishment for his crime.]

Inasmuch, however, as Lo has now already died in prison, there is no need to discuss his case further. [Here, as earlier (cases 157.4 and 164.1), the Board's insistence upon determining a precise penalty for the offender, even though he has already died, is noteworthy.]

This Department finds, according to sub-statute [Boulais 1341a], that if a son has been killed and the parents are bribed [by the killer] to hush the matter up, their punishment, irrespective of the amount of the bribe, shall be 100 blows of the heavy bamboo. [This sub-statute contradicts and supersedes a previous statute (Boulais 1340), stating that the parents' punishment for this offense depends upon the size of the bribe accepted by them.]

Again, we find that if a knavish fellow is bribed by a criminal to go to the authorities in place of the criminal and assume the latter's guilt, then should investigation show the fellow to be unrelated to the criminal, and should the criminal furthermore be eventually captured, the punishment for the fellow assuming the guilt shall be one degree less than that for the criminal's own offense. [This is still another clause in the same sub-statute cited above, Boulais 1532a.]

The present case concerns Mrs. Lo née P'eng and her son, Lo Hsi-hua, who, besides committing numerous robberies, had also once pushed her to the ground and hurt her. The clan head, Lo Shao-ch'eng, accordingly gave the son a beating from which he died. Then, fearing to report his deed to the authorities, he gave Mrs. Lo silver to induce her to take the crime upon her own head. [In contrast to life exile which, as we have seen, was the clan leader's basic sentence for this beating, Mrs. Lo's penalty for beating to death a "disobedient" son would either be 100 blows of the heavy bamboo if the beating were done in an "unreasonable" manner (Boulais 1420) or no penalty at all if it were done "reasonably," even though eventually resulting in death (Boulais 1421).]

The sub-statute on assuming another person's guilt specifies no penalty for a parent who, when his son is killed, accepts a bribe from the killer to assume the killer's guilt. However, the fact that the son of the present case had pushed his mother to the ground is in itself already enough to make him deserving of death. If, then, she really ordered someone else to beat the son for her so that he died, it is provided by statute [Boulais 1421] that she would receive no punishment.

Mrs. Lo's acceptance of a bribe for assuming guilt in the death of her son has circumstantial similarities to the offense covered in the sub-statute cited above on parents who accepted a bribe for remaining silent when their son is killed. From this it follows that Mrs. Lo should be sentenced according to this sub-statute.

The governor-general of Szechuan, on the other hand, has sentenced Mrs. Lo to penal servitude under the sub-statute on knavish fellows who accept bribes from criminals for going to the authorities in place of the criminals and assuming guilt. [This clause of Boulais 1532a provides, as we have seen, a one-degree lesser punishment for the acceptor of the bribe than for the actual criminal. Three years penal servitude is one degree less than Lo Shaoch'eng's basic penalty of life exile for the death of Mrs. Lo's son.] This sentence, however, fails to differentiate Mrs. Lo's offense from that committed by an ordinary person [in which no relationship is involved]. Therefore it requires correction.

Mrs. Lo should be sentenced under the above-cited sub-statute which states that if a son has been killed, and the parents are bribed to hush the matter up, their punishment, irrespective of the amount of the bribe, shall be 100 blows of the heavy bamboo. She should, in addition, be permitted to redeem this penalty by monetary payment. [On this privilege for women, see Boulais 40. The redemption fee for 100 blows of the heavy bamboo is the nominal sum of 0.75 ounces of silver. See table in Boulais, p. 11.]

210. EXTORTION PRACTICED BY MEMBERS OF AN OFFICIAL'S HOUSEHOLD
[Statutory References: Staunton 350, Boulais 1545]

Case 210.2, 1818. Leading Case.
Reported in HAHL 22.50/25b.

The governor of Shansi has reported the case of Chang Lin, a man from another province who, while gatekeeper for the district magistrate of Lin-fen hsien, maintained external criminal connections. Using his position, he tried to get a money changer to accept for exchange more than 300 ounces of substandard silver. Upon being rebuffed, he took steps to get the money changer locked up.

Because this act differs in no way from extortion as practiced by rapacious government underlings, it would be improper to permit Chang Lin leniency simply because he failed to get the money. He should, therefore, be sentenced in accordance with the sub-statute [Boulais 1541a] which stipulates that extortion

practiced by the personal servants of an official is to be punished
in the same way as extortion practiced by rapacious government
underlings. The latter offense, when it is in the amount of ten or
more ounces of silver, is punishable by military exile [at a nearby
frontier], which punishment, in the case of Chang Lin, is to be
reduced by one degree to 100 blows of the heavy bamboo and
three years penal servitude.

[Here the Board of Punishments, after denying that Chang
should enjoy leniency, nevertheless reduces his statutory punishment by one degree (on such reduction, see Chapter III, section
9). Presumably, it acts thus because the offender failed in his attempted extortion. Properly speaking, it should have applied the
relevant sub-statute analogically rather than directly.]

[What are here referred to as personal servants (ch'ang sui) are
the personally employed and personally paid servitors of an official (see case 41.7), whereas rapacious underlings (tu yi) are
minor governmental functionaries (messengers, guards, clerks)
who work for him in his official capacity and are salaried by the
state. For the several penalties (varying with the sums extorted)
specified for extortion by rapacious government underlings, see
Boulais 1522. In translating 1522, however, Boulais' reliance upon
an abbreviated version of the Chinese text has led him into a serious error. The result is that he caps the stated highest penalty of
military exile for extortion of ten or more ounces of silver by a
still higher penalty of strangulation after the assizes, allegedly for
extorting 120 ounces. In actual fact, this higher penalty has nothing to do with the earlier penalties, and instead should go at the
end of the following paragraph, in which penalties are listed (of
which this is the highest) for extortions that push the victim into
selling his offspring into slavery.]

*Case 210.3, 1814. Leading Case from the Department for
Chihli of the Board of Punishments.*
Reported in HAHL 22.50/25b–26a.

The Salt Gabelle Administration at Ch'ang-lu [an old name for
Tientsin] has submitted a memorial concerning the following
case.

Kuo Ning had been a personal servant (ch'ang sui) of the magistrate of Te-chou. When Lü Wen-ch'eng [probably a wealthy salt merchant, though this is not stated] was put under detention, Kuo approached Hu Pa, a yamen clerk, and asked him to try to straighten matters out. For this a bribe was demanded of 3,000 ounces of silver, but before Lü could pay it, he died under detention.

Lü's own case, despite his criminal readiness to bribe clerks and servants with huge sums of money, is closed by his death. Kuo Ning and Hu Pa, however, should both, under the sub-statute on extortion by rapacious government underlings, be sentenced to military exile at a nearby frontier, this being the penalty provided by this sub-statute [Boulais 1522] for the extortion of ten or more ounces of silver. [For the way in which Boulais has mistranslated this sub-statute, see preceding case.]

Another person involved in the case is the servitor Meng Ch'eng, who put Lü in fetters without any authority, in order to press him for money. Under the sub-statute on custodians who fetter persons without authority and thereby bring them to death or injury [Boulais 1675a], Meng Ch'eng should be sentenced to two months wearing of the cangue and military exile in a malarial region. [Unlike 1675, which concerns the maltreatment of prisoners while in prison, this sub-statute concerns their maltreatment while being transported from one place to another. It applies, furthermore, only to the maltreatment of prisoners guilty of crimes entailing penal servitude or life exile, but not capital crimes. Unfortunately, our text gives us no further information about Lü Wen-ch'eng himself and the circumstances of his case.]

214. MEMORIALS TO THE THRONE WHICH ARE DECEPTIVE AND DIVERGE FROM THE TRUTH
[Statutory References: Staunton 357, Boulais 1558]

Case 214.1, 1813. Metropolitan Leading Case from the Department for Mukden of the Board of Punishments.
Reported in HAHL 23.51/2b–3a.

The general commandant of the gendarmerie of Peking has reported in a memorial that Yüan Wen-kuei filed a petition suggesting that all evil rascals, knaves, thieves, and robbers should be permanently imprisoned; that the city walls should be built higher and the buildings immediately adjoining them on the outside should be razed; that all persons who enter and leave the city should be given iron talleys as permits; and that all merchants should be given licenses of authority. [One wonders what were the immediate circumstances at this time in Peking which inspired these suggestions.]

Under the statute on submitting memorials to the throne which are deceptive and diverge from the truth [Boulais 1558], Yüan Wen-kuei is now sentenced to 100 blows of the heavy bamboo and three years penal servitude.

[Of the three cases translated in this section, only this one is an application of the pertinent statute, Boulais 1558, while the other two are judged by quite a different statute, Boulais 826, providing a lighter punishment. The reasons for the differing treatments are not spelled out.]

Case 214.3, 1816. Metropolitan Leading Case from the Department for Hunan and Hupei of the Board of Punishments.
Reported in HAHL 23.51/3a.

The Censorate [in Peking] has memorialized concerning Wang Hsi, a dismissed official who was recently liberated after having undergone deportation. Since his return, Wang has repeatedly been submitting various proposals in the hope of regaining official employment.

It would not be suitable merely to sentence Wang to the 100 blows of the heavy bamboo provided by statute [Boulais 826] for crafty persons who seek advancement by inserting artful words and an insinuating manner into their memorials. The punishment of the statute, therefore, should in this case be increased by one degree, making for Wang Hsi a sentence of 60 blows of the heavy bamboo and one year penal servitude.

Case 214.4, 1815. Metropolitan Leading Case from the Department for Chekiang of the Board of Punishments.
Reported in HAHL 23.51/3a.

The general commandant of the gendarmerie of Peking has made a report concerning Hsi Wan-chen. Hsi first submitted a petition suggesting reforms in the administration of the Salt Gabelle. This petition resulted in the Office of the Gendarmerie memorializing to have him deported to his native place. Then he drafted other reform proposals concerning the administration of the government's granaries and treasuries, and with these he even personally approached the emperor in a roadside encounter at Ch'ang-hsin-tien [a small town in the southwest suburbs of Peking]. Following investigation, the Office of the Gendarmerie had him again deported to his native place. Now, however, he is once more back in Peking and has submitted further proposals concerning the expanded organization of the populace into *p'ai* and *chia* security units. [To facilitate police supervision, the Ch'ing government organized the populace into units known as *p'ai* (10 households each), *chia* (100 households each), and *pao* (1,000 households each).] The Office of the Gendarmerie has in turn transmitted these proposals to the Board of Punishments.

This Board now finds that Hsi Wan-chen should be sentenced to 100 blows of the heavy bamboo under the statute [Boulais 826] on crafty persons who seek advancement by inserting artful words and an ingratiating manner into their memorials. He is also to be deported once more to his native place and there restrained from returning to the capital.

222. SEXUAL VIOLATIONS
[Statutory References: Staunton 366, Boulais 1580–1594]

Case 222.16, 1812. Memorandum.
Reported in HAHL 23.52/5b–6a.

The governor-general of Chihli has reported a case in which Fan Yü-ch'üan tried unsuccessfully to rape a girl of fourteen, Li Erh-chieh. In view of the girl's youth and immaturity, Fan feared the rape would be difficult to carry out. He therefore started by thrusting his finger into her vagina, causing flow of blood.

The girl and her father both maintain that the rape was unachieved, and a midwife who has examined the girl likewise attests her still to be a virgin. The governor-general has accordingly sentenced Fan Yü-ch'üan to exile [at a distance of 3,000 li] under the statute [Boulais 1582] on attempted but unsuccessful rape. This sentence being in accord with the facts, it is appropriate to request a confirmatory reply. [Loss of virginity would, of course, seriously undermine the girl's chances for marriage. Had the rape been achieved, it would, under the same statute, have been punishable by strangulation after the assizes.]

Case 222.31, 1819. Leading Case.
Reported in HAHL 23.52/8b.

The governor-general of Chihli has memorialized concerning a case in which Chang Wen-t'ung, perceiving the clear white countenance of Chao T'ao-ch'i, a boy of twelve, decided with Shih Chin-ts'ai to commit successive sodomies upon the boy. The act was achieved.

By analogy to the sub-statute on successive consummated rapes by more than one man of a respectable woman [Boulais 1587a], Chang Wen-t'ung, as ringleader, is now sentenced to immediate decapitation, and Shih Chin-ts'ai, as accomplice, to strangulation after the assizes.

[Note the heavier penalty here for two or more men who successively commit rape (or sodomy), as compared with that for ordinary rape (see last case). It is curious that the Board of Punishments feels obliged to make analogical use of a sub-statute on rape in order to settle a case of sodomy, rather than going directly to Boulais 1588, wherein precisely the same penalties are specified for "evil individuals who, assembled in a group, abduct and forcibly commit sodomy upon the son or younger brother of a respectable person." The only apparent objection to applying the latter sub-statute to the present case—and it seems a weak one— is that the offenders in this case were only two in number, and it is unstated that they actually abducted their victim.]

223. TOLERATION BY A SPOUSE OF A WIFE'S OR CONCUBINE'S INFIDELITY

[Statutory References: Staunton 367, Boulais 1595–1598]

Case 223.2, 1818. Leading Case.
Reported in HAHL 23.52/18a.

The governor of Honan has reported a case in which Wang Hei-kou sold his wife to Li Ts'un-ching to become the latter's wife. Investigation shows that Wang's act was prompted by poverty and illness, which gave him no alternative. Thus it differs from the selling of a wife done without due cause. His wife, moreover, has no natal family to which to go, so that were her marriage dissolved as provided by statute, this would be detrimental to feminine morality. [See Boulais 1597, which states that if a husband sells his wife to another man, each of the three parties is to receive 100 blows of the heavy bamboo, the wife's marriage to her first husband is to be dissolved, and she is to be returned to her natal family.]

After careful consideration of the circumstances, this Board finds that the wife should be permitted to remain with the second husband Li Ts'un-ching, and that Wang Hei-kou should not be required to surrender the gift-money paid to him.

[Here the Board refuses to apply the provisions of the relevant statute (Boulais 1597) on the legal ground that the sale of a wife, if compelled by material need, is not the same as such sale done "without due cause" (*wu ku*). (It should be noted that this represents the Board's own reasoning; the statute itself makes no express reference to sales "with or without due cause." That Wang did indeed come from a lowly family and was therefore poor, is strongly suggested by his personal name, Hei-kou, which literally means "black dog," and is scarcely the kind of name that a person of substance would have.) No doubt the Board's judgment was prompted in part by humanitarian considerations. Perhaps even more important in its eyes, however, was the fact that dissolution of the wife's marriage would leave her no family to which to go. (Cf. Boulais 633 which, after setting out the causes justifying a husband in divorcing his wife, then provides that even though the husband has grounds for divorce, he may not send her off if she has no living parents or other close relatives to receive her back again.) From a Confucian point of view, the existence in society of women who live alone without a family is highly undesirable; to quote the Board, it is "detrimental to feminine morality" (*shih chieh*). The Board's leniency is further demonstrated by its readiness to let Wang keep the gift-money which had been paid him. This directly contradicts the statute, which states (in a clause omitted in the Boulais version) that such money is to be confiscated by the state.]

Case 223.3, 1817. Metropolitan Leading Case from the Department for Fukien of the Board of Punishments.
Reported in HAHL 23.52/18a.

The general commandant of the gendarmerie of Peking has reported and transferred to this Department a case in which Ch'ü Ta seized and had sexual relations with the wife of Ch'en Wu. In this case, Ch'ü Ta has accordingly been sentenced to life exile for forcible seizure of a woman. [The difficulty here is that the punishment for such an offense, according to the relevant statute, Boulais 606, is strangulation after the assizes. A sub-statute, Boulais 608, adds that if the seized woman has been recovered before being violated, the penalty is to be reduced by one degree (that is, it then becomes life exile). This variant, however, does not seem to fit the present case.]

Remaining for consideration is the fact that the husband, Ch'en Wu, tolerated the relationship of his wife with Ch'ü Ta, which, according to the relevant sub-statute [Boulais 1595], properly means that her marriage with Ch'en ought to be dissolved. It also appears, however, that Ch'en's toleration of the affair sprang from fear of Ch'ü Ta's strength and fierceness and was thus dictated by coercion. Moreover, according to what Ch'en Wu himself says, were his children to remain solely in his care after dissolution of the marriage, his straitened circumstances would make it impossible for him to care for them alone, so that the consequences would be disastrous. [The fact that the children in such a situation are normally to remain with the father is not explicitly stated in Boulais 1595 simply because, in a Confucian society, it is taken for granted that a primary reason for having children is so that they may perpetuate the paternal family line.]

Consideration of the basic circumstances leads us to the decision that both Mrs. Ch'en and the children should return to her husband and resume living with him. [Here again, as in the preceding case, we find the Board of Punishments not applying the statute according to its strict letter in order to handle a difficult social situation.]

*Case 223.4, 1814. Metropolitan Leading Case from the Depart-
ment for Szechuan of the Board of Punishments.*
Reported in HAHL 23.52/18a.

The Censorate of the North City of Peking has transferred to
this Department a case involving Ch'iu Kuei, who was originally
the wife of Wang Pao. Wang, because of poverty, arranged with
his wife's father to fabricate a report that he, Wang, had died, so
that he might in this way sell his wife as a concubine to P'an Shou-
lin. Later, however, when P'an learned the facts, P'an's own wife
reviled and beat Ch'iu Kuei, who ran away.

Under the statute [Boulais 1597] concerning the buying or selling of a woman, Wang Pao, P'an Shou-lin, and Ch'iu Kuei are
each to receive 100 blows of the heavy bamboo.

[It will be remembered from case 223.2 that this statute further
provides that the woman is to be divorced from her original husband and returned to her natal family. Two further points deserve notice in the present case: (1) The Board fails to allot any
penalty to the wife's father (whose name is not even mentioned),
despite his connivance in the matter. (2) The Board's insistence
upon the letter of the law contrasts strongly with its lenience in
the two preceding cases. In case 223.2, in particular, it will be remembered that poverty was, as in the present case, the compelling reason for selling the wife. Perhaps the Board's changed attitude here is prompted by Wang's deceit in having fabricated a report of his death.]

*Case 223.5, 1815. Metropolitan Leading Case from the Depart-
ment for Kiangsu of the Board of Punishments.*
Reported in HAHL 23.52/18a.

The Censorate of the North City of Peking has transferred to
this Department a case in which Yang Ching-jung sold his wife
through a go-between to Li T'ing-chih, who took her as his wife
in ignorance of the fact that she already had a husband.

In accordance with the statute on selling women [Boulais
1597], the first husband, Yang, and his wife are both to receive

100 blows of the heavy bamboo. His wife, however, is to continue living with her new husband, Li.

[This case raises three problems: (1) Despite the unqualified statement in Boulais 1597 that the buyer is to receive 100 blows of the heavy bamboo, the Board here provides no punishment at all for the buyer, Li. This is probably because he took her in ignorance of the fact that Mrs. Yang was already married, though no such contingency is expressly recognized as an excuse in the statute. In case 223.4, was not the buyer innocent and yet punished? Is this because he kept the woman after discovering she was not widowed? (2) The Board even permits Li to keep the woman, and this despite the provision in Boulais 1597 that such a woman, having been divorced from her original husband, is to return to her own natal family. (3) Likewise, the Board provides no punishment for the go-between in the sale, despite the statement in Boulais 1597 that such a go-between is to receive a punishment one degree less than that of the principals (90 blows of the heavy bamboo).]

224. INCEST
[Statutory References: Staunton 368, Boulais 1599–1606]

Case 224.10, 1821. Leading Case.
Reported in HAHL 23.52/22b.

The governor of Shantung has reported a case in which Chang Yung-pao had sexual relations with the daughter of his fifth-degree younger cousin, Chang Yung-ch'ao. When the affair was discovered, the girl committed suicide.

Chang Yung-pao is now sentenced to 100 blows of the heavy bamboo and three years penal servitude, this being the penalty provided by sub-statute [Boulais 1334] for a man whose fornication with a consenting woman, on being discovered, leads to her committing suicide out of shame. Furthermore, he is to wear the cangue for 40 days, as specified in the sub-statute [Boulais 1603] which adds this punishment to the basic penalty for fornication, when such occurs between members of the same clan whose relationship to each other lies beyond the five degrees of mourning.

[Because Chang's relationship to his distant younger cousin was the fifth degree, his relationship to the latter's daughter lay entirely outside of the five degrees of mourning. The basic penalty for sexual relations between such distant clan members (in the absence of other complicating factors, such as suicide by the woman) is stated by Boulais 1599 (a statute) to be 100 blows of the heavy bamboo. Apparently this punishment was later felt to be inadequate. Hence, under Boulais 1603 (a sub-statute), it was supplemented, as we have just seen, by 40 days of the cangue. Such relatively heavy punishment indicates how strong was the principle of clan exogamy in China.]

Case 224.22, 1817. Leading Case.
Reported in HAHL 23.52/26a.

The governor of Shansi has memorialized concerning a case in which Mrs. Li née Chang, after having been widowed for many years, happened to hear of someone getting married in her neighborhood, which so aroused licentious thoughts in her that she enticed Li Ming-tse, a son of her deceased husband through a former marriage, to have sex relations with her.

Li had been reared by Mrs. Li during his childhood, and in allowing himself nonetheless to be enticed by her, he showed complete disregard for her status as a stepmother. Both persons are thus equally guilty of a licentious behavior destructive of the primary human relationships. The Code, however, [rather surprisingly] contains no article dealing with sexual relations between a son and his stepmother. Therefore Mrs. Li and Li Tseming, subject to final approval from the throne, are both now sentenced to immediate decapitation by analogy to the statute [Boulais 1601] providing this penalty for fornication between a man and the wife of his paternal uncle.

228. SEXUAL VIOLATIONS COMMITTED DURING MOURNING OR BY BUDDHIST OR TAOIST MONKS

[Statutory References: Staunton 372, Boulais 1624–1627]

Case 228.2, 1820. Leading Case.
Reported in HAHL 24.53/19a–b.

The governor of Kiangsu, with reference to the case in which Chang Ts'ung-wei killed three persons within the same family, has memorialized concerning the sexual relationship existing at that time between Li Chiu-hsien, a Taoist monk, and Chang's wife, Mrs. Chang née Fu.

According to statute [Boulais 1581], adultery with a married woman is punishable by 90 blows of the heavy bamboo. Furthermore, according to sub-statute [Boulais 1626], a Buddhist or Taoist monk who commits adultery with a married woman receives a penalty two degrees higher than the foregoing 90 blows, that is to say, he receives 60 blows of the heavy bamboo and one year penal servitude. Besides this, he must also first wear the cangue for two months at the entrance to his monastery.

Inasmuch as Li Chiu-hsien is over the age of 70, he is permitted, according to sub-statute [Boulais 131], to redeem this punishment by a monetary payment. However, he must also return to lay status. [The table in Boulais, p. 11, indicates the nominal sum of 0.15 ounces of silver as the redemption fee for one year penal servitude, but fails to give the amount for two months wearing of the cangue.]

As for Mrs. Chang, she is sentenced to [100 blows of] the heavy bamboo and [one month] wearing of the cangue, this being the penalty under the sub-statute [Boulais 1590] on ordinary adultery involving either soldiers or civilians.

Case 228.3, 1820. Leading Case.
Reported in HAHL 24.53/19b.

The prefect of Mukden has reported a case in which Sun Fu-chin, a Taoist monk, intimidated Mrs. Ch'ü née Chang into having sex relations with him and also, to facilitate matters, beat and intimidated Mrs. Ch'ü's husband until he gave his assent.

Truly, such debauchery conforms with the sub-statute [Boulais 1169] on vicious scoundrels who repeatedly and wantonly commit molestations against decent people. Therefore, under this sub-statute, Sun Fu-chin is now sentenced to military exile [at the farthest distance of 4,000 li]. However, as he is a Taoist monk, he should also fulfill the punishment provided by law for his basic offense. This requirement means that [prior to exile] he is to wear the cangue for two months. [We have seen in the preceding case that Boulais 1626 requires a Buddhist or Taoist monk guilty of sex relations with a married woman to precede his year of penal servitude by wearing the cangue for two months at the entrance to his monastery. Cf. also case 89.2, where what is essentially the same offense, but committed within the actual precincts of a temple, is for that reason punished considerably more severely.]

230. OFFICIALS WHO CONSORT WITH PROSTITUTES
[Statutory References: Staunton 374, Boulais 1619]

Case 230.1, 1829. From the Peking Gazette.
Reported in HAHL 24.53/20a–b.

The Board of Punishments has presented a memorial concerning Ts'ao Liu-tien who, when an official awaiting appointment as a district magistrate, consorted with an entertainer and, upon the entertainer's death from over-drinking, secretly moved the corpse outside the Peking city walls and tried to conceal the matter.

Imperial Rescript of January 11, 1829: Ts'ao Liu-tien's conduct in consorting and drinking with an entertainer was reprehensible, but it became really abandoned when, upon the entertainer's death from over-drinking, he offered bribes to officials to hush the matter up. Let Ts'ao Liu-tien be stripped of official rank and deported to a military post, where, through efficacious labor, he may atone his crime.

As for Ts'ao K'un, he, by consorting with entertainers while awaiting appointment as an intendant, has shown himself lacking in moral restraint and has disgraced his position as an official. Let him be stripped of official rank as a public warning. Concerning other details of the case, let them be disposed of in accordance with what has been deliberated by the Board of Punishments.

[This case presents several ambiguities and irregularities, caused by the fact that it comes to us as a summary in the *Peking Gazette* rather than as a more detailed report by the Board of Punishments itself: (1) No statute or sub-statute is cited for the sentences given. Obviously, there is no application here of Boulais 1619, the basic statute for this section, since that statute merely provides 60 blows of the heavy bamboo for officials who consort with prostitutes. (2) Ts'ao K'un's role in the affair is unclear, and we do not know whether he was a companion of Ts'ao Liu-tien in the search for pleasure. Whether the two men were related is also not known. (3) Nor can we be certain of the sex of the "entertainer," an ambiguous term chosen deliberately to translate the Chinese terms *yu* or *yu-ling*. The dictionary meaning of both these terms is "actor," but their connotations also include clowns, comedians, and other members of the entertainment world, conceivably female as well as male. Women were not allowed to act in the Chinese theater at this period, but the fact that the statute under which this case is classified refers to prostitutes certainly suggests that the "entertainer" in this case was a woman.]

235. ACCIDENTAL FIRE
[Statutory References: Staunton 382, Boulais 1645–1648]

Case 235.1, 1796. Memorandum.
Reported in HAHL 24.53/27b–28a.

The governor of Fukien has memorialized concerning a case in which the prison at Hai-ch'eng hsien caught fire, resulting in the death of nine persons. He has recommended penal servitude for the prison's warden, inspector, and guards.

This Board finds that Mrs. Lin née Wu, an inmate of the prison, had an attack of stomach ache and therefore asked her maid, who was with her, to boil some medicine in the cell. The latter dumped the charcoal embers from the stove [probably a small portable brazier] upon the ground, where, blown by the wind, they started a fire which burned out two sections of the prison. Among those killed were three prisoners involved in prosecutions, including Mrs. Lin herself, three robbers, and Mrs. Lin's maid, the latter's small daughter, and the infant son born by Mrs. Lin herself [possibly within the prison].

The Provincial Court of Fukien has sentenced the prison's warden, as well as the inspector and guards who were on duty that night, all to penal servitude.

We find that the very fact that a prison is a place of confinement makes it particularly easy to supervise. How then could any-one have been left free to scatter burning embers from a stove at random, thus causing a fire that killed nine persons? Warden Ho Yen-ping, Inspector Wang Chang, and Guards Ch'en Yüan and Hsü Wu-lin have all been derelict in their duty, and their fault is inexcusable. There can be no exemption for any of them from the penal servitude to which they have been sentenced.

[This case is exceptional in that no statute is cited when passing sentence. Since the warden *et al.* were guilty of negligence rather than of actually setting the fire themselves, they were probably sentenced by analogy to Boulais 1646, specifying 80 blows of the heavy bamboo and two years penal servitude for persons acci-dentally setting fire to government administrative buildings (which would include prisons), granaries, or treasuries.]

Case 235.2, 1822. Metropolitan Leading Case from the Depart-ment for Shensi of the Board of Punishments.
Reported in HAHL 24.53/28a.

The Imperial Household Department has submitted a memorial concerning the accidental burning of the Imperial Library.

It has been found that Tseng Lu, a paperhanger who was re-papering in the building, was unfamiliar with and did not use the proper procedure for preparing oil paper; as a result, excessive oiliness of the paper induced spontaneous combustion, thus set-ting the building on fire. Although a fire so produced is not the same as fire actually lighted by accident by someone, and al-though the Imperial Library is not the same as a palace building proper (*kung-ch'üeh*), nonetheless the Library does in fact lie within the Forbidden City [the great walled enclosure in the cen-ter of Peking containing the imperial palaces] and thus differs from an ordinary government office (*ya-shu*).

[*Kung-ch'üeh* is the general term for all palace buildings in-tended for the residence of the emperor and his court, including the great throne room used by him for mass audiences (com-parable to the reception room in a private residence). *Ya-shu* is a term equivalent to yamen; hence, it signifies any kind of adminis-trative governmental building. The Imperial Library, despite its name, was regarded as pertaining to the administrative rather than the residential side of court life. It was located near the southwest corner of the Forbidden City, far away from the residential sections of that walled complex of buildings, where it was administered by the Imperial Household Department as one of several imperial service organs, such as the Imperial Dispensary, Imperial Construction Office, and others. Thus the Imperial Library was a kind of *ya-shu* or administrative organ, even though its exclusive concern with court matters, and its consequent location within the Forbidden City, differentiated it from, and placed it on a higher level than, ordinary *ya-shu* in other parts of Peking or in the provinces.]

Tseng Lu, therefore, should now be sentenced under the statute [Boulais 1645] which provides strangulation after the assizes for one who accidentally sets fire to imperial palace buildings (*kung-ch'üeh*), which sentence, however, may for Tseng be reduced by one degree to 100 blows of the heavy bamboo and life exile at a distance of 3,000 li.

[It would certainly seem that the difference between *ya-shu* and *kung-ch'üeh*, plus the reduction of statutory penalty, would require the statute to be applied analogically rather than directly. The HAHL editors append the following note: "Any oil paper, when heaped in layers within a confined space, may undergo spontaneous combustion if, during its preparation, manganese oxide has been admixed. This matter deserves examination." I am uncertain that this term is the correct equivalent for *t'u tzu* but have been unable to find any other. See B. E. Read and C. Pak, *A Compendium of Minerals and Stones Used in Chinese Medicine,* 2d ed. (Peiping: Peking Natural History Bulletin, 1936), no. 61.]

236. ARSON
[Statutory References: Staunton 383, Boulais 1649–1653]

Case 236.1, 1824. Memorandum.
Reported in HAHL 24.54/1a.

The governor-general of Chihli has reported a case in which Huo Kuei-ssu deliberately set fire to the threshing-yard of Ch'en Heng-jui, from which the fire spread to adjoining houses.

We have noted a case which came to this Board from the Board of Punishments of Manchuria in 1821 and which concerned a beggar named Kuo Lao-wu. When this beggar tried to extort money from somebody, another man, Liu Wen-ping, threatened to hand the beggar over to the authorities and warned people not to give him grain. The beggar, in retaliation, set fire to the firewood and grain in Liu's threshing-yard, from which the fire spread not only to Liu's own house but to other houses adjoining, destroying a total of 33 room-sections. [The basic principle of Chinese architecture is the use of vertical wooden columns set along the walls, on top of which rest horizontal beams which in turn support the roof. A *chien* or room-section is the floor space between one such column and the next. A single room, if small, may be co-extensive with a single *chien*, but if large it may comprise two, three, or even more successive *chien*. Traditionally, the size of Chinese houses has been calculated in terms of the number of *chien* rather than the number of rooms. For another instance of a rebuffed beggar committing arson, see case 239.7.]

Because of the seriousness of this offense, the Board of Punishments of Manchuria sentenced the beggar to military exile with two months wearing of the cangue under the sub-statute [Boulais 1169] on scoundrels who repeatedly and wantonly commit molestations against decent people. When, however, the case came to the Board of Punishments in Peking, this sentence was changed to two months wearing of the cangue plus 100 blows of the heavy bamboo and life exile at a distance of 3,000 li, under the sub-statute specifically covering the crime of deliberately setting fire to the firewood and straw in someone's threshing-yard. [In Boulais 1652, which gives only an abbreviated version of this sub-statute, the particular clause here cited is omitted.]

In the present case, Ch'en Heng-jui's refusal to sell soy bean-curd to Huo Kuei-ssu on credit, coupled with his public aspersion of Huo in the village, caused Huo to vent his anger by deliberately setting fire to the wheat straw in Ch'en's threshing-yard. From there the fire spread until it destroyed 37 thatched houses, including that of Ch'en himself.

We find this act extremely malicious and one that accords very closely with the crime of beggar Kuo. In the latter case, as we have noted, the Manchurian Board's original sentence of military exile under the sub-statute on malicious scoundrels was changed by the Peking Board to life exile, using the sub-statute on setting fire to someone's threshing-yard. In the present case, on the other hand, the Provincial Court of Chihli has itself used the latter sub-statute to sentence Huo to life exile, and for us now [simply because of the horrible nature of the crime] to change this sentence back to military exile under the sub-statute on scoundrels would be inconsistent. After careful scrutiny, therefore, we find that the Provincial Court has acted in conformity with the proper sub-statute, so that it seems appropriate to send a confirmatory reply.

Imperial Endorsement: Although the 37 houses of the present case amount to considerably more than the 33 room-sections of the other, it must be assumed that in both cases the offender was equally unaware of the distance to which his fire might spread. For this reason it is permissible to send a confirmatory reply.

[This endorsement seems to run counter to what is a prevailing feature of Chinese law: the attempt, whenever possible, to measure morality in precise quantitative terms. For another imperial statement which likewise opposes this trend, see case 172.4.]

237. DOING WHAT OUGHT NOT TO BE DONE [23]
[Statutory References: Staunton 386, Boulais 1656]

Case 237.1, 1819. Metropolitan Leading Case.
Reported in HAHL 24.54/7b.

The Department for Hunan and Hupei of the Board of Punishments has presented a memorial concerning Ch'i-ch'eng-ê, a [Manchu] hereditary officer of the Light Chariot, third class, who was deeply grateful to his teacher, Chao Ch'un-liang, both for the latter's long guidance and for his willingness on one occasion to lend Ch'i-ch'eng-ê money to repay a debt. When Chao died, therefore, Ch'i-ch'eng-ê entertained the idea of committing sui-

---

[23] We have encountered this catch-all statute, Boulais 1656, many times in these cases. It provides a convenient means for punishing actions which, though nowhere specifically prohibited by the Code, are nevertheless deemed reprehensible by the authorities. For this purpose it provides 80 blows of the heavy bamboo for more serious offenses and 40 blows of the light bamboo for those of a minor nature.

cide so as to follow and serve his teacher in the next world. He accordingly wrote a statement of intent which he presented to the head of his Banner so as to obviate the need for any investigation of his death.

The Code provides no penalty for someone proposing to commit suicide to honor his teacher. However, we find that Ch'i-ch'eng-ê should now be sentenced, under the statute on doing what ought not to be done [Boulais 1656], to the heavier penalty therein provided of 80 blows of the heavy bamboo. As a holder of official status, he is permitted, according to sub-statute [Boulais 69 and 71], the privilege of monetary redemption. In view of his stupid behavior, however, it would be impolitic to allow him to continue serving in his former position. We therefore request the throne for an imperial rescript, stating that Ch'i-ch'eng-ê should be handed over to the commander of his Banner in order there to be kept under official surveillance.

Case 237.3, 1883. Leading Case.
Reported in HAHL New Supplement 40.14/2a.

The governor of Kiangsi has submitted a memorial containing a report from the Board of Rites concerning the civil service examinations held in Kiangsi in 1882. In these examinations a discrepancy was found between the "red" and "black" versions of the examination paper of one candidate. [In order to prevent possible bias that might arise if the correctors of examination papers could recognize the handwriting of the candidates, the original versions of these papers (written in black ink) were copied in red ink by professional copyists, and these copies then went to the correctors. (In the red copies the names of candidates were also replaced by numbers.) After the papers had been evaluated, the copies were then compared with the originals for possible discrepancies.]

Ch'en Ch'eng-hsüan, the copyist, has been found to be quite careless. He miscopied the two characters *yung yung* ["employ the employable," an allusion to the "K'ang Kao" chapter in the *Documents Classic*], thereby requiring them to be scratched out and altered. Likewise he let a paper weight rest on the two characters *yu ch'ih* ["still slow"] appearing in the original paper, so that he failed to copy them at all.

This miscopying, although it did not affect the final outcome for the candidate, constitutes gross carelessness. Hence the request is made [to the throne] that Ch'en Ch'eng-hsüan, under the statute on doing what ought not to be done [Boulais 1656], should receive the heavier penalty therein provided of 80 blows of the heavy bamboo. This, however, may be commuted to dismissal from his position.

As for the examination candidate himself, the original version of his paper has been carefully compared with the copy, and investigation has revealed him to be completely ignorant of the circumstances whereby the changes occurred. There is therefore no need to institute deliberations concerning him.

239. WRONGDOERS WHO RESIST ARREST [24]
[Statutory References: Staunton 388, Boulais 1658–1661]

Case 239.7, 1827. Memorandum.
Reported in HAHL 24.54/12b.

The governor of Kueichow has reported a case in which Chou Li-jang slashed to death two scoundrels, Mou Ying and Mou Wei-lin.

This Board finds, according to sub-statute [Boulais 154], that if, in a homicide case, the homicide does not, according to law, require the requital [of a life for a life], but merely a penalty of military or life exile or of penal servitude, then the offender, even if he has caused the death of two persons, will, according to statute [Boulais 153], be liable for only one of them. To this the Official Commentary adds: "An example is the unauthorized killing of a wrongdoer guilty of a crime deserving penal servitude [or more]."

[This is one of the rare instances of the Official Commentary covering a sub-statute. The sub-statute is a particular application to homicide of the general principle enunciated in Boulais 153,

---

[24] This section deals not only with wrongdoers who resist apprehension by the duly constituted authorities or by a private individual but also, conversely, with private individuals who, during or after the apprehension of a wrongdoer, take the law into their own hands and kill or injure the wrongdoer.

according to which a person simultaneously guilty of two or more offenses is liable only for the most serious one among them or, if they be all equally serious, for only one of them. The principle does not extend, however, to the killing of two members of the same family, on which see case 161.3. From this we may conclude that the two Mous killed in the present case were not joint family members, despite their common surname. For the concept of "requital" (*ti*) of a life for a life, see cases 164.1 and 2, 185.1, etc.]

In the present case, Chou had already repeatedly suffered deceitful extortion from the two Mous when, in a sudden burst of rage, he slashed them to death. Moreover, the two Mous had likewise repeatedly practiced extortion upon two other persons, Li Lao-ta and Hsiang P'ai-tzu. Thus they truly were vicious scoundrels (*hsiung-ô kun-t'u*), so that Chou, when he killed them, did not thereby commit a capital offense [see below]. Hence, as already indicated, he should be held liable for a single killing only.

The Kueichow Provincial Court has accordingly sentenced Chou Li-jang to maximum [three years] penal servitude under the sub-statute [Boulais 1659b] providing this penalty for an injured party who, having been causelessly molested and harmed by a scoundrel, kills that scoundrel in a burst of rage at the very moment [of arrest]. Because this judgment accords with the sub-statute, it is proper to request a confirmatory reply. [This sub-statute is a corollary to Boulais 1169 (see cases 6.2, 8.1, 148.2, etc.), which provides military exile at the farthest distance of 4,000 li for scoundrels (*kun-t'u*) who repeatedly commit molestations against respectable people.]

Case 239.14, 1816. Leading Case.
Reported in HAHL 24.54/16a.

The governor-general of Chihli has reported a case in which P'ang Chen-te, having importunately begged Huan Ta-lu for food and having been refused, committed arson against Huang out of spite. [See also 236.1 for another case of a rebuffed beggar committing arson.] Huang thereupon apprehended P'ang and intended to bring him before the authorities. Being stopped by rain, however, he tied P'ang to a tree, where P'ang, soaked by the rain, died from exposure.

This outcome had not been anticipated by the offender, who, furthermore, had been subjected to arson and begging. Huang Ta-lu, therefore, should be sentenced to 100 blows of the heavy bamboo and life exile at a distance of 3,000 li, this being a one-degree reduction from the penalty provided by sub-statute for an injured party who, having suffered arson from a grudge-bearing scoundrel, kills the scoundrel, but not immediately. [That is, he did not kill him in the heat of passion. The sub-statute here cited is simply a continuation of the sub-statute cited in the preceding case, Boulais 1659b. The judgment in this case seems lenient compared with that in the case following. Theoretically, the sub-statute should have been applied analogically rather than directly in order to permit the one-degree reduction of punishment.]

Case 239.15, 1809. Memorandum.
Reported in HAHL 24.54/16a.

The governor of Shensi has memorialized concerning a case in which Liao Wu stabbed Hsiung Ta-ts'ai so that he died.

This Board finds, according to sub-statute, that if an injured party, having been causelessly molested by a scoundrel, kills that scoundrel in a burst of rage, he is to be sentenced to 100 blows of the heavy bamboo and three years penal servitude. If, however, his act of killing does not occur at once [not during the heat of passion], he is to be sentenced, as he would be for the unauthorized killing of a wrongdoer, to strangulation after the assizes. [Here again is the same sub-statute, Boulais 1659b, cited in the two preceding cases. For unauthorized killing (*shan sha*), see case 51.1.]

It should be noted that only the repeated molestations which the scoundrel commits against the injured party himself are to be taken into consideration when adjudging the guilt of the latter for having been induced to kill the scoundrel. Molestations by the scoundrel of other persons may not thus be taken into consideration.

In the present case, Hsiung had frequently squeezed money for drink out of Liao and had also seized for himself Liao's bed-quilt and jacket. Such conduct, however, still falls short of viciousness.

[What constitutes viciousness (*ch'eng-hsiung ch'ing-shih*) is not defined either in the above-cited sub-statute or in its corollary, Boulais 1169 (sub-statute providing military exile for vicious scoundrels who repeatedly molest respectable people). The latter, however, in its second portion (omitted by Boulais), states that neither random (sporadic) instances of extortion nor repeated but petty monetary exactions can be accounted as viciousness. Persons guilty of such acts, therefore, may not be convicted of being scoundrels under the general provisions of Boulais 1169 but may only be separately tried for each individual offense under the various pertinent statutes or sub-statutes.]

The fact that Hsiung also seized and sold an ox belonging to the Tsou Ying family, or that he unsuccessfully tried to rape Mrs. P'eng née Wang, has nothing to do with Liao Wu himself. Yet the governor of Shensi has sentenced Liao under the above-cited sub-statute on persons who kill a vicious scoundrel. In so doing he has violated the meaning of the sub-statute. Hsiung's actual offense against Liao was seizure of Liao's bed-quilt and jacket, which is an act falling under the crime of plundering. [Plundering (*ch'iang-to*), when it involves only small amounts of booty and is committed without a gang and without use of dangerous weapons, is punishable by three years of penal servitude (see Boulais 1093), that is, by far less than the military exile prescribed by Boulais 1169 for conviction as a scoundrel.]

Liao, however, assembled other men with whom he attacked Hsiung. Then, after having already rendered Hsiung helpless so that he could be taken to the authorities, Liao unexpectedly slashed him so that he died. This certainly constitutes unauthorized killing (*shan sha*).

Therefore, Liao Wu should now be resentenced under the statute which, for the unauthorized killing of a wrongdoer done after that wrongdoer has already been apprehended, prescribes the same punishment as for killing in an affray, namely, strangulation after the assizes.

[See Boulais 1659, which, however, omits the second half of the statute here cited. Note that the sentence Liao finally receives is the same as he would have received from the governor, though deriving from a different law. The Board's insistence upon finding exactly the right law under which to convict Liao, irrespective of the sameness of the resulting punishment, is exemplified also in case 183.1.]

[The Board's argument that the only criterion for adjudging an individual to be a scoundrel, at least with respect to another given individual, must be the vicious acts committed by him against that particular individual and no one else, runs counter to the Board's findings in case 239.7, where, on the contrary, it explicitly cites as additional evidence the acts also committed by the alleged scoundrel against other outside persons. The argument likewise runs counter to the concept of the scoundrel underlying Boulais 1169, wherein what makes a scoundrel a scoundrel is deemed to be his behavior toward society as a whole, and not necessarily only toward one of its individuals (see especially cases 6.2 and 8.1). It might be argued in rebuttal, however, that whereas the concern of Boulais 1169 is the scoundrel's position in society at large, that of the other sub-statute centers merely upon the relationship between the scoundrel and the other individual who kills him. The careful balance sheet drawn by the Board in the present case (but not in case 239.7) between these two concerned individuals perhaps reflects the ancient Chinese belief (see especially case 164.1) that human crime represents a disruption of the total cosmic order, reparation of which requires in each instance achievement of a new balance by carefully offering requital for whatever the crime has previously destroyed.]

241. ESCAPEES FROM PENAL SERVITUDE OR EXILE
[Statutory References: Staunton 390, Boulais 1664]

Case 241.9, 1815. Memorandum from the Department for Hunan and Hupei of the Board of Punishments.
Reported in HAHL 26.57/13b–14a.

The military governor of Kirin has reported the case of Wang Lung-yüan, a criminal who, after escaping from deportation, turned himself in to the authorities.

This Department finds, according to sub-statute, that if a criminal, having had his original death sentence for robbery reduced to deportation, should then escape from his place of deportation, but subsequently, because of fear of punishment, should surrender himself again to the authorities, he is to be spared from death and returned instead to his original place of deportation.

[See Boulais 122a, which, because of its clause on surrender, is placed under the section on voluntary confession (see case 17.1) rather than, as might be expected, under the present section. Were the escaped criminal to be recaptured instead of surrendering himself, he would be liable, upon receipt of an imperial rescript of approval, to the same death penalty to which his crime of robbery had originally condemned him. See Boulais 1664a.]

The present case is one in which Wang Lung-yüan, having originally been sentenced to death for committing robbery with violence, but then having had this sentence reduced to deportation, was accordingly deported to Kirin in 1788. There he was given as a slave to Shu-lun-t'ai [presumably a Manchu] but, escaping from him, remained at large until 1803, when he was recaptured. Through imperial grace he was then spared the punishment [of death] for his escape, and was returned instead to his former master. Because of personal friction, however, he was thereafter again transferred to Ninguta [still farther northeast in Manchuria], and there given as a slave to [another Manchu] Ma-na-erh. In 1813, as a result of the new arrangements made for Heilungkiang deportees, Wang's punishment was changed to life exile within China proper at a distance of 3,000 li [from his existing location at Ninguta]. It was accordingly decided that he should be sent to Kiangsu.

[These new arrangements, which applied to the neighboring province of Kirin as well as to Heilungkiang itself, are recounted in the following case 241.10 (untranslated), and, with full details, in case 27.12 (also untranslated; see HAHL 4.6/10a–12a). The reasons for them (the cold climate of the two Manchurian provinces, and especially the overcrowding of them with deportees owing to increased banditry and piracy in South China) are recounted in an edict of 1812, for which see *Ta Ch'ing hui-tien shih-li* (Taipei 1963 reprint of 1899 edition), 746/4b–5a. The new arrangements provided that many future deportees, instead of going to Manchuria, were to be sent to Sinkiang, and many deportees already in Manchuria were to be transferred to other areas. The latter included men who, like Wang, had been guilty of violent robbery and had been deportees in Manchuria for more than 20 years; these were to have their remaining sentence reduced to 3,000 li life exile within China proper.]

In the tenth month of the same year (1813), however, before Wang had yet been sent to Kiangsu, he again succeeded in escaping, this time remaining at large until the sixth month of the present year (1815), when he voluntarily surrendered himself to the authorities.

Thus the offender was recaptured after his first escape, but then, owing to imperial grace, was spared from punishment for escaping. Following his second escape, he himself surrendered voluntarily, thereby meeting the conditions stipulated in the sub-statute cited above, according to which a criminal whose original death sentence has been changed to deportation, and who escapes but then, out of fear of resulting punishment, voluntarily surrenders, is to be exempted from such punishment. This means, for Wang, that he should now be sent to Kiangsu, as originally intended.

The military governor of Kirin, on the other hand, [has overlooked the voluntary surrender and therefore] has sentenced Wang under another sub-statute stating that if a criminal escapes while undergoing life exile at a distance of 3,000 li, his sentence is to be increased to military exile. This judgment is in error and should be corrected.

[The Board's judgment is based on the fact that at the time of Wang's second escape, his status had already changed from that of deportee to that of criminal undergoing 3,000 li exile, even though he had not yet actually been sent to the new place of exile. The sub-statute used by the military governor is Boulais 1664b. Its penalty—military exile at the nearest distance of 2,000 li—is one degree higher than ordinary life exile at a distance of 3,000 li.]

[This case, besides illustrating the operation of the principle of voluntary confession or surrender (see case 17.1), also has interest as showing that the penal machinery of deportation was not necessarily immutable. Thus we find that a man originally sentenced to death not only had this sentence reduced to deportation, but, while a deportee, succeeded in escaping twice for a duration of more than 15 years. (It is a pity we are told nothing of how he existed during this period.) Then, instead of being executed for escaping, he ended up by being transferred to one of China's choicest provinces, Kiangsu (wherein lie Nanking and Shanghai).]

243. JAILOR'S NEGLIGENCE RESULTING IN ESCAPE OF PRISONERS
[Statutory References: Staunton 392, Boulais 1664c]

Case 243.5, 1822. Leading Case.
Reported in HAHL 26.58/14a.

The governor-general of Chihli has reported the escape from prison of the prisoner Wang Tuan-ch'ing.

This Board finds that Wang had been deported at the petition of his father. [See Boulais 1505, which states that if a parent accuses a son before the authorities of repeated disobedience, the son, at the parent's request, will be sent into military exile in a malarial region.] While en route to exile, he escaped but then was recaptured [and subsequently escaped again, this time from prison]. These events happened prior to [this year's] great imperial amnesty [relieving the offender of his original sentence of exile, if not of the onus for having then escaped].

Investigation indicates that the offender's father is now ready to receive him back again. Moreover, there is no article in the Code punishing a guiltless prisoner who escapes. [That is, a prisoner who becomes guiltless by reason of. amnesty. Therefore, the offender, despite his escapes, which ordinarily would bring increases to his original sentence, may be permitted to return to his father without further punishment.]

As for Fan Jo-k'un and the other prison guards [who had Wang in custody], they should now all be sentenced to the heavier penalty provided under the statute on doing what ought not to be done [Boulais 1656; see also sec. 237 above], namely 80 blows of the heavy bamboo.

[For a prisoner who escapes while en route to exile, the punishment (depending upon the number of days elapsing before recapture) ranges up to 100 blows of the heavy bamboo (Boulais

1664); for escape from prison, the penalty for the prisoner is a two-degree addition to his original sentence (Boulais 1662). In the present case, both kinds of escape took place prior to the general amnesty which freed the offender from his original sentence. (That it did not free him from the penalties for escaping seems indicated by the fact that the Board ignores the amnesty in its deliberations upon the escapes.) How then could the Board possibly argue that the offender was already "guiltless" when he made his escapes, and that these therefore did not constitute additional offences? (This reasoning seems clearly implied by the Board's statement that there is no punishment for an escaping prisoner who is guiltless.)]

[Again, the punishment for jailors who allow a prisoner to escape is, according to the statute under which this case is classified (Staunton 392; not in Boulais), only two degrees less than that of the escaping prisoner himself. Why then does the Board ignore this statute and sentence the jailors instead under the much lighter catch-all statute on doing what ought not to be done?]

[Obviously, the Board is eager to close the case with a minimum of damage to all parties. One reason, perhaps, is the rather vague basis (parental complaints of filial disobedience) upon which the son was sentenced to exile in the first place. Most probably, however, the father's present readiness to take the son back is of really decisive importance. Without this readiness, in fact, the son's sentence of exile for disobedience would, according to sub-statute (Boulais 93), be among those explicitly excluded from the provisions of amnesties.]

248. HARSH TREATMENT OF PRISONERS
[Statutory References: Staunton 398, Boulais 1675]

Case 248.2, 1821. Leading Case from the Department for Chihli of the Board of Punishments.
Reported in HAHL 27.59/5b–6a.

The prefect of the metropolitan prefecture of Peking has memorialized concerning Sun To, a tax registry clerk, and Hu

Tzu-ch'eng, a government underling belonging to the municipal administration. Sun, on being arrested for having levied excessive taxes, was placed under Hu's custody. Thereupon Hu, acting on his own initiative, chained Sun to the bars of his window. Yeh Wen, a guard, seized this opportunity to make demands for money upon Sun, who, as a result, took his own life by hanging himself from his chain.

It was not Yeh, however, who privately ordered Sun to be put in chains. Thus there is a difference between his act and the pressing of extortionate demands that lead to suicide. Therefore Yeh Wen should be sentenced under the sub-statute [abbreviated in Boulais 1522] providing strangulation [after the assizes] for rapacious government underlings whose extortionate demands result in the suicide of the victim, with, however, a one-degree reduction of this penalty for Yeh to 100 blows of the heavy bamboo and life exile at a distance of 3,000 li.

[Here the Board distinguishes between so-cha, a demand, usually monetary, pressed without the use of threats and intimidation, as against ho-cha, an extortionate demand which does include threats and intimidation. Yeh, the Board maintains, was guilty only of the former act, inasmuch as it was not he who had manacled and thus intimidated Sun. In view of Sun's suicide, the distinction may seem rather tenuous, but it provides the basis for reducing Yeh's sentence to less than death. In doing this, the Board should have applied the sub-statute analogously rather than directly.]

As for Hu Tzu-ch'eng, he was guilty merely of holding the prisoner in an illegal form of custody and not of treating him with unreasonable harshness. Therefore, his sentence should be one degree less than that of strangulation [after the assizes] which is provided under the statute [Boulais 1675] on treating a prisoner with unreasonable harshness, so that he dies. That is to say, his sentence, like that of Yeh Wen, should be 100 blows of the heavy bamboo and life exile at a distance of 3,000 li.

[Here again the Board makes a rather fine distinction between Hu's treatment of the prisoner (putting him in chains so that he ultimately commits suicide) and the statutory offense of treating a prisoner with unreasonable harshness (fei li ling-nüeh). The distinction becomes sharper when we read the fuller citation of Boulais 1675 in the next case, where striking and injuring the prisoner, so that he dies, are specifically mentioned as forms of unreasonable harshness. In its disposal of Hu, as of Yeh, the Board should have applied the statute analogically.]

Case 248.3, 1819. Leading Case.
Reported in HAHL 27.59/6a.

The Department for Anhui of the Board of Punishments submits a memorial concerning Chang Fu-lu, a government underling of a district office who was assigned custody over Yen Wenpin when the latter was held for investigation because of having written some queer characters. Chang, on his own initiative, placed handcuffs on Yen at night and only removed them during the daytime. Even though he was clearly notified that Yen was to be released on bail the following morning, he still held Yen in chains and handcuffs for fear he might escape. Yen, as a result, believing himself to be held on a very serious charge, committed suicide by hanging himself from his chain.

This Department finds that Yen's writing of queer characters was merely a result of rural ignorance and stupidity. Thus it was quite proper to release him after his interrogation in return for a reliable guarantee. Chang, as a lowly menial, was incapable of deep understanding, so that he thought the queer characters were connected with some kind of heterodox ideology. This led him to take special measures on his own initiative to prevent what he believed to be an important criminal from escaping. In this way he caused an ignorant citizen to commit suicide out of fear of punishment.

By analogy, therefore, to the statute [Boulais 1675] on jailors who treat prisoners with unreasonable harshness, striking and injuring them, and thus bringing about their death, Chang Fu-lu should be given a sentence one degree less than that of strangulation [after the assizes] as therein provided. That is to say, he should receive 100 blows of the heavy bamboo and life exile at a distance of 3,000 li.

[This case, like some earlier ones (92.1, 133.1–3, etc.), illustrates the fear in imperial China of anything which, being out of the ordinary, might therefore be deemed subversive.]

Case 248.4, 1813. Leading Case.
Reported in HAHL 27.59/6a.

The governor-general of Chihli has reported a case in which Wang Ming-ch'ien, a local constable, received an assignment to investigate and apprehend the slayer of a certain person. On learning through interrogation that Ch'ang Te had permitted a certain suspect to go free, Wang, without reporting to his superiors, took it upon himself, together with Chai Tien-pang, to chain Ch'ang Te hand and foot so as to take him into the city. This arrest led Ch'ang to kill himself, in a burst of indignation, by jumping into a well.

Wang Ming-ch'ien is now sentenced, by analogy to the substatute on guards who, while transporting prisoners, put manacles on them and press them to the point where they commit suicide, to two months wearing of the cangue, to be followed by military exile in a malarial region.

[See Boulais 1675a, the original text of which details various other kinds of mistreatment leading to suicide, such as beating the prisoners, taking their money, depriving them of money. Why the offender is here punished more severely than in the two preceding cases is not clear. In the absence of further reference to his assistant, Chai Tien-pang, we must assume that the latter was, as an accessory (see Boulais 110), given a sentence one degree less than that of Wang himself.]

257. JURISDICTION EXERCISED BY TRIBUNALS OF DIFFERENT LEVELS [25]
[Statutory References: Staunton 411, Boulais 1692–1694]

Case 257.2, 1793. Memorandum.
Reported in HAHL 27.59/14a.

The Department for Fukien of the Board of Punishments finds, with regard to capital cases referred to this Board from the provinces, that two procedures may arise:

(1) If, while a given case is still under consideration, a supple-

[25] This section has to do with what kinds of cases are to be settled at what levels, beginning with sentences involving bambooing only, which are settled at the district (*hsien*) level, and culminating with capital cases, which go to Peking and must receive final approval from the emperor.

mental report comes from the province of origin announcing the death of the principal defendant, and if the remaining defendants have been recommended by the provincial court for sentences of military or life exile, a report concerning them should still be sent from the province to the Board so that the Board may dispose of their cases. If, on the other hand, the sentences recommended for the remaining defendants consist of penal servitude or less, a request should be directed to this Board for permission to recall the original report and dispose of the case at the provincial court level.

(2) However, this Department has been unable to find any leading case providing precedent for the situation in which, while a capital case is being considered by this Board, a supplemental report comes from the province of origin announcing the escape of the principal defendant and in which the sentences recommended by the provincial court for the remaining defendants do not exceed penal servitude. After joint deliberation, we have reached the conclusion that, in such a situation, if the principal be subsequently recaptured, it then becomes necessary for the provincial court to prepare a new report containing a recommended sentence which takes into account the additional fact of the defendant's escape. During the interim prior to the issuance of that report, the previous report remains null and void as if the defendant had died.

The governor of Fukien has recently memorialized concerning a case in which Huang Mao-hsi killed Ma Liu-ling. According to a report just received from the governor, the offender has managed to escape while being sent back to his native place from trial in the provincial capital. The only other offender in the case is a Mrs. Chang née Ma, who was privy to Huang's act. For her the governor has recommended penal servitude, redeemable, since she is a woman, by a monetary payment [see Boulais 40]. It would seem, under the procedure suggested above, that the report containing the original indictment may now be replaced and the case closed [at the provincial level with the sentencing of Mrs. Chang, unless and until the principal offender is recaptured, when an entirely new report concerning him should be submitted].

259. UNLAWFUL ADMINISTRATION OF PUNISHMENT [26]
[Statutory References: Staunton 413, Boulais 1696]

Case 259.1, 1802. Memorandum.
Reported in HAHL 27.60/2b–3a.

The governor of Shantung has reported a case in which Yen Huai-che, a sergeant of the military post at Kuan-ch'eng, whipped a gambler, Chin Lien-shan, causing his death.

It being the depth of winter, when riffraff are likely to gather at certain spots for gambling, Yen was on the lookout for them as he led a patrol outside the city. During the night the patrol did indeed encounter a group of gamblers at a certain enclosure, among them Chin Lien-shan. Yen ordered his men to arrest the gamblers and take them into the city to be dealt with by the district magistrate. Chin Lien-shan, however, vigorously objected with a stream of vile language. Yen thereupon ordered two soldiers to pull down Chin's trousers and a third, Chang Ching, to whip him. It being dark and fearing that the tip of the whip might accidentally touch and injure Chin's testicles, Yen therefore ordered the beating to be done with the lash folded in two. After five lashes, however, Chin became even more abusive, so that Yen ordered another five lashes. This excessive whipping inflicted severe injuries on Chin's buttocks and thighs, which, together with the unexpected fact that he was a sufferer from tuberculosis, caused him to die within a short space of time.

On examination, this Board finds that when Chin objected strongly to the arrest with vile language, Yen should merely have informed the district magistrate accordingly, so that the latter might at his discretion have dealt with Chin more severely. Instead of this, however, Yen had a soldier beat him with a whip folded in two, thereby causing death. Such an act surely constitutes beating done in an illegal (*fei fa*) manner.

By analogy to the statute on supervisory officials who, in the

---

[26] For an analysis of the thirty-odd cases contained in this section of HAHL, see Judy Feldman Harrison, "Wrongful Treatment of Prisoners: A Case Study of Ch'ing Legal Practice," *Journal of Asian Studies*, 23:227–244 (1964).

course of their public duties, beat someone in an illegal manner, thus causing death, the governor of Shantung has sentenced Yen Huai-che to 100 blows of the heavy bamboo and three years penal servitude, and likewise has sentenced Yen's subordinate soldier, Chang Ching, who actually did the beating, to a one-degree lesser punishment of 90 blows and two and one half years penal servitude. These sentences being in accord with the offenses, it is proper to request a confirmatory reply.

[Boulais 1696 fails to include that portion of the statute here cited. The statute's general topic is the improper administering of punishments (either judicial or disciplinary) by officials. More specifically, it provides the following penalties in case of improper punishment resulting in death (see also Harrison, pp. 229–230): (1) An official who administers punishment in a manner not according to law (*pu ju fa*), thereby causing death, is liable to 100 blows of the heavy bamboo. "Not according to law" means, according to the Shen Chih-ch'i Commentary, violation of the proper legal procedure when administering punishment, administering punishment at places other than those legally provided for this purpose, or using an instrument of punishment which, while legal in itself, is improper under the circumstances (for example, the heavy bamboo, when used to carry out a punishment for which the light bamboo is legally specified). (2) Any supervisory official who, in the course of his public duties, administers punishment in a manner which is illegal (*fei fa*), thereby causing death, is liable to 100 blows of the heavy bamboo and three years penal servitude. "Supervisory official" (*chien-lin kuan*) here means an official (either civilian or military) possessing the duly constituted authority to supervise various administrative activities (the building of dikes or drilling of troops are two of innumerable examples); in the course of his supervision such an official may be obliged to inflict disciplinary punishment on those under him. "Illegal" is explained as signifying, for example, the beating of a victim on parts of the body other than that area (the buttocks) reserved by law for punishment or beating him with an oversized stick, or knife, or other instrument not legally sanctioned. This, then, is an offense considerably more serious than administering punishment "not according to law." In both categories, the subordinate who physically administers the punishment at the behest of his superior officer receives a penalty one degree less than does the latter. (3) Should an official, whether in a judicial or supervisory capacity, administer punishment which is "according to law" (*yi fa*), that is, carried out in accordance with correct legal procedure but which nevertheless results in the death of the recipient, the official is then not to be held liable.]

[It is obvious in the present case that the Board of Punishments regarded Yen's beating of the gambler as falling under the second of the above three articles of the statute, the article on illegal (*fei fa*) punishing, because it employs this term to describe Yen's use of a double-folded whip and sentences him accordingly. However, the article cites this offense only with reference to "supervisory officials who, in the course of their public duties," find it necessary to punish persons directly under their own supervision. In the present case, Yen did in fact exercise supervisory authority over the members of his own patrol but did not have similar authority over the gambler who was his victim. Toward the latter his right was merely that of arrest, but not of punishment. Although such reasoning does not explicitly appear, we may strongly suspect that it underlies the decision to apply this article of the statute to the offender only analogically and not directly. Similar reasoning is found in case 259.8 (untranslated), which in important respects parallels the present case. See exposition in Harrison, pp. 239–240 (where, however, the case is numbered as 7 instead of 8).]

[The Board's initial criticism of Yen for having administered the whipping on his own authority ("Yen should merely have informed the district magistrate") makes this seem at first sight to be its primary basis for sentencing him. At once, however, the Board goes on to mention the use of the double-folded whip and to equate this with a beating done in an "illegal" (*fei fa*) manner. We may therefore deduce that had the whip not been thus folded, the beating in itself might well have been regarded as falling into the less serious category of punishments administered "not in accordance with law" (*pu ju fa*). Harrison's analysis of the case is therefore confusing and contradictory when she says, p. 237: "Since the officer's duty was only to transfer the prisoner to the magistrate for punishment, the Board held that it was an *illegal* beating" (our emphasis), or when she says (p. 238): ". . . the beating itself was *legal* [our emphasis] . . . The basis of the punishment was the failure of the military officer to transfer the case to the proper authorities."

Case 259.2, 1825. Leading Case.
Reported in HAHL 27.60/3a.

The governor-general of Chihli has reported a case in which Kuo Fu-jen, having quarreled while trying to recover a debt, brought the matter before Li Ch'ung-shen, a sergeant of the military post at Pai-t'a. Li at first thought he would refer the case to the district magistrate but because it was the last day of the year [when the court would not be open for civil cases], and because the debt was small, he decided to mediate matters himself. Accordingly, he had Kuo Fu-jen and Kuo's son, Kuo Wu, summoned for questioning.

[We can only speculate as to why he did not also summon the delinquent debtor. Debts traditionally had to be settled before the New Year in China, which explains why Kuo attempted to collect at this time. Probably Li did not believe that the debtor could or would pay and therefore summoned the two Kuos in order to urge them to forget the matter, at least temporarily. Such urging would explain why the elder Kuo later became unruly.]

During the discussion, however, the elder Kuo became recalcitrant and obstreperous, whereupon Li ordered one of his soldiers, Yin Kao-sheng, to give him ten blows of the heavy bamboo. When the son, Kuo Wu, objected to this, Li ordered another soldier, Ch'en Wang, likewise to give the son twenty-five blows. So enraged did the elder Kuo become that he went home and hanged himself.

The governor-general has recommended that Li Ch'ung-shen should, for his offense, receive 100 blows of the heavy bamboo, by analogy to the statute on pressing a person into committing suicide.

[See Boulais 1323. Why the governor-general felt he could apply the statute only analogically rather than directly is unclear. The statute states that whoever makes demands upon another person (for example, in matters concerning marriage, sale of land, or payment of debt), thereby pressing him into suicide, is to receive 100 blows. It then states more specifically that the same penalty applies to officials and subordinate functionaries who, to advance some private matter, apply pressure on someone with the same result. Probably the governor-general's judgment was based on the opinion that Li's attempt to settle Kuo's case fell within the public (administrative) sphere and thus was not a private matter.]

On examination, this Board finds that Li Ch'ung-shen did not, as a petty military officer, possess the requisite authority for conducting inquiries, in spite of which he took it upon himself to handle the Kuo case and in so doing subjected both father and son to undue punishment. Although it is true that the elder Kuo died through his own hand, it is nonetheless a fact that his death was, in the final analysis, induced by the undue punishment he had received from Li.

It is accordingly appropriate to judge Li Ch'ung-shen by analogy to the sub-statute on innocent persons whose deaths result from undue punishment [torture] received in the course of judicial examination. This sub-statute states that the penalty for causing death in this way is the same as that in the statute on death caused by beating someone in an illegal manner. Thus, Li should receive 100 blows of the heavy bamboo and three years penal servitude and should pay the family of the deceased ten ounces of silver for funeral expenses.

[What is here cited is the concluding portion of a sub-statute whose earlier articles, but not this concluding article, appear in Boulais 1676. The statute on beating in an illegal manner, to which the sub-statute refers, is likewise omitted by Boulais, though it properly forms part of Boulais 1696. It has been discussed in detail in the preceding case. Why the sub-statute is used here analogically rather than directly to sentence Li is explainable on two grounds: (1) The sub-statute has to do with the mishandling of judicial procedures by persons who are duly constituted authorities, whereas Li, as we have seen, had no authority at all to handle investigations. (2) The sub-statute concerns itself with death resulting directly from undue punishment or torture, whereas Kuo's death by suicide was only the indirect result of his beating.]

As for Yin Kao-sheng [the soldier who beat Kuo], he is to receive the heavier punishment which is provided by the statute on doing what ought not to be done, namely, 80 blows of the heavy bamboo.

[See Boulais 1656 for this already frequently cited catch-all statute. The present judgment raises two questions: (1) If Yin Kao-sheng is punished for giving 10 blows to Kuo Fu-jen, why is not the other soldier, Ch'en Wang, likewise punished for giving 25 blows to Kuo's son, Kuo Wu? The answer, presumably, is that the elder Kuo's beating led to suicide whereas the younger Kuo's beating did not. (2) Whereas the guilty soldier in this case is given only 80 blows under the statute on doing what ought not to be done, the preceding case involves another soldier who was similarly guilty of beating a man at the command of his superior officer, for which he was given 90 blows plus two and one half years penal servitude on the basis of the same statute there used to sentence his commanding officer (and here used to sentence the commanding officer Li). Why the difference? An answer is provided in the following case in this series, 259.3 (not translated), in which case 259.1 and the present case are both discussed. (See also analysis in Harrison, p. 239.) Therein we are told that the soldier who inflicted the beating in case 259.1 was more guilty than the soldier who does the same in the present case, because the beating in 259.1 was so severe as in itself to cause death, whereas the beating in the present case was not itself fatal but merely induced suicide. (By the same token, however, the Board of Punishments should in the present case have accepted the governor-general's recommendation that the principal in the case, Li Ch'ung-shen, should be sentenced under the statute on pressing someone into committing suicide and therefore given only 100 blows. Yet, as we have seen, it refused to do this.)]

260. CITATION OF STATUTE WHEN IMPOSING SENTENCE [27]
[Statutory References: Staunton 415, Boulais 1696a]

Case 260.1, 1870. General Circular.
Reported in HAHL New Supplement 40.16/3a–4b.

The Board of Punishments reports to the throne that errors of fact occur in the memorial of the governor of Honan on a case which, having initially reached Peking from Honan in the form of an accusation, was then sent back by the Board to Honan for trial. In a case involving the suicide of a woman after a fight, it is essential to establish the exact facts of death and whether or not foul language was used, as well as to impose sentence in strict accord with the relevant statutes or sub-statutes. Especially with regard to cases first sent to Peking and then returned for trial, there is no place for undue leniency or favoritism.

The case involves Chang Erh-huan and an unrelated woman, Mrs. Chang née Chu, who lived in neighboring villages and between whom there had been no previous enmity. One day Chang Erh-huan, together with his father and the rest of his family, was in the fields cutting and carrying wheat. Mrs. Chang came by with her infant grandson to pick up any wheat that might have fallen along the way. Chang Erh-huan's father shouted to her to stop, and in the ensuing quarrel she butted him with her head. Chang Erh-huan then rushed into action with a flail with which he hit and wounded her on the head. Thereupon Chang's uncle intervened to break up the fight, and Mrs. Chang then returned home with her grandson, where her daughter-in-law tried to soothe her. Still enraged, however, Mrs. Chang soon rushed off again to Chang Erh-huan's house to get even with him. Finding nobody there because all the Changs were still in the fields, she in her passion hanged herself from a beam of the house. On returning home, one of Chang Erh-huan's brothers found the body

---

[27] This statute provides 30 blows of the light bamboo for any official who fails to cite a relevant statute or sub-statute relied on when imposing sentence. Forbidden for this purpose is the citation of any imperial edict issued merely to dispose of a particular case and not intended to become a lasting legal principle.

hanging there and summoned a passerby to help take it down. When Mrs. Chang's daughter-in-law heard this, she too tried to kill herself by jumping into a well but was rescued. By the time the case reached the district magistrate, the accused Chang Erh-huan had already fled.

Mrs. Chang's son, Chang Chün-hsi, had been absent at the time. When he returned, he could not believe that his aged mother would have surrendered life so easily. On learning that the entire Chang family had been together in the fields at the time, he began to suspect that they might have banded together to kill his mother and then have strung her on a rope in their house to make it seem that she had hanged herself. The coroner might have been bribed to disregard the wounds, and the passerby who had helped cut down the body might likewise have been bribed to give false testimony. With all this in mind, he lodged an accusation with the magistrate.

Chang Erh-huan, however, still remained at large, and Mrs. Chang's son suspected that the yamen clerks might have been bribed into being lax. Failing to get any action, he prepared a report with added details which he took to Peking and there presented to the Censorate. Thereafter the case was sent back to Honan. Chang Erh-huan was then apprehended and at the trial admitted everything.

The governor of Honan has accordingly sentenced Chang by analogy to the sub-statute [Boulais 1327a] which provides 100 blows of the heavy bamboo and three years penal servitude for one who, in beating another, inflicts non-serious but eventually fatal injuries which induce the victim to commit suicide before the injuries take effect. This penalty the governor has, in the case of Chang, reduced by one degree to 90 blows and two and one half years penal servitude.

[Application of the sub-statute analogically rather than directly permitted this reduction to be made. It covers five categories of beating, each causing the victim to commit suicide: (1) beating which inflicts serious and fatal injury; (2) beating which causes permanent crippling or comparable injury; (3) beating inflicting injury which, though not itself serious, eventually proves fatal (for example, through infection); (4) beating which inflicts serious but non-fatal injury; (5) beating which inflicts neither serious nor fatal injury. The penalty for either (1) or (2) is military exile at a nearby frontier; for (3) or (4) it is as specified in the text above; for (5) it is 60 blows of the heavy bamboo and one year penal servitude. Why the governor selects (3) to sentence Chang is unclear because there is no stated indication that Chang's wounding of Mrs. Chang with the flail would have proved fatal.]

As for Mrs. Chang's son, Chang Chün-hsi, the governor has sentenced him to 100 blows of the heavy bamboo under the statute [Boulais 1459, discussed below] on presenting accusations which prove to be false.

We have carefully examined this case and would raise the following points:

(1) When Mrs. Chang was quarreling with Chang Erh-huan's father, many of the latter's family were also present, and at least one among them might have been expected to stop the trouble. Why was the criminal in such a hurry to use his flail on Mrs. Chang?

(2) When Mrs. Chang later went to the Chang household to get even with the criminal, she must surely have been verbally exploding with rage. Why did nobody nearby hear her, and why was the house completely empty? If all the Changs were away in the fields, the house would surely have been locked. How, then, was Mrs. Chang able to enter it and hang herself there?

(3) Mrs. Chang's daughter-in-law had no part in the fight. Why then, as soon as she heard of her mother-in-law's death, did she herself try to jump into a well? It is hard to believe there were not some ulterior circumstances behind both women's readiness to abandon life.

(4) When Chang Chün-hsi returned after being away from home, his father and wife certainly told him the true facts about his mother's death. Why did he repeatedly try to present accusations?

(5) Why did the chief criminal, Chang Erh-huan, remain at large for three years and then fall into the hands of the authorities only after Chang Chün-hsi presented his accusation in Peking?

(6) Chang Chün-hsi has accused the court clerk and the head of the court police of deliberately neglecting to arrest the criminal. This accusation need not necessarily be completely false.

(7) The passerby who helped take down the corpse is a most important witness, yet he always managed to stay away from the trial on plea of illness and so never underwent interrogation.

(8) It was never ascertained at the original investigation whether the rope used for the hanging was brought by the victim to the Chang house or was part of the Chang household property.

The disposition of this case has been hasty and devious. The sentencing of Chang Erh-huan in terms of the sub-statute cited above, but with a one-degree reduction of penalty, can in no way be accounted a truly judicial decision. As for Chang Chün-hsi, the inherent doubts surrounding his mother's death, coupled with the continuing failure to arrest Chang Erh-huan and his own repeated failures to gain a personal hearing, all induced him to go directly to Peking to present his charges. In so doing he was motivated by a filial concern which differentiates him from those who for personal ends seek to implicate others in their accusations. Our investigation has already revealed that there is truth in his charges. From all this it naturally follows that his conviction should be voided. Yet the governor, while sentencing Chang to maximum bambooing under the statute on making false accusations, has failed to make any investigation of the clerk and police officer accused by Chang of malfeasance. This Board finds it impossible to go along with this. The governor should be commanded to conduct a new trial in order to determine the precise facts and then, in accordance with law, to render a judgment which may be submitted to us for renewed consideration.

There is a further matter on which we beg Your Majesty's attention. The statute cited above [Boulais 1459], under which the presenting of an accusation which proves to be false is punishable by 100 blows of the heavy bamboo, has reference to such an act *only* when effected by stopping the imperial chariot or beating the complaint drum.

[One could present an accusation by catching the emperor's attention when he was on the road or by petitioning him in the capital. The complaint drum (*teng-wen ku*, also known by other names) had its origin in legendary antiquity when, supposedly, such a drum stood in front of the ruler's palace. Any aggrieved person could, by beating this drum, summon an attendant who would straightway transmit his grievance to the ruler. The existence, and even the occasional use, of such a drum is well known for historical times, and the clause in our statute referring to it and the imperial chariot (*ch'e chia*) goes back, with only minor verbal changes, to the T'ang Code (book 24, article 13). For a dramatic instance of the use of the drum in the year 1426, see Charles O. Hucker, *The Censorial System of Ming China*, p. 100. In Ch'ing times, the drum no longer stood within the palace grounds (where it would have been inaccessible to the ordinary man) but at the entrance to the Transmission Office, an agency which received and transmitted memorials and petitions intended for the emperor, and which was located not far southwest of the great Gate of Heavenly Peace (on which see Part One, Chapter IV, section 2). We may suspect that by the nineteenth century very few people ever thought of trying to secure justice either by "stopping the imperial chariot" or by beating the complaint drum; yet see case 214.4 for an instance of the former act in 1815.]

Thus what is covered by this statute differs from ordinary acts of bypassing the immediate judicial authorities in order to present one's accusation before a higher tribunal. This is why the statute not only imposes a [minimum] penalty of bambooing for any act of false accusation falling under its jurisdiction but goes on to provide correspondingly heavier penalties for false allegations of offenses for which the stated penalties exceed maximum bambooing. [The statute further provides remission of all penalty if, on the other hand, the accusation proves to be correct.] This means that the statute is *not* intended merely as a means of concluding a case by imposing a beating.

[It is evident, both here and in case 171.3, where the same statute occurs, that its main function in Ch'ing times was indeed that of discouraging importunate plaintiffs from bringing their accusations to Peking—a function made possible only by the practice of ignoring the clause referring to the chariot and drum when citing the statute. So strong had his reinterpretation of the statute become by the nineteenth century that it leads both

Staunton and Boulais to mistranslate the clause in question. Thus *ch'e chia,* a well known technical designation for the emperor's chariot (and thereby for the emperor himself when traveling), is rendered by Staunton 332 as "an officer of justice in his public progress," and by Boulais 1459 as "le mandarin . . . hors de son tribunal." Only Philastre (*Le Code annamite,* article 301) translates correctly as "voitures du souverain." When, in the text below, the Board of Punishments demands that the ignored clause always be included in citations of the statute, it is obviously not motivated by love of tradition. Its interest in the clause is solely as a limitation upon further improper use of the statute.]

Of the accusations which reach Peking from the provinces, eight or nine in ten have to do with corrupt clerks. Although many are no doubt trumped up, yet genuine cases of injustice are also not uncommon. If the governors-general and governors would really handle cases conscientiously and straightforwardly, lawsuits would naturally diminish and there would be nothing like the number of accusations which in recent years have come to Peking from the provinces. Of the cases reported to us, hardly one in ten has been thoroughly investigated in advance so as to determine the truth or falsity of the charges. For the most part matters are smoothed over just to bring the case to an end. Serious items are commonly played down while trivial ones are played up. Inconclusive statements appear, such as that "behind the accusation lies some motivation" or "it is impossible to explain where the suspicions may lead." Also common is the practice, when taking testimony at a trial, of blunting the force of the charges by the use of oblique phraseology.

All these things happen because the judge is ready to treat what is true as false. Being deprived thereby of adequate means for silencing the plaintiff and fearful lest the latter bring counter accusations, the judge is unready to use against him the statute on [deliberately] making false accusations which call for increased penalties. [See Boulais 1474, which states that a false imputation of a crime to another will result in punishment for the imputor either two or three degrees more severe than the punishment which the imputed crime itself would merit (depending upon the seriousness of the imputed crime). Since this statute carries severe penalties and has to do with accusations which are deliberately fabricated, any conviction made under it is subject to careful scrutiny at higher judicial levels. By contrast, it is relatively easy for a judge to dispose of an obstreperous plaintiff merely by sentencing him under Boulais1459 (ignoring its limiting reference to the emperor) because this statute carries a relatively minor penalty and does not require the judge to find that the accusations deemed by him to be false were deliberately fabricated by the plaintiff.]

Thus, it commonly happens that cases which a judge deems to be baseless are conveniently settled by him through sentencing the plaintiff to maximum bambooing under the statute on accusations which prove to be false. In so doing, no mention is made of that part of the statute limiting such incorrect accusations to those presented by persons who stop the imperial chariot or beat the complaint drum.

As a result, cases of injustice have no means of being corrected whereas knavery is encouraged. Not only is this detrimental to law in general, but more particularly it makes empty words out of the statute concerning false accusations for which increased penalties are in order [Boulais 1474], or the statute concerning accusations of two or more crimes, the more serious of which proves to be false [Boulais 1478]. The effect upon governmental administration and popular morality alike is profound.

We beg Your Majesty to issue an order to the governors-general, governors, military governors, military lieutenant-governors, and metropolitan prefects, instructing them that hereafter whenever a case initially submitted to Peking is then transmitted to them for trial, they are to handle it with justice. If its charges are found accurate, the grievances must be redressed; if found wrong, the false accusations must be punished. Should there be extenuating circumstances, no obstacles should be placed upon possible mitigation of punishment. When, however, citation is made of the statute on presenting accusations which prove to be false, the habitual omission of the clause on stopping the imperial chariot or beating the complaint drum cannot possibly be permitted, simply in order thus to facilitate the disposition of the case.

Imperial Rescript: Let it be as has been deliberated.

262. FEMALE WRONGDOERS
[Statutory References: Staunton 420, Boulais 1698–1703]

Case 262.3, 1831. Memorandum.
Reported in HAHL 27.60/14b–15a.

The Department for Shantung of the Board of Punishments
finds, according to statute [Boulais 1700], that if a woman who is
pregnant becomes guilty of a capital crime, punishment shall not
be applied to her until 100 days after the birth of her child.
However, according to a sub-statute [Boulais 1703a], if a woman
who is pregnant commits a crime for which the sentence is death
by slicing, the total period following the birth before the execution shall be one month. Here the reference of the statute is to
capital punishment generally, whereas the sub-statute refers only
to one kind of capital punishment, namely death by slicing,
which, because the crimes covered are so heinous, may not
properly be delayed unduly.

In the present case, Mrs. Han née Chang injured her father-in-
law by mischance so that he died. For this she was originally sentenced to death by slicing. [See discussion at end of case.] By
imperial rescript, however, this sentence was then changed to
immediate decapitation.

Now, because Mrs. Han has given birth to a child while in
prison, the governor of Shantung asks whether her execution shall
take place only one month after the birth as under her original
sentence, or 100 days afterward as under the revised sentence
issued by imperial rescript.

This Department finds that Mrs. Han's change of sentence now
places her in a different category from a criminal who is really
condemned to death by slicing. It follows that, in accordance
with the above-cited statute on pregnant women guilty of capital
crimes, her execution should not be carried out until 100 days
after the birth of her child. The governor should be informed by
fastest post so that he may act accordingly.

[To understand this case better, it is necessary to know what is
meant when it is said that Mrs. Han injured her father-in-law "by

mischance" so that he died. Unfortunately, the circumstances of the death are not detailed because this is not the point at issue before the Board of Punishments. From Boulais 1283, however, we know that to kill (or injure) by mischance (*wu*) means to have the intention of killing (or injuring) a given individual, but by mischance killing (or injuring) another individual instead. Care should be taken to differentiate the Chinese concept of homicide by mischance from what Western jurists would term homicide by mistake. "Mischance" occurs, for example, when a stone thrown at individual A hits individual B instead, owing either to the thrower's poor aim or the unexpected interposing of individual B in the line of fire. "Mistake" occurs when the thrower hurls his stone at what he believes to be individual A but finds that owing to faulty identification he has struck individual B instead.]

[Because killing (or injuring) by mischance involves deliberate intent (even though it reaches a victim other than the one intended), the penalty for it in the Ch'ing Code is the same as for ordinary homicide in an affray, namely, strangulation after the assizes. Homicide by mischance thus differs from "accidental" (*kuo-shih*) homicide, which, as we have seen (case 166.3), occurs unexpectedly through force of circumstances, involves no malicious intent, and therefore, though nominally also punishable by strangulation after the assizes, is actually commutable from this to a monetary payment.]

[Boulais 1419, wherein a son or his wife receive equal punishment for acts of violence by one or the other against his parents, specifies that if a wife kills a parent-in-law in an affray, she is to undergo death by slicing, whereas if the homicide is caused accidently (*kuo-shih*), she is to be exiled at a distance of 3,000 li. Nothing is said about killing by mischance (*wu*), which, therefore, is implicitly subsumed under the killing of the parent-in-law in an affray. This then explains how Mrs. Han was originally sentenced to death by slicing.]

[In 1813, however, a case occurred which, though it did not add a new sub-statute to the Code, did provide a formula for handling future cases in which a son or his wife killed a parent or parent-in-law by mischance. (The case is summarized in Boulais

1427, and cited *in extenso* in case 191.21, reported in HAHL 19.54/9b–10b.) In this case, Pai P'eng-ho had asked his sister-in-law for oil for his lamp, was refused, quarreled with her, and finally hurled a large clod of earth, which missed her but by mischance hit Pai's mother, who at that moment had appeared on the scene to admonish Pai. The mother fell to the ground, struck her head, and died. Pai was accordingly sentenced to death by slicing on the basis of Boulais 1419, but the Chia-ch'ing Emperor reduced the sentence to immediate decapitation on the grounds that the son had not intended to kill the mother and stated that similar consideration should be shown to future cases of the same sort. A number of cases in HAHL dealing with the killing by mischance of a parent or parent-in-law (see citations in case 191.21 and the several cases immediately following) illustrate the resulting reduction of death by slicing to immediate decapitation or even, in one or two instances, decapitation after the assizes. The present case provides of course yet a further illustration.]

[For general comment on this case, see end of Chapter VI. Here it need only be remarked that the price of filial piety and wifely submission in China, like the price of conventional morality in any other land, could sometimes come terribly high.]

263. IMPROPER EXECUTION OF SENTENCE
[Statutory References: Staunton 422, Boulais 1705a]

Case 263.1, 1826. General Circular.
Reported in HAHL 27.60/15a–b.

The governor of Anhui has memorialized concerning a case occurring in Fou-yang hsien, in which there was a mix-up in the executing of two criminals who had been sentenced to decapitation and strangulation respectively. This memorial has led to the issuing of an imperial edict on August 6 of this year, in which, with regard to the said case, there is the following statement:

Imperial Edict: "Recently there have been repeated errors in the execution of criminals sentenced to decapitation or strangulation. The cause lies always in the failure of the guards to maintain strict discipline, which, coupled with confusion caused by the milling crowds, has prevented a proper check of the condemned criminals. Cases of this kind have really become scandalous. The governors-general and governors, therefore, are informed that from now on they must strictly instruct the magistrates of their provinces that whenever criminals marked for execution at the autumn assizes have been assembled at the execution ground, guards fully sufficient for maintaining good order must be sent there in advance, and crowds of noisy spectators must be prohibited. Moreover, the commanding officer of the local garrison is personally to witness the executions, and not, as in the past, to show a frivolous attitude toward them. This edict is to be generally circulated for the information of those concerned." [The first portion of this edict has been omitted in translation to avoid duplication of what comes below.]

Concerning the present case, the Board of Punishments finds that Li T'ien-kang and Hsü Ssu-pen, two criminals condemned to decapitation and strangulation respectively, were being marched to execution, one of them in front of the other, under the respective custodies of guards P'an Li and P'ei Hsien. So great was the press of spectators, however, that the two prisoners reversed their proper positions by the time they reached the spot of execution, so that Hsü Ssu-pen, who should have been strangled, was wrongly decapitated by the executioner for decapitations, and Li T'ien-kang, who should have been decapitated, was wrongly strangled by the executioner for strangulations.

This error, though unintentional, resulted from the faulty way in which guards P'an Li and P'ei Hsien marched their prisoners. Because the guilt of the two guards is identical, they should each be sentenced to 100 blows of the heavy bamboo, by analogy to the statute on violation of imperial decrees, with, however, a one-degree increase of penalty, thus raising it for them to 60 blows of the heavy bamboo and one year penal servitude. [See Boulais 274 for this catch-all statute, which we have often previously encountered. Its citation analogically permits, of course, the one-degree increase of penalty.]

Inasmuch, however, as P'an Li is the sole adult son of his aged mother, his case should be examined and acted on accordingly. [Reference is to the provision (see Boulais 96 and 99) whereby a criminal who is the only adult son of aged parents may have his sentence of penal servitude or more commuted in various ways so that he may stay at home to care for the parents. See cases 42.1 and 83.1 for application of the principle, as here, to less than capital cases. According to Boulais 99, the commutation of P'an Li's sentence of 60 blows of the heavy bamboo and one year penal servitude would result in the same 60 blows plus one month wearing of the cangue.]

As for the two executioners, they merely knew that the first three prisoners were supposed to be decapitated and the four who followed to be strangled. Thus, without paying any attention to one another, each executed a man who should have been executed by the other. Because this error is due to negligence, they should each be sentenced to 80 blows of the heavy bamboo, this being the heavier penalty provided under the statute on doing what ought not to be done [Boulais 1656; for this catch-all statute, see especially cases 237.1 and 3]. In addition, however, they should also wear the cangue for two months and be dismissed from their jobs.

There are two other yamen employees who did not actually witness the executions but went to the execution ground the following day to collect the bodies, at which time they were the first to discover the mistake. Because they reported it at once and did nothing improper, there is no need to consider them further.

There remains the question of the district magistrate, Li Fu-ch'ing, and his military colleague, Lieutenant Hsü Huai-ch'ing. In his memorial on the case, the governor of Anhui has already recommended that these two men be stripped of official rank. Although both of them personally attended the executions, neither paid adequate attention to what went on, with the result that the mix-up occurred. Such negligence is not comparable to ordinary negligence, so that it would be impolitic to subject them merely to reduction of rank and transfer to another post, as provided in the regulations of the Board of Civil Office. [These regulations, the *Li-pu tse-li*, drawn up by the Board of Civil Office for its own disciplining of members of the civil service, are more detailed, within their particular sphere, than are the comparable statutes in the Code itself.]

In the Code itself, we find, according to statute [the statute on improper execution of sentence, under which the present section is classified], that the penalty for decapitating a criminal who ought by law to have been strangled or for strangling a criminal who ought to have been decapitated is only 60 blows of the heavy bamboo if the act is done deliberately and a three-degree reduction of this penalty [only 30 blows of the light bamboo] if committed through error. Moreover, since these penalties are provided for offenses committed by officials acting in an official rather than a private capacity, it is possible for them to be commuted to mere reductions of official salary.

[For offenses committed by officials in an "official" or "private" capacity, see case 4.2. According to the table in Boulais 70 of commutations for offenses committed by officials in an official capacity, 30 blows of the light bamboo are commutable to three months' forfeiture of salary and 60 blows of the heavy bamboo to one year's forfeiture of salary. It should be remembered that the salaries of Chinese officials were exceedingly low and commonly had to be supplemented by income derived from other, often *sub rosa*, sources.]

Penalties such as these are unduly light for such a serious offense. [They are, indeed, considerably attenuated from the corresponding penalties as given in the T'ang Code of 653 (*T'ang-lü shu-yi*, book 30, article 17), wherein one year of penal servitude is the punishment for improper execution when done deliberately, and 90 blows of the heavy bamboo when done through error.] By comparison, the penalties maintained by the Board of Civil Office are more severe, for they provide a one-degree reduction in official rank and transfer to another post for an official who erroneously permits a strangulation to take place when decapitation was called for, and a two-degree reduction of rank plus transfer to another post when the reverse error occurs—decapitation in place of strangulation.

The Board of Punishments, in its previous handling of such errors, has acted under the statute which provides maximum [three years] penal servitude for a supervisory official who, in the course of his official duties, has his subordinates administer punishment with a knife [or in another illegal manner], thereby causing death. [Boulais 1696 contains a part of the statute here cited, though not this particular portion, on which, however, see case 259.1. As in the above-cited Boulais 274, one may question whether the statute is really properly applicable to the kind of offense for which the Board of Punishments here uses it.] Such a penalty, however, seems excessive when compared with the regulations of the Board of Civil Office. Yet on the other hand, we find that these same regulations make no distinction in penalty between an error in execution affecting only a single criminal and such an error involving a mix-up between two criminals. In the case at bar, the governor of Anhui has proposed that both the district magistrate and the lieutenant be stripped of official rank. This is a more severe penalty [than that provided in the regulations of the Board of Civil Office, yet it is not too severe, as is Boulais 1696]; hence the governor's recommendation should be approved.

In view of the discrepancy between the Board of Punishments' previous handling of cases of this kind, and the corresponding regulations of the Board of Civil Office, we look forward toward the issuing of a general circular for all provinces, stating that henceforth, whenever an improper execution occurs involving a confusion between two prisoners, the civil or military official overseeing the execution is to be stripped of official rank. If, however, the improper execution affects only a single prisoner, the case is then to be transmitted to the Board of Civil Office for handling by it under its own usual regulations. [That is, there will then merely be a one-degree reduction in official rank for the official who has mistakenly allowed strangulation where decapitation is called for and a two-degree reduction for the contrary mistake. In the present case (which itself constitutes the general circular asked for), we see how the Board of Punishments arrives at what is essentially a new law on improper execution of sentence, thereby making the original statute on the subject virtually obsolete.]

[That the circumstances of this case are not unique is indicated by a case reported from Honan in the *Peking Gazette* of April 13, 1888. See *Translations of Peking Gazette from 1st January to 30th June, 1888* (reprinted from the *Chinese Times*, Tientsin: Tientsin Printing Co., 1888); p. 63. There we are told that a soldier from the local garrison, deputed to strangle a condemned prisoner, decapitated the man instead after he himself had become drunk. The penalty for the soldier was dismissal from the army and 100 blows of the heavy bamboo. Two gendarmes who were with him were each given 80 blows for failing to prevent the mistake, and the district magistrate and lieutenant in command of the local garrison were both dismissed from the civil service.]

Case 263.3, 1797. Memorandum.
Reported in HAHL 27.60/16a.

The Department for Shantung of the Board of Punishments finds, according to sub-statute, that when a governor-general or a governor recommends a "light" sentence [strangulation] in a capital case, but the Board of Punishments changes it to a "heavy" one [decapitation], the case must then go back to the Provincial Court for retrial. If, however, the recommended sentence is a "heavy" one [decapitation], but the Board changes it to one that is "light" [strangulation], then, provided the Board's opinion is solidly based, there is no need to remand the case for retrial. [See Boulais 1705b. The sub-statute states further that if there is "something suspicious" about the lighter sentence pronounced by the Board, it too, like a heavier one, must be remanded for retrial to the Provincial Court. However, the sub-statute says nothing as to how and by whom the Board's sentence is to be determined as either "solidly based" or "suspicious."]

This Department has now examined a case in which Cheng Yi attempted to steal from a certain Mrs. Li and, while resisting capture, wounded her with a knife. He failed to get any loot through his theft. The Provincial Court of Shantung has accordingly recommended strangulation for him under the sub-statute [Boulais 1080b] concerning a thief who, before obtaining any loot, flees from the scene with the property owner in pursuit, and wounds the latter with a knife while resisting capture. [The penalty prescribed by this sub-statute is actually strangulation after the assizes rather than simply strangulation.]

Although the thief failed to obtain any loot, his resistance to capture and wounding of the property owner occurred at the scene of the theft itself [and not during subsequent flight]. Hence it is this Board's judgment that the recommended sentence should be reversed and that Cheng Yi should be sentenced instead to decapitation after the assizes, under the statute [Boulais 1063] which provides this penalty for a thief who, when found in the act of stealing, resists capture and thus wounds the property owner.

[Presumably, the punishment imposed for resisting capture at the scene of the theft is more drastic than for doing the same while in flight because flight indicates the thief's desire to avoid violence—despite the fact that his desire is nullified by the property owner's pursuit. By comparison, the thief's failure to obtain loot would seem to have only secondary significance, even though it is a given condition in the sub-statute which, for this very reason, is used by the Shantung Court for sentencing Cheng Yi. The Board of Punishments, on the other hand, brushes this point aside and concentrates upon the fact that Cheng committed his violence at the scene of the theft, rather than during subsequent flight. It therefore sentences him under Boulais 1063 and quite properly so because the Code's Official Commentary on this statute states explicitly that the statute remains operative regardless of whether or not the culprit obtained loot through his theft.]

Because this punishment is heavier than that originally recommended, the case should, in accordance with the sub-statute cited earlier, be remanded to the Shantung Court for retrial.

264. GOVERNMENT CLERKS WRITING
DEPOSITIONS ON BEHALF OF LITIGANTS [28]
[Statutory References: Staunton 423, Boulais 1705c]

Case 264.1, 1831. General Circular Received from the Throne by the Department for Shantung of the Board of Punishments Reported in HAHL 27.60/16b.

Imperial Edict of January 19, 1831, issued in response to a memorial received from the Censor Circuit of Shantung:

---

[28] This statute forbids clerks to prepare such depositions (see also case 203.2 for the parallel prohibition of activities by private "litigation tricksters"), but here the statute, in what is really not a case at all, serves as a mere springboard for an imperial edict dealing with a related but not entirely identical topic.

Censor Pien Shih-yün has requested in a memorial that orders be given to clerks in provincial government offices to cease the practice of affixing their own endorsements to petitions that are submitted. Whenever such petitions, whether weighty or trivial, come before the offices of governors-general, governors, lieutenant-governors, judicial commissioners, directors of education, salt controllers, and grain intendants, they should be verified by these administrators in person without allowing their subordinate clerks to stir up abuses and confusion.

According to Censor Pien, in every provincial office receiving petitions relating to legal cases, the petitioner first goes to the clerk in charge of drafting documents to get his petition put in order. Concerning matters that ought to be accepted, the clerk will quite possibly write a negative rejection, whereas concerning other matters deserving rejection, he may equally possibly write an affirmative endorsement. This decision is then privately leaked to the person concerned prior to formal announcement. Ignorant people are thus readily deceived, and even private secretaries of the administrators may become harmfully involved.

[Below the level of administrators who were members of the civil service, local government offices commonly contained two sets of secretaries and clerks: (1) those paid by the government, who were permanently attached to the office and commonly were natives of the locality; (2) the top administrator's personal staff of private secretaries, paid out of his own pocket and accompanying him from one post to another. The personal loyalty of these men was used by him to check the entrenched local interests commonly represented by the permanent government staff. As can be imagined, not infrequently clashes of interest developed. The subject is admirably treated in T'ung-tsu Ch'ü, *Local Government in China under the Ch'ing*.]

There is no office anywhere where these abuses do not obtain, thereby bringing on adverse administrative consequences not to be belittled. This edict is therefore now issued so that each governor-general and governor may in turn transmit it to all local offices, with instructions that henceforth, whenever petitions are received, all of them, whether significant or insignificant, are to receive the careful personal attention of the administrators concerned. No clerk or private secretary is to be entrusted with the task of accepting or rejecting them, thus opening the door to subterfuges, deceptions, and irregularities. In this way the administrative process will be purged of accumulated abuses and acquire a sense of decorum.

[This edict typifies the eternal dilemma of bureaucracy: how to maintain an honest and efficient administration without killing its top men by overwork.]

265. UNAUTHORIZED CONSTRUCTION WORK
[Statutory References: Staunton 424, Boulais 1706–1708]

Case 265.1, 1807. Memorandum.
Reported in HAHL 27.60/16b–17a.

The Department for Kuangtung of the Board of Punishments finds, according to statute [Boulais 1708a], that if, in a given public construction project, the combined costs of labor and materials exceed the sum which had been allocated, the person responsible shall be punished as though guilty of pecuniary malfeasance. Again, the statute on pecuniary malfeasance [Boulais 1529] states that if a person is guilty of such malfeasance, the total sum he has taken is to be divided in half and the punishment made proportionate to the resulting amount. For example, if this resulting amount is [between 80 and] 100 ounces of silver, his penalty shall be 60 blows of the heavy bamboo and one year penal servitude. [See table in Boulais 1529, where the punishments for sums of one to 400 or more ounces of silver are listed, with a maximum punishment for the latter of three years penal servitude.]

Likewise, according to sub-statute [Boulais 1522a], if an official guilty of pecuniary malfeasance is really able, within a stipulated period, to restore entirely what he has taken, he shall then [depending on the length of the time period] be allowed either the same reduction or the total remission of punishment which is allowed under the corresponding circumstances for one who depletes a government account by juggling funds. [In contrast to pecuniary malfeasance (*tso tsang*), in which the money is taken for personal benefit, the juggling of government funds, here referred to, is done by the official concerned only in order to make good on some other government account with which he is connected or to carry out some government project. See Boulais 1528.] Finally, according to another sub-statute [Boulais 685], if a person, having juggled funds in a government treasury [to cover some other government account or project as just stated], is really able, within a one-year period, to restore the amount in its entirety, his punishment shall be altogether remitted, and if the amount juggled was less than 20,000 ounces of silver, he may be permitted to return to his position.

In the present case, Ch'en P'an-kuei, a naval first captain, who has since been dismissed, found he needed money to repair sails and other equipment of his boats and so diverted funds for this purpose from the payroll of his naval personnel. Furthermore, he was unable to remain within the established allocation for repairs, so that the repair bills resulted in a deficit of 398 ounces of silver. Although investigation has revealed no evidence that any funds were appropriated by him for personal use, his reckless expenditures are nonetheless a violation of law. He should, therefore, be punished under the first statute cited above stating that expenditures for public construction, when exceeding the allocated amount, are punishable as would be pecuniary malfeasance. Under the second statute cited above, giving the procedure for thus calculating punishment, the present offender's deficit of 398 ounces is to be divided in half; the resulting figure means a penalty for him of 60 blows of the heavy bamboo and one year penal servitude. [This seems to be a manifest error. One half of 398 is 199, and according to the table in Boulais 1529, any sum between 100 and 200 ounces of silver is punishable by 70 blows of the heavy bamboo and one and one half years penal servitude. To incur the lesser punishment of one year penal servitude, the sum involved must be over 80 but under 100 ounces.]

This Department finds, however, that the said former officer has, during the year since his dismissal, succeeded in completely repaying the deficit. Therefore, under the second of the two substatutes cited above, he should receive a remission of punishment and be restored to his former position.

This case is now transmitted to the Board of War so that, in accordance with its regulations, it may handle the cancellation of its earlier directive calling for his dismissal.

266. CONSTRUCTION NOT ACCORDING TO PLAN
[Statutory References: Staunton 426, Boulais 1710–1711]

Case 266.1, 1809. Leading Case.
Reported in HAHL 27.60/17a.

This case concerns a dike which was built in a river so as to create a reservoir for growing lotus, and which, because its foundations were laid on a silty bottom, gave way after completion, causing severe loss not only to government storehouses but also to the fields and houses of persons downstream.

The Department for Kiangsu of the Board of Punishments finds that a certain petty military officer, Ch'ien Yün, is the man who, with an eye to self-advancement, recklessly urged this faulty construction. Ch'ien Yün should be sentenced by analogy to the statute [Boulais 1710] which provides penalties up to penal servitude for a public construction made in violation of the proper plan; in his case, however, the penalty for so doing should be increased to hard labor in military exile in Ili.

[This, the severest of all kinds of exile, is a considerable jump from the maximum penalty of 100 blows of the heavy bamboo and three years penal servitude provided by Boulais 1710 for faulty public construction. Presumably, the Board bases the increase on the fact that it applies the statute analogically rather than directly. Normally, however, an increase thus brought about is for one degree only, whereas here, according to the standard formula used for calculating such increases, the rise is much more than one degree. See case 188.2, where again we encounter an unexpectedly large increase of penalty.]

[Conceivably, use here of the statute analogically may also indicate that no plan had been made in advance for the construction of the reservoir; totally unauthorized construction would usually be more serious than unauthorized departures from projects properly undertaken.]

267. MANUFACTURE OF SILKS BEARING FIGURES OF THE IMPERIAL DRAGON OR PHOENIX [29]
[Statutory References: Staunton 429, Boulais 1712]

Case 267.2, 1779. Source of Case Not Indicated.
Reported in HAHL 27.60/18a–b

This case concerns Wei Yü-chen, a licentiate of Kan-yü hsien in Kiangsu, now already deprived of his degree, who in preparing a biographical memoir of his deceased father, improperly made use of the word *shê* (amnesty).

[A licentiate (*sheng yüan*) is one who has passed the lowest of the several sets of civil service examinations. *Shê* generally means "to forgive, to remit, to pardon," but it also has the narrower technical meaning of "to amnesty" or "an amnesty." Because only the emperor had the right to declare an amnesty, use of this word when describing the actions of anyone else, especially someone acting in an administrative capacity, could by a suspicious government be construed as *lèse-majesté*, since it would suggest that the person was doing what only an emperor could do.]

Wei Yü-chen's father, who died in 1778, had been in charge of the local community granary, in which capacity he had allowed peasants who were poor to forgo their grain interest payments. When Wei prepared a biographical memoir of his father after death, he improperly used the word *shê* (to excuse, to amnesty) to describe the manner in which his father had "excused" (*shê*) the interest payments or payments of long overdue accounts of the peasants.

Wei's grandfather had, like himself, been a licentiate. By outsiders, however, he had been regarded as only fair in literary ability. To bolster the grandfather's literary reputation, therefore,

[29] The dragon (*lung*) and so-called phoenix (*feng*, actually a pheasant-like mythological bird) were, in imperial China, symbols of the emperor and empress respectively; hence the wearing of fabrics embroidered with them was forbidden to ordinary people. The present statute provides 100 blows of the heavy bamboo for anyone who without authority manufactures silks bearing the figures of dragons or phoenixes and 100 blows plus three years penal servitude for one who buys and contumaciously uses them; if he buys but does not use them, the punishment is reduced to 30 blows of the light bamboo. What is essentially the same statute, but slightly differently worded, appears also elsewhere in the Code under Boulais 837.

Wei wrote in the same biographical memoir that his grandfather had been the author of an unpublished work called *Sung-hsi-t'ang kao* (Draft writings from the hall west of the pinetree), that he had filled the east and west halls of his house with books, and that many of these bore his own handwritten marginal annotations.

Upon the publication of the biographical memoir, a secondary paternal uncle of Wei Yü-chen, to whom a copy had been sent, noticed the word *shê* in the text and informed Wei of its impropriety. Since the memoir had already been distributed, however, Wei could only reply in defense that impropriety was out of the question, since the word is found in one of the Confucian "Four Books" in the phrase, "forgive (*shê*) minor errors." [See *Analects*, XIII, 2, where Confucius, speaking about good government, lists among its desiderata the ability to "forgive minor errors."] Thereupon the uncle, fearing lest he himself might become involved in trouble, reported the matter to the local director of schools. The result was a personal visit to Wei of official representatives from the provincial capital. Their search of his house, however, revealed no trace of the book alleged by Wei to have been written by his grandfather, no treasonable annotations written in any books belonging to the household, and no large collections of books in the east and west halls, in which grain was stored instead.

On the other hand, the search did bring to light a genealogy of the Wei family in whose text the term *shih-piao* (table by generations) occurred. [This term first appears in Chinese literature as part of the title of the thirteenth chapter of the earliest of the dynastic histories, the *Shih chi* or *Historical Records* (composed ca. 85 B.C.). The chapter in question is entitled *San-tai shih-piao* or "Table by Generations of the Three Dynasties," and consists of a listing, in tabular form, of the rulers of the first three Chinese dynasties. Use of the term *shih-piao* in the genealogy of an ordinary family, therefore, might be construed as showing that in the eyes of the author of the genealogy, the successive generations of his family were comparable to the rulers of these ancient dynasties—obviously a subversive idea.]

This family genealogy was also found to contain statements similar to those in the biographical memoir concerning Wei's grandfather's ownership of numerous books, and his authorship of a work entitled *Sung-hsi-t'ang kao,* with the added information that a biographical preface to the latter work had been written by a certain scholar who was a native of Jih-chao hsien, Shantung. Inquiry among family relatives and friends, however, revealed no knowledge on any of these points, and further inquiry in Jih-chao hsien indicated that the scholar in question had long since died and that no one in his family knew of any compositions by him.

Under intensified questioning, Wei Yü-chen finally admitted that all the above statements concerning his grandfather had been concocted by himself in order to refute those who had belittled the grandfather's literary attainments, and that the prefatory biography and its attribution to the Shantung scholar were likewise inventions. Wei insisted, however, that the improper use of the word *shê* (amnesty) was entirely due to ignorance and not to any deliberate intention on his part.

It has been recommended [by the governor of Kiangsu] that Wei Yü-chen should not only be stripped of his licentiate degree (which has already been done), but that he should further be sentenced to 100 blows of the heavy bamboo under the statute on violation of imperial decrees [Boulais 274]. The wooden blocks used for printing the biographical memoir of his father and his family genealogy should be destroyed. However, since nothing offensive has been found in the other books belonging to him, they may be returned to him. [Here, as in case 263.1, the statute on violation of imperial decrees seems to be used in a somewhat loose manner to punish any less-than-major instance of *lèse-majesté.*]

This Board agrees that aside from the improper use of the terms *shê* and *shih-piao* in the biographical memoir and family genealogy respectively, no other trace of subversion has been found. It nevertheless regards such improper usage as constituting contumacious insubordination (*chien wang*), and hence as not comparable with the mere violation of imperial decrees. There is, however, no specific article in the Code covering insubordination of this kind. Hence the judgment must be based on analogy.

As the holder of an examination degree, Wei Yü-chen ought to know *something* at least about the meaning of words. Yet he made no effort to avoid contumaciously using the terms *shê* and *shih-piao,* from which it follows that his crime of contumacious insubordination should be judged by analogy to the statute [Boulais 1712] providing 100 blows of the heavy bamboo and three years penal servitude for the contumacious use of silks bearing the figures of the dragon or phoenix. This punishment is to serve as a warning to others.

As to Wei Yü-chen's secondary paternal uncle who reported the matter to the authorities, he in so doing was motivated by no feeling of enmity but was merely fearful that he himself might get into trouble. Hence there is no need to deliberate further concerning him.

We memorialize the throne for approval of this case.

[There is much of interest in this case. Politically, the fact that a man could be given three years penal servitude for what seems to have been an entirely unintentional misuse of terminology exemplifies the almost paranoic fear of sedition found among many of China's Manchu rulers during this age. (See also Chapter VI, section 4.) It is significant in this regard that the provincial governor would have been content to punish the culprit with 100 blows of the heavy bamboo and forfeiture of his examination degree (already, it would seem, a considerable penalty), whereas the Board of Punishments, being close to the throne in Peking, insisted on a still stronger punishment. The date of this case (1779) came during the height of the government-organized campaign against allegedly seditious writings (ca. 1774–1788)—a campaign so effective that it wiped out for posterity more than 1,500 separate works. See L. Carrington Goodrich, *The Literary Inquisition of Ch'ien-lung* (Baltimore, 1935). It should be stressed, however, that fear of sedition was by no means peculiar to the Manchus. In varying degrees it has characterized the Confucian state ever since its formation in the second century B.C. Likewise, the search for esoteric seditious meanings in seemingly innocent words and phrases is an ancient one.]

[Legally speaking, the age-old Chinese preoccupation with

sedition makes it strange that the Ch'ing Code contained no specific statute dealing with this kind of improper use of language. Failing such a statute, it would seem that the Board of Punishments might have done better than make analogical use of Boulais 1712 (the statute on dragons and phoenixes). Boulais 283, for example, deals with the lèse-majesté involved in another kind of improper use of language, namely the insertion in various kinds of official documents of words constituting the personal names of the reigning emperor or his dynastic predecessors, for which it provides penalties ranging up to 100 blows of the heavy bamboo. (The taboo on uttering or writing the personal names of reigning emperors or other famous individuals, such as Confucius, probably goes back in China to the ancient magical idea, found also in other cultures, that by manipulating the personal name of a given individual, one acquires the power to control or harm the individual himself.) Probably, however, the Board refused to consider this statute (just as it rejected Boulais 274, which had been recommended by the provincial governor), precisely because it wanted a sterner penalty for what it (or at least the Ch'ien-lung Emperor) regarded as a very serious offense. This is suggested by the Board's added remark that the punishment "is to serve as a warning to others."]

[Socially and psychologically, the victim's compulsive need to glorify his father and rehabilitate his grandfather's literary reputation reflects the emphasis in Confucian China upon literary attainment as *the* one means to achieve prestige and power via government service. It also reflects the psychological insecurity of a person who, no doubt ambitious himself, belonged to a family probably living just on the borderline dividing the privileged gentry from the great mass of commoners. The degree of licentiate held both by Wei and his grandfather was, it will be remembered, the lowest of all literary degrees. As such it did not suffice, without further higher degrees, to give access to the coveted ranks of the civil service. Probably even this lowest degree, moreover, had not been held by Wei's father, or it would certainly have been mentioned. The fact that he had been in charge of the local community granary (*shê ts'ang*) means nothing in this connection, since this kind of granary, in contrast to the government's granaries, was privately supported and privately staffed by local persons who were not members of the civil service. See Kung-chuan Hsiao, *Rural China, Imperial Control in the Nineteenth Century*, pp. 149 ff.]

[Finally, one may wonder about the motivation of Wei's secondary paternal uncle (actually his father's cousin) when he revealed Wei's literary error to the authorities and thereby plunged him into disaster. Did the uncle really do this, as asserted, simply in order to save his own skin? Or was he perhaps jealous of the praise lavished upon his deceased cousin in the biographical memoir? The very insistence by the Board of Punishments upon the uncle's lack of personal enmity may cause some persons perversely to suspect that there may have been more to the uncle's act of betrayal than appears upon the surface. However, his act is also understandable, though still reprehensible, when we remember that this was the very period when the government was busily searching the houses of private individuals for allegedly subversive literature.]

269. FAILURE TO REPAIR DIKES AT THE PROPER TIME
[Statutory References: Staunton 434, Boulais 1718–1720]

Case 269.1, 1812. Memorandum.
Reported in HAHL 27.60/21a–b.

The governor of Chihli has reported a case in which Li Chia-shen encouraged Sun P'u and others to organize mass opposition to government labor services.

This Board finds, according to sub-statute [Boulais 1719a], that if, while urgently needed [emergency] river conservancy work is in progress, someone fabricates loose talk which induces large numbers of workers to relax their efforts, the person responsible shall suffer decapitation after the assizes.

In the present case, it should be noted that in the villages flanking the dikes of the Yung-ting River [not far from Peking] there are certain men who, like Li Chia-shen, are known as emergency workers (*hsien fu*), each of whom enjoys the use of

6.5 *mou* of cultivatable land allotted by the government [about one acre]. Whenever river conservancy work becomes necessary, such as straightening out a bend in the channel, these men are called upon to dig and carry away the earth. For every "square" of earth [*t'u fang*, 10 cubic Chinese feet] thus handled, they are paid four *fen* [0.04 ounces of silver].

In the spring of last year so many squares had to be dug out that various workers staged a slowdown. Sun P'u, a local village representative, noticed the workers' unwillingness and consulted with Li Chia-shen, who conceived the idea of organizing mass opposition to the work. Li told Sun and others to ask for a reduction of work and, when this request was refused, to avoid further work by returning the money already paid them for the earth they had previously removed. Various other villages along the river began similar protests. Li, realizing that the matter might reach the law courts, told Sun and others to collect money from each worker for possible use. When this news reached the attention of the local military post head, he ordered Sun arrested, and Sun, while resisting arrest, injured one of the river-conservancy gendarmes.

The Provincial Court of Chihli has found that this particular conservancy project was a routine job of river dredging not involving any kind of emergency. Moreover, Li's plan for cutting down the work load by handing back the previous pay was conceived only after the workers themselves had relaxed their efforts and Sun P'u had come to him for advice. This is different from fabricating loose talk so as to impede urgently needed [emergency] conservancy work.

The Provincial Court has accordingly sentenced Li Chia-shen to life exile, a penalty one degree less than the decapitation prescribed by the above-cited statute for someone fabricating loose talk during the carrying out of urgently needed river conservancy work, thereby inducing large numbers of workers to relax their efforts. The Court has likewise sentenced Sun P'u, as an accessory, to penal servitude. [Under Boulais 110, an accessory receives a penalty one degree less than the principal. Because Li's penalty was probably exile at a distance of 3,000 li, a one-degree reduction of this (see Boulais 111 for the manner in which such reductions are calculated) would mean a penalty for Sun of three years penal servitude. Here again, as in many earlier cases, the sub-statute is applied directly rather than analogically, despite the reduction of penalty.]

However, because Sun resisted arrest, the Court has increased this basic penalty by two degrees, resulting in a final penalty for him of life exile. [A two-degree increase from three years penal servitude results in life exile at a distance of 2,500 li. Boulais 1658, after specifying such a two-degree increase for ordinary resistance to arrest, goes on to provide strangulation after the assizes for one who breaks the finger or toe of the person making the arrest or inflicts comparable injury. Because no mention is made of this point here, we must assume that the injury inflicted by Sun on the gendarme was less serious.]

This Board finds that though the workers themselves started the slowdown because of the great amount of earth they had to move, it was nevertheless Li Chia-shen who initiated for them the plan of asking for a reduction of work and returning the pay. He therefore cannot but be tried on the charge of instigating loose talk. However, the sub-statute which provides decapitation after the assizes for this offense very clearly has reference to river conservancy work of an urgent nature. Emergency work of this sort cannot be mentioned in the same breath with ordinary year-to-year dredging and repairing. Yet it is just such routine work that the Provincial Court has found to be involved in the present case, for which reason it has separately sentenced each of the two offenders to penalties which are less than that specified in the above-cited statute on fabricating loose talk. This Board finds these sentences to accord with the circumstances of the case, and therefore deems it appropriate to send back a confirmatory reply.

[This case may be compared with cases 87.1 and 87.2 as examples of incipient labor movements. In all of them, the labor leaders are harshly punished. The payment here to the workers of 0.04 ounces of silver for every 10 cubic feet of earth removed may be compared with the figure of 0.855 ounces of silver suggested in Boulais 1706 as the proper daily wage for a worker engaged in government construction projects. For such an amount to be earned by one of our river conservancy workers, he would have to handle more than 200 cubic feet of earth per day. We may deduce that the emergency workers along the Yung-ting River more than earned the one-acre plots allotted them by the government.]

270. ENCROACHMENT UPON PUBLIC THOROUGHFARES
[Statutory References: Staunton 435, Boulais 1721]

Case 270.1, 1820. Leading Case.
Reported in HAHL 27.60/21b.

The governor of Shansi has reported that Yen Wang-nien, while repairing his shop, erected a surrounding wall which encroached upon [probably touched] the wall of the eastern enclosure of the [Imperial Confucian] Academy of Learning.

By analogy to the statute on erecting buildings which encroach upon public thoroughfares [Boulais 1721], Yen Wang-nien is sentenced to 60 blows of the heavy bamboo, in addition to which he is to wear the cangue for one month.

[This case presumably took place in the capital of Shansi, Taiyuan. The statute is used analogically rather than directly because the offense of encroaching upon an imperial educational building is different from and obviously more serious than encroachment upon an ordinary thoroughfare and as such calls for something additional (in this case the wearing of the cangue) to the ordinary statutory penalty of 60 blows.]

Part Three

STATUTORY INTERPRETATION EXEMPLIFIED IN THE CASES

STATUTORY INTERPRETATION
EXEMPLIFIED IN THE CASES

Introduction

When judges apply statutes they usually have no doubts about
the meaning of the enacted words. In, for example, the Lindberg
kidnapping case the New Jersey judge had no occasion to grapple
with the legislature's statutory definition of kidnapping. Nevertheless, in any system of statutory law, cases that raise doubts
about the applicability of an enactment are bound to occur.

The reach of a statute can be understood about as well by a
foreign scholar as by a local legal pundit if the foreigner's cultural
environment is similar to that of the state where the statute was
enacted. In the United States the meaning of state statutes
readily crosses state boundaries. Law and its language, however,
are rooted in culture. The legal processes of peoples whose
cultures differ sometimes have seeming likenesses that engender a
false sense of understanding. The preconceptions of an outland
reader of reported cases may warp his understanding. Therefore
it is appropriate at the beginning of this essay on interpretation of
Chinese Ch'ing criminal statutes to warn the Western reader that
strands of our own background may impede our undertaking.

Western judges have, of course, been applying statutes to cases
for a long time. Statutes were, however, of minor importance
until modern legislation burgeoned in the nineteenth century. *Les
Cinq Codes* were promulgated in France in 1803 and 1804 and
inspired codification in most other countries of continental Europe. No doubt this surge of legislation enlivened the legislative
process even in those common law countries where codification
was abjured. One pressure that produced nineteenth-century
enactments was the eighteenth-century philosophic demand for
preformulated legal principles. Three Western advocates of "settling the law" before cases arose were especially influential.

David Hume championed fixed legal rules so that property rights would be stabilized and industry and commerce would flourish.[1] The role of law in society, as Hume would have it, required not only a system of settled principles, but also their literal interpretation. Hume thought that law-making judges (swayed by prejudice aroused by concrete cases) disrupt the social order and thus threaten prosperity. Hume's remedy for this evil was stated legal principles strictly construed. Whenever literalism of this sort is found in the *Hsing-an hui-lan*, it is motivated by different considerations and may, therefore, have a different impact. Commercial stability had, at least in theory, a low priority in traditional China; tradesmen were regarded with suspicion and commerce was restricted to minor enterprise. Business disputes rarely were settled by public officials; they were mediated in the privacy of guilds rather than in the yamens. The impetus given to inexorable legal processes by Western mercantilism and capitalistic industry was not at work in China.

Montesquieu also espoused promulgated law. His rationale, however, was quite different from Hume's. Legislation, in Montesquieu's system, was needed to effect a separation of powers between the maker of policy and the applier of the law. Great power is, he thought, susceptible of great abuse. If one arm of the government settles the law in advance of dispute and another arm applies it to cases that arise thereafter, the law will not be unduly favorable to powerful litigants and will not subvert the people's liberties.[2] Of course in this system no judge should substitute his predilections for the legislature's policies. It would seem, however, that judges applying legislative policies can effectuate their office in cases of doubt about the meaning of statutory words only by trying to search out the genuine intention of the legislator. Judges do their job well only if they try to discern and honor legislative purpose. A Chinese official applying the Ch'ing Code was also expected to discern its genuine meaning, but the system was designed neither to separate powers nor to protect citizens'

[1] David Hume, *A Treatise of Human Nature*, Vol. II, Book III (1740). See especially Part II, Sec. III–VI.
[2] Baron de Montesquieu, *The Spirit of Laws* (1748). See especially Book XI, Chap. VI.

liberties. Chinese legal processes were not affected by any such scheme of separation of powers.

Rousseau added a dimension to the function of Western legislation. In his view the proper authors of legal principles were no fewer than the entire citizenry expressing "the general will." The "particular will" of a judge who decides a case ad hoc is, according to Rousseau, likely to be unwise at best and tyrannical at worst. Only when the law was preformulated (by stating the general will before cases arose) did the deep-rooted and fair-minded wisdom of the people assure justice.[3] To the Chinese the idea of popular participation in framing statutes was unthinkable. Occasionally, there was a hint in Chinese political theory that wisdom lies in the people's collective mind. The proper Chinese lawgiver, however, is an emperor. The Ch'ing Code was not supposed to give form to popular justice; it was never challenged on the ground that it was framed by elite scholar–officials for imperial promulgation.

What, then, were the general ideas on the function of statutes that affected the Ch'ing officials' interpretation? The answer to this question is complex, and I can only attempt to make a few observations which may throw a little light on the subject.

There is significance of the first order in the recurring denomination by the Chinese of their penal laws as punishments (*hsing*) instead of as statutes (*fa* or *lü*). The term *hsing* occurs in early and late writings about law. The *Lü hsing* in the *Documents Classic* (from the fourth century B.C. or earlier) contains the word for statutes (*fa*); it shows, however, no concern for description, classification, or definition of kinds of criminal conduct; it is focused on the need to assign suitable punishments to acts already known to be criminal. Whenever any government undertakes for the first time to promulgate statutes it is likely to draw on unorganized prevailing ideas and practices; at the outset of any system of penal legislation, statutes usually formulate and regularize pre-existing law. In China, however, propriety had reached a high degree of systematization before penal statutes were first promulgated. Professor Bodde tells us that "In China, perhaps even more than in most other civilizations, the ordinary

[3] Jean Jacques Rousseau, *The Social Contract* (1762). See especially Book II.

man's awareness and acceptance of [ethical norms] was shaped far more by the pervasive influence of custom and the usages of propriety than by any formally enacted law." The ancient feudal king who speaks in the *Lü hsing* says, "Now when you tranquilize the people . . . what should you carefully attend to, if not the punishments?" [4] He discusses undue harshness and undeserved leniency in detail and urges "reverent carefulness" in assessing the right punishment for each wrongdoing.

Two millennia later we find the Chinese still preoccupied with fitting the punishment to the crime. The highest judicial body through much of the history of imperial China is called the *Hsing pu*, the Board of Punishments. The Board is concerned in nearly all of its cases with whether or not the accused has been sentenced to the right amount of punishment; the Board seldom feels that it is called on to consider whether or not the accused is guilty or innocent.

This focus on apt punishments has affected both the process of drafting Chinese statutes and the process of applying them. Professor Bodde, in discussing the Chinese need for punishments that fit the crime, says, "The [imperial] codes always endeavor to foresee all possible variations of any given offense and to provide specific penalties for each." The exact punishment for violating a statute is an integral part of that statute. A magistrate who finds an accused guilty of violating a statute is, in theory, given no discretion in sentencing; the proper sentence is the single punishment specified in the statute defining the crime. If all who violate a statute must be given the same punishment, and if that punishment is to fit all of their crimes, then all must have committed equally serious offenses. If the same kind and amount of punishment were provided for misdeeds of varying seriousness, some convicts would be punished too harshly or too leniently. The designers of the imperial codes tried to avoid unsuitable punishments by defining each crime narrowly and by providing separately for each possible variation.

When such a narrow statute needs interpretation, limited

[4] Bernhard Karlgren, tr., "The Book of Documents," *Bulletin of the Museum of Far Eastern Antiquities* (Stockholm, 1950), 22:76.

(rather than extended) application is likely to be appropriate. If a statute carrying a drastic penalty would, when interpreted literally, be applicable to both some serious wrongs and some less serious ones, judicial fidelity to the system is likely to call for an interpretation excluding the less serious wrongs. This kind of interpretation need never result in the acquittal of those guilty of the lesser offenses; later discussion will show that an alternative opportunity to sentence them to an appropriate lighter penalty always existed.

Similarly, when a statute calling for mild punishment would when interpreted literally apply both to minor wrongs and to some more serious ones, judicial fidelity to the system is likely to call for an interpretation excluding the more serious ones. Such an interpretation will not acquit the serious wrongdoers; there is always some other route to their more drastic punishment.

The Chinese view of imperial franchise tends to strengthen the importance of assessing criminal punishments that fit the crime. In remote antiquity it was believed that a ruler could retain the throne only as long as he was heaven's mandatary. Heaven withdrew its mandate whenever the ruler neglected to restore disrupted natural harmony. Natural harmony was thought to flow from both the moral order and physical orderliness. Crimes produce discord; once a crime is committed, harmony is restored only by suitable punishment. An inept punishment is as bad as, or worse than, none; it will not restore natural harmony; on the contrary, it will disrupt order still further.

In the third century B.C., the first Ch'in Emperor extended the tenets of the Legalist school to all of his empire. The Legalists did not approve of the practice of varying punishments on the basis of differences in the social and family status of either the wrongdoer or his victim. The Ch'in Emperor tried to promulgate laws which clearly identified and forbade various crimes, but he forwent complicated and minutely scheduled punishments based on finespun gradations of evil. The Legalist theory was that the population should be terrified away from wrongdoing by threats of severe punishment; the function of law, the Legalists thought, is not reconstitution of order after every human disturbance; it is prevention of human disorder by forehandedness.[5] The severity of the Ch'in punishments was one cause of the disaffection that doomed the dynasty to early demise.

The succeeding Han dynasty purported to set aside Legalism and return to milder Confucianism. In one respect, however, Confucianism was never restored. Professor Bodde has shown us that the Confucianists disliked preformulated rules of law and preferred the judgment of each case as it arose on an ad hoc basis. There were two reasons (one practical and one theoretical) why the Han and succeeding dynasties continued the Legalist practice of imperially promulgated criminal laws. (1) Before Ch'in and under "feudalism," princes who had local autonomy warred on each other—sometimes with the hope of conquering the whole empire. Imperial rule became solider by the establishment of a centrally controlled national government. One of the incidents of such a centralized government was a national system of criminal law and justice administered by local officials responsible to the emperor. All dynasties after the Ch'in continued this feature of Legalism. (2) Confucian society deemed itself based on the five major relations: father and son, ruler and subject, husband and wife, elder and younger brother, friend and friend. Under feudalism all these relations, including ruler–subject, were personal relations; even humble subjects were not utterly remote from their rulers. In unified China, however, most of the emperor's far-flung subjects could not aspire to so much as a glimpse of the walls surrounding the imperial palace. The relation of ruler and subject existed only through intermediacy of the emperor's surrogates. It was a palpable relationship only when the surrogate personified the emperor by acting on the emperor's instructions. Over the wide empire, then, application of law that had been promulgated by the emperor gave substance to the relationship between ruler and subject.

In two respects, however, law could be and was purged of the Legalist theory. (1) Legalist criminal statutes were inflexibly harsh—a serious defect from the Confucian point of view. Overly

[5] See J. J. L. Duyvendak, tr. *The Book of Lord Shang* (London, 1928), pp. 179–80, 278–80.

severe punishments offended heaven and threatened the emperor's mandate. (2) Punishment, as such, does not (in Confucian theory) *prevent* disruption of natural harmony; law is *restorative* once discord occurs. The Confucian emperor inspires good order by moral leadership and example. In Professor Bodde's description of the Confucian posture, *li* (principles of morals and propriety) are seen as preventive; they turn people away from evil; law is remedial; it functions only after evil is committed. If law can count only retrospectively, then its value is only restorative; if punishments are exacted to re-attune nature, punishments must be calculated to fit the crime.

Both of these Confucian aspects of punishment tend to divert draftsmen of statutes and the judicial officers away from trying to deter wrongs. Punishment is exacted not to teach that crime does not pay, it is levied to placate heaven. Of course, this attitude toward punishment is not held so exclusively that deterrence is always and entirely out of mind. From time to time in the *Hsing-an hui-lan* the judicial officers expressly try to make an example of a wrongdoer.[6] An unexpressed aim to deter wrongdoing through punishment may be an important aspect of the judicial process during the Ch'ing dynasty. Nevertheless the Ch'ing legal system follows after and is closely modeled on systems running back to the Han dynasty. The Ch'ing Code was written as a variant of the Ming Code, which, though different in arrangement and detail, more or less took its principles from the T'ang Code and codes based on the T'ang. The practice of fitting the punishment to the crime had put its mark on Chinese law for nearly two thousand years. The dynastic codes all narrowly described crimes (not criminals) and treated the gradations of the five punishments as a scale of retribution calculated to undo the harm done by the disrupter of good order.

[6] See case 93.1, in which the Imperial Clan Court requests "as a warning to others" that miscreants be deprived of their positions as nobles; case 124.1, in which a department of the Board of Punishments after discussing a lighter sentence says, "This would still not serve as an adequate public warning. Therefore Te-t'ai should be sentenced to two months wearing of the cangue, followed by deportation to Kirin as a slave"; case 159.3, in which a heavy penalty is recommended by the Board of Punishments to "serve as a warning to lewd and evil persons." Similar expressions are found in cases 17.1, 171.5, 172.4, and 267.2.

Anciently, it was thought by some scholars that threats of punishment would not deter. In the *Tao-te Ching* [7] the Taoist sage says, "The more laws and orders are made prominent, the more thieves and robbers there will be." He seems to be making a statement of fact, as well as espousing the policy of governmental inactivity prized by the Taoists and (to a lesser extent) by the Confucianists.[8] In any event the Legalist view that *drastic* penalties deter seems to play little part in Ch'ing dynasty statutory interpretation. The *Hsing-an hui-lan* cases exemplify a Board of Punishments more often concerned with assessing the most appropriate punishment rather than the most effective one. This concern is not based on a Humean desire for legal stability that will promote commerce, or on a Montesquieuean desire to protect liberty through dividing governmental power so that different men make and apply the law, or a Rousseauian hope of conforming law to the wisdom of the general will. The aim of the Board of Punishments seems to be the effectuation of imperial commands in such a way that the social order is vindicated and the supervisory obligations of ruler to subject are discharged.

Clear Statutes, Clearly Applicable

Often the application of a statute involves no subtle understanding of the goals of the legal system. In Li Mao-Erh's case (21.38), the accused raped a girl. He evaded the authorities for ten years before being brought to justice. The statutory punishment for rape is decapitation after the assizes. The Code's provisions concerning fugitives from justice are: (1) If the criminal has been guilty of a serious homicide calling for immediate execution, such execution is to be carried out unchanged following his capture. (2) If the criminal has been guilty of a lesser kind of homicide calling only for execution after the assizes, the sentence is, upon his capture, to be increased to immediate execution. (3) If, however, the criminal is guilty of an offense other than homicide for which the penalty, nonetheless, consists of execution after the assizes, such penalty is to be carried out fol-

[7] Chap. 57.
[8] Confucius, in *Analects*, XV, 4.

lowing the capture without any change. The defendant's flight was clearly an instance of the third statutory provision. The wisdom of legislation providing that non-homicidal capital offenders should not have their sentences increased because of their truancy seems obvious to the outsider; the drastic punishment of the original offense seems, to say the least, harsh enough. An observer familiar with post-conviction procedures applicable to those sentenced to execution after the assizes (which allow a wide range of sentence adjustment) can even better appreciate the soundness of the statutory provision abjuring automatic increase of punishment for eluding the authorities.

The aptness of a statutory punishment may be so patent that even the emperor's doubts become stilled. In Sun Shou-chih's case (147.2) the accused had assaulted and broken the thigh of a man whom he caught stealing his tree branches. The statutory punishment for inflicting such an injury is three years penal servitude. The victim was, however, a senior relative of the accused. Another statute provided that when a junior relative strikes a senior his punishment for such a battery is to be increased one degree. The provincial governor who forwarded this case, following this clear statutory direction, had increased the defendant's sentence to life exile. The emperor said that he had doubts about the increase, since the victim, by his own misconduct, had provoked the attack; the initial imperial endorsement ordered reconsideration of the sentence. The Board of Punishments took issue with the emperor! The Board pointed out that the statute on theft from relatives underpins the governor's sentence in two ways: (1) The statute reduces punishment when theft is from a relative—thus implying that this victim's theft was not a provocation so mitigating as would be a stranger's theft. (2) The statute provides that should a theft from a relative lead to killing or wounding, "priority is to be given to these more serious offenses"—thus clearly indicating, said the Board, that bodily harm to a senior relative involved in theft is graver than a similar injury inflicted on a stranger–thief. The family-theft statute is, of course, a reflection of traditional Chinese attitudes on family relations. To one who respects this tradition the words of the assault and battery statute increasing the penalty for striking a senior relative mean what they say. In his second endorsement, the emperor reluctantly, but with conviction, says, "It is only possible to grant a confirmatory reply for the earlier sentence as requested." Note that the Board boldly advised the emperor that he ought to stand fast to the meaning of his statute, that his passing whim ought to give way to his more soundly based statutory principle. The Board did not say, of course, that the emperor lacked power to rule capriciously; the Board meant only that proper imperial rule calls for fidelity to the meaning of the emperor's own sound laws.

Those at home in the intellectual climate can, in some cases, understand literal sense that might elude the outlander. In Wang Ssu's case (164.1) the defendant had participated in an attack resulting in two deaths. A confederate of the defendant died of illness in prison while he awaited trial for those homicides. The statutory effect of this death due to illness on the punishment of the living confederates is reduction from strangulation to life exile. Professor Bodde's discussion of *ti ming*, appended to the report of this case, sets out the long history of the Chinese practice of requiting a life to restore cosmic order. An understanding of the cultural background of the statute providing for this commutation is needed to make the statute mean convincingly what it literally says. Similarly, those statutes which provide that fathers who kill their sons shall receive little or no punishment make sense only to those who know about Chinese attitudes on filial piety.[9]

Literalism, however, has an independent force when no aspect of culture tends to challenge it. Su Lo-pi's case (9.1) may be an example. The principal defendant was a household slave. His bannerman master reported to the authorities that the defendant had been repeatedly drunk. He was, according to statute, unquestionably liable to deportation to military slavery at a frontier. Whether or not relatives accompanied a convicted husband into exile depended, at that time, on his wishes and his financial ability to pay for their travel. A statute, however, dealt specifically with deportation of bannermen's household slaves for drunkenness. It provided, "The slave's wife and children . . . *are* to be deported with him," all to become slaves to frontier troops.

[9] See cases 191.1, 159.2, 167.5, 263.3.

The statute makes some exceptions not applicable to this case and then continues, "In no event are [wives and children] to be permitted to continue in the services of their original master." A department of the Board of Punishments ignored this last clause and returned the slave–defendant's family to their original master. The department, in so doing, probably relied on an earlier case in which traveling expenses were not allowed to a family who wanted to accompany a deported slave. The Directorate of the Board reversed the decision and ordered his wife and children to accompany Su into exile. One can think of reasons for allowing exiled slaves less choice in disposing of their families than is permitted to banished commoners. These reasons, however, were not compelling to the department and its judicial forerunners on whose precedent the department relied. Let us suppose that the statutory provision, which gave the slave no option to leave his innocent children in conditions less rigorous than serving troops on the frontier, is not easily rationalized. We can, however, also assume that the statutory provision (which disfavored a lowly caste and provided valuable assistance to government troops at the frontier) was not so beyond reason that the imperial promulgator was unlikely to have meant what he said. The point then is that a statute not raising manifest doubts can have literal force even though it has no affirmative justification. The Directorate of the Board of Punishments was perturbed because departments, on this and other occasions, had casually disregarded the statute. The Directorate said, "The several departments . . . are requested to note that hereafter, whenever a slave may be reported . . . by his bannerman master for deportation, the slave's wife and children are always to accompany him in accordance with the sub-statute, thereby preventing any possible recurrence of inconsistent and erroneous judgments."

The force of literalism can occasionally compel anomalous decisions. In, for example, Huo Kuei-ssu's case (236.1) the defendant, who had been refused credit by a merchant, set fire to the merchant's threshing yard. The fire spread and burned down the merchant's house and thirty-six other dwellings. A statute provided the punishment of life exile for "deliberately setting fire to the firewood and straw in someone's threshing yard"—a literal description of the defendant's proven acts. An application of this statute, however, gives this defendant no more drastic punishment than would be that of an arsonist who burns up only a handful of straw. The destruction of thirty-seven houses could hardly be made light of as accidental aftermath for which the defendant was not to blame—especially in imperial China where our Western view that "the risk reasonably to be perceived defines the duty to be obeyed" [10] is thought far too lenient. The decision is difficult to reconcile with another arson case (235.2), in which Tseng Lu, a paperhanger, *negligently* brought about spontaneous combustion of oiled wallpaper and was punished by life exile for the consequent burning of the Imperial Library. The paperhanger was punished for his *negligence* as severely as was the spiteful arsonist whose *intentionally* set fire destroyed thirty-seven houses. Literalism in the latter case seems to overpower the potent principle requiring punishments to vary in proportion to the heinousness of the crime.

This instance of literalism had a special background. A provincial court had heard the case at an early stage; it apparently relied on an older case in which a fire spitefully set in a threshing yard had spread and destroyed thirty-three room-sections. That older case had been decided by the Manchurian Board of Punishments, where the arsonist was sentenced to military exile under a catch-all statute. When the older case came to Peking the threshing-yard arson statute was held to apply to it, and under that statute the sentence was reduced to life exile. This precedent influenced the Board of Punishments; they apparently wanted to avoid the inconsistency which would have resulted had it not been followed in the second case. The emperor, however, was bothered. In his rescript he pointed out that the destruction of thirty-seven houses is greater devastation than was the burning of thirty-three room sections. The emperor, however, then makes the unlikely and un-Chinese statement, "It must be assumed that in both cases the offender was equally unaware of the distance to which his fire might spread. For this reason it is permissible to send a confirmatory reply"—approving the underpunishment

[10] Cardozo, J., in *Palsgraph v. Long Island R. R. Co.*, 248 N.Y. 339, 162 N.E. 99 (1928).

called for by the threshing-yard arson statute that literally encompassed the case.

The Unreliability of Literalism

Wooden-headed insistence on statutory words is an unacceptable and usually rejected method of interpretation in virtually all judicial systems applying statute law. The following United States Supreme Court case is a good illustration. The Congress had passed this law: "If any person shall knowingly and wilfully obstruct or retard the passage of the mail" he shall be guilty of a crime. Federal authorities prosecuted a Kentucky sheriff for disobeying this statute when he arrested a mail-delivering postman. The sheriff acted under a warrant ordering him to arrest the postman for murder. The Supreme Court held the statute inapplicable. In his opinion, Mr. Justice Field said, "All laws should receive a sensible construction . . . The reason of the law . . . should prevail over its letter. The common sense of man approves the judgment mentioned by Puffendorf, that the Bolognian law which enacted that 'whoever drew blood in the streets should be punished . . .' did not extend to a surgeon who opened the vein of a person that fell down in the street in a fit. The same common sense accepts the ruling . . . that the statute of the first Edward II, which enacts that a prisoner who breaks out of prison shall be guilty of a felony, does not extend to a prisoner who breaks out when the prison is on fire . . . The act of Congress which punishes the obstruction . . . of . . . the mail does not apply to a case of temporary detention caused by the arrest of the carrier . . . for murder." [11]

The old saw about the Bolognian medic's sidewalk therapy not breaking the law against bloody violence merely sidesteps a silly pun—a pun which confuses a good samaritan with a bad actor. The same kind of pun is disdained in the case of the prisoner who extricated himself from a burning prison—to call his act a "jailbreak" would be a ridiculous play on words. Reasonable interpretation of the mail-obstruction statute is almost as obvious as these other examples; even so, the Kentucky sheriff's prosecution raised

[11] *United States v. Kirby,* 74 U.S. (7 Wall.) 482, 486–487 (1868).

a genuine issue. The Supreme Court decided the case properly only by going beyond nomenclature. The Congress did intend to cloak working postmen with a special legal immunity. The Court referred to values ingrained in our culture to decide that Congress did not intend to prefer rapid delivery of the mail over prompt arrest of postmen indicted for murder.

One can say glibly with Hilary: "The meaning of what is said is according to the motive for saying it: because things are not subject to speech, but speech to things." [12] It is not always so easy, however, to cope with legislative intentions at odds with the statutory words—especially when they have been promulgated in an alien environment. Although we can grasp the propriety of the practice of our own courts when they, on occasion, go beyond the literal meaning of statutes, nevertheless the presumption is that the legislature has intended the ordinary meaning of the words used. Judicial departures from everyday meanings of the statutory words enacted often raise suspicions of usurpation—suspicions of temerity rather than fidelity to law.

Sometimes, however, statutory texts contain clues to special meanings. In Ts'ai Ssu-ching's and Mai Shu-hsin's case (164.2), the two defendants entered an affray and each killed one of the eleven men slain. While they awaited trial two of their confederates, each of whom had also struck mortal blows, died of illness. A sub-statute on joint assaults provided that the death from illness before trial of either the original planner or a confederate who struck mortal blows shall have the effect of reducing the punishment of remaining confederates from strangulation to life exile. Taken alone, the wording of this statute seems to entitle the defendants to reduced sentences. However, the Code also provided that when a joint assault results in three or more deaths and when the original planner dies of illness awaiting trial, his death will not entitle his confederates to reduction of punishment. This second clause, viewed literally and in isolation, says nothing about our case in which the confederates who died awaiting trial were not original planners. However, the first statute, on which commutation rests, equates the deaths awaiting trial of confed-

---

[12] In *De Trin* IV, quoted in Saint Thomas Aquinas, *Summa Theologica*, Parts I–II, Q. 96, Art. 6.

erates and the death of the planner. The Board of Punishments saw no reason for not honoring this equation; the Board said that consistency required them to conclude that the second statute was intended to withhold the clemency of the first. The literal wording of neither statute, taken alone, would justify the Board's holding. The words of the first statute are literally applicable but are not applied. The words of the second statute are literally inapplicable but are determinative. When each of the statutes is read with the meaning of the other in mind, the Board's ruling comports with the intention of the statutes.[13]

It cannot be said, however, that the combination of the two statutes is purely a process of formal logic. If a Kentucky legislature should pass a statute reducing the sentences of mountaineer feudists when a slayer's confederate dies of illness while awaiting trial, the Kentucky courts could reasonably suspect that the whole statute was a typographical error. The logic of the Chinese case makes sense only in a Chinese setting with a background of the theory of life requital.

In Mrs. Chiao's case (159.1) the statutory meaning was more clearly affected by cultural factors. Mrs. Chiao's daughter-in-law caught her committing adultery. A quarrel ensued and Mrs. Chiao set upon the girl with a poker. The daughter-in-law tried to protect herself by seizing the poker. The two pulled back and forth. One end of the poker was sharp, and the girl was accidentally stabbed and she died. A statute punishes by three years penal servitude a mother-in-law guilty of "unreasonably beating a daughter-in-law and thereby causing her death." Two other statutes deal with mothers-in-law who slay their daughters-in-law; one punishes by decapitation after the assizes a *premeditated* killing to seal the mouth of a daughter-in-law who knows about her mother-in-law's adultery; the other punishes by life exile any mother-in-law who with *premeditation* unjustifiably beats her daughter-in-law to death. Since Mrs. Chiao did not premeditate the killing, neither of these statutes was applicable. But the problem that remained was whether or not the unreasonable beating statute was applicable. It was held not to be directly applicable. The mother-in-law daughter-in-law relationship in

[13] See also case 131.1.

imperial China was often contentious; frictions are generated in this relationship over the world, but they were intensified in China by the iron-handed discipline to which the younger women were subjected. Unmerited beatings were commonplace, but the commission of adultery by most mothers-in-law was unthinkable. The unreasonable beating statute, therefore, dealt with a frequent abuse of power by women who were usually chaste. To call Mrs. Chiao's beating unreasonable or unjustifiable is a laughable understatement rather than a serious categorization of the facts. This view of the meaning of unreasonable beating is supported inferentially by the severity of the punishment of decapitation after the assizes that was provided for adulteresses who kill with premeditation to seal their daughters-in-law's mouths. This punishment is more drastic than the punishment for other premeditated murders of girls by their mothers-in-law; that punishment is usually life exile—more lenient than the punishment provided for premeditated murder of a stranger. This leniency (which Professor Bodde has told us flows from the Chinese view of legal obligations within the family) is expressly withheld by statute when premeditated homicides are committed by an adulterous mother-in-law. The provincial governor held that Mrs. Chiao's adultery also disqualified her for the leniency of the unreasonable beating statute and sentenced her to 2,000 li life exile and, at the same time, disallowed the money redemption usually accorded to women sentenced to exile. A department of the Board of Punishments said, "Since this constitutes the heaviest suitable punishment, it would seem that approval may be given." The department seems to regret that, in the absence of premeditation, a capital penalty is out of line with the established system of severities. We can suppose that the governor and the department were not substituting their predilections for the law on unreasonable beating. They believed (in my view, as honestly as Mr. Justice Field believed in the inapplicability of the statute in the mail obstruction case) that the unreasonable beating statute was not intended to apply directly to the case at hand.

A knottier problem is raised by some cases involving the dangerous weapons statutes, which punished more drastically a fighter who uses a weapon like a sword than one who fights with a tool like a plowshare even though the wound inflicted by each is of equal seriousness.

In Liu Tien-cheng's case (175.8) several men mounted an affray. The defendant was unarmed at the outset, but during the fighting he picked up and used a small war club. Wounding with a dangerous weapon is punishable, according to statute, by military exile. The provincial court held that the statute was not applicable and gave a milder sentence. The Board of Punishments disagreed and sent the defendant into military exile. The Board said, "Inasmuch as the culprit did . . . use a dangerous weapon . . . the mere fact that he picked the weapon up on the spot cannot differentiate him from any other handler of such dangerous weapons."

A year later the Board thought the statute spoke differently. In Chang Ssu-wa's case (175.6) the defendant had wrested a mace from a foe and used it against him. The Board this time ruled that the dangerous weapons statute did not apply. The punishment meted out to the defendant was more lenient than the statutory punishment but more drastic than the defendant should have got if he had done the same damage with a sledgehammer. Part of the Board's opinion is at odds with their earlier views. The Board said, "Anyone possessing such a dangerous weapon is . . . not a law-abiding citizen, so that even though his use of the weapon . . . may lead to injury no greater than that caused by an ordinary knife . . . his offense . . . is nevertheless more serious . . . Any injury whatever, when caused by use of a dangerous weapon . . . is to be punished by military exile; even if no injury at all results, the penalty is still to be 100 blows . . . When, however, a dangerous weapon is used in an affray by one who does not himself initially possess the weapon but who seizes it during the affray from the hand of his opponent, it is evident that this act, if not resulting in injury, should not be punished by 100 blows . . . Nor, if it results in any kind of injury, should it therefore be punished by military exile."

These two dangerous weapon cases differ slightly. The *victim* in the earlier case did not enter the affray armed with the dangerous weapon; the victim in the later case did. The injury in the earlier case was, therefore, inflicted on a violator of the dangerous weapons statute. The Board, however, said in the second case that had the defendant hurt no one he would not have incurred the 100 blow statutory punishment for wielding a dangerous weapon. Holding the statute not directly applicable, therefore, is premised upon the defendant's fortuitous possession of the weapon and not upon the victim's lawlessness. The Board has, then, overruled its earlier decision.

The good sense of the second opinion appeals to Western readers, but this amenity is not ipso facto an assurance of the holding's fidelity to the meaning of the statute. An argument can be made for the Board's earlier literalness. Such an argument can be premised on the unmitigated evilness of intentional, even though fortuitous, use of a dangerous weapon. The later non-literal statutory construction does, however, probably come closer to respecting the meaning of the statute. Rebellion was a major concern of most Chinese emperors. Arms bearers are equipped for subversive activity. The American constitutional right to keep and bear arms would be unthinkable in China. No Chinese, from time out of mind, would agree with Judge Story's statement, "The right of the citizens to keep and bear arms has been justly considered the palladium of liberties of a republic; since it offers a strong moral check against the usurpation and arbitrary power of rulers, and will generally, even if these are successful in the first instance, enable the people to resist and triumph over them." [14] Western attitudes toward keeping weapons for self-defense are a far cry from Chinese attitudes. "Self-defense" is not found as a heading in the indexes of such standard works on Chinese criminal law as Boulais, Staunton, Alabaster, and Ch'ü. The dangerous weapon statute, in the cultural context of imperial China, was intended to fix punishment for men who bore arms; the statute was not enacted to deal with fighters who suddenly and accidentally became armed in the course of an affray.

Even though the Board held, in the later case, that the punishments provided for by the dangerous weapons statute were inapplicable, the Board did not ignore the fact that the defendant

[14] Joseph Story, *Commentaries on the Constitution of the United States*, III, 746 (1833).

wielded a dangerous weapon. The Board sentenced the defendant to a punishment more drastic than the statutory punishment for inflicting damage with an everyday tool though milder than that for using a dangerous weapon.

We will discuss later the extensive authority of Chinese judicial officers to levy and fix punishments when an evil deed is not a statutory crime. At this juncture, however, it is specially appropriate to point out that the judicial franchise to fix apt punishments when no statute is applicable can act as a check on the temptation to stretch the ambit of a statute to make it extend to an evildoer who will otherwise escape punishment.[15] The Chinese practice, of course, involves other disadvantages.

In a system, like the Chinese, in which a major aim is to make the punishment fit the crime, greatly mitigating or seriously aggravating circumstances are likely to raise doubts about the intention to cover a crime otherwise falling within the literal meaning of the words of the statute. In Chang Hsiao-hsü's case (208.4) the defendant told the authorities that he had killed a man. The defendant's brother, in fact, was the slayer. The statutory punishment for this sort of perjury was set at one degree less than the punishment assigned to the crime for which blame was taken. This defendant, however, had turned himself over to the authorities in obedience to his mother's command; the Board of Punishments, therefore, sentenced him to a punishment milder than the statutory one. The Board said, "He was acting under the pressure of his mother's orders. Hence his deed differs from that of an ordinary man" who violates the statute. A case of the opposite sort is Liu Wen-huan's case (206.8). The defendant had been ordered to look into the affairs of a certain district and during his investigation had discovered that the district's magistrate had padded his budget. He covertly tried to coax a bribe out

[15] See the U.S. Supreme Court's dilemma in *United States v. Hood*, 343 U.S. 148, 72 Sup. Ct. 568 (1952), a case in which the defendants were charged with disobeying a criminal statute forbidding solicitation of money "in consideration of the promise of support or use of influence in obtaining for any person any appointive office or place under the United States." The defendants promised their dupes appointments to non-existent offices; authority to create those offices had been granted to the President, but he had not exercised that authority. Unless the court held the statute applicable the defendants would escape punishment for their influence peddling. The court by a majority of 5–4 held the statute applicable.

of the magistrate. The extortion statute provides two different punishments: (1) 100 blows for an unsuccessful attempt to extort "in which no precisely stipulated sum . . . is involved"; (2) three years penal servitude when an attempt "does involve a precisely stipulated sum of money and is connected with a proposed evasion of the law." Since the defendant put no price on his silence his wrong was outside of the ambit of the second clause. The problem is applicability of the first clause, the wording of which seems to cover all extortion attempts not included in the second. Because of their utterly inadequate salaries, many (if not most) Chinese functionaries were often slow to perform official duties until they received a little gift. These bribes were not to induce illegal action; they were to overcome inertia and produce an otherwise legal result. This defendant's wrong in this case was more heinous than those routine squeezes; he was guilty of one of the two aggravating circumstances that, in the second clause, made extortion attempts a more serious offense; that is, he proposed a venal "evasion of the law." The Board of Punishments held that the first clause was inapplicable, and said, "It would obviously not be proper to sentence Liu under the sub-statute which merely provides bambooing." He got three years servitude.

Readers of these last two cases may get an inkling that the Board talked itself out of holding the statutes applicable because the statutory punishments happened to be untoward, rather than because the statutory definitions of crime were not intended to cover the misdeeds committed. That suspicion deepens in Mrs. Chang's case (12.2). She had previously been convicted of forcing women into prostitution and was then properly sentenced to the statutory punishment of life exile. She was allowed, however, to pay a redeeming fine under the statute authorizing this clemency to exiled women. Thereafter she again forced women into prostitution and was tried for this second offense. The statute applied when she was first convicted is literally applicable to the acts now before the Board; if the statutory punishment fitted the crime (viewed abstractly) the first time, it fits it the second. The crying social need in Mrs. Chang's second case is not, however, for punishment to restore natural harmony but is for punishment that will discourage further recidivism. The statutes authorized two alternatives: (1) Another sentence to exile, with leave to pay a monetary redemption. This alternative had already proved itself ineffective. (2) A sentence to exile with a proviso (as was done in Mrs. Chiao's case) against monetary redemption. This punishment is drastic, since it separates a woman permanently from family ties. The Board of Punishments rejected both of these statutory alternatives. Mrs. Chang was sentenced to three years imprisonment. The Board of Punishments said nothing about the possibility of sentencing her to *life exile* without monetary redemption. The Board did say, "Such a wicked woman should not, this time, be allowed to redeem her crime and should be made to suffer what she deserves." In this case, then, the Board has not applied an applicable statute but instead has given a more sensible punishment than either statutory alternative. The Board can, of course, be defended. It not only gave (from our point of view) a just sentence; we can also say that the statute did not deal, one way or another, with recidivism, and therefore—in a sense—the statute was inapplicable. But saying the statute was inapplicable proves too much; the statement proves that the punishment ought to fit the criminal when the standard Chinese view was that the punishment ought to fit the crime. In most cases, a punishment calculated to fit the crime does fit the criminal well enough (in the eyes of Chinese officials) to raise no problem. If the focus, however, were to be on punishment befitting the criminal (as it seems to be in Communist China) then the whole design of the Ch'ing Code would seem inept.[16]

Infidelity to statute is still more pronounced in some wife-selling cases. In Wang Pao's case (223.4) a husband "because of poverty" got his father-in-law both to give out a report that he had died and to sell his wife to another man. The husband, wife, and buyer were each sentenced to 100 blows under the statute providing for these punishments. Four years later in Wang Hei-kou's case (223.2) a husband again had sold his wife. The husband's act, it was reported, "was prompted by poverty and illness which gave him no other alternative." The Board of Punishments compassionately said that this husband's transaction "differs from

[16] See case 148.2.

the selling of a wife done without due cause." This compassion seems judicial, not legislative; it flows from the warm hearts of the Board's members, not from the intention of the Code. This lapse from fidelity to statute must have been prompted by the feeling that punishment in such cases is intolerable.[17] Perhaps the Code's unrealistic inflexibility on this topic grew out of a prudish lip service to an ideal that could not be realized in Ch'ing times. A similar accommodation to unrealistic divorce laws is common in Western countries.

Some infidelities to statute do not appear on the face of the report of the case. In Mrs. Tu née Chang's case (171.5) the defendant's treatment for an ill person was burning incense. The patient died. She was sentenced to 100 blows under one of the catch-all statutes (a subject for later discussion). Another statute punished with strangulation after the assizes sorcerers who use heterodox arts to treat illness and thereby cause death.[18] A department of the Board of Punishments wrote an opinion in which they said, "This Department finds that the suggested sentence errs on the side of over-severity, for though Mrs. Tu's wrong action led to injuries, she had no thought of deliberately doing harm." Their phrase, "the suggested sentence," probably refers to the punishment provided in the sorcery statute, but the department does not reveal just what penalty was suggested and does not advert to the sorcery statute. The department seems to substitute its own predilections for the conflicting mandate of the statute.[19]

Bolder departure from statute is found in a few cases in which the Board of Punishments quotes a statute and then ignores it. In Li Mao's case (190.2) a younger brother, acting on his uncle's orders, tried to disarm his drunken, knife-brandishing elder brother and struck him. The Board of Punishments quoted a statute calling for three years of penal servitude for younger brothers who strike elder brothers. The governor-general who forwarded the case recommended that his punishment be increased to life exile. The Board said that the defendant's action

<hr/>

[17] See cases 223.3 and 223.5.
[18] See case 171.12.
[19] See also case 89.2.

violated one of the five cardinal relationships and therefore the recommendation for increasing punishment should be accepted. The Board might have thought that because the defendant beat his elder brother with a stick the statute which dealt with beating without specifically covering cudgeling was not entirely applicable. This rationalization, however, is offered without confidence. The case seems to be one in which the Board gave the punishment it thought apt instead of the punishment provided for by statute.[20]

Covert departure from unmentioned statutes seems more anomalous than departure from statutes quoted but not followed. The latter practice may be based on the belief that wise departure from statute in appropriate cases is an expected (or even hoped-for) part of the system of government—on the belief that the statute was intended as an abstract approximation of the right penalty and that the scholar–judge, dealing with the unique case, might indeed develop an understanding not possible to the maker of abstract laws promulgating them without the particular case in mind. Such an attitude seems especially appropriate because most Chinese statutes are intended to cover so narrow a crime that departure from literalism and extemporization for the unthought-of case is constantly called for. Judicial officers who often properly hold the ambit of a statute does not coincide with its literal meaning can easily slip beyond this practice and, without seeing much difference, refuse to follow an applicable statute when to do so would produce an unwise punishment. This slippage is to be expected especially from judicial personnel who are unadvised by advocates acting as prosecutors and defense counsel.[21]

The emperor himself was dissatisfied with applicable statutory punishment in the case of the adulterous Mrs. Ch'en née Chang (172.4). The statute provided that a married daughter whose unchastity provokes her father to suicide should be strangled after the assizes. When a son or unmarried daughter gives a father similar provocation the punishment is immediate strangulation. The Ch'ien-lung Emperor thought that no distinction

---

[20] Compare the punishment of the magistrate and the lieutenant in case 263.1.
[21] See case 203.5.

should be made between unchaste daughters whose fathers destroy themselves on the basis of whether or not they are married —that the married daughters should be punished by immediate strangulation as well as the unmarried ones. He sentenced this defendant to immediate strangulation and ordered that the statute be changed accordingly. This case is hard to square with Sun Shou-chih's case (147.2) discussed above. In Sun's case, however, the emperor was espousing a capricious departure from statute based on an impulsive reaction to the aptness of the statutory punishment in the particular case. In Mrs. Ch'en's case the emperor's view was more principled and less intuitive, more addressed to a class of cases which he believed was ineptly punished than to the mitigating circumstances of a particular case.

At a later date both the Board of Punishments and the emperor were bothered about ad hoc departures from applicable statutes. In Staunton's translation of the Code, Section 415, we read, "In all tribunals of justice, sentence should be pronounced against offenders according to all the existing laws, statutes, and precedents applicable to the case, considered together, the omission of which in any respect shall be punished at least with 30 blows; when, however, any article of the law is found to comprise and relate to other circumstances besides those which have occurred in the case under consideration, so much of the law shall be acted on as is really applicable." In case 260.1 the Board, commenting on the case before it, says, "It is essential to establish the exact facts . . . , as well as to impose sentence in strict accord with the relevant statutes or sub-statutes." The complainant in the case had been sentenced by the governor to 100 blows for making an accusation that turned out to be unfounded. The Board said, "The statute cited above, under which the presenting of an accusation which proves to be false is punishable by 100 blows of the heavy bamboo, has reference to such an act *only* when effected by stopping the imperial chariot or beating the complaint drum . . . It commonly happens that cases which a judge deems to be baseless are conveniently settled by him through sentencing the plaintiff to maximum bambooing under the statute on accusations which prove to be false. In so doing, no mention is made of that part of the statute limiting such incorrect accusations to those presented by persons who stop the imperial chariot or beat the complaint drum . . . Not only is this detrimental to law in general, but more particularly it makes empty words out of the statute[s] . . . When . . . citation is made of the statute . . . the habitual omission . . . cannot possibly be permitted." The emperor responded, "Let it be as has been deliberated."

No Statute Applicable; The Role of Analogy

In the United States criminal convictions for serious crime are almost always based on statute. Unless a promulgated statute both defines the ambit of the crime and provides for a penalty, our courts rarely hold that an accusation of crime is proper. Our federal courts have no constitutional jurisdiction to entertain prosecutions for "common law crimes." In eighteen of the states the common law crimes have been abolished and replaced by statutory penal codes. In the other states the courts are still authorized, in theory, to declare conduct criminal, but the judges are reluctant in fact either to invent new crimes or to recognize ancient ones not codified; in these states common law convictions are found only against petty offenders and resulting punishments are usually only small fines.[22] An extreme example of the American aversion to criminal punishment not authorized by statute is found in United States v. Evans.[23] A federal statute forbade either landing or harboring an immigrant entering the country unlawfully. The penalty clause of the statute, however, defectively provided only that those convicted "shall be punished by a fine not exceeding $2,000 and be imprisoned for a term not exceeding five years for each and every alien so landed." No penalty for harboring was set forth. The United States Supreme Court refused to permit the conviction of one who harbored illegal entrants on the ground that, even though the Congress clearly intended to make his conduct criminal, the Congress had promulgated only a penalty for landing and not for harboring.

[22] See "Common Law of Crimes in the United States," *Columbia Law Review,* 47:1332 (1947). But see also *Commonwealth v. Mochan,* 177 Pa. Super. 454 (1955).
[23] 333 U.S. 483, 68 Sup. Ct. 634 (1948).

This holding evidences an attitude on the importance of personal liberty; we distrust the ability of judges to define crimes and set punishments extemporaneously because we fear that they may be biased against the person on trial and that they may therefore fail to be objective and even-handed.

No such view about liberty moved the Chinese. Nevertheless, there were some Chinese prosecutions not expressly provided for in the Code that failed for totally different reasons. In Wang Tuan-ch'ing's case (243.5) the governor reported that a convict, whose original crime was pardoned by imperial amnesty, escaped from prison before the amnesty was announced. The amnesty did not pardon prison breaks, which are, according to statute, punishable by a two-degree increase of the escaper's punishment for his original crime. The Board of Punishments held that since the amnesty cancelled out Wang's original crime he was not liable to punishment for the prison break. They said, "There is no article in the Code punishing a guiltless prisoner who escapes." These words are not, of course, based on the policy of requiring statutory authorization for criminal conviction. If the Board had been of the mind that punishment for this jailbreak was suitable and fitting, they would, no doubt, have levied it, even though no statute so ordered.[24]

Sometimes a statutory definition of a crime has, in context, an implied negative meaning as well as an express affirmative one. The case of Cheng Liu's wife (131.2) involved relatives of a traitor found guilty of high treason. A statute set out punishments for a sizable list of relatives of convicted traitors. In this case the traitor's brother was sentenced to immediate decapitation under

[24] Wang T'ing-hsüan's case (80.23), decided three years later, illustrates. The defendant produced a small amount of salt for his own consumption. This was no statutory crime. Nevertheless a salt examiner tried to arrest Wang. He resisted and injured the examiner. Resisting arrest, like prison break, is a statutory crime punishable by an increase of the punishment for the original crime by two degrees. Even though Wang committed no statutory crime before his resistance, he was sentenced to penal servitude for a year and a half. The impact on the Board of Wang T'ing-hsüan's misconduct in resisting arrest was, no doubt, stronger than Wang Tuan-ch'ing's quieter wrong of slipping away from prison. The Board in the arrest-resistance case, in any event, rationalized conviction and severe punishment, imposed with no statute applicable to the original charge and even though the statutory punishment for resisting arrest was not applicable to this case. But see below, the discussion of case 60.5 evidencing reluctance to apply an ad hoc judgment with full vigor.

the statute, and the traitor's wife and daughter were sent into slavery under the statute. The defendant in whom we are interested was the traitor's brother's wife. A department of the Board of Punishments says, "The statute says nothing about implicating the sister-in-law of a principal offender, and it is presumably for this reason that the governor . . . has not taken her into account in his deliberations." The department affirmed the governor's holding. This holding was rooted in the statute. An Aristotelian logician might say that a statute affirmatively punishing some relatives implies nothing—one way or the other—about unmentioned relatives. But a statute listing those relatives of a traitor implicated in his crime is not likely to be incomplete. The holding in this case is a legitimate use of the dangerous overgeneralization expressed by the Western canon of statutory interpretation, "Expressio unius exclusio alterius." [25]

Less obvious to us, but probably equally faithful to the meaning of a statute, is the holding in K'ung Ch'uan-li's case (191.2). The defendant's daughter committed adultery, eloped, was brought back home, left her husband a second time and "appealed to people" to find her a new husband. Her father killed her. A statute punishes by 100 blows fathers who *unreasonably* beat and kill disobedient daughters. The Board of Punishments said that when a father kills a licentious daughter, such killing cannot be called merely unreasonable. The Board reversed the provincial court's conviction and sentence to a bambooing, and acquitted the defendant. The Board holds in this case that legislation punishing unreasonable killing means that a father is guilty of no crime when he is not unreasonable in slaying his daughter. Such was the meaning of the statutory words in imperial China; this negative implication is, however, far from obvious to Westerners.

These instances of acquittal on accusations not expressly covered by the Code exemplify principles of limited scope;

[25] "The expression of one thing is the exclusion of another." See P'u Yung-sheng's case (194.5) in which the accused had come to his brother's defense and killed a man. A statute extended clemency to sons, grandsons, and wives who inflict injuries on those attacking their respective parents, grandparents, and husbands but did not mention brothers. The Board interpreted the statute to mean that the defendant was not entitled to clemency.

generally the Chinese harbor no aversion, in the absence of statute, either to judicial invention of crimes or to judicial setting of penalties. This aspect of the Chinese judicial officer's role reflects the history of a legal system which was *not* focused on the function of originating the norms of conduct but merely had the office of assigning proper punishments when readily recognizable misconduct occurred. Most Chinese statutes assign a single and invariable punishment for a narrowly described crime. Because the aptness of the described punishment depends on the enormity of the misdeed, the ambit of each statute usually is small. Although the Ch'ing Code contains thousands of clauses, the narrowness of each clause resulted in failure to deal in advance with many kinds of serious wrongdoing. Gaps in the Code were expected. The codifiers coped with substantive incompleteness in two ways: (1) They provided for judging unspecified wrongs by analogy to those that were defined in the Code. (2) They drafted some catch-all statutes of wide ambit.

The legal basis for the analogical use of specific statutes is translated by Staunton this way, "Section XLIV. *Determination of Cases Not Provided for by Any Existing Law.* From the impracticality of providing for every possible contingency, there may be cases to which no laws or statutes are precisely applicable; such cases may be determined, by an accurate comparison with others which are already provided for, and which approach most nearly to those under investigation, in order to ascertain afterwards to what extent an aggravation or mitigation of punishment would be equitable." [26] The statute provides for review of such punishments by "the superior magistrates" and by the emperor. A judicial officer's failure to search out analogies in a proper case was itself a crime, punishable as a willful deviation from justice.

Sometimes Chinese judicial officers use a statute by analogy when it appears (to Western lawyers) to apply directly to the facts of the case. In, for example, Wu Pao-wa's case (126.2) the defendant was traveling on a narrow path, driving a laden mule before him. He met head-on traffic; when he was summarily ordered to give way he churlishly whipped his mule forward until

---

[26] Note once again the stress on arriving at punishments that fit the crime.

it kicked a person to death. A statute punished by life exile the owner of a domestic animal "who deliberately releases the animal thereby causing homicide." The Board sentenced the defendant to life exile "by analogy to the statute." Similarly, in Mao Hua-hsia's case (165.5) the defendant spread ordure over the mouth and face of a victim who retched himself to death. A statute punished by strangulation "introducing foreign objects into someone's ears, nostrils, or other openings of the body, thereby leading to his death." The statute was held not directly applicable, but the defendant's crime was held to be analogous to the statutory offense.[27]

Compare these cases with the New Jersey case of State v. Provenzano.[28] Therein the defendant was indicted for disobeying a criminal statute providing that "any duly *appointed* representative" of a labor organization who accepts a bribe commits a misdemeanor. The defendant contended (in vain) that the statute did not apply to his duplicity because he was not an "appointed" official, but an "elected" one. The court said that "to accept the defendant's argument would be to find that the Legislature intended the application of the criminal statute to depend upon the mode of selection which each union may choose to adopt . . . So to hold would be to attribute sheer inanity to the Legislature . . . In providing that the representative be 'duly appointed' the Legislature meant only that the representative be in fact designated as such by the labor organization." If the New Jersey courts followed the practice of holding that a statute not quite applicable to a case could when close enough be used by analogy, the judges might not have held in Provenzano that the elected official was an appointed one. If they saw no ground for distinguishing between election and appointment they could, nevertheless, afford the narrow literalism of holding the statute not directly applicable since they could turn around and hold the

[27] See also Chang Hu-ni's case (21.40). The defendant killed a man, destroyed his corpse, and escaped detection for six years. A statute increased the punishment of any criminal who "remains a fugitive from justice" for an extended period. The Board held the statute inapplicable, because the defendant had hidden the corpse instead of himself, but the defendant's avoidance of prosecution was sensibly held to be analogous to the statutory offense of remaining a fugitive. See also case 162.1.

[28] 34 N.J. 318, 169 A.2d 135 (1961).

defendant had committed an analogous wrong and deserved the statutory punishment. Such logic voices respect for both the statutory words and the principle behind them.

The specific meaning of words, however, does not always readily come unglued from the general principle they exemplify. In any language and at any time some interpretations of statutes may resemble the reasoning of the New Jersey court in the Provenzano case. Somewhat comparable reasoning is found in Mrs. Lo née P'eng's case (208.5). The defendant's son had committed robberies and had struck her. The head of the defendant's clan beat the son who died from the beating. Since the punishment for killing a son was much milder than the punishment the clan head faced he was able to bribe the defendant to go to the authorities and say that she killed the boy. She was held guilty of disobeying a statute punishing parents whose son is killed and who "hush up the matter." This defendant's "speaking out" (her false confession) was held to constitute a "hushing up"—a very sensible decision, of course.

It would be a mistake to suppose that judicial authorization to use analogy can be gracefully exploited whenever a peripheral case may fall in a gap in the Code. In Chang Ch'ing's case (161.3) the defendant killed two fourth-degree cousins who had been traveling together. Their baggage and funds were, for the time being, intermingled. A statute said, "If two persons . . . are killed within a single family, the punishment for so doing is immediate decapitation and exposure of the head." The statutory definition of a single family is "those who live together" and "share their resources." A lesser punishment applies to the murder of two who are not members of a single family. The Board of Punishments did not have the alternative of using the single family statute by analogy. If the case were only analogous to, rather than directly within, the single family statute, another statute applied. The rationale used to subsume the case under the more drastic statute sounds more strained than the New Jersey court's reasoning that classified an elected officer as an appointed representative. The Board said, "Wu Teng-chü arranged with his fourth-degree younger cousin to go on a business trip together, during which time they traveled together and stayed overnight together. Between this and living together there is no essential difference. [!] The load carried [by the defendant-porter] was baggage belonging to both of them, and what he stole from them was likewise money belonging to both of them. They may thus be regarded as men who jointly shared their resources." The temporary nature of the travelers' close association is suppressed in this analysis. Severe punishment of the murderer was, in the eyes of the Board, suitable. The aptness of the punishment did have (and perhaps should have had) bearing on the applicability of the statute.

There are, of course, a large number of cases to which no statute is applicable, but which, nevertheless, raise problems closely analogous to those dealt with by statutes. Analogic use of a statute consists in judicial recognition of the principle exemplified by the statute and enforcement of that principle, even though the statute clearly does not extend to the case at hand. Wen-yüan's case (45.1) is a simple example. The Board of Punishments treated theft from a Buddhist monk by his disciple as analogous to theft by a junior member of a family from a senior member. Similarly, in Kuo Liang's case (134.1) the Board treated theft from a state temple as analogous to theft of objects used for imperial worship. In Liu Wu-shou's case (171.4) a shopkeeper's mistake in delivering to a customer a drug different from that purchased was treated as analogous to a doctor's mistake in administering to his patient a drug different from that called for. In Chang K'ai-p'eng's case (167.11) a man who starved his concubine and brought on a fatal disorder was treated as analogous to a murderer using force. In these cases the analogies seem close enough to justify the result in a system permitting punishment of those whose misconduct is much like some statutory crime.

The punishment meted out to these last four defendants convicted by analogy was the same as that they would have incurred had they violated the statutes directly. These four crimes, then, were held not only to be instances of wrongdoing analogous to the statutory crimes, they were also held to be wrongdoing of the same gravity as the statutory crimes. Sometimes, however, analogous wrongdoing is more or less heinous than the similar statutory crime. In Ch'ien Yün's case (266.1) the defendant was prosecuted for faulty construction of a dike, the collapse of which resulted in a flood that damaged both government storehouses and private property. The closest statutory crime was deviation from plans for public works. This defendant was not entrusted with the execution of planned construction; he was a petty military officer who, with an eye to advancement, had built an unplanned lotus pond. His botchery was held analogous to, but graver than the statutory crime; he was sentenced to a severe form of military exile rather than to the statutory punishment of servitude for three years.[29]

Hu Tzu-cheng's case (248.3) involved a wrong less grave than the analogous statutory offense. The defendant was a jailor. He thought a prisoner in his custody was held on very serious charges and used unreasonably extreme measures of restraint. As a result the prisoner hanged himself. A statute punished by strangulation after the assizes jailors who treated prisoners with unreasonable harshness, striking and injuring them, thus bringing about their deaths. A department of the Board of Punishments reduced the defendant's punishment for his less heinous offense to life exile.

One practice made sentencing less flexible. A convict given a reduced sentence usually got a "one-degree" reduction. This came to mean that some punishments were reduced to the next lower *kind* of punishment; a capital sentence reduced one degree became life exile; life exile reduced one degree became penal servitude for three years.[30] These reductions were considerable —so much so that, sometimes, even though leniency was desirable, the reduction would be much too great. In T'eng Ch'üan-ching's case (199.4) the defendant, attempting to save his son from punishment, made "wild accusations." His charges could be checked, it was thought, only by steaming the cadaver to bring out marks of injury. The ensuing post mortem disproved the

[29] See Yen Wan-nien's case (270.1). The defendant built a structure that encroached on an imperial academy. His wrong was held analogous to the statutory crime of encroaching on a public thoroughfare. The statutory punishment of 60 blows was thought too lenient, so the Board added wearing of the cangue for one month.

[30] See Chap. III, sec. 9, above. Compare case 52.3 in which a 100 blow punishment was reduced to 90—both of course would be inflicted with the heavy bamboo.

defendant's accusations. No statute expressly applied to such an interference with a dead body. A statute did, however, provide that destroying a corpse by burning it or throwing it in the water should be punished by life exile at a distance of 3,000 li. The Board of Punishments, by an analogy to that statute, approved a sentence of life exile at 3,000 li. If the Board had reduced the punishment "by one degree" the defendant would have been sentenced only to three years of penal servitude. Perhaps the Board thought the defendant's motive unimportant, and that steaming a corpse was virtual destruction. In fact the Board said, with apparent approval, "The Provincial Court of Shantung has taken the viewpoint that to cause a corpse to be needlessly steamed is as grievous an act as to mutilate or destroy it." Protection of a son against conviction of a crime is, however, an act of Confucian virtue. It seems probable that the Board did not reduce the defendant's punishment at all because a "one-degree reduction" would be much too lenient and therefore less apt than the statutory penalty. This kind of Hobson's choice, however, sometimes is so exercised that trivial distinctions between evils make great differences in punishment.

In Ni Tao-yüan's case (133.2) the defendant was guilty of copying and propagating non-canonical magical writings. "Fabricating" magical writings and spells was a statutory crime punishable by life exile. Since the defendant was not the author of the words he wrote, his punishment was reduced one degree to penal servitude for three years, even though he must have known he was both producing and disseminating intellectual contraband.[31]

---

[31] See Feng Hsüeh-chou's case (115.6). A statute forbade making and selling gunpowder to salt smugglers and set the punishment at military exile. The defendant made gunpowder but sold it to some one other than a salt smuggler, a variation which seems not to reduce greatly the gravity of his crime. His punishment was reduced one degree below the statutory punishment, three years of penal servitude. And see To Fu's case (195.2). The defendant violently demonstrated before the house of his superior officer to force him to rectify grievances of other soldiers. The Board of Punishments reduced his sentence one degree from military exile to three years of penal servitude—principally because he staged his disturbances before his superior's residence and did not quite commit the statutory crime of demonstrating in his superior's office. At the opposite pole is Chao P'an-ming's case (83.1) in which a palpable difference went unrecognized. The defendant embezzler was not quite guilty of the statutory crime of "falsely claim[ing] to have lost property entrusted to him." He told

Some analogies look far-fetched to Westerners and yet are apposite from the Chinese point of view. In Hsü Hsüeh-ch'uan's case (203.5) the defendant had prepared five legal documents for others. The statute against practicing law punished by a severe form of military exile "habitual litigation tricksters who conspire with government clerks, trick ignorant country folk, or practice intimidation or fraud." The statute does not seem to us to condemn the practice of law; it seems applicable merely to instances of pettifogging. The statute was not directly applicable to this defendant; the Board of Punishments said there was no proof that this defendant either conspired with government clerks, or tricked country folk, or practiced intimidation or fraud. More important, the statute does not seem to us to be based on any principle that can be extended to this defendant. However, intermeddling in legal matters had long been disapproved of in China; the statute punished drastically extreme forms of a kind of conduct known to Chinese to be wrong; the statute was in fact an exemplification of a Chinese principle that also condemns what this defendant did. His crime was not so evil as violations of the statute. It was, however, in cultural context, a clearly analogous wrong. The Board of Punishments so held and reduced the statutory punishment one degree to three years of penal servitude.

In Wang T'ing-chü's case (44.1) the defendant's practice of law never got started. He had announced publicly that he was available for tax consultations and to settle litigations, but he attracted no law business. The Board of Punishments drew an analogy to the statutory crime of falsely purporting to be the head of a local group of families. The statutory punishment for this crime was two years of penal servitude. The Board gave the defendant this amount of punishment—on the view, no doubt,

his entruster that he would have to consult his business partner before making repayment. The disappointment provoked the victim to commit suicide. The defendant had misused the funds in a speculation. The embezzlement statute provided that those who disobeyed it were to be given a one-degree reduction from the statutory punishment for theft of a sum equal to that embezzled. The statutory punishment for a theft provoking the victim to suicide is penal servitude for three years. The department sentenced the defendant to three years of penal servitude by analogy to this last statute, ignoring the principle implied by the statute treating embezzlement as an offense less grave than theft. I find it difficult to understand why the department that quoted the embezzlement statute ignored this clearly analogous provision.

that the defendant's analogous crime was as grave but no graver than the statutory crime. This punishment was penal servitude for one year less than that of the intermeddler in the last case. A two year punishment would have been unconventional had the Board drawn an analogy to the litigation trickster statute; in that statute the punishment assigned was exile; when an exile punishment is reduced it is almost invariably reduced by one degree to three years penal servitude. Therefore the Board, by drawing its analogy to another statute, came up with a more lenient and, in its eyes, a more appropriate punishment for a less heinous wrong.

All of the analogy cases discussed thus far can be looked on as judicial attempts to do what the codifiers would have done had they anticipated the facts that arose. The statutes used as a source of principles gave rational clues to how the codifiers would have wanted the cases decided; the analogies are genuine. But there are cases in which the Board's analogies seem quite strained. I do not mean, however, that they should not have been drawn—after all the analogy statute requires that gaps in the Code be dealt with on the basis of the closest analogy available.[32] In P'eng Lo-wan's case (165.3), a winning gambler dunned the loser who forlornly took off his clothes and gave them to the winner as collateral for payment of his losses. The cold drove the naked man to suicide. A statute punished by strangulation the crime of causing death by depriving anyone of his clothes. The prohibition appeared in the same section of the Code as the prohibition against forcing foreign objects into a victim's eyes, nostrils, or other openings of his body. This section was directed to violence and seems to have little bearing on the gambling case. The unfortunate gambler only slightly resembles a ruffian who disrobes someone. The strained analogy used may be better than none at all; a drop of wisdom may have trickled from the statute and given a criminal aspect to the defendant's conduct. The statutory punishment, however, did not fit the crime and the court reduced it by one degree from strangulation to life exile. If the Board had drawn no analogy at all, it might still have fitted

[32] George Thomas Staunton, tr., *Ta Tsing Leu Lee, Being the Fundamental Laws . . . of the Penal Code of China* (London, 1810), XLIV.

punishment of this crime into the Chinese system of severities. But if the Board takes, as a point of departure, a statutory punishment, even though the statutory crime resembles the defendant's crime only superficially, the court endows with palpability the question of equal or greater or lesser evilness. This practice, then, does seem to have power to focus Chinese judicial officers sharply on their most important function. Of course, when the practice evoked the answer that the analogous crime was greatly dissimilar in seriousness, the Board probably abandoned the analogy and looked for a closer one.

In Chang Fu-kuan's case (151.8) the defendant pried open a coffin to get at a ghost who possessed his delirious wife. His crime resembled only superficially the statutory offense of robbing graves. Nevertheless the Board of Punishments held that the statutory punishment for grave robbery was apt in this case.[33]

There is a limit to the usefulness of strained analogies; they are sometimes not only useless but also baneful. In Wei Yü-chen's case (267.2) the defendant, a shallow scholar, wrote a boastful biography of his dead father, referring to him in terms properly ascribed only to imperial figures. He should have known better and the governor aptly recommended that he be both stripped of his rank and (absent any statute directly applicable) given 100 blows under a catch-all statute. The Board of Punishments, however, analogized the crime to "contumacious use of silks bearing the figures of the dragon or phoenix." Such silks were proper only for the raiment of the emperor and empress. The statutory crime does superficially resemble the defendant's misdeed. Professor Bodde tells us that the case came up during the Ch'ien-lung Emperor's reign and when a determined imperial campaign against seditious writing had reached its apex. If the Board was trying to please the emperor by borrowing the statutory punishment of penal servitude for three years, it no doubt succeeded.

---

[33] Compare also Hsü Chiu's case (87.3) in which a grain dealer who acquired a substantial quantity of military rations by buying grain coupons from soldiers got the statutory punishment for "dishonest trading." The Board probably did not use the analogy to help it determine that the defendant was a wrongdoer. The Board's opinion, read in cultural context, is more properly a justification for giving a clearly guilty man the punishment of life exile at a distance of 3,000 li.

Although the defendant's inadvertent use of phraseology imputing a tinge of royalty to his ancestors is somewhat like intentionally sporting regal raiment, it seems to me less presumptuous.
Here, if the analogy was thought to help the Board determine the
appropriate severity of punishment, that reasoning may have
been in error.

There are, of course, opinions in which the Board postulates an
analogy merely to discharge the duty of searching out the nearest
statute. In Te-t'ai's case (124.1) the defendant, who held a job in
the imperial park, negligently let a tiger escape from a cage near
palace quarters. The tiger killed a man. An arguably analogous
statute punished by strangulation the act of improperly tying up
animals and thereby causing death; this statute contained a
proviso, however, allowing monetary redemption of the capital
punishment at a bargain price. The Imperial Household Department (which had submitted the case) said, with redemption in
mind, that this statutory punishment was overly lenient and that,
therefore, the statute was not directly applicable. This was sound
interpretation; the statute was, no doubt, intended to apply to
unsure haltering of domestic animals and not the graver negligent
mishandling of wild beasts. The statutory crime was, of course,
somewhat analogous to the defendant's misdeed, but if the Department recognized the analogy and then tried to increase the
punishment (which they already said was inadequate), the conventional increase would be a ruling denying the defendant
monetary redemption. Such a ruling would jump the punishment
from what was, in effect, a trivial fine to a death sentence. This
result was unpalatable. Another statute was seized on as analogous; it punishes the keeper of government animals who allows
them to perish; it provides for punishments varying with the
number of animals lost up to a maximum of penal servitude for
three years. After the Department called this statutory crime
analogous, it was unhappy with its penalty provisions and then
raised the punishment to a severe form of life exile—a conventional but not especially impressive exercise of the judicial process. This use of analogy was only a formal exercise; it played no
genuine part either in establishing the wrongfulness of the de-

fendant's misconduct or in fixing the severity of the defendant's punishment.[34]

The statute requiring the use of analogies when a case is not covered by the Code, provides that punishments based on analogy be submitted to the emperor for review. In such cases the Board of Punishments cannot urge the emperor to honor his own statutory definitions of crime, as the Board can when a specifically applicable statute has been violated. It is not surprising, then, to find that the emperor has felt especially free to change punishments assessed analogically by the Board.[35]

Catch-all Statutes

Criminal statutes in the United States usually authorize flexibility in sentencing. For example, the statutory punishment for, say, illegal sale of firearms could be a fine not less than $50 or more than $5,000, or imprisonment for not less than 30 days or more than 2 years, or both. Many definitions of crimes in our penal codes are so broad that they apply to misdeeds of varying seriousness. Because each of our statutes on homicide, theft, trespass, and so on, covers a gamut of crimes, a relatively short penal code can be comprehensive. A few unusually abstract definitions of American crimes cover much ground so vaguely that they raise doubts about constitutionality. A Virginia vagrancy statute, for example, said that "all persons who have no visible income lawfully acquired and who consort with idlers, gamblers . . . or persons engaged in illegal enterprise of any kind" are deemed vagrants and may be punished as for misdemeanor. The statute was challenged for vagueness but was held to be a valid exercise of police power.[36] Vagrancy was a petty crime at common law; its modern statutory counterparts are used to jail seamy char-

---

[34] See also case 12.2.

[35] See case 124.1, the tiger escape case, in which the emperor reduced a penalty of exile and cangue merely to cangue—as an act of imperial grace. And see case 134.1, the temple robbery case, in which the emperor reduced the penalty from immediate decapitation to decapitation after the assizes. The first of these two cases is an instance of executive clemency rather than judicial review; the emperor reduces a proper penalty. The second, however, is an instance of judicial review in which the emperor overrules the Board, not as a matter of grace, but to produce a sounder legal result.

[36] *Morgan v. Commonwealth*, 168 Va. 731, 191 S.E. 791 (1937).

acters for a few days. These laws are not prized by the champions
of civil liberties; when vague statutes permit drastic punishments
they may be struck down. The case of Lanzetta v. New Jersey [37]
involved a New Jersey statute providing, "Any person not engaged in any lawful occupation, known to be a member of a gang
of two or more persons, who has been convicted at least three
times of being a disorderly person, or who has been convicted of
any crime in this or any other state, is declared to be a gangster"
and may be fined not more than $10,000 or imprisoned for not
more than twenty years, or both. Some defendants who were
convicted under this statute attacked its constitutionality. The
United States Supreme Court held the statute unconstitutional
under the due process clause of the Fourteenth Amendment. The
Board of Punishments would not have applauded the sentiments
of Mr. Justice Butler in the opinion of the Lanzetta case. He said,
"All are entitled to be informed as to what the state commands or
forbids."

In Ch'i-ch'eng-ê's case (237.1) a grateful pupil contemplated
suicide to join his revered teacher who had died. He informed the
authorities of his plan so that his death would not need to be investigated. He changed his mind and was prosecuted for stupidly
bothering officialdom. No statute dealt specifically with this
crime; the Board of Punishments held that a catch-all statute
authorized his punishment. The statute made it a crime "to do
what ought not to be done" and stipulated 40 blows for lighter
offenses and 80 blows for heavier ones. This statute gives even
less warning than the American vagrancy statutes. And the two
penalties authorized are significantly different in quality as well
as quanitity; 40 blows are given with the light bamboo, 80 with
the heavy. Fortunately for this misguided scholar, he had official
status and was therefore allowed to escape 80 heavy blows by
monetary redemption.[38]

Freedom of the Chinese judiciary to extemporize on both the
occasion for and extent of punishment extends still further; other
catch-alls carry heavier punishments. In Wang Hsün's case
(82.6) the defendant was an army officer. He pledged his certifi-

[37] 306 U.S. 451, 59 Sup. Ct. 618 (1938).
[38] See also cases 237.3 and 263.1.

cate of office to secure repayment of a loan. He was sentenced to 100 blows under a statute on violating imperial decrees. This statute is interpreted to authorize punishment even though the wrongdoer has not violated any promulgated decree. One who does an act that the emperor would have forbidden had he thought about it disobeys this statute.[39]

Sometimes acts that seem innocuous were held to have violated the imperial decree statute. In Kuan Sung-t'ing's case (92.1) the defendant made profits by selling books to dealers and was sentenced to 100 blows for "violating imperial decrees." Perhaps facts that made his acts wrongful were accidentally omitted from the report or in some other way the criminality of his conduct escapes our Western eyes.

The still more drastic punishment of military exile is authorized by the statute on "vicious scoundrels who repeatedly create disturbances and without reason molest decent people." In Li Wei-t'ang's case (8.1) the defendant–official seduced his slave's mother. He came home, as propriety demanded, for a period of mourning after the death of his mother. He brought the seduced woman with him and sold her services as a prostitute. On three different occasions he resorted to various nasty ways of extorting small sums. He was sentenced to military exile under the scoundrel statute.[40]

In some cases the Board of Punishments classified the defendant's crime as merely analogous to the wrongdoing covered by a catch-all statute. This form of reasoning purports to justify a punishment more drastic or more lenient than the statutory punishment. Because the catch-all statutes are, of course, vague enough to have wide sweep, the device gave the Board great flexibility in sentencing defendants guilty of crimes not covered by, or closely analogous to, the narrower sections of the Code. In the case of P'an Li and P'ei Hsien (261.3) the statute on violating imperial decrees was used by analogy, so that punishment could be raised from the statutory 100 blows to penal servitude for a year.[41]

[39] See also case 171.5.
[40] A similar catch-all with a still more drastic punishment applied to bannermen. See case 6.2.
[41] See the provincial court's sentence in case 148.7, reducing the punishment of the scoundrel statute by using it analogically. Sometimes a vague catch-all is never-

The use of catch-alls, even when coupled with the flexibility of sentence by using them analogically, need not, however, result in arbitrary caprice. In Ch'eng Ch'ao-tsung's case (148.2) the defendant, a gambler, extracted a mortgage from a dupe to secure payment of a gambling debt. Threats to foreclose enraged the dupe's father who upbraided his son. The dupe committed suicide. No statute expressly prohibited this kind of extortion. The Board of Punishments carefully compared the defendant's acts with various forms of provoking suicide both by malicious prosecutions on the complaint of private individuals and by extortionate demands of rapacious governmental underlings. The Board gave weight to the age of the dupe and the voluntary nature of his initial entanglement. The scoundrel catch-all was held to be analogous. The statutory punishment of that catch-all—military exile—was adjudged apt, and the defendant was sentenced to that punishment.

None of the catch-all cases results in a death penalty. The Board of Punishments probably would not entertain the idea that judicial officers are authorized to send a man to death on the ground that his wrongful act was analogous to, but worse than, the crimes covered by a vague catch-all.

Clemency

Professor Bodde has described in Chapter IV the practices resulting in clemency for many of those whose death sentences were reconsidered at the assizes. These post-conviction procedures continued to refine the process of making punishments fit crimes. Clemency was usually dispensed at the assizes in conformity to established rules; many commutations were entered in routine cases decided by applying formulated standards. When more problematic cases came up, final judgments on them were seldom ad hoc; officials dealt with them systematically and judged them by consulting and applying principles. Compassion no doubt influenced both the shape of the categories of clemency

---

theless meaningful enough to be inapplicable to a defendant's crime. In such a case, if the severity of the statutory punishment is apt, the catch-all may be used "by analogy" and the defendant may be sentenced to the punishment specified by the statute. See case 89.1.

and the placement of individual cases in or outside those categories. Nevertheless, we must not underrate the technical force of the system by stressing compassion too much. Humaneness probably affected clemency much less than a desire to avoid inappropriate sentences. Many capital sentences classified as suitable for "deferred execution" were probably given for crimes for which the death penalty was merely a formal punishment, a conservative fiction covering the more sensible exile punishment, formal Legalism overlaying actual Confucianism. For example, the *norms* of filial piety (rather than compassion) influenced commutations of the punishment of only sons so that they could take care of aged parents or make sacrifices to their ancestors. Those same norms, in other circumstances, sent unfilial children to death by "immediate" strangulation or decapitation. Although the category "cases worthy of compassion" seems calculated to focus on unique extenuating circumstances, many of the cases in this category were subsumed under statutory rules formulating appropriate principles of commutation for the young, the aged, women, or the infirm. The ceremony of the emperor's vermillion markings is non-rational, but its basis is regularized charisma rather than sporadic caprice. By and large, the system of clemency after the assizes was structured and produced decisions in conformity to principle.[42]

Two clemency cases illustrate the unstated principle that a criminal who honors family obligations running counter to the criminal law should receive a commutation. In Lu Ch'üan-hai's case (194.3) two families engaged in a fight. The defendant's father was slain; the defendant thereafter killed two enemies who were brothers. The statutory punishment for an affray in which two members of the same family are killed is immediate strangulation. Neither the provincial court nor the Board of Punishments were of the view that the earlier killing of the defendant's father took the defendant's homicide out of the statute; requital of the deaths of the two brothers was clearly within the statute's intention. Nevertheless, both the provincial court and the Board recommended that the emperor reduce the punishment because the defendant avenged his father's death; the emperor commuted the

[42] But see case 159.3.

defendant's sentence to strangulation after the assizes—recognizing that a son avenging his father should be punished less severely than a stranger who kills two men who are brothers.

Pi Ch'i-chang's case (189.1) is similar to the last case. The principal defendant discovered that his younger brother was a robber. He "induced" his two nephews-once-removed to join him in drowning the robber. The nephews were, therefore, parties to the murder of their fourth degree senior relative—a statutory crime punishable by decapitation after the assizes. Another statute expressly reduced punishment to life exile whenever a junior relative's murder of his fourth degree senior is coerced by another senior relative. The governor did not read this statute as giving him authority to reduce punishment; he sentenced the juniors to decapitation but asked the Board of Punishments for permission to add his petition for clemency. The Board agreed, and approved the reduction.[43]

These last two cases should be contrasted with Sun Shou-chih's case (147.2). That was the case discussed earlier in which the emperor proposed to disregard a statute increasing the punishment for assault and battery committed by a junior relative on his senior. The emperor advocated a less drastic sentence because the victim started the trouble by stealing the defendant's property. The Board of Punishments pointed out to the emperor that, in the statutory scheme, theft from a relative is less serious than theft from a stranger, but wounding a senior is more serious than wounding a stranger. Therefore, the circumstances were only slightly mitigating and the crime was especially grave. It was the Board's view that clemency was not appropriate. The emperor agreed, and withdrew his proposal. In this case family theory was better supported by denying clemency, and principle won out over the emperor's impulse.

When, however, a defendant's crime runs against imperial interests the emperor's grace is less restrained. In Te-t'ai's case (124.1), discussed earlier, the defendant's criminal negligence resulted in a man-killing tiger's escape. The Imperial Household Department suggested to the Board of Punishments a sentence of

[43] A provincial court recommended statutory clemency in case 14.1; the statute in that case expressly allows only a petition for clemency at the provincial level.

the cangue for two months and deportation to Kirin as a slave. The emperor, "as an act of imperial grace," rescinded the deportation order. He made no attempt to rationalize his leniency. Imperial commutation was given to the defendants in Kuo Liang's case (134.1) in which two robbers who stole from a state temple were sentenced to immediate decapitation by analogy to the statutory punishment for stealing objects used in imperial worship. The emperor changed the sentence to decapitation after the Autumn Assizes. These two cases, then, do seem to run somewhat counter to the hypothesis that clemency is structured, and not ad hoc. Since, however, both defendants had erred against the emperor, they seemed to fall into an exception of small scope, justifiable, at least in part, by the conflicting stereotype of the emperor as benevolent—a stereotype that played a large role in inspiring imperial general amnesties. The emperor, of course, did not reduce punishments for all crimes against him; in Chi Erh's case (134.2), he affirmed the defendant's sentence to immediate decapitation for stealing yellow satins from an imperial temple.

Professor Bodde says that the statutes that authorized monetary redemptions of corporal punishments for defendants who were young or old or for women did not entitle them to clemency as a matter of right. He cites several cases involving defendants who seem to fall under those statutes in which the Board of Punishments countermands for cause monetary redemptions that otherwise would fall under these statutes. There is, however, an indication that some other statutory provisions for monetary redemption were invariably applied. These statutes do not authorize clemency because of the defendant's status, but on some other ground. The defendant was clearly guilty of accidental homicide in Wu Ch'i-li's case (166.3). The defendant's fireworks display set a grass fire that claimed four lives. The statutory punishment for accidental homicide is strangulation subject to monetary redemption. Both the governor and the Board of Punishments ruled (as a matter of course) that the defendant could redeem himself by paying the stated sum to the families of his victims.[44]

[44] A similar accident which killed many more people was proved in Liu Chen-yao's case (89.1). The defendant's fireworks display attracted a crowd. Seventeen

Two other statutes authorized commutation that was forthcoming as a matter of right. One provides that death by illness while awaiting trial of the planner of a joint affray entitles his codefendant who struck a mortal blow during the affray to a one-degree reduction in penalty. The governor held this statute applicable in Wang Ssu's case (164.1); the Board of Punishments affirmed without question. Another statute authorizes a one-degree reduction of punishment in some kinds of homicide cases when death occurs more than ten days after injury. The statute was applied to reduce punishment by the provincial court in Fang Hsiao-liu's case (169.1); the judgment was affirmed by the Board of Punishments. No petitions for clemency to higher

---

people were trampled to death when a cloudburst threw the crowd into a panic. The Board of Punishments did not decide that this was an accidental death case; it sentenced the defendant to 100 blows and a month of cangue by analogy to the imperial decrees catch-all without discussing any other alternative. Perhaps the Board thought of this case as entirely different from the four-death fireworks case; in the latter the defendant's fire got out of control and killed the victims; in this seventeen-death case the cloudburst intervened between the defendant's fireworks and the deaths. This distinction seems to me, however, to prove too much; if the defendant were not responsible for the panic he should not have been punished at all; if he were he should be held responsible for seventeen accidental deaths. My suspicion falls on the suitability of the punishment called for by the accidental death statute, but I am not sure whether it would have been too heavy or too light. If the 200-plus ounces of silver for redemption of seventeen deaths were more than the culprit could raise (which seems unlikely since he was probably wealthy), the statutory punishment would be, in effect, strangulation after the assizes, and much too harsh. If the silver were forthcoming without discommoding the defendant, the fine is an overly lenient punishment for the author of such a disaster. If, however, the ineptness of the punishment motivated the Board in rejecting the punishment, this result could be principled and justified, rather than ad hoc—for after all the statute had not contemplated accidental holocaust, but only a single death or so.

In Te-t'ai's case (124.1)—in which the tiger escaped and killed a man—had the department held that the negligent keeper broke the statute on death caused by improperly tying up animals, the punishment would have had to be strangulation, redeemable as a matter of right by paying 12.42 ounces of silver. This, the department thought, would have been the wrong result, both as a matter of law and as a matter of policy. In Mrs. Tu née Chang's case (171.5), the patient of an unqualified healer did not respond to her quackery and died. She was given 100 blows as a violator of imperial decrees. The department said, "Should she be sentenced *merely* (italics added) under the statute on doctors who kill patients [to strangulation after the assizes], the penalty for which, according to the statute, is commutable to monetary redemption, this would not suffice to serve as a public warning." Here again is a demonstration that monetary redemption is available under the medical malpractice statute as a matter of right—a result that could be avoided only by holding that the statute was inapplicable, which, of course, it was.

authorities were filed or thought needed in either of these cases.

In some cases an appearance of clemency is, in fact, not a reduction of an applicable statutory punishment; the ruling is a tacit holding that the statute is not directly applicable but can be used by analogy for punishing a lesser offense meriting a sentence more lenient than the statutory punishment. Ho-ch'i-erh-pu-ni's case (165.2) is a good example. The defendant was a guard whose job was to protect a mountain. He captured a thieving woodcutter whom he held for the authorities. He tied up his prisoner, threw the prisoners robe over him, and fastened the collar of the robe to the ground. The prisoner wriggled out of his robe and ran away but, lacking his robe, he died of exposure. A department of the Board of Punishments says the defendant should be sentenced "under the statute" on causing death by disrobing but with the sentence reduced from the statutory punishment of strangulation to life exile. The department did not think that the defendant had committed the statutory crime; it said that the prisoner's exposure "was of his own choosing"; obviously the department is using the statute analogically; its failure to say so was at most a slip of the pen. This pattern is repeated so often that one is led to suspect that the analogical use of the statutes was clearly understood by all who were concerned and the lack of express labels is of no consequence. In Wu Wen's case (185.1) the military governor requested that the defendant who attempted to kill a slave be held guilty "in accordance with the statute" on attempting to kill a commoner, but with a reduction of the statutory punishment of strangulation to life exile; he seems to be using the statute analogically. So a department of the Board understood, we suppose, because the department recommends a confirmatory reply without any further express statement on the relation of the statute to the crime. Instead the department merely discusses the suitability of the penalty recommended in the context of the system of severities.[45]

The Board of Punishments does, however, sometimes sentence a defendant, in spite of clear applicability of a statute, to less than the statutory punishment because of mitigating circumstances.

[45] See also cases 112.7, 133.1, 175.6, 199.7, 206.1, 208.4, 235.2, 239.14, 248.2, 269.1. For a similar tacitly analogical *increase* of a statutory punishment see case 159.1.

The Board said, in a general circular (case 260.1), "We beg Your Majesty to issue an order to . . . governors . . . instructing them that hereafter whenever a case initially submitted to Peking is then transmitted to them for trial, they are to handle it with justice. If its charges are found accurate, the grievances must be redressed; if found wrong, the false accusations must be punished. *Should there be extenuating circumstances, no obstacles should be placed upon possible mitigation of punishment.*" (Italics added.) The imperial rescript was: "Let it be as has been deliberated." This circular, then, embraces the principle of authorizing reductions of statutory punishments whenever mitigating circumstances occur. The circular relieves judicial authorities in one class of cases from strict adherence to statutory law; it, in fact, recognizes the desirability of judicial officers making an effort toward results in fitting punishments to crimes more refined than can be reached by following the provisions of advance promulgations. The circular was issued 1870—quite late in the period of our cases, which runs from 1738 to 1883. It could not, as such, have affected sentencing in many of our cases. Very few of our cases are, it seems to me, instances in which the defendant is given a sentence lighter than the statutory punishment when his crime falls within the meaning of a statute. Three cases, however, merit special discussion.

In Tsou San's case (87.2) the defendant, a boat tracker who worked for the grain transport administration, incited a group of fellow workers to demand higher pay from their supervising bannerman. A lieutenant ordered them to stop their demands. The defendant started a fracas, struck the lieutenant and tore his clothes. The statute says, "If rowdies among grain-boat trackers form a group to press for money, and this group attacks somebody, . . . their ringleader will be sent into military exile at a nearby frontier." The Board of Punishments sets about so describing the facts of this case that the defendant is put in a favorable light. The Board says, "Finding that food prices were rising to a point where his wages no longer met the cost of living, Tsou San got the idea of assembling a group of fellow trackers . . ." The Board also points out that the disturbance took place after the lighters were at their destination and therefore did not delay the transportation of grain. The defendant's measure was not, says the Board, "in the nature of an obstructionist act done in order to extort money. Thus he is still deserving of leniency." The Board does not purport to hold that the statute is not directly applicable and, therefore, to use it analogically; it would have had an awkward time had it tried to do so. The defendant is sentenced "under the sub-statute" but his punishment is reduced from life exile to penal servitude for three years—a clear case of judicial reduction of an applicable statutory punishment on slight grounds of mitigating circumstances.

In Chan Chin's case (60.5) the defendant's clan and the Yeh clan were at odds. The defendant saw a passing woman of the Yeh clan and ordered one of his own women to force her into his house, where he raped her. A statute prescribed strangulation for abducting and having sexual relations with a woman. The defendant formed his intention to rape the woman after she was brought to him. Apparently the fact that his sexual designs were entertained after the abduction was, in the eyes of the Board of Punishments, a mitigating circumstance, and the defendant was sentenced by reducing the strangulation statutory punishment by one degree to life exile. The difference between the gravity of planning an abduction and rape and of abducting and thereafter deciding to rape seems too slight to justify the defendant's reduced sentence. The Board does not purport to use the statute analogically. If the statute is applicable directly clemency seems capricious.

In Chou Heng-yü's case (143.2) the defendants dredged goods and wares out of a shipwreck. The owner of the wrecked vessel objected, but the defendants ignored his protests and continued their plunder. The statutory punishment for taking advantage of a "crisis" to plunder is life exile at a distance of 2,000 li. The Board of Punishments sentenced the defendants in accordance with this statute but reduced the punishment by one degree to penal servitude for three years. The Board said that since the vessel sank before the defendants commenced their looting (implying that the "crisis" was over) the defendants' acts cannot be called "plundering" which is carried out at the moment of crisis; the defendants' acts, nevertheless, had "the character of plundering." Why should the Board have punished this looting less severely than expropriation done earlier in the disaster? No good reason is evident, and this sentence, too, looks like capricious judicial clemency.

Conclusion

The few cases in our collection that can be viewed as instances of judicial whim are not surprising. More significant is the general conclusion that Ch'ing penal procedure was systematic, reasoned, and an ongoing effort to effectuate a few important policies; only rarely were these policies ignored.

The most steadfastly held principle that affected the penal system of imperial China was that the punishment meted out should fit each crime. This policy guided codifications, following one after another and building on each other for two thousand years. The codes were, for the most part, elaborate collections of narrowly described statutory crimes, each carrying a befitting punishment. The statutory crimes were scaled on the range of severities called the Five Punishments. The five main categories, themselves, changed a little, very slowly, over the centuries, but they and their sub-categories remained fairly constant through most centuries and throughout each dynasty. The collected specific statutory crimes with their assigned punishments gave elaborate social meaning to the range of severities; statutory punishments were carefully assigned, constantly compared and studied, and occasionally refined or changed. The system of statutes commanded great respect from judicial officers; virtually all of whom virtually all of the time tried to understand and apply the statute's genuine (which was not always its literal) meaning. Chinese judicial officers were as likely (or more likely) to honor their duty of fidelity to statute as the judges who applied statute law in any other system.

The specific guidance of the Chinese codes was not intended to be complete. Chinese judicial officers were expected to fill the gaps by using analogies and applying catch-alls. Whenever gaps were to be filled the system of specific statutes was itself, however, regarded as helpful and effective guidance. Even clemency was, by and large, systematic and structured. And, except when his personal affairs were concerned, the emperor himself usually respected the structure. It was not surprising, however, that, in a system which called for so much judicial creativity, occasionally those deciding cases substituted their on-the-spot judgment for the pre-stated meaning of the statute. What is surprising is that they did so so seldom. And when they did, they were rarely capricious; in nearly every instance they tried to remain true to the overall goal of punishment befitting the crime. Only occasionally does some competing value displace this goal. Once in a while the obdurate evilness of the criminal inspires a punishment calculated to discourage his future wrongdoing or disable him so that he can commit no further wrongs. Once in a while a widespread tendency to continued misbehavior by many people inspires punishment calculated to deter.

In one uncalculated way, however, Legalism triumphed over Confucianism. Any entanglement with the Chinese imperial penal system was a personal disaster. The long periods of imprisonment awaiting appeals, the venal cruelty of jailors and wardens, the interferences with normal family life and the involvement of the accused person's relatives added up to a terrifying experience—even when the final punishment was lenient. So the system operated Legalistically so to speak. It tended to terrify the public into good behavior, rather than to redress disharmony.

APPENDICES
BIBLIOGRAPHY
GLOSSARY
INDEX

Appendix A · LIST OF CITED
STATUTES AND SUB-STATUTES

The total number of translated cases in which citations appear is 190. In each entry, the initial number before the slant is that of the statute or sub-statute as numbered by Boulais in his translation of the Ch'ing Code. A prefixed asterisk shows it to be a sub-statute; otherwise it is a statute. The number following the slant is that of the corresponding page in the Chinese edition of the Code used for this volume (the 1964 Taipei reprint, with continuous pagination, of an 1873 edition of the Code). Thus every cited item from Boulais is readily identifiable with its Chinese original.

The letter *a* suffixed to the number of a statute or sub-statute (or rarely *b* or *c* if there are more than one such together) indicates that Boulais has not included this particular statute or sub-statute in his translation; if he had, it would come between the identical number in Boulais (minus the suffixed letter) and Boulais' next numbered item.

Each entry, following the colon, lists the case or cases in which the statute or sub-statute is cited. A prefixed asterisk designates a case wherein the statute or sub-statute is cited only in the translator's commentary; without the asterisk, it is to be understood as appearing in the main text itself. Example:

* 1423a/2827: * 159.1, 159.3, 191.2

The item (*1423a) is a sub-statute (asterisk), not a statute, and its letter (*a*) indicates that it is not actually included in the Boulais translation. If it were there, however, it would come between his numbered entries 1423 and 1424. Its corresponding pagination in the Chinese edition of the Code is 2827. The sub-statute is cited in the main text of two of the three listed cases (159.3, 191.2), but only in the translator's commentary to the third (*159.1).

At the end of this appendix, following the list of cited statutes and sub-statutes, three much briefer lists also appear. They consist of items other than statutes and sub-statutes that are also cited from Boulais in the cases and that come from his Tables, Observations, and Cases.

37/223–4: *8.1, 186.9
40/227: *208.5, *257.2

45/235–8: *131.1, *159.2, *160.15, *161.2, *162.1

1063/1953: *17.1, 263.3
*1080a/1988: 147.3
*1080b/1990–1: 141.16, 263.3
1093/2027: *143.9, *239.15
*1100/2035–6: 143.9
*1107/2050: 143.2
1117/2069: *144.17, *147.1
1119/2070–1: *4.3, *45.1, *87.3, *144.17, 147.1, 149.2
*1122a/2080–1: 144.7
*1128/2090: 83.1, 147.1
1154/2153–5: *147.1, 147.2, 147.3
*1159/2161: 147.3
1166/2165: *147.1
1167/2165: 147.1
*1169/2166–7: 6.2, 8.1, 148.2, 148.6, 148.7, 200.2, 200.4, 228.3, 236.1, *239.7, *239.15
*1170a/2172: 17.1
1171/2197: *8.1
1173/2197: 149.2
*1173a/2199–2200: 206.8
*1174/2201: 4.3
*1176/2211: *149.2
1180/2213–4: 150.21
1182/2214: 150.19
1183/2214–5: *150.21
*1185/2221–2: *17.1, 19.1, 172.3, *191.2
1193/2242–5: 199.4
*1194a/2258–9: 151.8, 151.11
1199/2279: *51.1, 152.2
1210a/2319–29: *144.17
1211/2335: 21.40, 159.1, 159.2, 161.2, *171.3, *185.1, *189.1
1212/2335–6: 185.1
1214/2336: 157.4, *159.2
*1216/2345–6: 157.4
1224/2371: *159.2, *172.4
1225/2371–72: 185.1
*1226a/2376: 159.1
1233/2395: *160.10, 160.15
*1235a/2401–3: *160.10
1238/2424–5: *51.1
1249/2447: *161.2, 161.3, 162.1
*1251a/2452–3: 194.3
*1252/2453: 161.3, 162.1, *194.3
1257/2479–80: *162.1
1263/2490: *165.5

1268/2497: *14.1, *17.1, *51.1, 126.1, *169.1, 183.1, 185.1, 187.1, 194.5, 199.5, *208.4
1269/2497: *169.1, *185.1
1270/2497: 164.1, 175.6, 184.1, 184.2, 191.2, 194.3
*1274a/2508: 169.1
*1275/2508–9: *164.1, 164.2
*1276a/2510–1: 164.1, 164.2
1281/2523: 165.2, 165.3, 165.4, 165.5, *167.11
1283/2527: *262.3
1285/2527–8: *166.2, 166.3, *171.3, 171.13
*1285a/2530: 166.1
*1286/2533: *166.2
*1287/2535: 152.4
1298/2563: 167.11
1302/2571: 168.1
*1307/2574–5: 168.1
*1311a/2580–1: 169.1
1312/2583: *166.2, 170.1, 170.2
1313/2583: *166.2
1316/2587: *166.2, 171.3, 171.4, 171.5, 171.13
*1318/2588: 171.12
1319/2591: *166.2
1323/2593: *148.6, 186.6, 259.2
1325/2593: 17.1, 172.3
*1325a/2597–8: 172.3
*1326/2598: 172.4
*1327/2599: *17.1
*1327a/2599–600: *17.1, 172.3, 185.3, 260.1
*1329/2603: *201.6
*1334/2605: *17.1, 224.10
1340/2631: *208.5
*1341a/2633–5: 208.5
1344–48/2641–3: 175.6, 186.8
1345/2642: *169.1
1346/2642–3: 175.9
1347/2643: 147.2, 166.2, 188.2
*1350a/2649–51: 175.6, 175.7, 175.8, 175.9
*1361/2665–6: *42.1, 166.2, 169.1, *208.5
*1369a/2689–90: 87.1
*1377/2706–7: 183.1, 183.3
1380/2709: 184.1, 184.2, *189.1

1675/3527: *210.3, 248.2, 248.3
*1675a/3528–9: 210.3, 248.4
1676/3539: 259.2
1682–91/3587–8: *162.1
1692–*94/3627–80: *257.2
1696/3707: 259.1, 259.2, 263.1
1696a/3715: *260.1
1700/3731: 262.3
*1703a/3735–6: 262.3
1705a/3741: 263.1
*1705b/3743: 263.3

1705c/3747: *264.1
1706/3751: *269.1
1708a/3752: 265.1
1710/3765: 266.1
1712/3783: 267.2
1716/3797–8: 50.1
*1719a/3808–9: 269.1
1721/3813: 270.1
*1725/3820: 52.2, 52.3
Unidentified: 186.8, 186.9

Other Citations from Boulais

1. *Introductory tables* (tables of the five punishments, five degrees of mourning, and others, which, not being numbered consecutively with Boulais' statutes and sub-statutes, are referred to instead by his page numbers, followed by corresponding pages in the Chinese text of the Code):

Table I, p. 4 (not in Chinese text): *8.1
Table III, pp. 11–14/139–148: *14.1, *124.1, *166.3, *171.3, *199.5, *208.5
Table IV, pp. 17–22/195–209: 147.3, 186.8, 186.9

2. *Observations* (numbered paragraphs of commentary by Boulais, scattered among his translations of statutes and sub-statutes, and not contained in Chinese text of Code):

69: *8.1, 237.1   412–413: *45.1   1256: *162.1
342: *220.4   704: *80.23   1528: *50.1, *265.1
364: *183.1   749–750: *86.1   1580: *201.6
386: *42.1   758: *88.1, *134.1   Note 5 on page 641: *199.4

3. *Cases* (numbered summaries of important cases, usually from *Hsing-an hui-lan*, appended by Boulais to each section of grouped statutes and sub-statutes):

124: 17.1   1321: *171.4
138: 14.1   1416: *191.1

Appendix B · LIST OF CITED
PUNISHMENTS AND RELATED DATA

Total cases: 190. Not all cases, of course, contain pronouncements of punishment. The number of cases for each punishment or other item is indicated within parentheses. The list includes: (a) punishments as finally pronounced (but not punishments suggested prior to final judgment); (b) exemptions from punishment and commutations to lesser substitute punishments (fines, dismissal from official position, and others, but not ordinary one- or two-degree reductions from regular statutory punishments); (c) special groups (women, officials, Manchus, and others) which often, though not invariably, receive distinctive legal treatment in these cases; (d) other data relevant to the making of penal decisions.

Light Bamboo (2)

40 blows: 40.1, 86.2

Heavy Bamboo (35)

60 blows (4): 40.1, 61.1, 150.19
    Plus one month cangue: 270.1
70 blows: 41.7
80 blows (6): 152.4, 183.3 (?), 243.5, 259.2
    Plus one month cangue: 93.2
    Plus loss of government job: 263.1
    Commuted to fine: 4.2
    Commuted to fine of 4 ozs. silver: 186.9
    Commuted to fine as an official: 237.1
    Commuted to loss of government job: 237.1
90 blows (2): 52.3
    Plus 25 days cangue: 89.1
100 blows (20): 45.1, 52.2, 92.1, 167.11, 171.3, 171.5, 191.2, 194.3, 214.4, 223.4, 223.5
    Plus one month cangue: 89.1, 228.2
    Plus two months cangue: 87.1, 87.2, 133.3
    Plus reparation of 160 ozs. of silver: 50.1
    Plus dismissal from official position: 82.6, 93.2, 196.1
    Commuted to fine: 50.1

Commuted to fine as a woman: 208.5
Commuted to fine as a minor: 8.1
Number of blows unspecified: 144.7

Penal Servitude (46)

One year (5): 115.8, 159.2, 172.3, 214.3, 263.1
Commuted to fine because offender over 70: 228.2
Official pays for sum he appropriated and case is dropped: 265.1
One and one half years: 44.1, 80.20
Two years: 175.9, 235.1 (?)
Two and one half years (4): 115.7, 150.21, 168.1 (?), 259.1
Three years (33): 60.5, 87.3, 89.2, 115.6, 133.1, 133.3, 141.16, 143.2,
    151.8, 152.2, 152.4, 157.4, 164.1, 169.1, 171.6, 175.6, 175.7, 185.3,
    186.9, 195.2, 203.2, 203.4, 203.5, 206.8 (supplemental cangue omitted
    as an official), 206.19, 208. 4, 210.2, 214.1, 239.7, 259.1, 259.2, 267.2
    Plus 40 days cangue: 224.10
    Commuted to fine as a woman: 257.2
    Commuted to staying at home to care for parents: 83.1
Total penal servitude (four years plus 100 blows of heavy bamboo):
    151.11, 199.7
Transportation reduced to two-year authorized penal servitude: 44.1

Life Exile (38)

Distance of 2,000 li (5): 88.1, 147.1 (supplemental tatooing omitted),
    147.2, 159.1, 190.2
Distance of 2,500 li: 269.1 (?)
Distance of 3,000 li (30): 19.1, 60.5, 87.3, 112.7, 126.1, 126.2, 149.2
    (supplemental tatooing omitted), 159.2, 164.1, 165.2, 165.3, 165.4,
    170.1, 184.2, 185.1, 188.2, 191.1, 198.9, 199.4, 201.6, 201.7, 201.8,
    201.9, 222.16, 235.2, 236.1, 239.14, 248.2, 248.3, 269.1 (?)
    Commuted to two months cangue and 100 blows whip as a
    Manchu: 170.2
    Commuted to staying at home to care for parents: 42.1
Distance unspecified: 14.1, 223.3

Military Exile (23)

Very near (2,000 li): 80.20, 208.5
Nearby frontier (2,500 li) (5): 141.16, 175.7, 175.8, 175.9, 210.3
    Commuted to fine because offender over 70: 199.5
    Commuted to fine, whip, and cangue, as a Manchu: 4.3
Distant frontier (3,000 li): 151.11
Farthest frontier (4,000 li) (7): 148.2, 148.6, 148.7, 191.2, 200.2, 200.4
    Plus two months cangue (but tatooing omitted): 8.1

Man who sells wife because of poverty: 223.2, 223.3
Sons of treasonable persons who are previously enslaved or adopted
  into another family: 131.1
Escaped criminal who is amnestied: 243.5
Man unfairly sentenced by provincial court: 237.1
Official who makes good on defalcations: 265.1
Commutations to lesser substitute punishments (22):
  Monetary redemption (13): 4.2, 8.1, 12.2, 166.3, 171.3, 171.4, 171.13,
    186.9, 199.5, 208.5, 228.2, 237.1, 257.2
  Staying at home to care for parents (4):
    From immediate decapitation: 11.1
    From 3,000 li exile: 42.1
    From three years penal servitude: 83.1
    From one year penal servitude: 263.1
  Through imperial grace from deportation to cangue: 124.1
  Through imperial grace from execution for escaping: 241.9
  As Manchu from exile to whip and cangue: 4.3, 170.2
  As official from 80 blows to one-degree reduction in rank: 59.1
Petitions for clemency (6): 11.1, 14.1, 42.1, 189.1, 191.1, 194.3
Imperial Amnesties and Acts of Grace (6): 124.1, 166.1, 187.1, 201.9,
  241.9, 243.5
Denials of commutation (8): 12.2, 61.1, 159.1, 159.3, 171.5, 171.6,
  201.9, 203.5

Special Groups before the Law

Women (20): 12.2, 19.1, 60.5, 159.1, 159.3, 160.10, 160.15, 171.5, 171.6,
  171.13, 172.4, 186.8, 186.9, 208.5, 224.10, 224.22, 228.2, 228.3, 257.2,
  262.3
Aged persons (4): 162.1, 199.5, 203.5, 228.2
Minors (4): 8.1, 14.1, 144.17, 194.5
Officials (20): 4.2, 6.2, 8.1, 41.7, 41.8, 49.1, 59.1, 82.6, 86.2, 87.3, 93.2,
  162.1, 195.2, 196.1, 206.8, 214.3, 230.1, 237.1, 263.1, 265.1
Degree holders (6): 44.1, 59.1, 88.1, 133.1, 200.4, 267.2
Buddhist and Taoist monks (8): 45.1, 89.2, 133.2, 148.7, 183.1, 183.3,
  228.2, 228.3
Concubines: 186.8, 186.9
Servants (5): 41.7, 41.8, 186.9, 210.2, 210.3
Slaves (5): 9.1, 41.7, 185.1, 185.3, 186.8
Bannermen (Manchus, Mongols, or Chinese) (6): 6.2, 9.1, 87.3, 126.1,
  186.9, 237.1
Manchus (10): 4.2, 4.3, 9.1, 61.1, 93.1, 124.1, 126.1, 170.2, 195.2 (?),
  237.1
Mongols: 6.2, 165.2
Muslims: 144.7

Appendix C · CHRONOLOGICAL DISTRIBUTION OF CASES

Distribution by Reigns

Total Cases: 190   Ch'ing Dynasty, A.D. 1644–1911

Reign Period	No. of Cases	Reign Period	No. of Cases
Shun-chih (1644–1661)	0	Tao-kuang (1821–1850)	69
K'ang-hsi (1662–1722)	0	Hsien-feng (1851–1861)	0
Yung-cheng (1723–1735)	0	T'ung-chih (1862–1874)	1
Ch'ien-lung (1736–1795)	13	Kuang-hsü (1875–1907)	3
Chia-ch'ing (1796–1820)	104	Hsüan-t'ung (1908–1911)	0

Distribution by Years

(Number of cases indicated within parentheses after each year)

Ch'ien-lung (1736–1795)
1738 (1): 190.2
1751 (1): 41.7
1779 (1): 267.2
1786 (1): 186.8
1788 (1): 87.1
1789 (1): 4.2
1791 (2): 19.1, 172.4
1792 (2): 51.1, 159.1
1793 (1): 257.2
1794 (1): 183.3
1795 (1): 184.1

Chia-ch'ing (1796–1820)
1796 (4): 131.2, 144.17, 147.2 235.1
1797 (1): 263.3
1798 (1): 59.1
1801 (1): 148.2
1802 (2): 186.9, 259.1
1803 (2): 8.1, 148.6
1806 (1): 185.1
1807 (1): 265.1
1809 (4): 167.5, 184.2, 239.15, 266.1
1810 (3): 21.38, 159.2, 175.9
1811 (2): 161.2, 199.4

1812 (7): 21.40, 157.4, 162.1, 171.3, 194.5, 222.16, 269.1
1813 (8): 134.2, 151.8, 152.2, 160.15, 166.3, 203.4, 214.1, 248.4
1814 (4): 143.9, 208.4, 210.3, 223.4
1815 (11): 115.6, 133.2, 133.3, 141.16, 152.4, 170.1, 170.2, 194.3, 214.4, 223.5, 241.9
1816 (12): 6.2, 115.8, 133.1, 160.10, 165.2, 171.4, 175.8, 185.3, 200.4, 201.6, 214.3, 239.14
1817 (9): 89.1, 134.1, 159.3, 171.6, 175.6, 183.1, 203.2, 223.3, 224.22
1818 (10): 9.1, 17.1, 89.2, 144.7, 150.21, 164.2, 171.5, 198.7, 210.2, 223.2
1819 (11): 11.4, 60.5, 80.20, 88.1, 112.7, 165.4, 167.11, 175.7, 222.31, 237.1, 248.3
1820 (10): 4.3, 124.1, 201.7, 201.8, 203.5, 203.7, 206.19, 228.2, 228.3, 270.1

Tao-kuang (1821–1850)
1821 (5): 126.1, 149.2, 199.7, 224.10, 248.2

1822 (9): 52.2, 52.3, 126.2, 150.19, 165.3, 198.9, 206.8, 235.2, 243.5

1823 (5): 115.7, 134.3, 143.2, 199.5, 200.2

1824 (6): 40.1, 131.1, 151.11, 165.5, 171.13, 236.1

1825 (3): 80.23, 87.2, 259.2

1826 (15): 11.1, 14.1, 45.1, 147.1, 147.3, 164.1, 166.1, 166.2, 168.1, 169.1, 187.1, 189.1, 191.1, 191.2, 263.1

1827 (4): 42.1, 44.1, 172.3, 239.7

1828 (4): 61.1, 148.1, 171.12, 188.2

1829 (3): 198.8, 208.5, 230.1

1830 (2): 12.2, 93.1

1831 (7): 41.8, 82.6, 86.2, 87.3, 201.9, 262.3, 264.1

1832 (3): 49.1, 92.1, 161.3

1833 (1): 50.1

1834 (2): 83.1, 93.2

Hsien-feng (*1851–1861*)
(No cases)

T'ung-chih (*1862–1874*)
1870 (1): 260.1

Kuang-hsü (*1875–1907*)
1881 (2): 195.2, 196.1
1883 (1): 237.3

Appendix D · GEOGRAPHICAL DISTRIBUTION OF CASES

Total cases number one hundred and ninety. The number of cases for each province is indicated within parentheses. Paired provinces are those governed by a single governor-general, making it impossible for cases coming through him to Peking to be more specifically assigned to a single province.

Peking (31): 4.3, 9.1, 40.1, 42.1, 52.2, 52.3, 59.1, 61.1, 82.6, 86.2, 87.3, 92.1, 93.1, 124.1, 134.3, 150.19, 171.5, 171.6, 186.8, 195.2 (?), 198.8 (?), 214.1, 214.3, 214.4, 223.3, 223.4, 223.5, 230.1, 235.2, 237.1, 248.2

Chihli (Hopei) (20): 4.2, 80.23, 87.2, 144.7, 151.11, 165.3, 165.4, 165.5, 168.1, 190.2, 203.7, 210.3, 222.16, 222.31, 236.1, 239.14, 243.5, 248.4, 259.2, 269.1

Shantung (19): 11.4, 89.2, 115.8, 131.1, 157.4, 159.3, 160.10, 166.2, 169.1, 188.2, 191.2, 196.1, 199.4, 200.2, 224.10, 259.1, 262.3, 264.1

Kiangsu (15): 14.1, 19.1, 87.1, 148.6, 148.7, 149.2, 150.21, 151.8, 170.1, 175.7, 194.5, 201.7, 228.2, 266.1 (?), 267.2

Honan (12): 21.40, 44.1, 83.1, 133.1, 171.12, 172.4, 175.8, 175.9, 187.1, 203.2, 223.2, 260.1

Fukien (9): 8.1, 60.5, 131.2, 152.2, 166.3, 183.1, 206.8, 235.1, 257.2

Anhui (8): 147.1, 159.1, 171.3, 200.4, 203.4, 203.5, 248.3 (?), 263.1

Kuangtung (8): 17.1, 115.6, 147.3, 164.2, 167.5, 189.1, 201.9, 265.1

Shansi (8): 147.2, 175.6, 198.7 (?), 199.7, 201.8, 210.2, 224.22, 270.1

Shensi (8): 41.8, 112.7, 126.2, 133.2, 161.2, 171.13, 172.3, 239.15

Szechuan (8): 11.1, 41.7, 50.1, 167.11, 171.4, 198.9, 201.6, 208.5

Chekiang (6): 88.1, 144.17, 148.2, 152.4, 162.1, 206.19

Kiangsi (5): 21.38, 49.1, 51.1, 89.1, 237.3

Hunan-Hupei (4): 80.20, 93.2, 143.2, 160.15

Hupei (4): 133.3, 141.16, 143.9, 159.2

Yunnan (4): 12.2, 115.7, 199.5, 208.4

Hunan (3): 45.1, 164.1, 166.1

Kueichow (3): 183.3 (?), 185.3, 239.7

Yunnan-Kueichow (1): 161.3

Kansu: none

Kuangsi: none

Appendix E · SOURCES OF CASES

Total cases: 190. Number of cases for each kind of source is indicated within parentheses. For explanation of the categories of sources, see Chap. V, sect. 2.

Leading Cases (83): 6.2, 40.1, 44.1, 45.1, 50.1, 60.5, 61.1, 80.20, 80.23, 82.6, 86.2, 87.2, 88.1, 89.1, 89.2, 92.1, 112.7, 115.6, 115.7, 115.8, 126.2, 133.1, 133.2, 133.3, 134.1, 134.2, 141.16, 143.2, 143.9, 144.7, 150.21, 151.8, 151.11, 152.2, 152.4, 160.15, 165.2, 165.3, 165.4, 165.5, 167.11, 170.1, 170.2, 171.4, 171.12, 171.13, 172.4, 175.7, 175.8, 185.3, 194.3, 195.2, 196.1, 198.9, 199.5, 199.7, 200.4, 201.6, 201.7, 201.8, 203.2, 203.4, 203.5, 206.8, 206.19, 208.4, 210.2, 210.3, 222.31, 223.2, 224.10, 224.22, 228.2, 228.3, 237.3, 239.14, 243.5, 248.2, 248.3, 248.4, 259.2, 266.1, 270.1

Metropolitan Leading Cases (18): 4.3, 42.1, 52.2, 52.3, 124.1, 134.3, 150.19, 171.5, 171.6, 186.8, 214.1, 214.3, 214.4, 223.3, 223.4, 223.5, 235.2, 237.1

Memoranda (69): 4.2, 9.1, 11.1, 11.4, 12.2, 14.1, 17.1, 19.1, 21.38, 21.40, 51.1, 83.1, 126.1, 131.1, 131.2, 144.17, 147.1, 147.2, 147.3, 148.2, 148.6, 148.7, 149.2, 157.4, 159.1, 159.2, 159.3, 160.10, 161.2, 161.3, 164.1, 164.2, 166.1, 166.2, 166.3, 167.5, 168.1, 169.1, 171.3, 172.3, 175.9, 183.1, 183.3, 184.1, 184.2, 185.1, 186.9, 187.1, 188.2, 189.1, 191.1, 191.2, 194.5, 199.4, 200.2, 201.9, 208.5, 222.16, 235.1, 236.1, 239.7, 239.15, 241.9, 257.2, 259.1, 262.3, 263.3, 265.1, 269.1

General Circulars (10): 41.7, 49.1, 59.1, 162.1, 175.6, 198.7, 203.7, 260.1, 263.1, 264.1

Peking Gazette (6): 41.8, 87.3, 93.1, 93.2, 198.8, 230.1

Collection of Seen Leading Cases (3): 8.1, 87.1, 190.2

Source Not Indicated: 267.2

Appendix F · K A O Y A O A N D
E A R L Y C H I N E S E L A W

In Chapter I, section 3, was presented the legend in which the Miao, a barbarian people living during the reign of the legendary Shun (traditionally twenty-third century B.C.), are said to have created five oppressive punishments (*hsing*), which they then called law (*fa*). It was further stated that this legend (found in the *Lü hsing* section of the *Shu ching* or *Documents Classic*) is probably the earliest Chinese explanation of the origin of law.

Another well-known tradition also exists, however, according to which the same ruler, Shun, appointed a model minister, Kao Yao, to have charge of criminal matters. One version of the tradition states that in this post Kao Yao administered the punishments (*hsing*) which Shun had "delineated," whereas another version asserts that it was Kao Yao himself who "made" these punishments.[1] Still a third text of the first century A.D. does not mention the punishments at all, but instead connects Kao Yao's judicial activities with a mythological animal known as the Hsieh-chai.[2]

What the Hsieh-chai looked like and how it was associated with Kao Yao may be seen from the two illustrations in this book. The first is an early twentieth-century woodblock engraving, showing the Hsieh-chai about to butt a suspect in a courtroom presided over by Kao Yao. The second is a "life-size" bronze figure of the Hsieh-chai, no doubt unique in the world today, which was made in 1962 by the Philadelphia sculptor Henry Mitchell and is now exhibited in the University of Pennsylvania Law School. From the bilingual inscription accompanying this statue we learn about the Hsieh-chai's magical ability to distinguish the guilty from the innocent, and the way in which Kao Yao consequently used it to judge uncertain cases by having it butt the guilty party.

If we compare the *Lü hsing*'s legend of the Miao with these Kao Yao traditions, three points emerge:

[1] For the first version, see the following sections in the *Shu ching* (Documents classic): *Shun tien* (Canon of Shun), *Ta Yü mo* (Counsels of the great Yü), and *Yi Chi* (Yi and Chi); tr. James Legge, in *The Chinese Classics*, 5 vols. (Hong Kong, 1960), III, 38–39, 44–45, 58–59, 86, 89–90. For the second version, see the *Chu-shu chi-nien* (Annals of the bamboo books), tr. Legge, in *The Chinese Classics*, III, p. 115 of the Prolegomena.

[2] See Wang Ch'ung (A.D. 27–ca. 100), *Lun heng* (Critical essays), Chap. 52; tr. Alfred Forke, *Lun-Heng*, 2 vols. (New York: Paragon Book Gallery reprint, 1962), II, 321.

1. The *Lü hsing* legend, as we have seen in Chapter I, section 3, supposedly dates from around 950 B.C. but was probably in actual fact written some centuries later, though not later than the fourth century B.C. This would at first sight make it later than the references to Kao Yao in the *Shu ching* and *Chu-shu chi-nien* because these purport to be contemporary or nearly contemporary with Kao Yao himself. The texts in which these references appear, however, most certainly cannot be anywhere as old as their alleged dating, and in all probability were actually written later than the *Lü hsing*.[3]

2. Whereas the *Lü hsing* explicitly mentions *fa*, written law, this word never appears in the Kao Yao references, which speak instead of *hsing*, punishments, or more specifically of *wu hsing*, the five punishments. This fact weakens any effort to associate Kao Yao with the legendary beginnings of written law, since *hsing*, as we have seen in Chapter I, section 3, primarily denotes the punishments as such, and only secondarily the written penal laws which came to embody these punishments.

3. The argument linking Kao Yao with written law is further weakened by the tradition associating him with the mythical Hsieh-chai, in which no written law is mentioned at all. Conceptually, this tradition points to a magical and therefore probably a pre-legal stage in human thinking. Although textually attested only in the late first century B.C., it is quite possible that it already existed at a much earlier time in oral form before then being recorded in writing.[4]

It seems reasonable to conclude, therefore, that Kao Yao's role in legend is not at all that of a lawgiver (a maker and user of written law), but rather that of a supernaturally aided dispenser of justice. It represents, in other words, a magical rather than a legal stage in human development. The legend attributing the origin of written law to the Miao barbarians, on the other hand, belongs to the early period of written law itself, so that it, rather than the Kao Yao traditions, truly represents the early Chinese attitude on the subject.

[3] It is impossible here to go into the extremely complex problem of the dating of the several references, other than to say of the *Ta Yü mo* section of the *Shu ching* that it has long been recognized as a forgery of the third or fourth century A.D., and of the *Chu-shu chi-nien* that it is questionable to what extent its present text agrees with the text originally bearing this name which was first recovered from a tomb toward the end of the third century A.D. The other *Shu ching* references are also "late," but very difficult to date exactly.

[4] That lengthy oral tradition does in fact lie behind some of the mythological themes which first appear in writings of the Han dynasty has already been suggested by Wolfram Eberhard of the University of California. See D. Bodde, "Myths of Ancient China," in Samuel N. Kramer, ed., *Mythologies of the Ancient World* (New York: Doubleday Anchor Books, and Chicago: Quadrangle Books, 1961), p. 381: "As Eberhard points out, the Han writers could and did utilize long-existent popular oral tradition to a greater extent than did the more aristocratically oriented writers of the [preceding] feudal age."

Appendix G · COSMIC HARMONY IN THE CH'ING DYNASTY

In Chapter I, section 11, we traced the historical development of the idea that death sentences are to be carried out only during autumn and winter (these being seasons of decay and death) and should be totally avoided during spring and summer (these being seasons of growth and life). It was pointed out that, beginning with the T'ang Code and extending through that of Ming, the periods of taboo were greatly extended, but that in the Ch'ing dynasty they were restricted again to the opening and closing months of spring–summer (the first and sixth lunar months) plus a period from ten days before until seven days after the Winter Solstice, and another period from five days before until three days after the Summer Solstice. This statement, although correct and confirmed by the Ch'ing Code (Boulais, nos. 35 and 1694), is seemingly contradicted by parallel statements in the "Legal Treatise" of the *Ch'ing shih-kao* (Draft history of the Ch'ing dynasty) and in the *Ta Ch'ing hui-tien* (Collected institutes of the Ch'ing dynasty).

At the root of the confusion is the failure of the sources and their commentators to distinguish clearly in every instance between two key terms: *t'ing hsing*, "halting of punishments," and *t'ing shen*, "halting of the hearing of cases." It is only the first of these that, properly speaking, refers to the taboo on the carrying out of death penalties. (*Hsing*, "punishments," means in this context "death punishments.") The second term, *t'ing shen*, refers simply to the closing of the courts during certain months and days of the year, which, as we shall see, were in Ch'ing times considerably more extended than the periods forbidden for actual executions. Sometimes our sources erroneously assume that *t'ing shen* includes the halting of executions as well as of hearings. By carefully distinguishing between the two terms we arrive at a much clearer picture, as indicated below, even though source discrepancies still remain in two or three places.

1. The hearing of cases is to be halted (*t'ing shen*) during the first, sixth, and tenth months, as well as during certain individual days: (a) the first two days of each month; (b) days of imperial audience, of state sacrifice, the emperor's birthday (a period of seven days), and days of imperial funerals; (c) festivals, including the first seven days of the New Year, the Lantern Festival (fifteenth day of the first

month), the Buddha's birthday (eighth day of the fourth month), the Dragon-boat Festival (fifth day of the fifth month), the Mid-autumn Festival (fifteenth day of the eighth month), the Climbing-on-high Festival (ninth day of the ninth month), and the period from the Putting Away of the Seals until the New Year (roughly the last ten days of the twelfth month).[1]

2. In addition, the hearing of civil suits (cases having to do with marriage, landed property, and the like) is halted during the agricultural season, that is, from the fourth through the seventh months. However, this halt does not apply to criminal cases.[2]

3. Executions are halted (*t'ing hsing*) during the first and sixth months and also from ten days before until seven days after the Winter Solstice and from five days before until three days after the Summer Solstice, as stated above. This halt applies to "immediate" executions as well as those taking place after the assizes.[3]

4. In Peking, if the rainy season (which normally occurs in July and August) is delayed and there is drought, executions are suspended until the drought is over (but this prohibition does not apply to executions in the provinces).[4]

The magical concept underlying this final prohibition is a very ancient one. In a decree issued April 5, A.D. 134, for example, the emperor proclaimed that because of prolonged drought, persons imprisoned in the capital, irrespective of the seriousness of their crimes, would not be subjected to judicial examination until rain fell. On June 13 of the same year, the drought having continued, another decree granted an amnesty to everyone in the empire subject to the death penalty downward, including even "those having such crimes as plotting rebellion and 'great refractoriness,' which do not [normally] warrant forgiveness."[5]

---

[1] Ch'ing "Legal Treatise," pp. 99–100; *Ta Ch'ing hui-tien*, 56:15 (under a rubric misleadingly entitled *t'ing hsing*, "halting of executions"; phrases used in the text indicate that only the halting of the hearing of cases is intended); Ch'ing Code, second sub-statute under sec. 421 (sec. entirely omitted by Boulais; if included, it would come between his 1694 and 1695). The (unofficial) Upper Commentary, in its listing of the days above the sub-statute, wrongly says of them that they are times when executions are halted (*t'ing hsing*).

[2] Ch'ing "Legal Treatise," p. 100, and *Ta Ch'ing hui-tien*, 56:7a–b.

[3] Ch'ing "Legal Treatise," p. 100; *Ta Ch'ing hui-tien*, 56:15; Ch'ing Code, Boulais, nos. 35 and 1694. The *Ta Ch'ing hui-tien* erroneously adds the tenth month to the first and sixth months, apparently through confusion with the fact that the hearing of court cases is halted during all three months.

[4] *Ta Ch'ing hui-tien*, 56:15b; Ch'ing Code, sub-statute 19 in the long series omitted by Boulais which, if included, would come between his 1694 and 1695.

[5] See *Hou Han shu* (History of the Later Han dynasty), 6:8b, and, for the second decree, Hulsewé, *Remnants of Han Law*, I, 244.

BIBLIOGRAPHY

A. Original Sources

Editions are not listed for works cited in the text by title only. For titles of now lost codes and other works, see Glossary, section A.

Ch'eng-an so-chien-chi 成案所見集 (Collection of seen leading cases), comp. Ma Shih-lin 馬世璘. Four successive collections, covering 1736-1805.

Chien-shih Commentary. See Wang K'en-t'ang Chien-shih.

Ch'ing "Legal Treatise." See Ch'ing shih-kao Hsing-fa chih chu-chieh.

Ch'ing shih-kao Hsing-fa chih chu-chieh 清史稿刑法志註解 ("Legal Treatise" from the Ch'ing Draft History with annotations), ed. Kuo-wu yüan, Fa-chih chü, Fa-chih shih yen-chiu shih 國務院法制局法制史研究室 (Legal Research Division, Bureau of Legal Affairs, Council of State). Peking: Fa-lü ch'u-pan-she 法律出版社 (Legal Publishing Co.), 1957.

Ch'iu Han-p'ing. See Li-tai hsing-fa chih.

Conspectus, Conspectus of Penal Cases. See Hsing-an hui-lan.

Dynastic histories. Unless otherwise specified, all references to dynastic histories are to the Ssu-pu pei-yao 四部備要 ed.

HAHL. See Hsing-an hui-lan.

Hsi yüan lu 洗冤錄 (Instructions to coroners), by Sung Tz'u 宋慈 Ca. 1250. For an English translation, see Giles (sec. C, 6, below).

Hsiao tzu lu 孝慈錄 (Record of filial piety and parental kindness). Preface by the Hung-wu Emperor 1374.

Hsien-hsing tse-li 現行則例 (Sub-statutes currently operative). 1679.

Hsing-an hui-lan 刑案滙覽 (Conspectus of penal cases). Shanghai:
T'u-shu chi-ch'eng chü 圖書集成局 (T'u-shu Chi-ch'eng
Publishing Co.), fang hsiu-chen pan-yin 仿袖珍板印
("Pocket-size edition"); ca. 1886, 40 ts'e. Includes the following
separate works:

> Hsing-an hui-lan, by Chu Ch'ing-ch'i 祝慶祺 and Pao Shu-
> yün 鮑書芸. 60 chüan, ts'e 1-28; preface by Pao 1834.

> Hsü-tseng 續增 Hsing-an hui-lan (Hsing-an hui-lan supplement),
> by Chu Ch'ing-ch'i and Pao Shu-yün. 16 chüan, ts'e 29-36;
> preface by Pao 1840.

> Hsin-tseng 新增 Hsing-an hui-lan (Hsing-an hui-lan new
> supplement), by P'an Wen-fang 潘文舫 and Hsü Chien-
> ch'üan 徐諫荃. 16 chüan, ts'e 37-40; preface by
> Ho Wei-chieh 何維楷 1886.

Hsing-fa chih. See "Legal Treatise."

Hsing-t'ung 刑統 (Penal repertory). A.D. 963.

Huai-nan-tzu 淮南子 (The Master of Huai-nan), ed. Liu Wen-tien
劉文典, Huai-nan hung-lieh chi-chieh 淮南鴻烈集解
(Huai-nan's great and illustrious [compositions] with collected
commentaries). Shanghai: Commercial Press, 1933.

"Legal Treatise." The monographs in many of the dynastic histories
entitled Hsing-fa chih 刑法志 (Treatise on penal law) are in
this book regularly cited as the "Legal Treatise" of a given
dynasty. For the edition used for the Ch'ing "Legal Treatise,"
see Ch'ing shih-kao Hsing-fa chih chu-chieh; for the edition used
for all other legal treatises, see Li-tai hsing-fa chih.

Li-pu tse-li 吏部則例 (Regulations of the Board of Civil Office).
1820.

Li-tai hsing-fa chih 歷代刑法志 (Legal treatises of successive
dynasties), ed. Ch'iu Han-p'ing 丘漢平. Changsha:
Commercial Press, 1938.

Lü hsing 呂刑 (Punishments of Lü). Ancient legal text contained in
   Shu ching 書經 (Documents classic). For an English translation,
   see Legge, III, 588-611 (sec. C, 2, below).

Pi-tuei t'iao-k'uan 比對條款 (Articles for matching [capital cases
   with their proper categories]). 1767; rev. ed. 1784.

Po-an ch'eng-pien 駁案成編 (Compilation of reversed cases), by
   Hung Pin 洪彬. 1767.

San-liu tao-li piao 三流道里表 (Table of road distances for the
   three degrees of life exile). 1743; Hupei ed. 1872. Page
   references are to Hupei ed.

Ta Ch'ing hui-tien 大清會典 (Collected institutes of the great
   Ch'ing dynasty). Taipei: Ch'i-wen ch'u-pan-she 啟文出版
   社 (Ch'i-wen Book Co.), 1963. Reprint of 1899 ed. with
   continuous pagination.

Ta Ch'ing hui-tien shih-li 事例 (Supplement to collected institutes of
   the great Ch'ing dynasty). Taipei: Ch'i-wen ch'u-pan-she, 1963.
   Reprint of 1899 ed. with continuous pagination.

Ta Ch'ing lü chi-chieh fu-li 律集解附例 (Great Ch'ing Code with
   collected commentaries and appended sub-statutes). 1646.

Ta Ch'ing lü chi-chu 輯註 (Great Ch'ing Code with collected
   commentaries), by Shen Chih-ch'i 沈之奇. Preface 1715.

Ta Ch'ing lü-li 律例 (Statutes and sub-statutes of the great Ch'ing
   dynasty). 1740.

Ta Ch'ing lü-li chu-chu kuang-hui ch'üan-shu 硃註廣彙全書
   (Expanded classification of complete writings written as a red
   commentary on statutes and sub-statutes of the great Ch'ing
   dynasty). 1706.

Ta Ch'ing lü-li hui-t'ung hsin-tsuan 會通新纂 (Comprehensive
   new edition of the Ta Ch'ing lü-li), ed. Yao Yü-hsiang 姚雨薌,

with original commentary by Shen Chih-ch'i 沈之奇 and added
commentary by Hu Yang-shan 胡仰山 . Peking, 1873.
Reprinted, Taipei: Wen-hai ch'u-pan-she 文海出版社
(Wen-hai Publishing Co.), 1964 in 5 vols. with continuous
pagination. Page references are to reprint.

Ta Ch'ing lü-li tseng-hsiu t'ung-tsuan chi-ch'eng 增修統纂集成
(Revised comprehensive compilation of the Ta Ch'ing lü-li), ed.
Yao Jun 姚潤, Jen P'eng-nien 任彭年 , T'ao Chün 陶駿 ,
and T'ao Nien-lin 陶念霖 , with original commentary by Shen
Chih-ch'i 沈之奇 . 1878.

Ta Ming hui-tien 大明會典 (Collected institutes of the great Ming
dynasty). Reprint of 1587 ed., Taipei: Tung-nan shu-pao-she
東南書報社 (Southeast Book Co.), 1963 with continuous
pagination.

Ta Ming lü 律 (Code of the great Ming dynasty). 1373-1374; rev. ed.
1397.

T'ang lü shu-yi 唐律疏義 (T'ang Code with commentary). A. D. 653.

T'ang yin pi-shih 棠陰比事 (Parallel cases from under the pear-tree),
comp. Kuei Wan-jung 桂萬榮 . 1211. For an English translation,
see van Gulik (sec. C, 1, below).

Wang K'en-t'ang Chien-shih 王肯堂箋釋 (Wang K'en-t'ang's
expository commentary). Preface 1612; rev. ed. Ku Ting 顧鼎 ,
preface by Ku 1689.

Wen-hsing t'iao-li 文刑條例 (Itemized sub-statutes for pronouncing
judgments). Comp. 1500 with later additions.

Wu-chün tao-li piao 五軍道里表 (Table of road distances for the
five degrees of military exile). 1772; Hupei ed. 1872. Page
references are to Hupei ed.

Yü-chung tsa-chi 獄中雜記 (Notes on prison life), by Fang Pao 方
苞 (1668-1749).

B. Studies in Chinese and Japanese

Chao Lo 趙洛. T'ien-an men 天安門 (The gate of heavenly peace). Peking: Pei-ching ch'u-pan-she 北京出版社 (Peking Publishing Co.), 1957.

Ch'en Ku-yüan 陳顧遠. Chung-kuo fa-chih shih 中國法制史 (History of Chinese legal institutions). Shanghai: Commercial Press, 1934.

Cheng Ching-yi 鄭競毅, comp. Fa-lü ta tz'u-shu 法律大辭書 (Large dictionary of legal terms). 3 vols.; Shanghai: Commercial Press, 1936.

Ch'eng Shu-te 程樹德. Chiu-ch'ao lü-k'ao 九朝律考 (Study of the codes of nine dynasties). 2 vols.; Shanghai: Commercial Press, 1927.

Hōsei-shi Gakkai 法制史學會 (Society for the Study of the History of Law), comp. Hōsei-shi bunken mokuroku, 1945-1959--Shōwa 20-34 法制史文獻目錄, 昭和 20-34 (Catalogue of works on the history of law, 1945-1959--Shōwa 20-34). Pp. 143-193; Tokyo: Sōbun-sha 創文社 (Sōbun Publishing Co.), 1962.

Hsü Tao-lin 徐道鄰. Chung-kuo fa-chih shih lun-lüeh 中國法制史論略 (Outline history of Chinese legal institutions). Taipei: Cheng-chung shu-chü 正中書局 (Cheng-chung Book Co.), 1953.

Hsüeh Yün-sheng 薛允升. Tu-li ts'un-yi 讀例存疑 (Concentration on doubtful matters while perusing the sub-statutes). Peking: Han mao chai 翰茂齋, 1905.

Liang Ch'i-ch'ao 梁啟超. Chung-kuo ch'eng-wen fa pien-chih chih yen-ko 中國成文法編制之沿革 (Changing phases in the compilation of Chinese written law). Taipei: Chung-hua shu-chü 中華書局 (Chung-hua Book Co.), 1957.

567

Niida Noboru 仁井田陞. Chūgoku hōsei-shi 中國法制史
(A history of Chinese law). Tokyo: Iwanami shoten 岩波書
店 (Iwanami Book Co.), 1952.

------Chūgoku hōsei-shi kenkyū 中國法制史研究 (A
study of Chinese legal history). 4 unnumbered vols.; Tokyo:
Tōkyō daigaku shuppankai 東京大學出版會 (Tokyo
University Press), 1959-1964. Each volume has brief English
resumé and subtitle in English:

>Criminal Law, 1959.
>
>Law of Land and Law of Transaction, 1960.
>
>Law of Slave and Serf, and Law of Family and Village, 1962.
>
>Law and Custom, Law and Morality, 1964.

------Criminal Law. See Niida Noboru, Chūgoku hōsei-shi kenkyū.

Shen Chia-pen 沈家本, Bequeathed Writings. See Shen Chia-pen,
Shen Chi-yi hsien-sheng yi-shu, chia pien.

------Shen Chi-yi hsien-sheng yi-shu, chia pien 沈寄簃先生
遺書甲編 (Bequeathed writings of Mr. Shen Chi-yi [Shen
Chia-pen], first series). Peking, n.d. [1929]. Reprinted, Taipei:
Wen-hai ch'u-pan-she 文海出版社 (Wen-hai Publishing Co.),
1964 in 2 vols. with continuous pagination. The following items
from this reprint are cited herein:

>Ch'ung-chün k'ao 充軍考 (A study of military exile),
>pp. 541-552.
>
>Fen k'ao 分考 (Separate studies); 17 chüan, pp. 30-229.
>
>Hsing-an hui-lan san-pien hsü 刑案滙覽三編序 (Preface
>to a third compilation of the Hsing-an hui-lan), pp. 976-977.
>
>Hsing-chü k'ao 刑具考 (A study of the instruments of
>punishment), pp. 508-520.
>
>Kuang-hui ch'üan-shu pa 廣彙全書跋 (Postface to the
>Kuang-hui ch'üan-shu), p. 998.

Lü-ling 律令 (Statutes and ordinances); 9 chüan, pp. 358-490.

Ming lü mu chien 明律目箋 (The title sections of the Ming
   Code explained), pp. 774-821.

Ssu-hsing chih shu 死刑之數 (The figures for the death
   penalty), pp. 532-533.

Tsung k'ao 總考 (Comprehensive study); 4 chüan, pp. 3-29.

Yung-cheng lü k'o-pen pa 雍正律刻本跋 (Postface to the
   printed edition of the Yung-cheng code), pp. 996-997.

Yang Hung-lieh 楊鴻烈.　Chung-kuo fa-lü fa-ta shih 中國法律
   發達史 (History of the development of Chinese law).　2 vols.;
   Shanghai:　Commercial Press, 1930.

Yü Ching-jang 于景讓.　"Shih ching chi" 釋荊棘 (The Ching and
   Chi plants elucidated); Ta-lu tsa-chih 大陸雜誌 (Continent
   magazine), 14.12:365-372 (June 30, 1957).

C. Selected Western Works on Pre-Republican Chinese Law

1. General

Browne, Gertrude R., tr., translation of Escarra (sec. C, 1), in Browne, tr., *Chinese Law* (Works Progress Administration, W.P. 2799; Seattle: University of Washington, 1936). Reprinted (Xerox), Cambridge, Mass.: Harvard University Law School and East Asian Research Center, 1961.

Bünger, Karl, "The Punishment of Lunatics and Negligents According to Classical Chinese Law," *Studia Serica,* 9:1–16 (1950).

Ch'ü, T'ung-tsu, *Law and Society in Traditional China* (Paris and The Hague: Mouton & Co., 1961).
On this very important book, see Chap. I, notes 1 and 10.

Escarra, Jean, *Le Droit chinois* (Peiping: Henri Vetch, 1936). For an English translation, see Browne (sec. C, 1).
Important as a pioneer work, but much of it now outmoded. A considerable part is on Republican China.

Gulik, R. H. van, tr., *T'ang-yin-pi-shih, "Parallel Cases from under the Pear-tree," a 13th-century manual of jurisprudence and detection* (Sinica Leidensia series, Vol. X; Leiden: E. J. Brill, 1956).
Translation of 144 cases from a compilation made in 1211. Chapter 3 of Introduction is an excellent account of Chinese imperial judicial procedure at the district level.

Needham, Joseph, "Human Law and the Laws of Nature in China and the West," in Needham, *Science and Civilisation in China,* II, 518–583 (London and New York: Cambridge University Press, 1956).
Brilliant but controversial discussion of topic of utmost philosophical, legal, and scientific importance.

Pelliot, Paul, "Notes de bibliographie chinoise, II. Le Droit chinois," *Bulletin de l'École Française d'Extrême Orient,* 9:123–152 (1909).
The works here discussed are in Chinese.

Schurmann, H. F., "Traditional Property Concepts in China," *Far Eastern Quarterly,* 15:507–516 (1956).

Schwartz, Benjamin, "On Attitudes toward Law in China," in Milton Katz, ed., *Government under Law and the Individual* (Washington, D.C.: American Council of Learned Societies, 1957), pp. 28–39.
Brief but perceptive survey.

Wu, John C. H., "Chinese Legal Philosophy: A Brief Historical Survey," *Chinese Culture,* 1.4:7–48 (April 1958).

2. Pre-Imperial China (before 221 B.C.)

Creel, H. G., "The Fa-chia: 'Legalists' or 'Administrators'?" *Bulletin of the Institute of History and Philology, Academia Sinica,* Extra Vol. IV, 607–636 (Taipei, 1961).

——, "The Meaning of *Hsing Ming*," in Soren Egerod and Else Glahn, eds., *Studia Serica Bernhard Karlgren Dedicata* (Copenhagen: Ejnar Munksgaard, 1959), pp. 199–211.

Duyvendak, J. J. L., tr., *The Book of Lord Shang* (London: Arthur Probsthain, 1928).
Fine translation, preceded by what is still the best introduction to the Legalist school.

Legge, James, tr., translation of *Lü hsing* (sec. A, above), in Legge, tr., *The Chinese Classics,* 5 vols. (Hong Kong: Hong Kong University Press, 1960), III, 588–612.

Liao, W. K., tr., *The Complete Works of Han Fei Tzu,* 2 vols. (London: Arthur Probsthain; Vol. I, 1939; Vol. II, 1959).
Moderately satisfactory translation of the outstanding theoretician of the Legalist school.

Maspero, Henri, "Le Serment dans la procédure judiciaire de la Chine antique," *Mélanges Chinois et Bouddhiques,* 3:257–317 (1934–35).
Brilliant study of judicial procedure in feudal China.

Pokora, Timoteus, "The Canon of Laws by Li K'uei, A Double Falsification," *Archiv Orientalni,* 27:96–121 (1959).

Vogel, Werner, "Die historischen Grundlagen des chinesischen Strafrechts," *Zeitschrift für Vergleichende Rechtswissenschaft,* 40:37–134 (1923).
Carefully organized pioneer survey, marred by traditional approach to dating of classical texts. Approximately two-thirds deals with pre-imperial China, while remainder is a translation of the "Legal Treatise" in the Han dynastic history (unfavorably commented on by Hulsewé, *Remnants of Han Law,* pp. 316–317 [sec. C, 3, below]).

3. Han Dynasty (206 B.C.–A.D. 220)

Hulsewé, A. F. P., *Remnants of Han Law,* Vol. I (Leiden: E. J. Brill, 1955).
Invaluable study on the first long-lived imperial dynasty. To be followed by a second volume.

4. Period of Disunity and Sui Dynasty (220–617)

Balazs, Étienne, tr., *Le Traité juridique du "Souei-chou"* (Leiden: E. J. Brill, 1954).
Outstanding translation of Sui "Legal Treatise," enhanced by translator's introduction and copious commentary.

572

5. T'ang Dynasty (618–906)

Bünger, Karl, *Quellen zur Rechtsgeschichte der T'ang-Zeit* (Monumenta Serica Monograph 9; Peiping, 1946).
Fundamental for any study of T'ang legal development. Translates "Legal Treatises" in the T'ang dynastic histories, but not the T'ang Code itself.

Deloustal, Raymond, tr., "La Justice dans l'ancien Annam," *Bulletin de l'École Française d'Extrême Orient* (Vols. 8–13, 1908–1913; Vol. 19, 1919; Vol. 22, 1922).
The code here translated of the Le dynasty in Annam, 1428–1786, is closely based on the T'ang Code of 653.

Gernet, Jacques, "La Vente en Chine d'après les contrats de Touen-houang (IXe–Xe siècles)," *T'oung Pao*, 45:295–391 (1957).
Careful study based on contemporary documents. Covers also early Sung dynasty.

Hulsewé, A. F. P., *Periodieke executie- en slachtverboden in de T'ang tijd en hun oorsprong* (Leiden: E. J. Brill, 1948).

Kennedy, George Alexander, *Die Rolle des Geständnisses im chinesischen Gesetz* (Berlin, 1939).
Translation of a section of T'ang Code dealing with the particularly Chinese legal concept of confession.

Ou Koei-hing, *La Peine d'après le code des T'ang* (Shanghai: Université l'Aurore, 1935).
Only systematic analysis of the as yet untranslated T'ang Code of 653, valuable despite deficiencies.

Thomas, F. W., "Law of Theft in Chinese Kansu: A IXth–Xth Century Fragment from Tun-huang," *Zeitschrift für vergleichende Rechtswissenschaft*, 50:275–287 (1936).

Twitchett, Denis C., "The Fragment of the T'ang Ordinances of the Department of Waterways Discovered at Tun-huang," *Asia Major*, new series, 6:23–79 (1957–58).
Some valuable information, but technical.

6. Sung Dynasty (960–1279)

Eichhorn, Werner, "Bemerkungen über einige nicht amnestiebare Verbrechen im Sung-Rechtswesen," *Oriens Extremus*, 8:166–176 (1961).

Giles, Herbert Allen, tr., "The 'Hsi Yüan Lu' or Instructions to Coroners," *China Review*, 3:30–38, 92–99, 159–172 (1874–75); reprinted, "Section of the History of Medicine," *Proceedings of the Royal Society of Medicine*, 17:59–107 (London, 1924).
Somewhat free translation of basic treatise on forensic medicine, compiled between 1241–1253.

Wilhelm, Helmut, "Der Prozess der A Yün," *Monumenta Serica*, 1:338–351 (1935).
Detailed account of a famed legal case of 1068.

7. Yuan (Mongol) Dynasty (1280–1368)

Aubin, Françoise, "Index de 'Un Code des Yuan' de P. Ratchnevsky," *Mélanges publiés par l'Institut des Hautes Études Chinoises*, 2:423–515 (1960).
Ratchnevsky, Paul, "Die mongolische Rechtsinstitution der Busze in der chinesischen Gesetzbegung der Yüan-Zeit," in Herbert Franke, ed., *Studia Sino-Altaica, Festschrift für Erich Haenisch zum 80. Geburtstag* (Wiesbaden: Franz Steiner Verlag, 1961), pp. 169–179.
———, tr., *Un Code des Yuan* (Paris: E. Leroux, 1937).
Good partial translation, with extensive introduction, of a code probably dating from 1331.
Riasanovsky, V. A., "Mongol Law and Chinese Law in the Yuan Dynasty," *Chinese Social and Political Science Review*, 20:266–289 (1936–37).

8. Ming Dynasty (1368–1643)

Franke, Wolfgang, "Ein Document zum Prozess gegen Yü Ch'ien im Jahr 1467," *Studia Serica*, 6:193–208 (1947).
Hucker, Charles O., *The Censorial System of Ming China* (Stanford: University of Stanford Press, 1966).

9. Ch'ing (Manchu) Dynasty (1644–1911)

Alabaster, Ernest, "Dips into an Imperial Law Officer's Compendium," *Monumenta Serica*, 2:426–436 (1936).
———, *Notes and Commentaries on Chinese Criminal Law* (London: Luzac, 1899).
Major work on Ch'ing law, but sometimes careless in scholarship and overly favorable in its evaluation.
Boulais, Gui, tr., *Manuel du code chinois* (Variétés sinologiques series, No. 55; Shanghai, 1924).
Translation of the Ch'ing Code cited in this book.
Brunnert, H. S. and V. V. Hagelstrom, *Present Day Political Organization of China* (Shanghai: Kelly & Walsh, 1912).
Chang Yü-chüan, "The Chinese Judiciary," *Chinese Social and Political Science Review*, 2.4:68–88 (December 1917).
Good but brief. See especially pp. 78–85 for Ch'ing appellate system. Another installment in 3:1–30 (1918) deals with the judiciary in Republican China.

Ch'ü, T'ung-tsu, *Local Government in China under the Ch'ing* (Cambridge, Mass.: Harvard University Press, 1962).

Valuable information on judicial procedure at the lowest administrative level. See especially Chap. VI, "Private Secretaries," and Chap VII, "Administration of Justice."

Cohen, Jerome Alan, "Chinese Mediation on the Eve of Modernization," *California Law Review*, 54:1201–1226 (1966).

Good summary of Ch'ing extra-legal organs and techniques of mediation.

Dawson, F. L., Jr., "Law and the Merchant in Traditional China: The Ch'ing Code, *Ta Ch'ing lü li*, and Its Implications for the Merchant Class," *Papers on China*, 2:55–92 (Harvard University, East Asian Research Center, 1948).

Fairbank, John K., and Ssu-yü Teng, "On the Types and Uses of Ch'ing Documents," in Fairbank and Teng, *Ch'ing Administration: Three Studies* (Cambridge, Mass.: Harvard University Press, 1960).

A useful glossary of names of documents is on pp. 74–106.

Feng Han-yi, "The Chinese Kinship System," *Harvard Journal of Asiatic Studies*, 2:141–275 (1937).

Helpful when dealing with cases involving family relationships.

Gray, John Henry, *China: A History of the Laws, Manners and Customs of the People*, 2 vols. (London: Macmillan & Co., 1878).

For comment on the lengthy account of Chinese judicial procedure and punishments contained in this characteristic 19th-century work (I, 29–74), see this book's Chap. III, note 51.

Harrison, Judy Feldman, "Wrongful Treatment of Prisoners: A Case Study of Ch'ing Legal Practice," *Journal of Asian Studies*, 23:227–244 (1964).

Analysis of 30 cases in *Hsing-an hui-lan* having to do with sec. 413 of the Ch'ing Code. See comments in this book's translated case 259.1.

Hoang, Pierre, *Le Mariage chinois au point de vue légal* (Variétés sinologiques series, No. 14; Shanghai, 1898). Rev. ed., 1915.

———, *Notions techniques sur la propriété en Chine* (Variétés sinologiques series, No. 11; Shanghai, 1897). 2d ed., 1920.

Hsiao, Kung-chuan, *Rural China, Imperial Control in the Nineteenth Century* (Seattle: University of Washington Press, 1960).

Much valuable information, though not directly on formal law.

Hsieh, Pao Chao, *The Government of China (1644–1911)* (Baltimore: Johns Hopkins Press, 1925).

Includes a chapter, "The Judiciary," but overly sketchy and out of date.

Jamieson, George, *Chinese Family and Commercial Law* (Shanghai: Kelly & Walsh, 1921).

Kroker, Edward, "The Concept of Property in Chinese Customary

Law," *Transactions of the Asiatic Society of Japan*, 3d series, 7:123–146 (1959).

This and next two items are based on early 20th-century surveys of local customary law, carried out by Ministry of Justice.

——, "Dienst- und Werkverträge im chinesischen Gewohnheits-recht," *Zeitschrift der Deutschen Morgenländischen Gessellschaft*, 107:130–160 (1957).

——, "Rechtsgewohneiten in der Provinz Shantung," *Monumenta Serica*, 14:215–302 (1955).

MacGowan, D. J., "On the Banishment of Criminals in China," *Journal of the North China Branch of the Royal Asiatic Society*, 3:293–301 (December 1859).

See extensive quotations in Chap. III, sec. 11.

McAleavy, Henry, "Certain Aspects of Chinese Customary Law in the Light of Japanese Scholarship," *Bulletin of the School of Oriental and African Studies*, 17:535–547 (London, 1955).

Based on early 20th-century Japanese surveys made in Taiwan.

Meadows, T. T., "Description of an Execution at Canton," *Journal of The Royal Asiatic Society*, 16:54–58 (1856).

See extensive quotations in Chap. III, sec. 11.

Meijer, M. J., *The Introduction of Modern Criminal Law in China* (Batavia [Jakarta]: Koninklijke Drukkerij de Unie, 1949).

Excellent study of legal reforms of first decade of 20th century, often cited in this book.

Möllendorff, P. G. von, "The Family Law of the Chinese," *Journal of the North China Branch of the Royal Asiatic Society*, new series, 27:131–190 (1892–93).

Parkes, Sir Harry S., article in *North-China Herald*, 557:51 (Shanghai, March 30, 1861).

See extensive quotations in Chap. III, sec. 11.

Philastre, P. L. F., tr., *Le Code annamite, nouvelle traduction complète, comprenant: Les commentaires officiels du Code, traduits pour la première fois; de nombreuses annotations extraites des Commentaires du Code chinois* . . . 2 vols. (Paris: E. Leroux, 1876). 2d ed., 1909 (adds a 20-page index). [In 1967, while the present volume was in press, a reprint of Philastre (2d ed.) was issued by the Ch'eng-wen Publishing Co., Taiwan.]

Sprenkel, Sybille van der, *Legal Institutions in Manchu China* (London: Athlone Press for the University of London, 1962).

Good sociological analysis based mostly on secondary sources.

Staunton, George Thomas, tr., *Ta Tsing Leu Lee, Being the Fundamental Laws . . . of the Penal Code of China* (London: Cadell & Davies, 1810).

Sun, E-tu Zen, "The Board of Revenue in Nineteenth-Century China," *Harvard Journal of Asiatic Studies*, 24:175–228 (1962–63).

576

————, tr. and ed., *Ch'ing Administrative Terms* (Cambridge, Mass.: Harvard University Press, 1961).

Williams, Edward T., "Witchcraft in the Chinese Penal Code," *Journal of the North China Branch of the Royal Asiatic Society*, new series, 38:61–95 (1907).

GLOSSARY

A. Names and Terms

This list covers the occurrence of technical names and terms both in Part I and the translated cases. As much as possible, the list confines itself to names and terms of legal significance. Hence it omits such widely known non-legal names as Lao Tzu, Hsün Tzu, and others. Likewise it omits the hundreds of proper names mentioned in the translated cases because it was felt that these would only diminish the value of the Glossary. A few titles (indicated by underlining) of now lost codes, writings, etc., have been listed here, but for most Chinese titles and authors mentioned in this volume, the reader should consult the Bibliography.

an 案 (case; leading case)

an-ch'a shih 按察使 (judicial commissioner)

an yi-tsuan li 案已纂例 (leading case selected for
　　redaction as a sub-statute)

cha wei 詐偽 (deceptions and frauds)

chan 斬 (decapitation)

chan-ts'ui 斬衰 (garb of unhemmed sackcloth)

chang 杖 (heavy bamboo)

Chang San-feng 張三丰 (name of sect leader)

ch'ang sui 長隨 (private servant of an official)

chao 照 (in the light of)

ch'ao shen 朝審 (Court Assizes)

ch'e chia 車罩 (imperial chariot)

ch'eng an 成案 (leading case)

ch'eng-hsiung ch'ing-shih 逞兇情事 (viciousness)

chi pien 極邊 (farthest frontier)

chi-tzu 繼子 (successor)

chia 家 (family, household)

chia 甲 (100 households)

577

chia, chia hao 枷號 (cangue)

ch'iang 强 (force, forcibly, to exert force)

ch'iang to 搶奪 (plunder; to plunder)

chiao 絞 (strangulation)

ch'ieh tao 竊盜 (thief, theft)

chien 簡 (mace)

chien 姦 (moral turpitude, sexual offense)

chien 間 (room-section)

chien hou 監候 (after the assizes)

chien jen 賤人 (mean persons)

chien-lin kuan 監臨官 (supervising official)

Chien-teng ch'u 減等處 (Office for the Reduction of
    Sentences)

chien wang 僭妄 (contumacious insubordination)

ch'ien hsi 遷徙 (transportation)

ch'ien hsi chun t'u 遷徙准徒 (transportation-authorized
    penal servitude)

ch'ien hsi pi liu chien pan chun t'u erh nien 遷徙比流減
    半准徒二年 (transportation reduced to two-year
    authorized penal servitude)

Ch'ien pu lang 千步廊 (Esplanade of a Thousand Paces)

chih chih 職制 (administrative regulations)

chih shu 制書 (imperial decree)

ch'ih 笞 (light bamboo)

Chin lü 晉律 (Chin Code)

chin pien 近邊 (nearby frontier)

Ch'in-chou fu 秦州府 (place name)

ching sui 精髓 (vital marrow)

Ch'ing li ssu 清吏司 (Supervisory Department)

Ch'ing-ming 清明 (Clear and Bright Festival)

ch'ing shih 情實 (circumstances deserving of capital
    punishment)

Ch'ing tang-fang 清檔房 (Manchu Record and Registry Office)

Chiu-chang lü 九章律 (Code in Nine Sections)

chiu ch'ing 九卿 (Nine Chief Ministries)

chiu k'u 廄庫 (stables and treasuries)

chiu lü 廄律 (statutes on stables)

ch'iu fa 囚法 (laws on criminals under detention)

ch'iu shen 秋審 (Autumn Assizes)

Ch'iu-shen ch'u 秋審處 (Office for the Autumn Assizes)

chou 州 (department)

Chu 註 (Commentary)

chu hsing 竹刑 (punishments inscribed on tablets of bamboo)

chu shih 主使 (instigator)

ch'u 楚 (kind of wood)

chun 准 (authorized; comparable)

chun t'u 准徒 (authorized penal servitude)

Ch'un-ch'iu chüeh-yü 春秋決獄 (Case Decisions Based on the Spring and Autumn Annals)

chung 忠 (loyalty)

chung 眾 (masses, large numbers of people)

chü fa 具法 (general laws)

Ch'ü-yang 曲陽 (place name)

chün-tzu 君子 (Superior Man)

ch'ung chün 充軍 (military exile)

erh-mu so pu chi, ssu-lü so pu tao 耳目所不及，思慮所不到 (what the ears and eyes do not reach; what thinking and planning do not arrive at)

fa 法 (law, model, pattern)

fa chia 法家 (School of Law, Legalists)

fa ch'ien 發遣 (deportation)

Fa ching 法經 (Canon of Laws)

fa chung 發塚 (violating tombs)

fan li 凡例 (General Principles)

Fan-yin ch'u 飯銀處 (Food Costs Office)

fei fa 非法 (illegal)

fei li 非理 (unreasonably)

fei li ling-nüeh 非理陵虐 (unreasonable harshness)

fen 分 (1/100 of 1 oz. of silver)

feng 鳳 (phoenix)

feng 風 (wind; air; infection)

fu 府 (prefecture)

fu 婦 (woman; married daughter)

fu chin 附近 (very near)

Fu-shan hsien 福山縣 (place name)

Han Fei Tzu 韓非子 (name of Legalist theoretician)

Han lü 漢律 (Han Code)

Han tang-fang 漢檔房 (Chinese Record and Registry Office)

ho cha 嚇詐 (extortionate demand)

ho ch'iang 禾槍 (grain spike)

hsiao 孝 (filial piety)

Hsiao chu 小註 (Small Commentary)

hsiao-kung 小功 (garb worked with less coarseness)

hsiao jen 小人 (petty man)

hsiao shih 梟示 (exposure of the head)

Hsieh-chai 獬豸 (name of mythical animal)

hsien 縣 (district)

hsien fu 險夫 (emergency worker)

hsien shen an 現審案 (metropolitan leading case)

Hsien-shen ch'u 現審處 (Court of Manchu Affairs)

Hsien-yu kung 顯佑宮 (Hall of the Glorious Protector)

hsin 信 (good faith)

hsing 刑 (punishment, capital punishment)

hsing lü 興律 (statutes on corvée levies)

hsing-ming 刑名 (punishment and name; performance and title)

Hsing pu 刑部 (Board of Punishments)

hsing shu 刑書 (books of punishment)

hsiung ch'i 兇器 (dangerous weapons)

hsiung-ô kun-t'u 兇惡棍徒 (vicious scoundrel)

hsü 序 (preface)

Hsü chen-jen 許真人 (Hsü the True Man)

Hsü Hsün 許遜 (name of person)

hu hun 戶婚 (the family and marriage)

hu lü 戶律 (statutes on the family)

huan chüeh 緩決 (deferred execution)

hui hsiao fa 會小法 (Assemblage of the Lesser Judiciary)

hui ta fa 會大法 (Assemblage of the Greater Judiciary)

Hung Kou 洪溝 (Great Gulch)

Hung-yang 紅陽 (Red Male)

jen 仁 (benevolence)

kai ssu 該司 (the said department)

K'ai-huang lü 開皇律 (Code of the K'ai-huang period)

k'ang 炕 (platform-bed)

kao-liang 高粱 (sorghum)

Kao Yao 皐陶 (name of mythical judge)

k'o chin 可矜 (worthy of compassion)

ku 故 (with intent, deliberately)

ku sha 故殺 (intentional killing)

kuai-tai 拐帶 (embezzlement)

Kuan Ti (Yü) 關帝 (羽) (God of War)

581

K'uei-chi 會稽 (place name)

kun-t'u 棍徒 (scoundrel)

kung 公 (official capacity)

kung-ch'üeh 宮闕 (palace building)

kuo-shih 過失 (accident, accidental, accidentally)

li 里 (1/3 of English mile; 110 households)

li 禮 (rites; polite behavior)

li 例 (precedent, sub-statute)

li-chia 里甲 (system for tax payment)

li chüeh 立決 (immediate)

Li K'uei 李悝 (name of ancient jurist)

liang jen 良人 (good or respectable person; commoner)

lien-lei 連累 (implicated)

ling 令 (ordinance)

ling ch'ih 凌遲 (death by slicing)

ling ch'ih 陵遲 (gradual slope)

liu 流 (life exile)

liu-yang ch'eng-ssu 留養承祀 (remaining at home
    to care for the parents or to perpetuate the ancestral
    sacrifices)

lü 律 (statute, code)

Lü-li kuan 律例館 (Statutes Commission)

lung 龍 (dragon)

Lung-en tien 隆恩殿 (Hall of Surpassing Kindness)

Miao 苗 (name of barbarian tribe)

ming 名 (terms)

ming li 名例 (terms and general principles)

mo 墨 (tatooing)

mou 畝 (about 1/6 of English acre)

mou 謀 (premeditation)

582

Mou-ch'in tien 懋勤殿 (Hall of Earnest Diligence)

na shu 納贖 (to pay a fine)

Nan-hsiung chou 南雄州 (place name)

niang-niang 娘娘 (fairy princess)

nü 女 (girl; unmarried daughter)

pa tao 八刀 (eight cuts)

pa yi 八議 (eight considerations)

p'ai 牌 (10 households)

pao 保 (1,000 households)

pao-chia 保甲 (registration system)

pao-lung wan 抱龍丸 (dragon-embracing pills)

Pao-ting fu 保定府 (place name)

pen ssu 本司 (this department)

P'eng-lai hsien 蓬萊縣 (place name)

pi 比 (in comparison with)

pi 逼 (pressure, pressingly, to exert pressure)

pi chao 比照 (in the light of comparison with)

P'iao-kao Lao-tsu 飄高老祖 (Patriarch Who Soars
    Aloft on the Whirlwind)

pien 鞭 (whip)

pien yüan 邊遠 (distant frontier)

Pin-chou fu 邠州府 (place name)

pu 部 (board, ministry)

pu-cheng shih 布政使 (financial commissioner)

pu fa 捕法 (laws on arrests)

pu ju fa 不如法 (not according to law)

pu wang 捕亡 (arrests and escapes)

pu ying chung 不應重 (not ought heavy)

San fa ssu 三法司 (Three High Courts)

San-tai shih-piao 三代世表 (Table by Generations of
   the Three Dynasties)

shan hsing 擅興 (unauthorized corvée levies)

shan sha 擅殺 (unauthorized killing)

shan shang 擅傷 (unauthorized injuring)

Shang chu 上註 (Upper Commentary)

shang ssu 上司 (upper hierarchy)

Shang Ti 上帝 (Lord on High)

Shang Yang 商鞅 (name of ancient Legalist)

shê 赦 (to forgive, to amnesty)

Shê hsien 歙縣 (place name)

shê ts'ang 社倉 (community granary)

shen 審 (judicial investigation, trial)

sheng 省 (province)

sheng yüan 生員 (licentiate)

shih 石 (about 2.75 English bushels)

shih chieh 失節 (detrimental to feminine morality)

shih ô 十惡 (Ten Abominations)

shih-piao 世表 (table by generations)

shih ssu 市司 (market supervisor)

Shu-hsiang 叔向 (name of ancient official)

shuo t'ieh 説帖 (memorandum)

so-cha 索詐 (a non-extortionate demand)

ssu 死 (death)

ssu 嗣 (perpetuator)

ssu 私 (private)

ssu-ma 緦麻 (garb of plain hempen cloth)

Ssu-wu t'ing 司務廳 (Chancery)

Sung-hsi-t'ang kao 松西堂稿 (Draft Writings from the
   Hall West of the Pine Tree)

sung kun 訟棍 (litigation stick, trickster)

ta-kung 大功 (garb worked with great coarseness)

Ta li ssu 大理寺 (Court of Revision)

Ta-yeh lü 大業律 (Code of the Ta-yeh Period)

Ta Yüan t'ung-chih 大元通制 (General Regulations of the Great Yuan Dynasty)

Tang-yüeh ch'u 當月處 (Record Office)

T'ang 堂 (Directorate)

tao 道 (circuit)

tao 盜 (theft)

tao fa 盜法 (laws on theft)

tao tsei 盜賊 (theft and violence)

Teng-chou fu 登州府 (place name)

teng-wen ku 登聞鼓 (complaint drum)

ti 抵 (requital)

Ti-ch'ao 邸抄 (Peking Gazette)

ti ming 抵命 (requital-life, requiting a life)

t'i 題 (to memorialize)

T'i-lao t'ing 提牢廳 (Office of Prisons)

tiao t'u 刁徒 (knavish fellow)

t'ieh ch'ih 鐵尺 (iron footrule)

T'ien-an men 天安門 (Gate of Heavenly Peace)

t'ing hsing 停刑 (halting of executions)

t'ing shen 停審 (halting of hearing of cases)

tou shih hua 豆石花 (bean-stone flowers)

tou sung 鬥訟 (conflicts and suits)

tsa fa 雜法 (miscellaneous laws)

tsa fan 雜犯 (miscellaneous offenses)

tsang 贓 (squeeze, loot)

Tsang-fa k'u 贓罰庫 (Treasury)

tsei fa 賊法 (laws on violence)

tsei tao 賊盜 (violence and theft)

tso tsang 坐贓 (pecuniary malfeasance)

tsou 奏 (to memorialize)

tsui jen 罪人 (wrongdoer)

tsun hsing 遵行 (circulars for compliance)

tsung 總 (total)

Tsung chu 總註 (General Commentary)

Tsung lun 總論 (General Remarks)

tsung t'u 總徒 (total penal servitude)

tu 度 (regulations)

Tu-ch'a yüan 都察院 (Censorate)

Tu-pu ch'ing-li ssu 督捕清吏司 (Supervisory
    Department on Arrests)

Tu-ts'ui so 督催所 (Expediting Office)

tu yi 蠹役 (rapacious underling)

t'u 徒 (penal servitude)

t'u fang 土方 (10 cubic Chinese feet)

t'u tzu 土子 (manganese oxide?)

tuan yü 斷獄 (trial and imprisonment)

Tung-ch'ang fu 東昌府 (place name)

Tung Chung-shu 董仲舒 (name of Han Confucian)

Tung ling 東陵 (Eastern Mausolea)

t'ung 同 (jointly)

T'ung-chou fu 同州府 (place name)

t'ung hsing 通行 (general circular)

t'ung hsing yi-tsuan li 通行已纂例 (general circular
    selected for redaction as a sub-statute)

t'ung mou 同謀 (joint conspiracy)

t'ung-yang hsi 童養媳 (girl brought up in future
    husband's family)

tzu 子 (son; child)

Tzu-ch'an 子產 (name of ancient minister)

tzu-ts'ui 齊衰 (garb of hemmed sackcloth)

tz'u tzu 刺字 (tatooing)

wei chin 衛禁 (Imperial Guard and prohibitions
  [relative to the imperial palace])

wei li 威力 (intimidating power)

Wei lü 魏律 (Wei Code)

wu 誤 (by mischance)

wu fu 五服 (five degrees of mourning)

wu hsing 五刑 (five punishments)

wu ku 無故 (without cause)

Wu-tang 武當 (sect name)

Wu T'ing-fang 伍廷芳 (name of statesman)

ya-shu 衙署 (government office)

Yang Liang 楊倞 (name of commentator)

yen chang 烟瘴 (in a malarial region)

yi 依 (in reliance on)

yi 義 (social rightness)

yi chia 一家 (one family)

Yi-chou fu 沂州府 (place name)

yi fa 依法 (according to law)

yi-tzu 義子 (charity child or son)

yin 因 (cause, antecedent causal act)

yu, yu ling 優伶 (entertainer)

yu ch'ih 猶遲 (still slow)

yung yung 庸庸 (employ the employable)

yü kou 予勾 (to give a hook to, to check off)

Yü ling 裕陵 (Yü Mausoleum)

yüan mou 原謀 (original planner)

B. Section Titles in the <u>Hsing-an hui-lan</u>

This section supplies the Chinese characters for all division and section titles listed in the "Table of Cases" at the beginning of Part II.

I.   Ming-li   名例

4.   Chih-kuan yu fan   職官有犯

6.   Fan-tsui mien fa-ch'ien   犯罪免發遣

8.   Wu kuan fan-tsui   無官犯罪

9.   Liu-ch'iu chia-shu   流囚家屬

11.   Fan-tsui ts'un-liu yang ch'in   犯罪存留養親

12.   Kung yüeh hu chi fu-jen fan tsui   工樂戶及婦人犯罪

14.   Lao hsiao fei-chi shou-shu   老小廢疾收贖

17.   Fan-tsui tzu-shou   犯罪自首

19.   Fan-tsui kung-t'ao   犯罪共逃

21.   Fan-tsui shih-fa tsai-t'ao   犯罪事發在逃

II.   Li lü   吏律

A.   Chih chih   職制

B.   Kung shih   公式

40.   Lou-shih yin-hsin   漏使印信

III.   Hu lü   戶律

A.   Hu yi   戶役

41.   Jen-hu yi chi wei ting   人戶以籍為定

42.   Li ti-tzu wei-fa   立嫡子違法

44.   Chin ko chu pao-li chang   禁革主保里長

45.   Pei-yu ssu-shan yung-ts'ai   卑幼私擅用財

B.   T'ien-chai   田宅

49.   Jen so-chih mai t'ien-chai   住所置買田宅

50.   Ch'i-hui ch'i-wu chia-se teng   棄毀器物稼穡等

51.   Shan-shih t'ien-yüan kua-kuo   擅食田園瓜菓

588

       C. Hun-yin 婚姻

52. Nan-nü hun-yin 男女婚姻

59. Ch'ü pu-min fu-nü wei ch'i-ch'ieh 娶部民婦女為妻妾

60. Ch'iang-chan liang-chia ch'i-nü 強占良家妻女

61. Ch'ü yüeh-jen wei ch'i-ch'ieh 娶樂人為妻妾

       D. Ts'ang-k'u 倉庫

       E. K'o-ch'eng 課程

80. Yen fa 鹽法

       F. Ch'ien-chai 錢債

82. Wei-chin ch'ü-li 違禁取利

83. Fei-yung shou-chi ts'ai-ch'an 費用受寄財產

       G. Shih-ch'an 市廛

86. Shih-ssu p'ing wu-chia 市司平物價

87. Pa-ch'ih hang-shih 把持行市

IV. Li lü 禮律

       A. Chi-ssu 祭祀

88. Hui ta ssu ch'iu-t'an 毀大祀邱壇

89. Hsieh-tu shen-ming 褻瀆神明

       B. Yi-chih 儀制

92. Shou-tsang chin-shu 收藏禁書

93. Shih yi 失儀

V. Ping lü 兵律

       A. Kung wei 宮衛

       B. Chün-cheng 軍政

112. Chi-pien liang-min 激變良民

115. Ssu-tsang ying-chin chün-ch'i 私藏應禁軍器

       C. Kuan-ching 關津

       D. Chiu-mu 廄牧

124. Mu-yang ch'u-ch'an pu ju fa 牧養畜產不如法

126. Ch'u-ch'an yao-t'i jen 畜產咬踢人

    E. Yu-yi 郵驛

VI. Hsing lü 刑律

    A. Tsei-tao 賊盜

131. Mou-fan ta-ni 謀反大逆

133. Tsao yao-shu yao-yen 造妖書妖言

134. Tao ta ssu shen yü-wu 盜大祀神御物

141. Ch'iang-tao 强盜

143. Pai-chou ch'iang-to 白晝搶奪

144. Ch'ieh-tao 竊盜

147. Ch'in-shu hsiang tao 親屬相盜

148. K'ung-ho ch'ü-ts'ai 恐嚇取財

149. Cha-ch'i kuan-ssu ch'ü-ts'ai 詐欺官私取財

150. Lüeh jen lüeh-mai jen 略人略賣人

151. Fa chung 發塚

152. Yeh wu-ku ju jen-chia 夜無故入人家

    B. Jen-ming 人命

157. Mou-sha jen 謀殺人

159. Mou-sha tsu-fu-mu fu-mu 謀殺祖父母父母

160. Sha-ssu chien-fu 殺死姦夫

161. Sha yi-chia san-jen 殺一家三人

162. Ts'ai sheng che-ko jen 採生折割人

164. Tou-ou chi ku-sha jen 鬬毆及故殺人

165. Ping-ch'ü jen fu-shih 屏去人服食

166. Hsi-sha wu-sha kuo-shih sha-shang jen

    戲殺誤殺過失殺傷人

167. Fu ou-ssu yu-tsui ch'i-ch'ieh 夫毆死有罪妻妾

168. Sha tzu-sun chi nu-pei t'u lai jen 殺子孫及奴婢圖賴人

169. Kung-chien shang jen 弓箭傷人

170. Ch'e-ma sha-shang jen 車馬殺傷人

590

171. Yung-yi sha-shang jen 庸醫殺傷人

172. Wei-pi jen chih ssu 威逼人致死

    C. Tou-ou 鬭毆

175. Tou-ou 鬭毆

183. Ou shou-yeh shih 毆受業師

184. Wei-li chih-fu jen 威力制縛人

185. Liang-chien hsiang-ou 良賤相毆

186. Nu-pei ou chia-chang 奴婢毆家長

187. Ch'i-ch'ieh ou fu 妻妾毆夫

188. T'ung-hsing ch'in-shu hsiang-ou 同姓親屬相毆

189. Ou ta-kung yi-hsia tsun-chang 毆大功以下尊長

190. Ou ch'i-ch'in tsun-chang 毆期親尊長

191. Ou tsu-fu-mu fu-mu 毆祖父母父母

194. Fu-tsu pei ou 父祖被毆

    D. Ma-li 罵詈

195. Ma chih-shih chi pen-kuan chang-kuan
罵制使及本管長官

196. Tso-chih t'ung-shu ma chang-kuan
佐職統屬罵長官

    E. Su-sung 訴訟

198. T'ou ni-ming wen-shu kao jen tsui 投匿名文書告人罪

199. Wu-kao 誣告

200. Kan-ming fan-yi 干名犯義

201. Tzu-sun wei-fan chiao-ling 子孫違犯教令

203. Chiao-so tz'u-sung 教唆詞訟

    F. Shou-tsang 受贓

206. Kuan-li shou-ts'ai 官吏受財

208. Yu-shih yi-ts'ai ch'ing-ch'iu 有事以財請求

210. Chia-jen ch'iu-so 家人求索

    G. Cha-wei 詐偽

214. Tui-chih shang-shu cha pu yi shih
對制上書詐不以實

591

H.　Fan-chien　犯姦

222.　Fan-chien　犯姦

223.　Tsung-jung ch'i-ch'ieh fan-chien

縱容妻妾犯姦

224.　Ch'in-shu hsiang-chien　親屬相姦

228.　Chü-sang chi seng-tao fan-chien

居喪及僧道犯姦

230.　Kuan-li su-ch'ang　官吏宿娼

　　I.　Tsa fan　雜犯

235.　Shih-huo　失火

236.　Fang-huo ku-shao jen fang-wu　放火故燒人房屋

237.　Pu ying wei　不應為

　　J.　Pu-wang　捕亡

239.　Tsui-jen chü-pu　罪人拒捕

241.　T'u-liu jen t'ao　徒流人逃

243.　Chu-shou pu-chüeh shih-ch'iu　主守不覺失囚

　　K.　Tuan-yü　斷獄

248.　Ling-nüeh tsui-ch'iu　陵虐罪囚

257.　Yü-ssu chüeh-ch'iu teng-ti　有司決囚等第

259.　Chüeh-fa pu ju fa　決罰不如法

260.　Tuan-tsui yin lü-ling　斷罪引律令

262.　Fu-jen fan-tsui　婦人犯罪

263.　Tuan-tsui pu-tang　斷罪不當

264.　Li-tien tai-hsieh chao-ts'ao　吏典代寫招草

VII.　Kung lü　工律

　　A.　Ying-tsao　營造

265.　Shan tsao-tso　擅造作

266.　Tsao-tso pu ju fa　造作不如法

267.　Chih-tsao wei-chin lung-feng wen tuan-p'i

織造違禁龍鳳文段疋

B. Ho-fang 河防

269. Shih-shih pu-hsiu ti-fang 失時不修隄防
270. Ch'in-chan chieh-tao 侵占街道

INDEX

Excluded from this index are the names of the persons appearing in the translated cases in Part Two, as well as the statistical data presented in Appendixes A-E.

598 INDEX

Pennsylvania Paperbacks